Chinese Taiwanese & Korean
125 Motorcycles
Service and Repair Manual

by Matthew Coombs

(4871 - 336 - 3AO2)

Models covered

This manual provides generic coverage for 125 cc engined models from AJS, Baotian, Bashan, Better, Branson, Chituma, CPI, Dadyw, Dafier, Dayang, Dayun, Feiying, Francis-Barnett, FYM, Geely, Giantco, Haotian, Hartford, HMC (Herald), Hongdou, Honley, Honling, Huoniao, Hyosung, Jialing, Jianshe, Jinlun, Kaisar, Keeway, Kinlon, Kinroad, Kreidler, Kymco, Lexmoto, Lifan, Loncin, Mash, Moto Roma, Pioneer, POR, Pulse, Romet, Qingqi, Sanya, SFM, Shineray, Sinnis, Sinski, Skygo, Skyjet, Sky Team, Sukida, Sumoto, Superbyke, TMEC, Venture, Vulcan, Wangye, Warrior, WK, Wuyang, Xgjao, Xingyue, Yamasaki, Yuan, Zennco, Zhongneng, Znen, ZongShen, ZY Motor.

© Haynes Group Limited 2015

A book in the **Haynes Service and Repair Manual Series**

ABCDE
F

ISBN **978 0 85733 920 1**

British Library Cataloguing in Publication Data
A catalogue record for this book is available from the British Library.

Library of Congress Control Number 2014958877

Printed in India

Haynes Group Limited
Sparkford, Yeovil, Somerset BA22 7JJ, England

Haynes North America, Inc
2801 Townsgate Road, Suite 340, Thousand Oaks, CA 91361

Disclaimer

Contents

The Tip Of A (Very Big) Iceberg

by Julian Ryder

As China is the World's most populous country, it should come as no surprise that the Chinese motorcycle industry is very big indeed. Nevertheless, the sheer size of the numbers involved takes the breath away. In the first half of 2009 China's motorcycle factories produced just under 12-million machines – and this as the industry recovered from the worldwide financial crisis. Unbelievably, those numbers disguise a year-on-year decline in output of 7.5%. China makes around half of the world's motorcycles.

How many Chinese bike manufacturers are there? Probably over 100 actually making complete motorcycles but there are known to be over 2000 companies making everything from complete engines to individual components. The five largest companies, Guangdong, Chongqing, Zhejiang, Jiangsu and Henan, account for over 85% of this output.

Recent 'one vehicle, one VIN' legislation is the most visible attempt by government to bring order to what has been a surprisingly anarchic situation. This may be a side-effect of China joining the World Trade Organisation at the end of 2001, since when its tariffs and internal subsidies have been open to scrutiny. One would have expected central government to have a master plan for the industry from which there would be no deviation but this has not been the case until 2010. Small, unregulated companies copied domestic and foreign designs in a totally unregulated market. The wilder excesses of the free market have been curbed although factories that make one component, say wheels, will still deal with their neighbours who make engines, frames, and so on, and knock-up their own complete machines. However, the Chinese Chamber of Commerce at a January '10 meeting embarked on a plan to put some structure into their motorcycle industry. A three-part plan was formulated with the main objectives being: 'steady exports, market expansion, and structural adjustment.'

On the export front, all four Japanese companies have arrangements with one or other of the biggest Chinese manufacturers. Suzuki, for instance, is in partnership with the Grand River Group as Guangdong is also known. This joint venture saw an astounding 2.8-million bikes produced by the end of 2009. Much of the work with Suzuki is for other markets, notably Indonesia and Brazil. The Chinese factories manufacture the motorcycles but supply them in the form of 'knock-down' kits, which are then assembled in the end-user country to comply with local legislation on imports. When you consider that Yamaha sell over one-million bikes a year in Indonesia alone, you begin to understand the importance of this sort of business. On the home market, there is a drive to get motorcycles out into the Chinese countryside, at present the vast majority are sold in the big cities.

There is also a very realistic understanding of how the Chinese industry is viewed in the outside world. Try this for a quote from the President of the China Motorcycle Chamber of Commerce: 'overall poor image, low value-added products, independent innovation capacity is weak.'

There is no doubt, however, that the big companies, especially those in partnership with the Japanese factories, are capable of manufacturing to very high standards. GRG's factories for its domestic market-leading Haojue brand bikes, for instance, were awarded ISO9000 certification as long ago as 1997. The next step is obvious; it has to be the design and production of larger motorcycles for foreign markets. The question is how, especially as big bikes are not allowed on the roads at home. It is now worth going back fifty years and contemplating the fledgling Japanese industry and what it did when faced with a similar dilemma. It went racing. In 1954, six years after the founding of the Honda Motor Company, Soichiro Honda announced his intention to race in the Isle of Man TT with a machine of his own design. It took another five years but they got there, won a team award at their first attempt and took the first of over 180 TT victories in 1961. It is worth remembering that when Mr Honda told the world he was going racing, his company were the largest manufacturer of lightweight motorcycles in the world but they were only sold on the domestic market.

Two of China's million sellers have already put a toe in the water, but only using their name. Zongshen, the eighth biggest maker ran Suzuki GSX-R1000s to win the 2002 World Endurance Championship. At the time, most journalists thought Zongshen was a tyre manufacturer, and indeed they are. It's just that they also make a million bikes a year. They also ran a 250cc team for Chinese riders, based in France and using Aprilias. When MotoGP went to China for the first time in 2005 it was noticeable that the banners celebrating Zongshen's world title singularly failed to mention the word 'Suzuki'. China's second biggest brand, Loncin, also had its name on the side of a 125 GP team that was previously badged as Malaguti and is in reality based on Honda crankcases.

The firm that looked most likely to follow the Honda route and field their own machines in GP was, naturally, the biggest one, GRG. In 2009 they entered the 125cc class with their own bike. No less a person than John Surtees fronted the effort but the project was let down badly by its (non-Chinese) engine supplier and the team did not see out the season. Nevertheless, the Chinese company was fully aware that racing was the perfect way to educate its engineers. Remember the remark about 'independent innovation being weak'? Racing is one way to cure that problem.

The problem of image was also addressed by the China International Motorcycle & Parts Trade Fair – CIMAMotor – in Chongqing, the first truly national motorcycle trade show in the country for ten years. The fair is in the heart of China's motorcycle industry, the area accounts for about one-third of the country's production. As well as selling parts and complete bikes, one of CIMAMotor's stated ambitions was to build bridges with overseas manufacturers and facilitate technology transfer. It is one reason why, like Japanese motorcycles fifty years earlier, Chinese two-wheelers are improving so rapidly.

Production line at the Haojue factory

0•4 Acknowledgements

Our thanks are due to the importer and parts specialist Llexeter Ltd of Exeter, Premier Motorcycles of Southampton and GV Bikes of Taunton, who supplied the machines featured in the illustrations throughout this manual. We are also grateful to Llexeter for providing the model photographs used on the front cover and in particular to Paul Wakely for providing advice and technical assistance on the manual's content.

We are grateful to the UK importers who supplied literature or technical advice: AJS Motorcycles Ltd, E P Barrus Ltd (Hyosung), Hartford Industrial Co Ltd, Jinlun UK, Masco Ltd (Kymco), Moore Large & Co Ltd (Sym), MotoGB (Keeway and Daelim), Superbyke Ltd.

We would also like to thank NGK Spark Plugs (UK) Ltd for supplying the colour spark plug condition photographs, the Avon Rubber Company for supplying information on tyre fitting and Draper Tools Ltd for some of the workshop tools shown. Julian Ryder wrote the introduction 'The Tip of a (Very Big) Iceberg'.

About this Manual

The aim of this manual is to help you get the best value from your motorcycle. It can do so in several ways. It can help you decide what work must be done, even if you choose to have it done by a dealer; it provides information and procedures for routine maintenance and servicing; and it offers diagnostic and repair procedures to follow when trouble occurs.

We hope you use the manual to tackle the work yourself. For many simpler jobs, doing it yourself may be quicker than arranging an appointment to get the motorcycle into a dealer and making the trips to leave it and pick it up. More importantly, a lot of money can be saved by avoiding the expense the shop must pass on to you to cover its labour and overhead costs. An added benefit is the sense of satisfaction and accomplishment that you feel after doing the job yourself.

References to the left or right side of the motorcycle assume you are sitting on the seat, facing forward.

We take great pride in the accuracy of information given in this manual, but motorcycle manufacturers make alterations and design changes during the production run of a particular motorcycle of which they do not inform us. No liability can be accepted by the authors or publishers for loss, damage or injury caused by any errors in, or omissions from, the information given.

Identification numbers and buying spare parts

Frame and engine numbers

The frame serial number is stamped into the frame, generally on the right-hand side of the steering head. The engine serial number is stamped into the crankcase. Both of these numbers should be recorded and kept in a safe place so they can be given to law enforcement officials in the event of a theft. There is also a VIN plate on the frame, and this has the model code and frame number stamped into it.

The frame and engine serial numbers, and where present the colour code, should also be kept in a handy place (such as with your driver's licence) so they are always available when purchasing or ordering parts for your machine.

The frame number is stamped into the steering headstock

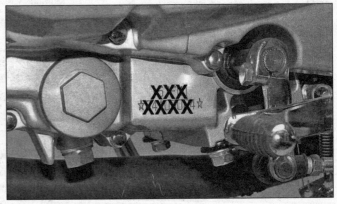
The engine number is stamped into crankcase

Buying spare parts

Once you have found all the identification numbers, record them for reference when buying parts. Provide the parts supplier with as much information as you can, and where possible, take the worn part to the supplier so direct comparison with the new component can be made.

There are several routes to obtaining new parts. If a dealer network exists, parts can be obtained over the counter or by mail order. If no dealer network exists you may need to contact the importer for guidance on how to obtain spares. Note that specialist mail order companies can supply parts for a wide range of models.

Certain components, such as chains and sprockets, tyres, spark plugs, lubricants and fluids can be obtained from virtually any aftermarket motorcycle accessory stockist.

Used parts can be obtained from breakers yards for roughly half the price of new ones, but you can't always be sure of what you're getting. Once again, take your worn part to the breaker for direct comparison, or when ordering by mail order make sure that you can return it if you are not happy.

Note: *The Pre-ride checks outlined in your Owner's Handbook cover those items which should be inspected before riding the scooter.*

Professional mechanics are trained in safe working procedures. However enthusiastic you may be about getting on with the job at hand, take the time to ensure that your safety is not put at risk. A moment's lack of attention can result in an accident, as can failure to observe simple precautions.

There will always be new ways of having accidents, and the following is not a comprehensive list of all dangers; it is intended rather to make you aware of the risks and to encourage a safe approach to all work you carry out on your bike.

Asbestos

● Certain friction, insulating, sealing and other products - such as brake pads, clutch linings, gaskets, etc. - contain asbestos. Extreme care must be taken to avoid inhalation of dust from such products since it is hazardous to health. If in doubt, assume that they do contain asbestos.

Fire

● Remember at all times that petrol is highly flammable. Never smoke or have any kind of naked flame around, when working on the vehicle. But the risk does not end there - a spark caused by an electrical short-circuit, by two metal surfaces contacting each other, by careless use of tools, or even by static electricity built up in your body under certain conditions, can ignite petrol vapour, which in a confined space is highly explosive. Never use petrol as a cleaning solvent. Use an approved safety solvent.

● Always disconnect the battery earth terminal before working on any part of the fuel or electrical system, and never risk spilling fuel on to a hot engine or exhaust.
● It is recommended that a fire extinguisher of a type suitable for fuel and electrical fires is kept handy in the garage or workplace at all times. Never try to extinguish a fuel or electrical fire with water.

Fumes

● Certain fumes are highly toxic and can quickly cause unconsciousness and even death if inhaled to any extent. Petrol vapour comes into this category, as do the vapours from certain solvents such as trichloro-ethylene. Any draining or pouring of such volatile fluids should be done in a well ventilated area.
● When using cleaning fluids and solvents, read the instructions carefully. Never use materials from unmarked containers - they may give off poisonous vapours.
● Never run the engine of a motor vehicle in an enclosed space such as a garage. Exhaust fumes contain carbon monoxide which is extremely poisonous; if you need to run the engine, always do so in the open air or at least have the rear of the vehicle outside the workplace.

The battery

● Never cause a spark, or allow a naked light near the vehicle's battery. It will normally be giving off a certain amount of hydrogen gas, which is highly explosive.

● Always disconnect the battery ground (earth) terminal before working on the fuel or electrical systems (except where noted).
● If possible, loosen the filler plugs or cover when charging the battery from an external source. Do not charge at an excessive rate or the battery may burst.
● Take care when topping up, cleaning or carrying the battery. The acid electrolyte, evenwhen diluted, is very corrosive and should not be allowed to contact the eyes or skin. Always wear rubber gloves and goggles or a face shield. If you ever need to prepare electrolyte yourself, always add the acid slowly to the water; never add the water to the acid.

Electricity

● When using an electric power tool, inspection light etc., always ensure that the appliance is correctly connected to its plug and that, where necessary, it is properly grounded (earthed). Do not use such appliances in damp conditions and, again, beware of creating a spark or applying excessive heat in the vicinity of fuel or fuel vapour. Also ensure that the appliances meet national safety standards.
● A severe electric shock can result from touching certain parts of the electrical system, such as the spark plug wires (HT leads), when the engine is running or being cranked, particularly if components are damp or the insulation is defective. Where an electronic ignition system is used, the secondary (HT) voltage is much higher and could prove fatal.

Remember...

✗ **Don't** start the engine without first ascertaining that the transmission is in neutral.

✗ **Don't** suddenly remove the pressure cap from a hot cooling system - cover it with a cloth and release the pressure gradually first, or you may get scalded by escaping coolant.

✗ **Don't** attempt to drain oil until you are sure it has cooled sufficiently to avoid scalding you.

✗ **Don't** grasp any part of the engine or exhaust system without first ascertaining that it is cool enough not to burn you.

✗ **Don't** allow brake fluid or antifreeze to contact the machine's paintwork or plastic components.

✗ **Don't** siphon toxic liquids such as fuel, hydraulic fluid or antifreeze by mouth, or allow them to remain on your skin.

✗ **Don't** inhale dust - it may be injurious to health (see Asbestos heading).

✗ **Don't** allow any spilled oil or grease to remain on the floor - wipe it up right away, before someone slips on it.

✗ **Don't** use ill-fitting spanners or other tools which may slip and cause injury.

✗ **Don't** lift a heavy component which may be beyond your capability - get assistance.

✗ **Don't** rush to finish a job or take unverified short cuts.

✗ **Don't** allow children or animals in or around an unattended vehicle.

✗ **Don't** inflate a tyre above the recommended pressure. Apart from overstressing the carcass, in extreme cases the tyre may blow off forcibly.

✔ **Do** ensure that the machine is supported securely at all times. This is especially important when the machine is blocked up to aid wheel or fork removal.

✔ **Do** take care when attempting to loosen a stubborn nut or bolt. It is generally better to pull on a spanner, rather than push, so that if you slip, you fall away from the machine rather than onto it.

✔ **Do** wear eye protection when using power tools such as drill, sander, bench grinder etc.

✔ **Do** use a barrier cream on your hands prior to undertaking dirty jobs - it will protect your skin from infection as well as making the dirt easier to remove afterwards; but make sure your hands aren't left slippery. Note that long-term contact with used engine oil can be a health hazard.

✔ **Do** keep loose clothing (cuffs, ties etc.

and long hair) well out of the way of moving mechanical parts.

✔ **Do** remove rings, wristwatch etc., before working on the vehicle - especially the electrical system.

✔ **Do** keep your work area tidy - it is only too easy to fall over articles left lying around.

✔ **Do** exercise caution when compressing springs for removal or installation. Ensure that the tension is applied and released in a controlled manner, using suitable tools which preclude the possibility of the spring escaping violently.

✔ **Do** ensure that any lifting tackle used has a safe working load rating adequate for the job.

✔ **Do** get someone to check periodically that all is well, when working alone on the vehicle.

✔ **Do** carry out work in a logical sequence and check that everything is correctly assembled and tightened afterwards.

✔ **Do** remember that your vehicle's safety affects that of yourself and others. If in doubt on any point, get professional advice.

● If in spite of following these precautions, you are unfortunate enough to injure yourself, seek medical attention as soon as possible.

OHV overhead valve single –
157FMI (air-cooled), 156MI-2B (liquid-cooled), 156FMI-B (air-cooled with balancer)

Developed from the Honda CG125 engine
Refer to Chapter 2A

AJS CR-3-125; **Baotian** BT125; **Bashan** Vixen 125; **Better** BT125; **Branson** BM125, BM125 Sport, BM125 Retro; **Chituma** CTM125-C; **CPI** SUV125, XR125; **Dayang/Dayun** DY125; **Feiying** FY125; **FYM** FY125; **Geely** JL125-2 Crusader; **Giantco** Warrior, Swift, Trooper, Bronco, Knight, Hunter; **Haotian** HT125-8 Vixen, HN125-4F; **Hartford** HD125L Legion, HD125S Super, VR125H, X, Z; **Hongdou** QLM125 Classic, HD125-GY2; **Honling** HL125-9; **Huoniao** HN125-4F, HN125-8; **Jialing** JH125 GY-3, JL125; **Jinlun** JL125-C, JL125-Y/XR; **Kaisar** KS125-23 (XTR), KS125-3 Destiny RX, KS125GY-3A; **Keeway** Speed 125, Superlight 125; **Kinlon** JL125 GY, JL125-7; **Kinroad** XT125GY Explorer, XT125-16 Cyclone, XT125-18 Typhoon, XT125-19; **Kymco** CK125; **Lexmoto** HT125-4F Arrow, KS125-23 XTR, HT125-8 Vixen, ZS125-30 Arizona, ZS125-50 Ranger; **Lifan** LF125GY, Apollo, LF125-J Mirage, LF125-14F King/Arizona/Heritage, LF125-30 Blazer/Sprint/Samurai, LF125GY-3A Grit, LF125-15, City X 125; **Loncin** JL125 GY-3; **Pioneer** XF125 L-4B Nevada/Torro, XF125-10V; **POR** Apache 125; **Romet** RM125, K125, Z125, ZK125; **Qingqi** QM125L-4B Renegade, QM125-10E Jet, QM125-10R Buffalo; **Sanya** SY125-11; **Shineray** XY125-10A, XY125 GY-5E; **Sinnis** Heist 125; **Sinski** XSJ125-6B; **Skygo** (see Lifan); **Skyjet** SJ125-3, SJ125-23; **Skyteam** ST125-Y, ST125 SM/TR, Cougar, ACE 125, Cobra 125, V-Raptor 125; **Sukida** SK125, SK125 GY; **Sumoto** SM125 GY; **Superbyke** SBS125, RCC 125, RBP125; **TMEC** MT125-1; **Venture** XT3 125; **Vulcan** Custom 125, Harrier 125; **Wangye** WY125-16C; **Warrior** Despatch 125; **Wuyang** WY125-16C; **Xgjao** XGJ125 GY-6, XGJ125-23; **Xingyue** XY125 GY; **Yamasaki** YM125-3; **Yuan** XGJ125-23 Renegade; **Zennco** YB125; **Zhongneng** ZN125-6, ZN125-8, ZN125-9; **ZongShen** ZS125 GY-A, ZS125 GY-10 Predator/Arktix, ZS125-24A, ZS125-30 Arizona/Dakota, ZS125-32, ZS125-50 Pursuit, ZS125-70; **ZY Motor** ZY125

OHC overhead cam single – K157FMI

Developed from the Suzuki GS125 engine
Refer to Chapter 2B

Dafier DFE125-8A; **Francis-Barnett** Kestrel; **HMC (Herald)** Classic 125; **Hyosung** RT125 Karion, RX125, XRX125 SM; **Keeway** TX125, RKS125, RKV125, Strike 125; **Kriedler** Enduro 125, Supermoto 125; **Lexmoto** DFE125-8A Street, Stockrider/Lowrider DFE125L, Adrenaline XFLM125 GY-2B; **Mash** Seventy-five Vintage; **Pioneer** XF125 GY-2B; **Pulse** XF125 GY-2B Adrenaline; **Qingqi** QM125-2F Ranger, QM125-2D, QM125-2C, QM125 GY-2D Tracker, QM125-2A; **SFM** ZZ125, ZX125, Roadster; **Sinnis** Trackstar, Stealth 125, Vista QM125-2C, Apache/Blade 125, Scrambler 125, Max II 125, Retrostar 125, Café 125; **Superbyke** RMX125, RMR125, RMZ125, RSR125; **Zennco** Bullet DFE125-8A

OHC overhead cam single – 154FMI

Developed from the Yamaha YBR125 engine
Refer to Chapter 2C

AJS JSM125, JS125 ECO-2 and JS125-6C Custom; **Honley** HD1, HD2, HD3; **Jianshe** JS125-6C; **Lexmoto** LSM125 (STR125YB), ZSF125; **Moto Roma** MRX125, SMX125; **Sinnis** JS125-6C, SC125, ST125, SP125; **WK** RT125

OHC overhead cam twin – 244FMI

Developed from the Honda CB125T engine
Refer to Chapter 2D

AJS Eos-125, Daytona, Regal Raptor DD125E, NAC12 (NKT); **Dadyw** DD125-E Regal Raptor; **Jialing** JH125-33; **Jinlun** JL125-13; JL125-11 Texan; **Sinnis** Cruisestar 125; **Superbyke** Ridgerider 125; **WK** Cruiser 125; **Znen** ZN125-6 Storm

The engines described on the previous page are developments of those fitted to Japanese models. The model specific manuals shown here are a source of additional information, although care should be taken when using data and settings.

Book No. 0433

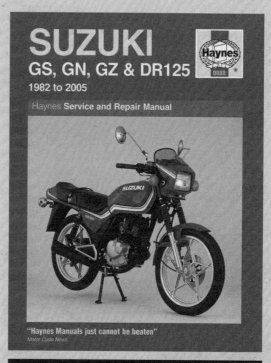

Book No. 0888

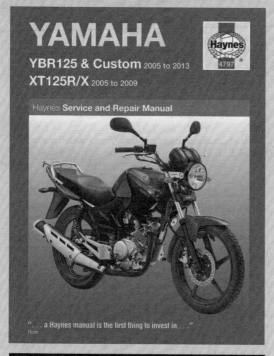

Book No. 4797

Book No. 0571

Engine oil level

Before you start:
✔ Start the engine and let it idle for 3 to 5 minutes.
Caution: Do not run the engine in an enclosed space such as a garage or workshop.
✔ Stop the engine and support the motorcycle upright on level ground. Allow it to stand for a few minutes for the oil level to stabilise.

The correct oil:
● Modern, high-revving engines place great demands on their oil. It is very important that the correct oil for your bike is used.
● Always top up with a good quality motorcycle oil of the specified type and viscosity and do not overfill the engine.
● Do not use engine oil designed for car use.

Oil type	API grade SG or SH
Oil viscosity	SAE 5W30, 10W30, 10W40 or 10W50

Caution: Do not use chemical additives or oils labelled 'ENERGY CONSERVING' – such additives or oils could cause clutch slip.

Bike care:
● If you have to add oil frequently, check the engine joints, oil seals and gaskets for oil leakage. If not, the engine could be burning oil, in which case there will be white smoke coming out of the exhaust (see *Fault Finding*).

Engines with an oil level dipstick

1 The oil level dipstick is incorporated with the oil filler cap on the right-hand side of the engine. Unscrew the cap . . .

2 . . . and wipe the dipstick clean.

3 Insert the dipstick so that the cap contacts the engine, but do not screw it in.

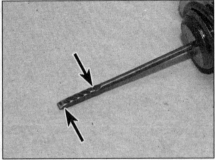

4 Remove the dipstick and check the oil mark - it should lie between the upper and lower level lines (arrowed) or within the hatched section, according to type.

5 If the level is on or below the lower line or below the hatched area, top up the engine with the recommended grade and type of oil to bring the level almost up to the upper line or to the top of the hatched area. Do not overfill. Fit the cap, making sure making sure the O-ring is in its groove and in good condition.

Engines with an oil level inspection window

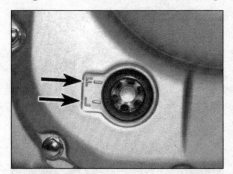

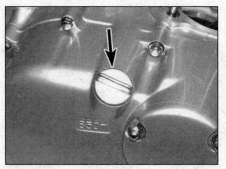

1 The oil level inspection window is located on the right-hand side of the engine. If necessary wipe the window so that it is clean. With the motorcycle vertical, the oil level should lie between the F (full) and L (low) lines (arrowed).

2 If the level is on or below the lower line, unscrew the oil filler cap (arrowed).

3 Top up the engine with the recommended grade and type of oil to bring the level almost up to the upper line on the inspection window. Do not overfill. Fit the filler cap, making sure the O-ring is in its groove and in good condition.

Coolant level (liquid-cooled engines)

⚠ *Warning: DO NOT remove the radiator pressure cap to add coolant. Topping up is done via the coolant reservoir tank filler. DO NOT leave open containers of coolant about, as it is poisonous.*

Before you start:

✔ Make sure you have a supply of coolant available (use either a pre-mixed coolant, or prepare a mix of 50% distilled water and 50% corrosion inhibited ethylene glycol anti-freeze).
✔ Always check the coolant level when the engine is cold.
✔ Support the motorcycle upright on level ground.

Bike care:

● It is important that anti-freeze is used in the system all year round, and not just in the winter. Do not top the system up using only water, as the system will become too diluted.
● Do not overfill the reservoir tank(s). If the coolant is significantly above the UPPER level line at any time, the surplus should be siphoned or drained off to prevent the possibility of it being expelled out of the overflow hose.
● If the coolant level falls steadily, check the system for leaks (see Chapter 1). If no leaks are found and the level continues to fall, it is recommended that the machine is taken to a dealer for a pressure test.

1 With the motorcycle vertical, the coolant level should lie between the upper and lower level lines marked on the reservoir.

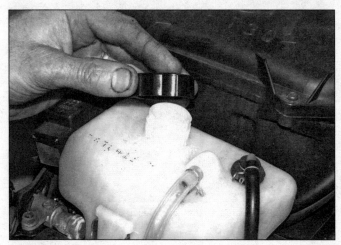

2 If the coolant level is on or below the LOWER line, remove the reservoir filler cap.

3 Top the reservoir up with the recommended coolant mixture to the UPPER level line, using a suitable funnel if required. Fit the cap.

Brake fluid level (disc brakes)

⚠️ **Warning: Brake hydraulic fluid can harm your eyes and damage painted surfaces, so use extreme caution when handling and pouring it and cover surrounding surfaces with rag. Do not use fluid that has been standing open for some time, as it is hygroscopic (absorbs moisture from the air) which can cause a dangerous loss of braking effectiveness.**

Before you start:

✔ The front brake fluid reservoir is on the right-hand handlebar.

✔ The rear brake fluid reservoir is between the seat and the swingarm on the right-hand side.

✔ Make sure you have the correct hydraulic fluid. DOT 4 is recommended.

✔ Wrap a rag around the reservoir to ensure that any spillage does not come into contact with painted surfaces.

Bike care:

● The fluid in the reservoir will drop very gradually as the brake pads wear down. If the reservoir requires repeated topping-up there is a leak somewhere in the system, which must be investigated immediately.

● Check for signs of fluid leakage from the hydraulic hose and/or brake system components – if found, rectify immediately (see Chapter 7).

● Check the operation of both brakes before taking the machine on the road; if there is evidence of air in the system (spongy feel to lever or pedal), it must be bled (see Chapter 7).

FRONT

1 Set the handlebars so the reservoir is level and check the fluid level through the window in the reservoir body – it must be above the LOWER level line (arrowed).

2 If the level is on or below the LOWER line, undo the two reservoir cover screws and remove the cover, diaphragm plate (where fitted), and diaphragm.

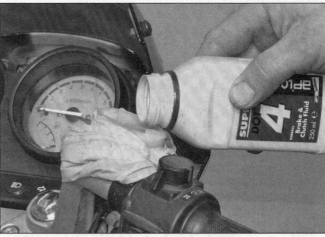

3 Top up with new clean DOT 4 hydraulic fluid. Do not overfill and take care to avoid spills (see Warning above).

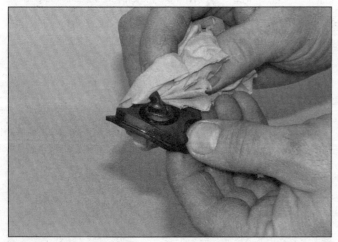

4 Wipe any moisture off the diaphragm with a tissue.

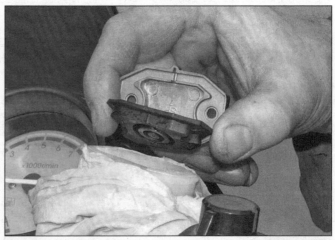

5 Ensure that the diaphragm is correctly seated before fitting the plate and cover. Secure the cover with its screws.

REAR

1 The rear brake fluid level is visible through the reservoir body – it must be between the UPPER and LOWER level lines (arrowed).

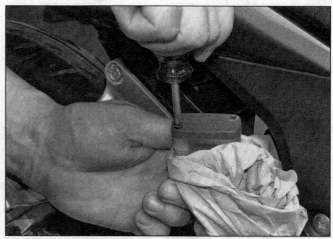

2 If the level is on or below the MIN line undo the reservoir cover screws and remove the cover, diaphragm plate and diaphragm – if necessary displace the reservoir to access them.

3 Top up with new clean DOT 4 hydraulic fluid, until the level is up to the MAX line. Do not overfill and take care to avoid spills (see **Warning** above).

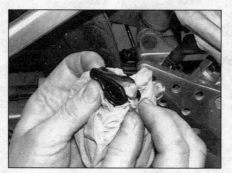

4 Wipe any moisture off the diaphragm with a tissue.

5 Ensure that the diaphragm is correctly seated before fitting the plate and cover. Secure the cover with its screws.

Suspension, steering and drive chain

Suspension and Steering:
● Check that the front and rear suspension operates smoothly without binding (see Chapter 1).
● Check that the steering moves smoothly from lock-to-lock.

Drive chain:
● Check that the chain isn't too loose or too tight, and adjust it if necessary (see Chapter 1).
● If the chain looks dry, lubricate it (see Chapter 1).

Legal and safety checks

Lighting and signalling:
● Take a minute to check that the headlight, tail light, brake light, licence plate light, instrument lights and turn signals all work correctly.
● Check that the horn sounds when the button is pressed.
● A working speedometer, graduated in mph, is a statutory requirement in the UK.

Safety:
● Check that the throttle grip rotates smoothly when opened and snaps shut when released, in all steering positions. Also check for the correct amount of freeplay (see Chapter 1).
● Check that the brake lever and pedal, clutch lever and gearchange lever operate smoothly. Lubricate them at the specified intervals or when necessary (see Chapter 1).
● Check that the engine shuts off when the kill switch is operated.

● Check that sidestand return springs hold the stand up securely when retracted.

Fuel:
● This may seem obvious, but check that you have enough fuel to complete your journey. If you notice signs of fuel leakage – rectify the cause immediately.
● Ensure you use the correct grade fuel – unleaded, minimum 91 RON.

Tyre checks

The correct pressures:

● The tyres must be checked when **cold**, not immediately after riding. Note that incorrect tyre pressures will cause abnormal tread wear and unsafe handling. Low tyre pressures may cause the tyre to slip on the rim or come off.

● Use an accurate pressure gauge. Many forecourt gauges are wildly inaccurate. If you buy your own, spend as much as you can justify on a quality gauge.

● Proper air pressure will increase tyre life and provide maximum stability and ride comfort – refer to your handbook, dealer or tyre manufacturer for the correct pressure for your bike and tyre.

Tyre care:

● Check the tyres carefully for cuts, tears, embedded nails or other sharp objects, and excessive wear. Riding a motorcycle with excessively worn tyres is extremely hazardous, as traction and handling are directly affected.

● Check the condition of the tyre valve and ensure the dust cap is in place. Also make sure the valve core is tight, especially if air pressure is lost – a special tool is needed for this, and some dust caps incorporate it (photo 4).

● Pick out any stones or nails which may have become embedded in the tyre tread. If left, they will eventually penetrate through the casing and cause a puncture.

● If tyre damage is apparent, or unexplained loss of pressure is experienced, seek the advice of a tyre fitting specialist without delay.

Tyre tread depth:

● At the time of writing UK law requires that tread depth must be at least 1 mm over 3/4 of the tread breadth all the way around the tyre, with no bald patches. Many riders, however, consider 2 mm tread depth minimum to be a safer limit. Refer to the tyre tread legislation in your country.

● Many tyres now incorporate wear indicators in the tread. Identify the location marking on the tyre sidewall to locate the indicator bar and replace the tyre if the tread has worn down to the bar.

1 Remove the dust cap from the valve and do not forget to fit it after checking the pressure.

2 Check the tyre pressures when the tyres are cold.

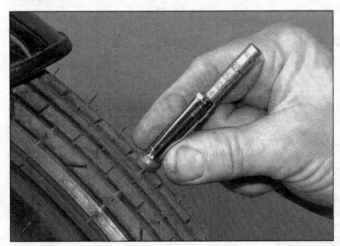

3 Measure tread depth at the centre of the tyre using a depth gauge.

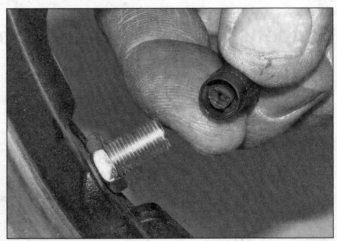

4 This dust cap incorporates the tool required for tightening the valve core.

Chapter 1
Routine maintenance and servicing

Contents

Degrees of difficulty

Easy, suitable for novice with little experience	**Fairly easy,** suitable for beginner with some experience	**Fairly difficult,** suitable for competent DIY mechanic	**Difficult,** suitable for experienced DIY mechanic	**Very difficult,** suitable for expert DIY or professional

Specifications

General torque settings according to thread size

5 mm bolt/nut	5 Nm
6 mm bolt/nut	10 Nm
8 mm bolt/nut	24 Nm
10 mm bolt/nut	35 Nm
12 mm bolt/nut	55 Nm

Note: *The intervals listed below are suggested as a guide for owners of machines with no handbook or service information provided by the manufacturer or dealer.*

Pre-ride

- [ ] See *'Pre-ride checks'* at the beginning of this manual for procedures.
- [ ] Check the coolant level (liquid-cooled engines only)
- [ ] Check the engine oil level
- [ ] Check the brake fluid level (models with disc brake(s))
- [ ] Check the tyre pressures, tread wear and condition
- [ ] Check that the machine is safe and legal to ride

Initial service from new

Note: *These two service intervals are performed once only, thereafter the machine is service according to the regular service schedule. Normally the initial service is performed by a dealer, but owners who have purchased the machine direct from the importer may like to carry out the initial service themselves.*

- [ ] After the first 300 miles (500 km) from new, change the engine oil and filter or clean the strainer (Section 14). Also check the tightness of all nuts, bolts and fasteners (Section 15) and check the drive chain tension (Section 1).
- [ ] After the first 600 miles (1000 km) from new, perform all the checks listed under the 'Every 3000 miles/5000 km heading below.

Every 300 miles (500 km)

- [ ] Check, adjust, clean and lubricate the drive chain (Section 1)

Every 3000 miles (5000 km)

Carry out all the items under the Pre-ride checks, plus the following:
- [ ] Check the spark plug (Section 2)
- [ ] Clean the air filter element and check the crankcase breather hose (Section 3)
- [ ] Check and adjust the valve clearances (Section 4)
- [ ] Check and adjust the engine idle speed (Section 5)
- [ ] Check the fuel system and hoses (Section 6)
- [ ] Check and adjust the throttle cable, and where fitted the choke cable (Section 7)
- [ ] Check the brake pads/shoes for wear (Section 8)
- [ ] Check the brake system and brake light switch operation (Section 8)
- [ ] Check and adjust the clutch cable freeplay (Section 9)
- [ ] Check the sidestand, centrestand where fitted, and starter interlock circuit (Section 10)
- [ ] Check the front and rear suspension (Section 11)

Every 3000 miles (5000 km) (continued)

- [ ] Check the condition of the wheels, wheel bearings and tyres (Section 12)
- [ ] Lubricate the clutch and brake levers, brake pedal, centrestand pivot (where fitted), sidestand pivot, and the throttle and choke cables (Section 13)
- [ ] Change the engine oil and filter or clean the strainer (Section 14)
- [ ] Check the tightness of all nuts, bolts and fasteners (Section 15)
- [ ] Check and adjust the steering head bearings (Section 16)
- [ ] Check the battery (Section 17)
- [ ] Check the cooling system on liquid-cooled models (Section 18)
- [ ] Check the air induction system where fitted (Section 19)

Every 6000 miles (10,000 km) or 12 months

Carry out all the items under the 3000 mile (5000 km) check, plus the following:
- [ ] Renew the spark plug(s) (Section 2)
- [ ] Fit a new air filter element (Section 3)
- [ ] Check the fuel strainer or filter (Section 6)

Every 12,000 miles (20,000 km)

Carry out all the items under the 6000 mile (10,000 km) check, plus the following:
- [ ] Re-grease the steering head bearings (Section 16)
- [ ] Re-grease the swingarm bushes (Section 11)

Every two years

- [ ] Change the brake fluid (Section 8)
- [ ] Change the coolant (liquid-cooled models) (Section 18)

Every four years

- [ ] Fit new brake hoses (Section 8)

Non-scheduled maintenance

- [ ] Fit new brake master cylinder and caliper seals (Section 8)
- [ ] Fit new fuel system hoses (Section 6)
- [ ] Change the front fork oil (Section 11)

1 This Chapter is designed to help the home mechanic maintain his/her motorcycle for safety, economy, long life and peak performance.

2 Deciding where to start or plug into the routine maintenance schedule depends on several factors. If your motorcycle has been maintained according to the warranty standards and has just come out of warranty, start routine maintenance as it coincides with the next mileage interval. If you have owned the machine for some time but have never performed any maintenance on it, start at the nearest interval and include some additional procedures to ensure that nothing important is overlooked. If you have just had a major engine overhaul, then start the maintenance routine from the beginning. If you have a used machine and have no knowledge of its history or maintenance record, combine all the checks into one large service initially and then settle into the specified maintenance schedule.

3 Before beginning any maintenance or repair, the machine should be cleaned thoroughly, especially around the oil filter/strainer and oil drain plug, valve cover, body panels, drive chain, suspension, wheels, etc. Cleaning will help ensure that dirt does not contaminate the engine and will allow you to detect wear and damage that could otherwise easily go unnoticed.

4 Certain maintenance information is sometimes printed on labels attached to the motorcycle. If the information on the labels differs from that included here, use the information on the label.

1 Drive chain and sprockets

Check chain slack

1 As the chain stretches with wear, adjustment will be necessary. A neglected drive chain won't last long and will quickly damage the sprockets. Routine chain adjustment and lubrication isn't difficult and will ensure maximum chain and sprocket life.

2 To check the chain, place the bike on its centrestand where fitted or on the sidestand if not. Make sure the transmission is in neutral. Make sure the ignition switch is OFF.

3 Push up on the bottom run of the chain and measure the slack midway between the two sprockets – there should be between 10 and 25 mm of slack (**see illustration**). Since the chain will rarely wear evenly, turn the rear wheel or push the bike forwards so that another section of chain can be checked – do this several times to check the entire length of chain, and mark the tightest spot.

Caution: Riding the bike with excess slack in the chain could lead to damage.

4 In some cases where lubrication has been neglected, corrosion and dirt may cause the links to bind and kink, which effectively shortens the chain's length and makes it tight (**see illustration**). Thoroughly clean and work free any such links, then highlight them with a marker pen or paint. Take the bike for a ride.

5 After the bike has been ridden, repeat the measurement for slack in the highlighted area. If the chain has kinked again and is still tight, replace it with a new one (see Chapter 7). A rusty, kinked or worn chain will damage the sprockets and can damage transmission bearings. If in any doubt as to the condition of a chain, it is far better to install a new one than risk damage to other components and possibly yourself.

6 Check the entire length of the chain for damaged rollers, loose links and pins, and on O-ring chains for missing O-rings, and replace it with a new one if necessary. **Note:** *It is good practise never to fit a new chain onto old sprockets, and never to use the old chain if you fit new sprockets – replace the chain and sprockets as a set.*

7 Inspect the drive chain slider on the front of the swingarm for excessive wear and damage and replace it with a new one if necessary.

Adjust chain slack

8 Set the tightest spot of the chain at the centre of its bottom run.

9 On drum brake models turn the rear brake freeplay adjuster nut anti-clockwise a few turns (**see illustration**). Where fitted slacken the nut on the brake torque arm bolt – there should be enough thread exposed between it and the split pin, but remove the pin if required, or if its ends are in the way (**see illustration**).

10 Where fitted remove the split pin from the end of the axle. Slacken the rear axle nut (**see illustration**).

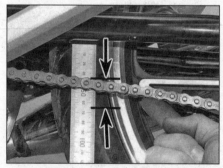

1.3 Push up on the chain and measure the slack

1.4 Neglect has caused the links in this chain to kink

1.9a Turn the nut (arrowed) a few turns anti-clockwise

1.9b Slacken the nut (A), removing the split pin (B) if required

1.10 Slacken the axle nut (arrowed)

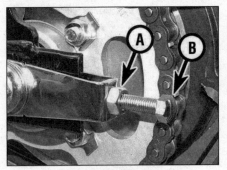

1.11a Type 1 - adjuster locknut (A), adjuster (B) . . .

1.11b . . . and alignment marker (C)

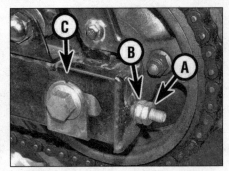

1.11c Type 2 - adjuster locknut (A), adjuster (B) and alignment marker (C)

11 Check the type of adjuster fitted to your model **(see illustrations)**. Slacken the locknut on each side of the swingarm and turn each adjuster evenly until the amount of freeplay specified in Step 3 is obtained at the centre of the bottom run of the chain.

12 Following adjustment, check that each chain adjustment marker is equally aligned with the index mark on each side of the swingarm. It is important the setting is the same on each side otherwise the rear wheel will be out of alignment with the front. Also make sure that the wheel is pushed fully forward in the swingarm slots. If there is a difference in the positions, adjust one of them so that its position is exactly the same as the other. Check the chain freeplay again and readjust if necessary.

13 When adjustment is complete, counter-hold the adjusters to prevent them turning and tighten the locknuts **(see**

1.15 Using a chain cleaning brush

illustration 1.11a or c)**. Tighten the axle nut. Recheck the adjustment as above, then make sure the wheel turns freely. Where removed fit the split pin into the axle, then bend its ends round – use a new one if necessary.

14 On drum brake models reset the rear brake adjuster (see Section 8, Step 19). Where fitted tighten the brake torque arm nut, then if removed fit a new split pin through the hole in the end of the bolt and bend its ends round **(see illustration 1.9b)**.

Clean and lubricate the chain

15 If required, wash the chain using a dedicated aerosol cleaner, or in paraffin (kerosene) or a suitable non-flammable or high flash-point solvent, using a soft brush to work any dirt out if necessary – specially shaped chain cleaning brushes are available from good suppliers **(see illustration)**. Wipe the cleaner off the chain and allow it to dry. If the chain is excessively dirty remove it from the machine and allow it to soak in the paraffin or solvent (see Chapter 7).

16 The best time to lubricate the chain is after the motorcycle has been ridden – when the chain is warm, the lubricant will penetrate the joints between the side plates better than when cold. Lubricate the chain with engine oil or a dedicated chain lube. If your bike has an O-ring chain note that the solvents used in some aerosol lubricants could damage the chain's sealing rings, so make sure you use a suitable one. Apply the lubricant to the area where the sideplates overlap – not the middle of the rollers **(see illustration)**.

> **HAYNES HiNT** *Apply the lubricant to the top of the lower chain run, so centrifugal force will work the oil into the chain when the bike is moving. After applying the lubricant, let it soak in a few minutes before wiping off any excess.*

> ⚠️ *Warning: Take care not to get any lubricant on the tyre or brake system components. If any of the lubricant inadvertently contacts them, clean it off thoroughly using a suitable solvent or dedicated brake cleaner before riding the machine.*

Check sprocket wear

17 Remove the front sprocket cover (see Chapter 7). Check the teeth on the front sprocket and the rear sprocket for wear **(see illustration)**. If the sprocket teeth are worn excessively, replace the chain and both sprockets with a new set. Check that the sprocket fasteners are tight.

2 Spark plug(s)

1 Make sure your spark plug socket is the correct size – a suitable one may be supplied if the bike comes with is a tool kit. Remove any body panels as required according to model for access to the spark plug (see Chapter 8). Where fitted, and if it restricts removal of the spark plug cap, undo the side trim cover screws and remove the cover **(see illustration)**.

1.16 Apply the lubricant to the overlapping sections of the sideplates

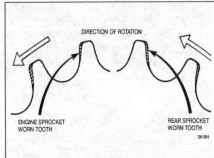

DIRECTION OF ROTATION

ENGINE SPROCKET WORN TOOTH

REAR SPROCKET WORN TOOTH

0618H

1.17 Check the sprockets in the areas indicated

2.1 Undo the screws (arrowed) and remove the trim cover

2.2 Pull the cap off the spark plug

2.4 Unscrew and remove the plug

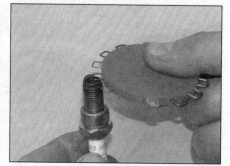

2.6a Using a wire type gauge to measure the spark plug electrode gap

2.6b Adjusting the gap using the fitting provided on the tool

2.9 Thread the plug into the head by hand to prevent cross-threading

2 Pull the cap off the spark plug (**see illustration**).
3 Clean the area around the base of the spark plug to prevent any dirt falling into the engine.
4 Using either the plug removing tool supplied in the bike's toolkit or a deep spark plug socket, unscrew and remove the plug from the cylinder head (**see illustration**).
5 Check the condition of the electrodes, referring to the spark plug reading chart at the end of this manual if signs of contamination are evident.
6 Clean the plug with a wire brush. Examine the tips of the electrodes – if a tip has rounded off, the plug is worn. Measure the gap between the two electrodes using a feeler gauge or a wire type gauge (**see illustration**). The gap should be as given in the Specifications section for

your model or as specified in your handbook if supplied, or around 0.7 mm if no specification can be found. If necessary adjust the gap by bending the side electrode (**see illustration**).
7 Check the threads, the washer and the ceramic insulator body for cracks and other damage.
8 If the plug is worn or damaged, or if any deposits cannot be cleaned off, replace the plug with a new one. If in any doubt as to the condition of the plug replace it with a new one – the expense is minimal.
9 Thread the plug into the cylinder head until the washer seats (**see illustration**). Since the cylinder head is made of aluminium, which is soft and easily damaged, thread the plug as far as possible by hand. Once the plug is finger-tight, the job can be finished with a

spanner on the tool supplied or a socket drive (**see illustration 2.4**). If a new plug is being installed, tighten it by 1/2 a turn after the washer has seated. If the old plug is being reused, tighten it by 1/4 turn after the washer has seated. Otherwise tighten it according to the instructions on the box. Do not over-tighten it.
10 Fit the spark plug cap, making sure it locates correctly onto the plug (**see illustration 2.2**). Install any removed body panels.

> **HAYNES HiNT** *Stripped plug threads in the cylinder head can be repaired with a Heli-Coil insert – see 'Tools and Workshop Tips' in the Reference section.*

3 Air filter

Caution: If the machine is continually ridden in wet or dusty conditions, the filter should be cleaned more frequently.
1 Access the air filter housing by removing the appropriate side panel, the seat, or the fuel tank (see Chapter 4), as required according to model.
2 Remove the air filter cover (**see illustrations**).

3.2a Air filter cover screws (arrowed) – typical example

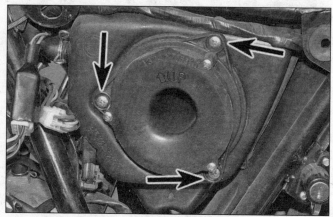

3.2b On this example undo the larger inner screws (arrowed), and note the UP mark

3.3a On this type the sponge element is in a plastic cage – remove the cage to clean the element

3.3b On this type the sponge element fits around the air intake

3.3c This type has a paper element in a cage

3 Remove the filter element **(see illustrations)**. Check it for damage and replace it with a new one if necessary.

4 On models with a sponge element **(see illustrations 3.3a and b)**, soak the element in solvent suitable for foam filters, then squeeze it dry – do not wring it out as it will be damaged. Allow the sponge to dry. Apply engine oil to the entire surface of the element, then squeeze out any excess – the element should be coated with oil but not dripping.

 Warning: Only using a high flash-point cleaning solvent to clean a sponge element. DO NOT use petrol or any other flammable liquid.

5 On models with a paper element **(see illustration 3.3c)** tap it on a hard surface to dislodge any dirt, then use compressed air to blow through it, directing the air in the opposite direction of normal flow **(see illustration)**.

6 Make sure any cover seal is properly seated. Fit the element into the housing **(see illustrations 3.3c, b and a)**. Fit the cover **(see illustrations 3.2b and a)**.

7 Install the side panel, fuel tank or seat as required.

8 Every so often remove the element and replace it with a new one whatever its apparent condition – the frequency of change will depend on amount of use and on climate and riding conditions – if the bike is constantly ridden in dusty or wet conditions the filter will need replacing more often than on bikes ridden only in clear conditions.

9 Check for a filter housing drain tube or collector, probably on the underside – if there is a tube that has a plug in it remove it and drain the tube, and if there is a collector which looks full remove, drain and clean it.

10 Check the crankcase breather hose between the engine and the air filter housing for signs of cracks, hardening and deformation, and replace it with a new one if necessary **(see illustration)**. Detach the hose from the engine and check that it is not full of emulsified oil – if it is, detach the hose at each end and clean it out.

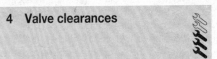

4 Valve clearances

Special tool: *A set of feeler gauges is necessary for this job* **(see illustration 4.6)**.

1 The engine must be completely cool for this maintenance procedure, so let the bike stand overnight before beginning.

2 Remove the spark plug(s) (see Section 2).

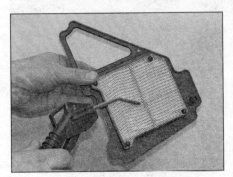

3.5 Using compressed air to clean a paper element

3 Where fitted unscrew the valve clearance adjuster access caps from the front and back of the cylinder head **(see illustration)**. Discard the O-rings – new ones should be used. Otherwise remove the valve cover (see Chapter 2).

4 The clearance for each valve can be measured when the valve is closed. To open and close the valves the engine must be turned. To turn the engine, place the motorcycle on the centrestand so that the rear wheel is off the ground, select a high gear, and rotate the rear wheel by hand in its normal direction of rotation while you watch the action of the rockers on the valves.

3.10 The crankcase breather hose (arrowed) is generally on top of the crankcase behind the cylinder

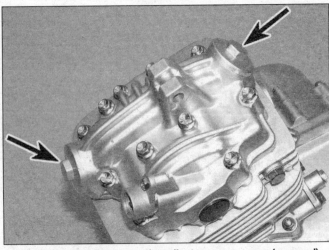

4.3 Where fitted unscrew the adjuster access caps (arrowed)

5 Turn the rear wheel until the end of the rocker above the valve being checked is at its highest point and the valve is closed – you should be able to feel some freeplay between them by moving the rocker with your fingers **(see illustration)**.

6 Insert a feeler gauge of the same thickness as the correct valve clearance (see below) in the gap between the rocker arm and the valve stem **(see illustrations)**. The intake valve(s) is/are on the back of the cylinder head and the exhaust valve(s) is/are on the front. The gauge should be a firm sliding fit – you should feel a slight drag when you pull the gauge out.

7 If the gap (clearance) is either too wide or too narrow, slacken the locknut on the adjuster in the rocker arm **(see illustration)**. Turn the adjuster as required using a screwdriver if the adjuster is slotted, or a very small spanner or a pair of pliers if not, until the gap is correct and the feeler gauge is a sliding fit. Hold the adjuster still and tighten the locknut. Recheck the clearance after tightening the locknut.

8 When all clearances are correct, either fit the access caps **(see illustration)**, or install the valve cover (see Chapter 2).

9 Install the spark plug(s) (Section 2). Check and adjust the idle speed (see Section 5).

Valve clearances

In the absence of valve clearance settings being provided in the owner's manual:

● *For OHV single cylinder engines and OHC twin cylinder engines, set the clearance for intake and exhaust valves to 0.08 mm.*

● *For OHC single cylinder engines, set the clearance for the intake valve to 0.08 mm and the exhaust valve to 0.15 mm.*

5 Idle speed

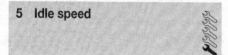

1 The idle speed should be around 1400 to 1500 rpm. It should be obvious if it is either too high or too low, especially if there is any sudden change (in which case the cause must be rectified). Make sure the spark plug(s) is/are in good condition (Section 2) and the air filter is clean (Section 3) before any adjustment is made.

5.3a Screw type idle speed adjuster (arrowed)

4.5 When the valve is closed you should feel freeplay in the rocker

4.7 Slacken the locknut and turn the adjuster with the gauge in place using a screwdriver or pliers until the gap is correct, then hold the adjuster while tightening the locknut

2 The engine should be at normal operating temperature, which is usually reached after 10 to 15 minutes of stop-and-go riding. Make sure the transmission is in neutral.

3 The idle speed adjuster is either a screw located on the side of the carburettor, or a knurled knob extending from it **(see illustrations)**. With the engine running, turn the screw until the engine idles at the speed specified in Step 1. Turn the screw clockwise to increase idle speed, and anti-clockwise to decrease it.

4 Snap the throttle open and shut a few times, then recheck the idle speed. If necessary, repeat the adjustment procedure. On completion check and adjust throttle cable freeplay (Section 7).

5 If a smooth, steady idle can't be achieved,

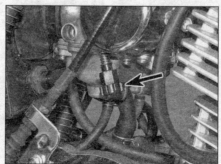

5.3b Knob type idle speed adjuster (arrowed)

4.6 Insert the feeler gauge between the base of the adjuster on the arm and the top of the valve stem as shown

4.8 On models with access caps make sure the O-rings (arrowed) are fitted, and smear them with grease

if not already done check the spark plug(s), air filter element and valve clearances (Sections 2, 3 and 4).

6 If that does not solve the problem check and adjust the pilot screw setting (Chapter 4). If the problem persists, there could be an air leak in the intake duct between the carburettor and the cylinder head, or a problem within the carburettor itself – refer to Fault Finding at the end of the book, and to Chapter 4.

6 Fuel system

Warning: Petrol (gasoline) is extremely flammable, so take extra precautions when you work on any part of the fuel system. Don't smoke or allow open flames or bare light bulbs near the work area, and don't work in a garage where a natural gas-type appliance is present. If you spill any fuel on your skin, rinse it off immediately with soap and water. When you perform any kind of work on the fuel system, wear safety glasses and have a fire extinguisher suitable for a Class B type fire (flammable liquids) on hand.

1 Remove the fuel tank (see Chapter 4). Check all the hoses from the fuel tank, the carburettor(s) and the air filter housing for signs of cracks, leaks, deterioration or damage. In particular check that there are no leaks from

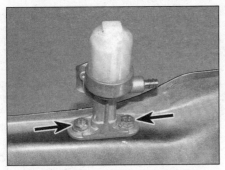

6.2a Make sure the fuel tap bolts (arrowed) . . .

6.2b . . . or nut (arrowed) . . .

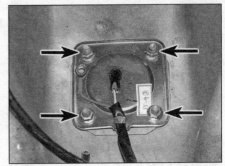

6.2c . . . and where fitted the level sensor nuts or bolts (arrowed) are tight

the fuel hose or hose unions. Make sure each hose is secure on its union at each end and retained by a clamp. Replace any hose that is cracked or deteriorated with a new one – refer to Chapter 4 if required.

2 Check the fuel tank for signs of fuel leakage. If the joint between the fuel tap and the tank, or where fitted between the fuel level sensor and the tank, is leaking, make sure the bolts or nut(s) are tight **(see illustrations)**. If the leak persists remove the tap or sensor and fit a new seal (see Chapter 4).

3 Inspect the carburettor, particularly around the float chamber on the bottom, for signs of leakage. If there are any leaks, remove the carburettor and fit new seals (see Chapter 4).

4 Check the fuel tap itself for leaks, and tighten any fasteners that are apparent.

5 If the tap has a bowl on its base there is probably a filter or strainer inside it **(see illustrations)**. Make sure the fuel tap is OFF, then unscrew the bowl. Drain any residual fuel. Check the condition of the filter or strainer and replace it with a new one if necessary.

6 Some models have a filter connected in the fuel hose between the tap and the carburettor, which should be replaced with a new one from time to time, and particularly if it looks dirty or if fuel starvation is suspected. Make sure the

fuel tap is OFF, then detach the hoses from the filter and remove it. The new filter should have an arrow on it that indicates the direction of fuel flow – fit the filter with the arrow pointing to the carburettor, not the tap, and make sure the hoses are secure.

7 Cleaning of the fuel strainer inside the tank is also advised after a particularly high mileage has been covered, and if fuel starvation is suspected and the filter is good. Remove the fuel tap from the tank to access the strainer (see Chapter 4). Flush the strainer through. Check the gauze for damage and replace it with a new one if necessary.

7 Throttle and choke cables

Throttle cable

1 With the engine off, make sure the throttle grip rotates smoothly and freely from fully closed to fully open with the front wheel turned at various angles. The grip should return automatically from fully open to fully closed when released.

2 If the throttle sticks, this is probably due to a cable fault. Remove the cable (see Chapter 4) and lubricate it (see Section 13). Check that the inner cable slides freely and easily in the outer cable. If not, replace the cable with a new one.

3 With the cable removed, make sure the throttle twistgrip rotates freely on the handlebar – dirt combined with a lack of lubrication can cause the action to be stiff. If necessary, where fitted remove the handlebar end-weight, then on all models slide the twistgrip off the handlebar. Clean any old grease from the bar and the inside of the tube. Smear fresh grease onto the bar, then refit the twistgrip, and the end-weight where removed. Install the cable, making sure it is correctly routed (see Chapter 4). If this fails to improve the operation of the throttle, the cable must be replaced with a new one. Note that in very rare cases the fault could lie in the carburettor (see Chapter 4).

4 With the throttle operating smoothly, and after the idle speed has been checked and if necessary adjusted (Section 5), check for a small amount of freeplay in the cable, measured in terms of the amount of twistgrip rotation before the throttle opens – there should be about 2 to 6 mm of free rotation

6.5a This tap has a filter (arrowed) threaded onto the base of the tap

6.5b This tap has a bowl (arrowed) with a strainer inside

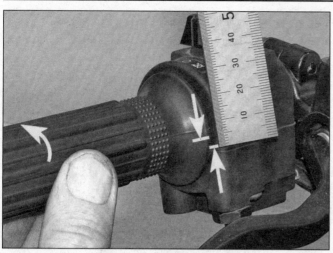

7.4 Throttle cable freeplay is measured in terms of twistgrip rotation

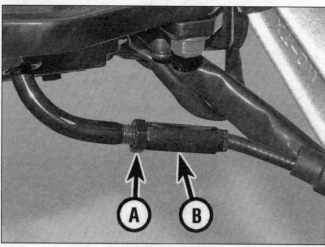

7.5a Adjuster locknut (A) and adjuster (B)

(see illustration). If it's incorrect, adjust the cable to correct it as follows.

5 Adjust freeplay using the adjuster in the throttle cable where it leaves the throttle/switch housing on the handlebar. Where fitted slide the rubber boot off the adjuster. Loosen the locknut and turn the adjuster in or out as required until the specified amount of freeplay is obtained **(see illustration)**, then retighten the locknut and if necessary fit the boot. If the adjuster has reached its limit check for a second adjuster at the carburettor end of the cable **(see illustration)** – if there is one, reset the handlebar end adjuster by threading it fully in (giving maximum freeplay), then adjust the cable at the carburettor end. Subsequent adjustment can now be made at the handlebar end. If there is no second adjuster replace the cable with a new one (see Chapter 4).

6 If the cable cannot be adjusted as specified, replace it with a new one (see Chapter 4). Check that the throttle twistgrip operates smoothly and snaps shut quickly when released.

⚠️ *Warning: Turn the handlebars all the way through their travel with the engine idling. Idle speed should not change. If it does, the cable may be routed incorrectly. Correct this condition before riding the bike.*

Choke

7 With the engine off, make sure the choke lever moves smoothly and freely.

8 If it is stiff or stuck, on models with a handlebar mounted lever that connects using a cable, this is probably due to a cable fault. Remove the cable (see Chapter 4) and lubricate it (see Section 13). Check that the inner cable slides freely and easily in the outer cable. If not, replace the cable with a new one. If the choke is still stiff or stuck with a new or lubricated cable, the fault is in the plunger in the carburettor. Remove the plunger for inspection (see Chapter 4).

9 Check for a small amount of freeplay in the lever before the cable opens the choke. If there is

none the choke could be permanently open, and if there is too much the choke might not open enough to be effective. Where fitted locate and loosen the cable adjuster locknut, and turn the adjuster in or out as required until there is a small amount of freeplay, then retighten the locknut **(see illustration 7.5a)**. If the cable does not have an adjuster loosen the cable holder screw and make sure the cable is set correctly in its holder, then retighten the holder screw **(see illustration)**.

10 If the choke is stiff or stuck on models with a lever mounted directly on the carburettor, remove it for inspection (see Chapter 4).

8 Brake system

1 A routine general check of the brake system will ensure that any problems are discovered and remedied before the rider's safety is jeopardised.

7.5b With this type of carburettor use the adjuster (arrowed) to set freeplay, in the opening cable on twin cable models (there should no freeplay in the closing cable)

7.9 Make sure the choke cable is set correctly in the holder (arrowed)

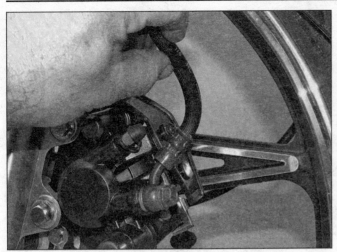

8.4 Twist and flex the hoses to check for cracks and deterioration

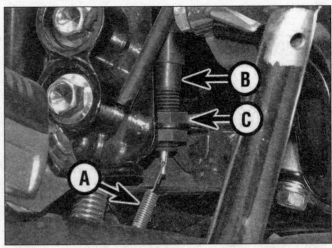

8.6 Make sure the spring (A) is attached and in good condition. To adjust the switch hold the body (B) and turn the adjuster ring (C) as required

Disc brakes

Brake system check

2 Make sure all brake component fasteners are tight. Check the brake lever (front) and pedal (rear) for improper or rough action, excessive play, bends, and other damage. Replace any damaged parts with new ones (see Chapter 7). Clean and lubricate the lever and pedal pivots if their action is stiff or rough (see Section 13).

3 Check the brake pads for wear (see Steps 8 and 9).

4 Make sure the fluid level in the reservoir is correct (see *Pre-ride checks*). Look for leaks at the hose connections and check for cracks in the hoses and unions **(see illustration)**. If the lever or pedal is spongy, bleed the brake (see Chapter 7).

5 Make sure the brake light works using both the front brake lever and the rear brake pedal. The light should come on after some of the freeplay in the lever or pedal is taken up but before the brake comes on. If the light doesn't come on at all first check the bulb, its holder and the wiring and connectors, and if they are good next check the switch (see Chapter 9).

6 If the rear brake light works but comes on too soon or is permanently on, or comes on or too late or not at all (and the bulb etc are good), the switch may need adjusting. Before making any adjustment check that the spring between the brake pedal and the switch is connected at each end and is not distorted or stretched **(see illustration)**. If adjustment is necessary, hold the switch and turn the adjuster ring on the switch body until the brake light is activated when required. If the brake light comes on too late or not at all, turn the ring clockwise (when looked at from the top) so the switch threads out of the bracket. If the brake light comes on too soon or is permanently on, turn the ring anti-clockwise so the switch threads into the bracket.

7 The 'at rest' position of the rear brake pedal in relation to the footrest should be set so the rear brake can be applied without excessive movement of the foot. To adjust the height slacken the clevis locknut on the master cylinder pushrod, then turn the pushrod using a spanner on the hex at the top of the rod until the pedal is at the desired height **(see illustration)**. On completion tighten the locknut.

Brake pad wear check

8 Visually check the amount of friction material remaining on each pad – there must be a minimum of 1 mm or the friction material must not be worn down level with the base of the wear limit groove **(see illustrations)**. Replace the pads with new ones when they are worn (see Chapter 6). On twin piston calipers also check that the pads are wearing evenly – uneven wear is indicative of a sticking piston, in which case the caliper should be overhauled (see Chapter 7).

9 If the pads are dirty or if you are in doubt as to the amount of friction material remaining, remove them for inspection (see Chapter 7). If the pads are excessively worn, check the brake discs (see Chapter 7).

Brake fluid change

10 The brake fluid should be changed every two years or whenever a master cylinder or caliper overhaul is carried out. Refer to Chapter 7 for details. Ensure that all the old fluid is pumped from the hydraulic system and that the level in the fluid reservoir is checked and the brakes tested before riding the motorcycle.

Brake hose

11 The hose will deteriorate with age and should be renewed regardless of its apparent condition (see Chapter 7).

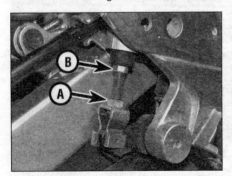

8.7 Loosen the locknut (A) and turn the hex (B) to adjust pedal height

8.8a Check the amount of friction material (arrowed) from the best vantage point

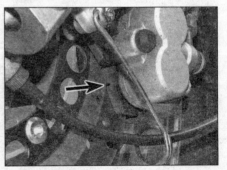

8.8b Most pads have a groove that serves as a wear indicator – the pad is worn when the groove is no longer visible

8.18a On Custom style models with a forward set pedal the switch (arrowed) is horizontal . . . .

8.18b . . . and a cable (arrowed) links the end of the spring to the pedal . . .

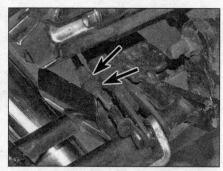

8.18c . . . with a provision for adjustment using the nuts (arrowed) that hold it in the bracket

12 Always replace the banjo union sealing washers with new ones when fitting a new hose. Refill the system with new brake fluid and bleed the system as described in Chapter 7.

Brake caliper and master cylinder seals

13 Brake system seals will deteriorate over a period of time and lose their effectiveness, leading to sticky operation of the brake master cylinder or the caliper, or fluid loss. Although seal replacement is not subject to a specific time or mileage interval, it is advised after a high mileage has been covered and particularly if fluid leakage or a sticking caliper action is apparent (see Chapter 7).

Drum brakes

Brake system check

14 Make sure all brake component fasteners are tight. Check the brake lever and pedal for improper or rough action, excessive play, bends, and other damage. Replace any damaged parts with new ones (see Chapter 7). Clean and lubricate the lever and pedal pivots if their action is stiff or rough (see Section 13). On models fitted with a cable linking the pedal to the drum instead of a rod make sure it is in good condition and lubricate it as well.
15 Check the brake shoes for wear (see Steps 21 and 22).
16 Make sure the cable or rod linking the lever or pedal to the drum is secure at each end, correctly adjusted (see below), and that there are no signs of fraying of cable ends.
17 Make sure the brake light works using both the front brake lever and the rear brake pedal. The light should come on after some of the freeplay in the lever or pedal is taken up but before the brake comes on. If the light doesn't come on at all first check the bulb, its holder and the wiring and connectors, and if they are good next check the switch (see Chapter 9).
18 If the rear brake light works but comes on too soon or is permanently on, or comes on or too late or not at all (and the bulb etc are good), the switch may need adjusting. Before making any adjustment check that the spring between the brake pedal and the switch is connected at each end and is not distorted or stretched **(see illustration 8.6)**. If adjustment is necessary,

hold the switch and turn the adjuster ring on the switch body until the brake light is activated when required. If the brake light comes on too late or not at all, turn the ring clockwise (when looked at from the top) so the switch threads out of the bracket. If the brake light comes on too soon or is permanently on, turn the ring anti-clockwise so the switch threads into the bracket **(see illustration)**. On Custom-style models with a footboard and forward set controls there is a cable between the spring and the pedal, and this may require adjustment or attention if the brake light cannot be made to function correctly as described above **(see illustration)**. First check that the cable is not loose or detached at either end, seized, or broken. If necessary remove the cable and either lubricate it (see Section 13) or replace it with a new one (see Chapter 7). If there is excessive freeplay in the cable adjust it using

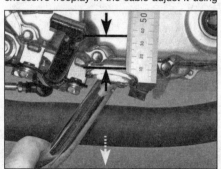

8.19a Measuring the amount of brake pedal freeplay

8.19c Cable operated drums have adjuster nuts (arrowed) at the pedal . . .

the nuts at the pedal end of the cable **(see illustration)**.
19 Check the amount of freeplay in the brake lever or pedal before the brake comes on – there should be about 10 to 20 mm free travel at the ball end of the front brake lever **(see illustration 9.3)** and 20 to 30 mm free travel in the toe of the brake pedal **(see illustration)**. If necessary adjust the free travel by turning the adjuster nut at the drum end of the brake cable or rod as required until the freeplay is correct **(see illustration)**. On models fitted with a cable linking the pedal to the drum instead of a rod the cable will have adjusters at each end, which will affect freeplay and need adjustment from time to time as well **(see illustrations)**. Now refer to Step 22 and check the amount of brake shoe wear. After adjustment check that there is no brake drag, then adjust the rear brake light switch (Step 18).

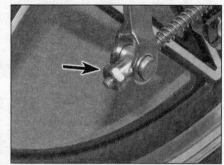

8.19b Adjust freeplay by turning the adjuster nut (arrowed)

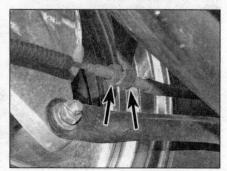

8.19d . . . and at the drum

8.20a Rear brake pedal position adjuster (arrowed) – conventional style pedal

8.20b Rear brake pedal position adjuster (arrowed) – Custom style pedal

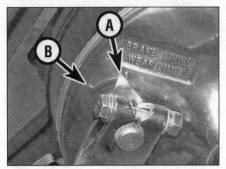

8.22 Brake shoe wear indicator (A) and limit line (B)

20 The 'at rest' position of the rear brake pedal in relation to the footrest or board should be set so that the rear brake can be applied without excessive movement of the foot. To adjust the height slacken the locknut on the stopper bolt, then turn the bolt until the pedal is in the desired position **(see illustrations)**. On completion tighten the locknut.

Brake shoe wear check

21 Make sure the amount of brake lever or pedal freeplay is correct (Step 19).
22 Apply the brake and check the position of the wear indicator on the brake arm in relation to the wear limit line on the brake plate **(see illustration)**. If the indicator has reached the limit line replace the brake shoes with new ones (see Chapter 7). With the shoes removed check the drum as described.

9 Clutch

1 Check that the clutch lever operates smoothly and easily.
2 If the clutch lever operation is heavy or stiff, remove the cable (see Chapter 2) and lubricate it (see Section 13). If the cable is still stiff, replace it with a new one. Install the lubricated or new cable (see Chapter 2).
3 With the cable operating smoothly,

check that it is correctly adjusted. Periodic adjustment is necessary to compensate for wear in the clutch plates and stretch of the cable. Check that there is 10 to 20 mm of free travel at the ball end of the clutch lever before the cable tensions and starts to disengage the clutch **(see illustration)**.
4 If adjustment is required, locate the adjusters – there is one where the cable goes into the lever bracket on the handlebar, and this is the first point of adjustment (Step 5). Trace the cable down to the engine to locate the lower adjuster, which will either be mid-way down the cable (Step 7) or at the cable fitting on the engine (Step 8).
5 At the lever bracket, where fitted pull the rubber boot off the adjuster. Loosen the adjuster lockring, then turn the adjuster in or out until the required amount of freeplay is obtained **(see illustration)**. To increase freeplay, thread the adjuster into the lever bracket. To reduce freeplay, thread the adjuster out of the bracket. Tighten the lockring on completion. Make sure that the slot in the

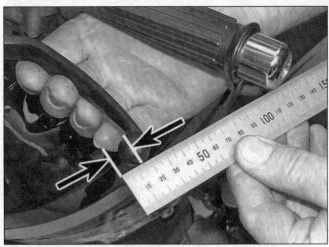

9.3 Measure the amount of freeplay at the clutch lever end as shown

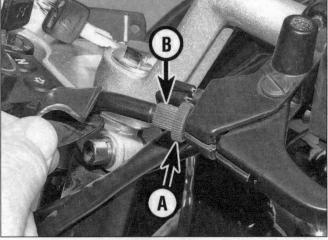

9.5 Slacken the lockring (A) and turn the handlebar adjuster (B) in or out as required

9.7 Slacken the locknut (A) and turn the in-line adjuster (B) in or out as required

9.8a Cable adjuster locknuts – OHV engine

adjuster and the lockring, are not aligned with the slot in the lever bracket – these slots are to allow removal of the cable, and if they are all aligned while the bike is in use the cable could jump out. Also make sure the adjuster is not threaded too far out of the bracket so that it is only held by a few threads – this will leave it unstable and the threads could be damaged. Tighten the lockring on completion, then where fitted relocate the rubber boot.

6 If all the adjustment has been taken up at the lever, thread the adjuster all the way in to give the maximum amount of freeplay, then back it out one turn – this resets the adjuster to its start point. Now set the correct amount of freeplay using the second adjuster (Step 7 or 8, depending on type).

7 On OHC engines with the adjuster in the cable, pull the boot back where fitted. Loosen the adjuster locknut, then turn the adjuster in or out until the required amount of freeplay is obtained **(see illustration)**. To increase freeplay, thread the adjuster towards

the locknut. To reduce freeplay, thread the adjuster away from the locknut. Make sure the adjuster is not threaded too far out so that it is only held by a few threads. Tighten the locknut on completion, then where fitted relocate the rubber boot.

8 On OHV and Twin engines slacken the locknuts, then reset the cable in the bracket as required until the freeplay at the lever end is as specified **(see illustrations)**. Tighten the locknuts on completion.

10 Sidestand, centrestand and starter safety circuit

1 Check the stand springs for damage and distortion **(see illustration)**. The springs must be capable of retracting the stand fully and holding it retracted when the motorcycle is in use. If a spring is sagged or broken it must be replaced with a new one.

2 Lubricate the stand pivot regularly (see Section 13).

3 Check the stands mounts for bends and cracks. Stands can often be repaired by welding.

4 On some models, the starter safety circuit comprises the neutral switch and the clutch switch, and prevents the engine from being started unless it is in neutral, or if it is in gear unless the clutch lever is pulled in. Check the circuit is working correctly.

5 On other models the starter safety circuit comprises the neutral switch, the clutch switch and the sidestand switch, and prevents the engine from being started unless it is in neutral, or if it is in gear unless the clutch lever is pulled in and the sidestand is up. Check the circuit is working correctly.

6 If the circuit does not operate as described, check the neutral switch, the clutch switch, the sidestand switch where fitted, the circuit diode, and the wiring between them (see Chapter 9).

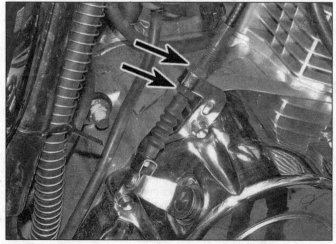

9.8b Cable adjuster locknuts – Twin engine

10.1 Check the stand springs

11.2 Compress and release the front suspension

11.8 Checking for play in the swingarm bushes

11.9 Checking for play in the rear shock mountings

11 Suspension

1 The suspension components must be maintained in top operating condition to ensure rider safety. Loose, worn or damaged suspension parts decrease the motorcycle's stability and control.

Front suspension check

2 While standing alongside the motorcycle, apply the front brake and push on the handlebars to compress the forks several times **(see illustration)**. See if they move up-and-down smoothly without binding. If binding is felt, the forks should be disassembled and inspected (see Chapter 6).
3 Where fitted, lift the fork gaiter. Inspect the fork inner tubes for scratches, corrosion and pitting which will cause premature seal failure – if the damage is excessive, new tubes should be fitted (see Chapter 6).
4 Inspect the area above the dust seal for signs of oil leakage, then carefully lever the seal up using a flat-bladed screwdriver and inspect the area around the fork seal. If leakage is evident, the seals must be replaced with new ones (see Chapter 6). If there is evidence of corrosion between the seal retaining ring and its groove in the fork outer tube spray the area with a penetrative lubricant, otherwise the ring will be difficult to remove if needed. Press the dust seal back into the top of the fork outer tube on completion.
5 Check the tightness of the fork clamp bolts in the yokes, and the fork top bolts, to be sure none have worked loose.

Rear suspension check

6 Inspect the rear shock absorber(s) for fluid leakage and tightness of the mountings. If leakage is found, the shock must be replaced with a new one (see Chapter 6).
7 With the aid of an assistant to support the bike, compress the rear suspension several times. It should move up-and-down freely without binding. If any binding is felt, the worn or faulty component must be identified and checked (see Chapter 6). The problem could

be due to either the shock absorber(s) or the swingarm pivot.
8 Support the motorcycle on an auxiliary stand so that the rear wheel is off the ground. Grab the swingarm and rock it from side-to-side – there should be no discernible movement at the rear **(see illustration)**. If there's movement or a slight clicking can be heard, check the swingarm and shock absorber mounting bolts and nuts are tight, then re-check for movement.
9 Next, grasp the top of the rear wheel and pull it upwards – there should be no discernible freeplay before the shock absorber(s) compress **(see illustration)**.
10 Any freeplay felt in either of check indicates worn bushes or bearings in the shock absorber(s) or swingarm. The worn components must be identified and replaced with new ones (see Chapter 6).
11 To make an accurate assessment of the swingarm bushes or bearings, remove the rear wheel (see Chapter 7) and the bolt(s) securing the shock absorber(s) to the swingarm (see Chapter 6). Grasp the rear of the swingarm with one hand and place your other hand at the junction of the swingarm and the frame. Try to move the rear of the swingarm from side-to-side. Any wear (play) in the bushes or bearings should be felt as movement between the swingarm and the frame at the front. If there is any play, the swingarm will be felt to move forward and backward at the front (not from side-to-side). If there is any play in the swingarm remove it for inspection (see Chapter 6).

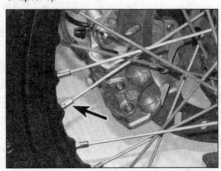

12.1 Turn the adjuster (arrowed) to set spoke tension

Front fork oil change

12 Although there is no set interval for changing the fork oil, note that the oil will degrade over a period of time and lose its damping qualities. Refer to Chapter 6 for details of fork removal, oil draining and refilling. The forks do not need to be completely disassembled to change the oil.

Rear suspension lubrication

13 Remove the swingarm, clean and re-grease the pivot bolt, spacers and bushes or bearings (see Chapter 6).

12 Wheels and tyres

Wire spoke wheels

1 Visually check the spokes for damage and corrosion. A broken or bent spoke must be replaced with a new one immediately because the load taken by it will be transferred to adjacent spokes which may in turn fail. Check the tension in each spoke by tapping each one lightly with a screwdriver and noting the sound produced – each should make the same sound of the correct pitch. Properly tensioned spokes will make a sharp pinging sound, loose ones will produce a lower pitch dull sound and tight ones will be higher pitched. If a spoke needs adjustment turn the adjuster at the rim using a spoke adjustment tool or an open-ended spanner **(see illustration)**.
2 Unevenly tensioned spokes will promote rim misalignment – refer to information on wheel runout in Chapter 7 and seek the advice of a dealer or wheel building specialist if the wheel needs realigning, which it may well do if many spokes are unevenly tensioned. Check front and rear wheel alignment as described in Chapter 7. Check that any wheel balance weights are fixed firmly to the wheel rim. If you suspect that a weight has fallen off, have the wheel rebalanced by a motorcycle tyre specialist.

Cast wheels

3 Cast wheels are virtually maintenance free, but they should be kept clean and checked

12.7 Checking for play in the rear wheel bearings

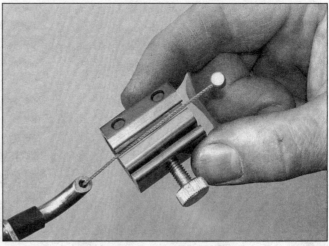

13.3a Fit the cable into the adapter . . .

periodically for cracks and other damage. Also check the wheel runout and alignment (see Chapter 7). Never attempt to repair damaged cast wheels; they must be replaced with new ones if damaged. Check that any wheel balance weights are fixed firmly to the wheel rim. If you suspect that a weight has fallen off, have the wheel rebalanced by a motorcycle tyre specialist.

Tyres

4 Check the tyre condition and tread depth thoroughly – see *Pre-ride checks*.

5 Make sure the valve cap is in place and tight. Check the valve for signs of damage. If tyre deflation occurs and it is not due to a slow puncture the valve core may be loose or it could be leaking past the seal – remove the cap and make sure the core is tight; if it is tight then it could be leaking – unscrew the core from the valve housing using a core removal tool and thread a new one in its place. A tool can be made quite easily by cutting a slot into the threaded end of a bolt using a hacksaw – the bolt must fit inside the valve housing and the slot must be deep enough to locate around the flat sides of the core and grip it.

Wheel bearings

6 Wheel bearings will wear over a considerable mileage and should be checked periodically to avoid handling problems.

7 Support the motorcycle upright using an auxiliary stand so that the wheel being examined is off the ground. When checking the front wheel bearings turn the handlebars to full lock on one side so you have something to push against. Check for any play in the bearings by pushing and pulling the wheel against the hub **(see illustration)**. Also rotate the wheel and check that it turns smoothly and without any grating noises.

8 If any play is detected in the hub, or if the wheel does not rotate smoothly (and this is not due to brake or transmission drag), remove the wheel and inspect the bearings for wear or damage (see Chapter 7).

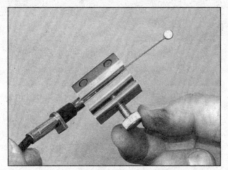

13.3b . . . and tighten the screw to seal it in . . .

13 General lubrication

Pivot points

1 Since the controls, cables and various other components of a motorcycle are exposed to the elements, they should be checked and lubricated periodically to ensure safe and trouble-free operation.

2 The footrest pivots, clutch and brake lever pivots, brake pedal pivot and sidestand and centrestand pivots should be lubricated frequently. In order for the lubricant to be applied where it will do the most good, the component should be disassembled (see Chapters 6 and 7). Next clean off any dirt and old grease, and remove any corrosion. A multi-purpose lithium based grease is good for most applications. An aerosol chain or cable lubricant can be applied to the pivot joint gaps and will usually work its way into the areas where friction occurs, so less disassembly of the component is needed (however it is always better to do so and clean off all corrosion, dirt and old lubricant first). If motor oil or light grease is being used,

13.3c . . . then apply the lubricant using the nozzle provided inserted in the hole in the adapter

apply it sparingly as it may attract dirt (which could cause the controls to bind or wear at an accelerated rate).

Cables

Special tool: *A cable lubricating adapter is necessary for this procedure* **(see illustration 13.3c)**.

3 To lubricate the cables, disconnect the relevant cable at its upper end, then lubricate it with a pressure adapter and aerosol lubricant **(see illustrations)**. See Chapter 4 for throttle and choke cable removal procedures, Chapter 2 for the clutch cable, and Chapter 7 for the drum brake cable (where fitted).

14 Engine oil and filter/strainer

> **Warning: Be careful when draining the oil, as the exhaust pipe, the engine, and the oil itself can cause severe burns.**

Oil change

1 Consistent routine oil changes are the single most important maintenance procedure

14.3a Unscrewing the oil filler cap – OHV engine

14.3b Oil filler cap (arrowed) – K157FMI OHC single engine

14.3c Oil filler cap (arrowed) – 154FMI OHC single engine

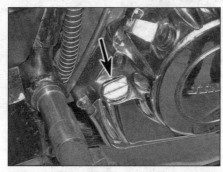

14.3d Oil filler cap (arrowed) – Twin engine

the engine so the oil will drain easily. Place the bike on its centrestand where fitted, or on the sidestand, and preferably on level ground – the object is to have the oil drain plug at the lowest point, so if it is on the underside of the engine and your bike only has a sidestand, use an auxiliary stand to support the bike upright.

3 Position a clean drain tray below the engine. Unscrew the oil filler cap to vent the crankcase and to act as a reminder that there is no oil in the engine **(see illustrations)**.

4 Unscrew the oil drain plug and allow the oil to flow into the drain tray **(see illustrations)**. Check the condition of the sealing washer on the drain plug and replace it with a new one if it is damaged or worn – it is highly advisable to use a new one whatever the condition of the old one. You may have to cut the old one off, depending on the type fitted. If the plug has a magnetic tip clean off any swarf.

5 When the oil has completely drained, fit the plug into the engine, preferably using a new sealing washer, and tighten it **(see illustration)**. Do not overtighten it as the threads in the engine are easily damaged.

6 Refill the engine to the proper level using the recommended type and amount of oil (see *Pre-ride checks)*. With the motorcycle vertical, the oil level should lie between the upper and lower level lines on the dipstick or inspection window (see *Pre-ride checks)*. Check the condition of the O-ring on the filler cap and replace it with a new one if it is damaged or worn. Install the filler cap **(see illustration 14.3a, b, c or d)**.

7 Start the engine and let it run for two or

you can perform. The oil not only lubricates the internal parts of the engine, transmission and clutch, but it also acts as a coolant, a cleaner, a sealant, and a protector. Because of these demands, the oil takes a terrific amount of abuse and should be replaced as specified

with new oil of the recommended grade and type.

2 Where fitted remove the fairing panels, belly-pan or sump guard as required according to model for access to the drain plug (see Chapter 8). Before draining the oil, warm up

14.4a Oil drain plug (arrowed) – OHV engine

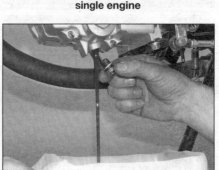

14.4b Oil drain plug (arrowed) – OHC single engine

14.4c Oil drain plug (arrowed) – 154FMI OHC single engine

14.4d Oil drain plug (arrowed) – Twin engine

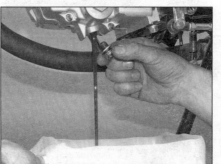

14.4e Unscrew the plug and allow the oil to completely drain

14.5 Install the drain plug using a new sealing washer

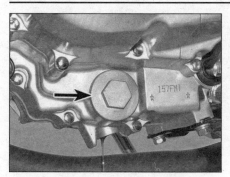

14.12a Unscrew the plug (arrowed) . . .

14.12b . . . and remove the spring . . .

14.12c . . . then withdraw the strainer

three minutes. Shut it off, wait a few minutes, then check the oil level. If necessary, add more oil to bring the level close to the upper line, but do not go above it.

8 Check around the drain plug for leaks. If a leak is evident and a new washer was not used, you will have to drain the oil again and fit a new washer. If a new washer was used then make sure the plug is tightened sufficiently, but take great care not to overtighten it and strip the threads. Where removed install the fairing panels, belly-pan or sump guard (see Chapter 8).

9 The old oil drained from the engine cannot be re-used and should be disposed of properly. Check with your local refuse disposal company, disposal facility or environmental agency to see whether they will accept the used oil for recycling. Don't pour used oil into drains or onto the ground.

Oil filter and/or strainer

OHV engines

10 At every second oil change remove and clean the strainer.

11 Drain the engine oil (see Steps 2 to 5).

12 Unscrew the strainer plug and withdraw the spring and strainer **(see illustrations)**. Discard the plug O-ring – a new one should be used.

13 Wash the strainer in solvent, making sure all debris is removed from the mesh **(see illustration)**. Check the mesh for holes and damage and replace it with a new one if necessary.

14 Fit the new O-ring onto the plug **(see illustration)**. Fit the strainer into the end of the spring and fit them back into the engine, then fit the plug and tighten it **(see illustrations)**.

Do not overtighten it as the threads in the engine are easily damaged.

15 On air-cooled models, after a significant mileage has been covered, or if there has been internal engine damage or there is evidence of oil sludge after draining the oil (see **Haynes Hint**), clean the centrifugal oil filter (see Chapter 2A, Section 16).

16 Refill the engine with oil (see Steps 6 to 8).

K157FMI OHC engine

17 At every second oil change remove the filter and replace it with a new one.

18 Drain the engine oil (see Steps 2 to 5). To avoid too much mess when removing the filter drain the filter chamber beforehand by undoing the plug below it **(see illustration)**. Discard the sealing washer. When the chamber

Check the old oil carefully – if it is very metallic coloured, then the engine is experiencing wear from break-in (new engine) or from insufficient lubrication. If there are flakes or chips of metal in the oil, then something is drastically wrong internally and the engine will have to be disassembled for inspection and repair. If there are pieces of fibre-like material in the oil, the clutch is experiencing excessive wear and should be checked.

14.13 Remove the debris from the mesh and check it for holes

14.14a Fit a new O-ring (arrowed)

14.14b Fit the strainer and spring into the engine . . .

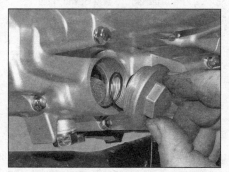

14.14c . . . then fit the plug

14.18 Unscrew the plug and drain the filter chamber, then fit a new sealing washer and install the plug

14.19 Unscrew the nuts (arrowed) and remove the cover, spring and filter

14.20a Fit a new O-ring over the lip (arrowed) . . .

14.20b . . . then fit the filter

has drained fit the plug using a new sealing washer and tighten it.

19 Unscrew the filter cover nuts and remove the cover and the spring, then withdraw the filter, noting which way round it fits **(see illustration)**. Note the O-ring on the inner end of the filter **(see illustration 14.20a)**. Discard the gasket (where fitted) and O-ring(s) – new ones must be used.

20 Fit a new O-ring over the lip in the filter housing **(see illustration)**. Fit the filter into the engine, making sure the end with the hole is innermost and it locates over the lip and against the O-ring **(see illustration)**.

21 Fit the new gasket and/or (according to type) O-ring onto the cover **(see illustration)**. Fit the spring and cover and tighten the nuts **(see illustration)**.

22 After a significant mileage has been covered, or if there has been internal engine

damage or there is evidence of oil sludge after draining the oil (see **Haynes Hint**), remove and clean the strainer as follows: unscrew the strainer cover bolts and remove the cover **(see illustration)**. Discard the O-ring – a new one must be used. Undo the strainer screws and remove the strainer **(see illustration)**. Wash the strainer in solvent and use an old toothbrush to remove any debris from the mesh. Check the mesh for holes and damage and replace it with a new one if necessary. Fit the strainer and tighten the screws. Fit the cover using a new O-ring and tighten the bolts **(see illustration)**.

23 Refill the engine with oil (see Steps 6 to 8).

154FMI OHC engine

24 This engine is fitted with an oil strainer and a centrifugal oil filter. After a significant mileage has been covered, or if there has been internal engine damage or there is evidence

of oil sludge or metal swarf after draining the oil (see *Haynes Hint*), remove and clean the strainer and fit a new oil filter.

25 Remove the clutch cover (see Chapter 2D) then withdaw the strainer from its location in the crankcase **(see illustration)**. Wash the strainer in solvent and use an old toothbrush to remove any debris from the mesh. Check the mesh for holes and damage and replace the strainer with a new one if necessary (see Chapter 2D, Section 17).

26 Follow the procedure in Chapter 2D, Sections 16 and 17, to remove and install the centrifugal oil filter.

27 Installation is the reverse of removal. Refill the engine with oil (see Steps 6 to 8).

Twin cylinder engines

28 Every 5,000 miles, or if there has been internal engine damage or there is evidence of oil sludge after draining the oil (see *Haynes*

14.21a Fit a new O-ring into the groove . . .

14.21b . . . then fit the spring over the lip and against the end of the filter

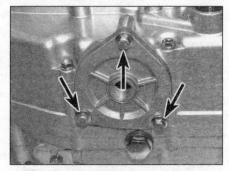

14.22a Unscrew the bolts (arrowed) and remove the cover

14.22b Undo the screws (arrowed) and remove the strainer

14.22c Fit the cover using a new O-ring

14.25 Location of the oil strainer (arrowed) – 154FMI type engine

14.30 Detach the strainer from the bottom of the pump, noting which way round it fits

16.4 Checking for play in the steering head bearings

Hint), remove and clean the strainer. Drain the engine oil (see Steps 2 to 5).

29 Remove the oil pump (see Chapter 2D, Section 18).

30 Detach the strainer from the bottom of the pump, noting which way round it fits **(see illustration)**.

31 Wash the strainer in solvent and use an old toothbrush to remove any debris from the mesh. Check the mesh for holes and damage and replace it with a new one if necessary.

32 Fit the strainer back onto the bottom of the pump so that when the pump is installed the thicker end of the strainer will face out **(see illustration 14.26)**.

33 Install the oil pump (see Chapter 2D, Section 18).

34 Refill the engine with oil (see Steps 6 to 8).

15 Nuts and bolts

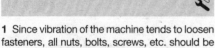

1 Since vibration of the machine tends to loosen fasteners, all nuts, bolts, screws, etc. should be periodically checked for proper tightness.

2 Pay particular attention to the following, referring to the relevant Chapter:

Spark plug(s)
Engine oil drain plug
Lever and pedal bolts
Footrest and stand bolts
Engine mounting bolts/nuts
Shock absorber bolts/nut; swingarm pivot
  bolt/nut
Handlebar clamp bolts
Front fork clamp bolts (top and bottom
  yoke), and fork top bolts (where fitted)
Steering stem nut
Front axle nut or bolt
Rear axle nut
Front and rear sprocket bolts/nuts
Brake caliper and master cylinder mounting
  bolts (disc brake)
Brake hose banjo bolts and caliper bleed
  valves (disc brake)
Brake disc bolts

Brake torque arm nuts (rear drum brake)
Exhaust system bolts/nuts

16 Steering head bearings

Freeplay check and adjustment

1 Steering head bearings can become dented, rough or loose during normal use of the machine. In extreme cases, worn or loose steering head bearings can cause steering wobble – a condition that is potentially dangerous.

Check

2 Raise the front wheel off the ground using an auxiliary stand placed under the engine. Always make sure that the bike is properly supported and secure.

3 Point the front wheel straight-ahead and slowly move the handlebars from lock to lock. Any dents or roughness in the bearing races will be felt and if the bearings are too tight the bars will not move smoothly and freely. Again point the wheel straight-ahead, and tap the front of the wheel to one side. The wheel should 'fall' under its own weight to the limit of its lock, indicating that the bearings are not too tight (take into account the restriction that cables and wiring may have). Check for similar movement to the other side.

4 Next, grasp the bottom of the forks and gently pull and push them forward and backward **(see illustration)**. Any looseness or freeplay in the steering head bearings will be felt as front-to-rear movement of the forks. If play is felt, adjust the bearings as described below.

> **HAYNES HiNT** *Make sure you are not mistaking any movement between the bike and stand, or between the stand and the ground, for freeplay in the bearings. Do not pull and push the forks too hard – a gentle movement is all that is needed. Freeplay between the tubes due to worn bushes can also be misinterpreted as steering head bearing play – do not confuse the two.*

Adjustment

5 As a precaution, remove the fuel tank (see Chapter 4), and where fitted the fairing – though not actually necessary, this will prevent the possibility of damage should a tool slip.

6 To turn the adjuster, and locknut if fitted, you will need either a C-spanner, or a drift to locate in one of the notches.

7 Slacken the fork clamp bolts in the top yoke **(see illustration)**. Slacken the steering stem nut or bolt **(see illustration)**.

8 Check for a locknut above the adjuster nut

16.7a Slacken the fork clamp bolt (arrowed) on each side . . .

16.7b . . . then slacken the steering stem nut or bolt (arrowed)

16.9a Using a C-spanner to tighten the head bearing adjuster nut

16.9b Using drift to tighten the head bearing adjuster nut

and see if there is a tabbed lockwasher locking them together– if there is (on most models there won't be), you will have to fully unscrew the steering stem nut or bolt and remove the washer where fitted, then lift the top yoke up off the forks in order to remove the lockwasher – if required displace the handlebars from the yoke first (see Chapter 6), and whatever your method lay or support the components forwards or to the side, using some rag as protection. If the lockwasher is above the locknut remove it then unscrew the locknut. If the washer is between them, unscrew the locknut then remove the washer. In either case note how the washer locates.

9 Turn the adjuster nut using a C-spanner located in one of the notches, either clockwise to tighten the head bearings or anti-clockwise to loosen them, and only moving it a small amount at a time **(see illustrations)**. After each small adjustment recheck the freeplay as described above (Step 4), before making further adjustments. The object is to set the adjuster nut so that the bearings are under a very light loading, just enough to remove any freeplay, but not so much that the steering does not move freely from side-to-side as described in the check procedure above.

Caution: Take great care not to apply excessive pressure because this will cause premature failure of the bearings.

10 Where removed fit the lock washer and the locknut in the reverse order of removal, and setting the washer tabs as noted. Fit the top yoke onto the steering stem. Fit the washer where removed, then the steering stem nut or

bolt. Install the handlebars if displaced (see Chapter 6).
11 Tighten the steering stem nut or bolt **(see illustration 16.7b)**. Now tighten both the fork clamp bolts **(see illustration 16.7a)**.
12 Check the bearing adjustment as described above and re-adjust if necessary.
13 If the bearings cannot be correctly adjusted, disassemble the steering head and check the bearings and races (see Chapter 6).
14 Install the fuel tank (see Chapter 4) and fairing (see Chapter 8) if removed.

Lubrication

15 Over a considerable time the grease in the bearings will be dispersed or will harden allowing the ingress of dirt and water.
16 The steering head should be disassembled periodically and the bearings cleaned and re-greased (see Chapter 6).

17 Battery

Note: *A standard type battery is fitted most models, but a maintenance free (MF) battery may be fitted to some. The batteries are easy to distinguish – standard ones have removable caps across the top and electrolyte level lines (marked UPPER and LOWER or MAX and MIN), while MF batteries do not, and are usually marked MF on the front. Identify the type of battery fitted on your bike before proceeding.*

Standard battery

1 Remove the seat or side cover as required according to model for access to the battery (see Chapter 8).
2 The electrolyte level is visible through the translucent battery case – with the bike upright it should be between the UPPER and LOWER or MAX and MIN level marks **(see illustration)**.
3 If the electrolyte is low, remove the battery (see Chapter 9). Remove the cell caps and fill each cell to the upper level mark with distilled water **(see illustrations)**. Do not use tap water (except in an emergency), and do not overfill. The cell holes are quite small, so use a small funnel or a clean plastic squeeze bottle with a small spout to add the water. Fit the cell caps.
4 The battery case should be kept clean to prevent current leakage, which can discharge the battery over a period of time (especially when it sits unused). Wash the outside of the case with a solution of baking soda and water. Rinse the battery thoroughly, then dry it.
5 Look for cracks in the case and replace the battery if any are found. If acid has been spilled on the frame or battery box, neutralise it with a baking soda and water solution, dry it thoroughly, then touch up any damaged paint.
6 If the motorcycle sits unused for long periods of time, remove the battery and charge it once every month to six weeks (see Chapter 9).
7 The condition of the battery can be assessed by measuring its specific gravity and open-circuit voltage (see Chapter 9).
8 Check the battery terminals and leads for corrosion. If corrosion is evident, clean the terminals and lead ends with a wire brush or knife and emery paper. Apply a thin coat of petroleum jelly (Vaseline) or a dedicated battery terminal spray to the connections to slow further corrosion.
9 Install the battery (see Chapter 9).

Maintenance free battery

Note: *Do not attempt to remove the battery caps to check the electrolyte level or battery specific gravity. Removal will damage the caps, resulting in electrolyte leakage and battery damage.*

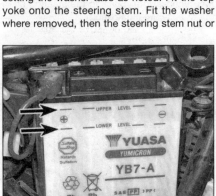

17.2 Make sure the level of the electrolyte is between the lines

17.3a Remove the cap from relevant cell(s) . . .

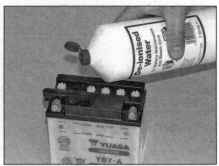

17.3b . . . and top up using distilled water if necessary

10 Remove the seat or side panel as required according to model for access to the battery (see Chapter 9).

11 Check the battery terminals and leads for tightness and corrosion. If corrosion is evident, clean the terminals and lead ends with a wire brush or knife and emery paper. Apply a thin coat of petroleum jelly (Vaseline) or a dedicated battery terminal spray to the connections to slow further corrosion.

12 If the machine is not in regular use, disconnect the battery and give it a refresher charge every month to six weeks (see Chapter 9).

13 The condition of the battery can be assessed by measuring its open-circuit voltage (see Chapter 9).

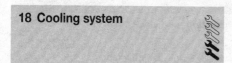

18 Cooling system

⚠ **Warning: The engine must be cool before beginning this procedure.**

1 On water-cooled engines a pump incorporated in the clutch cover, circulates coolant around the cylinder head and block and through a radiator where it is cooled. On a number of air-cooled engines an oil cooler is fitted to the front of the engine and oil circulates through this to cool it. The radiator or oil cooler are mounted in front of the engine.

2 Check the radiator or oil cooler and hoses for evidence of leaks. Make sure the hose clips are tight. Examine each hose along its entire length and at the unions and joints. Look for cracks, abrasions and other damage. Squeeze each hose at various points to see whether they are dried out or hard **(see illustration)**. They should feel firm, yet pliable, and return to their original shape when released. If necessary, replace them with new ones (see Chapter 3).

18.2 Check the hoses for cracks

18.4 Clean the radiator fins and straighten any bent ones

3 If leaks are noted in the radiator or cooler core replace it with a new one (see Chapter 3).

4 Check the radiator or cooler fins for mud, dirt and insects, which may impede the flow of air. If the fins are dirty, remove the radiator or cooler (see Chapter 3) and clean it using water or low pressure compressed air directed through the fins from the inner side of the radiator. If the fins are bent or distorted, straighten them carefully with a screwdriver **(see illustration)**. If airflow is restricted by bent or damaged fins over more than 20% of the surface area, replace the radiator or cooler with a new one.

5 On water-cooled models you must check the level of coolant regularly (see *Pre-Ride Checks*), and every so often you should drain the system and refill it with fresh coolant (see Chapter 3). Also check for any signs of oil or coolant leakage, or an emulsified mixture of both, coming from the drain tube connected to the water pump on the right-hand side of the engine **(see illustration)** – leakage indicates failure of one or both of the seals on the pump shaft. If there is coolant leakage the mechanical seal fitted behind the pump impeller has failed, and if there is oil leakage the oil seal has failed, while an emulsified mixture of both seals indicates failure of both seals. Refer to Chapter 3 for pump removal and seal replacement.

6 If problems such as overheating and/or loss of coolant occur of which there is no obvious cause, remove the pressure cap from the radiator filler neck by rotating it anti-clockwise until it reaches the stop **(see illustration)**. If you hear a hissing sound (indicating there is still pressure in the system), wait until it stops. Now press down on the cap and continue turning it until it can be removed. Check the cap seal for cracks and other damage. If in doubt about the cap's condition, have it tested by a dealer or fit a new one – the cost is minimal but it performs a crucial role.

19 Air induction system

1 To reduce the amount of unburned hydrocarbons released in the exhaust gases, an air induction system is fitted to all UK market models. Under normal running conditions the system allows filtered air to be drawn into the exhaust where it mixes with the exhaust gases, causing any unburned particles of the fuel in the mixture to be burnt. This process changes a considerable amount of hydrocarbons and carbon monoxide into relatively harmless carbon dioxide and water.

18.5 Check the hose (arrowed) for leakage (kickstart version shown)

18.6 Remove the pressure cap as described

19.2 Air induction system control valve (arrowed) and hoses

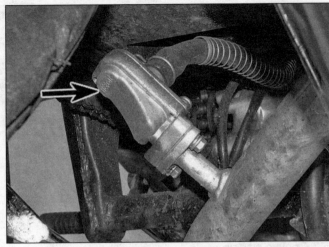

19.3 Air induction system reed valve (arrowed) and hose

2 On some models the system has a control valve, incorporating both a diaphragm valve and a reed valve, with the diaphragm valve actuated by vacuum taken off the intake duct between the carburettor and engine **(see illustration)**. Under normal operating conditions, the diaphragm valve is open allowing filtered air (sourced either from the filter housing or via a pipe incorporating its own cartridge filter) to be drawn through via the reed valve and either into the air passage through the cylinder block and/or head to the exhaust port, or directly into the top of the exhaust downpipe. When the throttle is closed the vacuum created in the intake duct closes the diaphragm valve, preventing exhaust popping on overrun. The reed valve prevents the flow of exhaust gases back up the cylinder head passage and into the air filter housing.

3 Alternatively filtered air, sourced in the same way as above, is drawn constantly via a reed valve directly into the front of the exhaust silencer – again the reed valve prevents the flow of exhaust gases back into the air filter **(see illustration)**.

4 The system is not adjustable and requires little maintenance. Check that the hoses are not kinked or pinched, are in good condition and are securely connected at each end. Replace any hoses that are cracked, split or generally deteriorated with new ones.

5 Refer to Chapter 4 for further information on the system and for checks if it is believed to be faulty.

20 Cam chain tension – K157FMI single and 244FMI twin engines

1 Most engines will have an automatic cam chain tensioner which is self adjusting and requires no maintenance. However early versions of these engines may be fitted with a tensioner that requires manual adjustment from time to time – a rattly cam chain is a sure indication. If you are not sure whether the tensioner on your engine is adjustable or not refer to Step 2 or 3 and to Chapter 2B or 2D according to engine and check the illustrations in the relevant Section of the Chapter – if the tensioner on your engine does not look like the one shown but has the adjuster described in Step 2 or 3 then you have the earlier type. If still in doubt ask your dealer.

2 On single cylinder engines the tensioner is on the left-hand side of the engine and protrudes from the back of the cylinder block, just above the crankcase – remove any body panels as required according to model for access (see Chapter 8). Hold the head of the bolt protruding from the side of the tensioner body and slacken the locknut, then turn the bolt anti-clockwise until the tensioner plunger is released and takes up any slack. Tighten the bolt, then hold it and tighten the locknut.

3 On twin cylinder engines the tensioner is inside the engine, and the adjuster protrudes from the back of the cylinder block, just below the carburettors – remove any body panels as required according to model for access (see Chapter 8). Slacken the nut on the stud protruding from the block until the tensioner slider is released and takes up any slack, then retighten the nut.

4 If the cam chain is still noisy after adjustment, or if it is noisy and your engine has an automatic tensioner, refer to Chapter 2B or 2D according to engine type and check the tensioner, its blade and the cam chain for wear and damage.

Chapter 2A
Engine, clutch and transmission – OHV engines

Contents

Degrees of difficulty

Easy, suitable for novice with little experience 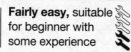	**Fairly easy,** suitable for beginner with some experience	**Fairly difficult,** suitable for competent DIY mechanic	**Difficult,** suitable for experienced DIY mechanic	**Very difficult,** suitable for expert DIY or professional

Specifications

General

Type	Four-stroke single, overhead valve
Capacity	124 cc
Bore	56.5 mm
Stroke	49.5 mm
Compression ratio	9.0 to 1
Cooling system	Air-cooled (157FMI) or liquid-cooled (156MI-2B)
Lubrication	Wet sump, trochoid pump
Clutch	Wet multi-plate
Transmission	Five-speed constant mesh
Final drive	Chain and sprockets

Torque settings

General settings (thread size given)

5 mm bolt/nut	5 Nm
6 mm bolt/nut	10 Nm
8 mm bolt/nut	24 Nm
10 mm bolt/nut	35 Nm
12 mm bolt/nut	55 Nm

Specific settings

Rocker assembly bolts	12 Nm
Cylinder head nuts and bolt	29 Nm
Alternator rotor bolt	30 Nm

Left view of the air-cooled OHV engine (type 157FMI)

Right view of the air-cooled OHV engine (type 157FMI)

1 General information

The engine/transmission unit has a single cylinder and is of unit construction (**see illustrations**). It is based on the Honda CG125 engine. A gear driven camshaft operates two lower rocker arms that lift the pushrods, and these in turn operate the upper rockers arms that open the two valves. The crankcase divides vertically. The engine is air-cooled on most models (type 157FMI, or 156FMI-B with balancer shaft), but some are liquid-cooled (type 156MI-2B). On most models the engine has both a kickstart mechanism and an electric starter motor, but on liquid-cooled engines the space occupied by the kickstart mechanism has been used to accommodate the water pump.

The crankcase incorporates a wet sump, pressure-fed lubrication system which uses a single rotor trochoidal oil pump that is gear-driven off the primary drive gear on the right-hand end of the crankshaft. Oil is filtered by a strainer in the side of the crankcase, and on air-cooled versions by a centrifugal oil filter on the right-hand end of the crankshaft. On liquid-cooled versions with a kickstart mechanism the centrifugal filter is removed to make way for the water pump.

The alternator is on the left-hand end of the crankshaft. The ignition timing trigger is on the outside of the alternator rotor, and the pick-up coil is mounted in the alternator cover along with the stator.

Power from the crankshaft is routed to the transmission via the clutch. The clutch is of the wet, multi-plate type and is gear-driven off the crankshaft. The clutch is operated by cable. The transmission is a five-speed constant-mesh unit. Final drive to the rear wheel is by chain and sprockets.

2 Component access

Operations possible with the engine in the frame

The components and assemblies listed below can usually be removed without having to remove the engine from the frame, though there may be the odd exception to the rule depending on the frame design of your model.

If a number of areas require attention at the same time, removal of the engine is recommended as it is not that difficult.

Valve cover
Rockers arms, pushrods and valves
Cylinder head
Cylinder block and piston
Camshaft and lower rockers
Clutch
Water pump (156MI-2B engine)

Left view of the air-cooled OHV engine with balancer shaft (type 156FMI-B)

Right view of the air-cooled OHV engine with balancer shaft (type 156FMI-B)

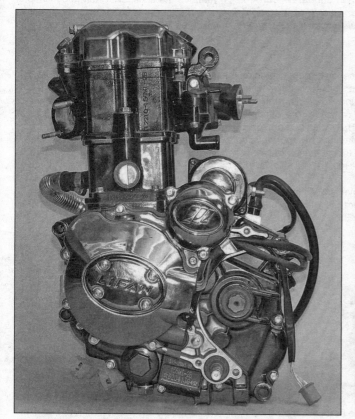

Left view of the liquid-cooled OHV engine (type 156MI-2B)

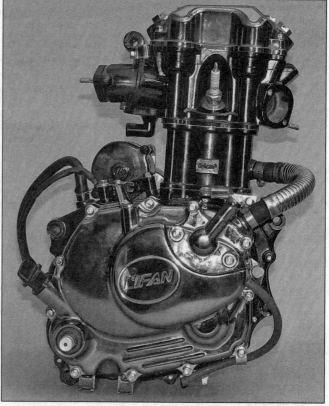

Right view of the liquid-cooled OHV engine (type 156MI-2B)

Oil pump, oil strainer and oil filter
Primary drive gear
Gearchange mechanism
Alternator
Starter clutch
Starter motor

Operations requiring engine removal

It is necessary to remove the engine from the frame to gain access to the following components.

Crankshaft, connecting rod and bearings
Transmission shafts and bearings
Balancer shaft (where fitted)
Selector drum and forks
Kickstart mechanism

3 Cylinder compression test

Special tool: *A compression gauge is required to perform this test.*

1 Poor engine performance may be caused by leaking valves, incorrect valve clearances, a leaking head gasket, or worn pistons, piston rings or cylinder walls. A cylinder compression check will highlight these conditions and can also indicate the presence of excessive carbon deposits in the cylinder head.

2 The only tools required are a compression gauge (there are two types, one with a threaded end and if necessary an adapter to fit the spark plug hole in the cylinder head, the other has a rubber seal which is pressed into the spark plug hole to create a seal – the threaded adapter type is preferable), and a spark plug socket. Depending on the outcome of the initial test, a squirt-type oil can may also be needed.

3 Make sure the valve clearances are correctly set (see Chapter 1).

4 Run the engine until it is at normal operating temperature. Remove the spark plug (see Chapter 1). Fit the plug back into the plug cap and ground the plug against the engine away from the plug hole – if the plug is not grounded the ignition system could be damaged.

5 Fit the gauge into the spark plug hole **(see illustration)** – if the rubber cone type is used keep the gauge pressed onto the hole throughout the test to maintain a good seal.

6 With the ignition switch ON, the throttle held fully open and the spark plug grounded, turn the engine over on the starter motor until the gauge reading has built up and stabilised **(see illustration)**.

7 Check the reading on the gauge – a good engine should show around 150 to 190 psi (10 to 13 Bar).

8 If the reading is low, it could be due to a worn cylinder bore, piston or rings, loose cylinder head nuts and/or failure of the cylinder head gasket, or worn valve seats. To determine which is the cause, pour a small quantity of engine oil into the spark plug hole

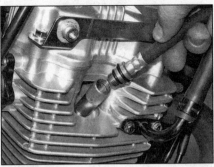

3.5 Thread the gauge hose directly into the spark plug hole or into an adapter as shown if required

to seal the rings, then repeat the compression test. If the figures are noticeably higher the cause is a worn cylinder, piston or rings. If there is no change the cause is a leaking head gasket or worn valve seats.

9 If the reading is high there could be a build-up of carbon deposits in the combustion chamber. Remove the cylinder head and scrape all deposits off the piston and the cylinder head.

4 Engine removal and installation

Caution: The engine is heavy. Engine removal and installation should be carried out with the aid of an assistant; personal injury or damage could occur if the engine falls or is dropped.

Removal

1 Support the bike either on its centrestand or using an auxiliary stand so it is upright, making sure it is on level ground. Work can be made easier by raising the machine to a suitable working height on an hydraulic ramp or a suitable platform. Make sure the motorcycle is secure and will not topple over, and tie the front brake lever to the handlebar to prevent it rolling forwards.

2 Where fitted remove any fairing panels, belly-pan or sump guard as required according to model (see Chapter 8).

3.6 Hold the throttle open and turn the engine over until the reading on the gauge has stabilised

3 If the engine is dirty, particularly around its mountings, wash it thoroughly. This will make work much easier and rule out the possibility of caked on lumps of dirt falling into some vital component.

4 Drain the engine oil (see Chapter 1). On liquid-cooled engines drain the cooling system, then remove the radiator along with its hoses (see Chapter 3).

5 Disconnect the negative (–) lead from the battery (see Chapter 9).

6 Remove the fuel tank (see Chapter 4). Either remove the carburettor, or alternatively detach it from the engine and leave it in the engine bay with its cables and hoses still connected (see Chapter 4). Either way, plug the engine intake duct with clean rag.

7 Remove the exhaust system (see Chapter 4). On models with an air induction system that routes the air through the cylinder head or block, disconnect the air hose from its union, and if necessary remove the control valve along with the hose and its bracket to minimise obstruction during engine removal (see Chapter 4).

8 Either remove the gearchange lever or displace the linkage arm (according to type), making an alignment mark with the shaft if there is none visible so it be correctly installed later **(see illustration)**. Where fitted remove the kickstart lever (again marking the alignment), and if fitted unscrew the stop bracket bolts and remove the bracket **(see illustrations)**.

9 Remove the front sprocket cover (see Chapter 7). Create maximum slack in the

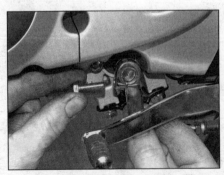

4.8a Unscrew the bolt and draw the linkage arm or lever off

4.8b Unscrew the bolt (arrowed) and draw the kickstart lever off

4.8c Unscrew the bolts (arrowed) and remove the bracket

4.9 Disengage the chain from the sprocket

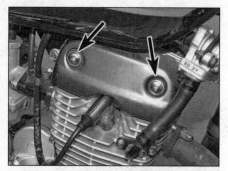

4.10a Undo the screws (arrowed) and remove the cover

4.10b Pull the cap off the spark plug

drive chain (see Chapter 1), then if required (for example if you intend to separate the crankcase halves) remove the front sprocket (see Chapter 7), or if not then slip the chain off the front sprocket **(see illustration)**.

10 Where fitted, and if it restricts removal of the spark plug cap, undo the side trim cover screws and remove the cover **(see illustration)**. Pull the cap off the spark plug **(see illustration)**. Release the lead from any clamp on the intake duct and secure it clear of the engine.

11 Where fitted detach the tachometer cable **(see illustration)**.

12 Detach the clutch cable and position it clear of the engine (see Section 15).

13 If required, remove the starter motor (see Chapter 9). If you want to leave the starter motor in situ, pull back the rubber cover on its

terminal, then unscrew the nut and disconnect the lead **(see illustration)** – spray it with some penetrating fluid first if it is corroded. Also unscrew the bolt securing the engine earth lead and detach the lead **(see illustration)** – if it is not secured by one of the starter motor bolts as shown here then it will most likely be secured by one of the crankcase bolts.

14 Trace the alternator, pick-up coil and neutral switch wiring from the left-hand side of the engine and disconnect it at the connectors **(see illustrations)**. Release the wiring from any clamps or ties that will restrict it when removing the engine.

15 Detach the crankcase breather hose **(see illustration)**.

16 Remove the individual footrests or the complete footrest assembly as required according to model (see Chapter 6) – this will

depend on the type fitted and whether they will get in the way when lifting the engine out.

17 Position an hydraulic or mechanical jack under the engine with a block of wood between the jack head and sump **(see**

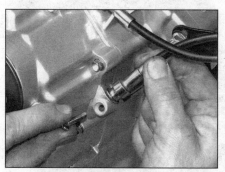

4.11 Undo the screw and detach the cable

4.13a Pull back the boot, unscrew the nut (arrowed) and detach the lead

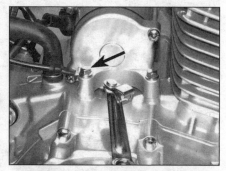

4.13b Unscrew the bolt (arrowed) and detach the lead

4.14a Trace the wiring (arrowed) . . .

4.14b . . . and disconnect the relevant connectors

4.15 Release the clamp and detach the hose (arrowed)

illustration). Make sure the jack is centrally positioned so the engine will not topple in any direction when the last mounting bolt is removed. Raise the jack to take the weight of the engine, but make sure it is not lifting the bike and taking the weight of that as well. The idea is to support the engine so that there is no pressure on any of the mounting bolts once they have been slackened, so they can be easily withdrawn. Note that it may be necessary to alter the position of the jack as some of the bolts are removed to relieve the stress transferred to the other bolts.

18 Take a look around the engine and identify the mounting bolts and nuts and any brackets and spacers that hold the engine in the frame **(see illustrations)**. Note that there are variations to those shown depending on manufacturer and model. After removing a bolt fit any associated washers, spacers, brackets and wiring clamps back onto it in their correct order, then thread the nut on to secure them, and finally tag the bolt according to its position.

19 First go round and unscrew the nuts with their washers (where fitted) from the bolts,

then slacken any bolts that don't have nuts on them.

20 Check that the engine is properly supported by the jack. Withdraw the mounting bolts and remove any washers, spacers and brackets.

21 Check that all wiring, cables and hoses are free and clear The engine can now be removed from the frame (see **Caution** above).

Installation

Note: *It is advisable to smear copper grease onto the engine mounting bolt shafts, not the threads, to prevent the possibility of them seizing in the engine or frame due to corrosion.*

22 Manoeuvre the engine into position in the frame and on the jack to align all the mounting bolt holes, making sure that all cables and wiring are correctly routed and do not get trapped **(see illustration 4.17)**. Note that it may be necessary to adjust the jack as some of the bolts are installed and tightened to realign the other bolt holes.

23 Install the mounting bolts along with any washers, spacers, brackets and wiring

clamps, then fit the nuts and tighten them finger-tight **(see illustrations 4.18c, b and a)**.

24 Now go round and tighten all the engine mounting bolts and nuts.

25 Remove the jack from under the engine.

26 The remainder of the installation procedure is the reverse of removal, noting the following points:

● *When fitting the kickstart and gearchange levers onto their shafts align the marks noted or made on removal **(see illustrations 4.8a and b)**.*
● *Use a new gasket on the exhaust pipe.*
● *Make sure all wires, cables and hoses are correctly routed and connected, and secured by any clips or ties.*
● *Refill the engine with oil to the correct level (see Chapter 1 and Pre-ride checks). On liquid-cooled engines refill the cooling system (see Chapter 3).*
● *Adjust the throttle and clutch cable freeplay.*
● *Adjust the drive chain (see Chapter 1).*
● *Start the engine and check that there are no oil leaks, or coolant leaks on liquid-cooled engines. Adjust the idle speed (see Chapter 1).*

4.17 Support the engine with a jack as shown

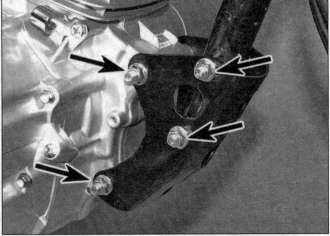

4.18a Front mounting bracket nuts/bolts (arrowed)

4.18b Upper mounting bracket nuts/bolts (arrowed)

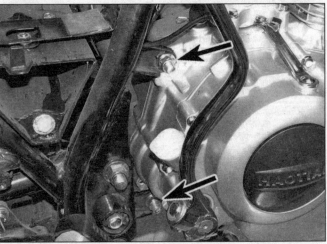

4.18c Upper and lower rear mounting bolts/nuts (arrowed)

5 Engine overhaul information

1 Before beginning the engine overhaul, read through the related procedures to familiarise yourself with the scope and requirements of the job. Overhauling an engine is not all that difficult, but it is time consuming. Check on the availability of parts and make sure that any necessary special tools are obtained in advance.

2 Most work can be done with a decent set of typical workshop hand tools, although a number of precision measuring tools are required for inspecting parts to determine if they are worn.

3 To ensure maximum life and minimum trouble from a rebuilt engine, everything must be assembled with care in a spotlessly clean environment.

Disassembly

4 Before disassembling the engine, thoroughly clean and degrease its external surfaces. This will prevent contamination of the engine internals, and will also make the job a lot easier and cleaner. A high flash-point solvent, such as paraffin (kerosene) can be used, or better still, a proprietary engine degreaser such as Gunk. Use old paintbrushes and toothbrushes to work the solvent into the various recesses of the casings. Take care to exclude solvent or water from the electrical components and intake and exhaust ports.

 Warning: The use of petrol (gasoline) as a cleaning agent should be avoided because of the risk of fire.

5 When clean and dry, position the engine on the workbench, leaving suitable clear area for working. Gather a selection of small containers, plastic bags and some labels so that parts can be grouped together in an easily identifiable manner. Also get some paper and a pen so that notes can be taken. You will also need a supply of clean rag, which should be as absorbent as possible.

6 Before commencing work, read through the appropriate section so that some idea of the necessary procedure can be gained. When removing components note that great force is seldom required. In many cases, a component's reluctance to be removed is indicative of an incorrect approach or removal method – if in any doubt, re-check with the text.

7 When disassembling the engine, keep 'mated' parts together (parts that have been in contact with each other during engine operation). These 'mated' parts must be refitted so they run together in the rebuilt engine.

8 A complete engine stripdown should be done in the following general order with reference to the appropriate Sections.

Remove the valve cover
Remove the rocker assembly and pushrods
Remove the cylinder head
Remove the cylinder block and piston
Remove the starter motor (see Chapter 9)
Remove the clutch
Remove the primary drive gear
Remove the oil pump
Remove the gearchange mechanism
Remove the alternator and starter clutch (see Chapter 9)
Separate the crankcase halves
Remove the kickstart mechanism (where fitted)
Remove the selector drum and forks
Remove the transmission shafts
Remove the crankshaft, and where fitted the balancer shaft

Reassembly

9 Reassembly is accomplished by reversing the general disassembly sequence.

6 Valve cover

Note: *The valve cover can be removed with the engine in the frame. If the engine has been removed, ignore the steps which do not apply.*

Removal

1 Remove any fairing panels or covers as required according to model for access to the valve cover (see Chapter 8).
2 Remove the fuel tank (see Chapter 4).

6.3 Undo the screws (arrowed) and remove the trim cover

6.6 Fit a new seal into the groove

3 Where fitted undo the side trim cover screws and remove each cover (**see illustration**).
4 Unscrew the valve cover bolts and remove the trim cover brackets where fitted (**see illustration**). Lift the cover off the cylinder head (**see illustration 6.7**). If it is stuck, do not try to lever it off with a screwdriver. Tap it gently around the sides with a rubber hammer or block of wood to dislodge it. Note any washers for the bolts.
5 Remove the rubber seal from the cover; if damaged, deformed or deteriorated, replace it with a new one (**see illustration 6.6**).

Installation

6 Fit the seal into the groove in the cover, using a new one if necessary (**see illustration**).
7 Position the valve cover on the cylinder head, making sure the seal stays in place (**see illustration**). Install the cover bolts with their washers (where fitted) and tighten them.
8 Install the remaining components.

7 Rocker assembly and pushrods

Note: *The rocker assembly and pushrods can be removed with the engine in the frame.*

Removal

1 Remove the spark plug (see Chapter 1). Remove the valve cover (see Section 6).
2 Remove the timing inspection cap and the crankshaft end cap from the alternator cover on the left-hand side of the engine (see

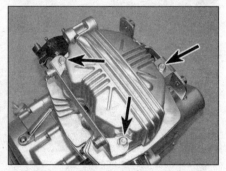
6.4 Unscrew the bolts (arrowed) and remove the valve cover

6.7 Fit the cover onto the head

7.2a Remove the crankshaft end cap (A) and the timing inspection cap (B) . . .

7.2b . . . which on some versions is secured by four bolts (arrowed)

illustrations). Check the condition of the cap O-rings and replace them with new ones if necessary.

3 The engine must be turned so that the piston is at TDC (top dead centre) on its compression stroke. Turn the engine using a suitable socket on the alternator rotor bolt, in an anti-clockwise direction only, until the line next to the T mark on the rotor aligns with the static timing mark, which is a notch in the inspection hole rim **(see illustrations)**. There should now be some freeplay in each rocker arm (i.e. they are not contacting the valve stem). If not, rotate the engine anti-clockwise one full turn (360°) until the line next to the T

mark again aligns with the static timing mark, and there is some freeplay in the rockers.

4 Unscrew the bolts securing the rocker assembly and remove the washers **(see illustration)**. Lift the rocker assembly off the head, noting how the cupped inner end of each arm locates onto the head of its pushrod.

5 Withdraw the pushrods, and mark the top of the front one F and the rear one R so they will be installed in the correct position and the same way up **(see illustration)**.

Inspection

6 Check the rocker arms for heat discoloration

(blue appearance). Check for freeplay between each rocker arm and its shaft **(see illustration)**. The arms should move freely with a light fit but no appreciable freeplay. Replace the assembly with a new one if necessary.

7 Check the bottom of each clearance adjuster and the top of each valve stem **(see illustration)**. Check the cupped sections and the tops and bottoms of the pushrods. If damage is noted or wear is excessive, the rocker assembly, pushrods and valves must be replaced with new ones.

8 Make sure each pushrod is straight by rolling it on a flat surface such as a piece of glass.

7.3a Turning the engine anti-clockwise . . .

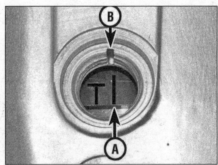

7.3b . . . align the line (A) on the rotor with the notch (B)

7.4 Unscrew the bolts (arrowed) and remove the rocker assembly

7.5 Withdraw the pushrods

7.6 Check for freeplay between the arm and shaft

7.7 Check all points of contact between the rockers, pushrods and valves

Installation

9 Lubricate each pushrod with molybdenum disulphide oil (a 50/50 mixture of molybdenum disulphide grease and engine oil). Fit them into the engine the same way up and in the same bore they were removed from **(see illustration 7.7)**.

10 Make sure the engine timing marks are aligned as described in Step 3.

11 Fit the rocker assembly onto the head, locating the inner cupped end of each rocker onto the top of its pushrod **(see illustration)**. Fit the bolts with their copper washers and tighten them evenly and a little at a time to 12 Nm using a torque wrench **(see illustration)**.

12 Turn the engine anti-clockwise through two full turns and check that the pushrods, rockers and valves all move as they should **(see illustration 7.3a)**.

13 Check the valve clearances and adjust them if necessary (see Chapter 1).

14 Install the timing inspection cap and crankshaft end cap using new O-rings if required, and smear the O-rings and the cap threads with clean oil **(see illustrations)**.

15 Install the valve cover (see Section 6). Install the spark plug (see Chapter 1).

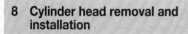

8 Cylinder head removal and installation

Note: *The cylinder head can be removed with the engine in the frame. If the engine has been removed ignore the steps that do not apply.*

8.2 Coolant temperature sensor (arrowed)

8.5b ... and where fitted remove the pushrod guide (arrowed)

7.11a Fit the assembly, locate the cups over the pushrods

7.14a Fit the caps using new O-rings (arrowed) if required ...

Removal

1 Remove the carburettor and the exhaust system (see Chapter 4). On models with an air induction system that routes the air through the cylinder head or block, disconnect the air

8.5a Unscrew the nuts (arrowed) ...

8.6 Carefully lift the head up off the block

7.11b Fit the bolts with their washers

7.14b ... and smear them with oil

hose from its union, and if necessary remove the control valve along with the hose and its bracket as required to minimise obstruction to cylinder head removal (see Chapter 4).

2 On liquid-cooled versions drain the cooling system (see Chapter 3). Disconnect the wire from the temperature sensor **(see illustration)**. Either remove the thermostat housing (see Chapter 3). Release the clamps securing the hoses to the housing and detach them.

3 Remove the rocker assembly and pushrods (see Section 7).

4 Unscrew the bolt on the side of the head and remove the washer **(see illustration 8.14)**.

5 Unscrew the four cylinder head nuts evenly and a little at a time in a criss-cross pattern **(see illustration)**. Remove the washers (two on models with a pushrod guide, four on models without), and where fitted the pushrod guide **(see illustration)**.

6 Lift the cylinder head up off the block **(see illustration)**. If the head is stuck, tap around the joint faces with a soft-faced mallet. Do not attempt to free it by inserting a screwdriver between the head and block mating surfaces – you'll damage them.

7 Remove the cylinder head gasket and discard it as a new one must be used **(see illustration 8.11)**. If they are loose, remove the dowels, and the O-ring (where fitted) around one of them, from the cylinder block or the underside of the cylinder head **(see illustration 8.10)**.

8 Check the cylinder head gasket and the mating surfaces on the cylinder head and cylinder block for signs of leakage, which

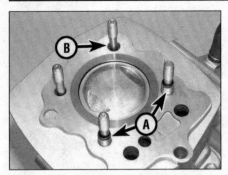

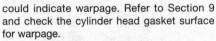

8.10 Fit the dowels (A) over the studs. Some models have a third dowel with an O-ring around it over stud (B)

8.11 Fit the gasket over the dowels and onto the block

8.14 Fit the side bolt with its washer

could indicate warpage. Refer to Section 9 and check the cylinder head gasket surface for warpage.

9 Clean all traces of old gasket material from the cylinder head and cylinder block. If a scraper is used, take care not to scratch or gouge the soft aluminium. Be careful not to let any of the gasket material fall into the cylinder bore or the oil and coolant passages. Refer to Section 10, Step 15 and check the studs are tight.

Installation

10 Lubricate the cylinder bore with engine oil. If removed, fit the dowels into the cylinder block **(see illustration)**. Fit a new O-ring (where fitted) around the one dowel.

11 Ensure both cylinder head and cylinder block mating surfaces are clean. Lay the new head gasket over the studs and onto the block, locating it over the dowels and making sure all the holes are correctly aligned **(see illustration)**. Never reuse the old gasket.

12 Carefully fit the cylinder head over the studs and onto the block, making sure it locates correctly onto the dowels **(see illustration 8.6)**.

13 Fit the washers, and where removed the pushrod guide, over the studs, then fit the cylinder head nuts finger-tight **(see illustrations 8.5b and a)**. Now tighten the nuts evenly and a little at a time in a criss-cross pattern to 29 Nm using a torque wrench.

14 Fit the bolt and washer into the side of the head and tighten to 29 Nm **(see illustration)**.

If the bolt won't thread in, check the slot in the end of the camshaft is vertical, and turn it or wiggle it if necessary using a screwdriver (if necessary turn it 180º so it is the other way up – this may help the threads to engage) (see Section 20).

15 Install the pushrods and rocker assembly (see Section 7).

16 On liquid-cooled versions install the thermostat housing if removed (see Chapter 3). If not, fit the hoses onto their unions and secure them with the clamps. Connect the wire to the temperature sensor **(see illustration 8.2)**. Refill the cooling system (see Chapter 3).

17 Install the carburettor and the exhaust system (see Chapter 4). Install the air induction system components (see Chapter 4).

9 Cylinder head and valve overhaul

1 Because of the complex nature of this job and the special tools and equipment required, most owners leave servicing of the valves, valve seats and valve guides to a professional.

2 With the correct tools (a valve spring compressor is essential – make sure it is suitable for motorcycle work), you can also remove the valves and associated components from the cylinder head, clean them and check them for wear to assess the extent of the work needed, and, unless seat cutting or guide

replacement is required, grind in the valves and reassemble them in the head.

3 A dealer service department or specialist can replace the guides and re-cut the valve seats.

4 After the valve service has been performed, be sure to clean the head very thoroughly before installation to remove any metal particles or abrasive grit that may still be present from the valve service operations. Use compressed air, if available, to blow out all the holes and passages.

Disassembly

5 Before proceeding, arrange to label and store the valves along with their related components in such a way that they can be returned to their original locations without getting mixed up. Labelled plastic bags or a plastic container with two compartments are ideal.

6 Compress the valve spring on the first valve with a spring compressor, making sure it is correctly located onto each end of the valve assembly **(see illustration)**. On the top of the valve the adaptor needs to be about the same size as the spring retainer – if it is too small it will be difficult to remove and install the collets **(see illustration)**. On the underside of the head make sure the plate on the compressor only contacts the valve and not the soft aluminium of the head **(see illustration)** – if the plate is too big for the valve, use a spacer between them. Do not compress the springs any more than is absolutely necessary.

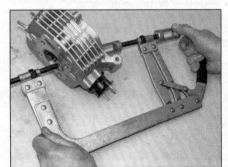

9.6a Using a valve spring compressor

9.6b Make sure the compressor locates correctly both on the top of the spring retainer . . .

9.6c . . . and on the bottom of the valve

9.7a Remove the collets . . .

9.7b . . . the spring retainer . . .

9.7c . . . the springs . . .

7 Remove the collets, using a magnet or a screwdriver with a dab of grease on it **(see illustration)**. Carefully release the valve spring compressor and remove the spring retainer, noting which way up it fits, the springs and the valve **(see illustrations)**. Mark the top of each spring with a dab of paint so they can be installed the same way up. If the valve binds in the guide and won't pull through, push it back into the head and deburr the area around the collet groove with a very fine file or whetstone **(see illustration)**.

8 Pull the valve stem seal off the top of the valve guide with pliers and discard it (the old seals should never be reused), then remove the spring seats noting which way up they fit **(see illustrations)**.

9 Repeat the procedure for the other valve. Remember to keep the parts for each valve together so they can be reinstalled in the same location.

10 Clean the cylinder head with solvent and dry it thoroughly. Compressed air will speed the drying process and ensure that all holes and recessed areas are clean. **Note:** *Do not use a wire brush mounted in a drill motor to clean the combustion chambers as the head material is soft and may be scratched or eroded away by the wire brush.*

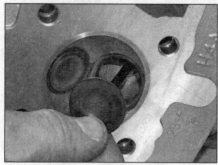

9.7d . . . and the valve

11 Clean the valve springs, collets, retainers and spring seats with solvent and dry them thoroughly. Do the parts from one valve at a time so that no mixing of parts between valves occurs.

12 Scrape off any deposits that may have formed on the valve, then use a motorised wire brush to remove deposits from the valve heads and stems. Again, make sure the valves do not get mixed up.

Inspection

13 Inspect the head very carefully for cracks

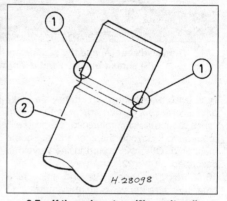

9.7e If the valve stem (2) won't pull through the guide, deburr the area (1) above the collet groove

and other damage. If cracks are found, a new head is required.

14 Using a precision straight-edge and a feeler gauge check the head gasket mating surface for warpage. Take six measurements, one along each side and two diagonally across. If the head is warped beyond 0.1 mm consider having it skimmed or resurfaced.

15 Examine the valve seats in the combustion chamber and the corresponding surface on

9.8a Pull the old seal off the valve stem . . .

9.8b . . . then use a magnet to remove both spring seats

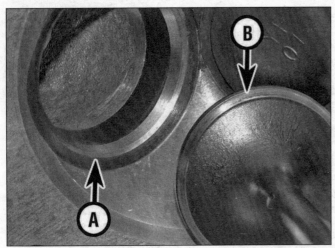

9.15 The valve seat (A) and the seating surface on the valve face (B) should be clean and uniform in width

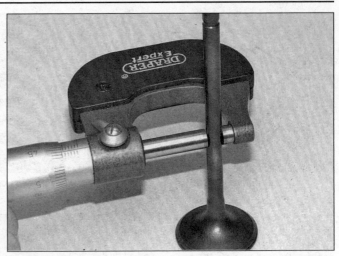

9.16a Measure the valve stem diameter with a micrometer

each valve **(see illustration)**. If they are badly pitted, cracked or burned, or if the width varies around its circumference, the head will require work beyond the scope of the home mechanic. Otherwise grind in the valves as described in Step 22.

16 Working on one valve and guide at a time, measure the valve stem diameter **(see illustration)**. Clean the valve's guide using a guide reamer to remove any carbon build-up – insert the reamer from the underside of the head and turn it clockwise only. Now measure the inside diameter of the guide (at both ends and in the centre of the guide) with a small bore gauge, then measure the gauge with a micrometer **(see illustration)**. Measure the guide at the ends and at the centre to determine if they are worn in a bell-mouth pattern (more wear at the ends). Subtract the stem diameter from the valve guide diameter to obtain the valve stem-to-guide clearance. If the stem-to-guide clearance exceeds 0.12 mm (intake) or 0.14 mm (exhaust) renew the valve; if this doesn't restore the clearance, renew the guide – this is a task for a dealer. Repeat for the other valve.

17 Carefully inspect each valve face, stem and collet groove area for cracks, pits and burned spots.

18 Rotate each valve and check for any obvious indication that it is bent, in which case it must be replaced with a new one. Check the end of the stem for pitting and excessive wear. The presence of any of the above conditions indicates the need for valve servicing.

19 Check the end of each valve spring for wear and pitting. Valve springs will sag (reduce in length) over time and the extent of this can only be measured by comparing their lengths with that of a new spring **(see illustration)**. Also place the spring upright on a flat surface and check it for bend by placing a ruler against it, or alternatively lay it against a set square. If the bend in any spring is excessive, it must be replaced with a new one.

20 Check the spring seats, retainers and collets for obvious wear and cracks. Any questionable parts should not be reused, as extensive damage will occur in the event of failure during engine operation.

21 If the inspection indicates that no overhaul work is required, the valve components can be reinstalled in the head.

Reassembly

22 Unless a valve service has been performed, before installing the valves in the head they should be ground in (lapped) to ensure a positive seal between the valves and seats. This procedure requires coarse and fine valve grinding compound and a valve grinding tool (either hand-held or drill driven – note that some drill-driven tools specify using only a fine grinding compound). If a grinding tool is not available, a piece of rubber or plastic hose can be slipped over the valve stem (after the valve has been installed in the guide) and used to turn the valve.

23 Apply a small amount of coarse grinding compound to the valve face **(see illustration)**. Smear some molybdenum disulphide oil (a 50/50 mixture of molybdenum disulphide grease and engine oil) to the valve stem, then slip the valve into the guide **(see illustration 9.7d)**. **Note:** *Make sure each valve is installed in its correct guide and be careful not to get any grinding compound on the valve stem.*

24 Attach the grinding tool to the valve and rotate the tool between the palms of your

9.16b Measure the valve guide with a small bore gauge, then measure the bore gauge with a micrometer

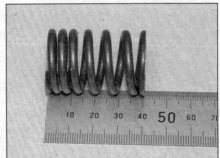

9.19 Measure the free length of the valve springs and check them for bend

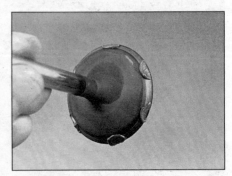

9.23 Apply small dabs of the paste around the circumference of the valve

9.24 Using a valve lapping tool

9.28 Fit the outer and inner spring seats

9.29a Fit a new valve stem seal . . .

9.29b . . . and press it squarely into place using a deep socket of the appropriate size

9.31 Make sure each collet has located in its groove in the top of the valve stem

9.33 Tap the top of the valve stem to ensure correct seating of the collets

hands **(see illustration)**. Use a back-and-forth motion (as though rubbing your hands together) rather than a circular motion (i.e. so that the valve rotates alternately clockwise and anti-clockwise rather than in one direction only). If a motorised tool is being used, take note of the correct drive speed for it – if your drill runs too fast and is not variable, use a hand tool instead. Lift the valve off the seat and turn it at regular intervals to distribute the grinding compound properly. Continue the grinding procedure until the valve face and seat contact area is of uniform width, and unbroken around the entire circumference **(see illustration 9.15)**.

25 Carefully remove the valve and wipe off all traces of grinding compound, making sure none gets in the guide. Use solvent to clean the valve and wipe the seat area thoroughly with a solvent soaked cloth.

26 Repeat the procedure with fine valve grinding compound, then use solvent to clean the valve and flush the guide, and wipe the seat area thoroughly with a solvent soaked cloth. Repeat the entire procedure for the other valve. On completion thoroughly clean the entire head again, then blow through all passages with compressed air. Make sure all traces of the grinding compound have been removed before assembling the head.

27 Coat the valve stem with molybdenum disulphide oil (a 50/50 mixture of molybdenum disulphide grease and engine oil), then install it into its guide, rotating it slowly to avoid damaging the seal **(see illustration 9.7d)**. Check that the valve moves up-and-down freely in the guide.

28 Working on one valve at a time, lay the spring seats in place in the cylinder head **(see illustration)**.

29 Fit a new valve stem seal onto the guide, using finger pressure, a stem seal fitting tool or an appropriate size deep socket, to push the seal squarely onto the end of the valve guide until it is felt to clip into place **(see illustrations)**.

30 Next, install the springs, the same way up as marked on removal **(see illustration 9.7c)**. Fit the spring retainer, with its shouldered side facing down so that it fits into the top of the springs **(see illustration 9.7b)**.

31 Apply a small amount of grease to the collets to help hold them in place. Compress the valve springs with a spring compressor, making sure it is correctly located onto each end of the valve assembly (see Step 6) **(see illustrations 9.6a, b and c)**. Do not compress the springs any more than is necessary to slip the collets into place. Locate each collet in turn into the groove in the valve stem using a screwdriver with a

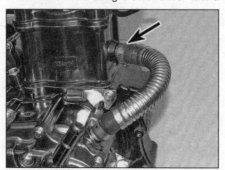

10.1 Release the clamp (arrowed) and detach the hose

dab of grease on it **(see illustration)**. Carefully release the compressor, making sure the collets seat and lock in the retaining groove.

32 Repeat the procedure for the other valve.

33 Support the cylinder head on blocks so the valves can't contact the work surface, then tap the end of each valve stem lightly to seat the collets in their grooves **(see illustration)**.

> **HAYNES HINT** *Check for proper sealing of the valves by pouring a small amount of solvent into each of the valve ports. If the solvent leaks past any valve into the combustion chamber the valve grinding operation on that valve should be repeated.*

34 After the cylinder head and camshaft holder have been installed, check the valve clearances and adjust as required (see Chapter 1).

10 Cylinder block

Note: *The cylinder block can be removed with the engine in the frame. If the engine has been removed ignore the steps that do not apply.*

Removal

1 On liquid-cooled models drain the cooling system (see Chapter 3). Release the clamp securing the coolant hose to the block and detach it, being prepared with a rag to catch any residual coolant **(see illustration)**.

10.3 Unscrew the bolts (arrowed)

10.4 Carefully lift the block up off the crankcase

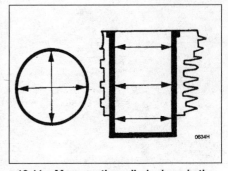

10.11a Measure the cylinder bore in the directions shown . . .

2 Remove the cylinder head (see Section 8).
3 Unscrew the cylinder block bolts and remove the washers where fitted (see illustration).
4 Pull the cylinder block up off the crankcase until the bottom half of the piston is exposed, but do not yet lift it all the way off (see illustration). If the block is stuck, tap around the joint faces with a soft-faced mallet – do not attempt to free it by inserting a screwdriver between the block and crankcase mating surfaces as you'll damage them. Stuff some clean rag around the connecting rod to protect and support it and the piston, and to prevent anything falling into the engine. Now lift the block up off the piston and remove it.
5 Remove the base gasket and discard it as a new one must be used.

6 If loose, remove the dowels from the crankcase or the underside of the cylinder block (see illustration 10.16a).
7 If required remove the lower rockers (see Section 20).
8 Clean all dirt and old gasket material and any sealant from the cylinder block and crankcase. If a scraper is used, take care not to scratch or gouge the soft aluminium. Be careful not to let any of the gasket material fall into the engine.

Inspection

Note: *Do not attempt to separate the cylinder liner from the cylinder block.*
9 Check the cylinder walls carefully for scratches and score marks.

10 Using a precision straight-edge and feeler gauges, check the block top surface for warpage. Take six measurements, one along each side and two diagonally across. If the block is warped beyond 0.1 mm consider having it skimmed or resurfaced.
11 Using a telescoping bore gauge and a micrometer, check the dimensions of the cylinder to assess the amount of wear, taper and ovality. Measure near the top (but below the level of the top piston ring at TDC), centre and bottom (but above the level of the oil ring at BDC) of the bore, both parallel to and across the crankshaft axis (see illustrations). The difference in measurements shouldn't exceed 0.1 mm. If the cylinder is worn, oval or tapered beyond the service limit check with your dealer whether oversize sets of pistons and rings are available, in which case it can be re-bored.
12 Also use the bore diameter, measured at the top of the bore, together with the piston diameter to determine piston-to-bore wear (see Section 11).

Installation

13 If removed install the lower rockers (see Section 20).
14 Check that the mating surfaces of the cylinder block and crankcase are free from oil, sealant and pieces of old gasket.
15 Check that all the studs are tight in the crankcase. If any are loose, or need to be replaced with new ones, remove them. Clean their threads and smear them with clean engine oil. Fit them into the crankcase and tighten them using a stud tool, or by threading two nuts onto the top of the stud and tightening them together so they are locked on the stud, then tighten the stud by turning the upper of the two nuts (see illustration).
16 Fit the dowels over the studs and into the crankcase and push them firmly home (see illustration). Apply a dab of RTV sealant to the short sections of crankcase mating surface that the block sits on (see illustration).
17 Lay the new base gasket in place, locating

10.11b . . . using a telescoping gauge, then measure the gauge with a micrometer

10.15 Studs can be tightened using two nuts locked together

10.16a Fit the dowels (arrowed)

10.16b Put a dab of sealant (arrowed) on each section of crankcase joint . . .

it over the dowels **(see illustration)**. The gasket can only fit one way, so if all the holes do not line up properly it is the wrong way round. Never re-use the old gasket.

18 Rotate the crankshaft so that the piston is at its highest point (top dead centre). Make sure the piston ring end gaps are positioned 120° apart before fitting the cylinder block.

19 Lubricate the cylinder bore, piston and piston rings with clean engine oil.

20 Carefully lower the block over the studs and onto the piston until the crown fits into the bore, holding the underside of the piston to prevent it dropping, and making sure it enters the bore squarely and does not get cocked sideways **(see illustration 10.4)**.

21 Carefully compress and feed each ring into the bore as the cylinder is lowered **(see illustration)**. If necessary, use a soft mallet to gently tap the cylinder down, but do not use force if it appears to be stuck as the piston and/or rings will be damaged.

22 When the piston and rings are correctly located in the bore, remove the rag from around the piston. Now press the cylinder block down onto the base gasket, making sure the dowels locate.

23 Fit the cylinder block bolts, with their washers where fitted, and tighten them **(see illustration 10.3)**.

24 Turn the crankshaft to check that everything moves as it should.

25 Install the cylinder head (see Section 8).

26 On liquid-cooled models connect the coolant hose and tighten the clamp (see illustration 10.1). Refill the cooling system (see Chapter 3).

11 Piston

Note: *The piston can be removed with the engine in the frame.*

Removal

1 Remove the cylinder block (see Section 10). Check that the holes into the crankcase and the pushrod tunnel are completely blocked with rag.

2 Look for a mark on the piston crown and

10.17 . . . then fit the new gasket

note which way it faces – the piston must be installed the same way round. The piston on the engine shown is marked IN, denoting the intake side (rear) of the piston, though sometimes an EX may be marked on the exhaust (front) side, or a punch mark is used, and this could be on either side **(see illustration)**. If no mark is visible make your own, either an F or EX at the front, or R or IN at the rear, as preferred.

3 Carefully prise out the circlip on one side of the piston using needle-nose pliers or a small flat-bladed screwdriver inserted into the notch **(see illustration)**. Push the piston pin out from the other side to free the piston from the connecting rod **(see illustration)**. Remove the other circlip and discard them as new ones must be used.

> **HAYNES HiNT**
> *If a piston pin is a tight fit in the piston bosses, heat the piston using a heat gun – this will expand the piston sufficiently to release its grip on the pin. If the piston pin is particularly stubborn, extract it using a drawbolt tool, but be careful to protect the piston's working surfaces.*

4 Using your thumbs or a piston ring removal and installation tool, carefully remove the rings from the pistons **(see illustrations 12.6, 12.5b, 12.3c, b and a)**. Piston rings are brittle and break easily, so care is needed. Do not nick or gouge the pistons in the process. The upper surface of the top and second rings

10.21 Carefully feed each ring into the bore as you lower the block

should be marked at one end, but mark them if not so they can installed the same way up if being re-used **(see illustration 12.5a)**. Keep the old rings and note any markings so the new rings can be matched to them for correct installation.

5 Scrape all traces of carbon from the top of the piston. A hand-held wire brush or a piece of fine emery cloth can be used once most of the deposits have been scraped away. Do not, under any circumstances, use a wire brush mounted in a drill motor to remove deposits from the pistons; the piston material is soft and will be eroded away by the wire brush.

6 Use a piston ring groove cleaning tool to remove any carbon deposits from the ring grooves. If a tool is not available, a piece broken off an old ring will do the job. Be very careful to remove only the carbon deposits. Do not remove any metal and do not nick or gouge the sides of the ring grooves.

7 Once the deposits have been removed, clean the piston with solvent and dry it thoroughly. Make sure the oil return holes below the oil ring groove are clear.

Inspection

8 Carefully inspect the piston for cracks around the skirt, at the pin bosses and at the ring lands. Normal piston wear appears as even, vertical wear on the thrust surfaces. If the skirt is scored or scuffed, the engine may have been suffering from overheating and/or abnormal combustion, which caused excessively high operating temperatures. Also check that the circlip grooves are not damaged.

11.2 Note the mark on the piston and which way it faces

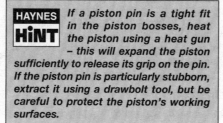

11.3a Prise out the circlip using a suitable tool in the notch . . .

11.3b . . . then push out the pin and separate the piston from the rod

11.10 Measure the piston diameter with a micrometer at the bottom of the skirt

11.11a Fit the pin into the piston and feel for any freeplay

11.11b Feel for freeplay between the middle of the pin and the small-end of the connecting rod

11.15 Use new circlips and make sure they locate correctly

9 A hole in the top of the piston, in one extreme, or burned areas around the edge of the piston crown, indicate that pre-ignition or knocking under load have occurred. If you find evidence of any problems the cause must be corrected or the damage will occur again (see *Fault Finding* in the *Reference* section).

10 Check the piston-to-bore clearance by measuring the bore diameter (see Section 10), then measure the piston about 6 mm up from the bottom of the skirt and at 90° to the piston pin axis **(see illustration)**. Subtract the piston diameter from the bore diameter to obtain the piston-to-bore clearance. If it is greater than 0.1 mm, the piston must be replaced with a new one (assuming the bore itself is within limits).

11 Apply clean engine oil to the piston pin, insert it into the piston and check for any freeplay between the two **(see illustration)**. Repeat the freeplay check between the middle of the pin and the connecting rod small-end **(see illustration)**.

Installation

12 Inspect and install the piston rings (see Section 12).

13 Lubricate the piston pin, the piston pin bore and the connecting rod small-end bore with molybdenum disulphide oil (a 50/50 mixture of molybdenum disulphide grease and clean engine oil).

14 When fitting the piston onto the connecting rod make sure the mark on the piston crown

faces the correct side of the engine (see Step 2).

15 Fit a *new* circlip into one side of the piston (do not reuse old circlips). Line up the piston on the correct connecting rod and insert the piston pin from the other side **(see illustration 11.3b)**. Secure the pin with the other *new* circlip **(see illustration)**. When fitting the circlips, compress them only just enough to fit them in the piston, and make sure they are properly seated in their grooves with the open end away from the removal notch.

16 Install the cylinder block (see Section 10).

12 Piston rings

1 Always replace the piston rings with new ones when an engine is being overhauled.

2 Refer to Section 11 and remove the old rings. Keep the old rings in order so that any markings on the new rings can be matched up.

3 Install the oil control ring (lowest on the piston) first. It is composed of three separate components, namely the expander and the upper and lower side-rails. Slip the expander into the groove, making sure the ends don't overlap, then fit the lower side-rail **(see illustrations)**. Do not use a piston ring installation tool on the side-rails as they may be damaged. Instead, place one end of the side-rail into the groove between the expander and the ring land. Hold it firmly in place and slide a finger around the piston while pushing the rail into the groove. Next, fit the upper side-rail in the same manner **(see illustration)**. Check that the ends of the expander have not overlapped.

4 After the three oil ring components have been installed, check to make sure that both the upper and lower side-rails can be turned smoothly in the ring groove.

5 The upper surface of the top and second rings should be marked at one end (usually with a letter or letters), and these marks must

12.3a Fit the oil ring expander in its groove . . .

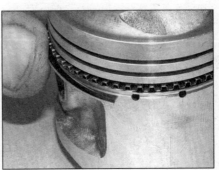

12.3b . . . then fit the lower side rail . . .

12.3c . . . and the upper side rail on each side of it

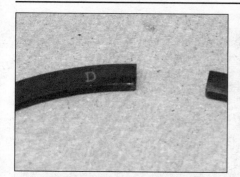

12.5a Note the marking on the two compression rings which must face up – the second ring shown here is marked D and is darker than the top ring

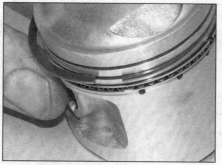

12.5b Install the second ring (marked D) . . .

12.6 . . . and the top ring (marked DY) as described

face up **(see illustration)**. Install the second (middle) ring next. Fit the ring into the middle groove in the piston **(see illustration)**. Do not expand the ring any more than is necessary to slide it into place. To avoid breaking the ring, use a piston ring installation tool.

6 Finally, install the top ring in the same manner into the top groove in the piston **(see illustration)**. Make sure the mark is facing up.

7 Once the rings are correctly installed, check they move freely without snagging and stagger their end gaps 120° apart.

13 Alternator, starter clutch and gears

Note: *The starter clutch is mounted on the back of the alternator rotor. They can be removed with the engine in the frame. If the engine has been removed, ignore the steps that do not apply.*

Alternator check

1 Checking of the charging system is covered in Chapter 9.

Starter clutch check

2 The operation of the starter clutch can be checked while it is in situ. Remove the starter motor (see Chapter 9). Check that the starter drive gear is able to rotate freely anti-clockwise as you look at it via the starter motor aperture, but locks when rotated clockwise. If not, the starter clutch is faulty and should be removed for inspection.

Removal

3 Remove any fairing panels as required according to model (see Chapter 8).

4 Drain the engine oil (see Chapter 1). Remove the front sprocket cover (see Chapter 7).

5 Trace the alternator and pick-up coil wiring from the cover on the left-hand side of the engine and disconnect it at the connectors **(see illustrations 4.14a and b)**. Slacken the wiring clamp bolt enough to free the wiring.

6 Unscrew the starter drive gear cover bolts and remove the cover **(see illustration)**.

Discard the O-ring – a new one must be used. Grasp the end of the drive gear shaft and remove the shaft/gear assembly as one **(see illustration)** – note the outer washer on the end of the shaft. If required slide the outer washer, the gear and the inner washer off the shaft.

7 Working in a criss-cross pattern, evenly slacken the alternator cover bolts, noting which fits where – on the engine photographed, the bolt inside the drive gear housing was a different colour, and the top bolt next to the timing mark inspection cap/hole had sealant on its threads **(see illustrations 13.25c and d)**. **Note:** *As each bolt is removed, store it in its relative position in a cardboard template of the cover (see illustration 21.6b). This will ensure all bolts are returned to their original locations on reassembly.* Draw the cover off the engine, noting that it will be restrained by the force of the rotor magnets,

and be prepared to catch any residual oil **(see illustration 13.25b)**. Remove and discard the gasket **(see illustration 13.25a)**. Remove the dowels from either the cover or the crankcase if loose.

8 Remove the idle/reduction gear, noting the thrust washer on each end of the shaft **(see illustration)**.

9 To remove the rotor bolt it is necessary to stop the rotor from turning. The best way is to use a commercially available rotor strap, taking care to avoid the raised trigger for the pick-up coil on the outside of the rotor **(see illustration)**. If a strap is not available and the engine is in the frame, try placing the transmission in gear and having an assistant apply the rear brake hard. With the rotor locked or held unscrew the bolt.

10 To remove the rotor from the shaft it is necessary to use a rotor puller – several are commercially available, but make sure you

13.6a Unscrew the bolts (arrowed) and remove the cover

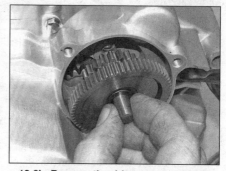

13.6b Remove the drive gear assembly

13.8 Remove the idle/reduction gear and thrust washers (arrowed)

13.9 Using a rotor strap to hold the rotor while unscrewing the bolt

13.10 Using a multi-application commercial puller that threads into the rotor hub

13.11 Remove the Woodruff key (arrowed) if it is loose

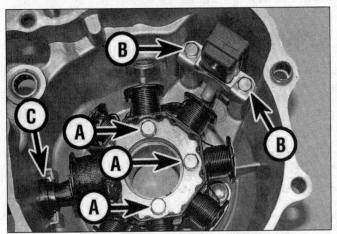

13.12 Unscrew the stator bolts (A) and the pick-up bolts (B), and free the grommet (C)

13.13 Check the operation of the starter clutch as described

buy the right one as shown. Thread the puller into the rotor, then hold the rotor as before and tighten the puller until the rotor is displaced from the shaft **(see illustration)**. If the rotor is very tight heat around the centre hub using a hot air gun, then tap the end of the puller.

11 Slide the starter driven gear off the end of the crankshaft **(see illustration 13.19)**, or remove it from the starter clutch if it came away with it – you will need to twist it anti-clockwise to release it **(see illustration 13.13)**. Remove the Woodruff key from its slot in the crankshaft if it is loose (see illustration). If required detach the starter clutch from the rotor (see Step 15).

12 To remove the stator and pick-up coil from the cover, you first need to release and remove the terminal pins from the wiring connectors to allow the wiring to be draw through its hole (note that on some models the pick-up coil is a separate component with separate wiring, but on most they are wired together and come as an assembly). Before doing so make a note of which wire goes where as they must be reinstalled in the same location. Unscrew the rotor and pick-up coil bolts as required then lift them out of the

cover, releasing the wiring grommet and drawing the wiring through **(see illustration)**.

Starter clutch inspection

13 With the rotor face down on a workbench and the starter driven gear in the starter clutch, check that the gear rotates freely anti-clockwise and locks against the rotor clockwise **(see illustration)**. If it doesn't, remove the starter driven gear, rotating it anti-clockwise as you do.

14 Check the condition of the rollers and the corresponding surface on the driven gear hub **(see illustration)**. If the rollers are damaged, marked or flattened at any point, remove them along with the plungers and springs, noting how they fit, and replace them with new ones, if available (if not, remove the starter clutch from the rotor (Step 15) and replace the whole assembly with a new one) **(see illustrations)**.

15 To remove the starter clutch from the

13.14a Check the rollers and hub for wear and damage

13.14b Remove the rollers . . .

13.14c . . . plungers and springs

13.15 Starter clutch bolts (arrowed)

13.16 Check the bush (arrowed) for wear

back of the alternator rotor hold the rotor using a holding strap and unscrew the three bolts **(see illustration)**. Clean the threads of the bolts and on installation apply a suitable non-permanent thread locking compound.

16 Check the bush in the starter driven gear hub and its bearing surface on the crankshaft **(see illustration)**. If the bush shows signs of excessive wear (the groove in the surface of the bush for holding the oil will be barely visible) replace the driven gear with a new one. Check the condition of the oil seal in the crankcase and replace it with a new one if necessary (though it is good practice to fit a new one as a matter of course) – lever the old one out using a seal hook or screwdriver. Press the new one in or tap them in using a socket, with the marked side facing out, and making sure they enter square.

17 Check the teeth of the starter motor drive shaft, the starter drive gear, the idle/reduction gear, and the starter driven gear. Replace the gears and/or starter motor as required if worn or chipped teeth are discovered on related gears. Also check the gear shafts for damage, and check that the drive gear is not a loose fit on its shaft. Check the idle/reduction shaft ends and the bearings they run in for wear, and similarly check the middle section of the drive gear shaft and the bearings in the gear **(see illustrations)**. The availability of

13.17a Check the idle/reduction gear shaft and bearings (arrowed) . . .

13.17b . . . and the drive gear shaft and bearings (arrowed)

individual components and bearings depends on manufacturer, so check with your dealer.

Installation

18 If removed fit the springs, plungers and rollers into the starter clutch, making sure they locate correctly **(see illustrations 13.14c and b)**. Apply clean engine oil to the rollers.

19 Lubricate the outside of the starter driven gear hub on each side and the bush in its centre with clean engine oil, then slide the gear onto the crankshaft with the narrower section of hub facing in, and fitting it into the crankcase seal **(see illustration)**.

20 Clean the tapered end of the crankshaft

and the corresponding mating surface on the inside of the rotor with a suitable solvent. Fit the Woodruff key into its slot in the crankshaft if removed **(see illustration 13.11)**.

21 Make sure that no metal objects have attached themselves to the magnet on the inside of the rotor. Slide the rotor onto the shaft, making sure the groove on the inside is aligned with and fits over the Woodruff key, and fit the starter clutch over the driven gear, rotating the gear clockwise as you do so to spread the rollers and allow it to enter **(see illustration)**. Make sure the key does not become dislodged. Give the rotor hub a gentle tap with a soft mallet to seat it.

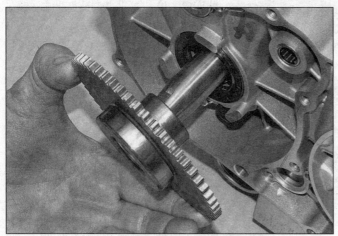

13.19 Slide the gear onto the shaft

13.21 Slide the rotor onto the shaft, aligning the cut-out with the Woodruff key, and turning the driven gear

13.22a Fit the bolt . . .

13.22b . . . and tighten it to the specified torque

13.25a Make sure the dowels (arrowed) are in place, then fit the new gasket

13.25b Fit the cover onto the dowels

13.25c Fit the coloured bolt into the drive gear housing . . .

13.25d . . . and apply sealant to the upper bolt

13.26a Fit the shaft, locating the pin in the cut-out

13.26b Fit the inner washer . . .

13.26c . . . the drive gear . . .

13.26d . . . and the outer washer

22 Fit the bolt and tighten it to 30 Nm, using the method employed on removal to prevent the rotor from turning **(see illustrations)**.
23 Lubricate the idle/reduction gear shaft ends with oil and make sure the thrust washer is fitted on each end **(see illustration 13.8)**. Fit the gear with the larger pinion innermost, meshing its teeth with the driven gear.

24 If removed clean the stator and pick-up coil wiring grommet and apply some fresh sealant, then feed the wiring through the hole in the alternator cover and seat the grommet. Fit the stator and coil into the cover **(see illustration 13.12)**. Apply a suitable thread locking compound to the bolts, and tighten them. Fit the wiring terminal pins back into their original locations in the connector, making sure they are securely retained by the tabs.
25 Before fitting the cover install the neutral switch if removed (see Chapter 9). Fit the dowels into the crankcase if removed, then locate a new gasket onto the dowels **(see illustration)**. Install the alternator cover, noting that the rotor magnets will forcibly draw the cover/stator on, making sure it locates onto the dowels **(see illustration)**. Fit the cover bolts – fit the longer bolts where the dowels are fitted, and if applicable to your engine (see Step 7) fit the coloured bolt in the drive gear housing and apply some sealant to the bolt adjacent the timing mark inspection cap **(see illustrations)**. Tighten the bolts evenly in a criss-cross sequence.
26 Lubricate the drive gear shaft with oil and fit it into its bore, locating the pin in the cut-out **(see illustration)**. Slide the inner washer on **(see illustration)**. Fit the drive gear with the small pinion innermost, meshing its teeth with the outer pinion on the idle/ reduction gear and with the starter motor shaft **(see illustration)**. Fit the outer washer **(see illustration)**. Fit the starter drive gear cover

13.26e Fit the cover using a new O-ring (arrowed)

14.6a Clutch cover bolts (arrowed) – air-cooled engine without balancer shaft

using a new O-ring and tighten the bolts **(see illustration)**.

27 Reconnect the wiring at the connectors – make sure it is correctly routed, then tighten the clamp bolt **(see illustration 4.14b and a)**.

28 Replenish the engine oil. Install the front sprocket cover (see Chapter 7). Install any body panels as required according to model.

14 Clutch

Note: *The clutch can be removed with the engine in the frame. If the engine has been removed, ignore the steps that don't apply.*

Clutch removal

1 Remove any fairing panels as required

according to model (see Chapter 8). Also remove the exhaust, brake pedal, footrest or footrest assembly where they prevent removal of the clutch cover (see Chapters 4 and 5).

2 Drain the engine oil (see Chapter 1).

3 On liquid-cooled models drain the coolant (see Chapter 3). Release the clamps securing the coolant hoses to the water pump and detach the hoses.

4 Where fitted undo the tachometer cable retaining screw and draw the cable out **(see illustration 4.11)**. Detach the clutch cable and position it clear (see Section 15).

5 Where fitted remove the kickstart lever, making an alignment mark with the shaft if there is none visible so it can be correctly installed later **(see illustration 4.8b)**. Unscrew the lever stop bracket bolts and remove the bracket **(see illustration 4.8c)**.

6 Working evenly in a criss-cross pattern, unscrew the clutch cover bolts, noting any

washers or brackets with the bolts, and noting which length bolts fit where **(see illustrations)**. **Note:** *As each bolt is removed, store it in its relative position in a cardboard template of the cover (see illustration 21.6b). This will ensure all bolts and anything fitted with them are returned to their original locations on reassembly.* Remove the cover, being prepared to catch any residual oil. Remove the gasket and discard it. Remove the two dowels from either the cover or the crankcase if they are loose.

7 Remove the centrifugal oil filter (see Section 16) – note that on liquid-cooled models with a kickstart mechanism this is not fitted (the water pump is in its place). On engines with a balancer shaft remove the oil pump driven sprocket (see Section 19). Remove the drive chain and slide the drive sprocket off the shaft, noting which way round it fits **(see illustrations 17.4a and b)**.

8 Remove the pushrod and its guide **(see**

14.6b Clutch cover bolts (arrowed) – air-cooled engine with balancer shaft

14.6c Clutch cover bolts (arrowed) – liquid-cooled engine with kickstart

14.8a Withdraw the pushrod and guide

14.8b Unscrew the bolts (arrowed) as described

14.9 Remove the circlip from the end of the shaft

illustration). Remove the bearing from the lifter plate if it is loose **(see illustration 14.25c).** Working in a criss-cross pattern, gradually slacken the clutch spring bolts until pressure is released **(see illustration).** To prevent the assembly from turning, cover it with a rag and hold it securely – the bolts are not very tight. If available, have an assistant hold the clutch while you unscrew the bolts. Remove the bolts, lifter plate and springs **(see illustrations 14.25b and a).**

9 Remove the circlip **(see illustration).** Discard it and use a new one on installation.

10 Note the fitting of the friction plate tabs in the clutch housing slots for your engine – on most models all the tabs on all the plates are aligned in the deep slots, however on the

kickstart liquid-cooled engine photographed the tabs of the outermost friction plate locate in shallow slots in the housing offset from the deep slots. Draw the complete clutch plate assembly off using the pressure plate posts **(see illustration).** Unless the plates are being replaced with new ones, keep the assembly together. To disassemble it place the clutch centre face down and remove the pressure plate from the back **(see illustration 14.21c).** Remove the clutch friction and plain plates, noting how they fit and keeping them in order **(see illustrations 14.21b and a).**

11 Turn the splined washer to unlock the splines and slide it off the shaft **(see illustration).** Draw the clutch housing off the shaft **(see illustration).** On engines with a

balancer shaft slide the spacer off the shaft **(see illustration).**

Inspection

12 After an extended period of service the clutch friction plates will wear and promote clutch slip. Measure the thickness of each friction plate using a Vernier caliper **(see illustration).** If the friction material shows obvious signs of wear (or is worn down to less than 2.6 mm), the plates smell burnt or are glazed, the friction plates must be replaced with a new set.

13 The plain plates should not show any signs of excess heating (bluing). Check for distortion using a flat surface and feeler gauge **(see illustration).** If any plate is warped

14.10 Draw the complete clutch plate assembly off the shaft

14.11a Turn the washer to unlock it and slide it off . . .

14.11b . . . then remove the clutch housing . . .

14.11c . . . and where fitted the spacer

14.12 Measuring clutch friction plate thickness

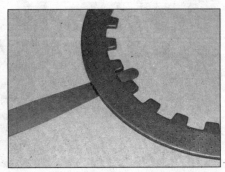

14.13 Check the plain plates for warpage

14.14 Measure the free length of the clutch springs and check them for bend

14.15a Check the friction plate tabs and housing slots . . .

14.15b . . . and the plain plate teeth and centre slots as described

more than 0.2 mm, or shows signs of bluing, all plain plates must be replaced with a new set.

14 Measure the free length of each clutch spring using a Vernier caliper **(see illustration)**. Place each spring upright on a flat surface and check it for bend by placing a ruler against it, or alternatively lay it against a set square. If any spring has sagged in comparison to the others, or if the bend in any spring is excessive, replace all the springs as a set.

15 Inspect the friction plates and the clutch housing for burrs and indentations on the edges of the protruding tabs on the plates and/or the slots in the housing **(see illustration)**. Similarly check for wear between the inner teeth of the plain plates and the slots in the clutch centre **(see illustration)**. Wear of this nature will cause clutch drag and slow disengagement during gear changes as the plates will snag when the pressure plate is lifted. With care a small amount of wear can be corrected by dressing with a fine file, but if this is excessive the worn components should be renewed.

16 Inspect the contact surfaces of the clutch

housing and the bearing surface of the kickstart driven pinion which locates on the input shaft. If there are any signs of wear, pitting or other damage the affected parts must be replaced with new ones. Check the teeth of the primary driven gear on the back of the clutch housing and the corresponding teeth of the primary drive gear on the crankshaft **(see illustration)**. Replace the clutch housing and/or primary drive gear with a new one if worn or chipped teeth are discovered – refer to Section 17 for the primary drive gear.

17 Check the lifter plate and its bearing for signs of wear or damage and roughness **(see illustration 14.25c)**. Check that the bearing outer race is a good fit in the centre of the lifter, and that the inner race rotates freely without any rough spots. Check the pushrod and the cam on the release mechanism shaft for signs of wear or damage **(see illustration)**. Replace any parts necessary with new ones.

18 Check the release mechanism in the clutch cover for a smooth action. If the action is stiff or rough, remove the split pin then withdraw the shaft and remove the cam and spring, noting how they locate, and the

14.16 Check the primary drive and driven gear teeth

O-ring **(see illustration)**. Lubricate the release mechanism shaft with molybdenum disulphide oil (a 50/50 mixture of molybdenum disulphide grease and engine oil) and the O-ring with grease before installing the shaft. Make sure the return spring ends and cam locate correctly.

19 Clean and check the kickstart shaft oil seal and the shaft bore in the cover. The seal can be replaced by levering the old one out with a

14.17 Check the ends of the pushrod and the lifter cam (arrowed) in the cover

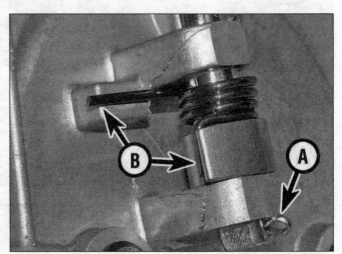

14.18 Remove the split pin (A) to release the shaft. Note the fitting of the return spring ends (B)

seal hook or screwdriver and pressing the new one in **(see illustrations)**. Similarly check the crankshaft end seal **(see illustration)**. Where fitted also check the tachometer drive shaft and its seal **(see illustration)**.

Installation

20 Remove all traces of old gasket from the crankcase and clutch cover surfaces.

21 If the clutch plate assembly was disassembled, coat each clutch plate with engine oil, then build up the plates on the clutch centre, starting with a friction plate, then fit a plain plate, then alternating plain and friction plates until all are installed **(see illustrations)**. Fit the pressure plate into the back of the pack, making sure its castellations engage with the clutch centre **(see illustration)**. Grasp the pack and turn it on its side, then pull on the pressure plate posts and check for any freeplay between the clutch plates – there should be none; if there is, it means the pressure plate has not located properly. Align the tabs of the friction plates.

22 On engines with a balancer shaft slide the spacer onto the shaft **(see illustration 14.11c)**. Fit the clutch housing onto the shaft **(see illustration 14.11b)**. Slide the splined washer on, then turn it in the groove so the splines lock the washer on the shaft **(see illustrations)**.

23 Fit the clutch plate assembly into the clutch housing, locating the friction plate tabs in the slots as noted before removal (see

14.19a Lever out the seal . . .

14.19b . . . and press a new one into place

14.19c Check the crankshaft seal (arrowed) . . .

14.19d . . . and the tachometer drive shaft (arrowed)

Step 10) **(see illustration 14.10)** – if applicable to your engine, offset the tabs of the outermost friction plate and locate them in the shall slots.

24 Fit a new circlip into the groove in the shaft **(see illustration)**.

25 Fit the clutch springs, lifter plate and bolts and tighten them evenly and a little at a time

14.21a Fit a friction plate . . .

14.21b . . . then a plain plate, and so on

14.21c Fit the pressure plate, making sure the castellations engage

14.22a Slide the washer on . . .

14.22b . . . then turn it in the groove to lock it on the shaft

14.24 Make sure the circlip locates correctly in the groove

in a criss-cross sequence **(see illustrations)**. Fit the bearing into the lifter plate if removed, and lubricate it with oil **(see illustration)**. Fit the pushrod and its guide **(see illustration 14.8a)**.

26 On engines with a balancer shaft slide the oil pump drive sprocket onto the shaft, then loop the drive chain around it **(see illustrations 17.4b and a)**. Install the oil pump driven sprocket (see Section 19). On all except liquid-cooled engines with a kickstart mechanism install the centrifugal oil filter (see Section 16).

27 Fit the two dowels into the crankcase if removed, then fit a new gasket, locating it over the dowels **(see illustration)**. Lubricate the centrifugal oil filter piece or crankshaft end (according to engine type) with oil, and make sure the seal it fits into in the cover is installed **(see illustration 14.19c)**. Install the cover, on liquid-cooled engines turning the water pump impeller as required to ease engagement of its gear **(see illustration)**. Install all the bolts finger-tight, then tighten them evenly and a little at a time in a criss-cross pattern **(see illustration 14.6a, b or c)**.

28 Reconnect the clutch cable (see Section 15) then adjust freeplay (see Chapter 1). Where

fitted connect the tachometer cable, aligning the slot in the end with the drive tab, and secure it with the screw **(see illustration 4.11)**.

29 On liquid-cooled models fit the coolant hoses onto their unions on the water pump and secure them with the clamps. Refill the cooling system (see Chapter 3).

30 Fill the engine with the correct amount and type of oil (see Chapter 1). Where fitted install the kickstart lever stop bracket and lever **(see illustrations 4.8c and b)**, and any other removed components as required according to model.

14.25a Fit the springs . . .

14.25b . . . and the lifter plate, and tighten the bolts as described

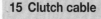

15 Clutch cable

1 Where fitted pull back the rubber boot covering the adjuster at the handlebar end of the cable. Fully slacken the lockring on the adjuster at the handlebar end of the cable, then thread the adjuster fully in **(see illustration)**. This provides freeplay in the cable and resets the adjuster to the beginning of its span.

14.25c Fit the bearing into the plate

14.27a Locate the new gasket over the dowels (arrowed) . . .

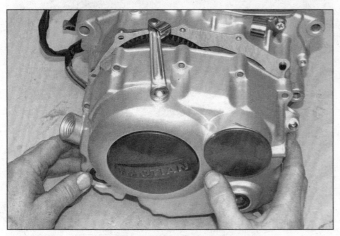

14.27b . . . then fit the cover

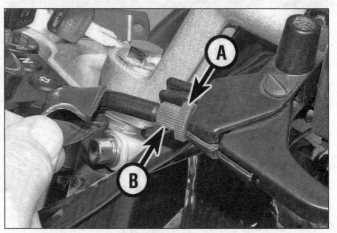

15.1 Pull back the boot, slacken the lockring (A) and turn the adjuster (B) in

15.3a Thread the rear nut (arrowed) off . . .

15.3b . . . then free the cable end from the arm . . .

15.3c . . . and slip the cable out of the bracket

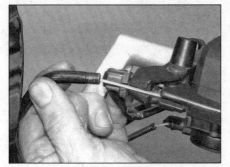

15.4a Free the outer cable from the adjuster . . .

15.4b . . . and the inner cable from the lever

5 Installation is the reverse of removal. Apply grease to the cable ends. Make sure the cable is correctly routed through its guides. Adjust the amount of clutch lever freeplay (see Chapter 1).

16 Centrifugal oil filter

Note: *The centrifugal oil filter is not fitted on liquid-cooled engines with a kickstart mechanism (the water pump is in its place). It can be removed with the engine in the frame.*
1 Remove the clutch cover (see Section 14, Steps 1 to 6).

Check and cleaning

2 Undo the filter cover screws and remove the cover – place some rag below to catch the residual oil **(see illustration)**. Discard the gasket – a new one must be used.
3 Clean out the filter – any dirt and debris should be found around the perimeter.
4 Make sure the sprung oil piece in the cover moves smoothly and freely against the spring. If necessary replace them with new ones – they are secured by a pin on the inside **(see illustration)**.

2 Remove any fairing side panel as required according to model to access the cable holder on the right-hand side of the engine (see Chapter 8).
3 Slacken the rear nut on the clutch cable adjuster and thread it off, then thread the front nut fully up the adjuster **(see illustration)**. Free the cable end from the release arm then draw the adjuster forward out of the bracket and slip the inner cable out the side **(see illustrations)**.
4 Align the slots in the adjuster and lockring at the handlebar end of the cable with that in the lever bracket, then pull the outer cable end from the socket in the adjuster and release the inner cable from the lever **(see illustrations)**. Remove the cable from the machine, noting its routing.

> **HAYNES HiNT**
> *Before removing the cable from the bike, tape the lower end of the new cable to the upper end of the old cable. Slowly pull the lower end of the old cable out, guiding the new cable down into position. Using this method will ensure the cable is routed correctly.*

16.2 Undo the screws (arrowed) and remove the cover

16.4 Withdraw the pin (arrowed) to release the oil piece and spring

16.7a Use a peg spanner to unscrew the nut

16.8 Slide the filter off the shaft

5 Fit a new gasket onto the cover, then fit the cover and tighten the screws.

Removal

6 Undo the filter cover screws and remove the cover – place some rag below to catch the residual oil **(see illustration 16.2)**. Discard the gasket – a new one must be used.

7 To unscrew the nut a 24 mm peg spanner, such as the one shown, is needed **(see illustration)** – these are commercially available from good suppliers of specialist motorcycle tools. Alternatively one can be made by cutting castellations into an old socket **(see Tool Tip)**. You also need to counter-hold the shaft to prevent it turning while slackening the nut – a good way to do this is to wedge a stout piece of rag or strap or a piece of 2 mm

16.7b Aluminium plate (arrowed) can be used to jam gears together

16.9 Make sure the washer is the correct way round

aluminium plate (DO NOT use steel) between the teeth of the primary drive and driven gears where they mesh at the top as shown **(see illustration)**. Alternatively, if the engine is in the frame, select a high gear and hold the rear brake on hard to lock the crankshaft. Unscrew the nut and remove the washer, noting which way round it fits. Remove the rag, strap or plate if used.

8 Slide the filter off the shaft **(see illustration)**.

Installation

9 Installation is the reverse of removal. Fit the washer with the OUTSIDE mark facing out **(see illustration)**. Lock the shaft to tighten the nut, but if using rag, strap or plate place it between the gear teeth on the underside, unless your

TOOL TiP

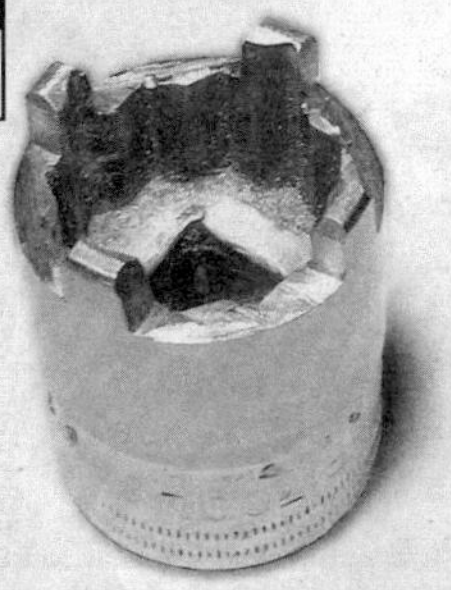

A peg spanner can be made by cutting castellations into a socket of the correct size using a hacksaw.

engine has a balancer shaft in which case it can be placed between the balancer drive and driven gears at the top.

17 Primary drive gear

Note: *The primary drive gear can be removed with the engine in the frame.*

Removal

1 Remove the clutch cover (see Section 14, Steps 1 to 6).

2 On all except liquid-cooled kickstart engines remove the centrifugal oil filter (see Section 16).

3 On liquid-cooled kickstart engines unscrew the primary drive gear nut using the tool and method described in Section 16, Step 7. Remove the washer, noting which way round it fits.

4 On engines with a balancer shaft remove the oil pump driven sprocket (see Section 19, Step 4). Remove the drive chain and slide the drive sprocket off the shaft, noting which way round it fits **(see illustrations)**.

5 Slide the primary drive gear off the shaft, noting which way round it fits **(see illustration)**.

17.4a Remove the drive chain . . .

17.4b . . . and slide the sprocket off

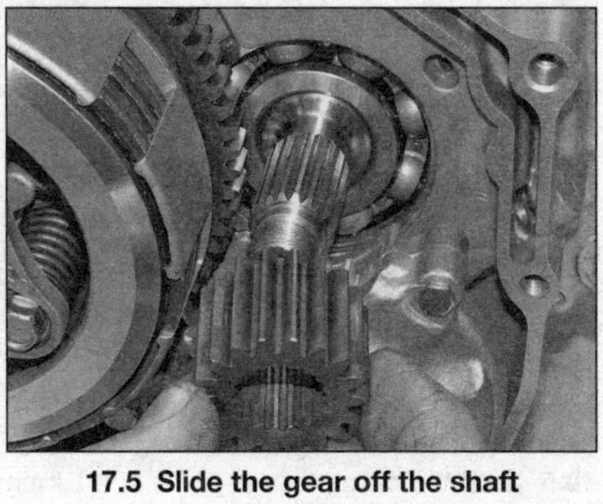

17.5 Slide the gear off the shaft

17.6 Fit the gear with the side with the chamfer (arrowed) facing in

Installation

6 Slide the gear onto the shaft with its chamfered end facing in **(see illustration)**.

7 On engines with a balancer shaft slide the oil pump drive sprocket onto the shaft, then loop the drive chain around it **(see illustrations 17.4b and a)**. Install the oil pump driven sprocket (see Section 19, Step 17).

6 On liquid-cooled kickstart engines fit the washer with the OUTSIDE mark facing out **(see illustration 16.9)**. Lock the shaft

to tighten the nut, but if using rag, strap or plate place it between the gear teeth on the underside.

7 On all except liquid-cooled kickstart engines install the centrifugal oil filter (see Section 16).

8 Install the clutch cover (see Section 14, Steps 27 to 30).

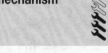

18 Gearchange mechanism

Note: *The gearchange mechanism can be removed with the engine in the frame. If the engine has been removed ignore the steps that don't apply.*

Removal

1 Make sure the transmission is in neutral. Remove the gearchange lever or displace the linkage arm, making an alignment mark with the shaft if there is none visible so it can be correctly installed later **(see illustration 4.8a)**.

2 Remove the clutch (see Section 14).

3 Note how the gearchange shaft centralising spring ends fit on each side of the lug on the

casing, and how the pawls on the selector arm locate onto the ribs on the front of the cam plate. Grasp the end of the shaft and withdraw the shaft/arm assembly **(see illustration)**. Note the washer fitted on the shaft.

4 Note how the stopper arm spring ends locate and how the roller on the arm locates in the neutral detent on the selector drum cam plate, then unscrew the stopper arm bolt and remove the arm and the spring, noting how they fit **(see illustration)**.

5 If the crankcases are being separated, unscrew the cam plate bolt and remove the plate, noting how it locates on the pin in the end of the drum **(see illustration)**. Remove the pin if it is loose **(see illustration 18.9a)**.

Inspection

6 Check the selector arm for cracks, distortion and wear of its pawls, and check for any corresponding wear on the ribs on the cam plate **(see illustration)**. Also check the stopper arm roller and the detents in the cam plate for any wear or damage, and make sure the roller turns freely. Replace any components that are worn or damaged with

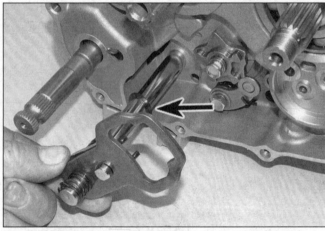

18.3 Withdraw the shaft/arm assembly, noting the washer (arrowed)

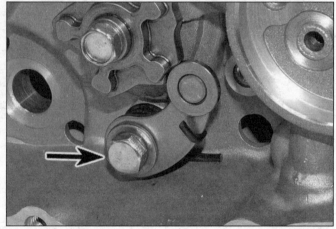

18.4 Unscrew the bolt (arrowed) and remove the arm

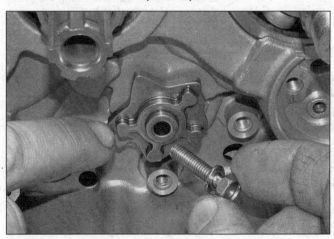

18.5 Hold the cam plate to prevent it turning and unscrew the bolt

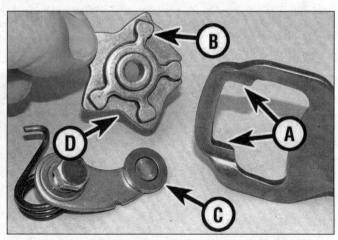

18.6 Check the selector arm pawls (A) and cam plate ribs (B), and the stopper arm roller (C) and cam plate detents (D)

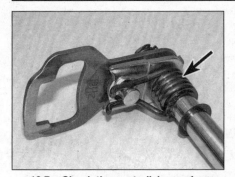

18.7a Check the centralising spring (arrowed) . . .

18.7b . . . the selector arm spring (arrowed) . . .

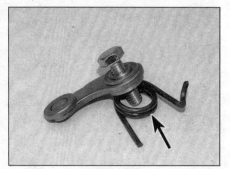

18.7c . . . and the stopper arm spring (arrowed)

new ones. If required (and not already done), refer to Step 5 for removal of the cam plate, and to Step 9 for installation.

7 Inspect the shaft centralising spring, the selector arm spring and the stopper arm return spring for fatigue, wear or damage **(see illustrations)**. If any is found, they must be replaced with new ones. To replace the shaft spring, slide the washer off, then release the circlip and slide it off, then slide the other washer off, followed by the spring, noting how its ends locate. Fit the new spring, locating the ends on each side of the tab. Fit the washer, circlip and washer – use a new circlip if the old one distorted on removal. To replace the selector arm spring release the circlip securing it then slide it off – again use a new circlip on installation if necessary.

8 Check the gearchange shaft is straight and look for damage to the splines. If the shaft

is bent you can attempt to straighten it, but if the splines are damaged the shaft must be replaced with a new one. Also check the condition of the shaft oil seal in the left-hand side of the crankcase. If it is damaged, deteriorated or shows signs of leakage it must be replaced with a new one (though it is best to fit a new one as a matter of course). Lever out the old seal with a seal hook or screwdriver **(see illustration)**. Press or drive the new seal squarely into place using your fingers, a seal driver or suitable socket **(see illustration)**.

Installation

9 If removed, fit the cam plate locating pin into the end of the selector drum **(see illustration)**. Locate the cam plate onto the pin **(see illustration)**. Apply a suitable non-permanent thread locking compound to the bolt and tighten it **(see illustration 18.5)**.

10 Assemble the stopper arm components **(see illustration 18.7c)**. Apply a suitable non-permanent thread locking compound to the bolt **(see illustration)**. Install the arm, locating the roller onto the neutral detent on the camplate and making sure the spring ends are positioned correctly **(see illustration 18.4)**. Tighten the bolt.

11 Check that the shaft centralising spring is properly positioned **(see illustration 18.7a)**. Apply some grease to the lips of the gearchange shaft oil seal in the left-hand side of the crankcase. Slide the shaft into place and push it all the way through the case until the splined end comes out the other side **(see illustration 18.3)**. Locate the selector arm pawls over the cam plate and the centralising spring ends onto each side of the locating lug on the crankcase **(see illustration)**.

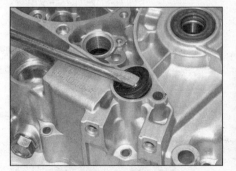

18.8a Lever out the seal . . .

18.8b . . . and press a new one into place

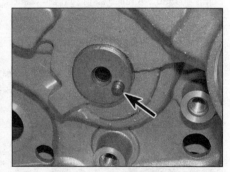

18.9a Fit the pin (arrowed) if removed . . .

18.9b . . . then fit the plate, locating the hole over the pin

18.10 Threadlock the bolt and fit the stopper arm

18.11 Make sure the spring ends locate correctly on each side of the lug (arrowed)

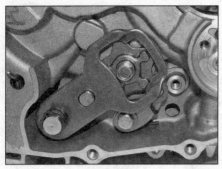

18.12 Make sure everything is correctly located

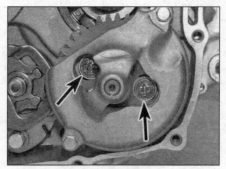

19.3a Align the holes, undo the screws (arrowed) and remove the pump

19.3b Remove the O-rings (arrowed)

12 Check that all components are correctly positioned **(see illustration)**.

13 Install the clutch (see Section 14).

14 Slide the gearchange lever or linkage arm onto the shaft, aligning it as marked on removal **(see illustrations 4.8a)**. Fit the pinch bolt and tighten it.

19 Oil pump

Note: *The oil pump can be removed with the engine in the frame.*

Removal

1 Remove the clutch cover (see Section 14, Steps 1 to 6).

2 On all except liquid-cooled kickstart engines remove the centrifugal oil filter (see Section 16).

3 On engines without a balancer shaft turn the pump gear so the holes align with the pump screws **(see illustration)** – to turn the gear, on all except liquid-cooled kickstart engines slide the primary drive gear off the shaft **(see illustration 17.5)**, then turn the gear by hand; on all liquid-cooled kickstart engines first remove the spark plug to reduce compression (see Chapter 1), then turn the clutch housing. Undo the two screws securing the pump, and remove it from the crankcase. If you cannot undo the screws using conventional tools,

19.4a Unscrew the bolts (arrowed) and remove the cover

unscrew the gear cover bolts and remove the cover **(see illustration 19.5)**, then use an impact screwdriver to jar them loose – if the engine is out of the frame turn it on its left-hand side and support it securely on wooden blocks to do this. Remove the O-rings and discard them **(see illustration)** – new ones must be used.

4 On engines with a balancer shaft unscrew the two bolts and remove the sprocket cover **(see illustration)**. Unscrew the sprocket nut, then slip the sprocket off the shaft and disengage it from the chain. If required remove the drive chain and slide the drive sprocket off the shaft, noting which way round it fits **(see illustrations 17.4a and b)**. Unscrew the bolts and remove the pump **(see illustration)**.

19.4b Unscrew the nut and remove the driven sprocket

Inspection

Note: *When removing the rotors from the oil pump, look for punch marks and note whether they face into or out of the pump body. The marks serve as a guide to which way round to fit the rotors on installation. Refitting the rotors in their original positions will ensure that mated surfaces continue to run together. If there are no marks, make your own, or keep the rotors a particular way up, to ensure they are correctly installed.*

5 On engines without a balancer shaft, if not already done when removing the pump unscrew the two bolts and remove the gear cover **(see illustration)**.

6 Undo the rotor cover screw(s) and remove

19.4c Unscrew the bolts (arrowed) and remove the pump

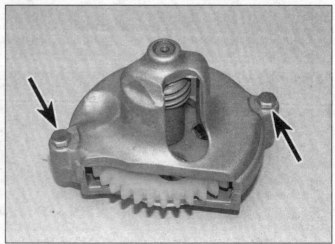

19.5 Unscrew the bolts (arrowed) and remove the cover

19.6a Pump cover screws (arrowed) – engines with gear driven pump

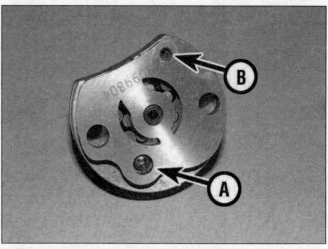

19.6b Pump cover screw (A) and locating pin (B) – engines with chain driven pump

the cover, and the gasket where fitted **(see illustrations)**. Discard the gasket – a new one must be used. Remove the inner and outer rotors, noting which way round they fit **(see illustrations 19.9c and b)**. Withdraw the drive shaft **(see illustration 19.9a)**.

7 Clean all the components in solvent.

8 Inspect the pump body and rotors for scoring and wear. If any damage, scoring or uneven or excessive wear is evident, replace the components with new ones.

9 Fit the drive shaft into the pump **(see illustration)**. Fit the inner rotor over the shaft,

aligning the flats **(see illustration)**. Fit the outer rotor **(see illustration)**.

10 Check that there isn't excessive clearance between the inner rotor tip and the outer rotor by measuring it with a feeler gauge **(see illustration)**. No more than 0.2 mm should be allowed.

11 Measure the clearance between the outer rotor and the pump body with a feeler gauge **(see illustration)**. Any more than 0.35 mm is excessive.

12 Lay a straight-edge across the rotors and the pump body and, using a feeler

gauge, measure the rotor end-float (the gap between the rotors and the straight-edge **(see illustration)**. End-float shouldn't exceed 0.15 mm.

13 Check the pump drive gear and shaft for wear or damage, and replace it with a new one if necessary. If wear and/or broken teeth are found on the gear check the primary drive gear teeth as well (Section 17). Also check the tachometer worm drive on the outer end of the shaft, and the corresponding drive on the tachometer shaft in the clutch cover.

14 If the pump is good, make sure all the

19.9a Fit the gear . . .

19.9b . . . then fit the inner rotor . . .

19.9c . . . and outer rotor

19.10 Measure the inner rotor tip-to-outer rotor clearance as shown

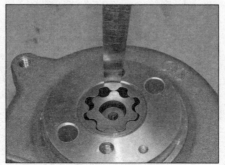

19.11 Measure the outer rotor-to-body clearance as shown

19.12 Measure rotor end-float as shown

19.14a Fit a new gasket where necessary . . .

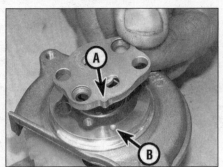

19.14b . . . then fit the cover, aligning the projection (A) with the mark (B) on covers with two screws . . .

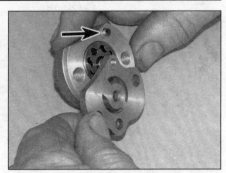

19.14c . . . and locating the hole over the pin (arrowed) on covers with a single screw

components are clean, then lubricate them with new engine oil and reassemble the pump as described in Step 9. Fit the rotor cover, using a new gasket where removed, aligning the projection with the mark on the pump (cover with two screws) or locating the hole over the pin (cover with a single screw) and tighten the screw(s) **(see illustrations)**. On engines without a balancer shaft fit the gear cover and tighten the bolts **(see illustration)**.

15 Rotate the pump shaft by hand and check it turns the rotors smoothly and freely.

Installation

16 On engines without a balancer shaft fit two new O-rings around the oil passage holes in the crankcase **(see illustration 19.3b)**. Fit the pump, making sure the O-rings stay in

place **(see illustration)**. Align the holes in the gear with the screw holes as before **(see illustration 19.3a)**. Apply some threadlock to the screw threads and tighten them. Slide the primary drive gear onto the shaft with the chamfered end innermost **(see illustration 17.6)**.

17 On engines with a balancer shaft fit the pump and tighten its bolts **(see illustration)**. If removed slide the oil pump drive sprocket onto the shaft, then loop the drive chain round it **(see illustrations 17.4b and a)**. Engage the chain in the sprocket, then locate the sprocket on the shaft, aligning the flats **(see illustration)**. Apply some threadlock to the threads and tighten the nut **(see illustration)**. Fit the sprocket cover and tighten the bolts **(see illustration)**.

18 On all except liquid-cooled kickstart engines install the centrifugal oil filter (see Section 16).

19 Install the clutch cover (see Section 14, Steps 27 to 30).

20 Camshaft and lower rockers

Note: The camshaft and lower rockers can be removed with the engine in the frame.

Removal

Lower rockers

1 Remove the cylinder block (see Section 10).

19.14d Fit the gear cover

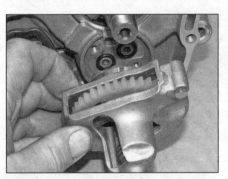

19.16 Fit the pump onto the crankcase (engine without balancer shaft)

19.17a Fit the pump onto the crankcase (engine with balancer shaft)

19.17b Align the flats between the sprocket and shaft . . .

19.17c . . . and apply threadlock to the shaft

19.17d Fit the cover

20.2a Lever the shaft out past the O-ring . . .

20.2b . . . then withdraw it, collecting the wave washer (arrowed) . . .

20.2c . . . and the rockers

2 Use a small flat-bladed screwdriver to prise the rocker shaft out as far as the O-ring, then withdraw it and collect the wave washer and two rockers, keeping them in order and the correct way round **(see illustrations)** – fitting them back onto the shaft is the best way. Discard the shaft O-rings – a new one must be used.

Camshaft

3 Remove the cylinder block (see Section 10).
4 Remove the alternator and starter driven gear (see Section 13).
5 Lever out the crankshaft oil seal using a flat-bladed screwdriver or seal hook **(see illustration)** – this is necessary as it obscures

the camshaft gear timing marks. Discard the seal – a new one must be used.
6 Unscrew the shaft retainer plate bolt and remove the plate and the spring **(see illustrations)**.
7 Turn the crankshaft to align the timing marks on the cam drive and driven gears **(see illustration)**. Withdraw the shaft and lift the gear out of the crankcase **(see illustration)** – note that there is a thrust washer that fits between the inner face of the shaft flange and the gear hub, which if not stuck to either by oil could drop if not retrieved. Discard the O-ring – a new one must be used.

Inspection

8 Clean all components.
9 Check the bushes in the cam driven gear

(see illustration) – the oil grooves should be clearly visible. Slide the shaft into the bushes and check for any freeplay between them. If the grooves are worn shallow or non-existent and there is excessive freeplay replace the gear/cam assembly with a new one. Re-check for freeplay between the shaft and the new bushes, and if necessary also replace the shaft with a new one.
10 Check the cam surfaces and rocker pads for heat discoloration (blue appearance), score marks, chipped areas, flat spots and pitting. If damage is noted or wear is excessive, the cam assembly and/or rockers must be replaced with new ones.
11 Check the pushrod ends and their seats in the lower rockers for damage and wear and replace with new ones if necessary.

20.5 Lever the oil seal out

20.6a Unscrew the bolt and remove the plate . . .

20.6b . . . and spring

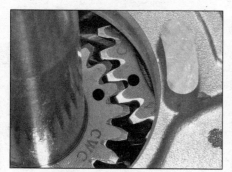

20.7a Align the marks . . .

20.7b . . . then withdraw the shaft and remove the gear

20.9 Check the bushes (arrowed) as described

20.12 Check or freeplay between the rockers and the shaft

20.14a Align the marks and locate the gear . . .

20.14b . . . then fit the shaft with its O-ring (A) and thrust washer (B) . . .

20.14c . . . and push it all the way in

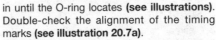

20.16 Fit a new crankcase oil seal

it in until the O-ring locates **(see illustrations 20.2c and b)**.
21 Check that both rockers move freely. Realign the shaft if necessary so the line on its outer end is vertical – if it isn't the cylinder head bolt will not thread into the shaft.
22 Install the cylinder block (see Section 10).

21 Crankcase separation and reassembly

Note: *To separate the crankcase halves, the engine must be removed from the frame.*

Separation

1 To access the crankshaft and connecting rod assembly, balancer shaft (where fitted), transmission shafts, selector drum and forks, kickstart mechanism (where fitted), and all related bearings, the crankcase must be split into its two halves.
2 Before the crankcases can be separated the engine must be removed from the frame (see Section 4), and the following components must be removed:

Starter motor (Chapter 9)
Oil strainer (Chapter 1)
Valve cover (Section 6)
Rocker assembly and pushrods (Section 7)
Cylinder head (Section 8)
Cylinder block (Section 10)
Piston (Section 11)
Alternator, starter clutch gears (Section 13)
Neutral switch (Chapter 9)
Clutch (Section 14)
Centrifugal oil filter (all except liquid-cooled kickstart engines) (Section 16)
Primary drive gear (Section 17)
Balancer shaft drive and driven gears (where fitted) (Section 28)
Gearchange mechanism (Section 18)
Oil pump (Section 19)
Camshaft (Section 20)

3 Unscrew the plunger assembly bolt **(see illustration)**. Withdraw the plunger body, retrieving the plunger and spring if they don't come with it. Discard the O-ring – a new one must be used.
4 Unscrew the right-hand crankcase bolt, noting the clutch cable bracket **(see illustration)**.

12 Check for freeplay between each rocker arm and the shaft **(see illustration)**. The arms should move freely with a light fit but no appreciable freeplay. Replace the arms and/or shaft with new ones if they are worn.

Installation

Camshaft

13 Lubricate the cam driven gear bushes and the cam with clean engine oil. Fit a new O-ring onto the shaft and smear it with oil **(see illustration 20.14b)**. Fit the thrust washer onto the shaft.
14 Turn the crankshaft so the timing mark on the drive gear is pointing up. Locate the driven gear in the crankcase with its timing mark facing down and engage it with the drive gear so the marks align **(see illustration)**. Slide the shaft through the gear and locate its inner end in its bore, then push the shaft

in until the O-ring locates **(see illustrations)**. Double-check the alignment of the timing marks **(see illustration 20.7a)**.
15 Locate the spring in the end of the shaft then fit the retainer plate and tighten the bolt **(see illustrations 20.6b and a)**.
16 Fit a new oil seal into the crankcase, pressing it in with your fingers or tapping it into place if necessary **(see illustration)**.
17 Install the cylinder block (see Section 10).
18 Install the alternator and starter driven gear (see Section 13).

Lower rockers

19 Lubricate the rocker shaft and rocker pads with clean engine oil. Fit a new O-ring onto the shaft and smear it with oil.
20 Align the shaft so the line on its outer end and therefore the threaded hole are vertical, then slide it through the hole and each rocker, in turn, and finally through the wave washer, then locate the inner end in its bore and push

21.3 Unscrew the bolt (arrowed) and withdraw the plunger

21.4 Unscrew the bolt (arrowed) and remove the bracket

21.6a Left-hand crankcase bolts (arrowed)

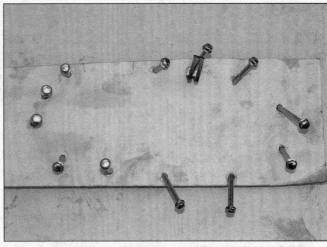

21.6b Example of a cardboard template used for holding the crankcase bolts

5 Lay the engine on its right-hand side on wooden blocks so the shafts are clear of the bench.

6 Unscrew the left-hand crankcase bolts evenly, a little at a time and in a criss-cross sequence until they are finger-tight, then remove them (see illustration). Note: *As each bolt is removed, store it in its relative position in a cardboard template of the crankcase halves (see illustration). This will ensure all bolts are returned to their original locations on reassembly.*

7 Carefully lift the left crankcase half off the right half, using a soft-faced hammer to tap around the joint to initially separate the halves if necessary (see illustration). Note: *If the halves do not separate easily, make sure all fasteners have been removed. Do not try and separate the halves by levering against the crankcase mating surfaces as they are easily scored and will leak oil in the future if damaged. If the halves separate then bind make sure they are coming apart parallel to each other, and if necessary gently tap the right-hand half back down to level them up and start again. The left-hand crankcase half will come away leaving the crankshaft, transmission shafts, selector drum and forks, and the kickstart mechanism in the right-hand half.*

8 Note the thrust washers on the left-hand end of each transmission shaft and on the kickstart shaft – if they are not there they are stuck to the bearings in the crankcase, in which case retrieve then and fit them back onto the shafts (see illustration 21.12). Remove the gasket. Remove the two locating dowels from the crankcase if they are loose (they could be in either half) (see illustration 21.14b).

9 Refer to Sections 22 to 27 for the removal and installation of the components housed within the crankcases.

10 Remove all traces of old gasket from the crankcase mating surfaces.

Reassembly

11 Make sure the crankcase mating surfaces are clean and dry.

12 Ensure that all components and their bearings are in place in the right-hand crankcase half, and that all bearings and new oil seals are in the left-hand half (see Section 18 for the gearchange shaft oil seal and Section 25 for the transmission output shaft seal). Make sure the thrust washers are in place on the left-hand ends of the transmission shafts and the kickstart shaft (see illustration).

13 Generously lubricate the crankshaft and

transmission shaft bearings and gears and the selector fork shafts and fork ends and the tracks in the selector drum with clean engine oil, then use a rag soaked in high flash-point solvent to wipe over the mating surfaces of both crankcase halves to remove any traces of oil.

14 Apply a smear of suitable RTV sealant to each side of the cylinder liner bore (see illustration). If removed, fit the two locating dowels into the right-hand crankcase half (see illustration). Fit a new gasket, locating it over the dowels.

21.7 Carefully separate the crankcase halves

21.12 Make sure the thrust washers (arrowed) are fitted

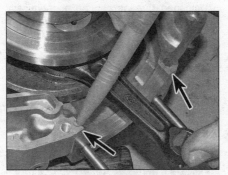

21.14a Apply sealant (arrowed) to the edges of the bore

21.14b Make sure the dowels (arrowed) are in place, then fit the gasket

21.19 Cut the gasket bridge flush with the crankcase

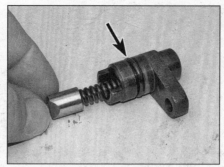

21.21a Fit the O-ring (arrowed), plunger and spring

21.21b Make sure the chamfered edge of the plunger is at the top

15 Check again that all components are in position **(see illustration 21.12)**. Carefully fit the left-hand crankcase half down onto the right-hand crankcase half, making sure the shaft ends and dowels locate correctly and that the cases remain square to each other **(see illustration 21.7)**. If necessary gently tap the case down using a soft mallet, but do not use force – if the cases do not join easily there is something wrong, in which case lift the case off and investigate.

16 Check that the left-hand crankcase half is correctly seated all round. Clean the threads of all the crankcase bolts.

Caution: The crankcase halves should fit together without being forced. If the casings are not correctly seated, remove the left-hand crankcase half and investigate the problem. Do not attempt to pull them together using the crankcase bolts as the casing will crack and be ruined.

17 Install the left-hand crankcase bolts finger-tight at first, then tighten them evenly and a little at a time in a criss-cross sequence **(see illustration 21.6a)**.

18 Support the engine upright and fit the right-hand bolt along with the clutch cable bracket **(see illustration 21.4)**.

19 Cut the section of gasket that bridges the cylinder liner bore flush with the crankcases **(see illustration)**.

20 With all crankcase bolts tightened, check that the crankshaft and transmission shafts rotate smoothly and easily. Check that the transmission shafts rotate freely and independently in neutral, then rotate the selector drum by hand (fit the cam plate on its right-hand end to do this – see Section 18) and select each gear in turn whilst rotating the input shaft. If there are any signs of undue stiffness, tight or rough spots, or of any other problem, the fault must be rectified before proceeding further.

21 Fit a new O-ring into the groove in the plunger assembly body and smear it with oil **(see illustration)**. Fit the spring and plunger into the body. Fit the assembly into the crankcase with the chamfered edge of the plunger facing up **(see illustration)**. Apply fresh threadlock to the bolt and tighten it.

22 Install all other removed assemblies in a reverse of the sequence given in Step 2.

22 Crankcases and bearings

Crankcases

1 After the crankcases have been separated, remove the crankshaft, balancer shaft (where fitted), the selector drum and forks and the transmission shafts, and the kickstart mechanism (where fitted), referring to the relevant Sections of this Chapter.

2 Clean the crankcases thoroughly with new solvent and dry them with compressed air. Blow out all oil passages with compressed air.

3 Remove all traces of old gasket from the mating surfaces. Clean up minor damage to the surfaces with a fine sharpening stone or grindstone.

Caution: Be very careful not to nick or gouge the crankcase mating surfaces or oil leaks will result. Check both crankcase halves very carefully for cracks and other damage.

4 Small cracks or holes in aluminium castings can be repaired with an epoxy resin adhesive as a temporary measure or with one of the low temperature welding kits. Permanent repairs can only be done by TIG (tungsten inert gas or heli-arc) welding, and only a specialist in this process is in a position to advise on the economy or practical aspect of such a repair. If any damage is found that can't be repaired, replace the crankcase halves as a set.

5 Damaged threads can be economically reclaimed using a diamond section wire insert, which is easily fitted after drilling and re-tapping the affected thread.

6 Sheared studs or screws can usually be removed with extractors, which consist of a tapered, left-hand thread screw of very hard steel. These are inserted into a pre-drilled hole in the stud, and usually succeed in dislodging the most stubborn stud or screw. If a stud has

Refer to Tools and Workshop Tips for details of installing a thread insert and using screw extractors.

sheared above its bore line, it can be removed using a conventional stud extractor which avoids the need for drilling.

7 Install all components and assemblies, referring to the relevant Sections of this and the other Chapters, before reassembling the crankcase halves.

Bearing information

8 The crankshaft and transmission shaft bearings should all be replaced with new ones as part of a complete engine overhaul, or individually as required due to wear or failure.

9 Bearing failure occurs mainly because of lack of lubrication, the presence of dirt or other foreign particles, overloading the engine, break-up of one or more of the bearing components due to fatigue, or corrosion. Regardless of the cause of bearing failure, it must be corrected before the engine is reassembled to prevent it from happening again.

10 The bearings should rotate smoothly, freely and quietly, there should be no rough spots, and there should be no excessive play between the inner and outer races, or between the inner race and the shaft it fits on, or between the outer race and its housing in the crankcase.

11 Dirt and other foreign particles get into the engine in a variety of ways. They may be left in the engine during assembly or they may pass through filters or breathers, then get into the oil and from there into the bearings. Metal chips from machining operations and normal engine wear are often present. Abrasives are sometimes left in engine components after reconditioning operations, especially when parts are not thoroughly cleaned using the proper cleaning methods. The best prevention for this cause of bearing failure is to clean all parts thoroughly and keep everything spotlessly clean during engine reassembly. Regular oil changes are also recommended.

12 Lack of lubrication or lubrication breakdown has a number of interrelated causes. Excessive heat (which thins the oil), overloading and oil leakage all contribute to lubrication breakdown. Blocked oil passages will starve a bearing of lubrication and destroy it.

13 Riding habits can have a definite effect on

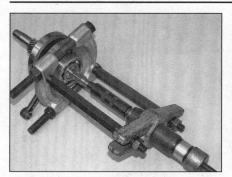

22.17a Removing a main bearing from the crankshaft using a puller

22.17b On the left-hand end the gear (arrowed) must be removed

bearing life. Full throttle low, speed operation, or labouring the engine, puts very high loads on bearings. Short trip riding leads to corrosion of bearings, as insufficient engine heat is produced to drive off the condensed water and corrosive gases produced. These products collect in the engine oil, forming acid and sludge. As the oil is carried to the engine bearings, the acid attacks and corrodes the bearing material.

14 Incorrect bearing installation during engine assembly will lead to bearing failure as well. To avoid bearing problems, clean all parts thoroughly before reassembly, and lubricate the new bearings with clean engine oil during installation.

Bearing removal and installation

Note: *If the correct bearing removal and installation tools are not available take the crankcases and crankshaft to a dealer – do not risk damaging either the cases or the crankshaft.*

Crankshaft (main) bearings

15 If the crankshaft (main) bearings have failed, excessive rumbling and vibration will be felt when the engine is running.

16 Separate the crankcase halves (Section 21) and remove the crankshaft (Section 23).

17 To remove the main bearings from the crankshaft, use an external bearing puller as shown, to draw them off **(see illustration)**. Take care to protect the end of the crankshaft by using the correct size adapter or a suitable spacer between them. When removing the left-hand bearing either remove the camshaft drive gear first (again using a puller or if necessary an hydraulic press), or draw it off along with the bearing **(see illustration)**. To ease removal heat the gear first using a hot air gun, but try not to heat the crankshaft as well.

18 Smear the inside of the new bearings with clean oil and fit them with the marked side facing out. Drive the bearing squarely on until it seats using a tubular driver that bears only on the inner race. Cooling or freezing the crankshaft (using a fridge, freezer or freeze spray) and heating the bearing inner race using a hot air gun will ease installation. Fit the camshaft drive gear, with its marked side facing out, in the same way, or if necessary using an hydraulic press.

Connecting rod (big-end) bearing

19 If the connecting rod (big-end) bearing has failed, there will be a pronounced knocking noise when the engine is running, particularly under load and increasing with engine speed.

Refer to Section 23, Step 4 for checks that can be made.

20 The connecting rod and its bearing are generally an integral part of the crankshaft assembly which usually comes as a pressed-up unit – individual components are sometimes available (depending on the manufacturer), but even if they are, disassembling and reassembling the crankshaft should only be undertaken by a suitably equipped specialist workshop. If the big-end bearing fails the best thing to do is replace the crankshaft/connecting rod assembly with a new one (see Section 23), but check with your dealer for advice.

Balancer shaft bearings

21 If the balancer bearings have failed, excessive rumbling and vibration will be felt when the engine is running.

22 Separate the crankcase halves (Section 21) and remove all assemblies within (see Step 1).

23 To remove the bearings from the crankcase, heat the bearing housing with a hot air gun, then tap the bearing out from the outside of the crankcase using a bearing driver or a suitable socket **(see illustration 22.27)**.

24 Smear the outside of the new bearing with clean oil and fit it with its marked side towards the inside of the engine, then heat the housing again and drive the bearing squarely in until it seats using a driver or socket that bears only on the outer race **(see illustration 22.29)**.

Transmission shaft bearings

25 If the transmission bearings have failed, excessive rumbling and vibration will be felt when the engine is running **(see illustrations)**.

26 Separate the crankcase halves (Section 21) and remove all assemblies within (see Step 1).

27 To remove the input shaft bearing from the right-hand crankcase and the output shaft bearing from the left-hand crankcase, heat

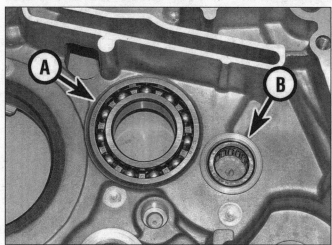

22.25a Transmission input shaft bearing (A) and output shaft bearing (B) – right-hand crankcase half

22.25b Transmission input shaft bearing (A) and output shaft bearing (B) – left-hand crankcase half

22.27 Drive the bearings out from the outside

22.28a Fit the expander into the bearing . . .

22.28b . . . and use the slide-hammer attachment to remove the bearing

the bearing housing with a hot air gun, then tap the bearing out from the outside of the crankcase using a bearing driver or a suitable socket on the inner race **(see illustration)**.

28 To remove the input shaft bearing from the left-hand crankcase and the output shaft bearing from the right-hand crankcase, an expanding knife-edge bearing puller with slide-hammer attachment may be required. First heat the bearing housing with a hot air gun and see whether the bearing will drop out. If not fit the expanding end of the puller behind the bearing, then turn the puller to expand it and lock it **(see illustration)**. Attach the slide-hammer to the puller, then hold the crankcase firmly down and operate the slide-hammer to jar the bearing out **(see illustration)**.

29 Smear the outside of the new bearing with clean oil and fit it with its marked side towards the inside of the engine, then heat the housing again and drive the bearing squarely in until it seats using a driver or socket that bears only on the outer race **(see illustration)**.

23 Crankshaft and connecting rod

Note: *To remove the crankshaft the engine must be removed from the frame and the crankcase halves separated.*

Removal

1 Remove the engine from the frame (see Section 4) and separate the crankcase halves (see Section 21).

2 Grasp the crankshaft and lift it out of the crankcase **(see illustration)**. If the shaft is stuck, use a soft-faced hammer and gently tap on the right-end.

Inspection

3 Clean the crankshaft with solvent. If available, blow the crank dry with compressed air. Check the camshaft drive gear for wear or damage **(see illustration 22.17b)**. If any of the gear teeth are excessively worn, chipped or broken, a new gear must be fitted (see Section 22, Step 17). If wear or damage is found, also inspect the driven gear on the camshaft. Where fitted, similarly check the balancer gears.

4 Hold the crankshaft still and check for any radial (up and down) play in the big-end bearing by pushing and pulling the rod against the crank **(see illustration)**. If the play is excessive refer to Section 22, Steps 19 and 20.

5 Refer to Section 11 and check the connecting rod small-end and piston pin for wear.

6 Have the rod checked for twist and bend by a dealer if you are in doubt about its straightness.

7 Refer to Section 22 and check the crankshaft (main) bearings.

Installation

8 Carefully lower the crankshaft into the right-hand crankcase, making sure the connecting rod is aligned between the cylinder block studs, and the shaft seats correctly **(see illustration 23.2)**.

9 Check that the crankshaft rotates freely and easily.

10 Reassemble the crankcase halves (see Section 21).

24 Selector drum and forks

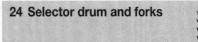

Note: *To remove the selector drum and forks the engine must be removed from the frame and the crankcases separated.*

Removal

1 Remove the engine from the frame (see Section 4) and separate the crankcase halves (see Section 21).

2 Before removing the selector forks check for any identification marks and note which way they face so the forks can be installed correctly – on the engine photographed the left-hand fork is marked SL-L, with the mark facing left, the centre fork SL-C facing left, and the right-hand fork SL-R facing right **(see**

22.29 Drive the bearings in from the inside

23.2 Lift the crankshaft out

23.4 Check for any radial play in the big-end bearing

24.2 Note the identification letters on the forks

24.3 Withdraw the shaft

24.4 Move the forks aside and remove the drum

illustration). If no letters are visible, mark them yourself using a felt pen. The R and L forks fit into the output shaft and the C fork fits into the input shaft.

3 Support the selector forks and withdraw the shaft **(see illustration)**. Pivot each fork out of its groove in the selector drum.

4 Remove the selector drum **(see illustration)**. Slide each fork out of its pinion and remove them **(see illustrations 24.10c, b and a)**. Once removed, slide the forks back onto the shaft to keep them in the correct order and way round.

Inspection

5 Inspect the selector forks for any signs of wear or damage, especially around the fork ends where they engage with the groove in the

pinion. Check that each fork fits correctly in its pinion groove **(see illustration)**. Check closely to see if the forks are bent. If the forks are in any way damaged they must be replaced with new ones.

6 Check that the forks fit correctly on the shaft **(see illustration)**. They should move freely with a light fit but no appreciable freeplay. Replace the forks and/or shaft with new ones if they are worn. Check that the fork shaft holes in the casing are neither worn nor damaged.

7 Check the selector fork shaft is straight by rolling it along a flat surface. A bent rod will cause difficulty in selecting gears and make the gearchange action heavy. Replace the shaft with a new one if it is bent.

8 Inspect the selector drum grooves and

selector fork guide pins for signs of wear or damage **(see illustration)**. If either component shows signs of wear or damage the fork(s) and drum must be replaced with new ones.

9 Check that the selector drum rotates freely in each crankcase half and has no sign of freeplay between it and the casing.

Installation

10 Lubricate each fork with oil. Locate each fork in turn in its pinion groove, making sure they are correctly positioned – see Step 2 **(see illustrations)**.

11 Lubricate the selector drum ends with clean engine oil. Fit the selector drum into the crankcase **(see illustration 24.4)**. Rotate it so that the hole for the neutral switch contact pin points to the bottom of the crankcase.

24.5 Check the fit of each fork in its pinion . . .

24.6 . . . and on its shaft

24.8 Check the guide pins and their grooves in the drum

24.10a Fit the right-hand fork . . .

24.10b . . . the centre fork . . .

24.10c . . . and the left-hand fork

24.12 Locate the fork guide pins in the drum

25.3 Lift the transmission shafts out together

25.4 Remove and discard the oil seal

12 Pivot each fork round to locate its guide pin in its groove in the selector drum, lifting the fork and its pinion where necessary **(see illustration)**.
13 Lubricate the selector fork shaft with oil. With all three forks installed and aligned slide the shaft through each and into its bore in the crankcase **(see illustration 24.3)**.
14 Reassemble the crankcase halves (see Section 21).

25 Transmission shaft removal and installation

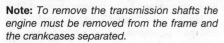

Note: *To remove the transmission shafts the engine must be removed from the frame and the crankcases separated.*

Removal

1 Remove the engine from the frame (see Section 4) and separate the crankcase halves (see Section 21).
2 Remove the selector drum and forks (see Section 24).
3 Grasp the input shaft and output shaft together and lift both shafts out of the crankcase – hold the bottom pinion on each shaft to prevent it dropping off **(see illustration)**. If the shafts are stuck, use a soft-faced hammer and gently tap on their ends. Note that there is a thrust washer on the right-hand end of the output shaft which may stick to the crankcase or fall off as you remove the shaft – retrieve the washer and fit it back onto the shaft.

25.7 Drive the new seal into place using a seal driver or socket

4 Prise the output shaft oil seal out of the left-hand crankcase using a seal hook or screwdriver **(see illustration)**. Discard the seal as a new one must be used.
5 If necessary, the transmission shafts can be disassembled and inspected for wear or damage (see Section 26).
6 Refer to Section 22 and check the transmission shaft bearings.

Installation

7 Press or drive a new output shaft oil seal into the left-hand crankcase and lubricate its lips with grease **(see illustration)**.
8 Make sure the thrust washer is on the right-hand end of the output shaft **(see illustration 26.18b)** and that it stays in place when installing the shafts – stick it in place with some grease to prevent it falling off.
9 Join the shafts together on the bench so their related gears are engaged. Grasp the shafts together, holding the pinions on the right-hand end of the each shaft to prevent them dropping off, and fit them into the right-hand crankcase, locating the shaft ends in the bearings **(see illustration 25.3)**.
10 Make sure both transmission shafts are correctly seated and their related pinions are correctly engaged.
11 Install the selector drum and forks (see Section 24).
12 Position the gears in the neutral position and check the shafts are free to rotate easily and independently (i.e. the input shaft can turn whilst the output shaft is held stationary) before proceeding further. Also check that

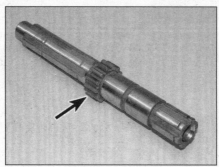

26.6 1st gear pinion (arrowed) is part of the input shaft

each gear can be selected by turning the input shaft with one hand and the selector drum with the other.
13 Make sure the thrust washers are in place on the left-hand end of each transmission shaft **(see illustration 21.12)**.
14 Reassemble the crankcase halves (see Section 21).

26 Transmission shaft overhaul

1 Remove the transmission shafts from the crankcase (see Section 25). Always disassemble the transmission shafts separately to avoid mixing up the components.

 HAYNES HINT *When disassembling the transmission shafts, place the parts on a long rod or length of stiff wire to keep them in order and facing the proper direction.*

Input shaft

Disassembly

2 Slide the kickstart mechanism driven pinion off the right-hand end of the shaft, followed by the thrust washer **(see illustrations 26.19b and a)**.
3 Slide the thrust washer and the 2nd gear pinion off the left-hand end of the shaft – mark the outer face of the pinion so it can be installed the same way round **(see illustrations 26.18b and a)**. Slide the 5th gear pinion off the shaft, followed by the splined washer **(see illustrations 26.17b and a)**.
4 Remove the circlip securing the 4th gear pinion, then slide the pinion off the shaft **(see illustrations 26.16b and a)**.
5 Remove the circlip securing the 3rd gear pinion, then slide the splined washer and the pinion off the shaft **(see illustrations 26.15c, b and a)**.
6 The 1st gear pinion is integral with the shaft **(see illustration)**.

Inspection

7 Wash all of the components in clean solvent and dry them off.

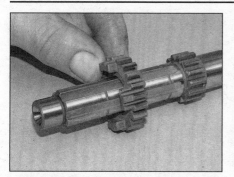

26.15a Slide the 3rd gear pinion . . .

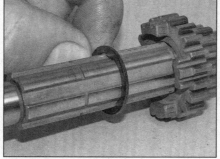

26.15b . . . and the washer onto the shaft . . .

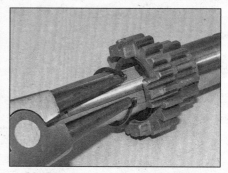

26.15c . . . and secure them with the circlip . . .

8 Check the gear teeth for cracking, chipping, pitting and other obvious wear or damage. Any pinion that is damaged as such must be replaced with a new one.

9 Inspect the dogs and the dog holes in the gears for cracks, chips, and excessive wear especially in the form of rounded edges. Make sure mating gears engage properly. Replace the paired gears as a set if necessary.

10 Check for signs of scoring or bluing on the pinions, bushes and shaft. This could be caused by overheating due to inadequate lubrication. Check that all the oil holes and passages are clear. Replace any damaged pinions.

11 Check that each pinion moves freely on the shaft but without undue freeplay. Where fitted check the pinion bushes for wear – the oil retaining holes should be clearly visible. If not the bushes are worn.

12 The shaft is unlikely to sustain damage unless the engine has seized, placing an unusually high loading on the transmission, or the machine has covered a very high mileage. Check the surface of the shaft, especially where a pinion turns on it, and replace the shaft if it has scored or picked up, or if there are any cracks. Damage of any kind can only be cured by replacement.

13 Check the washers and circlips and replace any that are bent or appear weakened or worn. Use new ones if in any doubt. Note that it is good practice to renew all circlips when overhauling gearshafts.

Reassembly

14 During reassembly, apply molybdenum disulphide oil (a 50/50 mixture of molybdenum disulphide grease and clean engine oil) to the mating surfaces of the shaft, pinions and bushes. When installing the circlips, do not expand their ends any further than is necessary. Install the stamped circlips and washers so that their chamfered side faces away from the thrust side.

15 Slide the 3rd gear pinion onto the shaft with its dogs facing away from the integral 1st gear **(see illustration)**. Slide the splined washer onto the shaft, then fit the circlip, making sure that it locates correctly in the groove in the shaft **(see illustrations)**.

16 Slide the 4th gear pinion onto the shaft with the selector fork groove facing the 3rd gear pinion **(see illustration)**. Fit the circlip, making sure it is locates correctly in its groove in the shaft **(see illustrations)**.

17 Slide the splined washer onto the shaft, followed by the 5th gear pinion, making sure its dogs face the 4th gear pinion **(see illustrations)**.

26.15d . . . making sure it locates properly in its groove

26.16a Slide the 4th gear pinion onto the shaft . . .

26.16b . . . then fit the circlip . . .

26.16c . . . making sure it locates properly in its groove

26.17a Slide the washer on . . .

26.17b . . . followed by the 5th gear pinion

26.18a Slide the 2nd gear pinion on . . .

26.18b . . . then fit the thrust washer

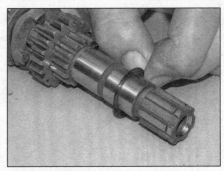

26.19a Slide the thrust washer on . . .

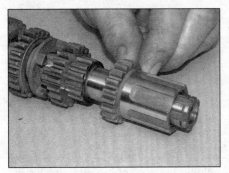

26.19b . . . followed the kickstart pinion

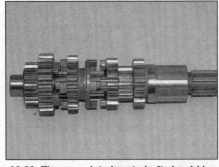

26.20 The complete input shaft should be
as shown

26.28a Slide the 2nd gear pinion on . . .

18 Slide the 2nd gear pinion onto the shaft with its previously marked side facing outwards **(see illustration)**. Fit the thrust washer onto the end of the shaft **(see illustration)**.

19 Slide the thrust washer onto the right-hand end of the shaft, followed by the kickstart mechanism driven pinion **(see illustrations)**.

20 Check that all components have been correctly installed **(see illustration)**.

Output shaft

Disassembly

21 Slide the thrust washer off the right-hand end of the shaft, followed by the kickstart intermediate pinion – mark the outer face of

the pinion so it can be installed the same way round **(see illustrations 26.33b and a)**.

22 Slide the thrust washer off the right-hand end of the shaft, followed by the 1st gear pinion, the thrust washer and the 3rd gear pinion **(see illustrations 26.32c, b and a, and 26.31)**.

23 Release the circlip securing the 4th gear pinion then slide the splined washer and the pinion off the shaft **(see illustrations 26.30c, b and a)**.

24 Slide the 5th gear pinion off the shaft **(see illustrations 26.29)**.

25 Slide the thrust washer off the left-hand end of the shaft, followed by the 2nd gear pinion **(see illustrations 26.28b and a)**.

Inspection

26 Refer to Steps 7 to 13 above.

Reassembly

27 During reassembly, apply molybdenum disulphide oil (a 50/50 mixture of molybdenum disulphide grease and clean engine oil) to the mating surfaces of the shaft, pinions and bushes. When installing the circlips, do not expand the ends any further than is necessary. Install the stamped circlips and washers so that their chamfered side faces away from the thrust side.

28 Slide the 2nd gear pinion onto the left-hand end of the shaft with its recessed side facing in, then fit the thrust washer **(see illustrations)**.

26.28b . . . then fit the thrust washer

26.29 Slide the 5th gear pinion onto the shaft

26.30a Slide the 4th gear pinion onto the shaft . . .

26.30b . . . followed by the washer . . .

26.30c . . . and secure them with the circlip . . .

29 Slide the 5th gear pinion onto the shaft with its selector fork groove facing away from the 2nd gear pinion **(see illustration)**.

30 Slide the 4th gear pinion onto the shaft (dogs facing away from the 5th gear pinion), followed by the splined washer

(see illustrations). Fit the circlip, making sure it locates correctly in its groove **(see illustrations)**.
31 Slide the 3rd gear pinion onto the shaft, with its selector fork groove facing the 4th gear pinion **(see illustration)**.
32 Slide the thrust washer onto the shaft, followed by the 1st gear pinion, with its flat side facing out **(see illustrations)**. Fit the thrust washer onto the end of the shaft **(see illustration)**.
33 Slide the kickstart intermediate pinion onto the shaft (previously marked side facing outwards), then fit the thrust washer onto the end of the shaft **(see illustrations)**.
34 Check that all components have been correctly installed **(see illustration)**.

26.30d . . . making sure it locates in the groove

26.31 Slide the 3rd gear pinion onto the shaft

26.32a Slide the thrust washer on . . .

26.32b . . . followed by the 1st gear pinion

26.32c Slide the thrust washer onto the shaft

26.33a Slide the kickstart pinion on . . .

26.33b . . . then the thrust washer

26.34 The complete output shaft should be as shown

27 Kickstart mechanism

Note: *To remove the kickstart mechanism the engine must be removed from the frame and the crankcases separated.*

Removal

1 Remove the engine from the frame (see Section 4) and separate the crankcase halves (see Section 21).
2 Remove the crankshaft, (see Section 23), the selector drum and forks, (Section 24) and the transmission shafts (Section 25).
3 Make a careful note of how the various components of the mechanism are positioned, and how the return spring end hooks into the hole in the crankcase **(see illustration)**.
4 Unhook the spring end and remove the kick start assembly **(see illustration 27.16a)**. Note that there is a thrust washer on the right-hand end of the shaft which may stick to the crankcase or fall off as you remove the shaft – retrieve the washer and fit it back onto the shaft **(see illustration 27.12e)**.

Inspection, disassembly and reassembly

5 Inspect all components for wear and damage. Do not disassemble the shaft

27.3 Note how the return spring end locates (arrowed)

unless there is a problem with it and/or a new component is required. If disassembly is required, keep all components in the correct order and way round.
6 Remove the thrust washer from the left-hand end of the shaft **(see illustration 27.14h)**. Release the circlip, then slide the cam piece off, followed by the thrust spring and the thrust washer **(see illustrations 27.14f, e, d and c)**.
7 Slide the engagement gear off the shaft, noting its alignment **(see illustration 27.14b and a)**.
8 Release the circlip, then slide the thrust washer, the drive gear and the thrust washer off **(see illustrations 27.13c, b and a)**.
9 Note how the inner end of the return spring and the retainer are located on the

27.9 Note how the spring end and retainer fit before removing them

right-hand end of the shaft **(see illustration)**. Remove the thrust washer, then turn the spring retainer and slide it off **(see illustrations 27.12e and c)**. Release the spring end from its hole and slide it off, followed by the thrust washer **(see illustrations 27.12b and a)**.
10 Clean all components in solvent. Check again for wear and damage and replace components with new ones as required.
11 Check the condition of the shaft oil seal in the clutch cover. If it is damaged, deteriorated or shows signs of leakage it must be replaced with a new one (though it is best to fit new ones whatever the apparent condition) – lever out the old seal with a seal hook or screwdriver **(see illustration 14.19a)**. Press or drive the new seal squarely into place using your fingers, a seal driver or suitable socket **(see illustration 14.19b)**.
12 Slide the thrust washer onto the right-hand end of the shaft, then fit the spring with its hooked end facing away from the thrust washer, and locating the straight end in the hole in the shaft **(see illustrations)**. Slide the spring retainer on, sliding it past the spring end in the shaft via the slot, then turn it and locate the spring in the cut-out as shown **(see illustrations)**. Slide the thrust washer against the retainer **(see illustration)**.
13 Slide the drive gear on, followed by the thrust washer, then fit the circlip, making

27.12a Slide on the thrust washer . . .

27.12b . . . then fit the spring, locating the end in the hole

27.12c Fit the retainer past the spring . . .

27.12d . . . then turn it so the spring end sits in the cut-out

27.12e Fit the thrust washer

27.13a Slide the drive gear . . .

27.13b . . . and the thrust washer on . . .

27.13c . . . then fit the circlip . . .

sure it locates correctly in the groove **(see illustrations)**.

14 Slide the engagement gear on, aligning the punch mark on its plain end with that on the

shaft **(see illustrations)**. Fit the thrust washer and the thrust spring **(see illustrations)**. Fit the cam piece, aligning it as shown in relation to the dog on the engagement gear **(see**

illustration). Fit the circlip into its groove, then fit the thrust washer **(see illustrations)**.

15 Check that all components have been correctly installed.

27.13d . . . making sure it locates in the groove

27.14a Slide the engagement gear on . . .

27.14b . . . aligning the marks

27.14c Fit the thrust washer . . .

27.14d . . . and the thrust spring

27.14e Fit the cam piece . . .

27.14f . . . and secure it with the circlip . . .

27.14g . . . making sure it locates in the groove

27.14h Fit the thrust washer

27.16a Insert the kickstart assembly . . .

27.16b . . . hooking the spring end in the hole (arrowed)

27.16c Align engagement gear and cam piece as shown

Installation

16 Hold the right-hand crankcase half upright and slide the kickstart shaft into its bore, making sure the thrust washer stays in place, and hooking the return spring end into the hole (see illustrations). Do not fully seat the inner end against the crankcase – you need to keep the protruding sections on the cam piece and engagement gear above the level of the crankcase mating surface. Now turn them against the tension of the return spring until the engagement gear and cam piece are aligned as shown (see illustration), then seat the shaft so they are held in position.

17 Install the transmission shafts (Section 25), the selector drum and forks (Section 24) and the crankshaft (see Section 23).

28 Balancer shaft

Note: *The balancer shaft drive and driven gears can be removed with the engine in the frame. To remove the balancer shaft the engine must be removed from the frame and the crankcases separated. The driven gear nut has a left-hand thread, which means it must be undone by turning it clockwise and tightened by turning it anti-clockwise.*

Removal

1 Remove the clutch cover (see Section 14, Steps 1 to 6).

2 Remove the spark plug (see Chapter 1).

3 To unscrew the driven gear nut a 24 mm peg spanner, such as the one shown in Section 16 is needed.

4 First use the peg spanner to turn the balancer shaft anti-clockwise until the dot on the driven gear aligns with that on the drive gear (see illustration 28.16c) – on installation of the gears these marks must be aligned.

5 You now need to lock the shaft to prevent it turning while slackening the nut – a good way to do this is to wedge a stout piece of rag or strap or a piece of 2 mm aluminium plate (DO NOT use steel) between the teeth of the drive and driven gears where they mesh at the bottom – this will lock them together to prevent them turning. Alternatively, if the engine is in the frame, select a high gear and hold the rear brake on hard to lock the crankshaft. Unscrew the nut turning it CLOCKWISE (it has a left-hand thread). Remove the rag, strap or plate if used. Remove the washer, noting which way round it fits (see illustration 28.15b). Slide the balancer driven gear off the shaft (see illustration 28.15a). Remove the Woodruff key from its slot if loose.

6 Remove the primary drive gear (see Section 17).

7 Remove the clutch (see Section 14).

8 Slide the balancer drive gear off the crankshaft (see illustration 28.16b). Remove the Woodruff key from its slot if loose (see illustration 28.16a).

9 Remove the engine from the frame (see Section 4) and separate the crankcase halves (see Section 21).

10 Lift the balancer shaft out of the crankcase.

Inspection

11 Check the gear teeth for cracking, chipping, pitting and other obvious wear or damage. If either pinion is damaged it must be replaced with a new one.

12 Refer to Section 22 and check the bearings.

Installation

13 Fit the longer end of the balancer shaft into its bearing in the right-hand crankcase.

14 Join the crankcase halves (see Section 21). Fit the engine into the frame now if preferred (see Section 4), or when fully assembled.

15 Fit the Woodruff key in its slot in the balancer shaft if removed. Slide the balancer driven gear onto the balancer shaft with its shouldered side facing in, locating its slot over the Woodruff key (see illustration). Fit the washer with its chamfered side facing in, then thread the nut on ANTI-CLOCKWISE and tighten it finger-tight (see illustration). Turn

28.15a Fit the key (arrowed) in its slot, then fit the gear onto the shaft and over the key

28.15b Fit the washer and the nut

28.16a Fit the key (arrowed) in its slot and turn the shaft so it is aligned as shown

28.16b Fit the drive gear, aligning the dots between the gears

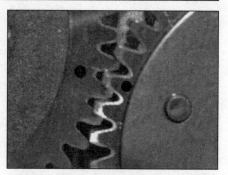

28.16c Make sure the dots are exactly aligned

the gear so that the dot is positioned roughly between the 9 and 10 o'clock position.

16 Fit the Woodruff key in its slot in the crankshaft if removed. Turn the crankshaft so the key is roughly at the 9 o'clock position **(see illustration)**. Slide the balancer drive gear onto the crankshaft, locating its slot over the Woodruff key, and making any minor adjustment to the position of either the crankshaft and/or the balancer shaft as required so the dots on the gears are in exact alignment **(see illustrations)**.

17 Install the clutch (see Section 14).

18 Install the primary drive gear (see Section 17).

19 Lock the balancer shaft to tighten the driven gear nut – if using rag, strap or plate placing it between the drive and driven gear teeth where they mesh at the top and tightening the nut ANTI-CLOCKWISE **(see illustration)**.

20 Install the clutch cover (see Section 14, Steps 27 to 30).

21 Install the spark plug (see Chapter 1).

29 Running-in procedure

1 Make sure the engine oil, and on

liquid-cooled models the coolant level, are correct (see *Pre-ride checks*). Make sure there is fuel in the tank.

2 Turn the engine kill switch to the ON position and shift the gearbox into neutral. Turn the ignition ON. Set the choke.

3 Start the engine and allow it to run at a moderately fast idle until it reaches operating temperature.

⚠️ *Warning: If the oil pressure warning light doesn't go off, or it comes on while the engine is running, stop the engine immediately.*

4 If a lubrication failure is suspected, stop the engine immediately and try to find the cause. If an engine is run without oil, even for a short period of time, severe damage will occur.

5 Check carefully that there are no oil (or coolant) leaks and make sure the transmission and controls, especially the brakes, function properly before road testing the machine.

6 Treat the machine gently for the first few miles to make sure oil has circulated throughout the engine and any new parts installed have started to seat.

7 Even greater care is necessary if a new piston and rings or a new cylinder have been fitted, and the bike will have to be run in as when new. This means greater use of the transmission and a restraining hand on the

28.19 Lock the gears as shown and tighten the nut

throttle until at least 300 miles (500 km) have been covered. There's no point in keeping to any set speed limit – the main idea is to keep from labouring the engine and to gradually increase performance up to the 300 mile (500 km) mark. Experience is the best guide, since it's easy to tell when an engine is running freely.

8 Upon completion of the road test, and after the engine has cooled down completely, recheck the valve clearances (see Chapter 1) and check the engine oil and, where applicable, coolant levels (see *Pre-ride checks*).

Notes

Chapter 2B
Engine, clutch and transmission – K157FMI OHC single engines

Contents

Degrees of difficulty

Easy, suitable for novice with little experience 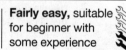	Fairly easy, suitable for beginner with some experience	Fairly difficult, suitable for competent DIY mechanic	Difficult, suitable for experienced DIY mechanic	Very difficult, suitable for expert DIY or professional

Specifications

General

Type	Four-stroke single
Capacity	124 cc
Bore	57.0 mm
Stroke	48.8 mm
Compression ratio	9.5 to 1
Cooling system	Air cooled
Lubrication	Wet sump, trochoid pump
Clutch	Wet multi-plate
Transmission	Five-speed constant mesh
Final drive	Chain and sprockets

Torque settings

General settings (thread size given)

5 mm bolt/nut	5 Nm
6 mm bolt/nut	10 Nm
8 mm bolt/nut	24 Nm
10 mm bolt/nut	35 Nm
12 mm bolt/nut	55 Nm

Specific settings

Alternator rotor nut	30 to 40 Nm
Camshaft holder bolts	10 Nm
Clutch nut	30 to 50 Nm
Cylinder head nuts	
8 mm nuts	15 to 20 Nm
6 mm nuts	10 Nm
Cylinder block nuts	10 Nm
Primary drive gear nut	40 to 60 Nm

Type K157FMI engine left view

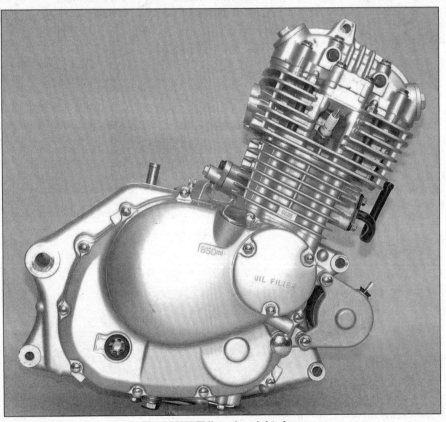

Type K157FMI engine right view

1 General information

The engine/transmission unit is an air-cooled single cylinder of unit construction. It is based on the Suzuki GS125 engine and known as the type K157FMI **(see illustrations)**. The two valves are operated by rocker arms actuated by a single overhead camshaft which is chain driven off the left-hand end of the crankshaft. The crankcase divides vertically.

The crankcase incorporates a wet sump, pressure-fed lubrication system which uses a single rotor trochoidal oil pump that is gear-driven off the right-hand end of the crankshaft. Oil is filtered by a conventional filter housed in the front of the clutch cover on the right-hand side of the engine.

The alternator is on the left-hand end of the crankshaft. The trigger for the ignition timing is on the outside of the alternator rotor, and the pick-up coil is mounted in the alternator cover along with the stator.

Power from the crankshaft is routed to the transmission via the clutch. The clutch is of the wet, multi-plate type and is gear-driven off the crankshaft. The clutch is operated by cable. The transmission is a five-speed constant-mesh unit. Final drive to the rear wheel is by chain and sprockets.

The electric starter motor is on the front of the engine, and on many models there is also a kickstart mechanism on the right-hand side.

2 Component access

Operations possible with the engine in the frame

The components and assemblies listed below can usually be removed without having to remove the engine from the frame, though there may be the odd exception to the rule depending on the frame design of your model.

If a number of areas require attention at the same time, removal of the engine is recommended as it is not that difficult.

Camshaft and rockers
Cylinder head
Cylinder block and piston
Clutch
Kickstart drive and idle gears
Primary drive gear
Oil pump
Gearchange mechanism
Alternator
Starter clutch
Cam chain, tensioner and blades
Starter motor

Operations requiring engine removal

It is necessary to remove the engine from the frame to gain access to the following components.

Crankshaft, connecting rod and bearings
Transmission shafts and bearings
Selector drum and forks
Kickstart shaft

3   Cylinder compression test

Special tool: *A compression gauge is required to perform this test.*

1 Poor engine performance may be caused by leaking valves, incorrect valve clearances, a leaking head gasket, or worn piston, piston rings or cylinder bore. A cylinder compression check will highlight these conditions and can also indicate the presence of excessive carbon deposits in the cylinder head.

2 The only tools required are a compression gauge (there are two types, one with a threaded end and if necessary an adapter to fit the spark plug hole in the cylinder head, the other has a rubber seal which is pressed into the spark plug hole to create a seal – the threaded adapter type is preferable), and a spark plug socket. Depending on the outcome of the initial test, a squirt-type oil can may also be needed.

3 Refer to Chapter 2A, Section 3, for details of the test.

4   Engine removal and installation

Caution: The engine is heavy. Engine removal and installation should be carried out with the aid of an assistant; personal injury or damage could occur if the engine falls or is dropped.

Removal

1 Support the bike either on its centrestand or using an auxiliary stand so it is upright, making sure it is on level ground. Work can be made easier by raising the machine to a suitable working height on an hydraulic ramp or a suitable platform. Make sure the motorcycle is secure and will not topple over, and tie the front brake lever to the handlebar to prevent it rolling forwards.

2 Where fitted remove any fairing panels, belly-pan or sump guard as required according to model (see Chapter 8).

3 If the engine is dirty, particularly around its mountings, wash it thoroughly. This will make work much easier and rule out the possibility of caked on lumps of dirt falling into some vital component.

4 Drain the engine oil (see Chapter 1).

5 Disconnect the negative (–) lead from the battery (see Chapter 9). Also disconnect the engine earth lead, usually secured by one of the crankcase bolts.

6 Remove the fuel tank (see Chapter 4). Either remove the carburettor, or alternatively detach it from the engine and leave it in the engine bay with its cables and hoses still connected (see Chapter 4). Either way, plug the engine intake duct with clean rag.

7 Remove the exhaust system (see Chapter 4). On models with an air induction system that routes the air through the cylinder head or block, disconnect the air hose from the pipe, and if necessary remove the control valve along with the hose and its bracket as required according to model to minimise obstruction to engine removal (see Chapter 4). Also detach the pipe from the head or block if required – a new gasket or O-ring (according to model) will be needed.

8 Make a mark where the slot in the gearchange lever or linkage arm (according to type) aligns with the shaft. Unscrew the pinch bolt and slide the lever or arm off the shaft. Where fitted remove the kickstart lever (again marking the alignment).

9 Remove the front sprocket cover (see Chapter 7). Create maximum slack in the drive chain (see Chapter 1), then if required (for example if you intend to separate the crankcase halves) remove the front sprocket (see Chapter 7), or if not then slip the chain off the front sprocket.

10 Pull the spark plug cap off the plug and secure it clear of the engine.

11 Where fitted detach the tachometer cable.

12 Detach the clutch cable and position it clear of the engine (see Section 15).

13 If required, remove the starter motor (see Chapter 9). If you want to leave the starter motor in situ, pull back the rubber cover on its terminal, then undo the screw and disconnect the lead – spray it with some penetrating fluid first if it is corroded.

14 Trace the alternator, pick-up coil and neutral switch wiring from the left-hand side of the engine and disconnect it at the connectors. Release the wiring from any clamps or ties that will restrict it when removing the engine.

15 Detach the crankcase breather hose.

16 Remove the individual footrests or the complete footrest assembly as required according to model (see Chapter 6) – this will depend on the type fitted and whether they will get in the way when lifting the engine out.

17 Position an hydraulic or mechanical jack under the engine with a block of wood between the jack head and sump. Make sure the jack is centrally positioned so the engine will not topple in any direction when the last mounting bolt is removed. Raise the jack to take the weight of the engine, but make sure it is not lifting the bike and taking the weight of that as well. The idea is to support the engine so that there is no pressure on any of the mounting bolts once they have been slackened, so they can be easily withdrawn. Note that it may be necessary to alter the position of the jack as some of the bolts are removed to relieve the stress transferred to the other bolts.

18 Take a look around the engine and identify the mounting bolts and nuts and any brackets

and spacers that hold the engine in the frame, and also whether the bottom sections of the frame can be removed – there are variations depending on manufacturer and model. After removing a bolt fit any associated washer(s), spacer(s). bracket(s) and wiring clamp(s) back onto it in their correct order, then thread the nut on to secure them, and finally tag the bolt according to its position.

19 First go round and unscrew the nuts with their washers (where fitted) from the bolts, then slacken any bolts that don't have nuts on them.

20 Check that the engine is properly supported by the jack. Withdraw the mounting bolts and remove any washers, spacers, frame sections and brackets.

21 Check that all wiring, cables and hoses are free and clear The engine can now be removed from the frame (see **Caution** above).

Installation

Note: *It is advisable to smear copper grease onto the engine mounting bolt shafts, not the threads, to prevent the possibility of them seizing in the engine or frame due to corrosion.*

22 Manoeuvre the engine into position in the frame and on the jack to align all the mounting bolt holes, making sure that all cables and wiring are correctly routed and do not get trapped. Note that it may be necessary to adjust the jack as some of the bolts are installed and tightened to realign the other bolt holes.

23 Install the mounting bolts along with any washers, spacers, brackets and wiring clamps, then fit the nuts and tighten them finger-tight.

24 Now go round and tighten all the engine mounting bolts and nuts.

25 Remove the jack from under the engine.

26 The remainder of the installation procedure is the reverse of removal, noting the following points:

● *When fitting the kickstart and gearchange levers onto their shafts align the marks noted or made on removal.*
● *Use a new gasket on the exhaust pipe.*
● *Make sure all wires, cables and hoses are correctly routed and connected, and secured by any clips or ties.*
● *Refill the engine with oil to the correct level (see Chapter 1 and Pre-ride checks).*
● *Adjust the throttle and clutch cable freeplay.*
● *Adjust the drive chain (see Chapter 1).*
● *Start the engine and check that there are no oil leaks. Adjust the idle speed (see Chapter 1).*

5   Engine overhaul information

1 Before beginning the engine overhaul, read through the related procedures to familiarise yourself with the scope and requirements of the job. Overhauling an engine is not all that difficult, but it is time consuming. Check on the availability of parts and make sure that

6.2 Unscrew the cap bolt (arrowed) and withdraw the spring

6.3 Unscrew the mounting bolts (arrowed) and withdraw the tensioner

any necessary special tools are obtained in advance.

2 Most work can be done with a decent set of typical workshop hand tools, although a number of precision measuring tools are required for inspecting parts to determine if they are worn.

3 To ensure maximum life and minimum trouble from a rebuilt engine, everything must be assembled with care in a spotlessly clean environment.

Disassembly

4 Before disassembling the engine, thoroughly clean and degrease its external surfaces. This will prevent contamination of the engine internals, and will also make the job a lot easier and cleaner. A high flash-point solvent, such as paraffin (kerosene) can be used, or better still, a proprietary engine degreaser such as Gunk. Use old paintbrushes and toothbrushes to work the solvent into the various recesses of the casings. Take care to exclude solvent or water from the electrical components and intake and exhaust ports.

 Warning: The use of petrol (gasoline) as a cleaning agent should be avoided because of the risk of fire.

5 When clean and dry, position the engine on the workbench, leaving suitable clear area for working. Gather a selection of small containers, plastic bags and some labels so that parts can be grouped together in an easily identifiable manner. Also get some paper and a pen so that notes can be taken. You will also need a supply of clean rag, which should be as absorbent as possible.

6 Before commencing work, read through the appropriate section so that some idea of the necessary procedure can be gained. When removing components note that great force is seldom required, unless specified (checking the specified torque setting of the particular bolt being removed will indicate how tight

it is, and therefore how much force should be needed). In many cases, a component's reluctance to be removed is indicative of an incorrect approach or removal method – if in any doubt, re-check with the text.

7 When disassembling the engine, keep 'mated' parts together (parts that have been in contact with each other during engine operation). These 'mated' parts must be refitted so they run together in the rebuilt engine.

8 A complete engine stripdown should be done in the following general order with reference to the appropriate Sections.

> Remove the camshaft
> Remove the cylinder head
> Remove the cylinder block and piston
> Remove the starter motor (see Chapter 9)
> Remove the clutch
> Remove the oil pump
> Remove the primary drive gear
> Remove the gearchange mechanism
> Remove the alternator and starter clutch
> (see Chapter 9)
> Separate the crankcase halves
> Remove the kickstart shaft (where fitted)
> Remove the selector drum and forks
> Remove the transmission shafts
> Remove the crankshaft

Reassembly

9 Reassembly is accomplished by reversing the general disassembly sequence.

6 Cam chain tensioner

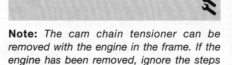

Note: The cam chain tensioner can be removed with the engine in the frame. If the engine has been removed, ignore the steps that do not apply.

Removal

1 Remove any fairing panels or covers as required according to model for access to the tensioner on the left-hand side of the engine (see Chapter 8).

2 Unscrew the tensioner cap bolt and remove the spring **(see illustration)**. Discard the O-ring – a new one must be used.

3 Unscrew the tensioner mounting bolts and withdraw the tensioner from the engine **(see illustration)**.

4 Remove the gasket and discard it – a new one must be used.

5 Remove all traces of old gasket from the tensioner and cylinder block mating surfaces.

Inspection

6 Do not attempt to dismantle the tensioner.

7 Lift the ratchet from the plunger and check that the plunger moves smoothly and freely in and out of the tensioner body **(see illustration 6.9)**. Release the ratchet and check that the plunger can move freely out of the body but locks when pushed back in.

Installation

8 Ensure the tensioner and cylinder block mating surfaces are clean and dry.

9 Lift the ratchet and push the plunger fully into the tensioner **(see illustration)**.

6.9 Lift the ratchet and push the plunger in

10 Fit a new gasket onto the tensioner body **(see illustration)**. Fit the tensioner with the UP mark at the top, then insert the bolts with their washers and tighten them.

11 Fit a new O-ring onto the tensioner cap bolt. Fit the spring over the bolt, then fit them into the tensioner and tighten the bolt – as you do so you should hear the plunger being pushed out over the ratchet mechanism **(see illustration)**.

12 Install any removed fairing panels or covers as required according to model (see Chapter 8).

6.10 Install the tensioner using a new gasket

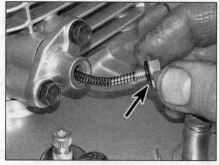

6.11 Fit a new O-ring (arrowed) and the spring then tighten the cap

7 Camshaft and rocker arms

Note: *The camshaft and rockers can be removed with the engine in the frame. If the engine has been removed ignore the steps that do not apply.*

Removal

1 Remove any fairing panels or covers as required according to model for access to the valve cover (see Chapter 8).

2 Remove the fuel tank (see Chapter 4).

3 Remove the spark plug (see Chapter 1).

4 Detach the tachometer cable from the drive housing. Undo the drive housing screw and draw the housing out **(see illustration)** – you may need to carefully prise it out using a

screwdriver to overcome the O-ring. Discard the O-ring – a new one must be used.

5 Remove the upper engine mounting bolt (that passes through the top of the engine), and detach the mounting brackets from the frame.

6 Unscrew the valve clearance adjuster access caps from the front and back of the cylinder head **(see illustration)**. Discard the O-rings – new ones must be used.

7 Remove the crankshaft end cap and the timing inspection cap from the alternator cover on the left-hand side of the engine **(see illustration)**. Check the condition of the sealing washer and O-ring and replace them with new ones if necessary.

8 The engine must be turned to position the piston at top dead centre (TDC) on its

compression stroke so that the valves are closed. Turn the engine anti-clockwise using a suitable socket on the alternator rotor nut until the index line on the rotor aligns with the pointer next to the inspection hole, and there is some freeplay in each rocker arm (i.e. they are not contacting the valve stem) **(see illustrations)**. If there is no play in either rocker, rotate the engine anti-clockwise one full turn (360°) until the index line on the rotor again aligns with the pointer – there should now be freeplay in each rocker.

9 Remove the cam chain tensioner (see Section 6).

10 Unscrew the camshaft holder bolts evenly and a little at a time in a criss-cross sequence until all are loose, then remove them, noting which fits where as they are different lengths,

7.4 Undo the screw (arrowed) and withdraw the tacho drive

7.6 Unscrew the adjuster access caps (arrowed)

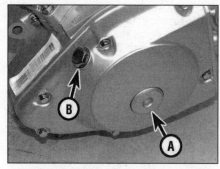

7.7 Remove the crankshaft end cap (A) and the timing inspection cap (B)

7.8a Turn the engine anti-clockwise . . .

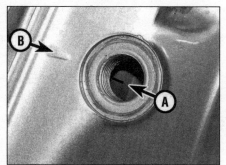

7.8b . . . until the line (A) on the rotor aligns with the index mark (B) . . .

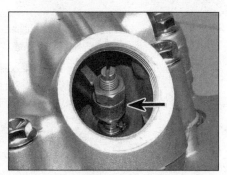

7.8c . . . and there is some freeplay in each rocker (arrowed)

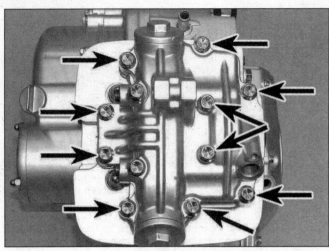

7.10 Camshaft holder bolts (arrowed)

7.12a Bend the locking tabs back off the bolts

and noting the two with sealing washers **(see illustration)**. Note that new washers should be used on installation. Do not remove the rocker shaft bolts at this stage. **Note:** *As each bolt is removed, store it in its relative position in a cardboard template of the camshaft holder* **(see illustration 20.8b)**. *This will ensure all bolts are returned to their original locations on reassembly.*

11 Lift the camshaft holder off the cylinder head, using a soft-faced hammer to gently tap around the edges to break the seal **(see illustration 7.32a)**. Remove the end cap from the holder or head **(see illustration 7.31d)**. Remove the two dowels from the holder or head if loose **(see illustration 7.31c)**.

12 Bend back the locking tabs on the camshaft sprocket bolt retainer **(see illustration)** – turn the engine as before to expose each bolt in turn, and keep a finger on the camshaft to hold it in place. Counter-hold the alternator rotor nut and unscrew the bolts, again turning the engine for access. Slip the sprocket off the end of the camshaft, noting how it locates on the pin (and making sure the pin does not come out and drop down the cam chain tunnel), and hold it while lifting the camshaft and drawing it out **(see illustration)**. Remove the sprocket – prevent the chain from dropping down its tunnel by securing it with a piece of wire.

13 While the camshaft is out do not rotate the crankshaft – the chain may drop down and bind between the crankshaft and case, which could damage these components. Place a rag over the cylinder head.

14 Remove the camshaft retainer ring from its groove in either the head or the camshaft **(see illustration)**.

15 Mark each rocker arm according to its location in the holder. Working on one rocker at a time, unscrew the rocker shaft bolt and remove the washer **(see illustration)**. Hold the rocker arm and draw the shaft out, then remove the rocker and collect the wave washer **(see illustrations 7.23a and b)**. Slide the rocker and washer back onto its shaft to prevent mixing them up – both shafts and rocker arms are identical and are therefore interchangeable, but mark them according to their location so they can be installed in their original position. Repeat the procedure for the other rocker arm and shaft. Discard the sealing washers – new ones should be used.

16 Clean all traces of sealant from the camshaft holder and cylinder head mating surfaces, and from the camshaft end cap – place a rag in the cam chain tunnel to prevent any bits dropping in. Clean the camshaft, rockers and shafts. Blow the camshaft oil passages out with compressed air.

Inspection

17 Inspect the bearing surfaces on the camshaft holder and cylinder head and the corresponding journals on the camshaft. Look for score marks, deep scratches and evidence of heat discoloration (blue appearance) and spalling (a pitted appearance). Check the oil passages for clogging. Note that if there is evidence of oil starvation the cause must be rectified before the engine is reassembled.

18 Check the camshaft lobes and the contact pads on the rocker arms for heat discoloration, score marks, chipped areas, flat spots and spalling.

19 Inspect the cam chain guide and tensioner blade (see Section 8).

20 Except in cases of oil starvation, the cam chain should wear very little. If the chain has stretched excessively, which makes it difficult to maintain proper tension, or if it is stiff or the links are binding or kinking, replace it with a new one (see Section 8). Check the sprocket for wear, cracks and other damage, and replace it with a new one if necessary. If the sprocket teeth are worn, the cam chain is also worn, and so probably is the sprocket on the crankshaft. If severe wear is apparent, the entire engine should be disassembled for inspection.

21 Check the bottom of each clearance

7.12b Detach the sprocket and remove the camshaft

7.14 Remove the retainer ring

7.15 Unscrew the bolt, then use pliers to withdraw the shaft

7.22 Check for freeplay between each arm and its shaft

7.23a Fit a new O-ring (arrowed), then position the rocker and insert the shaft . . .

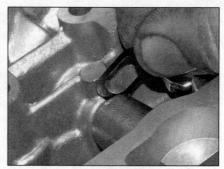

7.23b . . . and fit the wave washer

adjuster on each rocker and the top of each valve stem. If damage is noted or wear is excessive, the rocker arms and valves must be replaced with new ones as required.

22 Check for freeplay between each rocker arm and its shaft in the centre **(see illustration)**. The arms should move freely with a light fit but no appreciable freeplay. Similarly check for freeplay between the shaft ends and the bores in the holder. Replace the arms and/or shafts with new ones if they are worn.

Installation

23 Slacken the valve clearance adjuster locknuts and thread the adjusters anti-clockwise to create maximum clearance. Fit a new O-ring onto each rocker shaft. Lubricate each shaft and arm with molybdenum disulphide oil if available (a 50/50 mixture of molybdenum disulphide grease and engine oil), or clean engine oil if not. Working on one rocker at a time, position the arm in its correct location and slide its shaft nearly all the way through, aligning it so the bolt hole is vertical in the holder, then fit the wave washer between the inner end of the rocker bore and the holder wall before sliding the shaft fully home **(see illustrations)**. Fit the shaft bolt with its washer, turning the shaft for correct alignment as required, and tighten the bolt **(see illustration 7.15)**. Check that the rocker moves freely on the shaft. Repeat for the other rocker.

24 Fit the camshaft retainer ring into its groove in the head **(see illustration 7.14)**.

Fit the sprocket locating pin into its hole if removed **(see illustration)** – stick it with grease if you think it is likely to drop out.

25 Make sure the index line on the alternator rotor aligns with the pointer next to the inspection hole so the piston is at TDC (see Step 8) **(see illustration 7.8b)** – if you need to turn the engine to realign the marks hold the cam chain up and keep it taught as you do.

26 Lubricate the camshaft bearings and the camshaft lobes.

27 Fit the camshaft sprocket into the chain so the hole for the locating pin is just forward of centre at the top **(see illustration)**. Align the camshaft so the index lines in its left-hand end are parallel with the head mating surface **(see illustration 7.27c)**, with the locating pin at the top and the cam lobes pointing down, and lay it on the head, locating the sprocket on its end and seating the groove over the

7.24 Fit the sprocket locating pin

retaining ring **(see illustration 7.12b)**. Seat the sprocket against the flange, locating the pin in the hole **(see illustration)**. Now check that the timing marks on the rotor are correct (see Step 8), and correspondingly the index lines on the end of the camshaft are parallel with the head **(see illustration)**. Fit the sprocket bolt retainer, making sure the curved bridging section between the two holes covers the sprocket locating pin, then thread in one bolt and tighten it finger tight **(see illustration)**. Now turn the engine (keep a finger on the camshaft to hold it in place while you do so) and fit the other bolt, and fully tighten it, counter-holding the alternator rotor. Turn the engine again and fully tighten the first bolt. Turn the engine again to realign the timing marks.

28 Use a piece of wooden dowel or other suitable tool to press on the back of the cam

7.27a Engage the sprocket in the chain with the pin hole (arrowed) as shown

7.27b Fit the sprocket, locating the pin (arrowed) in the hole

7.27c The index lines on the end of the camshaft must be parallel with the head mating surface

7.27d Make sure the locating pin (arrowed) is retained by the bridging section

7.29 Bend the tabs up against the bolts

7.31a Apply sealant to the mating surface . . .

7.31b . . . and to each cut-out

chain tensioner blade via the tensioner bore in the cylinder block to ensure that any slack in the cam chain is taken up in the rear run of the chain. At this point check that the timing marks are still in **exact** alignment as described in Step 27 **(see illustrations 7.8b and 7.27c)**. Note that it is easy to be slightly out (one tooth on the sprocket) without the marks appearing drastically out of alignment. If the marks are out unscrew the sprocket bolts and slide the sprocket off the camshaft, then reposition the sprocket in the chain as required, fit the sprocket back into the chain and onto the camshaft, and check the marks again.

29 When you are completely satisfied that the timing is correct bend the edges of the sprocket bolt retainer up against a flat on each bolt, turning the engine as required **(see illustration)**. Now turn the engine back to its

TDC position, making sure the camshaft lobes point down not up.

Caution: If the marks are not aligned exactly as described, the valve timing will be incorrect and the valves may strike the piston, causing extensive damage to the engine.

30 Pour a small amount of engine oil into the well below the camshaft lobes.

31 Clean the mating surfaces of the cylinder head and camshaft holder with solvent. When dry apply a smear of RTV sealant to the cylinder head surface, and also to the cut-outs for the camshaft end cap in both the head and the holder **(see illustrations)**. Fit the two dowels if removed **(see illustration)**. Fit the end cap onto the head **(see illustration)**.

32 Fit the camshaft holder onto the head, locating it over the dowels **(see illustration)**.

Check that the holder is seated all round, then fit the bolts in their correct locations, using new sealing washers with the two inner bolts **(see illustration)**. Tighten the bolts evenly and a little at a time in a criss-cross pattern, starting with the two inner bolts with sealing washers, tightening them all to 10 Nm.

33 Install the cam chain tensioner (see Section 6).

34 Set the valve clearances (see Chapter 1).

35 Turn the engine anti-clockwise through two full turns and check everything moves correctly. Recheck the valve clearances.

36 Fit the adjuster access caps using new O-rings smeared with grease **(see illustration)**.

37 Fit the timing inspection cap and crankshaft end cap using a new sealing washer and O-ring if required, and smear the O-ring with grease **(see illustration)**.

7.31c Fit the dowels (arrowed) . . .

7.31d . . . and the end cap

7.32a Fit the holder onto the head

7.32b Use new sealing washers with these bolts

7.36 Fit the caps using new O-rings

7.37 Fit the caps using a new sealing washer and O-ring

7.38 Fit a new O-ring (arrowed) onto the drive housing

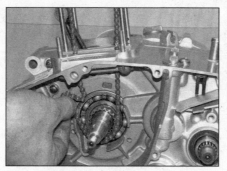

8.3 Removing the cam chain

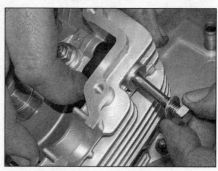

8.5a Unscrew the bolt . . .

38 Install the tachometer drive housing using a new O-ring smeared with grease **(see illustration)**. Connect the cable.
39 Fit the upper engine mounting brackets and bolts.
40 Install the spark plug (see Chapter 1). Install all remaining components. Check and adjust the idle speed (see Chapter 1).

8   Cam chain, tensioner blade and guide blade

Note: *The cam chain and its blades can be removed with the engine in the frame. If the engine has been removed ignore the steps that do not apply.*

Removal

Cam chain

1 Remove the camshaft (see Section 7).
2 Remove the alternator rotor and starter clutch driven gear (see Section 13).
3 Draw the cam chain off the crankshaft sprocket and out of the engine **(see illustration)**.

Tensioner blade

4 Remove the camshaft (see Section 7).
5 Unscrew the tensioner blade pivot bolt, noting the washer **(see illustration)**. Draw the blade out of the top of the cylinder head **(see illustration)**.

Guide blade

6 Remove the cylinder head (see Section 9).

7 Draw the guide blade out of the top of the cylinder block, noting how it locates **(see illustration)**.

Inspection

Cam chain

8 Check the chain for binding, kinks and any obvious damage and replace it with a new one if necessary. Check the camshaft and crankshaft sprocket teeth for wear and replace the cam chain, camshaft sprocket and crankshaft with new ones if necessary – the drive sprocket is part of the crankshaft.

Tensioner and guide blades

9 Check the sliding surface and edges of the blades for excessive wear, deep grooves, cracking and other obvious damage, and replace them with new ones if necessary.

Installation

10 Installation of the chain and blades is the reverse of removal. Make sure the bottom of the guide blade sits in its seat and the lugs near its top locate in the cut-outs in the cylinder block **(see illustration)**. Lubricate the tensioner blade pivot bolt with clean oil and do not forget its washer **(see illustration 8.5b)**.

9   Cylinder head

Note: *The cylinder head can be removed with the engine in the frame. If the engine has been removed ignore the steps that do not apply.*

Removal

1 Remove the fuel tank and exhaust system (see Chapter 4).
2 On models with an air induction system that routes the air through the cylinder head or block, disconnect the air hose from the pipe, and if necessary remove the control valve along with the hose and its bracket as required according to model to minimise obstruction to cylinder head removal (see Chapter 4). Also detach the pipe from the head or block if required – a new gasket or O-ring (according to model) will be needed.
3 Either remove the carburettor, or alternatively detach it from the engine and leave it in the engine bay with its cables and hoses still connected (see Chapter 4). Either way, plug the engine intake duct with clean rag.
4 Remove the camshaft (see Section 7).
5 Remove the cam chain tensioner blade (see Section 8).
6 The cylinder head is secured by two 6 mm nuts on the left-hand side, and by four 8 mm nuts on the top. Of the four 8 mm nuts three are domed and the rear left one is plain. On the engine photographed all four nuts were fitted with copper sealing washers, but parts catalogues for other models show that the front left and rear right washers are sealing washers (either copper or aluminium), and the front right and rear left are steel. Note that copper or aluminium washers should be replaced with new ones, while steel washers can be reused.

8.5b . . . and withdraw the blade

8.7 Draw the guide blade out, noting how it locates

8.10 Make sure the lugs locate in the cut-outs

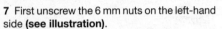

9.7 Unscrew the 6 mm nuts (arrowed)

9.8 Unscrew the 8 mm nuts (arrowed)

9.9 Carefully lift the head up off the block

7 First unscrew the 6 mm nuts on the left-hand side (**see illustration**).

8 Unscrew the 8 mm nuts 1/4 a turn at a time in a criss-cross pattern until they are all loose, then remove them (**see illustration**). Remove the washers.

9 Hold the cam chain up and lift the cylinder head up off the block, then pass the cam chain down through the tunnel (**see illustration**). Do not let the chain fall into the engine – lay it over the front or back of the block and secure it with a piece of wire. If the head is stuck, tap around the joint faces with a soft-faced mallet. Do not attempt to free it by inserting a screwdriver between the head and block mating surfaces – you'll damage them.

10 Remove the cylinder head gasket and discard it as a new one must be used. If they are loose, remove the dowels from the cylinder block or the underside of the cylinder head (**see illustration 9.16**). On models with an air induction system that routes the air through the cylinder block, if there is an O-ring for the air passage remove it – a new one should used. On these models also make sure when ordering a new gasket that it comes with a hole for the air passage.

11 Check the cylinder head gasket and the mating surfaces on the cylinder head and cylinder block for signs of leakage, which could indicate warpage. Refer to Section 10 and check the cylinder head gasket surface for warpage.

12 Clean all traces of old gasket material from the cylinder head and cylinder block. If a scraper is used, take care not to scratch or gouge the soft aluminium. Be careful not to let

any of the gasket material fall into the cylinder bore or the oil passages.

13 If required unscrew the intake duct bolts and remove the duct. Discard the O-ring – a new one must be used.

Installation

14 If removed fit a new O-ring smeared with grease into the groove in the intake duct, then fit the intake duct onto the head and tighten the bolts.

15 If removed, fit the dowels into the cylinder block (**see illustration 9.16**). Where removed fit the air passage O-ring. Make sure the cam chain guide blade is correctly seated (see Section 8).

16 Ensure both cylinder head and cylinder block mating surfaces are clean. Lay the new head gasket onto the block, locating it over the dowels and making sure all the holes are correctly aligned (**see illustration**). Never reuse the old gasket.

17 Carefully fit the cylinder head onto the block, feeding the cam chain up through the tunnel as you do, and making sure it locates correctly onto the dowels (**see illustration 9.9**). Secure the chain in place with a piece of wire to prevent it from falling back down.

18 Fit the washers, using new sealing washers, onto the correct studs (see Step 6). Fit the 8 mm nuts, plain nut to the rear left stud, and tighten them finger-tight (**see illustration**). Now tighten the nuts evenly and a little at a time in a criss-cross pattern sequence to a torque of 15 to 20 Nm.

19 Fit the 6 mm nuts to the left-hand side and tighten them to 10 Nm (**see illustration 9.7**).

If the cylinder block was also removed, now tighten the cylinder block nuts to 10 Nm (**see illustration 11.2**).

20 Install the cam chain tensioner blade (see Section 8).

21 Install the camshaft (see Section 7).

22 Where fitted, and if removed, fit the air induction system pipe onto the cylinder block or head using a new gasket or O-ring and tighten the bolts. Fit the hose and control valve as required according to removal (see Chapter 4).

23 Install the carburettor, exhaust system and fuel tank (see Chapter 4).

10 Cylinder head and valve overhaul

Refer to Chapter 2A, Section 9 for this procedure. The only difference is in the spring seat, which is a shaped one-piece seat as opposed to two individual seats.

11 Cylinder block

Note: *The cylinder block can be removed with the engine in the frame.*

Removal

1 Remove the cylinder head (see Section 9). Remove the cam chain guide blade (see Section 8).

2 Unscrew the cylinder block nuts (**see illustration**).

9.16 Fit the dowels (arrowed) then lay the new gasket on the block

9.18 Make sure the washers and nuts are correctly fitted

11.2 Unscrew the nuts (arrowed)

11.3 Carefully lift the block up off the crankcase

11.8 Studs can be tightened using two nuts locked together

11.10 Lay the new gasket over the dowels (arrowed) and onto the crankcase

3 Keeping the cam chain taut pull the cylinder block up off the crankcase until the bottom half of the piston is exposed, but do not yet lift it all the way off **(see illustration)**. If the block is stuck, tap around the joint faces with a soft-faced mallet – do not attempt to free it by inserting a screwdriver between the block and crankcase mating surfaces as you'll damage them. Stuff some clean rag around the connecting rod to protect and support it and the piston, and to prevent anything falling into the engine. Similarly stuff some rag into the cam chain tunnel, then pass the chain down through the block and lay it on the rag. Now lift the block up off the piston and remove it.

4 Remove the base gasket and discard it as a new one must be used. If loose, remove the dowels from the crankcase or the underside of the cylinder block **(see illustration 11.10)**.

5 Clean all traces of old gasket material and any sealant from the cylinder block and crankcase. If a scraper is used, take care not to scratch or gouge the soft aluminium. Be careful not to let any of the gasket material fall into the engine.

Inspection

Note: *Do not attempt to separate the cylinder liner from the cylinder block.*

6 Refer to Chapter 2A, Section 10.

Installation

7 Check that the mating surfaces of the cylinder block and crankcase are free from oil, sealant and pieces of old gasket.

8 Check that all the studs are tight in the crankcase. If any are loose, or need to be replaced with new ones, remove them. Clean their threads and smear them with clean engine oil. Fit them into the crankcase and tighten them using a stud tool, or by threading two nuts onto the top of the stud and tightening them together so they are locked on the stud, then tighten the stud by turning the upper of the two nuts **(see illustration)**.

9 Fit the dowels over the studs and into the crankcase and push them firmly home **(see illustration 11.10)**. Apply a dab of RTV sealant to the short sections of crankcase mating surface that the block sits on.

10 Lay the new base gasket in place, locating it over the dowels **(see illustration)**. The gasket can only fit one way, so if all the holes do not line up properly it is the wrong way round. Never re-use the old gasket.

11 Rotate the crankshaft so that the piston is at its highest point (top dead centre). Make sure the piston ring end gaps are positioned 120° apart.

12 Lubricate the cylinder bore, piston and piston rings with clean engine oil.

13 Carefully lower the block over the studs and onto the piston until the crown fits into the bore, holding the underside of the piston if you are not using a support to prevent it dropping, and making sure it enters the bore squarely and does not get cocked sideways **(see illustration 11.3)**.

14 Carefully compress and feed each ring into the bore as the cylinder is lowered **(see illustration)**. If necessary, use a soft-faced mallet to gently tap the cylinder down, but do not use force if it appears to be stuck as the piston and/or rings will be damaged.

15 When the piston and rings are correctly located in the bore, remove the rag from around the piston, taking care not to let the cam chain drop – pass it up through the block and secure it using some wire. Now press the cylinder block down onto the base gasket, making sure the dowels locate.

16 Fit the cylinder block nuts and tighten them finger-tight **(see illustration 11.2)**.

17 Hold the block and turn the crankshaft to check that everything moves as it should.

18 Install the cylinder head (see Section 9).

11.14 Carefully feed each ring into the bore as you lower the block

12 Piston and piston rings

Note: *The piston can be removed with the engine in the frame.*

1 Refer to the procedure in Chapter 2A, Sections 11 and 12.

13 Alternator, starter clutch and gears

Note: *The starter clutch is mounted on the back of the alternator rotor. They can be removed with the engine in the frame. If the engine has been removed, ignore the steps which do not apply.*

Alternator check

1 Checking of the charging system is covered in Chapter 9.

Starter clutch check

2 The operation of the starter clutch can be checked while it is in situ. Remove the starter motor (see Chapter 9). Check that the starter idle/reduction gear is able to rotate freely clockwise as you look at it via the starter motor aperture, but locks when rotated anti-clockwise. If not, the starter clutch is faulty and should be removed for inspection.

Removal

3 Remove any fairing panels as required according to model (see Chapter 8).

4 Drain the engine oil (see Chapter 1). Remove the front sprocket cover (see Chapter 7).

5 Trace the alternator and pick-up coil wiring from the cover on the left-hand side of the engine and disconnect it at the connectors **(see illustration 13.6)**. Release the wiring from the clamp.

6 Working in a criss-cross pattern, evenly slacken the alternator cover bolts, noting which fits where as there are different lengths **(see**

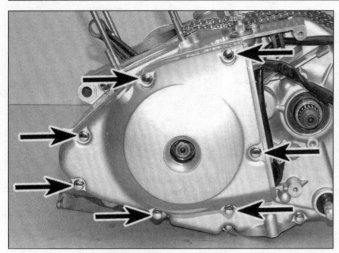

13.6 Alternator cover bolts (arrowed)

13.7 Withdraw the shaft with the spacer and remove the gear

illustration). Note: *As each bolt is removed, store it in its relative position in a cardboard template of the cover* **(see illustration 20.8b for example)**. *This will ensure all bolts are returned to their original locations on reassembly.* Draw the cover off the engine, noting that it will be restrained by the force of the rotor magnets, and be prepared to catch any residual oil. Remove and discard the gasket **(see illustration 13.25)**. Remove the dowel from either the cover or the crankcase if loose.

7 Withdraw the idle/reduction gear shaft with its spacer and remove the gear **(see illustration)**.
8 To remove the rotor nut it is necessary to prevent the rotor turning by counter-holding it using a spanner on the rotor boss flats. With the rotor held unscrew the nut **(see illustration)**.
9 To remove the rotor from the shaft it is necessary to use a rotor puller – several are commercially available, but make sure you buy the right one as shown. Thread the puller

onto the rotor, then hold the puller body and tighten the bolt until the rotor is displaced from the shaft **(see illustrations)**. If the rotor is very tight, remove the puller, heat around the rotor boss using a hot air gun, then refit and tighten the puller and if necessary tap the end of it.
10 Slide the starter driven gear off the end of the crankshaft if it didn't come off with the rotor, or remove it from the starter clutch if it came away with it – you will need to twist it anti-clockwise to release it **(see illustration 13.19)**.
11 Remove the Woodruff key from its slot in the crankshaft if it is loose **(see illustration)**. If required detach the starter clutch from the rotor (see Step 15).
12 To remove the stator and pick-up coil from the cover, undo the screws then lift them out, releasing the wiring grommet **(see illustration)**.

Starter clutch inspection

13 With the rotor face down on a workbench and the starter driven gear in the starter clutch, check that the gear rotates freely anti-clockwise and locks against the rotor

13.8 Counter-hold the rotor and unscrew the nut

13.9a Thread the puller onto the rotor boss . . .

13.9b . . . then hold it while tightening the bolt

13.11 Remove the key (arrowed) if loose

13.12 Undo the screws (arrowed) and remove the stator and pick-up coil

13.13 Check the operation of the clutch as described

13.14a Check the rollers and hub for wear and damage

13.14b Remove the rollers . . .

13.14c . . . plungers and springs

13.15 Starter clutch bolts (arrowed)

13.16 Check the bush (arrowed) for wear

clockwise **(see illustration)**. If it doesn't, remove the starter driven gear, rotating it anti-clockwise as you do.

14 Check the condition of the rollers or sprags (according to type fitted) and the corresponding surface on the driven gear hub **(see illustration)**. If rollers are fitted and they are damaged, marked or flattened at any point, remove them along with the plungers and springs, noting how they fit, and replace them with new ones, if available **(see illustrations)**. If not, or if a sprag assembly is fitted, remove the starter clutch from the rotor (Step 15) and replace the whole assembly with a new one.

15 To remove the starter clutch from the back of the alternator rotor hold the rotor using a holding strap and unscrew the three bolts **(see illustration)**. Clean the threads of the bolts and on installation apply a suitable non-permanent thread locking compound.

16 Check the bush in the starter driven gear

hub and its bearing surface on the crankshaft **(see illustration)**. If the bush shows signs of excessive wear (the grooves in the surface of the bush for holding the oil will be barely visible) replace the driven gear with a new one.

17 Check the teeth of the starter motor drive shaft, the idle/reduction gear, and the starter driven gear. Replace the gears and/or starter motor as required if worn or chipped teeth are discovered on related gears. Also check the gear shaft and spacer for damage, and check that the gear is not a loose fit on its shaft. Check the shaft ends and the bores they run in for wear.

Installation

18 Where applicable and if removed fit the springs, plungers and rollers into the starter clutch, making sure they locate correctly **(see illustrations 13.14c and b)**. Apply clean engine oil to the rollers or sprags, according to type.

19 Lubricate the outside of the starter driven

gear hub with clean engine oil, then fit the gear into the clutch, turning it anti-clockwise as you do **(see illustration)**.

20 Smear some oil onto the flat section of the crankshaft that the driven gear runs on **(see illustration)**. Clean the tapered end of the crankshaft and the corresponding mating surface on the inside of the rotor with a suitable solvent. Fit the Woodruff key into its slot in the crankshaft if removed **(see illustration 13.11)**. If the camshaft has been removed make sure the cam chain is correctly seated around its sprocket.

21 Make sure that no metal objects have attached themselves to the magnet on the inside of the rotor. Slide the rotor onto the shaft, making sure the groove on the inside is aligned with and fits over the Woodruff key **(see illustration)**. Make sure the key does not become dislodged. Give the rotor hub a gentle tap with a soft mallet to seat it.

13.19 Fit the gear into the clutch body

13.20 Lubricate the flat section (A) and clean the tapered section (B)

13.21 Slide the rotor onto the shaft, aligning the cut-out with the Woodruff key

13.22a Fit the nut . . .

13.22b . . . and tighten it to the specified torque

13.25 Make sure the dowel (arrowed) is in place, then fit the new gasket

22 Fit the nut and tighten it to 30 to 40 Nm, using the method employed on removal to prevent the rotor from turning **(see illustrations)**.

23 Lubricate the idle/reduction gear shaft with oil. Fit the gear with the smaller pinion innermost, meshing its teeth with the driven gear, then slide in the shaft and slide on the spacer **(see illustration 13.7)**.

24 If removed clean the stator and pick-up coil wiring grommet and apply some fresh sealant, then fit the stator and coil into the cover and seat the grommet **(see illustration 13.12)**. Apply a suitable thread locking compound to the screws, and tighten them.

25 Before fitting the cover install the neutral switch if removed (see Chapter 9). Fit the dowel into the crankcase if removed, then locate a new gasket onto it **(see illustration)**. Install the alternator cover, noting that the rotor magnets will forcibly draw the cover/stator on, making sure it locates onto the dowel. Fit the cover bolts in their correct locations and tighten them evenly in a criss-cross sequence **(see illustration 13.6)**.

26 Reconnect the wiring at the connectors – make sure it is correctly routed and secured by the clamp.

27 Replenish the engine oil. Install the

front sprocket cover (see Chapter 7). Install any body panels as required according to model.

14 Clutch

Note: *The clutch can be removed with the engine in the frame. If the engine has been removed, ignore the steps that don't apply.*

Clutch removal

1 Remove any fairing panels as required according to model (see Chapter 8). Also remove the exhaust, brake pedal, footrest or footrest assembly if they get in the way of removing the clutch cover, again as required according to model (see Chapters 4 and 5).

2 Drain the engine oil and remove the filter (see Chapter 1).

3 Where fitted remove the kickstart lever, making an alignment mark with the shaft if there is none visible so it can be correctly installed later.

4 Working evenly in a criss-cross pattern, unscrew the clutch cover bolts, noting any washers or brackets with the bolts, and noting

which length bolts fit where **(see illustration)**. **Note:** *As each bolt is removed, store it in its relative position in a cardboard template of the cover* **(see illustration 20.8b for example)**. *This will ensure all bolts are returned to their original locations on reassembly.* Remove the cover, being prepared to catch any residual oil. Remove the gasket and discard it. Remove the two dowels from either the cover or the crankcase if they are loose **(see illustration 14.31a)**. On models with a kickstart mechanism check whether the thrust washer on the end of the shaft is in place – if not it is probably stuck to the clutch cover, in which case retrieve it and slide it onto the shaft.

5 Working in a criss-cross pattern, gradually slacken the clutch spring bolts until pressure is released **(see illustration)**. To prevent the clutch from turning, cover it with a rag and hold it securely – the bolts are not very tight. If available, have an assistant hold the clutch while you unscrew the bolts. Remove the bolts, springs and the pressure plate **(see illustration 14.27)**.

6 Withdraw the short pushrod assembly, noting the thrust washer (where fitted) and bearing **(see illustration)**. Using a magnet draw the long pushrod out of the transmission

14.4 Unscrew the bolts (arrowed) and remove the clutch cover

14.5 Unscrew the bolts as described and remove the springs

14.6a Withdraw the short pushrod assembly . . .

14.6b . . . and the long pushrod

14.7 Remove the clutch plates as a pack

input shaft, noting which way round it fits **(see illustration)**.

7 Grasp the complete clutch plate assembly and draw it out **(see illustration)**. Unless the plates are being replaced with new ones, keep the assembly together. If you are going to remove the primary drive gear, refer to Section 16 and slacken the nut now.

8 Where present bend the clutch nut lockwasher tab off the nut **(see illustration)** – note that on some models a different type of lockwasher (such as Belleville or spring) may be fitted. To unscrew the clutch nut, the input shaft must be locked – this can be done in several ways: if the engine is in the frame, engage 5th gear and have an assistant hold the rear brake on hard with the rear tyre in firm contact with the ground; alternatively, and if the engine has been removed, a commercially available clutch holding tool (as shown) can be used to stop the clutch centre from turning **(see illustration)**. Unscrew the nut and remove the washer, noting how it fits. Check the condition of the washer and replace it with a new one if necessary.

9 Slide the clutch centre off the shaft **(see illustration 14.22b)**. Slide the outer thrust washer off the shaft **(see illustration 14.22a)**.

14.8a Where applicable bend the tab off the nut

10 Slide the clutch housing off the shaft and remove the centre spacer **(see illustration 14.21b and a)**. Slide the inner thrust washer off the shaft **(see illustration 14.20)**.

Inspection

11 After an extended period of service the clutch friction plates will wear and promote clutch slip. Measure the thickness of each friction plate using a Vernier caliper **(see illustration)**. If the friction material shows

14.8b Lock or hold the clutch and unscrew the nut – this shows a commercially available holding tool

obvious signs of wear (or is worn down to less than 2.6 mm), the plates smell burnt or are glazed, the friction plates must be replaced with a new set.

12 The plain plates should not show any signs of excess heating (bluing). Check for distortion using a flat surface and feeler gauge **(see illustration)**. If any plate is warped more than 0.1 mm, or shows signs of bluing, all plain plates must be replaced with a new set.

13 Measure the free length of each clutch spring

14.11 Measuring clutch friction plate thickness

14.12 Check the plain plates for warpage

14.13 Measure the free length of the clutch springs and check them for bend

14.14a Check the friction plate tabs and housing slots . . .

14.14b . . . and the plain plate teeth and centre slots as described

(see illustration). Place each spring upright on a flat surface and check it for bend by placing a ruler against it, or alternatively lay it against a set square. If any spring has sagged in comparison to the others, or if the bend in any spring is excessive, replace all the springs as a set.

14 Inspect the friction plates and the clutch housing for burrs and indentations on the edges of the protruding tabs on the plates and/or the slots in the housing (see illustration). Similarly check for wear between the inner teeth of the plain plates and the slots in the clutch centre (see illustration). Wear of this nature will cause clutch drag and slow disengagement during gear changes as the plates will snag when the pressure plate is lifted. With care a small amount of wear can be corrected by dressing with a fine file, but if this is excessive the worn components should be renewed.

15 Inspect the contact surfaces of the clutch housing, the spacer and the input shaft, and

check for freeplay between them (see illustration 14.21a). If there are any signs of wear, pitting or other damage, or the clutch housing bush has worn so the oil wells are only just or are not visible, the affected parts must be replaced with new ones. Check the teeth of the primary driven gear on the back of the clutch housing and the corresponding teeth of the primary drive gear on the crankshaft (see illustration). Replace the clutch housing and/or primary drive gear with a new one if worn or chipped teeth are discovered – refer to Section 16 for the primary drive gear. Where fitted also check the teeth on the kickstart mechanism driven gear and the corresponding teeth on the idle gear on the end of the transmission output shaft and the drive gear on the kickstart shaft (see Section 19).

16 Check the pressure plate and the short pushrod bearing for signs of wear or damage and roughness (see illustration 14.6a). Check the long pushrod for signs of wear or damage

and make sure it is straight. Replace any parts necessary with new ones.

17 Check the release mechanism in the crankcase for a smooth action. To remove the shaft, first detach the cable (see Section 15). Note the alignment of the arm, making a mark if none is visible, then undo the clamp bolt and lift the arm off. Undo the retaining washer screw and remove the washer (see illustration). Carefully dig the oil seal out using a pointed tool, taking care not to damage the crankcase. Withdraw the shaft, noting the washer. Discard the oil seal and fit a new one on installation. Check the pushrod contact surface, the shaft itself and the bores it turns in for damage. On installation lubricate the shaft with molybdenum disulphide oil (a 50/50 mixture of molybdenum disulphide grease and engine oil). Do not forget the washer, and fit a new oil seal. Make sure the arm is correctly aligned on the shaft. Connect the cable.

18 Clean and check the crankshaft end seal in the clutch cover (see illustration). The seal can be replaced by levering the old one out with a seal hook or screwdriver and pressing the new one in. Where fitted Similarly check the kickstart shaft oil seal and the shaft bore.

Installation

19 Remove all traces of old gasket from the crankcase and clutch cover surfaces.

20 Slide the inner thrust washer onto the shaft (see illustration).

21 Smear the spacer (inside and out) and the clutch housing bush with clean engine oil (see illustration). Fit the spacer into the bush.

14.15 Check related gear teeth for wear and damage

14.17 Undo the screw and remove the retainer

14.18 Crankshaft end seal

14.20 Slide the inner thrust washer onto the shaft

14.21a Lubricate the spacer and bush then slide the spacer in . . .

14.21b . . . and slide the housing onto the shaft

14.22a Slide the outer thrust washer . . .

14.22b . . . and the centre onto the shaft

Slide the housing onto the shaft making sure that the teeth of the primary driven gear, and where fitted the kickstart driven gear on the back of the housing, engage with those of the primary drive gear and where fitted the kickstart idle gear (see illustration).

22 Slide the outer thrust washer onto the shaft, followed by the clutch centre (see illustrations).

23 Fit the lockwasher as noted on removal according to type, where fitted locating its machined tab against the flat side of the clutch centre boss (see illustration). Thread the clutch nut on. (see illustration) Using the method employed on removal to lock the input shaft, tighten the nut to 30 to 50 Nm (see illustration). Where necessary bend the rim of the washer up against one of the flats on the nut to lock it (see illustration). If you need to tighten the primary drive gear nut, do so now (Section 16).

24 Coat each clutch plate with engine oil. Build up the plates in the housing, starting with a friction plate, then a plain plate, then alternating friction and plain plates until all are installed (see illustrations).

25 Push the long pushrod into the hole in the shaft with the longer thin section going in first (see illustration 14.6b).

26 Fit the bearing and thrust washer, onto the outer end of the short pushrod, then fit the inner end into the shaft (see illustration 14.6a).

27 Fit the pressure plate, making sure the castellations locate in the clutch centre (see illustration). Hold the pressure plate and

check for any gaps between the clutch plates – there should be none; if there are, it means the pressure plate has not located properly.

28 Fit the clutch springs and bolts and tighten the bolts evenly and a little at a time in a criss-cross sequence (see illustration 14.5).

29 Counter-hold the outer end of the short pushrod using a screwdriver and slacken the locknut, then turn the pushrod in until light

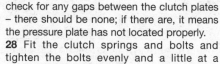

14.23a Where present, locate the washer tab in the flat section (arrowed)

14.23b Thread the nut on . . .

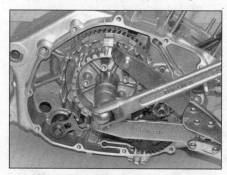

14.23c . . . and tighten it to the specified torque

14.23d Where applicable bend the tab up against the nut

14.24a Fit a friction plate first . . .

14.24b . . . then a plain plate and so on

14.27 Fit the pressure plate, engaging the castellations

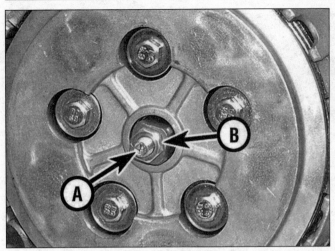

14.29 Clutch plate freeplay adjuster screw (A) and locknut (B)

14.31a Locate the new gasket over the dowels (arrowed) . . .

resistance is felt, then turn it out 1/4 to 1/2 a turn (see illustration). Hold the pushrod so it can't turn and tighten the locknut. This setting is important as there must be some freeplay between the rods when the clutch is engaged. Reconnect the cable (Section 15).

30 If not already done refer to Step 18 and

fit a new crankshaft oil seal, and where fitted kickstart shaft oil seal into the clutch cover. Also make sure the thrust washer is on the end of the kickstart shaft.

31 Fit the two dowels into the crankcase if removed, then fit a new gasket, locating it over the dowels (see illustration). Fit the cover (see illustration). Install all the bolts finger-tight, fitting a new sealing washer with the bolt adjacent to the oil filler cap, and making sure the longer bolt is in its correct position (see illustration), then tighten them evenly and a little at a time in a criss-cross pattern.

32 Where fitted slide the kickstart lever onto the shaft, making sure it is aligned as noted on removal. Fit the bolt and tighten it.

33 Install all remaining components as required according to model (see Step 1).

34 Fit the oil filter and fill the engine with the correct amount and type of oil (see Chapter 1 and *Pre-ride checks*).

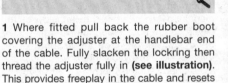

15 Clutch cable

1 Where fitted pull back the rubber boot covering the adjuster at the handlebar end of the cable. Fully slacken the lockring then thread the adjuster fully in (see illustration). This provides freeplay in the cable and resets the adjuster to the beginning of its span.

2 Remove any fairing panels as required according to model to access the cable holder on the right-hand side of the engine and the release mechanism arm on the left (see Chapter 8).

3 Slacken the inner nut on the clutch cable adjuster on the engine and thread it off, then thread the front nut fully up the adjuster. Free the cable end from the release arm then draw the adjuster out of the bracket and slip the inner cable out the top.

14.31b . . . then fit the cover . . .

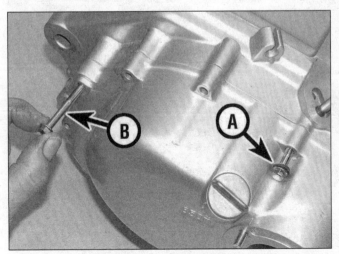

14.31c . . . fitting a new sealing washer onto the bolt (A), and fitting the long bolt (B) as shown

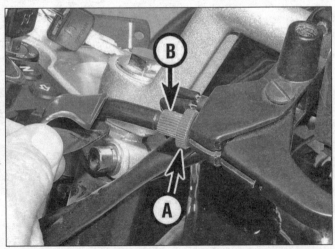

15.1 Pull back the boot, slacken the lockring (A) and turn the adjuster (B) in

4 Align the slots in the adjuster and lockring at the handlebar end of the cable with that in the lever bracket, then pull the outer cable end from the socket in the adjuster and release the inner cable from the lever **(see illustrations)**. Remove the cable from the machine, noting its routing.

> **HAYNES HiNT** *Before removing the cable from the bike, tape the lower end of the new cable to the upper end of the old cable. Slowly pull the lower end of the old cable out, guiding the new cable down into position. Using this method will ensure the cable is routed correctly.*

5 Installation is the reverse of removal. Apply grease to the cable ends. Make sure the cable is correctly routed through its guides. Adjust the amount of clutch lever freeplay (see Chapter 1).

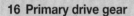

16 Primary drive gear

Note: *The primary drive gear can be removed with the engine in the frame.*

Removal

1 Remove the clutch plates (see Section 14, Steps 1 to 7).

15.4a Free the outer cable from the adjuster . . .

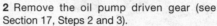

2 Remove the oil pump driven gear (see Section 17, Steps 2 and 3).
3 Bend back the tab on the primary drive gear lockwasher **(see illustration)**. To unscrew the primary drive gear nut wedge a stout piece of rag or rolled up strap, or if available a piece of aluminium plate (DO NOT use steel), between the teeth of the primary drive and driven gears where they mesh at the bottom – this will lock them together to prevent them turning. Slacken the primary drive gear nut, turning it CLOCKWISE (it has a left-hand thread). Remove the rag, strap or plate.
4 Remove the remainder of the clutch assembly (Section 14, Step 8 to 10).
5 Unscrew the primary drive gear nut and remove the washer **(see illustrations)**. Slide the oil pump drive gear off the end of the crankshaft, then slide the primary drive gear

15.4b . . . and the inner cable from the lever

off, noting which way round they fit and how they locate on the Woodruff key **(see illustrations 16.7 and 16.6)**. Remove the key from its slot **(see illustration)**.

Installation

6 Fit the Woodruff key into its slot in the crankshaft **(see illustration 16.5c)**. Slide the primary drive gear onto the shaft, with its chamfered inner side facing in, and aligning it so the cut-out locates over the key **(see illustration)**.
7 Slide the oil pump drive gear onto the shaft, with its chamfered side facing in, and aligning it so the cut-out locates over the key **(see illustration)**.
8 Fit the washer, locating its inner tab in the key slot **(see illustration 16.5b)**. Fit the

16.3 Bend the tab off the nut

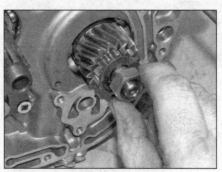

16.5a Unscrew the nut . . .

16.5b . . . and remove the washer, noting how the tab locates

16.5c Remove the key from its slot

16.6 Fit the primary drive gear with the chamfered side facing in, locating it over the key

16.7 Fit the oil pump drive gear with the chamfered side facing in, locating it over the key

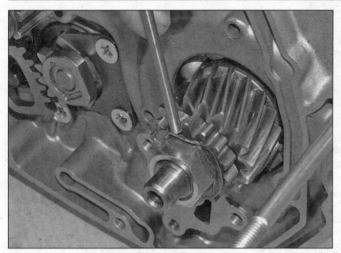

16.10 Bend the rim up against the nut

17.3a Remove the E-clip . . .

17.3b . . . and slide the gear off – note the alignment of the bent up tab of the primary drive gear lockwasher

17.3c Withdraw the pin from the shaft

nut and tighten it finger-tight **(see illustration 16.5a)**.

9 Fit the clutch housing and clutch centre and tighten the clutch nut (see Section 14, Steps 19 to 23).

10 Wedge the stout piece of rag, strap or aluminium plate where the primary drive and driven gear teeth mesh at the top and tighten

17.4 Undo the screws (arrowed) and remove the pump

the primary drive gear nut ANTI-CLOCKWISE to 40 to 60 Nm. Bend up the exposed rim of the washer against one of the flat sides of the nut **(see illustration)**.

11 Fit the oil pump driven gear (see Section 17, Step 15).

12 Install the remainder of the clutch assembly (see Section 14, from Step 24).

17 Oil pump

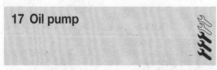

Note: *The oil pump can be removed with the engine in the frame.*

Removal

1 Remove the clutch cover (see Section 14, Steps 1 to 4).

2 Turn the crankshaft using a spanner or socket on the primary drive gear nut to align the raised section of the lockwasher rim with the teeth of the oil pump driven gear **(see**

illustration 17.3b) – this allows the teeth to slide past the washer.

3 Remove the E-clip securing the oil pump driven gear, then draw the gear off the shaft and remove the drive pin **(see illustrations)**.

4 Undo the three screws securing the pump, and remove it from the crankcase **(see illustration)**. If you cannot undo the screws using conventional tools, use an impact screwdriver to jar them loose – if the engine is out of the frame turn it on its left-hand side and support it securely on wooden blocks to do this.

Inspection

Note: *When removing the rotors from the oil pump, note whether any punch marks face into or out of the pump body. The marks serve as a guide to which way round to fit the rotors on installation. Refitting the rotors in their original positions will ensure that mated surfaces continue to run together. If there are no marks, make your own, or keep the rotors a particular way up, to ensure they are correctly installed.*

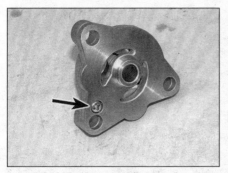

17.5 Undo the screw (arrowed) and remove the cover

17.8a Fit the outer rotor . . .

17.8b . . . the inner rotor . . .

5 Undo the rotor cover screw and remove the cover **(see illustration)**. Withdraw the shaft, noting how the drive pin locates in the inner rotor **(see illustration 17.8c)**. Remove the inner and outer rotors, noting which way round they fit **(see illustrations 17.8b and a)**.
6 Clean all the components in solvent.
7 Inspect the pump body and rotors for scoring and wear. If any damage, scoring or uneven or excessive wear is evident, replace the components with new ones.
8 Fit the outer and inner rotors into the pump **(see illustrations)**. Fit the shaft into the inner rotor, locating the drive pin in the cut-out **(see illustration)**.
9 Check the pump driven gear and shaft for wear or damage, and replace it with a new

one if necessary. If wear and/or broken teeth are found on the gear check the drive gear teeth as well (Section 16).
10 If the pump is good, make sure all the components are clean, then lubricate them with new engine oil and reassemble the pump as described in Step 8. Fit the rotor cover and tighten the screw **(see illustration)**.
11 Rotate the pump shaft by hand and check it turns the rotors smoothly and freely.

Installation

12 Fit the pump onto the crankcase **(see illustration)**. Apply some threadlock to the screw threads and tighten them.
13 Make sure the primary drive gear nut lockwasher is aligned as in Step 2. Fit the

oil pump driven gear drive pin into its hole **(see illustration 17.3c)**. Fit the gear, locating the slot in its inner face over the pin **(see illustration 17.3b)**. Secure the gear with the E-clip **(see illustration)**.
14 Install the clutch cover (see Section 14, Steps 30 to 34).

18 Gearchange mechanism

Note: *The gearchange mechanism can be removed with the engine in the frame. If the engine has been removed ignore the steps that don't apply.*

Removal

1 Make sure the transmission is in neutral. Remove the gearchange lever or displace the linkage arm, making an alignment mark with the shaft if there is none visible so it can be correctly installed later.
2 Remove the clutch (see Section 14).
3 Note how the gearchange shaft centralising spring ends fit on each side of the pin in the casing, and how the teeth on the selector arm engage with those on the pawl holder. Grasp the end of the shaft and withdraw the shaft/arm assembly **(see illustration)**.
4 Undo the screws securing the pawl lifter plate and holder guide plate to the crankcase

17.8c . . . and the drive shaft, locating the pin in the cut-outs

17.10 Fit the cover onto the pump

17.12 Fit the pump and threadlock the screws

17.13 Fit the E-clip into the groove in the end of the shaft

18.3 Withdraw the shaft/arm assembly, noting how it fits

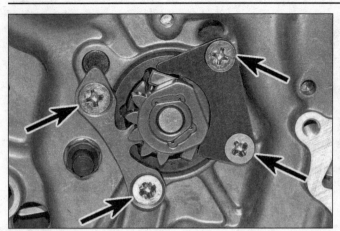

18.4 Undo the screws (arrowed) and remove the pawl lifter plate and the holder guide plate

18.5 Hold the pawls so they won't fly out when removing the holder

and remove them **(see illustration)**. If you cannot undo the screws using conventional tools, use an impact screwdriver to jar them loose – if the engine is out of the frame turn it on its left-hand side and support it securely on wooden blocks to do this.

5 The pawls are spring-loaded in the holder. Before removing the holder, place a finger over each pawl to prevent them from springing out

18.7 Make sure the spring is not fatigued

(see illustration). Remove the holder along with the pawls. Place the holder on a bench and carefully release the pawls, noting how they and their pins and springs fit.

6 Note that the stopper arm and detent plate are inside the crankcases, which will have to be separated for access to them (see Section 20).

Inspection

7 Inspect the shaft centralising spring for fatigue, wear or damage **(see illustration)**. If any is found, the spring must be replaced with a new one. Also check that the spring locating pin in the crankcase is tight. If it is loose, remove it and apply a non-permanent thread locking compound to its threads, then tighten it.

8 Check the gearchange shaft is straight and look for damage to the splines or arm teeth. If the shaft is bent you can attempt to straighten it, but if the splines or teeth are damaged the shaft must be replaced with a new one.

9 Check the condition of the shaft oil seal in the left-hand side of the crankcase. If it is damaged or deteriorated it must be replaced

with a new one, though it is best to fit a new one as a matter of course). Lever out the old seal using a seal hook or screwdriver **(see illustration)**. Drive the new seal squarely into place, with its marked side facing out, using a seal driver, a suitable socket, or a piece of wood as shown **(see illustration)**.

10 Check the pawl holder, pawls, pins and springs, and the pawl cut-outs in the end of the selector drum, for wear and damage. Replace worn or damaged parts with new ones.

Installation

11 Fit the springs, pins and pawls into the holder **(see illustrations)**. Make sure the rounded end of each pawl fits into the rounded cut-out in the holder, and that the pins locate correctly in the cut-outs in the pawls, with the wider edge of the cut-out facing the holder teeth. It will be necessary to hold each pawl assembly in place while the holder is installed in the end of the selector drum.

12 Fit the holder with its teeth facing back and down as shown so that they will align

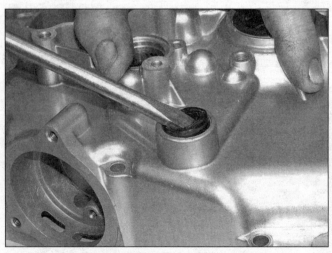

18.9a Lever out the old gearchange shaft seal

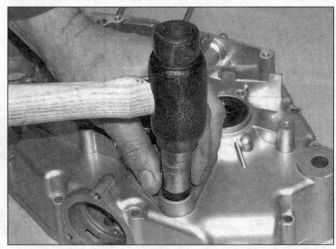

18.9b Fit the new seal and drive it in, setting it flush with the crankcase

18.11a Fit the springs . . .

18.11b . . . the pins . . .

18.11c . . . and the pawls, with the wider edge on the side of the holder teeth

centrally with the teeth on the shaft arm when it is installed **(see illustration 18.5)**. Apply a suitable non-permanent thread locking compound to the pawl lifter and holder guide plate screws, then fit the plates and tighten the screws **(see illustration 18.4)**.

13 Apply a smear of grease to the lips of the gearchange shaft seal in the left-hand side of the crankcase.

14 If removed, slide the centralising spring onto the gearchange shaft and locate the spring ends each side of the pin on the arm **(see illustration 18.7)**. Smear clean engine oil over the shaft then carefully slide it into the engine **(see illustration 18.3)**, making sure the centralising spring ends locate correctly on each side of the pin on the crankcase, and engage the shaft arm teeth centrally with the teeth of the pawl holder.

15 Check that all components are correctly positioned **(see illustration)**. Install the clutch (see Section 14).

16 Slide the gearchange lever or linkage arm onto the shaft, aligning it as marked on removal. Fit the pinch bolt and tighten it.

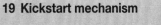

19 Kickstart mechanism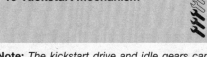

Note: *The kickstart drive and idle gears can be removed after removing the clutch. To remove the kickstart shaft the engine must be removed from the frame and the crankcases separated.*

Removal

1 Remove the clutch (see Section 14).

2 Slide the outer thrust washer, the drive gear and the inner thrust washer off the kickstart shaft.

3 Release the circlip securing the idle gear on the end of the transmission output shaft and remove the outer thrust washer, the gear (noting which way round it fits – mark its outer face as a reminder), and the inner thrust washer. Discard the circlip and use a new one on installation.

4 Separate the crankcase halves (see Section 20).

5 Inside the crankcase, note how the return spring ends locate. Release the circlip from the left-hand end of the shaft. Slide the spring guide off. Carefully release the hooked end of the spring from its lug on the crankcase and allow it to unwind, then release the straight end from its hole in the shaft and slide the spring off. Discard the circlip and use a new one on installation.

6 Withdraw the shaft from the outside of the crankcase. Slide the thrust washer, thrust spring and ratchet off the left-hand end – note how the punch mark on the ratchet aligns with that on the shaft.

7 If required unscrew the stopper plate and ratchet guide plate bolts and remove the plates, noting how they fit.

Inspection

8 Clean all the components in solvent.

9 Check the ratchet teeth and those on the drive gear with which it engages for wear and damage. Also check the splines in the ratchet and those on the shaft. Also check the drive gear teeth, the idle gear teeth and the driven gear teeth on the back of the clutch housing. Check the bushes in the drive and idle gears for wear.

10 Check the return spring and thrust spring for wear and damage.

11 If any components are worn or damaged they must be replaced with new ones.

Installation

12 Clean the threads of the stopper plate and ratchet guide plate bolts. Apply some fresh threadlock, then fit the plates and tighten the bolts.

13 Align the punch mark on the ratchet with that on the kickstart shaft, then slide the ratchet onto the left-hand end with the ratchet teeth facing the right, and slide it all the way along the splines. Slide the compression spring against the ratchet then fit the thrust washer.

14 Slide the kickstart shaft into the crankcase from the outside, engaging the ratchet arm under the plate.

15 Slide the return spring onto the left-hand end of the shaft with its hooked end innermost, and locate the hook in its recess. Grasp the straight end of the spring firmly with pliers and

18.15 The installed assembly should be as shown

tension it clockwise until the end can be fitted in the hole in the shaft. Slide the spring guide onto the shaft and into the spring, aligning the slot with the spring end in the shaft. Fit a new circlip, making sure it locates correctly in the groove.

16 Join the crankcase halves (see Section 20).

17 Slide the inner thrust washer onto the end of the transmission output shaft, then fit the idle gear with is shaped side facing in. Fit the outer thrust washer then secure them with a new circlip, making sure it locates correctly in the groove.

18 Slide the inner thrust washer onto the kickstart shaft, followed by the drive gear with its ratchet teeth facing in, and the outer thrust washer.

19 Install the clutch (see Section 14).

20 Crankcase separation and reassembly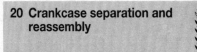

Note: *To separate the crankcase halves, the engine must be removed from the frame.*

Separation

1 To access the crankshaft and connecting rod assembly, transmission shafts, selector drum and forks, kickstart mechanism (where fitted), and all related bearings, the crankcase must be split into its two halves.

2 Before the crankcases can be separated the engine must be removed from the frame

20.3a Unscrew the bolt . . .

20.3b . . . and remove the spring . . .

20.3c . . . and plunger

20.4a Bend back the tabs . . .

20.4b . . . then unscrew the bolts (arrowed) and remove the retainer

20.4c Draw the spacer out of the seal and off the shaft

(see Section 4), and the following components must be removed:

Starter motor (Chapter 9)
Cam chain tensioner (Section 6)
Camshaft and rocker arms (Section 7)
Cylinder head (Section 9)
Cylinder block (Section 11)
Piston (Section 12)
Alternator, starter clutch gears (Section 13)
Neutral switch (Chapter 9)
Clutch (Section 14)
Primary drive gear (section 16)
Oil pump (Section 17)
Gearchange mechanism (Section 18)

3 Unscrew the neutral plunger bolt and withdraw the spring and plunger (see illustrations). Discard the sealing washer – a new one must be used.

4 Bend back the locking tabs on the transmission output shaft oil seal retainer, then unscrew the bolts and remove the retainer (see illustrations). Slide the spacer off the end of the shaft (see illustration). Remove the O-ring from inside the spacer – a new one must be fitted (see illustration 20.25a).

5 On models with a kickstart mechanism refer to Section 19, Steps 2 and 3 and remove the drive and idle gear components.

6 On models without a kickstart mechanism, and where fitted, release the circlip on the end of the transmission output shaft and remove the thrust washer.

7 Lay the engine on its right hand side on wooden blocks so the shafts are clear of the bench.

8 Unscrew the left-hand crankcase bolts evenly, a little at a time and in a criss-cross sequence until they are finger-tight, then remove them (see illustration). **Note:** *As each bolt is removed, store it in its relative position in a cardboard template of the crankcase halves, along with the wiring clamp fitted with one bolt (see illustration). This will ensure all bolts are returned to their original locations on reassembly.*

20.8a Crankcase bolts (arrowed) – note the wiring clamp with the bolt (A)

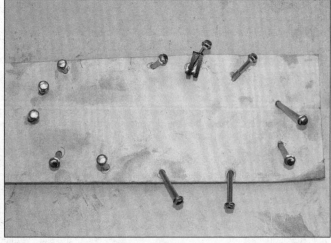

20.8b Make a cardboard template like the one shown to store the bolts

20.10 Carefully separate the crankcase halves

20.16 Make sure all components, and the two dowels (arrowed), are installed

9 Carefully turn the engine over so it rests on its left-hand side, again on blocks so the shafts are clear of the bench.

10 Carefully lift the right crankcase half off the left half, using a soft-faced hammer to tap around the joint to initially separate the halves if necessary **(see illustration)**. If necessary heat around the right-hand crankshaft main bearing using a hot-air gun, and while lifting the right-hand crankcase have an assistant **gently** tap the ends of the crankshaft and transmission shafts using a soft mallet. **Note:** *If the halves do not separate easily, make sure all fasteners have been removed. Do not try and separate the halves by levering against the crankcase mating surfaces as they are easily scored and will leak oil in the future if damaged. If the halves separate then bind make sure they are coming apart parallel to each other, and if necessary gently tap the right-hand half back down to level them up and start again.* The right-hand crankcase half will come away leaving the crankshaft, transmission shafts, and selector drum and forks in the left-hand half. Where fitted the kickstart mechanism comes away with the right-hand half. On the engine photographed the right-hand main bearing came away in the crankcase, but on some it may stay on the crankshaft.

11 Note the thrust washer on the right-hand end of the transmission output shaft – if it is not there it is stuck to the bearing in the crankcase, in which case retrieve it and fit it

back onto the shaft **(see illustration 20.16)**. On engines that have a needle bearing in the crankcase (instead of a ball bearing) for the right-hand end of the transmission output shaft there is also a bush, which if not on the end of the shaft with the thrust washer will be in the bearing in the crankcase.

12 Remove the two locating dowels from the crankcase if they are loose (they could be in either half) **(see illustration 20.16)**.

13 Refer to Sections 21 to 24 for the removal and installation of the components housed within the crankcases.

14 Remove all traces of old sealant from the crankcase mating surfaces.

Reassembly

15 Make sure the crankcase mating surfaces are clean and dry. Clean the threads of all the crankcase bolts.

16 Ensure that all components and their bearings and new oil seals (see Section 18 for the gearchange shaft oil seal and Section 24 for the transmission output shaft seal) are in place in the left-hand crankcase half. Make sure that all bearings, and where fitted the kickstart mechanism, are in the right-hand half. Make sure the thrust washer is in place on the right-hand end of the transmission output shaft, and on engines with a needle bearing the bush is also fitted on the end of the shaft. If removed, fit the two locating dowels into the left-hand crankcase **(see illustration)**.

17 Generously lubricate the crankshaft and transmission shaft bearings and gears and the selector fork shafts and fork ends and the tracks in the selector drum with clean engine oil, then use a rag soaked in high flash-point solvent to wipe over the mating surfaces of both crankcase halves to remove any traces of oil.

18 Apply a smear of suitable RTV sealant to the right-hand crankcase mating surface **(see illustration)**.

19 Check again that all components are in position **(see illustration 20.16)**. Carefully fit the right-hand crankcase down onto the left-hand crankcase, making sure the shaft ends and dowels locate correctly and the cases remain square to each other **(see illustration 20.10)**. If the right-hand main bearing is in the crankcase and does not want to slide onto the crankshaft gently tap it on using a socket that bears on the inner race of the bearing, and similarly tap the inner races of the transmission shaft bearings if necessary **(see illustration)**. If the main bearing is on the crankshaft and the crankcase does not want to seat over it heat the housing with a hot-air gun. Do not use force – if the cases do not join easily there is something wrong, in which case lift the case off and investigate.

20 Check that the right-hand crankcase half is correctly seated all round. Carefully turn the engine over so it rests on its right-hand side, again on blocks so the shafts are clear of the bench.

Caution: The crankcase halves should fit together without being forced. If the casings are not correctly seated, remove the right-hand crankcase half and investigate the problem. Do not attempt to pull them together using the crankcase bolts as the casing will crack and be ruined.

21 Thread the crankcase bolts into the left-hand side finger-tight at first, not forgetting the wiring clamp, then tighten them evenly and a little at a time in a criss-cross sequence **(see illustration 20.8a)**.

22 With all crankcase bolts tightened, check that the crankshaft and transmission shafts rotate smoothly and easily. Check that the transmission shafts rotate freely and independently in neutral, then rotate the selector drum by hand and select each gear in turn whilst rotating the input shaft. If there are any signs of undue stiffness, tight or rough spots, or of any other problem, the fault must be rectified before proceeding further.

23 On models without a kickstart mechanism, where removed fit the thrust washer onto the end of the transmission output shaft, then fit a new circlip, making sure it locates correctly in the groove.

24 On models with a kickstart mechanism refer to Section 19, Steps 17 and 18 and install the idle and gear drive components.

25 Fit a new O-ring smeared with oil into the groove inside the output shaft spacer **(see**

20.18 Apply the sealant to the perimeter mating surface, making sure none blocks the oil passages

20.19 Gently tap on the inner race to ease the bearing onto the crankshaft if required

20.25a Fit a new O-ring (arrowed), and make sure the grooved rim of the spacer faces into the engine

20.25b Bend the tabs against the bolts

21.17 Removing a main bearing from the crankshaft using a puller

illustration). Slide the spacer onto the shaft and into the seal. Fit the output shaft oil seal retainer and tighten the bolts **(see illustration 20.4b)**, then bend the tabs up against them **(see illustration)**.

26 Slide the neutral plunger and spring into the crankcase **(see illustrations 20.3c and b)**. Fit the bolt using a new sealing washer **(see illustration 20.3a)**.

27 Install all other removed assemblies in a reverse of the sequence given in Step 2.

21 Crankcases and bearings

Crankcases

1 After the crankcases have been separated, remove the selector drum and forks, the transmission shafts, and the crankshaft, and the kickstart shaft (where fitted), referring to the relevant Sections of this Chapter.

2 Clean the crankcases thoroughly with new solvent and dry them with compressed air. Blow out all oil passages with compressed air.

3 Remove all traces of old sealant from the mating surfaces. Clean up minor damage to the surfaces with a fine sharpening stone or grindstone.
Caution: Be very careful not to nick or gouge the crankcase mating surfaces or oil leaks will result. Check both crankcase halves very carefully for cracks and other damage.

4 Small cracks or holes in aluminium castings can be repaired with an epoxy resin adhesive as a temporary measure or with one of the low temperature welding kits. Permanent repairs can only be done by TIG (tungsten inert gas or heli-arc) welding, and only a specialist in this process is in a position to advise on the economy or practical aspect of such a repair. If any damage is found that can't be repaired, replace the crankcase halves as a set.

5 Damaged threads can be economically reclaimed using a diamond section wire insert, for example of the Heli-Coil type (though there are other makes), which are easily fitted after drilling and re-tapping the affected thread.

6 Sheared studs or screws can usually be removed with extractors, which consist of a tapered, left-hand thread screw of very hard steel. These are inserted into a pre-drilled hole in the stud, and usually succeed in dislodging the most stubborn stud or screw. If a stud has sheared above its bore line, it can be removed using a conventional stud extractor which avoids the need for drilling.

 HAYNES HiNT *Refer to Tools and Workshop Tips for details of installing a thread insert and using screw extractors.*

7 Install all components and assemblies, referring to the relevant Sections of this and the other Chapters, before reassembling the crankcase halves.

Bearing information

8 The crankshaft and transmission shaft bearings should all be replaced with new ones as part of a complete engine overhaul, or individually as required due to wear or failure.

9 Bearing failure occurs mainly because of lack of lubrication, the presence of dirt or other foreign particles, overloading the engine, break-up of one or more of the bearing components due to fatigue, or corrosion. Regardless of the cause of bearing failure, it must be corrected before the engine is reassembled to prevent it from happening again.

10 The bearings should rotate smoothly, freely and quietly, there should be no rough spots, and there should be no excessive play between the inner and outer races, or between the inner race and the shaft it fits on, or between the outer race and its housing in the crankcase.

11 Dirt and other foreign particles get into the engine in a variety of ways. They may be left in the engine during assembly or they may pass through filters or breathers, then get into the oil and from there into the bearings. Metal chips from machining operations and normal engine wear are often present. Abrasives are sometimes left in engine components after reconditioning operations, especially when parts are not thoroughly cleaned using the

proper cleaning methods. The best prevention for this cause of bearing failure is to clean all parts thoroughly and keep everything spotlessly clean during engine reassembly. Regular oil changes are also recommended.

12 Lack of lubrication or lubrication breakdown has a number of interrelated causes. Excessive heat (which thins the oil), overloading and oil leakage all contribute to lubrication breakdown. Blocked oil passages will starve a bearing of lubrication and destroy it.

13 Riding habits can have a definite effect on bearing life. Full throttle low, speed operation, or labouring the engine, puts very high loads on bearings, as insufficient engine heat is produced to drive off the condensed water and corrosive gases produced. These products collect in the engine oil, forming acid and sludge. As the oil is carried to the engine bearings, the acid attacks and corrodes the bearing material.

14 Incorrect bearing installation during engine assembly will lead to bearing failure as well. To avoid bearing problems, clean all parts thoroughly before reassembly, and lubricate the new bearings with clean engine oil during installation.

Bearing removal and installation

Note: *If the correct bearing removal and installation tools are not available take the crankcases and crankshaft to a dealer – do not risk damaging either the cases or the crankshaft.*

Crankshaft (main) bearings

15 If the crankshaft (main) bearings have failed, excessive rumbling and vibration will be felt when the engine is running.

16 Separate the crankcase halves (Section 20) and remove all assemblies within (see Step 1).

17 To remove a main bearing from the crankshaft, use an external bearing puller as shown, to draw them off **(see illustration)**. Take care to protect the end of the crankshaft by using the correct size adapter or a suitable spacer between them. To ease removal heat the bearing first using a hot air gun, but try not to heat the crankshaft as well.

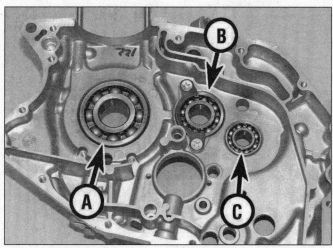

21.24a Main bearing (A), transmission input shaft bearing (B) and output shaft bearing (C) – right-hand crankcase half

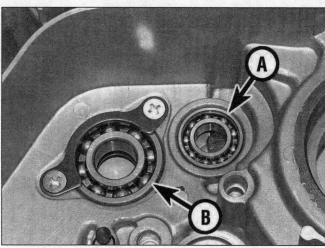

21.24b Transmission input shaft bearing (A) and output shaft bearing (B) – left-hand crankcase half

18 To remove a main bearing from the crankcase, heat the bearing housing with a hot air gun, then tap the bearing out from the outside of the crankcase using a bearing driver or a suitable socket on the inner race **(see illustrations 21.24a and 21.27)**.

19 Fit the new bearings according to how they were removed, i.e. if the left-hand bearing was on the crankshaft, fit the new one onto the crankshaft, not into the crankcase, and if the right-hand bearing came away in the crankcase, fit the new on into the crankcase, not onto the crankshaft.

20 To fit a bearing onto the crankshaft, smear the inside with clean oil and fit it with the marked side facing out. Drive the bearing squarely on until it seats using a tubular driver that bears only on the inner race. Cooling or freezing the crankshaft (using a fridge, freezer or freeze spray) and heating the bearing inner race using a hot air gun will ease installation.

21 To fit a bearing into the crankcase, smear the outside of the new bearing with clean oil and fit it with its marked side facing towards the inside of the engine, then heat the housing and drive the bearing squarely in until it seats using a driver or socket that bears only on the outer race.

Connecting rod (big-end) bearing

22 If the connecting rod (big-end) bearing has failed, there will be a pronounced knocking noise when the engine is running, particularly under load and increasing with engine speed. Refer to Section 22, Step 5 for checks that can be made.

23 The connecting rod and its bearing are generally an integral part of the crankshaft assembly which usually comes as a pressed-up unit – individual components are sometimes available (depending on the manufacturer), but even if they are, disassembling and reassembling the crankshaft should only be undertaken by a suitably equipped specialist workshop. If the big-end bearing fails the best thing to do is replace the crankshaft/connecting rod assembly with a new one (see Section 22), but if preferred check with your dealer for advice.

Transmission shaft bearings

24 If the transmission bearings have failed, excessive rumbling and vibration will be felt when the engine is running **(see illustrations)**.

25 Separate the crankcase halves (Section 20) and remove all assemblies within (see Step 1).

26 Remove the retainers securing the right-hand bearing for the input shaft and the left-hand bearing for the output shaft – each is secured by two counter-sunk screws **(see illustrations 21.24a and b)**. If you can't release the screws using a conventional screwdriver use an impact driver, and support the crankcase on a wooden block under the bearing.

27 To remove both shaft bearings from the right-hand crankcase and the output shaft bearing from the left-hand crankcase, heat the bearing housing with a hot air gun, then tap the bearing out from the outside of the crankcase using a bearing driver or a suitable socket on the inner race **(see illustration)**.

28 To remove the input shaft bearing from the left-hand crankcase, an expanding knife-edge bearing puller with slide-hammer attachment may be required. First heat the bearing housing with a hot air gun and see whether the bearing will drop out. If not fit the expanding end of the puller behind the bearing, then turn the puller to expand it and lock it **(see illustration)**. Attach the slide-hammer to the puller, then hold the crankcase firmly down and operate the slide-hammer to jar the bearing out **(see illustration)**.

21.27 Drive the bearings out from the outside

21.28a Fit the expander into the bearing . . .

21.28b . . . and use the slide-hammer attachment to remove the bearing

21.29 Drive the bearings in from the inside

22.3a Heat around the main bearing housing . . .

22.3b . . . then lift the crankshaft out, but wear gloves!

29 Smear the outside of the new bearing with clean oil and fit it with its marked side towards the inside of the engine, then heat the housing again and drive the bearing squarely in until it seats using a driver or socket that bears only on the outer race **(see illustration)**.
30 If the bearing retainer screw heads were deformed on removal use new ones. If they can be reused clean the threads, then apply some fresh threadlock. Fit the retainers and tighten the screws.

22 Crankshaft and connecting rod

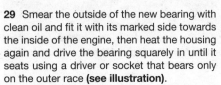

Note: *To remove the crankshaft the engine must be removed from the frame and the crankcase halves separated.*

Removal

1 Remove the engine from the frame (see Section 4) and separate the crankcase halves (see Section 20).
2 Remove the selector drum and forks (Section 23) and the transmission shafts (Section 24).
3 Heat around the left-hand main bearing housing using a hot-air gun, then grasp the crankshaft and lift it out of the crankcase **(see illustrations)**. If the shaft is stuck, thread the alternator rotor nut on its left-hand end then use a soft-faced mallet and gently tap on the nut, supporting the inside of the crankcase on wooden blocks high enough so the crankshaft

is just clear of the bench and can't go far should it suddenly release and drop out.

Inspection

4 Clean the crankshaft with solvent. If available, blow the crank dry with compressed air.
5 Hold the crankshaft still and check for any radial (up and down) play in the big-end bearing by pushing and pulling the rod against the crank **(see illustration)**. If the play is excessive refer to Section 21, Step 23.
6 Refer to Chapter 2A, Section 11 and check the connecting rod small end and piston pin for wear.
7 Have the rod checked for twist and bend by a dealer if you are in doubt about its straightness.
8 Refer to Section 21 and check the crankshaft (main) bearings.

Installation

9 Heat around the left-hand main bearing housing using a hot-air gun, then carefully lower the crankshaft into the crankcase, making sure the connecting rod is aligned between the cylinder block studs, that the bearing enters the housing squarely, and seats correctly **(see illustration 22.3a and b)**. If necessary thread the primary drive gear nut onto the right-hand end of the shaft and gently tap it using a soft-faced mallet so you are sure the bearing has seated in its housing, using more heat if required.
10 Check that the crankshaft rotates freely and easily.

11 Install the transmission shafts (Section 24) and the selector drum and forks (Section 23).
12 Reassemble the crankcase halves (see Section 20).

23 Selector drum and forks

Note: *To remove the selector drum and forks the engine must be removed from the frame and the crankcases separated.*

Removal

1 Remove the engine from the frame (see Section 4) and separate the crankcase halves (see Section 20).
2 Before removing the selector forks check for any identification marks and note which way they face so the forks can be installed correctly. If no letters are visible, mark them yourself using a felt pen. On the engine photographed all forks were marked the same, with the marks facing left, and while the centre fork is different the right and left forks are identical and so could get mixed up. The right and left forks fit into the output shaft and the centre fork fits into the input shaft.
3 Support the selector forks and withdraw the shafts **(see illustration)**. Pivot each fork out of its groove in the selector drum.
4 Unhook the stopper arm return spring from its post, then pivot the arm so the roller is clear of the selector drum **(see illustration)**.

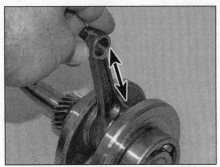

22.5 Check for any radial play in the big-end bearing

23.3 Withdraw the shafts

23.4a Unhook the spring and pivot the stopper arm away from the drum

23.4b Move the forks aside and remove the drum

23.6 Unscrew the bolt (arrowed) and remove the arm

23.7 Check the fit of each fork in its pinion . . .

23.8 . . . and on its shaft

23.10 Check the guide pins and their grooves in the drum

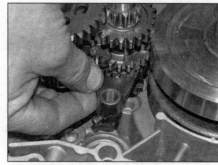

23.14a Fit the centre fork . . .

Remove the drum (see illustration). Note the stopper plate, its locating pin and the thrust washer on the left-hand end of the drum and take care they do not drop off (see illustration 23.15c, b and a).
5 Slide each fork out of its pinion and remove them (see illustrations 23.14c, b and a). Once removed, slide the forks back onto the correct shafts to keep them in the correct order and way round.
6 Unscrew the stopper arm bolt and remove the arm (see illustration).

Inspection

7 Inspect the selector forks for any signs of wear or damage, especially around the fork ends where they engage with the groove in the pinion. Check that each fork fits correctly in its pinion groove (see illustration). Check closely to see if the forks are bent. If the forks are in any way damaged they must be replaced with new ones.

8 Check each fork fits correctly on its shaft (see illustration). They should move freely with a light fit but no appreciable freeplay. Replace the forks and/or shafts with new ones if they are worn. Check that the fork shaft holes in the casing are neither worn nor damaged.
9 Check each selector fork shaft is straight by rolling it along a flat surface. A bent rod will cause difficulty in selecting gears and make the gearchange action heavy. Replace the shaft with a new one if it is bent.
10 Inspect the selector drum grooves and selector fork guide pins for signs of wear or damage (see illustration). If either component shows signs of wear or damage the fork(s) and drum must be replaced with new ones.
11 Check that the selector drum rotates freely in each crankcase half and has no sign of freeplay between it and the casing.
12 Check the stopper arm roller and the

cams on the stopper plate for wear. Make sure the roller turns freely. Check the spring for deformation and stretch and replace it with a new one if necessary.

Installation

13 Clean the threads of the stopper arm bolt. Apply some fresh threadlock, then fit the arm and tighten the bolt (see illustration 23.6). Do not hook the spring up yet, and make sure the roller is clear of the selector drum bore.
14 Lubricate each fork with oil. Locate each fork in turn in its pinion groove, making sure they are correctly positioned – see Step 2 (see illustrations).
15 Fit the thrust washer, locating pin and stopper plate onto the selector drum, coating each with grease so they stick in place and won't drop off when fitting the drum, and locating the cam with the cut-out over the pin (see illustrations). Lubricate the

23.14b . . . the left-hand fork . . .

23.14c . . . and the right-hand fork

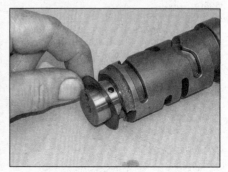

23.15a Fit the thrust washer . . .

23.15b . . . and the locating pin . . .

23.15c . . . then fit the stopper camplate, locating the cut-out (arrowed) over the pin

23.16 Locate the guide pins and align the forks, then fit the shafts

selector drum ends with clean engine oil. Fit the selector drum into the crankcase **(see illustration 23.4b)**. Rotate it so that the hole for the neutral switch contact pin points to the bottom of the crankcase. Pivot the stopper arm across so the roller seats against the stopper plate, then hook the spring onto its post **(see illustrations 23.4a and 23.6)**.

16 Lubricate the selector fork shafts with oil. Pivot each fork around to locate its guide pin in its groove in the selector drum, lifting the fork and its pinion where necessary, and slide the shafts through and into their bores in the crankcase **(see illustration and 23.3)**.

17 Reassemble the crankcase halves (see Section 20).

24 Transmission shaft removal and installation

Note: *To remove the transmission shafts the engine must be removed from the frame and the crankcases separated.*

Removal

1 Remove the engine from the frame (see Section 4) and separate the crankcase halves (see Section 20).

2 Remove the selector drum and forks (see Section 23).

3 Grasp the input shaft and output shaft together and lift both shafts out of the crankcase **(see illustration)**. If the shafts are stuck, use a soft-faced hammer and gently tap on the protruding outer end of the output shaft.

4 Prise the output shaft oil seal out of the left-hand crankcase using a seal hook or screwdriver **(see illustration)**. Remove the washer **(see illustration)**. Discard the seal as a new one must be used.

5 If necessary, the transmission shafts can be disassembled and inspected for wear or damage (see Section 25).

6 Refer to Section 21 and check the transmission shaft bearings.

Installation

7 Fit the washer against the output shaft bearing in the left-hand crankcase **(see**

illustration 24.4b). Press or drive a new oil seal into the crankcase and lubricate its lips with grease **(see illustration)**.

8 Join the shafts together on the bench so their related gears are engaged. Grasp the shafts together and fit them into the left-hand crankcase, locating the shaft ends in the bearings **(see illustration 24.3)**.

9 Make sure both transmission shafts are correctly seated and their related pinions are correctly engaged.

10 Install the selector drum and forks (see Section 23).

11 Position the gears in the neutral position and check the shafts are free to rotate easily and independently (i.e. the input shaft can turn whilst the output shaft is held stationary) before proceeding further. Also check that each gear can be selected by turning the input shaft with one hand and the selector drum with the other.

24.3 Lift the transmission shafts out together

24.4b . . . and remove the washer

12 Make sure the thrust washer is in place on the right-hand end of the output shaft, and on engines with a needle bearing the bush is also fitted on the end of the shaft.

13 Reassemble the crankcase halves (see Section 20).

25 Transmission shaft overhaul

1 Remove the transmission shafts from the crankcase (see Section 24). Always disassemble the transmission shafts separately to avoid mixing up the components. Two different types of gearshafts are fitted, type A with a combined 3rd/4th input shaft gear, and type B with separate input shaft gear pinions. Identify which type is fitted and follow the appropriate procedure.

24.4a Remove and discard the oil seal . . .

24.7 Drive the new seal into place using a seal driver or socket

HAYNES HiNT *When disassembling the transmission shafts, place the parts on a long rod or length of stiff wire to keep them in order and facing the proper direction.*

Input shaft

Disassembly – type A

2 The 2nd gear pinion is a press fit on the shaft. Draw it off it using a puller, with a suitable protective interface such as a bolt as shown between the puller bolt and the shaft end **(see illustrations)**. If the pinion is too tight for a puller, and heating the pinion with a hot air gun does not help, support the inner face of the gear and use an hydraulic press to press the shaft out **(see illustration)**.
3 Slide the combined 3rd/4th gear pinion off the shaft **(see illustration 25.20)**.
4 Release the circlip securing the 5th gear pinion, then slide the pinion off the shaft **(see illustrations 25.19b and a)**.
5 The 1st gear pinion is integral with the shaft **(see illustration)**.

Disassembly – type B

6 The 2nd gear pinion is a press fit on the shaft **(see illustrations 25.2a and b)**. Draw it off it using a puller, with a suitable protective interface such as a bolt as shown between the puller bolt and the shaft end. If the pinion is too tight for a puller, and heating the pinion with a hot air gun does not help, support the inner face of the gear and use an hydraulic press to press the shaft out **(see illustration 25.2c)**.
7 Slide the 5th gear pinion off the shaft.
8 Release the circlip securing the 3rd gear pinion, then slide the pinion off the shaft.
9 Release the circlip securing the 4th gear pinion, then slide the pinion off the shaft.
10 The 1st gear pinion is integral with the shaft **(see illustration 25.5)**.

Inspection

11 Wash all of the components in clean solvent and dry them off.
12 Check the gear teeth for cracking, chipping, pitting and other obvious wear or damage. Any pinion that is damaged as such must be replaced with a new one.

25.2a Fit a bolt into the end of the shaft . . .

25.2c If necessary use an hydraulic press as shown

13 Inspect the dogs and the dog holes in the gears for cracks, chips, and excessive wear especially in the form of rounded edges. Make sure mating gears engage properly. Replace the paired gears as a set if necessary.
14 Check for signs of scoring or bluing on the pinions, bushes and shaft. This could be caused by overheating due to inadequate lubrication. Check that all the oil holes and passages are clear. Replace any damaged pinions.
15 Check that each pinion moves freely on the shaft but without undue freeplay. Where fitted check the pinion bushes for wear – the oil retaining holes should be clearly visible. If not the bushes are worn.
16 The shaft is unlikely to sustain damage unless the engine has seized, placing an unusually high loading on the transmission, or the machine has covered a very high mileage. Check the surface of the shaft, especially where a pinion turns on it, and replace the shaft if it has scored or picked up, or if there

25.2b . . . and set the puller up as shown

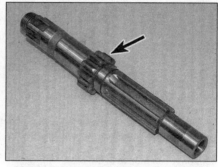

25.5 1st gear pinion (arrowed) is part of the shaft

are any cracks. Damage of any kind can only be cured by replacement.
17 Check the washers and circlips and replace any that are bent or appear weakened or worn. Use new ones if in any doubt. Note that it is good practice to renew all circlips when overhauling gearshafts.

Reassembly – type A

18 During reassembly, apply molybdenum disulphide oil (a 50/50 mixture of molybdenum disulphide grease and clean engine oil) to the mating surfaces of the shaft, pinions and bushes. When installing the circlips, do not expand their ends any further than is necessary. Install the stamped circlips and washers so that their chamfered side faces away from the thrust side.
19 Slide the 5th gear pinion onto the shaft with its dogs facing away from the integral 1st gear **(see illustration)**. Fit the circlip, making sure it is locates correctly in its groove in the shaft **(see illustrations)**.

25.19a Slide the 5th gear pinion onto the shaft . . .

25.19b . . . and secure it with the circlip . . .

25.19c . . . making sure it locates properly in its groove

20 Slide the combined 3rd/4th gear pinion onto the shaft with the larger (4th) gear pinion facing the 5th gear pinion **(see illustration)**.

21 Slide the 2nd gear pinion onto the shaft **(see illustration)**. Drive or press the gear onto the shaft until its sleeved section abuts the splined section of shaft using a suitable tubular drift or an hydraulic press **(see illustration)**.

22 Check that all components have been correctly installed **(see illustration)**.

Reassembly – type B

23 During reassembly, apply molybdenum disulphide oil (a 50/50 mixture of molybdenum disulphide grease and clean engine oil) to the mating surfaces of the shaft, pinions and bushes. When installing the circlips, do not expand their ends any further than is necessary. Install the stamped circlips and washers so that their chamfered side faces away from the thrust side.

24 Slide the 4th gear pinion onto the shaft with its dogs facing away from the integral 1st gear. Fit the circlip, making sure it is locates correctly in its groove in the shaft.

25 Slide the 3rd gear pinion onto the shaft with its selector fork groove facing the 4th gear pinion. Fit the circlip, making sure it is locates correctly in its groove in the shaft.

26 Slide the 5th gear pinion onto the shaft with its dogs facing the 3rd gear pinion.

27 Slide the 2nd gear pinion onto the shaft. Drive or press the gear onto the shaft until it butts the splined section using a suitable tubular drift or a hydraulic press.

28 Check that all components have been correctly installed.

Output shaft

Disassembly – type A

29 Slide the thrust washer off the right-hand end of the shaft, followed by the 1st gear pinion, the needle bearing, the thrust washer, and the 5th gear pinion **(see illustrations 25.44d,c, b and a, and 25.43)**.

30 Release the circlip securing the 4th gear pinion then slide the splined washer, the 4th gear pinion, the 3rd gear pinion and the thrust

25.20 Slide the 3rd/4th gear pinion onto the shaft

25.21b . . . then press it on as far as it will go

washer off the shaft **(see illustrations 25.42c, b and a, and 25.41b and a)**.

31 Release the circlip securing the selector dog, then slide the selector dog off the shaft **(see illustrations 25.40b and a)**.

32 Release the circlip securing the 2nd gear pinion, then slide the pinion off the shaft **(see illustrations 25.39b and a)**.

Disassembly – type B

33 Slide the bush and thrust washer off the right-hand end of the shaft, followed by the 1st gear pinion, the needle bearing, the thrust washer, and the 4th gear pinion.

34 Release the circlip securing the 3rd gear pinion, then slide the pinion and the thrust washer off the shaft.

35 Release the circlip securing the 5th gear pinion, then slide the pinion off the shaft.

36 Release the circlip securing the 2nd gear pinion, then slide the pinion off the shaft.

25.21a Fit the 2nd gear on as far as it will go . . .

25.22 The assembled input shaft should be as shown

Inspection

37 Refer to Steps 11 to 17 above.

Reassembly – type A

38 During reassembly, apply molybdenum disulphide oil (a 50/50 mixture of molybdenum disulphide grease and clean engine oil) to the mating surfaces of the shaft, pinions and bushes. When installing the circlips, do not expand the ends any further than is necessary. Install the stamped circlips and washers so that their chamfered side faces away from the thrust side.

39 Slide the 2nd gear pinion onto the right-hand end of the shaft with its recessed side facing in, then fit the circlip, making sure it locates correctly in its groove **(see illustrations)**.

40 Slide the selector dog onto the shaft with its fork groove facing away from the

25.39a Slide the 2nd gear pinion on . . .

25.39b . . . and secure it with the circlip . . .

25.39c . . . making sure it locates properly in its groove

25.40a Slide the selector dog on . . .

25.40b . . . and secure it with the circlip . . .

25.40c . . . making sure it locates properly in its groove

25.41a Slide the thrust washer onto the shaft . . .

25.41b . . . followed by the 3rd gear pinion

25.42a Slide the 4th gear pinion onto the shaft . . .

2nd gear pinion, then fit the circlip, making sure it locates correctly in its groove (see illustrations).

41 Slide the thrust washer onto the shaft followed by the 3rd gear pinion with its selector dogs facing the selector dog (see illustration).

42 Slide the 4th gear pinion onto the shaft with its recessed side facing away from the 3rd gear pinion, followed by the splined washer (see illustrations). Fit the circlip, making sure it locates correctly in its groove (see illustrations).

43 Slide the 5th gear pinion onto the shaft, with its selector fork groove facing the 4th gear pinion (see illustration).

25.42b . . . followed by the splined washer

25.42c . . . and secure them with the circlip . . .

25.42d . . . making sure it locates in the groove

25.43 Slide the 5th gear pinion onto the shaft

25.44a Slide the thrust washer on . . .

25.44b . . . followed by the needle bearing . . .

25.44c . . . then fit the 1st gear pinion onto the bearing . . .

44 Slide the thrust washer onto the shaft, followed by the needle bearing, then fit the 1st gear pinion, with its flat side facing out, onto the bearing **(see illustrations)**. Fit the thrust washer onto the end of the shaft **(see illustration)**.
45 Check that all components have been correctly installed **(see illustration)**.

Reassembly – type B

46 During reassembly, apply molybdenum disulphide oil (a 50/50 mixture of molybdenum disulphide grease and clean engine oil) to the mating surfaces of the shaft, pinions and bushes. When installing the circlips, do not expand the ends any further than is necessary. Install the stamped circlips and washers so that their chamfered side faces away from the thrust side.
47 Slide the 2nd gear pinion onto the right-hand end of the shaft with its recessed side facing in, then fit the circlip, making sure it locates correctly in its groove.
48 Slide the 5th gear pinion onto the shaft with its fork groove facing away from the 2nd

gear pinion, then fit the circlip, making sure it locates correctly in its groove.
49 Slide the thrust washer onto the shaft followed by the 3rd gear pinion with its dogs facing away from the 5th gear pinion. Fit the circlip, making sure it locates correctly in its groove.
50 Slide the 4th gear pinion onto the shaft with its fork groove facing the 3rd gear pinion.
51 Slide on the needle bearing, then fit the 1st gear pinion, with its flat side facing out, onto the bearing. Fit the thrust washer and bush onto the end of the shaft.
52 Check that all components have been correctly installed.

26 Running-in procedure

1 Make sure the engine oil level is correct (see *Pre-ride checks*). Make sure there is fuel in the tank.
2 Turn the engine kill switch to the ON position

and shift the gearbox into neutral. Turn the ignition ON. Set the choke.
3 Start the engine and allow it to run at a moderately fast idle until it reaches operating temperature.

 Warning: If the oil pressure warning light doesn't go off, or it comes on while the engine is running, stop the engine immediately.

4 If a lubrication failure is suspected, stop the engine immediately and try to find the cause. If an engine is run without oil, even for a short period of time, severe damage will occur.
5 Check carefully that there are no oil leaks and make sure the transmission and controls, especially the brakes, function properly before road testing the machine.
6 Treat the machine gently for the first few miles to make sure oil has circulated throughout the engine and any new parts installed have started to seat.
7 Even greater care is necessary if a new piston and rings or a new cylinder have been fitted, and the bike will have to be run in as when new. This means greater use of the transmission and a restraining hand on the throttle until at least 300 miles (500 km) have been covered. There's no point in keeping to any set speed limit – the main idea is to keep from labouring the engine and to gradually increase performance up to the 300 miles (500 km) mark. Experience is the best guide, since it's easy to tell when an engine is running freely.
8 Upon completion of the road test, and after the engine has cooled down completely, recheck the valve clearances (see Chapter 1) and check the engine oil level (see *Pre-ride checks*).

25.44d . . . and fit the thrust washer

25.45 The assembled output shaft should be as shown

Chapter 2C
Engine, clutch and transmission –
154FMI OHC single engines

Contents

Degrees of difficulty

Easy, suitable for novice with little experience	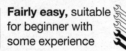	Fairly easy, suitable for beginner with some experience		Fairly difficult, suitable for competent DIY mechanic		Difficult, suitable for experienced DIY mechanic		Very difficult, suitable for expert DIY or professional	

Specifications

General

Type	Four-stroke single
Capacity	124 cc
Bore	54.0 mm
Stroke	54.0 mm
Cooling system	Air cooled
Lubrication	Wet sump, trochoid pump
Clutch	Wet multi-plate
Transmission	Five-speed constant mesh
Final drive	Chain and sprockets

Cylinder head

Warpage (max)	0.05 mm

Valves, guides and springs

Valve clearances	see Chapter 1

Cylinder bore

Ovality (out-of-round) (max)	0.01 mm
Taper (max)	0.05 mm

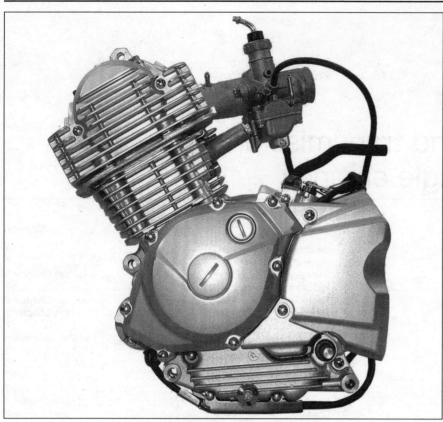

Type 154FMI engine left view

Torque settings

General settings (thread size given)

5 mm bolt/nut	5 Nm
6 mm bolt/nut	10 Nm
8 mm bolt/nut	24 Nm
10 mm bolt/nut	35 Nm
12 mm bolt/nut	55 Nm

Specific settings

Air induction system pipe bolts	10 Nm
Alternator cover bolts	10 Nm
Alternator rotor nut	70 Nm
Cam chain tensioner blade bolt	10 Nm
Cam chain tensioner cap bolt	8 Nm
Cam chain tensioner mounting bolts	10 Nm
Camshaft/rocker shaft retainer bolt	10 Nm
Camshaft sprocket cover bolts	10 Nm
Camshaft sprocket bolt	20 Nm
Clutch cover bolts	10 Nm
Clutch nut	60 Nm
Clutch spring bolts	6 Nm
Crankcase bolts	10 Nm
Cylinder head 8 mm bolts	22 Nm
Cylinder head 6 mm bolts	10 Nm
Engine mounting bolt nuts	
Front engine bracket-to-frame	55 Nm
All others	38 Nm
Intake duct bolts	10 Nm
Oil pressure check bolt	7 Nm
Primary drive gear nut	70 Nm
Starter clutch bolts	30 Nm
Stopper arm bolt	10 Nm

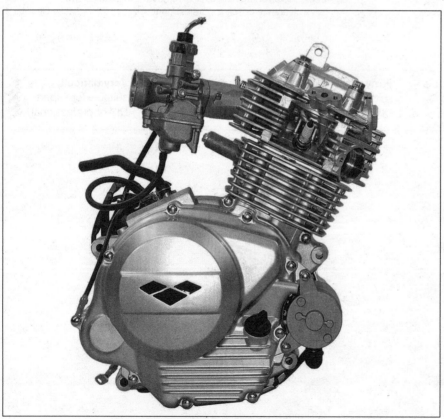

Type 154FMI engine right view

1 General information

The engine/transmission unit is an air-cooled single cylinder of unit construction. Manufactured by the Chinese Jianshe factory, it is based on the YamahaYBR125 engine and known as the type 154FMI **(see illustrations)**. The two valves are operated by rocker arms actuated by a single overhead camshaft which is chain driven off the left-hand end of the crankshaft. The crankcase divides vertically.

The crankcase incorporates a wet sump, pressure-fed lubrication system which uses a single rotor trochoidal oil pump that is gear-driven off the right-hand end of the crankshaft. Oil is filtered by a rotary filter on the crankshaft.

The alternator is on the left-hand end of the crankshaft. The crankshaft position sensor trigger for the ignition timing is on the outside of the alternator rotor, and the sensor is mounted in the alternator cover along with the stator.

Power from the crankshaft is routed to the transmission via the clutch. The clutch is of the wet, multi-plate type and is gear-driven off the crankshaft. The clutch is operated by cable. The transmission is a five-speed constant-mesh unit. Final drive to the rear wheel is by chain and sprockets.

2 Component access

Operations possible with the engine in the frame

The components and assemblies listed below can be removed without having to remove the engine from the frame. If however, a number of areas require attention at the same time, removal of the engine is recommended.

    Camshaft and rockers
    Cylinder head
    Cylinder block and piston
    Cam chain, tensioner and blades
    Clutch
    Oil pump and filter
    Gearchange mechanism
    Alternator
    Starter clutch
    Starter motor

Operations requiring engine removal

It is necessary to remove the engine from the frame to gain access to the following components.

    Balancer shaft
    Crankshaft, connecting rod and bearings
    Selector drum and forks
    Transmission shafts and bearings

3 Engine wear assessment

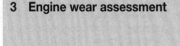

Cylinder compression check

Special tool: *A compression gauge is required to perform this test.*

1 Poor engine performance may be caused by leaking valves, incorrect valve clearances, a leaking head gasket, or a worn piston, piston rings or cylinder. A cylinder compression check will highlight these conditions and can also indicate the presence of excessive carbon deposits in the cylinder head.

2 The only tools required are a compression gauge (there are two types, one with a

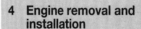

3.6 Unscrew the oil pressure check bolt (arrowed)

threaded adapter to fit the spark plug hole in the cylinder head, the other has a rubber seal which is pressed into the spark plug hole to create a seal – the threaded adapter type is preferable), and a spark plug socket. Depending on the outcome of the initial test, a squirt-type oil can may also be needed.

3 Refer to Chapter 2A, Section 3, for details of the check.

Engine oil pressure check

4 The engine has no oil pressure switch or level sensor and therefore there is no oil pressure or level warning light in the instrument cluster.

5 However, if there is any doubt about the performance of the engine lubrication system an oil pressure check must be carried out. This provides useful information about the state of wear of the engine.

6 First make sure the engine oil level is correct and confirm that the correct grade oil is being used (see *Pre-ride checks*). Make sure there are no obvious oil leaks from anywhere around the engine and that the oil drain plug is tight (see Chapter 1). Remove the oil pressure check bolt from the cylinder head **(see illustration)**. Have some rag to hand.

7 Start the engine and allow it idle, and watch the pressure check hole – oil should come out of the hole quite soon after starting the engine. When the oil appears stop the engine. If no oil has appeared after one minute, stop the engine immediately.

8 If no oil came out during the test, the pressure is significantly lower than it should

be or non-existent. This could mean that the oil pump or its drive mechanism is faulty, the filter is blocked, an oil passage is blocked, or there is other engine damage. Begin diagnosis by checking the oil strainer (see Chapter 1), then the filter and pump (see Section 17). If these items check out okay, the engine needs to be overhauled to clean out all oil passages.

9 On completion, fit the oil pressure check bolt into the cylinder head and tighten it to the torque setting specified at the beginning of the Chapter.

4 Engine removal and installation

Caution: The engine isn't particularly heavy, but the aid of an assistant is advised during this process.

Removal

1 Support the bike on its centrestand where fitted, or using an auxiliary stand, making sure it is on level ground. Work can be made easier by raising the machine to a suitable working height on an hydraulic ramp or a suitable platform. Make sure the motorcycle is secure and will not topple over, and tie the front brake lever to the handlebar to prevent it rolling forwards.

2 Where fitted, remove any fairing or bodywork panels as required to access wiring connectors and other engine related components (see Chapter 8).

3 Disconnect the negative (-) lead from the battery (see Chapter 9).

4 Remove the fuel tank (see Chapter 4).

5 If the engine is dirty, particularly around its mountings, wash it thoroughly. This will make work much easier and rule out the possibility of dirt falling into some vital component.

6 Drain the engine oil (see Chapter 1).

7 Pull the spark plug cap off the plug and secure the lead clear of the engine.

8 Undo the bolts securing the air induction system (AIS) union to the cylinder head and secure the union clear of the engine **(see illustration)**. Note the location of the aluminium gasket **(see illustration)**. Pull the AIS valve vacuum hose off its union on the intake duct **(see illustration)**.

4.8a Disconnect the AIS union . . .

4.8b . . . noting the location of the gasket

4.8c Disconnect the vacuum hose

4.9 Disconnect the engine earth lead

4.11 Detach the crankcase breather hose

4.12a Free the clutch cable end . . .

4.12b . . . and draw the cable out of the bracket

4.13 Gearchange lever pinch bolt

Remove the carburettor (see Chapter 4). Plug the intake on the engine with clean rag.

12 Create some slack in the clutch cable (see Chapter 1). Free the cable end from the release arm and draw the cable out of the bracket on the crankcase **(see illustrations)**. Position the cable clear of the engine.

13 Undo the pinch bolt and remove the gearchange lever **(see illustration)**.

14 Remove the footrest bracket complete with sidestand. On the left side first trace the sidestand switch wiring up to its connector and disconnect it **(see illustration)**. On the right side disconnect the brake rod from the operating arm on the brake backplate (see Chapter 7) to enable the brake pedal to be lowered for access to the footrest bracket rear mounting bolt – note that the brake light switch spring will require disconnecting from the pedal. Remove the rear mounting bolt from the footrest bracket on each side, then remove the lower rear engine mounting bolt which forms the footrest bracket front mounting **(see illustrations)**. Draw the footrest bracket and sidestand complete with its wiring away **(see illustration)**.

15 Undo the bolts securing the front sprocket cover and remove the cover, noting the location of the wiring from the neutral switch **(see illustration)**. Disconnect the drive chain at its spring link and rotate the rear wheel to draw the chain off the sprocket (see Chapter 7).

16 If required, remove the starter motor (see Chapter 9). If you want to leave the starter motor in situ, pull back the rubber cover on its

9 Where fitted, remove the kickstart lever, noting its position on the kickstart shaft. Disconnect the engine earth lead secured by the rear crankcase bolt, then refit the bolt for safekeeping **(see illustration)**.

10 Remove the exhaust system (see Chapter 4).

11 Release the clip securing the crankcase breather hose and detach the hose from the top of the crankcase **(see illustration)**.

4.14a Sidestand switch wiring connector

4.14b Remove the rear mounting bolt (arrowed) . . .

4.14c . . . and the lower rear engine mounting bolt

4.14d Lift off the footrest bracket/ sidestand assembly

4.15 Remove the front sprocket cover

4.16a Disconnect the lead from the starter motor terminal

4.16b Undo the bolts (arrowed) and remove the guard

4.17 Disconnect the wiring connectors

terminal, then undo the nut and disconnect the lead **(see illustration)**. Undo the crankcase bolts securing the lead guard from the underside of the engine and remove the guard **(see illustration)**. Secure the lead clear of the engine then refit the bolts for safekeeping.

17 Trace the alternator, pick-up coil and neutral switch wiring from the left-hand side of the engine and disconnect it at the connectors **(see illustration)**. Release the wiring from any clips of ties that will restrict it when removing the engine.

18 Position an hydraulic or mechanical jack under the engine with a block of wood between the jack head and sump. Make sure the jack is centrally positioned so the engine will not topple in any direction when the last mounting bolt is removed. Raise the jack to take the weight of the engine, but make sure it is not lifting the bike and taking the weight of that as well. The idea is to support the engine so that there is no pressure on any of the mounting bolts once they have been slackened, so they can be easily withdrawn. Note that it may be necessary to alter the position of the jack as some of the bolts are removed to relieve the stress transferred to the other bolts. **Note:** *Check which side the engine mounting bolts and bracket bolts are fitted, and keep any washers with their bolts.*

19 Unscrew the nuts from the front engine mounting bolts and the bolts securing the front bracket to the frame **(see illustration)**. Withdraw the bolts and remove the bracket **(see illustration)**.

20 Unscrew the nuts on the top engine mounting bolts and withdraw all three bolts and the two brackets **(see illustrations)**.

21 Unscrew the nut on the upper rear mounting bolt **(see illustration)**.

22 Check that the engine is properly supported by the jack. Check that all wiring, cables and hoses are free and clear.

23 Withdraw the upper rear mounting bolt. With the aid of an assistant, support the weight of the engine and remove the jack, then lift the engine clear of the frame (see *Caution* above).

Installation

24 Manoeuvre the engine into position in the frame and support it with a jack and block of wood. Align all the mounting bolt holes, making sure that all cables and wiring are correctly routed and do not get trapped. Note that it may be necessary to adjust the jack as

4.19a Undo the nuts and bolts . . .

some of the bolts are installed to realign the other bolt holes.

25 Referring to the removal procedure, fit all the mounting bolts and brackets, inserting the bolts from the same side from which they were removed. Install the footrest bracket (see Step 14). Fit all the nuts and tighten them finger-tight. Now, in reverse order of their slackening and removal (i.e. rear first, then top, then front), tighten the nuts to the torque settings specified at the beginning of the Chapter, counter-holding the bolt heads to prevent them turning.

26 Remove the jack from under the engine.

27 The remainder of the installation procedure is the reverse of removal, noting the following points:

● When fitting the gearchange lever onto the gearchange shaft, align the slot in the arm with the mark on the shaft.

● Use a new gasket on the exhaust pipe.

4.19b . . . and remove the front mounting bracket

4.20a Undo the nuts and bolts . . .

4.20b . . . and remove the top engine mounting brackets

4.21 Undo the nut on the upper rear mounting bolt

● When connecting the AIS pipe to the cylinder head, remember to fit the aluminium gasket.
● Make sure all wires, cables and hoses are correctly routed and connected, and secured by any clips or ties.
● Refill the engine with oil to the correct level (see Chapter 1 and *Pre-ride checks*).
● Adjust the throttle and clutch cable freeplay (see Chapter 1).
● Adjust the drive chain (see Chapter 1).
● Check the operation of the rear brake and brake light switch and adjust if necessary (see Chapter 1).
● Start the engine and check that there are no oil leaks. Adjust the idle speed (see Chapter 1).

5 Engine overhaul information

1 Before beginning the engine overhaul, read through the related procedures to familiarise yourself with the scope and requirements of the job. Overhauling an engine is not all that difficult, but it is time consuming. Check on the availability of parts and make sure that any necessary special tools are obtained in advance.
2 Most work can be done with a decent set of typical workshop hand tools, although a number of precision measuring tools are required for inspecting parts to determine if they are worn.
3 To ensure maximum life and minimum trouble from a rebuilt engine, everything must be assembled with care in a spotlessly clean environment.

Disassembly

4 Before disassembling the engine, thoroughly clean and degrease its external surfaces. This will prevent contamination of the engine internals, and will also make the job a lot easier and cleaner. A high flash-point solvent, such as paraffin (kerosene) can be used, or better still, a proprietary engine degreaser such as Gunk. Use old paintbrushes and toothbrushes to work the solvent into the various recesses of the casings. Take care to exclude solvent or water from the electrical components and intake and exhaust ports.

⚠ **Warning: The use of petrol (gasoline) as a cleaning agent should be avoided because of the risk of fire.**

5 When clean and dry, position the engine on the workbench, leaving suitable clear area for working. Gather a selection of small containers, plastic bags and some labels so that parts can be grouped together in an easily identifiable manner. Also get some paper and a pen so that notes can be taken. You will also need a supply of clean rag, which should be as absorbent as possible.
6 Before commencing work, read through the appropriate section so that some idea of the necessary procedure can be gained. When removing components note that great force is seldom required, unless specified (checking the specified torque setting of the particular bolt being removed will indicate how tight it is, and therefore how much force should be needed). In many cases, a component's reluctance to be removed is indicative of an incorrect approach or removal method – if in any doubt, re-check with the text.
7 When disassembling the engine, keep 'mated' parts together that have been in contact with each other during engine operation. These 'mated' parts must be reused or replaced as an assembly.
8 A complete engine stripdown should be done in the following general order with reference to the appropriate Sections.

Remove the cam chain tensioner
Remove the cylinder head
Remove the rockers and camshaft
Remove the cylinder block and piston
Remove the starter motor (see Chapter 9)
Remove the clutch
Remove the oil pump
Remove the gearchange mechanism
Remove the kickstart mechanism
Remove the alternator and starter clutch
Remove the cam chain and tensioner blade
Separate the crankcase halves
Remove the crankshaft and balancer shaft
Remove the selector drum and forks
Remove the transmission shafts

Reassembly

9 Reassembly is accomplished by reversing the general disassembly sequence.

6 Cam chain tensioner

Note: *The cam chain tensioner can be removed with the engine in the frame.*

Removal

1 Unscrew the tensioner cap bolt **(see illustration)**.
2 Unscrew the tensioner mounting bolts and washers and withdraw the tensioner from the engine **(see illustration)**.
3 Remove the gasket and discard it – a new one must be used on installation. Do not attempt to dismantle the tensioner.
4 Remove all traces of old gasket from the tensioner and cylinder block mating surfaces.

Inspection

5 Insert a small flat-bladed screwdriver in the end of the tensioner so that it engages the slotted plunger **(see illustration)**. Press on the end of the plunger and turn the screwdriver clockwise until the plunger is fully retracted. The plunger should move smoothly when wound into the tensioner. Now remove the screwdriver and release the plunger – it should spring out freely when released.

Installation

6 Using the screwdriver, retract the plunger fully and hold it in this position with the screwdriver.
7 Fit a new gasket onto the tensioner body. Install the tensioner and mounting bolts and tighten the bolts to the torque setting specified at the beginning of the Chapter, all the time keeping a hold on the screwdriver. Release and remove the screwdriver.
8 Tighten the cap bolt to the specified torque.

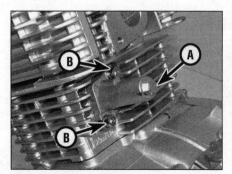

6.1 Unscrew the cap bolt (A) and mounting bolts (B) . . .

6.2 . . . and remove the cam chain tensioner

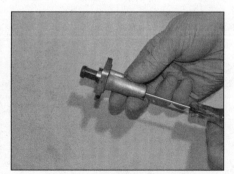

6.5 Insert a screwdriver and retract the plunger

7.6a Unscrew the bolts (arrowed) . . .

7.6b . . . and remove the sprocket cover

7.7 Unscrew both adjuster access caps

7 Cylinder head removal and installation

Note: *The cylinder head can be removed with the engine in the frame.*

Removal

1 Remove the fuel tank and exhaust system (see Chapter 4).

2 Follow the procedure in Section 4 and disconnect the air induction system (AIS) union from the cylinder head **(see illustrations 4.8a and b)**. Disconnect the AIS valve vacuum hose from the intake stub **(see illustration 4.8c)**.

3 Remove the spark plug (see Chapter 1).

4 Unscrew the nuts on the top engine mounting bolts and remove all three bolts and the two brackets **(see illustrations 4.20a and b)**. Remember which side the bolts are fitted from so they are installed the same way.

5 Remove or displace the carburettor (see Chapter 4). If required, remove the intake duct. Plug the engine intake with clean rag.

6 Unscrew the camshaft sprocket cover bolts and remove the cover **(see illustrations)**. Note the location of the cover O-ring and discard it as a new one must be fitted on reassembly.

7 Unscrew the valve clearance adjuster access caps from the front and back of the cylinder head **(see illustration)**. Discard the O-rings – new ones must be fitted on reassembly.

8 Unscrew the timing inspection cap and the crankshaft end cap from the alternator cover on the left-hand side of the engine **(see illustration)**. Check the condition of the cap O-rings and replace them with new ones if necessary.

9 The engine must be turned to position the piston at top dead centre (TDC) on its compression stroke so that the valves are

closed. Turn the engine anti-clockwise using a suitable socket on the alternator rotor nut until the index line on the rotor aligns with the pointer inside the inspection hole, and the index line on the camshaft sprocket is above the centre of the sprocket and aligned with the pointer on the top of the cylinder head **(see illustrations)**. There should now be some freeplay in each rocker arm (i.e. they are not contacting the valve stem) **(see illustration)**.

Note: *If the index line on the sprocket is below the centre, rotate the engine anti-clockwise one full turn (360°) until the index line on the rotor again aligns with the pointer inside the inspection hole – the index line on the sprocket will now be above the centre.*

10 Remove the cam chain tensioner (see Section 6).

11 Counter-hold the alternator rotor nut and unscrew the bolt securing the camshaft sprocket **(see illustration)**. Draw the sprocket

7.8 Remove the crankshaft end cap (A) and the timing inspection cap (B)

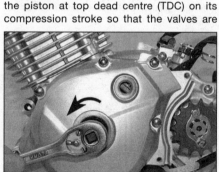

7.9a Turn the engine anti-clockwise using the rotor nut . . .

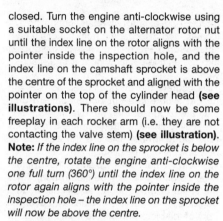

7.9b . . . until the line (A) on the rotor aligns with the pointer (B) . . .

7.9c . . . and the line (A) on the camshaft sprocket aligns with the pointer (B)

7.9d Check for freeplay in the rocker arms

7.11a Unscrew the bolt

7.11b Disengage the chain from the sprocket . . .

7.11c . . . and remove the sprocket. Note locating tab (arrowed)

off the end of the camshaft, noting how it locates, and disengage it from the chain **(see illustrations)**. Prevent the chain from dropping into the engine by securing it with a piece of wire.

12 Unscrew the cylinder head bolts 1/4 a turn at a time in a criss-cross pattern until they are all loose, then remove them, noting the sealing washers fitted with the 8 mm bolts **(see illustrations)**. Discard the washers as new ones should be used.

13 Hold the cam chain up and lift the cylinder head up off the block **(see illustration)**. Pass the chain down through the cylinder head – do not let it fall into the engine, lay it over the front of the block and secure it with a piece of wire. If the head is stuck, tap around the joint faces with a soft-faced mallet. Do not attempt to free it by inserting a screwdriver between the head and block mating surfaces – you'll

damage them. Stuff some clean rag into the cam chain tunnel in the block to prevent anything falling into the engine. Do not rotate the crankshaft – the chain may drop down and bind between the crankshaft and case, which could damage these components.

14 Remove the cylinder head gasket and discard it as a new one must be used **(see illustration)**. If they are loose, remove the dowels from the cylinder block or the underside of the cylinder head **(see illustration)**.

15 Check the cylinder head gasket and the mating surfaces on the cylinder head and cylinder block for signs of leakage, which could indicate warpage. Refer to Chapter 2A, Section 9 and check the cylinder head gasket surface for warpage.

16 Clean all traces of old gasket material from the cylinder head and cylinder block. If a scraper is used, take care not to scratch or

gouge the soft aluminium. Be careful not to let any of the gasket material fall into the cylinder bore or the oil passages.

Installation

17 Lubricate the cylinder bore with engine oil. If removed, fit the dowels into the cylinder block **(see illustration 7.14b)**. Make sure the cam chain guide blade is correctly seated (see Section 10).

18 Ensure both cylinder head and cylinder block mating surfaces are clean. Lay the new head gasket over the cam chain and blades and onto the block, locating it over the dowels and making sure all the holes are correctly aligned **(see illustration 7.14a)**. Never reuse the old gasket.

19 Carefully fit the cylinder head over the cam chain and cam chain blades and onto the block, making sure it locates correctly onto the dowels. Secure the chain in place with a piece of wire.

20 Apply engine oil to the threads, under the heads and onto both sides of the new sealing washers on the 8 mm bolts. Fit the bolts with their washers and tighten them finger-tight **(see illustration 7.12b)**. Apply a suitable sealant to the threads of the 6 mm bolts, then tighten them finger-tight. Now tighten the bolts evenly and a little at a time in the numerical sequence shown to the torque settings specified at the beginning of the Chapter **(see illustration)**.

21 Check that the index line on the alternator rotor aligns with the pointer inside the inspection hole **(see illustration 7.9b)**. Make

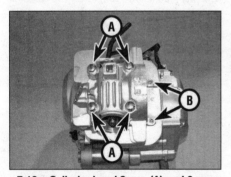

7.12a Cylinder head 8 mm (A) and 6 mm bolts (B)

7.12b Note the sealing washers

7.13 Carefully lift the head up off the block

7.14a Remove the cylinder head gasket

7.14b Remove the dowels if they are loose

7.20 Tighten the bolts as described in the order shown

7.21 Note position of the camshaft cut-out

8.2a Unscrew the bolt (arrowed) . . .

8.2b . . . and remove the camshaft retainer

sure the sprocket locating cut-out in the camshaft is at the bottom **(see illustration)**.

22 Align the camshaft sprocket with the end of the camshaft, ensuring that the index line on the sprocket is above the centre and aligned with the pointer on the top of the cylinder head **(see illustration 7.9c)**.

23 Engage the sprocket with the chain, making sure the crankshaft does not rotate, then fit the sprocket onto the camshaft, locating the tab on the sprocket in the cut-out in the end of the camshaft. Ensure that the front run of the chain between the camshaft and crankshaft sprockets is tight and that any slack is in the rear run so it will be taken up by the tensioner.

24 Fit the camshaft sprocket bolt with its washer and lightly tighten it **(see illustration 7.11a)**.

25 Use a piece of wooden dowel or other suitable tool to press on the back of the cam chain tensioner blade via the tensioner bore in the cylinder block. This will take up any slack in the rear run of the chain. Now check that the timing marks are still in **exact** alignment as described in Step 9 **(see illustrations 7.9b and c)**. Note that it is easy for the chain to be out by one tooth on the sprocket without the marks appearing drastically out of alignment. If the marks are not aligned exactly, unscrew the sprocket bolt and reposition the sprocket in the chain as required. Secure the sprocket on the camshaft and check the marks again.

Caution: If the marks are not aligned exactly as described, the valve timing will

be incorrect and the valves may strike the piston, causing extensive damage to the engine.

26 Install the cam chain tensioner (see Section 6).

27 Turn the engine anti-clockwise through two full turns and check again that all the timing marks still align (see Step 9).

28 Counter-hold the alternator rotor nut and tighten the camshaft sprocket bolt to the specified torque setting. Check the valve clearances and adjust them if necessary (see Chapter 1).

29 Pour a small amount of engine oil into the head via one of the valve clearance adjuster access holes so it fills the well below the camshaft lobes.

30 Fit the adjuster access caps using new O-rings smeared with grease **(see illustration 7.7)**. Fit the camshaft sprocket cover using a new O-ring smeared with grease and tighten the bolts to the specified torque **(see illustration 7.6b and a)**.

31 Fit the timing inspection cap and crankshaft end cap using new O-rings if required, and smear the O-rings with grease.

32 Install the spark plug (see Chapter 1).

33 If removed, fit the intake duct. Fit the carburettor (see Chapter 4).

34 Install the remaining components in the reverse order of removal. Tighten the top engine mounting bolts and the AIS pipe bolts to the specified torque settings.

35 Check and adjust the idle speed (see Chapter 1).

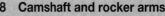

8   Camshaft and rocker arms

Note: *The camshaft and rockers can be removed with the engine in the frame.*
Special Tool: *A slide-hammer is required to remove the rocker shafts (see Step 4).*

Removal

1 Remove the cylinder head (see Section 7).

2 Unscrew the camshaft retainer bolt and remove the retainer, noting how it locates **(see illustrations)**.

3 Mark each rocker arm according to its location in the cylinder head as an aid to reassembly.

4 First remove the rocker shafts using a slide-hammer as follows. Thread an adapter into the end of the rocker shaft being removed, then fit the slide-hammer and draw the shaft out with repeated blows of the hammer **(see illustrations)**. Follow the same procedure to remove the other rocker shaft. Mark the rocker shafts according to location – they are different lengths and must be kept together with the appropriate rocker arm for inspection and installation.

5 Lift the rocker arms clear of the camshaft lobes – do not try to remove the arms at this stage. Thread the camshaft sprocket bolt partially into the end of the camshaft and use it to draw the camshaft out of the cylinder head **(see illustration)**. Note that the camshaft and bearings are fitted as an assembly.

8.4a Thread the adapter into the end of the shaft (arrowed) . . .

8.4b . . . then fit the slide-hammer and draw the shaft out

8.5 Pull the camshaft out using the sprocket bolt

8.6a Removing the intake rocker arm

8.6b Removing the exhaust rocker arm

6 Remove the rocker arms noting how they fit. On the engine used to illustrate this procedure, due to the internal design of the cylinder head, the intake arm was removed through the opening for the camshaft and the exhaust arm was removed through the valve adjuster access aperture **(see illustrations)**. Slide the rocker arms back onto their shafts to prevent mixing them up.

Inspection

7 Clean the camshaft, rockers and shafts. Blow the camshaft oil passages out with compressed air.
8 Check the camshaft bearings **(see illustration)**. The bearings must be a tight fit on the camshaft and they must turn smoothly with no play between the inner and outer races. Inspect the camshaft lobes for heat discoloration (blue appearance), score marks, chipped areas, flat spots and pitting **(see illustration)**.

9 If the bearings or camshaft are damaged or worn the assembly must be replaced with a new one.
10 Inspect the rocker arms for heat discoloration, score marks, chipped areas, flat spots and pitting where they contact the camshaft lobes **(see illustration)**. Similarly check the bottom of each clearance adjuster and the top of each valve stem. Check for freeplay between each rocker arm and its shaft **(see illustration)**. The arms should move freely with no appreciable freeplay.
11 If any component is worn or damaged it must be replaced with a new one. Note that the rocker arms and shafts should be renewed together and that the clearance adjusters are available separately.
12 The rocker shafts and the camshaft bearings should be a firm press fit in the cylinder head – if not it is likely the head

has worn and a bearing retaining compound should be used on reassembly.
13 Check the camshaft sprocket for wear, cracks and other damage, and replace it with a new one if necessary. If the sprocket teeth are worn, the cam chain is also worn, and so probably is the sprocket on the crankshaft (see Section 10). If severe wear is apparent, the entire engine should be disassembled for inspection.
14 Inspect the cam chain guide and tensioner blades (see Section 10).

Installation

15 Fit the rocker arms into the head as noted on removal with the adjusters on the outside, leaving clearance for the camshaft **(see illustrations 8.6b and a)**.
16 Lubricate the camshaft bearings with clean engine oil and the camshaft lobes with molybdenum disulphide oil. Insert the camshaft into the head and press the bearings all the way in to their housings. Ensure the rocker arms are clear of the cam lobes. Align the camshaft so the cut-out for the cam chain sprocket is pointing down **(see illustration)**.
17 Working on one rocker arm at a time, align the arm with the holes for the shaft with the inner end resting on the camshaft and press the shaft all the way in. If the shaft is tight, thread a suitable bolt in its end and tap the end of the bolt, but make sure everything is correctly aligned before doing so **(see illustration)**.
18 Make sure both rocker shafts and the camshaft are fully installed in the head. There

8.8a Check both camshaft bearings (arrowed) for wear

8.8b Inspect the camshaft lobes (arrowed)

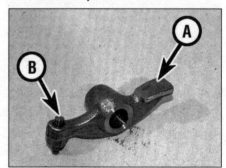

8.10a Inspect the rocker arms at (A) and the adjusters at (B)

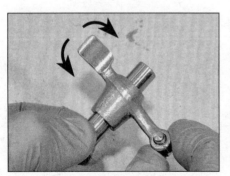

8.10b Check for freeplay between the rocker and the shaft

8.16 Align the cut-out (arrowed) as shown

8.17 Tap the rocker shaft into place

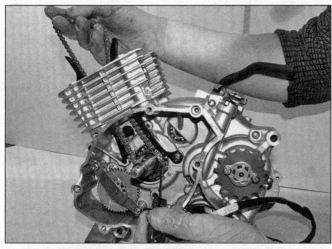

10.4a Disengage the chain from the crankshaft . . .

10.4b . . . and lift it out

should be a small amount of free movement in the shafts – check the valve clearances.

19 Apply some threadlock to the retainer bolt, then fit the retainer and tighten the bolt to the torque setting specified at the beginning of the Chapter **(see illustrations 8.2b and a)**.

20 Lubricate the rocker shafts via the valve clearance adjuster access holes with molybdenum disulphide oil (a 50/50 mixture of molybdenum disulphide grease and engine oil).

21 Install the cylinder head.

<h3>9   Cylinder head and valve overhaul</h3>

Refer to Chapter 2A, Section 9 for this procedure. The only difference is that the engines covered in this Chapter have only one valve spring per valve.

<h3>10 Cam chain, tensioner blade and guide blade</h3>

Note: *The cam chain and its blades can be removed with the engine in the frame.*

Removal

Cam chain

1 Remove the camshaft sprocket (see Section 7).

2 Remove the alternator rotor and starter clutch (see Section 13).

3 Mark one side of the chain with a dab of paint so that it can be installed the same way round.

4 Lift the chain off the crankshaft sprocket and out of the engine **(see illustrations)**.

Tensioner blade

5 Remove the cylinder head (see Section 7).

6 Remove the alternator rotor and starter clutch (see Section 13).

7 Unscrew the tensioner blade bolt, and draw the blade out of the top of the cylinder block noting which way round it fits **(see illustration)**. Note the pivot collar in the lower end of the blade **(see illustration)**.

Guide blade

8 Remove the cylinder head (see Section 7).

9 Note how the blade locates in the top front edge of the cam chain tunnel, and draw it out **(see illustrations)**.

Inspection

Cam chain

10 Except in cases of oil starvation, the cam

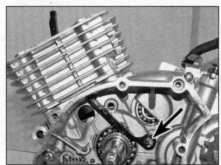

10.7a Location of the tensioner blade bolt

10.9a Location of the top end of the guide blade

chain should wear very little. If the chain has stretched excessively, which makes it difficult to maintain proper tension, or if it is stiff or the links are binding or kinking, replace it with a new one.

11 Check the camshaft sprocket teeth for wear and replace the cam chain and sprocket as a set. The crankshaft sprocket is an integral part of the crankshaft – if the teeth are worn or damaged a new crankshaft will have to be fitted **(see illustration 21.19)**.

Tensioner and guide blades

12 Check the sliding surface and edges of the blades for excessive wear, deep grooves,

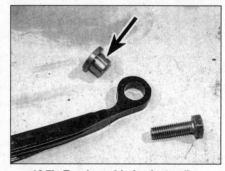

10.7b Tensioner blade pivot collar (arrowed)

10.9b Note how the guide blade fits

10.13 Location of the lower end of the guide blade

11.3 Support the piston as the block is lifted off

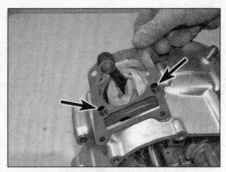

11.5 Remove the base gasket. Note the dowels (arrowed)

cracking and other obvious damage, and replace them with new ones if necessary.

Installation

13 Installation is the reverse of removal. Make sure the bottom of the guide blade sits in its seat **(see illustration)** and the lugs near its top locate in the cut-outs in the cylinder block. Lubricate the tensioner blade pivot collar with clean oil and install it with the wide end against the crankcase **(see illustration 10.7b)**. Apply threadlock to the bolt and tighten it to the torque setting specified at the beginning of the Chapter.

11 Cylinder block

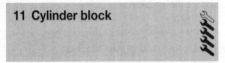

Note: *The cylinder block can be removed with the engine in the frame.*

Removal

1 Remove the cylinder head (see Section 7).

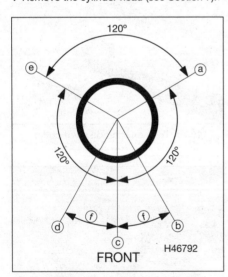

12.1 Piston ring installation details – stagger the ring end gaps as shown

a   Top ring
b   Upper side rail
c   Oil ring expander
d   Lower side rail
e   Second ring
f   20 mm measured at piston edge

2 Draw the cam chain guide blade out of the top of the cylinder block, noting how it locates **(see illustration 10.9b)**.

3 Hold the cam chain to prevent it falling into the engine and pull the block up off the crankcase, supporting the piston so the connecting rod does not knock against the engine **(see illustration)**. If the block is stuck, tap around the joint faces with a soft-faced mallet. Do not attempt to free it by inserting a screwdriver between the block and crankcase mating surfaces – you'll damage them. Lay the cam chain over the front of the crankcase and secure it with a piece of wire.

4 Stuff some clean rag into the cam chain tunnel and around the connecting rod to protect and support it and to prevent anything falling into the engine.

5 Remove the base gasket and discard it as a new one must be used **(see illustration)**. If they are loose, remove the dowels from the crankcase or the underside of the cylinder block.

6 Clean all traces of old gasket material from the cylinder block and crankcase. If a scraper is used, take care not to scratch or gouge the soft aluminium. Be careful not to let any of the gasket material fall into the engine.

Inspection

7 Refer to Chapter 2A, Section 10.

Installation

8 If removed, fit the dowels into the crankcase and push them firmly home **(see illustration 11.5)**.

9 Remove the rags from around the piston and the cam chain tunnel, taking care not to let the connecting rod fall against the rim of the crankcase. Lay the new base gasket in place, locating it over the dowels. Never re-use the old gasket.

10 Rotate the crankshaft so that the piston is at its highest point (top dead centre). It is useful to place a support under the piston so that it remains at TDC while the cylinder block is fitted.

11 Ensure the piston ring end gaps are positioned correctly **(see illustration 12.1)** and lubricate the cylinder bore, piston and piston rings with clean engine oil.

12 Carefully lower the block onto the piston,

making sure the piston enters squarely and does not get cocked sideways **(see illustration 11.3)**. Feed the cam chain up the tunnel and secure it with a piece of wire to prevent it falling back into the engine.

13 Compress and feed each ring into the bore as the block is lowered. If necessary, use a soft mallet to gently tap the block down, but do not use force if it appears to be stuck as the piston and/or rings will be damaged.

14 When the piston and rings are located in the bore, remove the support and press the block down onto the base gasket, making sure the dowels locate fully.

15 Install the cam chain guide blade, making sure the bottom of the blade sits in its seat and the lugs near its top locate in the cut-outs in the block **(see illustration 10.9a)**.

16 Install the cylinder head (see Section 7).

12 Piston and piston rings

Note: *The piston can be removed with the engine in the frame.*

1 Refer to the procedure in Chapter 2A, Sections 11 and 12, noting the following:

● The piston crown is marked with an arrow pointing towards the front (exhaust side) of the engine.

● On the engine covered in this Chapter, the top piston ring was marked ATG and the second ring was marked A.

● The piston ring end gaps should be staggered as shown **(see illustration)**.

13 Alternator, starter clutch and gears

Note: *The starter clutch is mounted on the back of the alternator rotor. The rotor can be removed with the engine in the frame. If the engine has been removed, ignore the steps which do not apply.*

Alternator check

1 Checking of the charging system is covered in Chapter 9.

13.6a Unscrew the cover bolts (arrowed)

13.6b Location of the cover dowels (arrowed)

Starter clutch check

2 The operation of the starter clutch can be checked while it is in situ. Remove the starter motor (see Chapter 9). Check that the idle/ reduction gear is able to rotate freely clockwise as you look at it via the starter motor aperture, but locks when rotated anti-clockwise. If not, the starter clutch is faulty and should be removed for inspection.

Removal

Special Tools: *A rotor strap and a puller are required to remove the alternator rotor (see Steps 7 and 8).*

3 Remove the front sprocket cover **(see illustration 4.15)**.

4 Drain the engine oil (see Chapter 1).

5 Trace the alternator and pick-up coil wiring from the left-hand side of the engine and disconnect it at the connectors **(see illustration 4.17)**. Release the wiring from any clips of ties and feed it down to the alternator cover.

6 Working in a criss-cross pattern, evenly slacken the alternator cover bolts noting where they fit **(see illustration)**. **Note:** *As each bolt is removed store it in its relative position in a cardboard template of the cover (see illustration 20.3 for example). This will*

ensure all bolts are returned to their original locations on reassembly. Draw the cover off the engine, noting that it will be restrained by the force of the rotor magnets, and be prepared to catch any residual oil. Remove and discard the gasket. Remove the dowels from either the cover or the crankcase if they are loose **(see illustration)**.

7 To undo the rotor nut it is necessary to stop the rotor turning using a commercially available rotor strap **(see illustration)**. Ensure the strap is tightened securely around the rotor then undo the nut with steady pressure. Remove the nut and washer **(see illustration)**.

8 To draw the rotor off the taper on the crankshaft, thread the legs of a three-legged puller into the holes in the rotor **(see illustrations)**. Assemble the rotor as shown and tighten the centre bolt – if the rotor is an extremely tight fit, strike the head of the centre bolt with a hammer to jar the taper free.

9 Lift off the alternator rotor and starter clutch assembly **(see illustration)**.

10 Remove the Woodruff key from its slot in the crankshaft if it is loose **(see illustration)**.

11 If the starter driven gear does not come away with the starter clutch, draw it off the

13.7a Holding the rotor with a rotor strap

13.7b Remove the rotor nut and washer

13.8a Thread the puller legs into the holes (arrowed)

13.8b Set-up for drawing the rotor off the crankshaft

13.9 The starter clutch (arrowed) is located on the back of the rotor

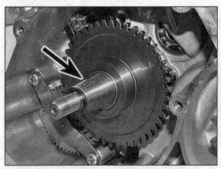

13.10 Location of the Woodruff key

13.11a Draw off the starter driven gear . . .

13.11b . . . and the thrust washer

crankshaft and remove the thrust washer **(see illustrations)**.

12 To remove the alternator stator and ignition pick-up coil, undo the bolts securing them to the inside of the cover. Ease the

wiring grommet out of the cover and lift the stator/pick-up coil out.

13 Undo the idle/reduction gear retainer screws and remove the retainer, then slide the gear off its shaft **(see illustrations)**.

Inspection

14 Lay the rotor face down on a workbench and, if it is separate, install the starter driven gear into the starter clutch body, twisting it anti-clockwise **(see illustration)**. Once installed, the gear should rotate freely anti-clockwise and lock against the clutch when turned clockwise **(see illustration)**. If it doesn't, remove the starter driven gear, rotating it anti-clockwise.

15 Check the condition of the rollers and the corresponding surface on the driven gear hub **(see illustrations)**. If any of the rollers are damaged, marked or flattened at any point, a new starter clutch will have to be fitted. If the rollers are jammed, ease them out carefully and remove the plungers and springs **(see illustrations)**. Wash all the components in suitable solvent and inspect them for wear and damage. Individual components are not

13.13a Undo the screws securing the retainer . . .

13.13b . . . and slide the gear off

13.14a Fit the driven gear into the clutch body

13.14b Check the operation of the clutch as described

13.15a Inspect the rollers . . .

13.15b . . . and the driven gear hub

13.15c Remove the rollers . . .

13.15d . . . plungers and springs

13.16 Stake the end of each bolt (arrowed) after tightening

available and if necessary a new starter clutch will have to be fitted.

16 To remove the starter clutch from the back of the alternator rotor hold the rotor using a holding strap and unscrew the three bolts. Discard the bolts – new ones should be used. On installation apply a suitable non-permanent thread locking compound to the bolts and tighten them to the torque setting specified at the beginning of the Chapter. Stake the ends of the bolts as shown using a punch **(see illustration)**.

17 Check the bush inside the hub of the starter driven gear and its bearing surface on the crankshaft. If the bush shows signs of excessive wear or damage, replace the driven gear with a new one.

18 Check the teeth of the idle/reduction gear and the corresponding teeth of the starter driven gear and starter motor drive shaft. Replace the gears and/or starter motor if worn or chipped teeth are discovered on related gears.

19 Check the idle/reduction gear shaft for damage and check that the gear is not a loose fit on it. The shaft is a press fit in the crankcase and should be renewed if necessary.

14.4 Unscrew the kickstart lever nut

Installation

20 Lubricate the idle/reduction gear shaft with clean engine oil. Slide the gear onto the shaft, meshing the teeth of the larger inner gear with those of the starter motor shaft. Fit the retainer and tighten its screws securely **(see illustration 13.13a)**.

21 Lubricate the starter clutch rollers with clean engine oil. Lubricate the outside of the starter driven gear hub, then fit the gear into the clutch, rotating it anti-clockwise **(see illustration 13.14a)**.

22 Slide the thrust washer onto the crankshaft and lubricate the inner end of the shaft with oil. Clean the crankshaft taper and the corresponding taper inside the alternator rotor with a suitable solvent. If removed, fit the Woodruff key into its slot in the crankshaft.

23 Make sure no metal objects have attached themselves to the rotor magnets. Align the slot inside the rotor hub with the key in the crankshaft and slide the rotor and starter clutch assembly onto the shaft making sure the teeth on the starter driven gear mesh with those on the idle/reduction gear. Press the assembly on firmly, then fit the washer and nut finger tight **(see illustration 13.7b)**.

24 Hold the rotor with a rotor strap as on removal and tighten the nut to the torque setting specified at the beginning of the Chapter.

14 Clutch

Note: *The clutch can be removed with the engine in the frame. If the engine has been removed, ignore the steps which don't apply.*

Removal

1 Drain the engine oil (see Chapter 1).
2 Remove the starter motor (see Chapter 9).
3 Remove the exhaust system (see Chapter 4).
4 Where fitted, unscrew the nut retaining the kickstart lever **(see illustration)**. Make an alignment mark between the lever and the shaft, then draw the lever off.
5 Remove the footrest bracket complete with sidestand (see Section 4, Step 14).
6 Working evenly in a criss-cross pattern, unscrew the clutch cover bolts **(see illustration)**. Note the engine earth lead secured by the bolt to the rear of the kickstart lever shaft **(see illustration 4.9)**. **Note:** *As each bolt is removed store it in its relative position in a cardboard template of the cover* **(see illustration 20.3 for example)**. *This will ensure all bolts are returned to their original locations on reassembly.* Draw the cover off, being prepared to catch any residual oil. Remove the gasket and discard it **(see illustration)**. Remove the two dowels from either the cover or the crankcase if they are loose.
7 Note the location of the crankshaft oil seal

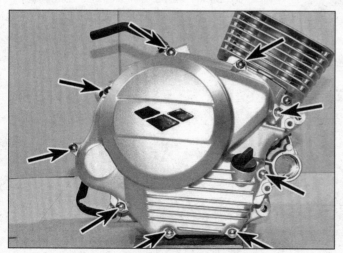

14.6a Unscrew the clutch cover bolts

14.6b Remove the cover gasket. Note location of dowels (arrowed)

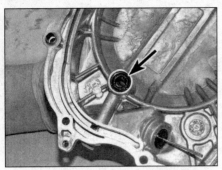

14.7 Location of the crankshaft oil seal

14.9 Slacken the clutch spring bolts gradually

14.10a Remove the clutch pressure plate

in the cover **(see illustration)**. If the seal is damaged or deteriorated it should be renewed although it is good practice to renew the seal whenever the cover is removed. Lever the old seal out with a seal hook or screwdriver. Press

14.10b Short pushrod and holder . . .

or drive the new seal squarely into place using your fingers, a seal driver or suitable socket.
8 Where fitted, check the kickstart shaft oil seal (see Section 19).
9 Working in a criss-cross pattern, gradually

14.10c . . . are secured by the locknut and washer

slacken the clutch spring bolts until pressure is released **(see illustration)**. To prevent the clutch from turning, cover it with a rag and hold it securely – the bolts are not very tight. Remove the bolts and springs.
10 Lift off the pressure plate noting how it locates on the clutch centre **(see illustration)**. Note the location of the short pushrod and holder – the assembly is secured in the pressure plate by a locknut and washer on the outside **(see illustrations)**. Using a magnet, draw the pushrod ball bearing out of the transmission input shaft **(see illustration)**. There is also a long pushrod inside the shaft but this will only come out of the left-hand end when the transmission shafts have to be removed (see Section 24 if required).
11 Grasp the complete clutch plate assembly and draw it out. Unless the plates are being replaced with new ones, keep the assembly together.
Note: If you are going to remove the primary drive gear, refer to Section 16 and slacken its nut now.
12 Bend the tab of the clutch nut lockwasher off the nut **(see illustration)**. Use a commercially available clutch holding tool to prevent the clutch centre from turning and loosen the clutch nut **(see illustration)**. Remove the nut and lockwasher, noting how the small tab on the washer locates in the cut-out in the clutch centre hub **(see illustration)**. Check the condition of the washer – if both large tabs have been used to lock the clutch nut a new lockwasher must be fitted on reassembly.
13 Slide the clutch centre and the outer thrust washer off the shaft **(see illustrations)**.

14.10d Remove the ball bearing for safe-keeping

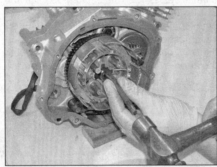

14.12a Bend back the lockwasher tab

14.12b Using a commercially available holding tool while loosening the clutch nut

14.12c Note how the lockwasher locates

14.13a Remove the clutch centre . . .

14.13b . . . the outer thrust washer . . .

14.14a . . . the clutch housing . . .

14.14b . . . and the inner thrust washer

14.16 Check the plain plates for warpage

14.18a Check the friction plate tabs and housing slots . . .

14.18b . . . and the plain plate teeth and centre slots as described

14 Slide the clutch housing and the inner thrust washer off the shaft **(see illustrations)**.

Inspection

15 After an extended period of service the clutch friction plates will wear and promote clutch slip. If the friction material on any of the plates has worn away, or if any of the plates smell burnt or are glazed, the friction plates must be replaced with a new set.

16 The plain plates should not show any signs of excess heating (bluing). Check for warpage using a flat surface and feeler gauges **(see illustration)**. If any plate is warped more than 0.1 mm, or shows signs of bluing, all plain plates must be replaced with a new set.

17 Measure the free length of the clutch springs. Place each spring upright on a flat surface and check it for bend by placing a ruler against it, or alternatively lay it against a set square. If any spring has sagged in comparison to the others or if the bend in any spring is excessive, replace all the springs as a set.

18 Inspect the friction plates and the clutch housing for burrs and indentations on the edges of the protruding tabs on the plates and/or the slots in the housing **(see illustration)**. Similarly check for wear between the inner teeth of the plain plates and the slots in the clutch centre **(see illustration)**. Wear of this nature will cause clutch drag and slow disengagement during gear changes as the plates will snag when the pressure plate is lifted. With care a small amount of wear can

be corrected by dressing with a fine file, but if this is excessive the worn components should be replaced with new ones.

19 Inspect the bearing surfaces of the clutch housing bush and the input shaft **(see illustration)**. If there are any signs of wear, pitting or other damage the affected parts must be replaced with new ones.

20 Check the pressure plate, pushrod assembly and ball bearing for signs of wear or damage **(see illustrations 14.10a, b and d)**. Replace any parts necessary with new ones.

21 Check the release arm in the left-hand side of the engine for a smooth action **(see illustration)**. If the action is stiff or rough, detach the cable (see Section 15), then withdraw the shaft and remove the spring, noting how its ends locate **(see illustration)**.

14.19 Check the bearing surface on the clutch housing bush

14.21a Check the action of the release arm

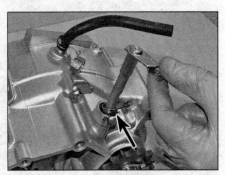

14.21b Withdraw the shaft and remove the spring (arrowed)

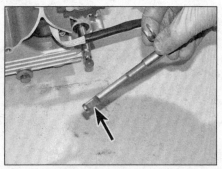

14.21c Inspect the contacting surface of
the shaft (arrowed)

14.22a Remove the circlip . . .

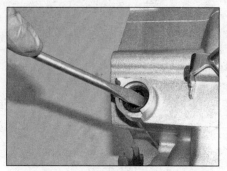

14.22b . . . then lever out the old seal

14.22c Hook spring around tab (arrowed)

14.23 Installed position of the release arm
and spring

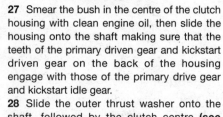

14.24 Primary driven gear (A) and kickstart
driven gear (B)

Inspect the contacting surface of the shaft for
wear and damage (see illustration).
22   Check the oil seal and clean the shaft bore
in the crankcase. To fit a new seal, first remove
the circlip, then lever the old one out with a
seal hook or screwdriver (see illustrations).
Press the new seal in, using a suitable socket
to drive it in if necessary, and secure it with a
new circlip. Position the spring above the seal
with the short end hooked around the tab on
the casing (see illustration).
23   Lubricate the shaft with molybdenum
disulphide oil (a 50/50 mixture of molybdenum
disulphide grease and engine oil) and the seal
lips with grease, then install the shaft and
hook the long end of the spring over the arm
(see illustration).
24   Check the teeth of the primary driven

gear on the clutch housing (see illustration)
and the corresponding teeth of the primary
drive gear on the crankshaft (see Section 16).
Replace the clutch housing and/or primary
drive gear with a new one if worn or chipped
teeth are discovered. Check for any rotational
play between the primary driven gear and the
clutch housing and replace the housing with a
new one if any is evident. Check the teeth on
the kickstart mechanism driven gear and the
corresponding teeth on the idle gear and the
slider gear (see Section 19).

Installation

25   Remove all traces of old gasket from the
crankcase and clutch cover surfaces.
26   Slide the inner thrust washer onto
the transmission input shaft (see illustration 14.14b). .

27   Smear the bush in the centre of the clutch
housing with clean engine oil, then slide the
housing onto the shaft making sure that the
teeth of the primary driven gear and kickstart
driven gear on the back of the housing
engage with those of the primary drive gear
and kickstart idle gear.
28   Slide the outer thrust washer onto the
shaft, followed by the clutch centre (see
illustrations 14.13b and a).
29   Fit the lockwasher, locating the small tab
in the cut-out (see illustration 14.12c). Thread
the clutch nut on. Using the clutch holding tool
to secure the clutch centre, tighten the nut to
the torque setting specified at the beginning
of the Chapter (see illustration 14.12b). Bend
one of the large lockwasher tabs down against
one of the flats on the nut (see illustrations).

14.29a Bend the lockwasher tab against the nut as shown

14.29b Correct position of the lockwasher tab

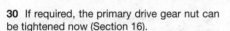

14.31a Fit a friction plate first . . .

14.31b . . . then a plain plate and so on

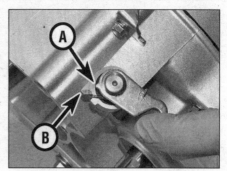

14.36 Make sure the pointer (A) aligns with the projection (B)

30 If required, the primary drive gear nut can be tightened now (Section 16).

31 Coat each clutch plate with engine oil. Build up the plates in the housing, starting with a friction plate, then a plain plate, then alternating friction and plain plates until all are installed **(see illustrations)**.

32 Push the ball bearing into the hole in the shaft **(see illustration 14.10d)**.

33 If removed fit the short pushrod, its holder, the washer and the locknut into the pressure plate **(see illustrations 14.10b and c)** – leave the locknut loose as the position of the pushrod will need to be adjusted.

34 Fit the pressure plate, inserting the pushrod in the shaft, and making sure the castellations locate in the clutch centre **(see illustration 14.10a)**. Hold the pressure plate and check for any gaps between the clutch plates – there should be none; if there are, it means the pressure plate has not located properly.

35 Fit the clutch springs and bolts and tighten the bolts evenly and a little at a time in a criss-cross sequence to the specified torque **(see illustration 14.9)**.

36 Check the set-up of the clutch pushrod. Push the release arm in fully – the pointer on the arm should align with the projection on the crankcase **(see illustration)**. If they do not align, counter-hold the outer end of the short pushrod using a screwdriver and slacken the locknut, then turn the pushrod as required until the pointer aligns correctly. Tighten the locknut. Re-check the alignment marks with the arm pushed in. This setting is important as there must be some freeplay between the long and short pushrods when the clutch is engaged. Reconnect the cable (Section 15).

37 Fit the two dowels into the crankcase if removed, then fit a new gasket, locating it over the dowels **(see illustration 14.6b)**. Fit the cover and install all the bolts finger-tight,

not forgetting the earth lead if the engine is in the frame (see Step 6). Tighten the bolts evenly and a little at a time in a criss-cross pattern to the specified torque.

38 Install the remaining components in the reverse order of removal.

39 Fill the engine with the correct amount and type of oil (see Chapter 1 and *Pre-ride checks*).

40 Check the operation of the rear brake (see Chapter 1).

15 Clutch cable

1 Refer to the procedure in Chapter 2B, Section 15, noting the following when disconnecting the cable at the engine end.

2 If necessary, slacken the cable adjuster locknut and screw the adjuster all the way in to provide extra freeplay in the cable. Draw the cable out of the bracket on the engine and detach the end from the release arm **(see illustrations 4.12a and b)**.

16 Primary drive gear

Removal

1 Follow the procedure in Section 14, Steps 1 to 8, and remove the clutch cover.

2 To loosen the primary drive gear nut wedge a stout piece of rag or a locking piece of soft aluminium or copper (DO NOT use steel) between the teeth of the primary drive and driven gears where they mesh at the top – this will lock them together to prevent them turning **(see illustration)**. Loosen the nut, then remove the rag or locking piece.

3 Unscrew the primary drive gear nut and remove the washer **(see illustrations)**.

4 Check for an assembly mark on the outer face of the drive gear – if no mark is visible, make your own with a dab of paint to aid reassembly. Slide the gear off the end of the crankshaft, noting how it locates on the Woodruff key **(see illustration)**. Remove the key from its slot.

16.2 Using a piece of soft metal (arrowed) to lock the gears while loosening the nut

16.3a Unscrew the nut . . .

16.3b . . . and remove the washer

16.4 Mark the gear to aid reassembly. Note Woodruff key (arrowed)

17.2 Location of identification mark

17.3 Remove the oil pump drive gear

17.4a Remove the E-clip . . .

17.4b . . . the plain washer and outer spring washer . . .

17.4c . . . and the pump driven gear

17.5 Remove the drive pin and inner spring washer (arrowed)

5 Refer to Section 17 for removal of the oil filter and pump.

Installation

6 Make sure the oil filter is fully installed on the crankshaft (see Section 17).
7 Fit the Woodruff key into its slot in the crankshaft.
8 Align the slot in the primary drive gear with the key, then slide the gear onto the shaft with its marked side facing out **(see illustration 16.4)**. Fit the washer and tighten the nut finger-tight.
9 Using the same method as on removal, lock the primary drive and driven gears together, this time at the bottom, and tighten the primary drive gear nut to the torque setting specified at the beginning of the Chapter.

10 Install the remaining components in the reverse order of removal.

17 Oil filter, strainer and oil pump

Note: *The oil pump can be removed with the engine in the frame. If the engine has been removed, ignore the steps which don't apply.*

Removal

1 Remove the clutch and the primary drive gear (see Sections 14 and 16).
2 The outer face of the centrifugal oil filter should be marked for identification – on the machine photographed it was stamped with

the letters TC **(see illustration)**. If no mark is visible, make your own with a dab of paint to aid reassembly. Slide the oil filter off the shaft, noting how it fits.
3 Slide the oil pump drive gear off **(see illustration)**.
4 Remove the E-clip securing the oil pump driven gear, then remove the plain washer and outer spring washer and the gear **(see illustrations)**. Note how the slot at the back of the gear locates over the drive pin in the pump shaft.
5 Remove the drive pin and the inner spring washer **(see illustration)**.
6 Undo the screws securing the pump and lift it off, noting how it locates against the crankcase **(see illustrations)**.
7 Remove the gasket and discard it – a new one must be used **(see illustration)**.

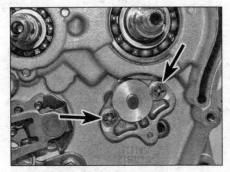

17.6a Undo the screws . . .

17.6b . . . and remove the pump

17.7 Location of the oil pump gasket

17.8 Oil strainer is a sliding fit

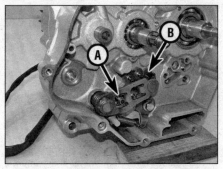

18.3 Centralising spring locating pin (A) and selector arm pawls (B)

18.4 Withdraw the gearchange shaft/arm assembly

8 Withdraw the oil strainer noting how it fits **(see illustration)**.

Inspection

Oil filter and strainer

9 The centrifugal oil filter is a sealed unit that should remain serviceable for an extremely high mileage unless there has been internal engine damage or there is evidence of oil sludge or metal swarf in the engine oil, in which case a new filter should be fitted.

10 Clean and inspect the strainer as described in Chapter 1, Section 14.

Oil pump

Note: *Not all manufacturers list parts for the pump – check with your supplier before disassembly.*

11 Rotate the pump shaft by hand and check that the internal rotors turn smoothly and freely. If necessary, wash the pump out with a suitable solvent, then dry it thoroughly and fill it with clean engine oil via the holes in the cover. Check the pump again – if the action is still poor, follow the procedure in Chapter 2B, Section 17, to inspect the internal components.

Installation

12 Fit the pump using a new gasket and tighten the screws securely **(see illustrations 17.6b and a)**.

13 Install the inner spring washer and the drive pin **(see illustrations 17.5)**. Centralise the pin in the shaft, then install the pump driven gear over the pin. Install the outer spring washer, the plain washer and the E-clip **(see illustrations 17.4c, b and a)**. **Note:** *The E-clip should be a firm fit on the shaft – if available, fit a new E-clip.*

14 Install the oil pump drive gear **(see illustrations 17.3)**.

15 Slide the centrifugal oil filter onto the shaft, aligning the tab in the centre with the slot in the crankshaft **(see illustration 17.2)**.

16 Install the primary drive gear and the clutch (see Sections 16 and 14).

17 Fit the oil strainer **(see illustration 17.8)**.

18 Gearchange mechanism

Note: *The gearchange mechanism can be removed with the engine in the frame. If the engine has been removed, ignore the steps which don't apply.*

Removal

1 Make sure the transmission is in neutral. Remove the clutch (see Section 14).

2 Make a mark where the slot in the gearchange lever aligns with the shaft. Unscrew the pinch bolt and slide the lever off the shaft **(see illustration 4.13)**. Wrap a single layer of thin insulating tape around the gearchange shaft splines to protect the left-hand oil seal when the shaft is removed.

3 Note how the gearchange shaft centralising spring ends fit on each side of the locating pin in the casing, and how the pawls on the selector arm locate onto the pins on the camplate end of the selector drum **(see illustration)**.

4 Grasp the shaft/arm assembly and withdraw it from the crankcase **(see illustration)**.

5 Note how the roller on the stopper arm locates in the neutral detent on the selector drum cam **(see illustration)**. Unscrew the stopper arm bolt and remove the arm and washer, and unhook the spring **(see illustration)**.

6 If the crankcases are being separated, or if otherwise required, undo the camplate screw, holding the selector drum with a tool as shown to prevent it turning **(see illustration)**. Remove the camplate, noting the two pins that locate the plate on the end of the selector drum **(see illustration)**. Remove the pins for safekeeping.

18.5a Stopper arm roller locates in neutral detent

18.5b Removing the stopper arm assembly

18.6a Hold the camplate to prevent it turning and unscrew the bolt

18.6b Note location of the two pins

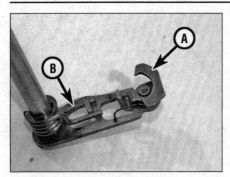

18.7 Inspect the pawls (A) and centralising spring (B)

Inspection

7 Check the selector arm for cracks, distortion and wear of its pawls, and check the shaft centralising spring for fatigue, wear or damage (see illustration).

8 Check for any corresponding wear on the pins on the selector drum camplate. Also check the stopper arm roller and the detents in the camplate for any wear or damage, and make sure the roller turns freely. Inspect the stopper arm return spring for fatigue, wear or damage.

9 Replace any components that are worn or damaged with new ones.

10 Ensure that the gearchange shaft is straight and look for damage to the splines. If necessary, fit a new shaft.

11 Check the condition of the shaft oil seal

in the left-hand side of the crankcase (see illustration 24.5). If it is damaged, deteriorated or shows signs of leakage it must be replaced with a new one, though it is advisable to fit a new one whatever the apparent condition. Lever out the old seal with a seal hook or screwdriver, then press or drive the new seal squarely into place using your fingers, a seal driver or suitable socket.

Installation

12 Fit the camplate locating pins into the end of the selector drum and install the camplate (see illustration 18.6b). Apply a suitable non-permanent thread locking compound to the camplate screw and tighten it (see illustration 18.6a) – hold the drum as on removal.

13 Apply a suitable non-permanent thread locking compound to the stopper arm bolt. Hook the stopper arm spring onto its post, then fit the stopper arm and tighten the bolt to the torque setting specified at the beginning of the Chapter (see illustration 18.5b and a). Ensure that the stopper arm roller is positioned in the neutral detent on the camplate (see illustration 18.5a).

14 Check that the shaft centralising spring is properly positioned (see illustration 18.7). Apply some grease to the lips of the gearchange shaft oil seal in the left-hand side of the crankcase. Slide the shaft into place and push it all the way through the case until the splined end comes out the other side, taking care not to damage the oil seal. Locate

the selector arm pawls onto the pins on the selector drum and the centralising spring ends onto each side of the locating pin in the crankcase (see illustration 18.3).

15 Remove the insulating tape from around the gearchange shaft splines. Slide the gearchange lever onto the shaft, aligning the slot with the punch mark, then tighten the pinch bolt.

16 Install the clutch (see Section 14).

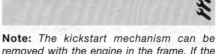

19 Kickstart mechanism

Note: *The kickstart mechanism can be removed with the engine in the frame. If the engine has been removed, ignore the steps which don't apply.*

Removal

1 Remove the clutch (see Section 14).

2 Release the outer circlip securing the idle gear and remove the outer washer, the gear, the inner washer, and if required the inner circlip (see illustrations). Discard the circlips as new ones should be used on reassembly.

3 Note how the return spring ends locate, then hold the end in the crankcase with pliers and remove the kickstart assembly (see illustration).

Inspection

4 Clean all the components in solvent.

19.2a Remove the outer circlip . . .

19.2b . . . the outer washer . . .

19.2c . . . the idle gear . . .

19.2d . . . the inner washer . . .

19.2e . . . and the inner circlip

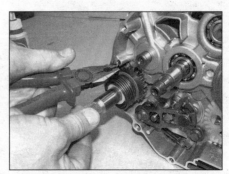

19.3 Removing the kickstart assembly – hold the spring end to prevent it uncoiling

19.5a Check the gears and splines for wear and damage . . .

19.5b . . . and check the bush (arrowed)

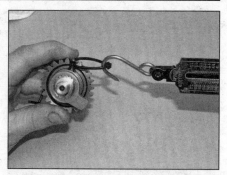

19.6 Check the force applied as the spring turns in the groove

19.8 Check the kickstart shaft oil seal (arrowed)

19.9a Locate the spring loop in the recess (arrowed) . . .

19.9b . . . and the return spring end in the hole as you fit the shaft

5 Check the teeth on the slider gear and the helical splines between the slider gear and the shaft for wear and damage **(see illustration)**. Also check the idle gear teeth and the driven gear teeth on the back of the clutch housing. Check the bush in the idle gear for wear **(see illustration)**.

6 Check the return spring and kick spring for wear and damage. If a spring gauge is available, check the force that can be applied to the kick spring before it spins in its groove in the gear **(see illustration)** – it should be 8 to 12 N.

7 If any components are worn or damaged they must be replaced with new ones. Remove the spacer, return spring, washer, slider gear and kick spring from the shaft, noting how they all fit. On reassembly make sure the bent end of the kick spring faces in **(see illustration 19.5a)**. Make sure the notch in the spacer for the return spring faces in and that the spring end locates in it.

8 Check the condition of the kickstart shaft oil seal in the clutch cover **(see illustration)**. If it is damaged, deteriorated or shows signs of leakage it must be replaced with a new one (though it is best to fit a new one whatever the apparent condition). Lever out the old seal with a seal hook or screwdriver. Press or drive the new seal squarely into place using your fingers, a seal driver or suitable socket.

Installation

9 Fit the kickstart mechanism onto the crankcase, locating the kick spring loop in the recess, and tensioning the return spring to locate its free end in the hole **(see illustrations)**.

10 If removed fit the new idle gear inner circlip into its groove, then fit the inner washer, the gear with its marked side facing out, the outer washer and the new outer circlip **(see illustrations 19.2e to a)**.

11 Install the clutch (see Section 14).

20 Crankcase separation and reassembly

Note: *To separate the crankcase halves, the engine must be removed from the frame.*

Separation

1 To access the crankshaft and connecting rod assembly, balancer shaft, transmission shafts, selector drum and forks, and their bearings, the crankcase must be split into its two halves.

2 Before the crankcases can be separated the following components must be removed:

Starter motor (Chapter 9)
Neutral switch/gear position switch (Chapter 9)
Cylinder head (Section 7)
Cam chain and blades (Section 10)
Cylinder block (Section 11)
Piston (Section 12)
Alternator (Section 13)
Clutch (Section 14)
Primary drive gear (Section 16)
Oil filter, strainer and pump (Section 17)
Gearchange mechanism (Section 18)
Kickstart mechanism (Section 19)

3 Make a cardboard template punched with holes to match all the bolts in the each crankcase half – as each crankcase bolt is removed, store it in its relative position in the template **(see illustration)**. This will ensure all bolts are installed in the correct location on reassembly.

4 Unscrew the crankcase bolts evenly, a little at a time and in a criss-cross sequence until they are finger-tight, then remove them – there are two bolts in the right-hand side and eight in the left, including the upper bolt that retains

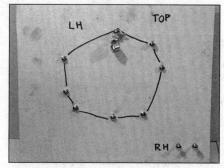

20.3 Make a cardboard template like the one shown to store the bolts

20.4a Right-hand crankcase bolts (arrowed)

20.4b Left-hand crankcase bolts (arrowed)

20.4c Note location of the clutch cable guide

the clutch cable guide **(see illustrations)**. **Note:** *As each bolt is removed, store it in its relative position in a cardboard template of the crankcase halves. This will ensure all bolts and washers are returned to their original locations on reassembly.*

5 Holding both halves of the crankcase place the engine on its left-hand side, laying it on wooden blocks so the shaft ends are clear of the bench. Carefully lift the right crankcase half off the left half **(see illustration)**. If the crankcase halves do not separate easily, first ensure all fasteners have been removed. Next, apply heat to the right-hand main bearing

housing with a hot air gun, tap around the joint with a soft-faced mallet and try lifting the right-hand half off again. **Note:** *If the halves do not separate easily, make sure all fasteners have been removed. Do not try and separate the halves by levering against the crankcase mating surfaces as they are easily scored and will leak oil in the future if damaged.* The right-hand crankcase half will come away leaving the balancer shaft, crankshaft, balancer shaft, transmission shafts and selector drum and forks in the left-hand half **(see illustration)**.

6 Remove the two locating dowels from the crankcase if they are loose – they could be in either half **(see illustration 20.5b)**.

7 Refer to Sections 22 to 26 for the removal and installation of the components housed within the crankcases.

Reassembly

8 Remove all traces of sealant from the crankcase mating surfaces. Clean the threads of all the crankcase bolts.

9 Refer to Sections 22 to 26 and double check that all components and their bearings, and the transmission output shaft oil seal, are in place in the left-hand crankcase half, and that all the relevant bearings are in the right-hand half.

10 Generously lubricate the crankshaft and transmission shaft bearings and gears and the selector fork shafts and fork ends and the tracks in the selector drum with clean engine oil, then use a rag soaked in high flash-point solvent to wipe over the mating surfaces of both crankcase halves to remove all traces of oil.

11 If removed, fit the two locating dowels into the right-hand crankcase half **(see illustration 20.5b)**.

12 Apply a small amount of suitable sealant to the mating surface of the left-hand crankcase half as shown, avoiding the oil passage in the top of the crankcase **(see illustration)**.

Caution: Apply the sealant only to the mating surfaces. Do not apply an excessive amount as it will ooze out when the case halves are assembled and may obstruct oil passages. Do not apply the sealant close to any of the oil passages.

13 Carefully fit the right-hand crankcase half down onto the left-hand half, making sure the shaft ends and dowels all locate correctly.

14 Check that the right-hand crankcase half is correctly seated, then fit the two bolts into the right-hand crankcase and tighten them finger-tight **(see illustration 20.4a)**. Grasp both halves of the crankcase and turn the engine over.

20.5a Carefully separate the crankcase halves

20.5b Location of the crankcase components. Note the dowels (arrowed)

20.12 Apply sealant to the mating surface, making sure none blocks the oil passage (arrowed)

Caution: The crankcase halves should fit together without being forced. If the casings are not correctly seated, remove the right-hand crankcase half and investigate the problem. Do not attempt to pull them together using the crankcase bolts as the casing will crack and be ruined.

15 Install the eight left-hand crankcase bolts, fitting the clutch cable holder with the uppermost bolt, and tighten them finger-tight **(see illustrations 20.4c and b)**. Stand the engine upright. Now tighten all the bolts evenly and a little at a time in a criss-cross sequence to the torque setting specified at the beginning of the Chapter.

16 With all crankcase fasteners tightened, check that the crankshaft, balancer shaft and transmission shafts rotate smoothly and easily. Check that the transmission shafts rotate freely and independently in neutral, then rotate the selector drum by hand (you will need to fit the camplate – see Section 18) and select each gear in turn whilst rotating the input shaft. If there are any signs of undue stiffness, tight or rough spots, or of any other problem, the fault must be rectified before proceeding further.

17 Install all other removed assemblies in a reverse of the sequence given in Step 2.

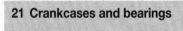

21 Crankcases and bearings

Crankcases

1 After the crankcases have been separated, remove the balancer shaft, the selector drum and forks, the transmission shafts and the crankshaft (see Sections 22 to 26).

2 Clean the crankcases thoroughly with solvent and dry them with compressed air. Blow out all oil passages with compressed air **(see illustrations)**.

3 Remove all traces of old gasket sealant from the mating surfaces. Clean up minor damage to the surfaces with a fine sharpening stone or grindstone.

Caution: Be very careful not to nick or gouge the crankcase mating surfaces or oil leaks will result. Check both crankcase halves very carefully for cracks and other damage.

4 Small cracks or holes in aluminium castings can be repaired with an epoxy resin adhesive as a temporary measure or with one of the low temperature welding kits. Permanent repairs can only be done by TIG (tungsten inert gas or heli-arc) welding, and only a specialist in this process is in a position to advise on the economy or practical aspect of such a repair. If any damage is found that can't be repaired, replace the crankcase halves as a set.

5 Damaged threads can be economically reclaimed using a diamond section wire insert, for example of the Heli-Coil type (though there

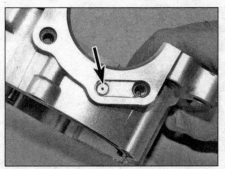

21.2a Clear the oil passages (arrowed) . . .

are other makes), which are easily fitted after drilling and re-tapping the affected thread.

6 Sheared studs or screws can usually be removed with extractors, which consist of a tapered, left-hand thread screw of very hard steel. These are inserted into a pre-drilled hole in the stud, and usually succeed in dislodging the most stubborn stud or screw. If a stud has sheared above its bore line, it can be removed using a conventional stud extractor which avoids the need for drilling.

HAYNES HiNT *Refer to Tools and Workshop Tips for details of installing a thread insert and using screw extractors.*

7 Install all components and assemblies, referring to the relevant Sections of this and the other Chapters, before reassembling the crankcase halves.

Bearing information

8 The crankshaft, balancer shaft, and transmission shaft bearings should all be replaced with new ones as part of a complete engine overhaul, or individually as required due to wear or failure.

9 Bearing failure occurs mainly because of lack of lubrication, the presence of dirt or other foreign particles, overloading the engine, break-up of one or more of the bearing components due to fatigue, or corrosion. Regardless of the cause of bearing failure, it must be corrected before the engine is reassembled to prevent it from happening again.

10 The bearings should rotate smoothly, freely and quietly, there should be no rough spots, and there should be no excessive play between the inner and outer races, or between the inner race and the shaft it fits on, or between the outer race and its housing in the crankcase.

11 Dirt and other foreign particles get into the engine in a variety of ways. They may be left in the engine during assembly or they may pass through filters or breathers, then get into the oil and from there into the bearings. Metal chips from machining operations and normal

21.2b . . . with compressed air

engine wear are often present. Abrasives are sometimes left in engine components after reconditioning operations, especially when parts are not thoroughly cleaned using the proper cleaning methods. The best prevention for this cause of bearing failure is to clean all parts thoroughly and keep everything spotlessly clean during engine reassembly. Regular oil changes are also recommended.

12 Lack of lubrication or lubrication breakdown has a number of interrelated causes. Excessive heat (which thins the oil), overloading and oil leakage all contribute to lubrication breakdown. Blocked oil passages will starve a bearing of lubrication and destroy it.

13 Riding habits can have a definite effect on bearing life. Full throttle low, speed operation, or labouring the engine, puts very high loads on bearings. Short trip riding leads to corrosion of bearings, as insufficient engine heat is produced to drive off the condensed water and corrosive gases produced. These products collect in the engine oil, forming acid and sludge. As the oil is carried to the engine bearings, the acid attacks and corrodes the bearing material.

14 Incorrect bearing installation during engine assembly will lead to bearing failure as well. To avoid bearing problems, clean all parts thoroughly before reassembly, and lubricate the new bearings with clean engine oil during installation.

Bearing removal and installation

Note: *If the correct bearing removal and installation tools are not available take the crankcases and crankshaft to a dealer – do not risk damaging either the cases or the crankshaft.*

Crankshaft (main) bearings

15 If the crankshaft (main) bearings have failed, excessive rumbling and vibration will be felt when the engine is running.

16 Separate the crankcase halves (Section 20) and remove the components housed within the crankcases (Sections 22 to 26). Follow the procedure in Step 10 to check the bearings.

17 To remove the right-hand main bearing from the crankcase, heat the bearing housing with a hot air gun, then tap the bearing out

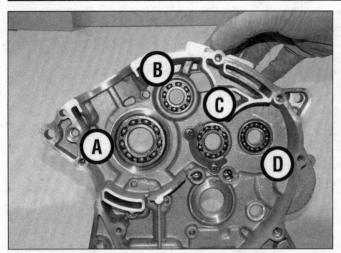

21.17 Crankshaft (main) bearing (A), balancer shaft bearing (B), input shaft bearing (C) and output shaft bearing (D) – right-hand crankcase half

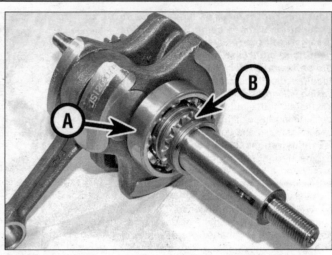

21.19 Left-hand crankshaft (main) bearing (A). Note cam chain sprocket (B)

from the outside of the crankcase using a bearing driver or a suitable socket **(see illustration)**.

18 Smear the outside of the new bearing with clean oil and fit it with its marked side towards the inside of the engine. Heat the housing and drive the bearing squarely in until it seats using a driver or socket that bears only on the outer race.

19 The left-hand main bearing is an integral part of the crankshaft assembly and is not available separately **(see illustration)**. If the bearing has failed a new crankshaft will have to be fitted.

20 Inspect the bearing housing in the crankcase **(see illustration)**. The bearing should be a tight fit in the housing (see Section 26). If the bearing has seized and the outer race has spun in the housing, the housing may be damaged. Seek specialist advice as to whether the crankcase is serviceable.

Connecting rod (big-end) bearing

21 If the connecting rod (big-end) bearing has failed, there will be a pronounced knocking noise when the engine is running, particularly under load and increasing with engine speed. Refer to Section 26 for checks that can be made.

Balancer shaft bearings

22 If the balancer shaft bearings have failed, excessive rumbling and vibration will be felt when the engine is running.

23 Separate the crankcase halves (Section 20) and remove the components housed within the crankcases (Sections 22 to 26). Follow the procedure in Step 10 to check the bearings.

24 To remove the right-hand bearing from the crankcase, heat the bearing housing with a hot air gun, then tap the bearing out from the outside of the crankcase using a bearing driver or a suitable socket **(see illustration 21.17)**.

25 Smear the outside of the new bearing with clean oil and fit it with its marked side towards the inside of the engine. Heat the housing and drive the bearing squarely in until it seats using a driver or socket that bears only on the outer race.

26 To remove the left-hand bearing **(see illustration)** lay the crankcase inside face down on the work bench and heat the bearing housing with a hot air gun until the bearing drops out. If it doesn't come out, refer to *Tools and Workshop Tips* in the *Reference* section and use an expanding knife-edge puller with slide-hammer attachment.

27 Follow the procedure in Step 25 to install the new bearing.

Transmission shaft bearings

28 If the transmission bearings have failed, excessive rumbling and vibration will be felt when the engine is running **(see illustrations 21.17 and 26)**.

21.20 Left-hand main bearing housing

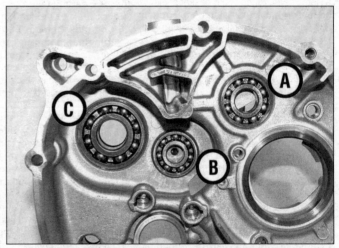

21.26 Balancer shaft bearing (A), input shaft bearing (B) and output shaft bearing (C) – left-hand crankcase half

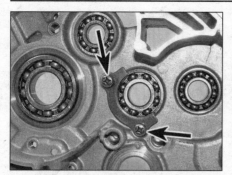

21.30 Screws (arrowed) secure input shaft retainer plate

29 Separate the crankcase halves (Section 20) and remove the components housed within the crankcases (Sections 22 to 26). Follow the procedure in Step 10 to check the bearings.

30 If required, undo the two screws securing the input shaft bearing retainer plate on the inside of the right-hand crankcase **(see illustration)**.

31 To remove the input shaft bearing from the right-hand crankcase and the output shaft bearings from each crankcase, follow the procedure in Step 24. Follow the procedure in Step 25 to install the new bearings.

32 If removed, apply a suitable non-permanent thread locking compound to the bearing retainer plate screws, then fit the plate and tighten the screws **(see illustration 21.30)**.

33 To remove the input shaft bearing from the left-hand crankcase, follow the procedure in Step 26. Follow the procedure in Step 25 to install the new bearing.

23.2 Location of the output shaft forks (A), input shaft fork (B) and selector drum (C)

23.3b Removing the output shaft selector fork assembly

22.2a Note alignment marks on the gears . . .

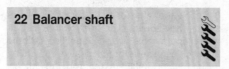

22 Balancer shaft

Note: *To remove the balancer shaft the engine must be removed from the frame and the crankcases separated.*

Removal

1 Remove the engine from the frame (see Section 4) and separate the crankcase halves (see Section 20).

2 Turn the crankshaft and balancer shaft until the punch marks on their respective gears are aligned – this is how they must be positioned on installation **(see illustration)**. Lift the balancer shaft out of the crankcase **(see illustration)**.

Inspection

3 Clean the balancer shaft with solvent. If

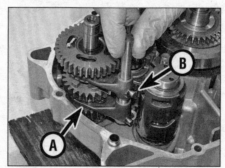

23.3a Location of the selector forks (A) and guide pins (B)

23.3c Keep the forks on the shaft in the correct order

22.2b . . . then lift out the balancer shaft

available, blow it dry with compressed air. Check the balancer driven gear for wear or damage. If any of the gear teeth are excessively worn, chipped or broken, the gear must be replaced with a new one. If wear or damage is found, also inspect the drive gear on the crankshaft **(see illustration 26.7)**.

4 Refer to Section 21 and check the balancer shaft bearings.

Installation

5 Carefully fit the balancer shaft into the left-hand crankcase, locating the shaft end in the bearing and aligning the punch mark on the driven gear tooth with that on the drive gear tooth on the crankshaft **(see illustration 22.2a)**.

6 Check that the crankshaft and balancer shaft rotate freely and easily.

7 Reassemble the crankcase halves (see Section 20).

23 Selector drum and forks

Note: *To remove the selector drum and forks the engine must be removed from the frame and the crankcases separated.*

Removal

1 Remove the engine (see Section 4) and separate the crankcase halves (see Section 20).

2 Before removing the selector forks, note the arrangement of the forks and selector drum **(see illustration)**. Note that each fork carries an identification letter. On the machine used to illustrate this procedure the output shaft forks were marked JR and JL and the input shaft fork was marked JC. All identification letters face the right-hand side of the engine. If no letters are visible, mark the forks with a dab of paint to avoid mixing them up and to aid reassembly.

3 Working on the transmission output shaft first, note how the forks fit into the grooves in the 4th and 2nd gear pinions and how the fork guide pins locate in the grooves in the selector drum **(see illustration)**. Withdraw the fork shaft from the left-hand casing and lift the assembly out **(see illustration)**. Keep the forks on the shaft in the correct order and way round **(see illustration)**.

23.4 **Remove the shaft for the input shaft fork**

23.5 **Lift out the selector drum**

23.6 **Location of the input shaft fork**

4 Withdraw completely the shaft for the input shaft fork **(see illustration)**. Note that this shaft is shorter than the one for the output shaft forks.

5 Withdraw the selector drum **(see illustration)**.

6 Note how the input shaft fork fits into the groove in the 3rd gear pinion **(see illustration)** then remove the fork and slide it back onto its shaft.

Inspection

7 Inspect the selector forks for any signs of wear or damage, especially around the fork ends where they engage with the groove in the pinion **(see illustration)**. Check closely to see if the forks are bent and ensure that each fork fits correctly in its pinion groove. If the forks are in any way damaged they must be replaced with new ones.

8 Check that the forks fit correctly on the shaft – they should slide freely with a light fit but no appreciable freeplay **(see illustration)**.

9 Check each selector fork shaft is straight by rolling it along a flat surface. A bent shaft will cause difficulty in selecting gears and make the gearchange action heavy. Replace the shaft with a new one if it is bent. Check that the fork shaft holes in the casings are neither worn nor damaged.

10 Inspect the selector drum grooves and selector fork guide pins for signs of wear or damage **(see illustration)**. If either component shows signs of wear or damage it must be renewed.

11 Check that the selector drum rotates freely in each crankcase half and has no sign of freeplay between it and the casing. Replace the drum and/or crankcases with new ones if they are worn.

Installation

12 Ensure that the transmission shafts are correctly installed (see Section 24).

13 Lubricate the ends and bore of each fork and the fork shaft with oil before installing it.

14 Locate the input shaft fork, marked JC, in its pinion groove, making sure it is the correct way up **(see illustration 23.6)**.

15 Lubricate the selector drum left-hand end with clean engine oil and install the selector drum in the crankcase. Lift the input shaft fork and locate its guide pin in the centre track in the drum then secure the fork with the fork shaft **(see illustration)**.

16 Locate the output shaft forks in their pinion grooves, JL lower, JR upper, making sure they are the correct way round **(see illustration 23.3b)**. Pivot each fork round to locate its guide pin in its groove in the selector drum then secure the forks with the fork shaft **(see illustration 23.3a)**. Ensure both fork shafts are pressed fully into the bores in the crankcase **(see illustration)**.

17 Reassemble the crankcase halves (see Section 20).

24 Transmission shafts and oil seal removal and installation

Note: *To remove the transmission shafts the engine must be removed from the frame and the crankcases separated.*

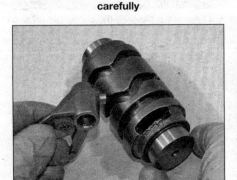

23.7 **Check the forks and fork ends carefully**

23.8 **There should be no freeplay between the forks and shaft**

23.10 **Check the guide pins and their grooves in the drum**

23.15 **Secure the input shaft fork (arrowed) with the shaft**

23.16 **Press the fork shafts fully home**

24.3 Lift the transmission shafts out together

24.4 Note how the pushrod is fitted

24.5 Output shaft oil seal (A). Note gearchange shaft seal (B)

Removal

1 Remove the engine from the frame and separate the crankcase halves (see Section 20).
2 Remove the balancer shaft and the selector drum and forks (see Sections 22 and 23).
3 Support the left-hand crankcase upright, then grasp the input and output shafts and lift them both out of the crankcase together **(see illustration)**. Note that there is a thrust washer on the left-hand end of the output shaft which may stick to the bearing or fall off as you remove the shafts – retrieve the washer and fit it back onto the shaft **(see illustration 25.20a)**.
4 Note the location of the long clutch pushrod inside the left-hand end of the input shaft **(see illustration)**. Note which way round the pushrod is fitted.
5 Prise the output shaft oil seal out of the left-hand crankcase using a seal hook or flat-bladed screwdriver **(see illustration)**. Discard the seal as a new one must be used.
6 If necessary, the transmission shafts can be disassembled and inspected for wear or damage (see Section 25).
7 Refer to Section 21 and check the transmission shaft bearings.

Installation

8 Press or drive the new output shaft seal into its housing until it is level with the rim of the housing **(see illustration 24.5)**. Grease the lips of the new seal.
9 Make sure the thrust washer is on the left-hand end of the output shaft **(see illustration 25.20a)** – stick it in place with

some grease to ensure it doesn't fall off during installation.
10 Ensure the long clutch pushrod is inserted fully into the left-hand end of the input shaft **(see illustration 24.4)**.
11 Lay the shafts together on the bench so their related gears are aligned **(see illustration)** then fit them into the left-hand crankcase, locating the shaft ends in the bearings **(see illustration 24.3)**. Make sure both transmission shafts are correctly seated and that their related pinions are correctly engaged **(see illustration)**.
12 Install the selector drum and forks and the balancer shaft (see Sections 23 and 22).
13 Position the gears in the neutral position and check the shafts are free to rotate easily and independently (i.e. the input shaft can turn whilst the output shaft is held stationary) before proceeding further. Also check that each gear can be selected by turning the input

shaft with one hand and the selector drum with the other.
14 Reassemble the crankcase halves (see Section 20).

Output shaft oil seal

15 If there is evidence of leakage from the oil seal in everyday use it can be replaced with a new one without having to separate the crankcase halves and remove the output shaft.
16 Remove the front sprocket (see Chapter 6).
17 Push one side of the seal in so it tilts, then prise out the other side **(see illustration)**.
18 Wrap some insulating tap around the splines on the end of the shaft **(see illustration)**. Grease the lips of the new seal. Slide the seal over the shaft and press it into its housing **(see illustration)**. Press or drive the seal in until it is level with the rim of the housing.

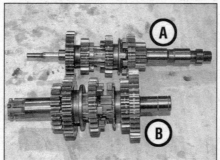

24.11a Align the input (A) and output (B) shafts

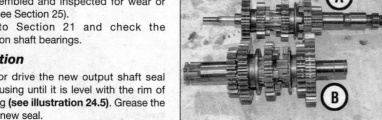

24.11b Check that the gear pinions engage correctly

24.17 Tilt the seal and lever it out

24.18a Wrap some tape around the shaft . . .

24.18b . . . then press the new seal into place

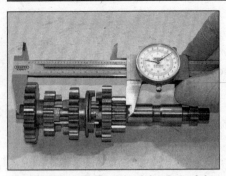

25.3 Measure the length of the gear pinion assembly

25.4a Using a puller to remove the 5th gear pinion – protect the shaft end (arrowed) as shown

25.4b Note raised shoulder on 5th gear pinion

25 Transmission shafts overhaul

1 Remove the transmission shafts from the crankcase (see Section 24). Always disassemble the transmission shafts separately to avoid mixing up the components **(see illustration 24.11a)**.

HAYNES HiNT *When disassembling the transmission shafts, place the parts on a long rod or thread a wire through them to keep them in order and facing the proper direction.*

Input shaft

Disassembly

2 Withdraw the long clutch pushrod from inside the left-hand end of the shaft **(see illustration 24.4)**.

3 Before disassembly, measure the distance between the outer faces of the 5th and 1st gear pinions as shown and record the result **(see illustration)**. When the pinions are reassembled on the shaft the distance must be exactly the same.

4 Draw the 5th gear pinion off the shaft using a puller – place a piece of soft metal such as a copper coin between the end of the shaft and the puller to protect the shaft **(see illustration)**. Note which way round the pinion fits **(see illustration)**.

5 Slide the 2nd and 3rd gear pinions off the shaft **(see illustrations)**.

6 Remove the circlip securing the 4th gear pinion, then slide the thrust washer and the pinion off the shaft **(see illustrations)**.

7 The 1st gear pinion is integral with the shaft **(see illustration)**.

Inspection

8 Wash all of the components in clean solvent and dry them off.

9 Check the gear teeth for cracking, chipping, pitting and other obvious wear or damage. Any pinion that is damaged must be replaced with a new one.

10 Inspect the dogs and the dog holes in the gears for cracks, chips, and excessive wear especially in the form of rounded edges (see

25.5a Slide off the 2nd . . .

25.5b . . . and 3rd gear pinions

25.6a Remove the circlip . . .

25.6b . . . then slide off the washer . . .

25.6c . . . and 4th gear pinion

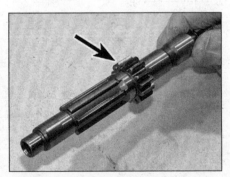

25.7 1st gear pinion (arrowed) is part of the shaft

25.10 Inspect the gear pinion dogs for wear and damage

25.15 Note location of circlip ends (arrowed)

25.20a Slide off the thrust washer . . .

illustration). Make sure mating gears engage properly. Replace the paired gears as a set if necessary.

11 Check for signs of scoring or bluing on the pinions and shaft. This could be caused by overheating due to inadequate lubrication. Check that all the oil holes and passages are clear. Check that each pinion moves freely on the shaft but without undue freeplay.

12 The shaft is unlikely to sustain damage unless the engine has seized, placing an unusually high loading on the transmission, or the machine has covered a very high mileage. Check the surface of the shaft, especially where a pinion turns on it, and replace the shaft if it has scored or picked up, or if there are any cracks.

13 Check the thrust washer and circlip and replace if they are bent or appear worn. Use new ones if in any doubt about their condition. Note that it is good practice to use new circlips when overhauling the transmission shafts.

Reassembly

14 During reassembly, apply molybdenum disulphide oil (a 50/50 mixture of molybdenum disulphide grease and clean engine oil) to the mating surfaces of the shaft and pinions. When fitting the circlip, do not expand its ends any further than is necessary, and position them between the raised splines on the shaft **(see illustration 25.15)**. Fit the circlip so that its chamfered side faces away from the thrust side, i.e. towards the pinion it secures.

15 Slide the 4th gear pinion onto the shaft with its dogs facing away from the integral 1st

25.20b . . . the 5th gear pinion . . .

25.20c . . . and the 2nd gear pinion

gear **(see illustration 25.6c)**. Slide the washer onto the shaft, then fit the circlip, making sure that it locates correctly in the groove in the shaft **(see illustration)**.

16 Slide the 3rd gear pinion onto the shaft with the selector fork groove facing the 4th gear pinion **(see illustration 25.5b)**.

17 Slide the 2nd gear pinion onto the shaft with its dogs facing the 3rd gear pinion **(see illustration 25.5a)**.

18 Press the 5th gear pinion onto the end of the shaft with the shouldered section towards the 2nd gear pinion **(see illustration 25.4b)**. This can be done in the jaws of large vice ensuring the ends of the shaft are protected from damage. Alternatively use an hydraulic press. As the gear is pressed on it is essential to repeatedly measure the distance between the outer faces of the 5th and 1st gear pinions until it is exactly as noted on disassembly

(see illustration 25.3). If the distance is too short the 5th gear pinion could press against the 2nd gear pinion and prevent it from turning freely. If you go too far, draw the 5th gear pinion back using the puller as on removal.

19 Fit the long clutch pushrod inside the left-hand end of the shaft **(see illustration 24.4)**. Check that all components have been correctly installed **(see illustration 24.11a)**.

Output shaft

Disassembly

20 Slide the thrust washer off the left-hand end of the shaft, followed by the 5th and 2nd gear pinions **(see illustrations)**.

21 Release the circlip securing the 1st gear pinion on the right-hand end of the shaft, and remove the thrust washer **(see illustrations)**.

22 Slide the 1st gear pinion off the shaft, followed by the 4th gear pinion **(see illustrations)**.

25.21a Remove the circlip . . .

25.21b . . . and the thrust washer

25.22a Slide off the 1st gear pinion . . .

25.22b . . . and 4th gear pinion

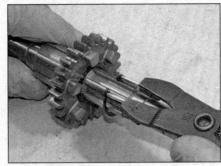

25.23a Remove the circlip . . .

25.23b . . . and the thrust washer

23 Release the circlip securing the 3rd gear pinion, then slide the thrust washer and pinion off the shaft (see illustrations).

Inspection

24 Refer to Steps 8 to 13 above.

Reassembly

25 During reassembly, lubricate the components and install the circlips as described in Step 14.

26 Slide the 3rd gear pinion onto the right-hand end of the shaft, with its dogs facing the right (see illustration 25.23c). Slide the washer onto the shaft, then fit the circlip, making sure it is locates correctly in its groove (see illustration 25.15).

27 Slide the 4th gear pinion onto the shaft, with its selector fork groove facing the 3rd gear pinion (see illustration 25.22b).

28 Slide the 1st gear pinion onto the shaft with the recessed face towards the 4th gear pinion (see illustration).

29 Slide the washer onto the shaft then fit the circlip, making sure it is locates correctly in its groove (see illustrations 25.21b and a).

30 Slide the 2nd gear pinion onto the left-hand end of the shaft with its selector fork groove facing the 3rd gear pinion (see illustration 25.20c).

31 Slide the 5th gear pinion onto the shaft with its dogs facing the 2nd gear pinion (see illustration 25.20b).

32 Slide the thrust washer onto the end of the shaft – smear it with grease to prevent it dropping off (see illustration 25.20a).

25.23c Slide off the 3rd gear pinion

33 Check that all components have been correctly installed (see illustration 24.11a).

26 Crankshaft and connecting rod

Note: *To remove the crankshaft the engine must be removed from the frame and the crankcase halves separated. The connecting rod is an integral part of the crankshaft assembly which comes as a pressed-up unit – individual components are not available.*

Removal

1 Remove the engine from the frame (see Section 4) and separate the crankcase halves (see Section 20).

25.28 Recessed face of the 1st gear pinion

2 Remove the balancer shaft, the selector drum and forks and the transmission shafts (see Sections 22 to 24)

3 The crankshaft assembly must be pressed out of the left-hand crankcase half – the left-hand crankshaft (main) bearing is an integral part of the crankshaft assembly and is a tight fit in the crankcase.

4 Support the crankcase on wooden blocks high enough so the crankshaft is just clear of the bench and can't fall far should it suddenly release and drop (see illustration). Screw the alternator rotor nut onto the crankshaft to protect the end and install a two-legged puller as shown; thread the legs into the holes provided in the crankcase and tighten the nuts on the top of the legs evenly (see illustration).

26.4a Support the crankcase on wooden blocks

26.4b Set-up for pressing the crankshaft out

5 Using a hot air gun, heat the crankshaft bearing housing and apply steady pressure on the crankshaft via the puller centre bolt. If the crankshaft does not release the bearing housing is not hot enough.

6 Once the crankshaft is free let the components cool before handling them.

Inspection

7 Clean the crankshaft with solvent. If available, blow the crank dry with compressed air. Check the balancer drive gear for wear or damage **(see illustration)**. If any of the gear teeth are excessively worn, chipped or broken, the crankshaft must be replaced with a new one. If wear or damage is found, also inspect the driven gear on the balancer shaft **(see illustration 22.2b)**. Similarly check the cam chain sprocket.

8 Hold the crankshaft still and check for any radial (up and down) play in the big-end bearing by pushing and pulling the connecting rod against the crank **(see illustration)**. If any play is detected the bearing has failed and a new crankshaft assembly will have to be fitted. **Note:** *Do not confuse radial play with side-to-side play – a small amount of side-to-side play in the big-end is acceptable.*

9 Refer to Chapter 2A, Section 11 and check the connecting rod small-end and piston pin for wear.

10 Have the rod checked for twist and bend by a dealer if you are in doubt about its straightness.

11 Refer to Section 21 and check the crankshaft (main) bearings.

Installation

Note: *When installing the crankshaft ensure the connecting rod is positioned so it sits in the opening for the cylinder bore.*

12 Ideally the crankshaft should be drawn into the left-hand crankcase using a similar set-up to the one used for removal **(see illustration 26.4b)**, this time with the nuts on the underside of the cross beam. An adapter will be required to connect the threaded end of the crankshaft to the puller centre bolt. Heat the bearing housing and draw the crankshaft bearing into the crankcase by applying steady pressure.

13 Alternatively, support the crankcase on wooden blocks and heat the bearing housing thoroughly. Use a freeze spray on the crankshaft bearing, then align the bearing squarely with the housing and tap the assembly into place using a deep socket that bears on the hub of the balancer drive gear **(see illustration)**. DO NOT hit on the end of the crankshaft and DO NOT use excessive force.

26.7 Inspect the teeth of the balancer shaft drive gear

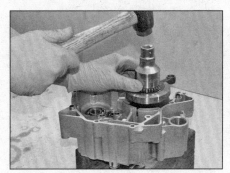

26.13 Use a hammer and socket to seat the crankshaft

If you do not have the tools or experience required take the crankcase and crankshaft to a dealer or specialist.

14 Check on the outside of the crankcase that the bearing is fully installed in its housing **(see illustration)**. Ensure the crankshaft rotates freely without binding.

15 Install the remaining components in the crankcases (see Steps 22 to 24).

16 Reassemble the crankcase halves (see Section 20).

27 Running-in procedure

1 Make sure the engine oil level is correct (see *Pre-ride checks*). Make sure there is fuel in the tank.

2 Turn the engine kill switch to the ON position and shift the gearbox into neutral. Turn the ignition ON. Operate the choke.

3 Start the engine and allow it to run at a moderately fast idle until it reaches operating temperature.

4 If a lubrication failure is suspected, carry out the oil pressure check described in Section 3.

26.8 Check for any radial play in the big-end bearing

26.14 Check that the crankshaft bearing (arrowed) is fully installed

If an engine is run without oil, even for a short period of time, severe damage will occur.

5 Check carefully that there are no oil leaks and make sure the transmission and controls, especially the brakes, function properly before road testing the machine.

6 Treat the machine gently for the first few miles to make sure oil has circulated throughout the engine and any new parts installed have started to seat.

7 Even greater care is necessary if a new piston and rings or a new cylinder have been fitted, and the bike will have to be run in as when new. This means greater use of the transmission and a restraining hand on the throttle until at least 300 miles (500 km) have been covered. There's no point in keeping to any set speed limit – the main idea is to keep from labouring the engine and to gradually increase performance up to the 300 miles (500 km) mark. Experience is the best guide, since it's easy to tell when an engine is running freely.

8 Upon completion of the road test, and after the engine has cooled down completely, recheck the valve clearances (see Chapter 1) and check the engine oil level (see *Pre-ride checks*).

Chapter 2D
Engine, clutch and transmission – twin cylinder engines

Degrees of difficulty

Easy, suitable for novice with little experience	**Fairly easy,** suitable for beginner with some experience	**Fairly difficult,** suitable for competent DIY mechanic	**Difficult,** suitable for experienced DIY mechanic	**Very difficult,** suitable for expert DIY or professional

Specifications

General

Type	Four-stroke twin cylinder
Capacity	124 cc
Bore	44.0 mm
Stroke	41.0 mm
Compression ratio	9.4 to 1
Cooling system	Air-cooled or liquid-cooled
Lubrication	Wet sump, trochoid pump
Clutch	Wet multi-plate
Transmission	Five-speed constant mesh
Final drive	Chain and sprockets

Torque settings

General settings (thread size given)

5 mm bolt/nut	5 Nm
6 mm bolt/nut	10 Nm
8 mm bolt/nut	24 Nm
10 mm bolt/nut	35 Nm
12 mm bolt/nut	55 Nm

Specific settings

Alternator rotor bolt	55 to 65 Nm
Camshaft sprocket bolts	17 to 23 Nm
Clutch nut	40 to 50 Nm
Crankcase bolts	10 to 14 Nm
Crankcase centre main bearing holder bolts/nut	10 to 14 Nm
Primary drive gear nut	45 to 60 Nm
Rocker holder (cylinder head) nuts	16 to 20 Nm

1 General information

The engine/transmission unit is a twin cylinder of unit construction. It is based on the Honda CB125T engine. The two valves per cylinder are operated by rocker arms actuated by a single overhead camshaft which is chain driven off the middle of the crankshaft. The crankcase divides vertically. The engine is air-cooled on most models (known as type 244FMI), but some are liquid-cooled.

The crankcase incorporates a wet sump, pressure-fed lubrication system which uses a single rotor trochoidal oil pump that is gear-driven off the right-hand end of the crankshaft. Oil is filtered by a mesh fitted to the pick-up on the oil pump.

The alternator is on the left-hand end of the crankshaft. The trigger for the ignition timing is on the outside of the alternator rotor, and the pick-up coil is mounted in the alternator cover along with the stator.

Power from the crankshaft is routed to the transmission via the clutch. The clutch is of the wet, multi-plate type and is gear-driven off the crankshaft. The clutch is operated by cable. The transmission is a five-speed constant-mesh unit. Final drive to the rear wheel is by chain and sprockets.

The electric starter motor is on the front of the engine, and on many models there is also a kickstart mechanism on the right-hand side.

2 Component access

Operations possible with the engine in the frame

The components and assemblies listed below can usually be removed without having to remove the engine from the frame, though there may be the odd exception to the rule depending on the frame design of your model.

If a number of areas require attention at the same time, removal of the engine is recommended as it is not that difficult.

Valve cover
Cam chain guide blade
Camshaft and rockers
Cylinder head (see Note in Section 11)
Cylinder block and pistons (see Note in Section 11)
Clutch
Oil pump
Primary drive gear
Gearchange mechanism
Kickstart mechanism (where fitted)
Alternator
Starter clutch
Starter motor

Operations requiring engine removal

It is necessary to remove the engine from the frame to gain access to the following components.

Crankshaft, connecting rods and bearings
Cam chain, tensioner and tensioner blade
Transmission shafts and bearings
Selector drum and forks

3 Cylinder compression test

Special tool: *A compression gauge is required to perform this test.*

1 Poor engine performance may be caused by leaking valves, incorrect valve clearances, a leaking head gasket, or worn pistons, piston rings or cylinder bores. A cylinder compression check will highlight these conditions and can also indicate the presence of excessive carbon deposits in the cylinder head.
2 The only tools required are a compression gauge (there are two types, one with a threaded end and if necessary an adapter to fit the spark plug hole in the cylinder head, the other has a rubber seal which is pressed into the spark plug hole to create a seal – the threaded adapter type is preferable), and a spark plug socket. Depending on the outcome of the initial test, a squirt-type oil can may also be needed.
3 Refer to Chapter 2A, Section 3, for details of the test – note both spark plugs should be removed when checking each cylinder.

4 Engine removal and installation

Caution: The engine is heavy. Engine removal and installation should be carried out with the aid of an assistant; personal injury or damage could occur if the engine falls or is dropped.

Removal

1 Support the bike either on its centrestand or

4.8 Make an alignment mark, then unscrew the bolt and draw the linkage arm or lever off

using an auxiliary stand so it is upright, making sure it is on level ground. Work can be made easier by raising the machine to a suitable working height on an hydraulic ramp or a suitable platform. Make sure the motorcycle is secure and will not topple over, and tie the front brake lever to the handlebar to prevent it rolling forwards.
2 Where fitted remove any fairing panels, belly-pan or sump guard, and engine protection bars as required according to model (see Chapter 8).
3 If the engine is dirty, particularly around its mountings, wash it thoroughly. This will make work much easier and rule out the possibility of caked on lumps of dirt falling into some vital component.
4 Drain the engine oil (see Chapter 1). On liquid-cooled engines drain the cooling system, then remove the radiator along with its hoses (see Chapter 3).
5 Disconnect the negative (–) lead from the battery (see Chapter 9). Also disconnect the engine earth lead, usually secured by one of the crankcase bolts.
6 Remove the fuel tank (see Chapter 4). Remove the carburettor(s) (see Chapter 4). Plug the engine intake duct(s) with clean rag.
7 Remove the exhaust system (see Chapter 4). On models with an air induction system that routes the air through the cylinder head or block, disconnect the air hose(s) from the pipe(s), and if necessary remove the control valve along with the hose(s) and its bracket

4.9 Disengage the chain from the sprocket

as required according to model to minimise obstruction to engine removal (see Chapter 4). Also detach the pipe(s) from the head or block if required – a new gasket(s) or O-ring(s) (according to model) will be needed.
8 Make a mark where the slot in the gearchange lever or linkage arm (according to type) aligns with the shaft **(see illustration)**. Unscrew the pinch bolt and slide the lever or arm off the shaft. Where fitted remove the kickstart lever (again marking the alignment).
9 Remove the front sprocket cover (see Chapter 7). Create maximum slack in the drive chain (see Chapter 1), then if required (for example if you intend to separate the crankcase halves) remove the front sprocket (see Chapter 7), or if not then slip the chain off the front sprocket **(see illustration)**.
10 Pull the spark plug caps off the plugs and secure them clear of the engine.
11 Where fitted detach the tachometer cable.
12 Detach the crankcase breather hose **(see illustration)**.
13 Detach the clutch cable and position it clear of the engine (see Section 17).
14 Trace the alternator, pick-up coil and neutral switch wiring from the left-hand side of the engine and disconnect it at the connectors **(see illustration)**. Release the wiring from any clamps or ties that will restrict it when removing the engine **(see illustration)**.
15 Remove the starter motor (see Chapter 9).
16 Remove the individual footrests or the complete footrest assembly as required

4.12 Release the clamp and detach the breather hose (arrowed)

4.14a Trace the wiring and disconnect the relevant connectors (arrowed) . . .

4.14b . . . and release any relevant cable-ties or clamps

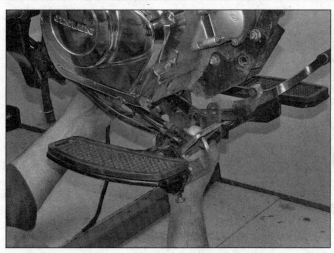

4.16 Removing the footboard assembly on a custom style bike

4.17 Support the engine as shown and described

according to model (see Chapter 6) – this will depend on the type fitted and whether they will get in the way when lifting the engine out **(see illustration)**.

17 Position an hydraulic or mechanical jack under the engine with a block of wood between the jack head and sump **(see illustration)**. Make sure the jack is centrally positioned so the engine will not topple in any direction when the last mounting bolt is removed. Raise the jack to take the weight of the engine, but make sure it is not lifting the bike and taking the weight of that as well. The idea is to support the engine so that there is no pressure on any of the mounting bolts once they have been slackened, so they can be easily withdrawn. Note that it may be necessary to alter the position of the jack as some of the bolts are removed to relieve the stress transferred to the other bolts.

18 Take a look around the engine and identify the mounting bolts and nuts and any brackets and spacers that hold the engine in the frame, and also whether the bottom sections of the frame can be removed – there are variations depending on manufacturer and model **(see illustrations)**. After removing a bolt fit any associated washer(s), spacer(s). bracket(s) and wiring clamp(s) back onto it in their correct order, then thread the nut on to secure them, and finally tag the bolt according to its position.

19 First go round and unscrew the nuts with their washers where fitted from the bolts, then slacken any bolts that don't have nuts on them.

20 Check that the engine is properly supported by the jack. Withdraw the mounting bolts and remove any washers, spacers, frame sections and brackets.

21 Check that all wiring, cables and hoses are free and clear. The engine can now be removed from the frame (see **Caution** above).

Installation

Note: *It is advisable to smear copper grease onto the engine mounting bolt shafts, not the threads, to prevent the possibility of them seizing in the engine or frame due to corrosion.*

22 Manoeuvre the engine into position in the frame and on the jack to align all the mounting bolt holes, making sure that all cables and wiring are correctly routed and do not get trapped. Note that it may be necessary to adjust the jack as some of the bolts are installed and tightened to realign the other bolt holes.

23 Install the mounting bolts along with any washers, spacers, brackets and wiring clamps, then fit the nuts and tighten them finger-tight.

24 Now go round and tighten all the engine mounting bolts and nuts.

25 Remove the jack from under the engine.

26 The remainder of the installation procedure is the reverse of removal, noting the following points:

● *When fitting the kickstart and gearchange levers onto their shafts align the marks noted or made on removal.*

● *Use a new gasket on the exhaust pipe.*

● *Make sure all wires, cables and hoses are correctly routed and connected, and secured by any clips or ties.*

● *Refill the engine with oil to the correct level (see Chapter 1 and Pre-ride checks). On liquid-cooled engines refill the cooling system (see Chapter 3).*

● *Adjust the throttle and clutch cable freeplay.*

● *Adjust the drive chain (see Chapter 1).*

● *Start the engine and check that there are no oil leaks, or coolant leaks on liquid-cooled engines. Adjust the idle speed (see Chapter 1).*

5 Engine overhaul information

1 Before beginning the engine overhaul, read through the related procedures to familiarise yourself with the scope and requirements of the job. Overhauling an engine is not all that

4.18a Typical front mounting bracket arrangement

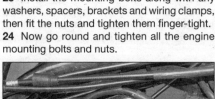

4.18b Typical upper mounting bracket arrangement

4.18c Upper and lower rear mounting bolts/nuts (arrowed)

difficult, but it is time consuming. Check on the availability of parts and make sure that any necessary special tools are obtained in advance.

2 Most work can be done with a decent set of typical workshop hand tools, although a number of precision measuring tools are required for inspecting parts to determine if they are worn.

3 To ensure maximum life and minimum trouble from a rebuilt engine, everything must be assembled with care in a spotlessly clean environment.

Disassembly

4 Before disassembling the engine, thoroughly clean and degrease its external surfaces. This will prevent contamination of the engine internals, and will also make the job a lot easier and cleaner. A high flash-point solvent, such as paraffin (kerosene) can be used, or better still, a proprietary engine degreaser such as Gunk. Use old paintbrushes and toothbrushes to work the solvent into the various recesses of the casings. Take care to exclude solvent or water from the electrical components and intake and exhaust ports.

 Warning: The use of petrol (gasoline) as a cleaning agent should be avoided because of the risk of fire.

5 When clean and dry, position the engine on the workbench, leaving suitable clear area for working. Gather a selection of small containers, plastic bags and some labels so

that parts can be grouped together in an easily identifiable manner. Also get some paper and a pen so that notes can be taken. You will also need a supply of clean rag, which should be as absorbent as possible.

6 Before commencing work, read through the appropriate section so that some idea of the necessary procedure can be gained. When removing components note that great force is seldom required, unless specified (checking the specified torque setting of the particular bolt being removed will indicate how tight it is, and therefore how much force should be needed). In many cases, a component's reluctance to be removed is indicative of an incorrect approach or removal method – if in any doubt, re-check with the text.

7 When disassembling the engine, keep 'mated' parts together (parts that have been in contact with each other during engine operation). These 'mated' parts must be refitted so they run together in the rebuilt engine.

8 A complete engine stripdown should be done in the following general order with reference to the appropriate Sections.

Remove the valve cover
Remove the camshaft
Remove the cylinder head
Remove the cylinder block and pistons
Remove the clutch
Remove the kickstart mechanism (where fitted)
Remove the oil pump
Remove the gearchange mechanism
Remove the primary drive gear

Remove the alternator and starter clutch (see Chapter 9)
Separate the crankcase halves
Remove the selector drum and forks
Remove the transmission shafts
Remove the crankshaft

Reassembly

9 Reassembly is accomplished by reversing the general disassembly sequence.

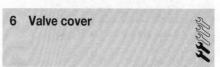

6 Valve cover

Note: *The valve cover can be removed with the engine in the frame. If the engine has been removed, ignore the steps which do not apply.*

Removal

1 Remove any fairing panels or covers as required according to model for access to the valve cover (see Chapter 8).

2 Remove the fuel tank (see Chapter 4).

3 Where fitted undo the side trim cover screws and remove each cover **(see illustration)**.

4 Unscrew the valve cover bolts, and where fitted remove the top trim cover **(see illustration)**. Lift the valve cover off the cylinder head **(see illustration 6.7a)**. If it is stuck, do not try to lever it off with a screwdriver. Tap it gently around the sides with a rubber hammer or block of wood to dislodge it. Note the sealing washers with the bolts – replace the washers with new ones if they have deteriorated or deformed.

5 Remove the rubber seal from the cover. If it is in any way damaged, deformed or deteriorated, replace it with a new one **(see illustration 6.6)**.

Installation

6 Fit the seal into the groove in the cover, using a new one if necessary **(see illustration)**.

7 Position the valve cover on the cylinder head, making sure the seal stays in place **(see illustration)**. Where removed fit the top trim cover. Install the cover bolts with their washers and tighten them **(see illustration)**.

8 Install the remaining components.

6.3 Undo the screws and remove the side covers

6.4 Unscrew the bolts (arrowed) and remove the cover

6.6 Fit a new seal into the groove

6.7a Fit the valve cover onto the head

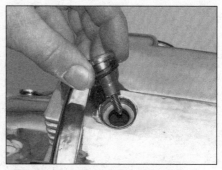

6.7b Fit the bolts with their sealing washers

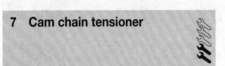

7.3a Withdraw the R-clip . . .

7.3b . . . and remove the tensioner

7 Cam chain tensioner

Note: *To remove the cam chain tensioner the engine must be removed from the frame and the crankcases separated. One of two types of tensioner may be fitted, depending on manufacturer. Type A has an upper mounting bolt and a locknut on the lower adjuster bolt, located on the back of the cylinder head and block respectively. Type B is self adjusting and has two mounting bolts (see illustration 11.7).*

Removal

1 Remove the engine from the frame (see Section 4) and separate the crankcase halves (see Section 22).

2 Remove the crankshaft (see Section 24).
3 Remove the R-clip from the tensioner blade pivot pin, and where fitted remove the washer **(see illustration)**. Slide the blade off the pin and remove the tensioner assembly, noting how it is positioned relative to the chain and the main bearing holder **(see illustration)**.

Inspection

4 Examine the tensioner assembly components for wear and damage. Check the tension of the spring. Check the sliding surface and edges of the blade for excessive wear, deep grooves, cracking and other obvious damage.
5 Before dismantling the tensioner check with your dealer on the availability of individual components, then either replace the complete assembly or individual components

accordingly, in which case carefully note or photograph how everything fits before dismantling it.

Installation

6 Installation is the reverse of removal. Lubricate the tensioner blade pivot and if necessary use a new R-clip.

8 Rocker assemblies

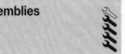

Note: *The rockers can be removed with the engine in the frame. If the engine has been removed ignore the steps that do not apply, but refit the alternator cover temporarily so that the timing marks can be accurately set.*

Removal

1 Remove the valve cover (see Section 6).
2 Remove the spark plugs (see Chapter 1).
3 Remove the crankshaft end cap and the timing inspection cap from the alternator cover on the left-hand side of the engine **(see illustration)**. Check the condition of the O-rings and replace them with new ones if necessary.
4 If both rocker assemblies are being removed, or if only the left-hand assembly is being removed, the engine must be turned to position the No. 1 (left-hand) piston at top dead centre (TDC) on its compression stroke so that its valves are closed. Turn the engine anti-clockwise using a suitable socket on the alternator rotor bolt until the index line on the rotor for the No. 1 piston aligns with the notch in the inspection hole rim, the notch in the left-hand end of the camshaft faces back and the index lines on the cam chain sprocket face forward and back (i.e. at 9 and 3 o'clock) parallel to the top of the cylinder head **(see illustrations)**. If the marks do not align as described, rotate the engine anti-clockwise one full turn (360°) until the index line on the rotor again aligns with the pointer – the marks should now be as described.

8.3 Remove the crankshaft end cap (A) and the timing inspection cap (B)

8.4a Turn the engine anti-clockwise . . .

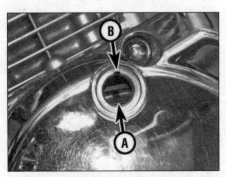

8.4b . . . until the line (A) on the rotor aligns with the notch (B) . . .

8.4c . . . and the notch (arrowed) . . .

8.4d . . . and the index lines (arrowed) on the sprocket are positioned as shown

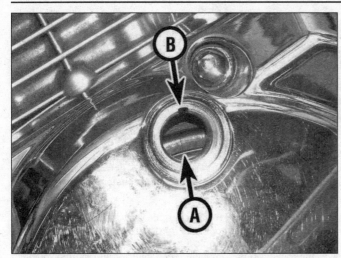

8.5a When the No. 2 cylinder is at TDC the line (A) on the rotor aligns with the notch (B) . . .

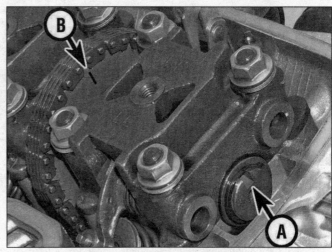

8.5b . . . and the notch (A) and sprocket index line (B) are positioned as shown

5 If only the right-hand rocker assembly is being removed, the engine must be turned to position the No. 2 (right-hand) piston at top dead centre (TDC) on its compression stroke so that its valves are closed. Turn the engine anti-clockwise using a suitable socket on the alternator rotor bolt **(see illustration 8.4a)** until the index line on the rotor for the No. 2 piston aligns with the notch in the inspection hole rim, the notch in the left-hand end of the camshaft faces up and the index lines on the cam chain sprocket face up and down (i.e. at 12 and 6 o'clock) perpendicular to the top of the cylinder head **(see illustrations)**. If the marks do not align as described, rotate the engine anti-clockwise one full turn (360°) until the index line on the rotor again aligns with the pointer – the marks should now be as described.

6 Before removing the rocker assemblies mark each holder L or R according to which side

of the engine it fits – they must be returned to their original position on reassembly. Note that each holder is already marked LF and LE – the LF mark faces the intake side (rear) of the engine and the LE mark faces the exhaust side (front) **(see illustration)**.

7 Unscrew the rocker assembly nuts (also serving as the cylinder head nuts) evenly and a little at a time in a criss-cross sequence, starting with the outer nuts and working to the inner ones if both holders are being removed, until all are loose, then remove them and their washers **(see illustration)**.

8 Lift each rocker assembly off the cylinder head **(see illustration)**. Remove the two dowels from each holder or the head if loose, noting which fits where as they are different lengths. If you are removing the rocker shafts and arms from the holders the long dowels must be removed from the

holders as they block withdrawal of the rear shafts.

9 Mark each rocker arm according to its location and its holder. Working on one rocker at a time, thread a 5 mm bolt into the rocker shaft to use as a handle, then hold the rocker

8.6 Note the markings on each rocker holder

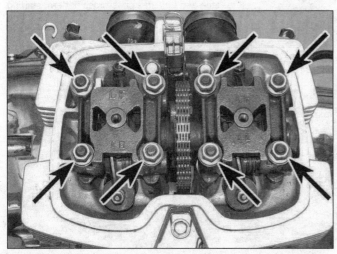

8.7 Unscrew the nuts (arrowed) as required and remove each rocker assembly

8.8 Lift the rocker assembly off, noting the short dowel (A) and long dowel (B)

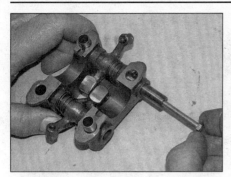

8.9 Withdraw the shaft using a bolt as a handle and remove the rocker and spring

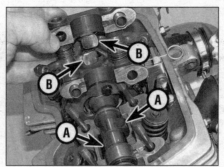

8.11 Check the lobes (A) and the rocker pads (B)

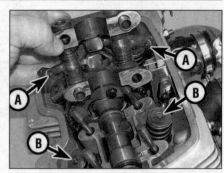

8.12 Check the adjusters (A) and the valve stems (B)

arm and draw the shaft out, and remove the rocker and collect the spring **(see illustration)**. Slide the rocker and spring back onto its shaft to prevent mixing components up – all shafts and rocker arms are identical and are therefore interchangeable, but mark them according to their location so they can be installed in their original position, so keeping mated parts running together. Repeat the procedure for the other rocker arm and shaft, and the other holder.

10 Clean the holders, rockers and shafts, taking care not to mix components up. Blow the oil passages out with compressed air.

Inspection

11 Check the camshaft lobes and the contact pads on the rocker arms for heat discoloration, score marks, chipped areas, flat spots and spalling **(see illustration)**. If damage is noted or wear is excessive new parts must be fitted.

12 Check the bottom of each clearance adjuster on each rocker and the top of each valve stem **(see illustration)**. If damage is noted or wear is excessive, the rocker arms and valves must be replaced with new ones as required.

13 Check for freeplay between each rocker arm and its shaft in the centre **(see illustration)**. The arms should move smoothly and freely with a light fit but no appreciable freeplay. Similarly check for freeplay between the shaft ends and the bores in the holder. Replace the arms and/or shafts with new ones if they appear worn.

14 Check the springs for deformation and replace them with new ones if necessary.

Installation

15 Work on one rocker and holder at a time, and make sure everything is returned to its original fitted position as noted on removal.

16 Slacken the valve clearance adjuster locknuts and thread the adjusters anti-clockwise to create maximum clearance. Lubricate each shaft and arm with molybdenum disulphide oil if available (a 50/50 mixture of molybdenum disulphide grease and engine oil), or clean engine oil if not. Fit the spring onto the arm as shown, then position the arm in its correct location, making sure the spring locates correctly, and slide its shaft all the way in **(see illustrations and 8.9)**. Check that the rocker moves freely on the shaft. Repeat for the other rockers.

17 Make sure the alternator rotor and camshaft timing marks are all aligned correctly according to your removal procedure (see Step 4 or 5).

18 Lubricate the camshaft lobes rocker arm contact pads.

19 If removed, fit the dowels (either into the holder or over the studs and into the cylinder head), making sure the short dowel is positioned for the front right stud and the long dowel for the rear left stud for each holder **(see illustration 8.8 and 8.20a)**.

20 Fit each rocker assembly onto the head, making sure the dowels locate correctly **(see illustration)**. Check that the holder is seated all round, then fit the washers and nuts **(see illustration)**. Tighten the nuts evenly and a little at a time in a criss-cross pattern, starting with the inner nuts and working to the outer if both holders were removed, tightening them all to 18 Nm.

21 Set the valve clearances (see Chapter 1).

22 Turn the engine anti-clockwise through

8.13 Check for freeplay between the arm and shaft

8.16a Fit the spring onto the rocker . . .

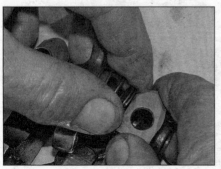

8.16b . . . then locate them in the holder and slide the shaft through

8.20a Fit the assembly over the studs

8.20b Fit the nuts with their washers and tighten as described

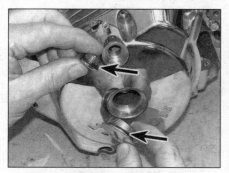

8.23 Fit the caps using new O-rings (arrowed) smeared with grease

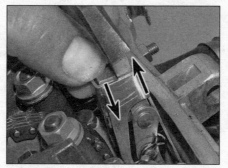

9.5a Pull the slider up and push the wedge down . . .

9.5b . . . and fit the pin when the hole is exposed

two full turns and check everything moves correctly **(see illustration 8.4a)**. Recheck the valve clearances.

23 Fit the timing inspection cap and crankshaft end cap using new O-rings, and smear them with grease **(see illustration)**.

24 Install the spark plugs (see Chapter 1).

25 Install the valve cover (see Section 6).

26 Check and adjust the idle speed (see Chapter 1).

9 Camshaft

Note: *The camshaft can be removed with the engine in the frame. If the engine has been removed ignore the steps that do not apply. One of two types of cam chain tensioner may be fitted, depending on manufacturer. Type A has an upper mounting bolt and a locknut on the lower adjuster bolt. Type B is self adjusting and has two mounting bolts.*

Removal

1 Remove the valve cover.

2 Remove the spark plugs (see Chapter 1).

3 Turn the engine so the No. 1 piston is at TDC on its compression stroke (see Section 8, Steps 3 and 4).

4 On engines with the Type A tensioner, slacken the locknut on the tensioner adjuster on the back of the cylinder block. Grasp the top of the tensioning slider using pliers and

pull it up as far as possible against the pull of the spring, then tighten the locknut to hold it there.

5 On engines with the Type B tensioner, first obtain a suitable nail or piece of wire at least 1 mm thick but no more than 2 mm, to use as a locking pin. Grasp the top of the tensioning slider using pliers and pull it up as far as possible against the pull of the spring while also pushing the front wedge down, and when the hole in the slider is visible insert the locking pin so it rests over the top of the wedge as shown **(see illustrations)**.

6 Remove the rocker assemblies (see Section 8).

7 Counter-hold the alternator rotor bolt and unscrew the camshaft sprocket bolts – turn the engine as before to expose each bolt in turn **(see illustration)**. With both bolts removed now turn the engine so one of the cut-outs in

9.7a Unscrew each camshaft bolt (arrowed) as described

the sprocket is at the top – this allows extra slack in the cam chain. Slip the sprocket off its mounting flange, then disengage the chain from it **(see illustrations)**.

8 Remove the camshaft **(see illustration)** – prevent the chain from dropping down its tunnel by securing it with a piece of wire or passing a rod through it. Remove the sprocket from the camshaft if required **(see illustration)**.

9 While the camshaft is out do not rotate the crankshaft unless necessary – the chain may drop down and bind between the crankshaft and case, which could damage these components. If you do need to turn the crank hold the chain up taut as you do so. Place a rag over the cylinder head.

10 Remove the bush from each end of the camshaft – the one on the left-hand end is secured by a circlip that has a washer fitted

9.7b Position the cut-out (arrowed) at the top and displace the sprocket . . .

9.7c . . . then disengage the chain . . .

9.8a . . . and remove the camshaft

9.8b Slip the sprocket off the shaft if required

9.10a The right-hand bush can be slipped off . . .

9.10b . . . remove the circlip (arrowed) and washer to release the left-hand bush

9.18 Apply some threadlock to each bolt before fitting it

behind it **(see illustrations)**. Mark each bush according to its end so it can be installed on the same end. Clean the camshaft and bushes.

Inspection

11 Inspect the bearing surfaces on the camshaft and bushes. Look for score marks, deep scratches and evidence of heat discoloration (blue appearance) and spalling (a pitted appearance). Note that if there is evidence of oil starvation the cause must be rectified before the engine is reassembled. Check that each bush is a good fit on its journal – they should turn smoothly and freely with a light fit but no appreciable freeplay. Fit new bushes if you are in any doubt.
12 Check the camshaft lobes and the contact pads on the rocker arms for heat discoloration, score marks, chipped areas, flat spots and spalling. If damage is noted or wear is excessive new parts must be fitted.
13 Check the cam chain sprocket for wear, cracks and other damage, and replace it with a new one if necessary. If the sprocket teeth are worn, the cam chain is also worn, and so probably is the sprocket on the crankshaft. If severe wear is apparent, the entire engine should be disassembled for inspection.
14 Check the cam chain (see Section 10).

Installation

15 Clean the thread of the camshaft sprocket bolts.
16 Make sure the index line on the alternator rotor aligns with the notch in the inspection hole rim so the No. 1 (left-hand) piston is at TDC (see Section 8, Step 4) **(see illustration 8.4b)** – if you need to turn the engine to realign the marks hold the cam chain up and keep it taut as you do. To make sure it is the No. 1 (left-hand) piston and not the No. 2 (right-hand) piston that is at TDC, hold a screwdriver in the spark plug hole and against the top of the piston while turning the engine and stop when it is at its highest point.
17 Lubricate the camshaft bushes and journals and the camshaft lobes with molybdenum disulphide oil if available (a 50/50 mixture of molybdenum disulphide

grease and engine oil), or clean engine oil if not. Fit each bush onto its correct end of the camshaft with the grooved rim facing in **(see illustration 9.10a)**. Fit the thrust washer against the left-hand bush then secure them a new circlip, making sure it locates correctly in the groove **(see illustration 9.10b)**.
18 Fit the sprocket onto the camshaft with the index lines facing the left-hand (notched) end **(see illustration 9.8b)**. Fit the camshaft onto the head with the notched end on the left, passing it through the chain, and aligning it so the notch faces back and is parallel to the head mating surface, and the lobes for the No. 1 cylinder valves are pointing down **(see illustration 9.8a)**. Make sure the locating pin on each end bush locates in its cut-out – the right-hand pin faces forwards and the left-hand pin faces back. Turn the sprocket so the index lines are parallel with the cylinder head mating surface, then pull up on the front run of the cam chain so it is taut and engage the chain on the sprocket **(see illustration 9.7c)** – at this stage due to the lack of slack you may not be able to fully engage the chain around the sprocket, but at least engage some teeth so the relative positions of the crankshaft and sprocket are correct for timing. Now you can turn the crankshaft, keeping the chain on the sprocket, until one of the cut-outs in the sprocket is at the top, allowing the sprocket to sit lower on the camshaft so the chain can be fully engaged **(see illustration 9.7b)**. Now turn the engine again and check that the marks on the rotor and sprocket are correct (see Section 8, Step 4) **(see illustrations 8.4b, c and d)**. Also check the camshaft is still correctly positioned, then mount the sprocket against the flange – if everything is correctly positioned the bolt holes should be aligned. Apply some thread locking compound to the sprocket bolts. Thread in one bolt and tighten it finger-tight. Now check that the timing marks on the rotor and camshaft and sprocket are correct (see Section 8, Step 4). Now turn the engine and fit the other bolt into the sprocket, and tighten it to 20 Nm, counter-holding the alternator rotor **(see illustration)**. Turn the engine again and tighten the first bolt to 20 Nm. Turn the engine again to realign the timing marks.
19 Use a piece of wooden dowel or other

suitable tool to press on the back of the cam chain tensioner blade via the tensioner bore in the cylinder block to ensure that any slack in the cam chain is taken up in the rear run of the chain. At this point check that the timing marks are still in **exact** alignment as described in Section 8, Step 4 **(see illustrations 8.4b, c and d)**. Note that it is easy to be slightly out (one tooth on the sprocket) without the marks appearing drastically out of alignment. If the marks are out unscrew the sprocket bolts and slide the sprocket off the camshaft, then reposition the sprocket in the chain as required, fit the sprocket back into the chain and onto the camshaft, and check the marks again. Make sure you are completely satisfied that the timing is correct before continuing. Leave the engine positioned at TDC for the No. 1 piston.
Caution: If the marks are not aligned exactly as described, the valve timing will be incorrect and the valves may strike the pistons, causing extensive damage to the engine.
20 Pour a small amount of engine oil into each well below the camshaft lobes.
21 Install the rocker assemblies (see Section 8).
22 On engines with the Type A tensioner, slacken the locknut on the tensioner adjuster until it releases and takes up the tension in the chain, then tighten the locknut.
23 On engines with the Type B tensioner, grasp the top of the tensioning slider using pliers and pull it up, then withdraw the locking pin and release the slider **(see illustration 9.5b)**.
24 Recheck the timing marks (see Section 8, Step 4) **(see illustrations 8.4b, c and d)**.
25 Set the valve clearances (see Chapter 1).
26 Turn the engine anti-clockwise through two full turns and check everything moves correctly **(see illustration 8.4a)**. Recheck valve clearances.
27 Fit the timing inspection cap and crankshaft end cap using new sealing O-rings if required, and smear them with grease **(see illustration 8.23)**.
28 Install the spark plugs (see Chapter 1).
29 Install the valve cover (see Section 6).
30 Check and adjust the idle speed (see Chapter 1).

10 Cam chain and guide blade

Note: *The cam chain guide blade can be removed with the engine in the frame. The cam chain, tensioner and its blade can only be removed once the crankcases have been separated.*

Removal

Cam chain

1 Remove the crankshaft (see Section 23).
2 Remove the cam chain tensioner (see Section 7).
3 Draw the cam chain off the crankshaft sprocket and out of the engine **(see illustration)**.

Guide blade

4 Remove the cylinder head (see Section 11).
5 Draw the guide blade out of the top of the cylinder block, noting how it locates **(see illustration)**.

Inspection

Cam chain

6 Check the chain for binding, kinks and any obvious damage and replace it with a new one if necessary. Check the camshaft and crankshaft sprocket teeth for wear and replace the cam chain, camshaft sprocket and crankshaft sprocket with a new set if necessary – the drive sprocket on the crankshaft is pressed on, so the crankshaft will have to be taken to a workshop or dealer equipped with an hydraulic press to remove it and to fit a new one. Note that if the chain is noisy when the engine is running, and there is nothing obviously wrong with it, then the fault could be in the tensioner (see Section 7).

Guide blade

7 Check the sliding surface and edges of

10.3 Disengage the cam chain from the sprocket and slip it out past the bearing holder

the blade for excessive wear, deep grooves, cracking and other obvious damage, and replace it with a new one if necessary.

Installation

Cam chain

8 Installation of the chain is the reverse of removal. Make sure the chain is correctly positioned in relation to the centre main bearing holder and tensioner pivot as shown before fitting the tensioner and check again before installing the crankshaft **(see illustration)**.

Guide blade

9 Installation of the guide blade is the reverse of removal. Make sure the bottom of the guide blade sits in its seat and the lugs near its top locate in the cut-outs in the cylinder block **(see illustration)**.

11 Cylinder head

Note: *Whether the cylinder head can be removed with the engine in the frame depends on the model of bike you have and the type*

10.5 Lift the guide blade out, noting now it locates

of frame used – check the clearance between the top of the engine and frame (after the valve cover has been removed) to see whether there is enough space for the cylinder head to be lifted up off the studs. If not, remove the engine (see Section 4). If the engine has been removed ignore the steps that do not apply.

Removal

1 Remove the fuel tank, exhaust system and carburettor(s) (see Chapter 4). Plug the engine intake duct(s) with clean rag. Release the spark plug leads from their guides on the intake duct(s) where fitted **(see illustration 11.13)**.
2 Remove the upper engine mounting bolt (that passes through the back of the head), and detach the mounting brackets from the frame **(see illustration 4.18b)**.
3 On models with an air induction system that routes the air through the cylinder head or block, disconnect the air hose(s) from the pipe(s), and if necessary remove the control valve along with the hose(s) and its bracket as required according to model to minimise obstruction to engine removal (see Chapter 4). Also detach the pipe(s) from the head or block if required – a new gasket(s) or O-ring(s) (according to model) will be needed.

10.8 Make sure the chain is correctly positioned in relation to the holder upper mounting lug (A) and the tensioner pivot (B)

10.9 Make sure the lugs (arrowed) locate in the cut-outs

11.7 Type B tensioner mounting bolts (arrowed)

11.8a Unscrew the 6 mm bolts (arrowed) – note that the rocker assemblies will have already been removed

11.8b The front bolt is secured by the captive nut

4 On liquid-cooled versions drain the cooling system (see Chapter 3). If the thermostat housing is mounted on the engine disconnect the wire from the temperature sensor. If required remove the thermostat housing (see Chapter 3). If not, release the clamps securing the hoses to the housing and detach them.

5 Remove the rocker assemblies (see Section 8) and the camshaft (see Section 9).

6 On engines with the Type A tensioner (see **Note** in Section 7), unscrew the locknut on the tensioner adjuster and remove the washer and O-ring. Unscrew the tensioner mounting bolt and remove the O-ring(s). Push the tensioner forwards until the adjuster stud is clear of its hole. Discard the O-rings – new ones should be used.

7 On engines with the Type B tensioner (see **Note** in Section 7), unscrew the mounting bolts, noting the washer(s) and O-rings **(see illustration)**. Discard the O-rings – new ones should be used.

8 The cylinder head is mainly secured by the rocker assembly nuts, which have already been removed. There are also three 6 mm bolts, one outside the head at the front and

two inside at the back **(see illustration)** – unscrew and remove these bolts, noting the captive nut in the cylinder block for the front bolt **(see illustration)**.

9 Hold the cam chain up and lift the cylinder head up off the block, then pass the cam chain down through the tunnel **(see illustration)**. Do not let the chain fall into the engine – lay it over the front or back of the block and secure it with a piece of wire. If the head is stuck, tap around the joint faces with a soft-faced mallet. Do not attempt to free it by inserting a screwdriver between the head and block mating surfaces – you'll damage them.

10 Remove the cylinder head gasket and discard it as a new one must be used. If they are loose, remove the dowels from the cylinder block or the underside of the cylinder head **(see illustration 11.15)**. On models with an air induction system that routes the air through the cylinder block, if there is an O-ring for the air passage remove it – a new one should used. On these models also make sure when buying the new gasket that it comes with a hole for the air passage.

11 Check the cylinder head gasket and the mating surfaces on the cylinder head and

cylinder block for signs of leakage, which could indicate warpage. Refer to Section 12 and check the cylinder head gasket surface for warpage.

12 Clean all traces of old gasket material from the cylinder head and cylinder block. If a scraper is used, take care not to scratch or gouge the soft aluminium. Be careful not to let any of the gasket material fall into the cylinder bore or the oil passages.

13 If required unscrew the intake duct nuts and remove the duct(s) and any spacing plate(s) and where fitted the HT lead guides **(see illustration)**. Discard the O-rings – new ones must be used. Make sure the studs are tight in the head. If loose, remove them, clean them and refit them using some threadlock – refer to Section 13, Step 8 for details on stud removal and tightening.

Installation

14 If removed fit new O-ring(s) smeared with grease into the grooves in the intake duct(s) and any spacing plate(s), then fit the intake duct(s) onto the head and tighten the nuts.

15 If removed, fit the dowels into the cylinder

11.9 Carefully lift the head up off the block

11.13 Intake duct nuts (A) – twin CV carb type shown. Note the HT lead guide (B)

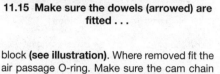

11.15 Make sure the dowels (arrowed) are fitted . . .

11.16 . . . and the gasket is the correct way up

11.19 Use new O-rings and do not forget any washers on the tensioner bolts/stud – Type B tensioner shown

block **(see illustration)**. Where removed fit the air passage O-ring. Make sure the cam chain guide blade is correctly seated (see Section 10).

16 Ensure both cylinder head and cylinder block mating surfaces are clean. Lay the new head gasket onto the block, locating it over the dowels and making sure all the holes are correctly aligned – where present the UP mark should read correctly **(see illustration)**. Never reuse the old gasket.

17 Carefully fit the cylinder head onto the block, feeding the cam chain up through the tunnel as you do, and making sure it locates correctly over the cam chain tensioner and onto the dowels **(see illustration 11.9)**. Secure the chain in place with a piece of wire to prevent it from falling back down.

18 Make sure the captive washer for the front 6 mm bolt is in place in the block **(see illustration 11.8b)**. Fit the bolts and tighten them finger-tight only at this stage **(see illustration 11.8a)**.

19 Secure the cam chain tensioner to the head using new O-rings on the bolts/stud, not forgetting the washer(s), as required according to type (see Step 6 or 7) **(see illustration)**. On engines with the type A tensioner refer to Section 9, Step 4, and pull up and lock the tensioning slider as described.

20 Install the camshaft (see Section 9) and the rocker assemblies (see Section 8).

21 Now tighten the 6 mm bolts **(see illustration 11.8a)**.

22 Remove the rag from the engine intake duct(s). Install the carburettor(s) (see Chapter 4).

23 Install the upper engine mounting bolt and brackets **(see illustration 4.18b)**.

24 Where fitted, and if removed, fit the air induction system pipe(s) onto the cylinder block or head using a new gasket(s) or O-ring(s) and tighten the bolts. Fit the hose(s) and control valve as required according to removal (see Chapter 4).

25 On liquid-cooled versions install the thermostat housing if removed (see Chapter 3). If not and where applicable, fit the hoses onto their unions and secure them with the clamps. Connect the wire to the temperature sensor. Refill the cooling system (see Chapter 3).

26 Install the exhaust system and fuel tank (see Chapter 4).

12 Cylinder head and valve overhaul

Refer to the procedure in Chapter 2A, Section 9. The only difference is in the valve spring seat. Some engines may have a separate seat for each spring, others may have one shaped seat for both springs.

13 Cylinder block

Note: *Whether the cylinder block can be removed with the engine in the frame depends on the model of bike you have and the type of frame used – check the clearance between the top of the engine and frame (after the valve cover has been removed) to see whether there is enough space for the cylinder head to be lifted up off the studs. If not, remove the engine (see Section 4). If the engine has been removed ignore the steps that do not apply.*

Removal

1 Remove the cylinder head (see Section 11). Remove the cam chain guide blade (see Section 10).

2 On liquid-cooled engines, release the clamp securing the coolant hose to the block and

13.3 Carefully lift the block up off the crankcase

detach it, being prepared with a rag to catch any residual coolant.

3 Keeping the cam chain taut, pull the cylinder block up off the crankcase, then pass the chain down through the block and lay it over the front **(see illustration)**. If the block is stuck, tap around the joint faces with a soft-faced mallet – do not attempt to free it by inserting a screwdriver between the block and crankcase mating surfaces as you'll damage them. Stuff some clean rag around each connecting rod to protect and support it and the piston, and to prevent anything falling into the engine. Similarly stuff some rag into the cam chain tunnel.

4 Remove the base gasket and discard it as a new one must be used. If loose, remove the dowels from the crankcase or the underside of the cylinder block **(see illustration)**.

5 Clean all traces of old gasket material and any sealant from the cylinder block and crankcase. If a scraper is used, take care not to scratch or gouge the soft aluminium. Be careful not to let any of the gasket material fall into the engine.

Inspection

Note: *Do not attempt to separate the cylinder liners from the cylinder block.*

6 Refer to Chapter 2A, Section 10.

Installation

7 Check that the mating surfaces of the cylinder block and crankcase are free from oil, sealant and pieces of old gasket.

8 Check that all the studs are tight in the

13.4 Remove the dowels (arrowed) if loose

13.8 Studs can be tightened using two nuts locked together

13.13 Carefully lower the block onto the No. 1 piston . . .

13.14 . . . and feed each ring into the bore as you lower the block

crankcase. If any are loose, or need to be replaced with new ones, remove them. Clean their threads and smear them with clean engine oil. Fit them into the crankcase and tighten them using a stud tool, or by threading two nuts onto the top of the stud and tightening them together so they are locked on the stud, then tighten the stud by turning the upper of the two nuts **(see illustration)**.

9 Fit the dowels over the studs and into the crankcase and push them firmly home **(see illustration 13.4)**. Apply a dab of RTV sealant to the short sections of crankcase mating surface that the block sits on.

10 Lay the new base gasket in place, locating it over the dowels. The gasket can only fit one way, so if all the holes do not line up properly it is the wrong way round. Never re-use the old gasket.

11 Rotate the crankshaft so that the No. 1 piston is at its highest point (top dead centre). Make sure the piston ring end gaps are positioned 120° apart before fitting the cylinder block (see Section 14). If possible, have an assistant to support the cylinder block while the piston rings are fed into the bore.

12 Lubricate the cylinder bores, pistons and piston rings with clean engine oil.

13 Carefully lower the block over the studs and onto the No. 1 piston until the crown fits into the bore, holding the underside of the piston if you are not using a support to prevent it dropping, and making sure it enters the bore squarely and does not get cocked sideways **(see illustration)**. Pass the cam chain up through the block and secure it using some wire.

14 Carefully compress and feed each ring into the bore as the cylinder is lowered **(see illustration)**. If necessary, use a soft mallet to gently tap the cylinder down, but do not use force if it appears to be stuck as the piston and/or rings will be damaged.

15 When the No. 1 piston and rings are correctly located in the bore, press the cylinder block down, pushing the piston down and so turning the crankshaft with it, so that the No. 2 piston rises to meet the block, and as it enters feed its rings in as with the first piston. When both pistons are correctly located in their bores push the block down onto the base gasket, making sure the dowels locate.

16 Fit the cam chain guide blade (see Section 10).

17 Hold the block down and turn the crankshaft to check that everything moves as it should.

18 Install the cylinder head (see Section 11).

19 On liquid-cooled models connect the coolant hose and tighten the clamp. Refill the cooling system (see Chapter 3).

14 Pistons and piston rings

Note: *Whether the pistons can be removed with the engine in the frame depends on the model of bike you have and the type of frame used – check the clearance between the top of the engine and frame (after the valve cover has been removed) to see whether there is enough space for the cylinder head to be lifted*

up off the studs. If not, remove the engine (see Section 4). If the engine has been removed ignore the steps that do not apply.

1 Refer to Chapter 2A, Sections 11 and 12. Note that on the engine photographed each piston was marked IN **(see illustration)**, which faces the intake side (rear) of the engine – also mark the pistons 1 and 2 or L and R according to side so they don't get mixed up and can be refitted to their original rods.

15 Alternator and starter clutch

Note: *The starter clutch is mounted on the back of the alternator rotor. They can be removed with the engine in the frame. If the engine has been removed, ignore the steps which do not apply.*

Alternator check

1 Checking of the charging system is covered in Chapter 9.

Starter clutch check

2 The operation of the starter clutch can be checked while it is in situ. Remove the alternator cover, starter clutch drive sprocket and chain (see Steps 3 to 8). Check that the starter driven sprocket is able to rotate freely clockwise as you look at, but locks when rotated anti-clockwise. If not, the starter clutch is faulty and should be removed for inspection.

Removal

3 Remove any fairing panels as required according to model (see Chapter 8).

4 Drain the engine oil (see Chapter 1). Remove the front sprocket cover (see Chapter 7).

5 Trace the alternator and pick-up coil wiring from the cover on the left-hand side of the engine and disconnect it at the connectors **(see illustration 4.14a)**. Release the wiring from any ties **(see illustration 4.14b)**, and from its cut-out above the front sprocket.

6 Working in a criss-cross pattern, evenly slacken the alternator cover bolts, noting which fits where as they vary in length **(see illustration)**. **Note:** *As each bolt is removed, store it in its relative position in a cardboard*

14.1 Note the mark on the piston and which way it faces

15.6a Unscrew the bolts (arrowed) and remove the cover . . .

15.6b . . . and disconnect the wiring connector

15.7a Draw the drive sprocket off the shaft . . .

15.7b . . . and remove the chain

template of the cover **(see illustration 22.3b)**. *This will ensure all bolts are returned to their original locations on reassembly.* Draw the cover off the engine, noting that it will be restrained by the force of the rotor magnets, and disconnect the neutral switch wiring connector **(see illustration)**.

7 Slip the drive sprocket off the end of the starter motor shaft and remove it along with the chain **(see illustrations)**.

8 Remove and discard the outer gasket **(see illustration 15.27)**. Remove the sprocket retainer from the backing plate **(see illustration)**.

9 To remove the rotor bolt it is necessary to prevent the rotor turning by counter-holding it using a rotor holder or strap. With the rotor held unscrew the bolt **(see illustration)**.

10 To remove the rotor from the shaft it is necessary to use a rotor puller – several are commercially available, but make sure you buy the right one as shown. Thread the puller into the rotor, then hold the rotor as before and tighten the puller until the rotor is displaced from the shaft **(see illustration)**. If the rotor is very tight, heat around the centre hub using a hot air gun, then tap the end of the puller **(see illustration)**.

11 Slide the starter driven sprocket off the end of the crankshaft if it didn't come off with the rotor **(see illustration)**. Remove the cover backing plate, then remove the inner gasket **(see illustration)**. Remove the dowels

15.8 Unscrew the bolt (arrowed) and remove the retainer, noting how it locates

15.9 Using a rotor strap to hold the rotor while unscrewing the bolt

15.10a This shows a multi-application commercial puller that threads into the rotor hub

15.10b Heat the hub if necessary to ease removal

15.11a Slide the sprocket off the crankshaft

15.11b Remove the backing plate and inner gasket

15.12 Remove the locating pin (arrowed) if loose

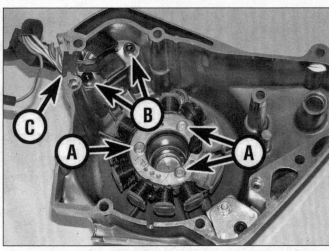

15.13 Unscrew the stator bolts (A) and the pick-up bolts (B), and free the grommet (C)

from the crankcase if loose **(see illustration 15.21a)**.

12 Note the rotor locating pin in the crankshaft and remove it if loose **(see illustration)**. If required detach the starter clutch from the rotor (see Step 16).

13 To remove the stator and pick-up coil from the cover, undo the bolts then lift them out, releasing the wiring grommet **(see illustration)**.

Starter clutch inspection

14 With the rotor face down on a workbench and the starter driven sprocket in the starter clutch, check that the sprocket rotates freely anti-clockwise and locks against the rotor clockwise **(see illustration)**. If it doesn't, remove the starter driven sprocket, rotating it anti-clockwise as you do.

15 Check the condition of the rollers and the corresponding surface on the driven sprocket hub **(see illustration)**. If the rollers are damaged, marked or flattened at any point, remove them along with the plungers and springs, noting how they fit, and replace them with new ones **(see illustrations)**.

16 To remove the starter clutch from the back of the alternator rotor hold the rotor using a

holding strap and unscrew the three bolts **(see illustration)** – note the locating pin. Clean the threads of the bolts and on installation apply a suitable non-permanent thread locking compound.

17 Check the bush in the starter driven gear hub and its bearing surface on the crankshaft **(see illustration)**. If the bush shows signs of excessive wear (the groove in the surface of the bush for holding the oil will be barely visible) replace the driven sprocket with a new one.

18 Check the condition of the oil seal on the hub **(see illustration 15.17)** and that in the

15.14 Check the operation of the clutch as described

15.15a Check the rollers and hub for wear and damage

15.15b Remove the rollers . . .

15.15c . . . plungers and springs

15.16 Starter clutch bolts (arrowed)

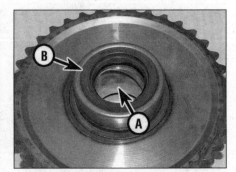

15.17 Check the bush (A) for wear. It is best to fit a new hub oil seal (B) . . .

15.18 . . . and crankcase oil seal (arrowed)

15.21a Fit the dowels (arrowed) and a new inner gasket . . .

15.21b . . . and the backing plate

crankcase **(see illustration)** and replace them with new ones if necessary (though it is good practice to fit new ones as a matter of course) – lever the old ones out using a seal hook or screwdriver. Press the new ones in or tap them in using a socket, with the marked side facing out, and making sure they enter square.

19 Check the splines of the starter motor drive shaft and in the drive sprocket, and check the drive and driven sprocket teeth and the chain. Replace the chain and sprockets and/or starter motor as required if worn or chipped teeth are discovered.

Installation

20 Where applicable and if removed fit the springs, plungers and rollers into the starter clutch, making sure they locate correctly **(see illustrations 15.15c and b)**. Apply clean engine oil to the rollers.

21 Fit the dowels into the crankcase if removed. Fit a new inner gasket, locating it over the dowels **(see illustration)**. Fit the cover backing plate, again locating it over the dowels **(see illustration)**.

22 Lubricate the outside of the starter driven sprocket hub on each side of the sprocket and the oil seal lips in the hub and crankcase with clean engine oil, then fit the sprocket into the clutch, turning it anti-clockwise as you do **(see illustration)**. Do not lubricate the bush on the inside.

23 Smear some oil onto the flat section of the crankshaft that the driven sprocket bush runs

on. Clean the tapered end of the crankshaft and the corresponding mating surface on the inside of the rotor with a suitable solvent. Fit the locating pin into its hole in the crankshaft if removed **(see illustration 15.12)**.

24 Make sure that no metal objects have attached themselves to the magnet on the inside of the rotor. Slide the rotor onto the shaft, making sure the groove on the inside is aligned with and fits over the locating pin **(see illustration)**. Give the rotor hub a gentle tap with a soft mallet to seat it.

25 Fit the rotor bolt and tighten it to 60 Nm, using the method employed on removal to prevent the rotor from turning **(see illustrations)**.

26 Clean the threads of the sprocket retainer bolt. Apply some fresh threadlock, then fit the

retainer as shown and tighten the bolt **(see illustration 15.8)**.

27 Fit a new outer gasket, locating it over the dowels **(see illustration)**.

28 Loop the chain around the driven sprocket, then fit the drive sprocket into the chain and slide it onto the starter motor shaft **(see illustrations 15.7b and a)**.

29 If removed clean the stator and pick-up coil wiring grommet and apply some fresh sealant, then fit the stator and coil into the cover and seat the grommet **(see illustration 15.13)**. Apply a suitable thread locking compound to the bolts, and tighten them.

30 Before fitting the cover install the neutral switch if removed (see Chapter 9). Install the alternator cover, connecting the neutral switch

15.22 Lubricate the outside of each hub (arrowed) then fit the sprocket into the clutch

15.24 Slide the rotor onto the shaft, aligning the cut-out with the pin

15.25a Fit the bolt . . .

15.25b . . . and tighten it to the specified torque

15.27 Fit the new outer gasket

15.30 Fit the cover, noting that it will be drawn on by the magnets

16.5 Unscrew the bolts (arrowed) and remove the cover

16.6 Unscrew the bolts (arrowed) as described

wiring as you offer it up **(see illustration 15.6b)**, and noting that the rotor magnets will forcibly draw the cover/stator on, making sure it locates onto the dowels **(see illustration)**. Fit the cover bolts in their correct locations and tighten them evenly in a criss-cross sequence **(see illustration 15.6a)**.

31 Reconnect the wiring at the connectors **(see illustration 4.14a)** – make sure it is correctly routed and secured, and the grommet is seated in its cut-out.

32 Replenish the engine oil. Install the front sprocket cover (see Chapter 7). Install any body panels as required according to model.

16 Clutch

Note: *The clutch can be removed with the engine in the frame. If the engine has been removed, ignore the steps that don't apply.*

Clutch removal

1 Remove any fairing panels as required according to model (see Chapter 8). Also remove the exhaust, brake pedal, footrest or footrest assembly if they get in the way of removing the clutch cover, again as required according to model (see Chapters 4 and 5).

2 Drain the engine oil (see Chapter 1). On liquid-cooled models drain the coolant (see Chapter 3). Release the clamps securing the coolant hoses to the water pump and detach the hoses.

3 Where fitted remove the kickstart lever, making an alignment mark with the shaft if there is none visible so it can be correctly installed later.

4 Detach the clutch cable and position it clear (see Section 17). Where fitted detach the tachometer cable.

5 Working evenly in a criss-cross pattern, unscrew the clutch cover bolts, noting the cable bracket and which length bolts fit where **(see illustration)**. **Note:** *As each bolt is removed, store it in its relative position in a cardboard template of the cover **(see illustration 22.3b)**. This will ensure all bolts are returned to their original locations on reassembly.* Remove the cover, being prepared to catch any residual oil – note the clutch pushrod and remove it for safekeeping **(see illustration 16.24a)**. Remove the gasket and discard it. Remove the two dowels from either the cover or the crankcase if they are loose. Note that there is a sprung oil nozzle located in the end of the crankshaft – make sure it has not come away with the cover, and refit it if it has, aligning the cut-out with the pin **(see illustration 16.24b)**.

6 Working in a criss-cross pattern, gradually slacken the clutch spring bolts until pressure is released **(see illustration)**. To prevent the assembly from turning, cover it with a rag and hold it securely – the bolts are not very tight. If available, have an assistant hold the clutch while you unscrew the bolts. Remove the bolts, lifter plate and springs **(see illustrations 16.23c and b)**. Remove the bearing from the lifter plate if it is loose **(see illustration 16.23a)**.

7 To unscrew the clutch nut a peg spanner, such as the one shown, is needed **(see illustration)** – these are commercially available from good suppliers of specialist motorcycle tools, but measure the nut to make sure you get the correct size. Alternatively one can be made by cutting castellations into an old socket **(see Tool Tip)**. You also need to counter-hold the shaft to prevent it turning while slackening the nut – select a high gear and use a clutch holding tool (again available from good suppliers of specialist motorcycle tools) to hold the front sprocket as shown **(see illustrations)**. Alternatively, if the engine is in the frame, select a high gear and hold the rear brake on hard. Unscrew the nut and remove the washer, noting which way round it fits.

TOOL TiP

A peg spanner can be made by cutting castellations into a socket of the correct size using a hacksaw.

16.7a Unscrew the clutch nut using a peg spanner

16.7b Counter-hold the sprocket using the reverse (pegged) side of a clutch holding tool . . .

16.7c . . . while unscrewing the nut

16.8 Draw the complete clutch plate assembly off the shaft

16.9a Turn the washer to unlock it and slide it off . . .

16.9b . . . then remove the clutch housing . . .

8 Draw the complete clutch plate assembly off using the pressure plate posts **(see illustration)**. Unless the plates are being replaced with new ones, keep the assembly together. To disassemble it place the clutch centre face down and remove the pressure plate from the back **(see illustration 16.19g)**. Remove the clutch friction and plain plates, noting how they fit and keeping them in order **(see illustrations 16.19f, e and d)** – note that the innermost friction plate has a larger internal diameter allowing it to sit round the anti-judder spring and its seat. Remove the anti-judder spring and seat, noting how they fit **(see illustrations 16.19b and a)**.

9 Turn the splined washer to unlock the splines and slide it off the shaft **(see illustration)**. Draw the clutch housing off the shaft **(see illustration)**. Remove the thrust washer **(see illustration)**.

Inspection

10 After an extended period of service the clutch friction plates will wear and promote clutch slip. Measure the thickness of each friction plate using a Vernier caliper **(see illustration)**. If the friction material shows obvious signs of wear (or is worn down to less than 2.6 mm), the plates smell burnt or are glazed, the friction plates must be replaced with a new set.

11 The plain plates should not show any signs of excess heating (bluing). Check for distortion using a flat surface and feeler gauge **(see illustration)**. If any plate is warped more than 0.2 mm, or shows signs of bluing, all plain plates must be replaced with a new set.

12 Measure the free length of each clutch spring using a Vernier caliper **(see illustration)**. Place each spring upright on a

flat surface and check it for bend by placing a ruler against it, or alternatively lay it against a set square. If any spring has sagged in comparison to the others, or if the bend in any spring is excessive, replace all the springs as a set.

13 Inspect the friction plates and the clutch housing for burrs and indentations on the edges of the protruding tabs on the plates and/or the slots in the housing **(see illustration)**. Similarly check for wear between the inner teeth of the plain plates and the slots in the clutch centre **(see illustration)**. Wear of this nature will cause clutch drag and slow disengagement during gear changes as the plates will snag when the pressure plate is lifted. With care a small amount of wear can be corrected by dressing with a fine file, but if this is excessive the worn components should be replaced with new ones.

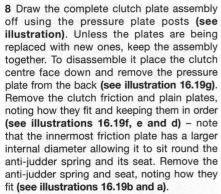

16.9c . . . and the thrust washer

16.10 Measuring clutch friction plate thickness

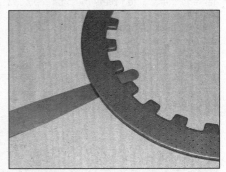

16.11 Check the plain plates for warpage

16.12 Measure the free length of the clutch springs and check them for bend

16.13a Check the friction plate tabs and housing slots . . .

16.13b . . . and the plain plate teeth and centre slots as described

16.14 Check the primary drive and driven gear teeth

16.16a Withdraw the shaft and remove the spring

16.16b Check the oil seal and bearings (arrowed)

16.16c Make sure the spring ends (arrowed) locate correctly

action is stiff or rough, withdraw the shaft and remove the spring, noting how its ends locate **(see illustration)**. Clean and check the condition of the oil seal and bearings and replace them with new ones if necessary **(see illustration)** – lever the oil seal out using a seal hook or screwdriver, then draw the bearings out using and internal expanding puller with slide-hammer attachment. Drive the new bearings and seal in using a suitable drift or socket. Lubricate the release mechanism shaft with molybdenum disulphide oil (a 50/50 mixture of molybdenum disulphide grease and engine oil) before installing it. Locate the spring then insert the shaft, making sure the straight end locates in the hole in the bottom of the shaft, and seat the hooked end over the lug in the cover **(see illustration)**. Fit the pushrod, turning the shaft so it is correctly aligned **(see illustration 16.24a)**. Check the mechanism works correctly – when turning the shaft the pushrod should move out.

17 Where fitted clean and check the kickstart shaft oil seal and the shaft bore in the cover. The seal can be replaced by levering the old one out with a seal hook or screwdriver and pressing the new one in. Where fitted also check the tachometer drive shaft and its seal **(see illustrations)**.

Installation

18 Remove all traces of old gasket from the crankcase and clutch cover surfaces.

19 If the clutch plate assembly was disassembled, fit the anti-judder spring seat, then fit the spring so its outer edge is raised off the seat. Coat each clutch plate with engine oil, then build up the plates on the clutch centre, starting with the inner friction plate that has a larger internal diameter so its sits around the anti-judder spring and seat, then fit a plain plate, then alternating standard friction and plain plates until all are

14 Inspect the contact surfaces of the clutch housing and the guide on the input shaft. If there are any signs of wear, pitting or other damage the affected parts must be replaced with new ones. Check the teeth of the primary driven gear on the back of the clutch housing and the corresponding teeth of the primary drive gear on the crankshaft **(see illustration)**. Replace the clutch housing and/or primary drive gear with a new one if worn or chipped teeth are discovered – refer to Section 19 for the primary drive gear.

15 Check the lifter plate and its bearing for signs of wear or damage and roughness **(see illustration 16.23a)**. Check that the bearing outer race is a good fit in the centre of the lifter, and that the bearing rotates freely without any rough spots. Check the pushrod and the cam on the release mechanism shaft for signs of wear or damage **(see illustration 16.24a)**. Replace any parts necessary with new ones.

16 Check the release mechanism in the clutch cover for a smooth action. If the

16.17a Lever out the seal . . .

16.17b . . . and press a new one into place

16.19a Fit the spring seat . . .

16.19b . . . then the spring . . .

16.19c . . . so its outer edge is raised off the seat

16.19d Fit the inner plate around the spring . . .

16.19e . . . then fit a plain plate . . .

16.19f . . . and a friction plate, and so on

installed **(see illustrations)**. Fit the pressure plate into the back of the pack, making sure its castellations engage with the clutch centre **(see illustration)**. Grasp the pack and turn it on its side, then pull on the pressure plate posts and check for any freeplay between the clutch plates – there should be none; if there is, it means the pressure plate has not located properly. Align the tabs of the friction plates.

20 Slide the thrust washer onto the shaft, followed by the clutch housing **(see illustrations 16.9c and b)**. Slide the splined washer on, then turn it in the groove so the splines lock the washer on the shaft **(see illustrations)**.

21 Fit the clutch plate assembly into the clutch housing, locating the friction plate tabs in the slots **(see illustration 16.8)**.

16.19g Fitting the clutch pressure plate

22 Fit the clutch nut lockwasher with its marked or chamfered face outwards **(see illustration)**. Thread the nut on and tighten

16.20a Slide the washer on . . .

it to 45 Nm, counter-holding the shaft as on removal **(see illustration)**.

23 Fit the bearing into the lifter plate if

16.20b . . . then turn it in the groove to lock it on the shaft

16.22a Fit the lockwasher . . .

16.22b . . . then the clutch nut

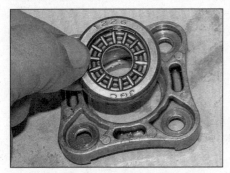

16.23a Fit the bearing into the plate

16.23b Fit the springs . . .

16.23c . . . and the lifter plate, and tighten the bolts as described

16.24a Turn the shaft and fit the pushrod end against its flat section

16.24b Make sure the sprung oil nozzle is in place

16.25a Fit the cover

removed, and lubricate it with oil **(see illustration)**. Fit the clutch springs, lifter plate and bolts and tighten them evenly and a little at a time in a criss-cross sequence **(see illustrations)**.

24 Fit the pushrod into the clutch cover, turning the shaft so it is correctly aligned **(see illustration)**. Make sure the oil nozzle and its spring are in the end of the crankshaft, and that the nozzle moves in and out freely against spring pressure **(see illustration)**.

25 Fit the two dowels into the crankcase if removed, then fit a new gasket, locating it over the dowels. Install the cover, making sure

the pushrod stays in place **(see illustration)**. Install all the bolts finger-tight, not forgetting the cable bracket, then tighten them evenly and a little at a time in a criss-cross pattern **(see illustration)**.

26 Reconnect the clutch cable (see Section 17) then adjust freeplay (see Chapter 1). Where fitted connect the tachometer cable.

27 On liquid-cooled models fit the coolant hoses onto their unions on the water pump and secure them with the clamps. Refill the cooling system (see Chapter 3).

28 Fill the engine with oil to the correct level (see Chapter 1 and *Pre-ride checks*). Where

fitted install the kickstart lever, and any other removed components.

17 Clutch cable

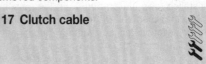

1 Where fitted pull back the rubber boot covering the adjuster at the handlebar end of the cable. Fully slacken the lockring on the adjuster at the handlebar end of the cable, then thread the adjuster fully in **(see illustration)**. This provides freeplay in the cable and resets the adjuster to the beginning of its span.

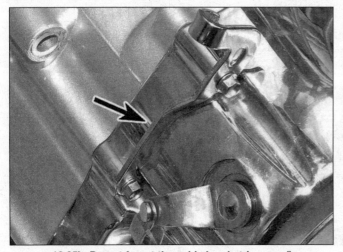

16.25b Do not forget the cable bracket (arrowed)

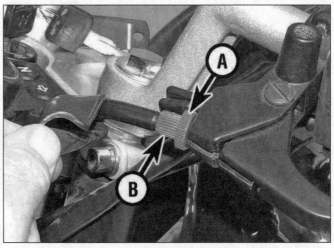

17.1 Pull back the boot, slacken the lockring (A) and turn the adjuster (B) in

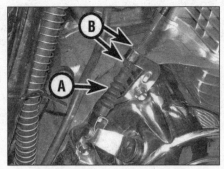

17.3a Pull the boot (A) down where fitted, then slacken the nuts (B) as described . . .

17.3b . . . then free the cable end from the arm . . .

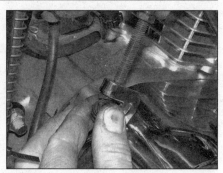

17.3c . . . and draw the cable out of the bracket

2 Remove any fairing panels as required to access the cable holder on the right-hand side of the engine (see Chapter 8).

3 Where fitted pull the rubber boot off the bottom of the cable adjuster **(see illustration)**. Slacken the bottom nut and thread it off, then thread the top nut fully up the adjuster **(see illustration)**. Free the cable end from the release arm then draw the adjuster out of the bracket and slip the inner cable out the side **(see illustration)**.

4 Align the slots in the adjuster and lockring at the handlebar end of the cable with that in the lever bracket, then pull the outer cable end from the socket in the adjuster and release the inner cable from the lever **(see illustrations)**. Remove the cable from the machine, noting its routing.

5 Installation is the reverse of removal. Apply grease to the cable ends. Make sure the cable is correctly routed through its guides.

Before removing the cable from the bike, tape the lower end of the new cable to the upper end of the old cable. Slowly pull the lower end of the old cable out, guiding the new cable down into position. Using this method will ensure the cable is routed correctly.

Adjust the amount of clutch lever freeplay (see Chapter 1).

18 Oil pump

Note: *The oil pump can be removed with the engine in the frame.*

Removal

1 Remove the clutch cover (see Section 16, Steps 1 to 5).

2 Turn the pump driven gear so the holes align with the pump screws **(see illustration)** – to turn the gear, first remove the spark plugs to reduce compression (see Chapter 1), then turn the clutch housing.

3 Undo the screws and remove the pump from the crankcase. If you cannot undo the screws using conventional tools, unscrew the gear cover bolts and remove the cover, then remove the gear and shaft, and use an impact screwdriver to jar them loose **(see illustrations)** – if the engine is out of the frame turn it on its left-hand side and support it securely on wooden blocks to do this.

4 Remove the O-ring from the crankcase and discard it **(see illustration 18.15)** – a new one

17.4a Free the outer cable from the adjuster . . .

17.4b . . . and the inner cable from the lever

18.2 Align the holes in the gear with the screws (arrowed)

18.3a Undo the bolts (arrowed) and remove the cover . . .

18.3b . . . and the gear . . .

18.3c . . . and use an impact driver

18.4 Remove the strainer

18.5 Undo the screw (arrowed) and remove the cover

18.8 Fit the shaft, aligning the flats

must be used. Remove the strainer from the bottom of the pump **(see illustration)**.

Inspection

Note: *When removing the rotors from the oil pump, look for any punch marks facing into or out of the pump body. The marks serve as a guide to which way round to fit the rotors on installation. Refitting the rotors in their original positions will ensure that mated surfaces continue to run together. If there are no marks, make your own, or keep the rotors a particular way up, to ensure they are correctly installed.*

5 Remove the cover, gear and shaft if not already done when removing the pump (see Step 3). Undo the rotor cover screw and remove the cover, noting how it locates on the pin **(see illustration)**. Remove the pin if loose. Remove the gasket where fitted and discard it – a new one must be used. Remove the inner

and outer rotors, noting which way round they fit.

6 Clean all the components in solvent. Clean the strainer, removing all debris from the mesh using an old toothbrush. Check the mesh for holes and damage and replace it with a new one if necessary.

7 Inspect the pump body and rotors for scoring and wear. If any damage, scoring or uneven or excessive wear is evident, replace the components with new ones.

8 Fit the outer and inner rotors into the pump. Fit the shaft into the pump, aligning the flats between it and the inner rotor **(see illustration)**.

9 Measure the clearance between the inner rotor tip and the outer rotor with a feeler gauge, no more than 0.2 mm is allowed **(see illustration)**.

10 Measure the clearance between the

outer rotor and the pump body with a feeler gauge; no more than 0.25 mm is allowed **(see illustration)**.

11 Check the pump driven gear and shaft for wear or damage, and replace them with new ones if necessary. If wear and/or broken teeth are found on the gear check the drive gear teeth as well (Section 19).

12 If the pump is good, make sure all the components are clean, then lubricate them with new engine oil and reassemble the pump as described in Step 8. Fit the rotor cover locating pin if removed. Fit the cover, along with a new gasket where removed, locating the cover on the pin, and tighten the screw **(see illustration 18.5)**.

13 Rotate the pump shaft by hand and check it turns the rotors smoothly and freely.

Installation

14 Fit the strainer back onto the bottom of the pump so that when the pump is installed the thicker end of the strainer will face out **(see illustration 18.4)**.

15 Fit a new O-ring onto the crankcase, then fit the pump, aligning the gear so the screw holes are exposed **(see illustration)**. Apply some threadlock to the screw threads and tighten them.

16 Fit the cover and tighten the bolts **(see illustration)**.

17 Install the clutch cover (see Section 16, Steps 24 to 28).

18.9 Measure the inner rotor tip-to-outer rotor clearance as shown

18.10 Measure the outer rotor-to-body clearance as shown

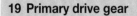

19 Primary drive gear

Note: *The primary drive gear can be removed with the engine in the frame.*

Removal

1 Remove the oil pump (see Section 18).

2 Remove the oil nozzle and its spring from the end of the crankshaft **(see illustration 16.24b)**.

3 To unscrew the primary drive gear nut wedge a stout piece of rag or rolled up strap, or if available a piece of aluminium plate (DO NOT use steel), between the teeth of the primary drive and driven gears where they

18.15 Place a new O-ring in the hole (arrowed) then fit the pump onto the crankcase

18.16 Fit the cover

19.3a An aluminium plate can be used to jam gears together to unscrew the nut

19.3b Align a cut-out in the clutch housing with the socket for clearance

mesh at the top (see illustration) – this will lock them together to prevent them turning. Slacken the primary drive gear nut – if you are using a thick walled socket and you can't get it to fit on the nut turn the crankshaft until one of the cut-outs for the friction plate tabs in the clutch housing aligns with the nut, providing extra clearance (see illustration). Remove the rag, strap or plate.

4 Remove the clutch (Section 16).

5 Unscrew the primary drive gear nut and remove the washer, noting which way round it fits (see illustrations). Slide the oil pump drive gear off the end of the crankshaft, then slide

the primary drive gear off (see illustrations). Note which way round the gears fit – unless there are obvious differences in the inner and outer faces it is best to mark the outer face to ensure they are fitted the same way round.

Installation

6 Slide the primary drive gear onto the shaft the same way round as noted on removal (see illustration 19.5c) – on the engine photographed the rimmed side of the gear faced in (see illustration).

7 Slide the oil pump drive gear onto the

shaft, again the same way round as noted on removal (see illustration 19.5b).

8 Fit the washer, with its marked or chamfered face outwards (see illustration 19.5a). Fit the nut and tighten it finger-tight.

9 Install the clutch (see Section 16).

10 Wedge the stout piece of rag, strap or aluminium plate where the primary drive and driven gear teeth mesh at the bottom and tighten the primary drive gear nut to 53 Nm (see illustration).

11 Fit the oil nozzle with its spring into the end of the crankshaft, aligning the cut-out with the pin in the shaft (see illustration 16.24b).

12 Install the oil pump (see Section 18).

---

20 Gearchange mechanism

Note: The gearchange mechanism can be removed with the engine in the frame. If the engine has been removed ignore the steps that don't apply.

Removal

1 Make sure the transmission is in neutral. Remove the gearchange lever or displace the linkage arm, making an alignment mark with

19.5a Unscrew the nut and remove the washer (arrowed)

19.5b Slide the oil pump drive gear off . . .

19.5c . . . then slide the primary drive gear off

19.6 The inner face of the gear was rimmed on this engine

19.10 Wedge the gears as shown when tightening the nut

20.3a Push the pawl plate away from the cam plate in the direction shown . . .

20.3b . . . and withdraw the shaft/arm assembly

20.4 Unscrew the bolt (arrowed) and remove the arm

20.5 Hold the cam plate to prevent it turning and unscrew the bolt (arrowed)

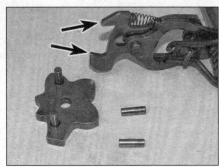

20.6a Check the selector arm pawls (arrowed) and cam plate pins . . .

the shaft if there is none visible so it can be correctly installed later **(see illustration 4.8)**.

2 Remove the clutch (see Section 16).

3 Note how the gearchange shaft centralising spring ends fit on each side of the lug on the casing, and how the pawls on the selector arm pawl plate locate onto the pins behind the cam plate. Grasp the bottom of the selector arm, then push the pawl plate away from the pins so it clears the cam plate and withdraw the shaft/arm assembly **(see illustrations)**.

4 Note how the stopper arm spring ends locate and how the roller on the arm locates in the neutral detent on the selector drum cam

plate, then unscrew the stopper arm bolt and remove the arm, washer and spring, noting how they fit **(see illustration)**.

5 If the crankcases are being separated, unscrew the cam plate bolt and remove the plate, noting how its pins locate in the holes in the end of the drum **(see illustration)**. Remove the other two pins from the drum **(see illustration 20.9a)**. The pins in the plate should stay in place.

Inspection

6 Check the selector arm and pawl plate for cracks, distortion and wear of the pawls, and

check for any corresponding wear on the pins **(see illustration)**. Also check the stopper arm roller and the detents in the cam plate for any wear or damage, and make sure the roller turns freely **(see illustration)**. Replace any components that are worn or damaged with new ones. If required (and not already done), refer to Step 5 for removal of the cam plate, and to Step 9 for installation.

7 Inspect the shaft centralising spring, the pawl plate spring and the stopper arm return spring for fatigue, wear or damage **(see illustration)**. If any is found, they must be replaced with new ones. To replace the shaft spring, slide it off, noting how its ends locate. Fit the new spring, locating the ends on each side of the tab. To replace the pawl plate spring compress it to release its ends from the lugs. When fitting the spring take care not to distort it. Also check that the centralising spring locating pin in the crankcase is tight. If it is loose, remove it and apply a non-permanent thread locking compound to its threads, then tighten it.

8 Check the gearchange shaft is straight and look for damage to the splines. If the shaft is bent you can attempt to straighten it, but if the splines are damaged the shaft must be replaced with a new one. Also check the condition of the shaft oil seal in the left-hand

20.6b . . . and the stopper arm roller and cam plate detents

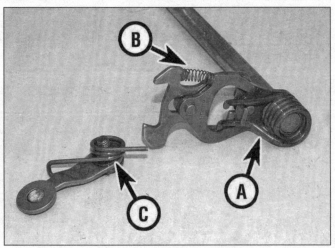

20.7 Check the centralising spring (A), the pawl plate spring (B) and the stopper arm spring (C)

20.8 Lever out the seal (arrowed) and press a new one into place

20.9b ... then fit the plate, locating its pins in the other holes

20.9a Fit the pins into the correct holes in the drum ...

20.9c Threadlock the cam plate bolt

12 Check that all components are correctly positioned **(see illustration)**.
13 Install the clutch (see Section 16).
14 Slide the gearchange lever or linkage arm onto the shaft, aligning it as marked on removal **(see illustrations 4.8)**. Fit the pinch bolt and tighten it.

21 Kickstart mechanism

Note: *The kickstart mechanism can be removed with the engine in the frame. If the engine has been removed, ignore the steps which don't apply.*

Removal

1 Remove the clutch cover (see Section 16, Steps 1 to 5).
2 Before removing the mechanism make a careful note of how the return spring ends locate, how the arm on the ratchet locates against the crankcase, and how the ratchet guide plate fits – pictures taken using a digital camera will be a good aid to correct reassembly.
3 Very carefully unhook the outer end of the return spring using strong pliers and slowly allow the spring to unwind, then remove the kickstart mechanism, noting how everything locates and fits.

Inspection

4 Clean all the components in solvent.
5 Check the ratchet teeth on both the ratchet and on the drive gear, and check the drive gear teeth and the idle gear teeth on the transmission output shaft for wear and damage. Also check the splines between the ratchet and the shaft.
6 Check the return spring and ratchet spring for wear and damage.
7 If any components are worn or damaged they must be replaced with new ones: on the outer end of the shaft remove the guide from inside the return spring, then pull the spring end out of its hole in the shaft and slide it off, followed by the thrust washer; on the inner end of the shaft remove the ratchet guide,

side of the crankcase **(see illustration)**. If it is damaged, deteriorated or shows signs of leakage it must be replaced with a new one (though it is best to fit a new one as a matter of course). Lever out the old seal with a seal hook or screwdriver. Press or drive the new seal squarely into place using your fingers, a seal driver or suitable socket.

Installation

9 If removed, fit the pins into their holes in the end of the selector drum **(see illustration)**. Fit the cam plate, locating its pins in the holes **(see illustration)**. Apply a suitable non-permanent thread locking compound to the bolt and tighten it **(see illustration)**.
10 Assemble the stopper arm components **(see illustration)**. Apply a suitable

non-permanent thread locking compound to the bolt. Install the arm, locating the roller onto the neutral detent on the selector drum and making sure the spring ends are positioned correctly **(see illustration 20.4)**. Tighten the bolt.
11 Check that the shaft centralising spring is properly positioned **(see illustration 20.7)**. Apply some grease to the lips of the gearchange shaft oil seal in the left-hand side of the crankcase **(see illustration 20.8)**. Slide the shaft into place and push it all the way through the case until the splined end comes out the other side, pushing the pawl plate down so it clears the cam plate then releasing it so it locates behind it, and locating the centralising spring ends onto each side of the locating pin in the crankcase **(see illustration)**.

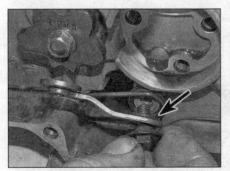

20.10 Threadlock the bolt, do not forget the washer (arrowed) and make sure the spring ends are correctly positioned

20.11 Push the pawl plate down to locate it behind the cam plate

20.12 Make sure everything is correctly located

then release the circlip and slide the ratchet spring and ratchet off, noting the alignment of its punch mark with that on the shaft. Release the snap ring then slide the thrust washer and drive gear off.

8 Check the condition of the shaft oil seal in the clutch cover. If it is damaged, deteriorated or shows signs of leakage it must be replaced with a new one (though it is best to fit a new one whatever the apparent condition) – lever out the old seal with a seal hook or screwdriver. Press or drive the new seal squarely into place using your fingers, a seal driver or suitable socket.

9 Slide the drive gear onto the inner end of the shaft with its ratchet teeth facing the inner end, followed by the thrust washer, then fit the circlip, making sure it locates correctly in the groove.

10 Slide the ratchet on, aligning the punch mark with that on the shaft, and with the teeth facing those on the drive gear. Fit the ratchet spring. Fit the circlip into its groove, then fit the ratchet guide with the guide plate facing the ratchet.

11 Slide the thrust washer onto the outer end of the shaft, then fit the spring with its hooked end facing away from the thrust washer, and locating the straight end in the hole in the shaft. Slide the spring guide on, sliding it past the spring end in the shaft via the slot.

12 Check that all components have been correctly installed.

Installation

13 Slide the kickstart shaft into its bore, making sure the ratchet guide stays on and locates in its cut-out, and the arm on the ratchet locates correctly against the crankcase lug, as noted on removal. Turn the shaft anticlockwise and check that it functions as it should, then reset it fully clockwise. Grasp the hooked end of the return spring securely with a pair of pliers and carefully turn it clockwise until the end can be hooked onto its post on the crankcase.

22.3a Left-hand crankcase bolts (arrowed)

14 Install the clutch cover (see Section 16, Steps 24 to 28).

22 Crankcase separation and reassembly

Note: *To separate the crankcase halves, the engine must be removed from the frame.*

Separation

1 To access the crankshaft and connecting rod assembly, transmission shafts, selector drum and forks, and all related bearings, the crankcase must be split into its two halves.

2 Before the crankcases can be separated the engine must be removed from the frame (see Section 4), and the following components must be removed:

Rocker assemblies (Section 8)
Camshaft (Section 9)
Cylinder head (Section 11)
Cylinder block (Section 13)
Pistons (Section 14)
Alternator rotor and starter driven sprocket
  (Section 15)
Starter motor (Chapter 9)
Neutral switch (Chapter 9)
Clutch (Section 16)

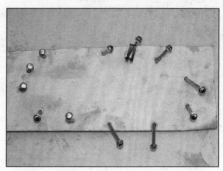

22.3b Example of a cardboard template used for holding the crankcase bolts

Oil pump (Section 18)
Primary drive gear (Section 19)
Gearchange mechanism (Section 20)
Kickstart mechanism (where fitted)
  (Section 21)

3 Unscrew the two crankcase bolts in the left-hand side **(see illustration)**. **Note:** As each bolt is removed, store it in its relative position in a cardboard template of the crankcase halves **(see illustration)**. This will ensure all bolts are returned to their original locations on reassembly.

4 Lay the engine on its left-hand side on wooden blocks so the shafts are clear of the bench.

5 Unscrew the eight crankcase bolts in the right-hand side evenly, a little at a time and in a criss-cross sequence until they are finger-tight, then remove them and store them in the template **(see illustration)**.

6 Carefully lift the right crankcase half off the left half, using a soft-faced hammer to tap around the joint to initially separate the halves **(see illustration)**. If necessary, while lifting the right-hand crankcase have an assistant **gently** tap the ends of the crankshaft and transmission shafts using a soft mallet. **Note:** *If the halves do not separate easily, make sure all fasteners have been removed. Do not try and separate the halves by levering against*

22.5 Right-hand crankcase bolts (arrowed)

22.6 Carefully separate the crankcase halves

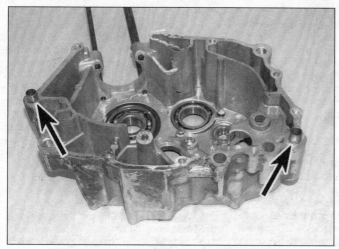

22.8 Remove the dowels (arrowed) if loose

22.12 Starter driven sprocket seal (A), transmission output shaft seal (B), gearchange shaft seal (C)

the crankcase mating surfaces as they are easily scored and will leak oil in the future if damaged. If the halves separate then bind make sure they are coming apart parallel to each other, and if necessary gently tap the right-hand half back down to level them up and start again. The right-hand crankcase half will come away leaving the crankshaft, transmission shafts, and selector drum and forks in the left-hand half.

7 Note the thrust washer on the right-hand end of the transmission output shaft – if it is not there it is stuck to the bearing in the crankcase, in which case retrieve it and fit it back onto the shaft.

8 Remove the gasket and discard it – a new one must be used. Remove the two locating dowels from the crankcase if they are loose (they could be in either half) **(see illustration)**.

9 Refer to Sections 23 to 26 for the removal and installation of the components housed within the crankcases.

10 Remove all traces of old sealant from the crankcase mating surfaces.

Reassembly

11 Make sure the crankcase mating surfaces are clean and dry. Clean the threads of all the crankcase bolts.

12 Ensure that all components and their bearings and new oil seals (see Section 15 for the starter driven sprocket seal, Section 26 for the transmission output shaft seal, and Section 20 for the gearchange shaft seal) are in place in the left-hand crankcase half **(see illustration)**. Make sure that all bearings are in the right-hand half. Make sure the thrust washer is in place on the right-hand end of the transmission output shaft. Make sure the cam chain is correctly positioned in relation to the crankshaft bearing housing and the cylinder bore cut-out **(see illustration 24.3)**. If removed, fit the two locating dowels into the left-hand crankcase **(see illustration 22.8)**.

13 Generously lubricate the crankshaft and transmission shaft bearings and gears and the

selector fork shafts and fork ends and the tracks in the selector drum with clean engine oil, then use a rag soaked in high flash-point solvent to wipe over the mating surfaces of both crankcase halves to remove any traces of oil.

14 Lay a new gasket onto the left-hand crankcase mating surface, locating it over the dowels.

15 Check again that all components are in position. Carefully fit the right-hand crankcase down onto the left-hand crankcase, making sure the shaft ends and dowels locate correctly and that the cases remain square to each other **(see illustration 22.6)**. If necessary gently tap the case down using a soft mallet, but do not use force – if the cases do not join easily there is something wrong, in which case lift the case off and investigate.

16 Check that the right-hand crankcase half is correctly seated all round.

Caution: The crankcase halves should fit together without being forced. If the casings are not correctly seated, remove the right-hand crankcase half and investigate the problem. Do not attempt to pull them together using the crankcase bolts as the casing will crack and be ruined.

17 Thread the crankcase bolts into the right-hand side finger-tight, then tighten them evenly and a little at a time in a criss-cross sequence to 12 Nm **(see illustration 22.5)**.

18 Carefully sit the engine upright. Fit the bolts into the left-hand side and tighten them to 12 Nm **(see illustration 22.3a)**.

19 With all crankcase bolts tightened, check that the crankshaft and transmission shafts rotate smoothly and easily. Check that the transmission shafts rotate freely and independently in neutral, then rotate the selector drum by hand and select each gear in turn whilst rotating the input shaft. If there are any signs of undue stiffness, tight or rough spots, or of any other problem, the fault must be rectified before proceeding further.

20 Install all other removed assemblies in a reverse of the sequence given in Step 2.

23 Crankcases and bearings

Crankcases

1 After the crankcases have been separated, remove the selector drum and forks, the transmission shafts and the crankshaft, referring to the relevant Sections of this Chapter.

2 Clean the crankcases thoroughly with new solvent and dry them with compressed air. Blow out all oil passages with compressed air.

3 Remove all traces of old gasket from the mating surfaces. Clean up minor damage to the surfaces with a fine sharpening stone or grindstone.

Caution: Be very careful not to nick or gouge the crankcase mating surfaces or oil leaks will result. Check both crankcase halves very carefully for cracks and other damage.

4 Small cracks or holes in aluminium castings can be repaired with an epoxy resin adhesive as a temporary measure or with one of the low temperature welding kits. Permanent repairs can only be done by TIG (tungsten inert gas or heli-arc) welding, and only a specialist in this process is in a position to advise on the economy or practical aspect of such a repair. If any damage is found that can't be repaired, replace the crankcase halves as a set.

5 Damaged threads can be economically reclaimed using a diamond section wire insert, for example of the Heli-Coil type (though there are other makes), which are easily fitted after drilling and re-tapping the affected thread.

6 Sheared studs or screws can usually be removed with extractors, which consist of a tapered, left-hand thread screw of very hard steel. These are inserted into a pre-drilled hole in the stud, and usually succeed in dislodging the most stubborn stud or screw. If a stud has sheared above its bore line, it can be removed using a conventional stud extractor which avoids the need for drilling.

 HAYNES HINT *Refer to Tools and Workshop Tips for details of installing a thread insert and using screw extractors.*

7 Install all components and assemblies, referring to the relevant Sections of this and the other Chapters, before reassembling the crankcase halves.

Bearing information

8 The crankshaft and transmission shaft bearings should all be replaced with new ones as part of a complete engine overhaul, or individually as required due to wear or failure.

9 Bearing failure occurs mainly because of lack of lubrication, the presence of dirt or other foreign particles, overloading the engine, break-up of one or more of the bearing components due to fatigue, or corrosion. Regardless of the cause of bearing failure, it must be corrected before the engine is reassembled to prevent it from happening again.

10 The bearings should rotate smoothly, freely and quietly, there should be no rough spots, and there should be no excessive play between the inner and outer races, or between the inner race and the shaft it fits on, or between the outer race and its housing in the crankcase.

11 Dirt and other foreign particles get into the engine in a variety of ways. They may be left in the engine during assembly or they may pass through filters or breathers, then get into the oil and from there into the bearings. Metal chips from machining operations and normal engine wear are often present. Abrasives are sometimes left in engine components after reconditioning operations, especially when parts are not thoroughly cleaned using the proper cleaning methods. The best prevention for this cause of bearing failure is to clean

all parts thoroughly and keep everything spotlessly clean during engine reassembly. Regular oil changes are also recommended.

12 Lack of lubrication or lubrication breakdown has a number of interrelated causes. Excessive heat (which thins the oil), overloading and oil leakage all contribute to lubrication breakdown. Blocked oil passages will starve a bearing of lubrication and destroy it.

13 Riding habits can have a definite effect on bearing life. Full throttle low, speed operation, or labouring the engine, puts very high loads on bearings. Short trip riding leads to corrosion of bearings, as insufficient engine heat is produced to drive off the condensed water and corrosive gases produced. These products collect in the engine oil, forming acid and sludge. As the oil is carried to the engine bearings, the acid attacks and corrodes the bearing material.

14 Incorrect bearing installation during engine assembly will lead to bearing failure as well. To avoid bearing problems, clean all parts thoroughly before reassembly, and lubricate the new bearings with clean engine oil during installation.

Bearing removal and installation

Note: *If the correct bearing removal and installation tools are not available take the crankcases and crankshaft to a dealer – do not risk damaging either the cases or the crankshaft.*

Crankshaft (main) bearings

15 If the crankshaft (main) bearings have failed, excessive rumbling and vibration will be felt when the engine is running. Note that the centre main bearing is part of the crankshaft assembly and is not available separately – if this bearing has failed a new crankshaft must be installed.

16 Separate the crankcase halves (Section 22) and remove all assemblies within (see Step 1).

17 Undo the screws securing the oil plate in the left-hand crankcase **(see illustration)**

– use an impact driver if necessary, making sure the crankcase is adequately supported on wooden blocks under the bearing. Remove the plate, then remove the O-ring from the oil passage. Discard the O-ring – a new one should be used.

18 To remove the outer main bearings from the crankcases, heat the bearing housing with a hot air gun, then tap the bearing out from the outside of the crankcase using a bearing driver or a suitable socket on the inner race **(see illustration 23.26)**.

19 To fit the bearings into the crankcase, smear the outside of the new bearing with clean oil, then heat the housing and drive the bearing squarely in until it seats using a driver or socket that bears only on the outer race **(see illustration 23.28)**.

20 Clean the threads of the oil plate screws. Fit a new O-ring onto the oil passage. Fit the plate, then apply some threadlock to the screws and tighten them **(see illustration 23.17)**.

Connecting rod (big-end) bearings

21 If a connecting rod (big-end) bearing has failed, there will be a pronounced knocking noise when the engine is running, particularly under load and increasing with engine speed. Refer to Section 24, Step 7 for checks that can be made.

22 The connecting rods and their bearings are generally an integral part of the crankshaft assembly which usually comes as a pressed-up unit – individual components are sometimes available (depending on the manufacturer), but even if they are, disassembling and reassembling the crankshaft should only be undertaken by a suitably equipped specialist workshop. If the big-end bearing fails the best thing to do is replace the crankshaft/connecting rod assembly with a new one (see Section 24), but if preferred check with your dealer for advice.

Transmission shaft bearings

23 If the transmission bearings have

23.17 Undo the screws (arrowed) and remove the plate and the O-ring

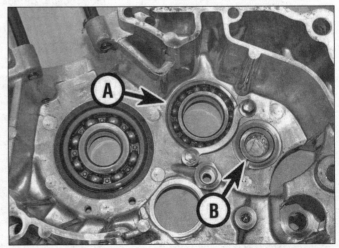

23.23a Transmission input shaft bearing (A) and output shaft bearing (B) – right-hand crankcase half

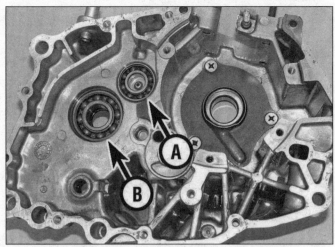

23.23b Transmission input shaft bearing (A) and output shaft bearing (B) – left-hand crankcase half

23.26 Drive the bearings out from the outside

23.27a Fit the expander into the bearing . . .

23.27b . . . and use the slide-hammer attachment to remove the bearing

failed, excessive rumbling and vibration will be felt when the engine is running **(see illustrations)**.

24 Separate the crankcase halves (Section 22) and remove all assemblies within (see Step 1).

25 Remove the retainer securing the right-hand bearing for the input shaft – it is secured by two bolts **(see illustration 23.23a)**.

23.28 Drive the bearings in from the inside

26 To remove the input shaft bearing from the right-hand crankcase and the output shaft bearing from the left-hand crankcase, heat the bearing housing with a hot air gun, then tap the bearing out from the outside of the crankcase using a bearing driver or a suitable socket on the inner race **(see illustration)**.

27 To remove the input shaft bearing from the left-hand crankcase and the output shaft bearing from the right-hand crankcase, an expanding knife-edge bearing puller with slide-hammer attachment may be required. First heat the bearing housing with a hot air gun and see whether the bearing will drop out. If not fit the expanding end of the puller behind the bearing, then turn the puller to expand it and lock it **(see illustration)**. Attach the slide-hammer to the puller, then hold the crankcase firmly down and operate the slide-hammer to jar the bearing out **(see illustration)**.

28 Smear the outside of the new bearing with clean oil, then heat the housing again and drive the bearing squarely in until it seats

using a driver or socket that bears only on the outer race **(see illustration)**.

29 Clean the threads of the bearing retainer bolts, then apply some fresh threadlock. Fit the retainer and tighten the bolts.

24 Crankshaft and connecting rods

Note: *To remove the crankshaft the engine must be removed from the frame and the crankcase halves separated.*

Removal

1 Remove the engine from the frame (see Section 4) and separate the crankcase halves (see Section 22).

2 Remove the selector drum and forks (Section 25) and the transmission shafts (Section 26).

3 Unscrew the main bearing holder bolts/nut

24.3 Main bearing holder bolts (A) and nut (B)

24.4 Lift the crankshaft out

– some engines will have six bolts, others five bolts and one nut on a stud **(see illustration)**.

4 Grasp the crankshaft and lift it out of the crankcase, bringing the cam chain and tensioner with it **(see illustration)**. If the shaft is stuck, thread the alternator rotor nut on its left-hand end then use a soft-faced mallet and gently tap on the nut, supporting the inside of the crankcase on wooden blocks high enough so the crankshaft is just clear of the bench and can't go far should it suddenly release and drop out.

5 Remove the cam chain tensioner (see Section 7) and separate the cam chain from the crankshaft **(see illustration 10.3)**.

Inspection

6 Clean the crankshaft with solvent. If available, blow the crank dry with compressed air.

7 Hold the crankshaft still and check for any radial (up and down) play in the big-end bearings by pushing and pulling the rods against the crank **(see illustration 22.5 in Chapter 2B)**. If the play is excessive refer to Section 23, Steps 21 and 22.

8 Refer to Chapter 2A, Section 11 and check the connecting rod small-end and piston pin for wear.

9 Have the rods checked for twist and bend by a dealer if you are in doubt about their straightness.

10 Refer to Section 23 and check the crankshaft (main) bearings.

Installation

11 Where a stud is fitted in the crankcase for the upper mounting lug on the main bearing holder, make sure it is tight. If it is loose, remove it, clean it and refit it using some threadlock – refer to Section 13, Step 8 for details on stud removal and tightening.

12 Fit the cam chain and the tensioner (see Section 7). Make sure they are both positioned

correctly in relation to each other and to the centre main bearing holder before installing the crankshaft **(see illustration 10.8)**.

13 Carefully lower the crankshaft into the crankcase, making sure the left-hand connecting rod is aligned between the cylinder block studs, that the centre main bearing holder is correctly aligned in relation to the crankcase so the cam chain is positioned on either side of the upper mounting lug with the tensioner blade against the rear run of the chain, with them all aligned between the studs, and the crankshaft enters the bearing squarely and seats correctly. If necessary thread the primary drive gear nut onto the right-hand end of the shaft and gently tap it using a soft-faced mallet so you are sure the crankshaft has seated in its bearing.

14 Clean the threads of the main bearing holder bolts/nut and stud, then apply some fresh threadlock and tighten them evenly and a little at a time in a criss-cross sequence to 12 Nm.

15 Check that the crankshaft rotates freely and easily.

16 Install the transmission shafts (Section 26) and the selector drum and forks (Section 25).

17 Reassemble the crankcase halves (see Section 22).

---

25 Selector drum and forks

Note: *To remove the selector drum and forks the engine must be removed from the frame and the crankcases separated.*

Removal

1 Remove the engine from the frame (see Section 4) and separate the crankcase halves (see Section 22).

2 Before removing the selector forks check

for any identification marks and note which way they face so the forks can be installed correctly – each fork is different. On the engine photographed the right-hand fork was marked R, with the mark facing right, the centre fork C facing left, and the left-hand fork L facing left. If no letters are visible, mark them yourself using a felt pen. The R and L forks fit into the output shaft and the C fork fits into the input shaft.

3 Support the selector forks and withdraw the shaft **(see illustration)**. Pivot each fork out of its groove in the selector drum then draw it out of its pinion on the transmission shaft and remove it **(see illustrations 25.12c, b and a)**. Once removed, slide each fork back onto the shaft to keep them in the correct order and way round.

4 Remove the drum **(see illustration 25.11a)**. Note the neutral switch contact plate on the left-hand end of the drum and take care it does not drop off or catch on something and distort **(see illustration 25.10)**.

Inspection

5 Inspect the selector forks for any signs of wear or damage, especially around the fork ends where they engage with the groove in the pinion. Check that each fork fits correctly in its

25.3 Withdraw the shaft and remove the forks

25.5 Check the fit of each fork in its pinion . . .

25.6 . . . and on its shaft

25.8 Check the guide pins and their grooves in the drum

25.10 Make sure the contact plate is correctly in place

25.11a Fit the drum, aligning the contact (arrowed) . . .

25.11b . . . with the neutral switch hole (arrowed)

pinion groove **(see illustration)**. Check closely to see if the forks are bent. If the forks are in any way damaged they must be replaced with new ones.

6 Check each fork fits correctly on the shaft **(see illustration)**. They should move freely with a light fit but no appreciable freeplay. Replace the forks and/or shaft with new ones if they are worn. Check that the fork shaft holes in the casing are neither worn nor damaged.

7 Check the selector fork shaft is straight by rolling it along a flat surface. A bent rod will cause difficulty in selecting gears and make the gearchange action heavy. Replace the shaft with a new one if it is bent.

8 Inspect the selector drum grooves and selector fork guide pins for signs of wear or damage **(see illustration)**. If either component shows signs of wear or damage the fork(s) and drum must be replaced with new ones.

9 Check that the selector drum rotates freely in each crankcase half and has no sign of freeplay between it and the casing.

Installation

10 If removed fit the neutral switch contact plate onto the drum, locating the hooked end in the cut-out **(see illustration)**.

11 Fit the selector drum into the crankcase with the contact for the neutral switch over the switch hole **(see illustrations)**.

12 Lubricate each fork with oil. Locate each fork in turn in its pinion groove, making sure each is correctly positioned (see Step 2), then pivot the fork round to locate its guide pin in its groove in the selector drum, lifting the fork and its pinion where necessary **(see illustrations)**.

13 Lubricate the selector fork shaft with oil

and slide it through each fork and into its bore in the crankcase **(see illustration 25.3)**.

14 Reassemble the crankcase halves (see Section 22).

26 Transmission shaft removal and installation

Note: *To remove the transmission shafts the engine must be removed from the frame and the crankcases separated.*

Removal

1 Remove the engine from the frame (see Section 4) and separate the crankcase halves (see Section 22).

2 Remove the selector drum and forks (see Section 25).

25.12a Fit the left-hand fork . . .

25.12b . . . the centre fork . . .

25.12c . . . and the right-hand fork

26.3 Lift the transmission shafts out together

3 Grasp the input shaft and output shaft together and lift both shafts out of the crankcase **(see illustration)**. If the shafts are stuck, use a soft-faced hammer and gently tap on the protruding outer end of the output shaft. If the thrust washer on the left-hand end of the input shaft and the spacer on the output shaft drop off or stick in the crankcase, retrieve them and fit them back onto the shafts.
4 Prise the output shaft oil seal out of the left-hand crankcase using a seal hook or screwdriver **(see illustration 22.12)**. Discard the seal as a new one must be used.
5 If necessary, the transmission shafts can be disassembled and inspected for wear or damage (see Section 27).
6 Refer to Section 23 and check the transmission shaft bearings.

Installation

7 Press or drive a new oil seal into the crankcase and lubricate its lips with grease **(see illustration 22.12)**.
8 Use some grease to stick the thrust washer on the left-hand end of the input shaft and the spacer on the output shaft to prevent them dropping off. Join the shafts together on the bench so their related gears are engaged. Grasp the shafts together and fit them into the left-hand crankcase, locating the shaft ends in the bearings **(see illustration 26.3)**.
9 Make sure both transmission shafts are correctly seated and their related pinions are correctly engaged.
10 Install the selector drum and forks (see Section 25).

27.4a This spacer replaces the thrust washer in illustration 26.28b of Chapter 2A

11 Position the gears in the neutral position and check the shafts are free to rotate easily and independently (i.e. the input shaft can turn whilst the output shaft is held stationary) before proceeding further. Also check that each gear can be selected by turning the input shaft with one hand and the selector drum with the other.
12 Make sure the thrust washer is in place on the right-hand end of the output shaft.
13 Reassemble the crankcase halves (see Section 22).

27 Transmission shaft overhaul

1 Remove the transmission shafts from the crankcase (see Section 26). Always disassemble the transmission shafts separately to avoid mixing up the components.
2 The transmission shafts fitted to the twin cylinder engine are the same as those fitted to the OHV engine covered in Section 26 in Chapter 2A, with only minor differences depending on whether a kickstart mechanism is fitted.
3 If your engine has a kickstart mechanism refer to Section 26 in Chapter 2A for details and illustrations. The only difference (and this will depend on the manufacturer of your engine) is in the bush for the 1st gear pinion on the output shaft – on the OHV engine in Chapter 2A the pinion has a fitted bush inside it and there is a thrust washer between the pinion and the 3rd gear opinion next to it, whereas on twin engines the 1st gear pinion has a shouldered bush that the pinion fits onto, with the shouldered section taking the place of the thrust washer.
4 If your engine does not have a kickstart mechanism refer to Section 26 in Chapter 2A for details and illustrations, but note that the part referred to as the kickstart mechanism driven pinion on the right-hand end of the input shaft is still there and will look similar, but without having pinion teeth. Also note that on the left-hand end of the output shaft a spacer replaces the thrust washer **(see illustration)**, and on the right-hand end, next in from the outer thrust washer a collared spacer replaces

27.4b This collared spacer replaces the kickstart pinion and thrust washer in illustrations 26.33a and 26.32c of Chapter 2A

the kickstart mechanism intermediate gear and the thrust washer between that and the 1st gear pinion – note that the wider side faces out **(see illustration)**. Also note that the difference in the 1st gear pinion bush, as described in Step 3, may be encountered.
5 When disassembling the shafts as long as you follow the advice given in the Haynes Hint and keep all parts in order and the correct way round there should be no room for error or confusion.

> **HAYNES HINT** *When disassembling the transmission shafts, place the parts on a long rod or length of stiff wire to keep them in order and facing the proper direction.*

28 Running-in procedure

1 Make sure the engine oil, and on liquid-cooled models the coolant level, are correct (see *Pre-ride checks*). Make sure there is fuel in the tank.
2 Turn the engine kill switch to the ON position and shift the gearbox into neutral. Turn the ignition ON. Set the choke.
3 Start the engine and allow it to run at a moderately fast idle until it reaches operating temperature.

> ⚠ *Warning: If the oil pressure warning light doesn't go off, or it comes on while the engine is running, stop the engine immediately.*

4 If a lubrication failure is suspected, stop the engine immediately and try to find the cause. If an engine is run without oil, even for a short period of time, severe damage will occur.
5 Check carefully that there are no oil (or coolant) leaks and make sure the transmission and controls, especially the brakes, function properly before road testing the machine.
6 Treat the machine gently for the first few miles to make sure oil has circulated throughout the engine and any new parts installed have started to seat.
7 Even greater care is necessary if new pistons and rings or a new cylinder block has been fitted, and the bike will have to be run in as when new. This means greater use of the transmission and a restraining hand on the throttle until at least 300 miles (500 km) have been covered. There's no point in keeping to any set speed limit – the main idea is to keep from labouring the engine and to gradually increase performance up to the 300 miles (500 km) mark. Experience is the best guide, since it's easy to tell when an engine is running freely.
8 Upon completion of the road test, and after the engine has cooled down completely, recheck the valve clearances (see Chapter 1) and check the engine oil and, where applicable, coolant levels (see *Pre-ride checks*).

Chapter 3
Cooling system

Contents

Degrees of difficulty

Easy, suitable for novice with little experience	**Fairly easy,** suitable for beginner with some experience	**Fairly difficult,** suitable for competent DIY mechanic	**Difficult,** suitable for experienced DIY mechanic	**Very difficult,** suitable for expert DIY or professional

Specifications

Coolant

Coolant type	50% distilled water, 50% corrosion inhibited ethylene glycol anti-freeze

General torque settings according to thread size

5 mm bolt/nut	5 Nm
6 mm bolt/nut	10 Nm
8 mm bolt/nut	24 Nm
10 mm bolt/nut	35 Nm
12 mm bolt/nut	55 Nm

1 General information

The liquid cooling system uses a water/anti-freeze coolant to carry away excess heat from the engine and maintain as constant a temperature as possible. The cylinder(s) is/are surrounded by a water jacket from which the heated coolant is circulated by thermo-syphonic action in conjunction with a water pump, which is driven either by the primary drive gear or the primary driven gear,

depending on engine and layout. The hot coolant from the engine passes upwards to the thermostat and through to the radiator. The coolant then flows across the core of the radiator, then to the water pump and back to the engine where the cycle is repeated.

A thermostat is fitted in the system to prevent the coolant flowing through the radiator when the engine is cold, therefore accelerating the speed at which the engine reaches normal operating temperature. A temperature gauge sensor mounted in the thermostat housing transmits information to the temperature gauge on the instrument panel. A cooling fan fitted to the back of the radiator on certain

models aids cooling in extreme conditions by drawing extra air through. The fan motor is controlled by a thermo-switch mounted in the right-hand side of the radiator.

The complete cooling system is partially sealed and pressurised, the pressure being controlled by a valve contained in the spring-loaded radiator cap. By pressurising the coolant the boiling point is raised, preventing premature boiling in adverse conditions. The overflow pipe from the system is connected to a reservoir into which excess coolant is expelled under pressure. The discharged coolant automatically returns to the radiator by the vacuum created when the engine cools.

Warning: Do not remove the pressure cap from the radiator when the engine is hot. Scalding hot coolant and steam may be blown out under pressure, which could cause serious injury. When the engine has cooled, place a thick rag, like a towel, over the pressure cap; slowly rotate the cap anti-clockwise to the first stop. This procedure allows any residual pressure to escape. When the steam has stopped escaping, press down on the cap while turning it anti-clockwise and remove it.

Caution: Do not allow anti-freeze to come in contact with your skin or painted surfaces of the motorcycle. Rinse off any spills immediately with plenty of water. Anti-freeze is highly toxic if ingested. Never leave anti-freeze lying around in an open container or in puddles on the floor; children and pets are attracted by its sweet smell and may drink it. Check with the local authorities about disposing of used anti-freeze. Many communities will have collection centres which will see that anti-freeze is disposed of safely.

Caution: At all times use the specified type of anti-freeze, and always mix it with distilled water in the correct proportion. The anti-freeze contains corrosion inhibitors which are essential to avoid damage to the cooling system. A lack of these inhibitors could lead to a build-up of corrosion which would block the coolant passages, resulting in overheating and severe engine damage. Distilled water must be used as opposed to tap water to avoid a build-up of scale which would also block the passages.

Some air-cooled bikes may be fitted with an oil cooler. After circulating through the engine, the oil passes through a cooler which acts in the same way as a radiator on a liquid-cooled engine. An oil cooling system has only the cooler itself and the hoses which connect it to the engine – it has no fan, temperature sensor or gauge, thermostat or reservoir.

2 Coolant change

Check

Warning: The engine must be cool before beginning this procedure.

1 Check the coolant level in the reservoir (see *Pre-ride checks*).

2 Remove any body panels as required according to model for access to the radiator at the front of the engine (see Chapter 8).

3 Remove the pressure cap from the radiator filler neck by turning it anti-clockwise until it reaches the stop **(see illustration)**. If you hear a hissing sound (indicating there is still pressure in the system), wait until it stops. Now press down on the cap and continue turning it until it can be removed.

2.3 Remove the pressure cap as described

4 Check the condition of the coolant in the system. If it is rust-coloured or if accumulations of scale are visible, drain, flush and refill the system with new coolant (see below). Check the cap seal for cracks and other damage. If in doubt about the pressure cap's condition, have it tested by a dealer or fit a new one – the cost is minimal but it performs a crucial role.

5 Check the antifreeze content of the coolant with an antifreeze hydrometer. If the system has not been topped-up with the correct coolant mixture (see *Pre-ride checks*) the coolant will be too weak to offer adequate protection. If the hydrometer indicates a weak mixture, drain, flush and refill the system (see below).

6 Fit the cap by turning it clockwise until it reaches the first stop then push down on it and continue turning until it can turn no further. Start the engine and let it reach normal operating temperature, then check for leaks again. As the coolant temperature increases, the electric fan (mounted on the back of the radiator) should come on automatically and the temperature should begin to drop. If it does not, refer to Section 3 and check the fan, fan switch and fan circuit.

7 If the coolant level is consistently low, and no evidence of leaks can be found, have the entire system pressure checked by a dealer.

Change the coolant

Warning: Allow the engine to cool completely before draining the coolant. Also, don't allow anti-freeze to come into contact

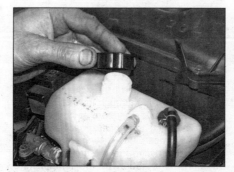

2.10 Remove the reservoir cap – typical reservoir shown

with your skin or the painted surfaces of the motorcycle. Rinse off spills immediately with plenty of water. Anti-freeze is highly toxic if ingested. Never leave anti-freeze lying around in an open container or in puddles on the floor; children and pets are attracted by its sweet smell and may drink it. Check with local authorities (councils) about disposing of anti-freeze. Many communities have collection centres which will see that anti-freeze is disposed of safely. Anti-freeze is also combustible, so don't store it near open flames.

Draining

8 Support the motorcycle upright on a level surface using an auxiliary stand.

9 Remove any fairing panels as required according to model for access to the radiator at the front of the engine and the water pump in the clutch cover on the right-hand side (see Chapter 8).

10 Remove the pressure cap (see Step 3). Also remove the coolant reservoir cap **(see illustration)**.

11 Position a suitable container beneath the water pump on the right-hand side of the engine. Unscrew the drain bolt and allow the coolant to completely drain from the system **(see illustration)**. Retain the old sealing washer for use during flushing. If there is no drain bolt release the clamp securing the radiator hose either to the pump or the bottom of the radiator, the detach the hose and drain the system – if you detach the hose from the radiator place its end lower than the water pump to ensure complete draining.

12 Disconnect the overflow hose from the back of the radiator filler neck and place it in the container to allow the reservoir to drain.

Flushing

13 Flush the system with clean tap water by inserting a hose in the radiator filler neck. Allow the water to run through the system until it is clear and flows out cleanly. If the radiator is extremely corroded, remove it (see Section 6) and have it cleaned by a specialist. Also flush the reservoir, then fit the radiator overflow hose back onto the filler neck.

14 Clean the drain hole in the water pump then install the drain bolt using the old sealing washer **(see illustration 2.11)**.

2.11 Cooling system drain bolt and its sealing washer

15 Fill the system to the base of the radiator filler neck with clean water mixed with a flushing compound. Make sure the flushing compound is compatible with aluminium components, and follow the manufacturer's instructions carefully. Fit the radiator cap.

16 Start the engine and allow it to reach normal operating temperature. Let it run for about ten minutes.

17 Stop the engine. Let it cool for a while, then cover the pressure cap with a heavy rag and turn it anti-clockwise to the first stop, releasing any pressure that may be present in the system. Once the hissing stops, push down on the cap and remove it completely.

18 Drain the system once again.

19 Fill the system with clean water, then fit the radiator cap and repeat Steps 16 to 18.

Refilling

20 Install the drain bolt using a new sealing washer and tighten it **(see illustration 2.11)**.

21 Fill the system to the base of the radiator filler neck with the proper coolant mixture (see this Chapter's Specifications). **Note:** *Pour the coolant in slowly to minimise the amount of air entering the system.* Fill the reservoir to the UPPER level line (see *Pre-ride checks)*. Carefully shake the bike to dislodge any trapped air.

22 Start the engine and allow it to idle for 2 to 3 minutes. Flick the throttle twistgrip part open 3 or 4 times, so that the engine speed rises to approximately 4000 to 5000 rpm, then stop the engine. Any air trapped in the system should bleed back to the radiator filler neck.

23 If necessary, top up the coolant level to the base of the radiator filler neck, then install the pressure cap. Also top up the coolant reservoir(s) to the UPPER level line.

24 Start the engine and allow it to reach normal operating temperature, then shut it off. Let the engine cool then remove the pressure cap as described in Step 3. Check that the coolant level is still up to the base of the radiator filler neck. If it's low, add the specified mixture until it reaches the base of the filler neck. Refit the cap.

25 Check the coolant level in the reservoir and top up if necessary.

26 Check the system for leaks. Install any removed body panels (see Chapter 8).

27 Do not dispose of the old coolant by pouring it down the drain. Instead pour it into a heavy plastic container, cap it tightly and take it into an authorised disposal site or service station – see *Warning* at the beginning of this sub-Section.

3 Cooling fan and fan switch

Note: *Not all liquid-cooled engines have a cooling fan on the back of the radiator.*

Cooling fan
Check

1 If the engine is overheating and the cooling fan isn't coming on, first check the fan fuse if fitted (see Chapter 9). If the fuse is good, check the switch as described below.

2 To test the cooling fan motor, locate the wiring connector by tracing the wiring from the fan motor, which is on the back of the radiator. Remove any body panel(s) and the fuel tank as required according to model (see Chapters 8 and 4). Disconnect the wiring connector. Using a 12 volt battery and two jumper wires with suitable connectors, connect the battery to the terminals on the fan side of the connector. Once connected the fan should operate. If it does not, and the wiring and connectors are all good, then the fan motor is faulty.

Replacement

 Warning: The engine must be completely cool before carrying out this procedure.

3 Remove the radiator (see Section 6).

4 If the fan switch wire is in the same loom as the fan motor, disconnect it from the switch **(see illustration)**. Undo the screws securing the fan assembly to the radiator, noting any earth wire, and remove the fan assembly.

5 Installation is the reverse of removal.

Cooling fan switch
Check

6 If the engine is overheating and the cooling fan isn't coming on, first check the fan motor fuse if fitted (see Chapter 9). If the fuse is

blown, check the fan circuit for a short to earth (see the wiring diagrams at the end of Chapter 9).

7 If the fuse is good, disconnect the wiring connector from the fan switch, which is usually in the back of the radiator on one side **(see illustration)** – remove any body panel as required for access (see Chapter 8). Using a voltmeter check for voltage at the wiring connector with the ignition ON – if there is more than one wire check both of them. There should be battery voltage, at one of the wires only on twin wire connectors. If there is no voltage trace the break or faulty connector. If there is voltage check that the switch is tight in the radiator. Next check the earth wire shows continuity to earth. If it doesn't locate the break or the detached wire or terminal and repair it. Make sure all connectors and terminals are clean.

8 If the wiring is good, or if the fan works but is suspected of cutting in at the wrong temperature or is on the whole time, remove the switch (Steps 10 and 11) and test it as follows: fill a small heatproof container with coolant and place it on a stove. Using some wire or other support suspend the switch in the coolant so that just the sensing head up to the threads is submerged, and with the head a minimum of 40 mm above the bottom of the container **(see illustration)**. Using an ohmmeter or continuity tester, connect the positive (+) probe of the meter to the wire terminal on the switch, and the negative (–) probe to the body of the sensor. Also place a thermometer capable of reading temperatures up to 130°C in the coolant so that its bulb is close to the sensor. **Note:** *None of the components should be allowed to directly touch the container.*

 Warning: This must be done very carefully to avoid the risk of personal injury.

9 Begin to heat the coolant, stirring it gently. Initially there should be no continuity, indicating that the switch is open or off. When the temperature reaches around 100°C, the switch should close (turn on) and there should be continuity on the meter. Keep heating to a few degrees above 100, then turn off the heat. As the coolant cools to around 100°C the

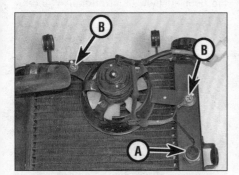

3.4 Disconnect the fan switch wire (A) if necessary, then undo the screws (B), noting the earth wire – typical arrangement shown

3.7 Typical fan switch and its wiring connector (arrowed)

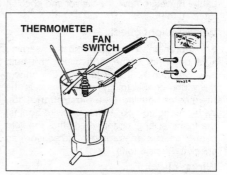

THERMOMETER
FAN SWITCH

3.8 Fan switch/temperature sensor test set-up

switch should open (turn off) and the meter should show no continuity. If there is more than a 5% error in the temperature at which the switch closes and opens, or if it shows continuity the whole time or no continuity the whole time, replace it with a new one (Steps 10 and 11).

Replacement

10 The switch is in the radiator. Drain the cooling system (see Section 2).

11 Disconnect the wiring connector from the switch **(see illustration 3.7)**. Unscrew the switch. Discard the O-ring or sealing washer as a new one must be used.

12 Installation is the reverse of removal. Fit a new O-ring or sealing washer onto the switch, and do not overtighten it. Fill the system with the specified coolant (see Section 2). Run the engine and check the switch for leaks and that it functions correctly.

---

4   Temperature gauge and sensor

Temperature gauge or warning light

1 The circuit consists of a sensor mounted in the thermostat housing **(see illustration 4.10)** and a gauge and/or warning light in the instrument cluster. The thermostat housing is bolted to the back of the cylinder head on the left-hand side of the engine on some OHV engines, but on others it may be remote from the engine, fitted in the coolant outlet hose between the cylinder head and the top of the radiator. Remove any body panels as required for access to both (see Chapter 8).

Gauge check

2 If the gauge needle does not move as the engine warms up, disconnect the wiring connector from the sensor in the thermostat housing **(see illustration 4.10)**. With the ignition on, touch the wire against the frame or engine and check that the needle moves around the gauge, then quickly disconnect the wire to avoid damaging the gauge. If the gauge moves remove the sensor and check it (Steps 6 to 9).

Warning light check

3 If the engine overheats and the warning light does not come, first check the bulb (see Chapter 9). If that is good disconnect the wiring connector from the sensor in the thermostat housing **(see illustration 4.10)**. With the ignition on, touch the wire against the frame or engine and check that the light comes on. If it does remove the sensor and check it (Steps 6 to 9).

Wiring check

4 If the gauge does not move or the warning light does not come in Step 2 or 3, check the wiring between the sensor and the gauge for continuity, referring to Chapter 9. Also check for continuity to earth between the sensor hex and the frame. If there is none make sure the sensor and the thermostat mounting bolt are tight. If that is good check for voltage at the wire to the gauge or warning light.

Replacement

5 The temperature gauge and/or warning light is/are part of the instrument cluster, which is covered in Chapter 9.

Temperature gauge sensor

Check

6 The sensor is mounted in the thermostat housing **(see illustration 4.10)**. Drain the cooling system (see Section 2).

7 Remove the sensor (see Steps 10 and 11 below).

8 Fill a small heatproof container with coolant and place it on a stove. Using some wire or other support suspend the sensor in the coolant so that just the sensing head up to the threads is submerged, and with the head a minimum of 40 mm above the bottom of the container **(see illustration 3.8)**. Using a multimeter set to test resistance for a temperature gauge or to test continuity for a warning light, connect the positive (+) probe of the meter to the terminal on the sensor, and the negative (–) probe to the body of the sensor. Also place a thermometer capable of reading temperatures up to 130°C in the coolant so that its bulb is close to the sensor. **Note:** *None of the components should be allowed to directly touch the container.*

 Warning: This must be done very carefully to avoid the risk of personal injury.

9 Begin to heat the coolant, stirring it gently. If a gauge is fitted, the resistance of the sensor as shown on the meter should fall as the temperature of the coolant rises. If a warning light is fitted, the meter should show no continuity (switch OFF) until the coolant reaches a temperature of around 100°C (no actual specifications are available), and then continuity should be shown (switch ON). Switch the heat off and allow the coolant to cool – as the temperature drops the resistance should increase or the meter should go from showing continuity to showing no continuity. If the results are not as described, then the sensor is probably faulty.

Replacement

 Warning: The engine must be completely cool before carrying out this procedure.

10 The sensor is mounted in the thermostat housing **(see illustration)**. Drain the cooling system (see Chapter 1).

11 Disconnect the sensor wiring connector. Unscrew and remove the sensor.

12 Apply a suitable sealant to the thread of the sensor, making sure none gets on the sensor head. Install the sensor and tighten it. Connect the wiring.

13 Refill the cooling system (see Section 2).

---

5   Thermostat and housing

---

1 The thermostat is automatic in operation and should give many years service without requiring attention. In the event of a failure, the valve will probably jam open, in which case the engine will take much longer than normal to warm up. Conversely, if the valve jams shut, the coolant will be unable to circulate and the engine will overheat. Neither condition is acceptable, and the fault must be investigated promptly.

Removal

Note: *The complete thermostat housing can be removed without removing the thermostat itself if required.*

 Warning: The engine must be completely cool before carrying out this procedure.

2 Drain the coolant (see Section 2). The thermostat housing is bolted to the back of the cylinder head on the left-hand side of the engine on some OHV engines, but on others it may be remote from the engine, fitted in the coolant outlet hose between the cylinder head and the top of the radiator.

3 To remove the thermostat, unscrew the two bolts securing the cover and detach it from the housing **(see illustrations)**. Withdraw

4.10 Typical temperature gauge sensor (arrowed)

5.3a Unscrew the bolts (arrowed) . . .

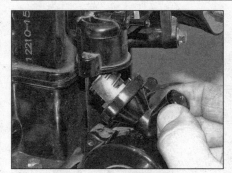

5.3b ... detach the cover ...

5.3c ... and remove the thermostat

5.4 Thermostat housing mounting bolt (arrowed)

the thermostat, noting how it fits **(see illustration)**.

4 To remove the thermostat housing, disconnect the temperature gauge sensor wiring connector **(see illustration 4.10)**. Release the hoses clamps and detach the hoses. Unscrew the bolt(s) securing the housing and detach it **(see illustration)** – if the housing bolts directly to the engine discard the O-ring on its union **(see illustration 5.9)**.

Check

5 Examine the thermostat visually before carrying out the test. If it remains in the open position at room temperature, it should be replaced with a new one.

6 Suspend the thermostat by a piece of wire in a container of cold water. Place a thermometer capable of reading temperatures up to 110°C in the water so that the bulb is close to the thermostat **(see illustration)**. Heat the water – the thermostat should open at around 75°C and be fully open at around 85°C. If not the thermostat is faulty and must be replaced with a new one. Also check that it closes again as the water cools.

7 In the event of thermostat failure, as an emergency measure only, it can be removed and the machine used without it (this is better than leaving a permanently closed thermostat in, but if it is permanently open, you might as well leave it in). **Note:** *Take care when starting the engine from cold as it will take much longer than usual to warm up.* Ensure that a new unit is installed as soon as possible.

Installation

8 To install the thermostat, first make sure the seal fitted around it or in a groove in the cover is in good condition, if not fit a new seal if available, or otherwise fit a new thermostat **(see illustration 5.3c)**. Smear some fresh coolant over the seal. Make sure the thermostat locates correctly, and where possible fit it with the jiggle pin hole at the top. Fit the cover onto the housing, then install and tighten the bolts **(see illustrations 5.3b and a)**.

9 To install the thermostat housing, fit a new O-ring where necessary, then fit the housing and tighten the bolt(s) **(see illustration)**. Fit the hoses and tighten the clamps. Connect the

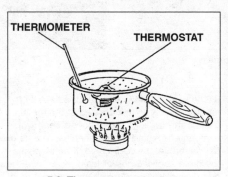

THERMOMETER

THERMOSTAT

5.6 Thermostat test set-up

temperature gauge sensor wiring connector.

10 Refill the cooling system with fresh coolant (see Section 2).

6 Radiator

Note: *If the radiator is being removed as part of the engine removal procedure, detach the hoses from their unions on the engine rather than on the radiator and remove the radiator with the hoses attached to it. Note the routing of the hoses.*

Removal

⚠️ **Warning: The engine must be completely cool before carrying out this procedure.**

6.3 Detach the hoses (arrowed) from each side of the radiator as required

5.9 Fit a new O-ring (arrowed) into the groove

1 Drain the coolant (see Section 2).

2 Where fitted disconnect the fan motor wiring connector and feed the wiring to the radiator, noting its routing.

3 Slacken the clamps securing the hoses to the radiator and detach them, noting which fits where **(see illustration)**.

4 Unscrew the radiator mounting bolts and manoeuvre the radiator out **(see illustration)**. Note the arrangement of any collars and rubber grommets in the radiator mounts. Replace the grommets with new ones if they are damaged, deformed or deteriorated.

5 If necessary, remove the cooling fan and fan switch from the radiator (see Section 3). Check the radiator for signs of damage and clear any dirt or debris that might obstruct air flow and inhibit cooling. If the radiator fins are badly damaged or broken the radiator must be replaced with a new one.

6.4 Locate and unscrew the radiator bolts (arrowed)

7.2 Drain hose (arrowed) fitted to some engines

7.5 Water pump cover bolts (arrowed)

Installation

6 Installation is the reverse of removal, noting the following.
- *Make sure any rubber grommets are in place.*
- *Make sure any bolt collars are correctly installed in the grommets.*
- *Make sure that where fitted the fan wiring is correctly connected.*
- *Ensure the coolant hoses are in good condition, and are securely retained by their clamps, using new ones if necessary.*
- *On completion refill the cooling system with fresh coolant as described in Section 2.*

Pressure cap check

7 If problems such as overheating or loss of coolant occur, check the entire system as described in Chapter 1. The radiator cap opening pressure should be checked by a dealer with the special tester required to do the job. If the cap is defective, or if you are in doubt or cannot get it tested, replace it with a new one – the expense is minimal.

7 Water pump

Check

1 The water pump is located in the clutch cover on the right-hand side of the engine. Remove any body panels as required for access (see Chapter 8). Visually check the area around the pump for signs of leakage.
2 To prevent leakage of water from the cooling system to the lubrication system and *vice versa*, two seals are fitted on the pump shaft. Below the pump housing there is a drain hole or hose **(see illustration)**. If either seal fails, the drain allows the coolant or oil to escape and prevents them mixing.

3 The seal on the water pump side is of the mechanical type which bears on the rear face of the impeller. The second seal, which is mounted behind the mechanical seal, is of the normal feathered lip type. If on inspection the drain shows signs of leakage remove the pump, and fit a new mechanical seal if there is coolant leakage, and a new oil seal as well if there is oil leakage or if the leakage is an emulsion-like mix of coolant and oil.

Removal

4 Drain the coolant (see Section 2).
5 Unscrew the pump cover bolts, noting which fits where, and remove the cover **(see illustration)**. Discard the O-ring as a new one must be used. Remove the dowels where fitted and if loose **(see illustration 7.20b)**.
6 Wiggle the water pump impeller back-and-forth and in-and-out **(see illustration)**. If there is excessive movement, remove and disassemble the pump. Also check for corrosion or a build-up of scale in the pump body.
7 Refer to Chapter 2A if you have an OHV single engine and to Chapter 2D if you have a twin cylinder engine, and remove the clutch cover.
8 Counter-hold the inner end of the pump shaft using a spanner on the flats, then

7.6 Check the impeller (arrowed) as described

unscrew the impeller, and remove the washer where fitted **(see illustration)**. Draw the shaft out from the inner side **(see illustration)**.
9 If required and where fitted release the circlip and remove the gear from the shaft, noting how it fits.

Seal and bearing replacement

Note: *Do not remove the seals and bearing(s) unless they need to be replaced with new ones – once removed they cannot be re-used.*
10 On some engines the seals and bearing(s) are fitted into a housing that itself fits into the clutch cover – if required carefully drive or lever the housing out using a screwdriver

7.8a Counter-hold the shaft and unscrew the impeller . . .

7.8b . . . then withdraw the shaft

7.10 Remove the housing from the cover – note the alignment of the tab (A) with the cut-out (B). Remove and discard the O-rings (C)

7.11 Mechanical seal (A) and oil seal (B)

7.18a Fit the washer if removed . . .

7.18b . . . and thread the impeller onto the shaft

and remove it **(see illustration)**. Discard the O-ring(s) – new ones must be used. On other engines the seals and bearing(s) fit directly into the cover.

11 To remove the mechanical seal, an expanding knife-edge bearing puller with slide-hammer attachment is useful, if available **(see illustration)**. Fit the expanding end of the puller behind the seal, then turn the puller to expand it and lock it. Attach the slide-hammer to the puller, then operate the slide-hammer to jar the bearing out. Alternatively drive the seal out using a suitable drift inserted from the inner side, through the bearing and oil seal.

12 Drive the oil seal out using a suitable drift inserted from the inner side, through the bearing. Note which way round the seal fits.

13 All models will have one bearing in the seal housing **(see illustration 7.8b)**. A second bearing may be fitted on the shaft, or the shaft end may run in a bush in the crankcase. Check the bearing(s) and/or bush for wear, excessive freeplay between it and the shaft, and smooth running of the bearing or of the shaft in the bush. If required drive the bearing out from the outer side of the housing or draw the bearing off the shaft and replace it/them with new

ones. If a bush is worn check for availability of a replacement with your dealer.

14 Fit the new oil seal and drive it in until it seats using a suitable socket.

15 Fit the new mechanical seal and drive it in until it seats using a suitable socket that bears only on the outer flange.

16 Check for a seal fitted in the inner face of the impeller and replace it with a new one if necessary.

Installation

17 If removed fit the gear onto the shaft and secure it with a new circlip **(see illustration 7.8b)**.

18 Fit the shaft through the bearing and seals, rotating it to ease its passage through **(see illustration 7.8b)**. Where removed fit the washer onto the outer end of the shaft **(see illustration)**. Thread the impeller on and tighten it, counter-holding the shaft end as before **(see illustration)**. Rotate the pump by hand to make sure it turns freely (but take into account the grip of the seals).

19 Refer to Chapter 2A or 2D, and install the clutch cover.

20 Smear the new cover O-ring with grease and fit it into its groove **(see illustration)**. Fit the cover dowels if removed **(see illustration)**. Fit the cover onto the pump **(see illustration)**.

7.20a Fit a new O-ring (arrowed) into the groove

7.20b Make sure the dowels (arrowed) are fitted

7.20c Make sure the different length bolts are in their correct places . . .

7.20d . . . and use a new sealing washer on the drain bolt

8.2 Coolant hose clamps (arrowed) – inlet hose from pump to cylinder block

9.3 Always use new O-rings (arrowed) to prevent leaks

Fit the bolts and tighten them. Use a new sealing washer on the drain bolt, where fitted **(see illustration)**.

21 Fill the engine with the correct amount and type of oil (see Chapter 1) and coolant (see Section 2). Run the engine to normal temperature and check that there are no leaks.

22 Install any body panels (See Chapter 8).

8 Coolant hoses and unions

Removal

1 Before removing a hose or its union, drain the coolant (see Section 2).

2 Use a screwdriver to slacken the larger-bore hose clamps, then slide them back along the hose and clear of the union spigot **(see illustration)**. The small-bore hoses are secured by spring clamps which can be expanded by squeezing their ears together with pliers.

Caution: The radiator unions are fragile. Do not use excessive force when attempting to remove the hoses.

3 If a hose proves stubborn, release it by rotating it on its union before working it off. If all else fails, cut the hose with a sharp knife. Whilst this means replacing the hose with a new one, it is preferable to buying a new radiator.

4 To remove a hose union unscrew the bolt(s) securing it and either pull it out of its bore or detach it from its mount. Discard the O-ring(s) – new one(s) must be used.

Installation

5 When fitting a union use new O-ring(s) smeared with grease. Make sure the union is fully pushed into its bore where relevant, the O-ring(s) seat correctly, and the union is secured by its bolt(s).

6 Slide the clamps onto the hose and then work the hose on to its union as far as the spigot where present.

 HAYNES HiNT *If the hose is difficult to push on its union, soften it by soaking it in very hot water, or alternatively a little soapy water on the union can be used as a lubricant.*

7 Rotate the hose on its unions to settle it in position before sliding the clamps into place and tightening them securely.

8 Refill the cooling system with fresh coolant (see Section 2).

9 Oil cooler and hoses

Note: *The oil cooler can be removed with the engine in the frame. If work is being carried out with the engine removed ignore the preliminary steps.*

Removal

1 Remove any body panels as required for access (see Chapter 8).

2 Drain the engine oil (see Chapter 1). Keep the container handy to catch any residual oil in the cooler and hoses.

3 To detach the pipes or hoses from either the engine or the cooler, unscrew the union bolts and detach the pipes or hoses, noting which fits where. Discard the sealing washers or O-rings as new ones must be used **(see illustration)**.

4 To remove the cooler, first detach the hoses from either the engine or the cooler as required. Unscrew the nuts and/or bolts securing the oil cooler, noting the arrangement of any collars and grommets, and remove the cooler.

5 Check the cooler for leaks and other damage. Check the cooler fins for mud, dirt and insects, which will impede the flow of air through it. If the fins are dirty, clean them using water or low pressure compressed air directed through from the rear face. If the fins are bent or distorted, straighten them carefully with a screwdriver. If the airflow is restricted by bent or damaged fins over more than 30% of the cooler's surface area, or if the cooler is leaking, replace it with a new one.

Installation

6 Installation is a reverse of the removal procedure, noting the following:
● *Make sure any rubber grommets are in place.*
● *Make sure any bolt collars are correctly installed in the grommets.*
● *Use a new O-ring on each flange type union **(see illustration 9.3)**, and use two new sealing washers on each banjo type union, one on each side.*
● *Refill the engine with oil (see Chapter 1 and Pre-ride checks). Make sure there are no leaks from the oil cooler hose unions when the engine is run.*

Chapter 4
Fuel system and exhaust

Contents

Degrees of difficulty

Easy, suitable for novice with little experience	Fairly easy, suitable for beginner with some experience	Fairly difficult, suitable for competent DIY mechanic	Difficult, suitable for experienced DIY mechanic	Very difficult, suitable for expert DIY or professional

Specifications

General torque settings according to thread size

5 mm bolt/nut. . . . .   5 Nm
6 mm bolt/nut. . . . .   10 Nm
8 mm bolt/nut. . . . .   24 Nm
10 mm bolt/nut. . . . .   35 Nm
12 mm bolt/nut. . . . .   55 Nm

1 General information and precautions

General information

The fuel system consists of the fuel tank, the fuel tap, fuel strainer and/or filter, fuel hose, carburettor(s) and control cables.

On single cylinder engines there is either a single carburettor with a sliding throttle valve, or a single CV carburettor. Twin cylinder engines are more likely to have two CV carburettors, but some are fitted with a single sliding carburettor that feeds both cylinders via a two-way manifold. For cold starting, there is a choke lever either on the left-hand side of the carburettor, or in the left-hand switch housing and connected to the carburettor(s) by cable.

Air is drawn into the carburettor via an air filter fitted in a housing behind the carburettor.

Some models either have a fuel gauge in the instrument cluster, or a low fuel warning light, each actuated by a level sensor inside the fuel tank.

Precautions

 Warning: Petrol (gasoline) is extremely flammable, so take extra precautions when you work on any part of the fuel system. Don't smoke or allow open flames or bare light bulbs near the work area, and don't work in a garage where a natural gas-type appliance is present. If you spill any fuel on your skin, rinse it off immediately with soap and water. When you perform any kind of work on the fuel system, wear safety glasses and have a fire extinguisher suitable for a class B type fire (flammable liquids) on hand.

2.1a Example of a manual tap with single hose and ON/OFF/RES lever

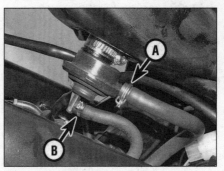

2.1b Example of an automatic tap with fuel hose (A), vacuum hose (B) and no lever

2.2 Release the clamp and detach the fuel hose

Always perform service procedures in a well-ventilated area to prevent a build-up of fumes.

Never work in a building containing a gas appliance with a pilot light, or any other form of naked flame. Ensure that there are no naked light bulbs or any sources of flame or sparks nearby.

Do not smoke (or allow anyone else to smoke) while in the vicinity of petrol (gasoline), or of components containing petrol. Remember the possible presence of vapour from these sources and move well clear before smoking.

Check all electrical equipment belonging to the house, garage or workshop where work is being undertaken (see the *Safety First!* section of this manual). Remember that certain electrical appliances such as drills, cutters etc. create sparks in the normal course of operation and must not be used near petrol (gasoline) or any component containing it. Again, remember the possible presence of fumes before using electrical equipment.

Always mop up any spilt fuel and safely dispose of the rag used.

Any stored fuel that is drained off during servicing work must be kept in sealed containers that are suitable for holding petrol (gasoline), and clearly marked as such; the containers themselves should be kept in a safe place. Note that this last point applies equally to the fuel tank if it is removed from the machine; also remember to keep its filler cap closed at all times.

Read the *Safety first!* section of this manual carefully before starting work.

2 Fuel tank and fuel tap

> **Warning: Refer to the precautions given in Section 1 before starting work.**

Fuel tank draining

1 Most models are fitted with a standard type 'gravity' tap with a manual lever for opening and closing and a single fuel hose - when the tap is turned on fuel flows under the force of gravity down to the carburettor(s) **(see illustration)**. Some models are fitted with an automatic vacuum-operated tap that has two hoses, one sourcing a vacuum from the intake duct when the engine turns over that acts on a diaphragm valve that opens and closes the tap, the other supplying the fuel to the carburettor(s) **(see illustration)**.

Manual (gravity) tap

2 Turn the fuel tap off. Have a rag ready to catch any residual fuel. Release the fuel hose clamp and detach the hose from the tap **(see illustration)**.
3 Connect a drain hose to the fuel outlet union on the tap and insert its end in a container suitable and large enough for storing the fuel. Turn the fuel tap to the 'RES' position and allow the tank to drain. When the tank has drained, turn the tap to the 'OFF' position.

Automatic (vacuum) tap

4 Have a rag ready to catch any residual fuel. Release the fuel hose clamp and detach the hose from the tap **(see illustration 2.1b)**. Also detach the vacuum hose.
5 Connect a drain hose to the fuel outlet union on the tap and insert its end in a container suitable and large enough for storing the fuel. Gradually apply a vacuum to the tap using a vacuum pump and auxiliary hose connected to the vacuum hose union until fuel starts to flow, then allow the tank to drain. When the tank has drained, release the vacuum and detach the hose.

Fuel tank

Removal

6 On models with a manual fuel tap turn the tap off. Make sure the filler cap is secure.
7 Remove the seat and any body panels as required according to model (see Chapter 8).
8 Have a rag ready to catch any residual fuel, then release the fuel hose clamp and detach the hose from the tap **(see illustration 2.2)**.
9 On models with an automatic tap also detach the vacuum hose **(see illustration 2.1b)**.
10 Unscrew the fuel tank bolt(s) and remove any washer(s) and other components necessary **(see illustration)**.
11 Raise the tank, then locate and disconnect the fuel level sensor wiring connector, and on models with a tank mounted instrument panel any related wiring connector(s) **(see illustrations)**. Also disconnect any drain and breather hoses.

2.10 Unscrew the bolt(s) and remove any washer(s), collar(s) and rubber support(s)

2.11a This model just has a fuel level sensor wiring connector (arrowed) . . .

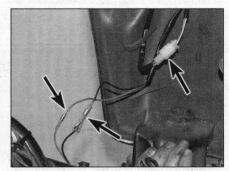

2.11b . . . this Custom model has a level sensor connector and gauge connectors (arrowed)

2.12 Carefully lift the tank away

2.13 Check the tank support rubbers (arrowed)

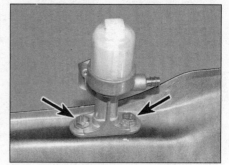

2.16a Fuel tap with mounting bolts (arrowed)

12 Draw the tank back and remove it **(see illustration)**.

13 Inspect the tank mounting rubbers for signs of damage or deterioration and replace them with new ones if necessary **(see illustration)**.

Installation

14 Installation is the reverse of removal, noting the following:

● *Make sure the wiring and any drain and breather hoses are securely connected.*
● *Make sure the tank rubbers are correctly fitted and all support components and washer(s) fitted with the mounting bolt(s) (see illustrations 2.13 and 2.10).*
● *Make sure the fuel hose is fully pushed onto the tap union and is secured by the clamp (see illustration 2.2). Where fitted make sure the vacuum hose is in good condition and securely connected (see illustration 2.1b).*
● *Turn the fuel tap ON (manual tap) and check that there is no sign of fuel leakage.*
● *Start the engine and check that there is no sign of fuel leakage.*

Fuel tap

Removal

15 Drain the fuel tank as described in Steps 2 to 5 according to type. Remove the tank (Steps 6 to 12). Make sure the filler cap is secure, then turn the tank over and rest it on some rag.

16 Undo the screws, bolts or nut securing

the tap to the tank and withdraw the tap **(see illustrations)**. Note any washers. Remove the sealing ring where fitted and discard it as a new one must be used.

17 Clean the strainer in solvent and remove any particles caught in the gauze. If there any tears or holes replace the strainer with a new one if available, or fit a new tap if not. If the tap has been leaking you can disassemble it and check for worn or damaged parts. Replace any found with new ones if available, or otherwise fit a new tap.

Installation

18 Where applicable fit a new sealing ring into the groove in the tap.

19 Fit the tap, making sure the sealing ring stays in place. Tighten the nut, or fit the screws or bolts with any washers and tighten them.

20 Install the fuel tank (see above).

Fuel tank cleaning and repair

21 All repairs to the fuel tank should be carried out by a professional who has experience in this critical and potentially dangerous work. Even after cleaning and flushing of the fuel system, explosive fumes can remain and ignite during repair of the tank.

22 If the fuel tank is removed from the bike, it should not be placed in an area where sparks or open flames could ignite the fumes coming out of the tank. Be especially careful inside garages where a natural gas-type appliance is located, because the pilot light could cause an explosion.

3 Fuel gauge or warning light and level sensor

⚠️ *Warning: Refer to the precautions given in Section 1 before starting work.*

Check

Models with fuel gauge

1 The circuit consists of the level sensor mounted in the fuel tank and the gauge mounted in the instrument cluster.

2 If the gauge does not work as it should first check the wiring between the sensor connector and the instrument cluster for continuity, referring to Chapter 9 for access to the instrument cluster wiring and for continuity testing details. If the wiring is good check the power supply.

3 If the wiring is good, remove the sensor (see Steps 10 to 12). Check that no fuel has entered the float due to a leak, and check that the arm moves up and down smoothly.

4 Connect the probes of an ohmmeter to the wire terminals on the sensor connector and check the resistance of the sensor with the float in both the FULL and EMPTY positions **(see illustrations)**. If the resistance does not change as you move the float, or the reading shows an open circuit (infinite resistance) replace the sensor with a new one.

5 If the sensor and all the wiring is good then it is likely the gauge is faulty – refer to Chapter

2.16b Fuel tap with union nut (arrowed)

3.4a Check the resistance with the float in the full position . . .

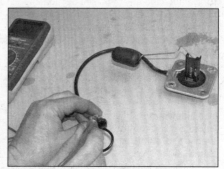

3.4b . . . and the empty position

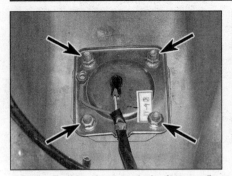

3.12a Fuel level sensor bolts (arrowed)

3.12b Take care when manoeuvring the float arm out

3.12c Remove the seal and fit a new one

9 for removal of the instrument cluster, and check with a dealer as to the availability of individual components. If the gauge is not available separately a new cluster will have to be fitted.

Models with warning light

6 The circuit consists of the sensor in the fuel tank, and the low level warning light in the instrument cluster.

7 If the warning light does not work, first check the bulb (see Chapter 9).

8 Disconnect the sensor wiring connector **(see illustration 2.11a)**. Short between the terminals in the loom side of the connector using an auxiliary piece of wire, with the ignition ON – the warning light should come on. If it doesn't check the wiring connector for a loose wire or corroded or broken terminal, then check the wiring between the sensor and the instrument cluster and to earth.

9 If the light does come on remove the sensor (see Steps 10 to 12). First make sure the float moves smoothly and freely on its rod. Next connect the probes of a continuity tester to the terminals in the sensor connector. With the sensor float at the top of its rod there should be no continuity. With it at the bottom there should be continuity. If not replace the sensor with a new one.

Replacement

 Warning: Refer to the precautions given in Section 1 before starting work.

10 Remove the fuel tank (see Section 2).

11 Make sure the cap is secure, then turn the tank over and lay it on a cushion of rags to protect it and soak up any fuel that may leak.

12 Unscrew the nuts or bolts securing the sensor and carefully manoeuvre it out of the tank, taking care not to snag the float arm, and noting which way it fits **(see illustrations)**. Discard the seal as a new one must be used **(see illustration)**. Fit a new seal onto the tank. Fit the sensor into the tank. Tighten the bolts evenly and a little at a time in a criss-cross pattern.

13 Install the tank (see Section 2), and check carefully that there are no leaks around the sensor before using the bike.

4 Carburettor overhaul notes

1 Poor engine performance, hesitation, hard starting, stalling, flooding and backfiring are all signs that carburettor maintenance may be required.

2 However these symptoms are often caused by ignition or electrical system malfunctions, or mechanical problems within the engine. Try to establish for certain that the carburettor is in need of maintenance before beginning an overhaul.

3 Check the fuel tap, strainer and/or filter, the fuel hose, the intake duct on the cylinder head and its joint clamps, the air filter, the ignition system, the spark plug(s), idle speed and valve clearances before assuming that a carburettor overhaul is required.

4 Most carburettor problems are caused by dirt particles, varnish and other deposits which build up in and block the fuel and air passages. Also, in time, gaskets and O-rings shrink or deteriorate and cause fuel and air leaks which lead to poor performance.

5 Before disassembling the carburettor, make sure you have some carburettor cleaner, a supply of clean rags, some means of blowing out the carburettor passages and a clean place to work.

6 When overhauling the carburettor, disassemble it completely and clean the parts thoroughly with the carburettor cleaning solvent and dry them with filtered, unlubricated compressed air. Blow through the fuel and air passages with compressed air to force out any dirt that may have been loosened but not removed by the solvent. Once the cleaning process is complete, reassemble the carburettor using new gaskets and O-rings.

Idle fuel/air mixture adjustment

7 Idle fuel/air mixture is set using the pilot screw **(see illustrations 6.7, 6.33 and 6.41)**. Adjustment of the pilot screw is not normally necessary and should only be performed if the engine is running roughly, stalls continually, or if the pilot screw has been turned or a new pilot screw has been fitted. Before adjusting

the pilot screw check all the items listed in Step 3.

8 If the pilot screw is removed during a carburettor overhaul, record its current setting by turning it in until it seats lightly, counting the number of turns necessary to achieve this, then unscrew it fully. On installation, turn the screw in until it seats lightly, then back it out the number of turns you've recorded.

9 Pilot screw adjustment must be made with the engine running and at normal working temperature. Stop the engine and screw the pilot screw in until it seats lightly, then back it out the number of turns specified at the beginning of this Chapter. Start the engine and set the idle speed to between 1400 and 1500 rpm using the idle speed adjustment screw (see Chapter 1).

10 Now turn the pilot screw outwards by ¼ turn at a time until the idle speed increases. Re-adjust the idle speed.

11 Now turn the pilot screw in until the idle speed drops by 50 rpm, noting exactly the amount of turn it takes. Now turn the pilot screw out by half that amount so it is set between the two parameters. Re-adjust the idle speed.

12 If it is not possible to achieve a satisfactory idle speed after adjusting the pilot screw, take the machine to a dealer and have the fuel/air mixture adjusted with the aid of an exhaust gas analyser. Also bear in mind that it is possible the problem is not down to the fuel system – ignition system causes should also be considered.

5 Carburettor removal and installation

 Warning: Refer to the precautions given in Section 1 before starting work.

Removal

1 Remove any body panels as required according to model (see Chapter 8).

2 Remove the fuel tank (see Section 2).

3 On models with a slide carburettor unscrew the top cap and draw the slide out, taking care

5.3 Unscrew the cap and draw the slide out

5.5a Slacken the clamp screw . . .

5.5b . . . and draw the air duct off

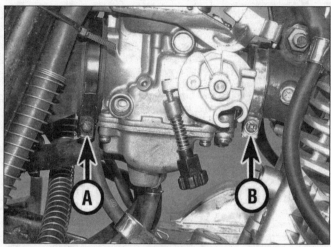

5.5c Carburettor air duct clamp screw (A) and intake duct clamp screw (B) – twin CV carbs

5.5d Unscrew the filter housing bolts (arrowed) and move the housing back to improve clearance

not to bend the needle **(see illustration)**. If required detach the throttle cable from it (see Section 7), or alternatively support it clear. Where fitted detach the choke cable (see Section 7).

4 On models with a CV carburettor detach the throttle cable(s), and where fitted, the choke cable (see Section 7).

5 Fully slacken the clamp screw(s) securing the air duct(s) to the carburettor(s) – note the orientation of the clamp(s) **(see illustrations)**. Pull the duct(s) off the carburettor(s) **(see illustration)** – if necessary and where possible unscrew the air filter housing bolts and manoeuvre the housing back to improve clearance **(see illustration)**.

6 If the carburettor is secured to the intake duct by nuts or bolts unscrew them, then detach the carburettor from the duct and remove any joint plate if fitted and O-ring(s) **(see illustrations)**. Ease the carburettor out to one side. **Note:** *Keep the carburettor level to prevent fuel spillage from the float chamber.*

7 If the carburettor(s) is/are secured to the intake duct(s) by clamps, slacken the clamp screw(s) **(see illustration 5.5c)**. Ease the carburettor out to one side **(see illustration)**. *Caution: Stuff clean rag into the cylinder head intake(s) after removing the carburettors, to prevent anything from falling in.*

5.6a Unscrew the nuts (arrowed) . . .

5.6b . . . then draw the carburettor out . . .

5.6c . . . and remove the O-ring (arrowed)

5.7 Removing a pair of CV carbs

5.8a Drain screw (arrowed) – single slide carb

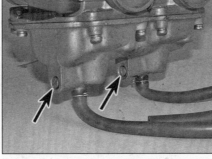

5.8b Drain screws (arrowed) – twin CV carbs

5.9a On this model detach the vacuum hose (A) and release the HT lead (B) . . .

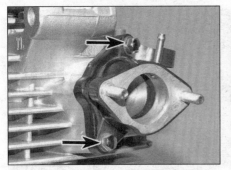

5.9b . . . then unscrew the bolts (arrowed) and remove the duct

5.10 Make sure the slide is correctly aligned as described

throttle cable(s), and where fitted the choke cable. Check the operation of the cable(s) and adjust them as necessary (see Chapter 1).
● On models with a slide carburettor make sure the slide is the correct way round when fitting it into the carburettor – normally one side of the piston is chamfered at the bottom, and this faces back towards the air intake, there is often a small guide pin in the carburettor which the cable removal slot locates over, and there is a short cut-out for the idle speed adjuster screw (see illustration).
● Check idle speed and adjust as necessary (see Chapter 1).

8 Place a suitable container below the float chamber(s), then slacken the drain screw(s) and drain all the fuel from the carburettor(s) **(see illustrations)**. Tighten the screw(s) once all the fuel has been drained.
9 If required detach any vacuum hose(s) and lead(s) from the intake duct(s), then unscrew the bolts securing the duct(s) to the cylinder head and remove it/them, along with any lead clamp(s) and joint plate(s) **(see illustrations)**. Discard the O-ring(s).

Installation

10 Installation is the reverse of removal, noting the following.
● Check for cracks or splits in the air duct and intake duct (if rubber), and replace them with new ones if necessary. If removed fit the intake duct(s) and any joint

plate(s) and lead clamp(s) using new O-ring(s) smeared with grease and tighten the bolts **(see illustration 5.9b)**. Connect the vacuum hose(s) and secure the HT lead(s) where fitted **(see illustration 5.9a)**.
● Where applicable make sure the carburettor(s) is/are fully engaged with the intake duct(s) –a squirt of WD40 or a smear of grease will ease entry. Otherwise fit a new O-ring onto the joint flange and joint plate where fitted **(see illustration 5.6c)**.
● Make sure the air duct(s) is/are fully engaged on the carburettor(s) when fitting the air filter housing, and tighten the clamp screw(s), after the filter housing bolts if disturbed **(see illustrations 5.5a, b, c and d)**.
● Refer to Section 7 for connection of the

6 Carburettor overhaul procedure and float height check

⚠ **Warning: Refer to the precautions given in Section 1 before starting work.**

1 There are two main types of carburettor used across the range of models covered in this manual, the slide carburettor and the CV carburettor. Of these main types the different manufacturers use different versions, so the illustrations may not be an identical match to the carburettor fitted on your bike. Therefore it is a good idea to make your own notes and/or take pictures using a digital camera.
2 Remove the carburettor (see Section 5). Detach the fuel hose, the vent hose and any other hoses as required according to model, noting which fits where. Check the condition of the hoses and replace them with new ones if they are damaged, deformed or deteriorated.

Slide carburettor

Disassembly

3 Undo the float chamber screws and detach it from the base of the carburettor **(see illustration)**. Note the seal and remove it if required – a new one should be used.
4 Push the float pivot pin out using a suitable tool and remove the float **(see illustration)**. Unhook the needle valve from the tab on the float, noting how it fits **(see illustration 6.24a)**.

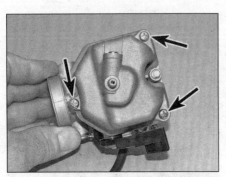

6.3 Undo the screws (arrowed) and remove the float chamber

6.4 Push the pin out and remove the float

6.5 Unscrew the pilot jet (arrowed)

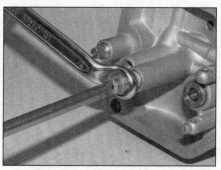

6.6a Unscrew the main jet . . .

6.6b . . . then unscrew the needle jet (arrowed)

5 Unscrew the pilot jet **(see illustration)**.
6 Counter-hold the needle jet using a spanner and unscrew the main jet, noting any washer **(see illustration)**. Unscrew the needle jet **(see illustration)**.
7 The pilot screw can be removed from the carburettor, but note that its setting must be precisely noted first (see **Haynes Hint**). Where fitted remove the anti-tamper plug. Unscrew and remove the pilot screw, along with its spring, washer and O-ring **(see illustration)**.

 To record the pilot screw's current setting, turn the screw in until it seats lightly, counting the number of turns necessary to achieve this, then fully unscrew and remove it. On installation, the screw is simply backed out the number of turns you've recorded.

8 If required, repeat Step 7 for the idle speed adjuster screw **(see illustration)**.
9 Where fitted undo the diaphragm valve cover screws and remove the cover and spring, then carefully lift the rim of the diaphragm and withdraw the needle **(see illustrations 6.36a and b)**.

Cleaning

Caution: Use only a dedicated carburettor cleaner or petroleum-based solvent for carburettor cleaning. Do not use caustic cleaners.
10 Clean the carburettor body, float chamber

and individual components according to the instructions on the cleaner container. Loosen and remove the varnish and other deposits using a nylon-bristle brush. Rinse then dry with compressed air.
11 Squirt carburettor cleaner through all of the fuel and air passages **(see illustration)**. Use a jet of compressed air to blow through all passages.
Caution: Never clean the jets or passages with a piece of wire or a drill bit, as they will be enlarged, causing the fuel and air metering rates to be upset.

Inspection

Note: *The availability of spare parts for the carburettor varies according to manufacturer – from some all components are listed as available, but even so your dealer may not stock them, and only be able to supply a complete carburettor. Other manufacturers do*

6.7 Pilot screw (arrowed) – on some carburettors it may be on the side

not supply any spare parts and only offer the complete carburettor.
12 If removed, check the tapered portion of the pilot screw and the spring and O-ring for wear or damage **(see illustration 6.41)**.
13 Check the carburettor body, float chamber, jet housings and cap for cracks, distorted sealing surfaces and other damage.
14 Insert the slide in the carburettor and check that it moves up and down smoothly. Check the surface of the slide and its bore for wear **(see illustration)**.
15 Release the needle retaining clip and withdraw the needle from the piston **(see illustration)**. Check the needle is straight. If you remove the E-clip, note which groove it fits into first, and return it to the same one. Make sure the retaining clip locates correctly on installation.
16 Check the tip of the float needle valve and the valve seat for wear which may affect their

6.8 Idle speed adjuster screw (arrowed)

6.11 Clean through all fuel and air jets and passages – air jets (arrowed)

6.14 Check the slide for wear

6.15 Release the retaining clip (arrowed) to remove the needle

6.16 Check the tip of the needle valve for wear

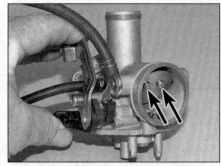

6.17 Check the mechanism and the butterfly screws (arrowed)

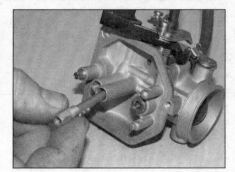

6.22a Thread the needle jet into its bore . . .

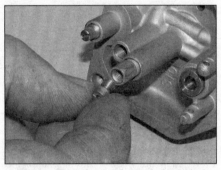

6.22b . . . then thread the main jet into the needle jet

6.23 Screw the pilot jet into its bore

6.24a Hook the needle valve onto the float . . .

ability to form a seal against the flow of fuel into the carburettor **(see illustration)**. Check the spring loaded rod in the valve operates correctly. Check the float for damage. This will usually be apparent by the presence of fuel inside the float.

17 Make sure the choke mechanism works correctly, and the choke butterfly screws (arrowed) are tight **(see illustration)**.

18 Where fitted check the diaphragm valve components, particularly looking for any holes or splits in the diaphragm – holding it up to a light will help reveal any. Make sure the spring is not distorted and the needle is straight.

Reassembly and float height check

Note: *When reassembling the carburettor(s), do not overtighten the carburettor jets and screws, as they are easily damaged.*

19 Where fitted insert the diaphragm needle in its passage then seat the rim of the diaphragm, making sure it is correctly aligned **(see illustration 6.36b)**. Fit the spring and the cover.

20 Fit the pilot screw (if removed) along with its spring, washer and O-ring, turning it in until it seats lightly **(see illustration 6.41)**. Now turn the screw out the number of turns previously recorded on removal. Fit a new anti-tamper plug where necessary.

21 Repeat Step 20 for the idle speed adjuster screw if removed **(see illustration 6.8)**. If you did not record the previous setting thread it in a little way, then reassemble and install the carburettor and make final adjustments to the idle speed with the engine running – refer to Chapter 1.

22 Screw the needle jet into the carburettor **(see illustration)**. Screw the main jet into the needle jet **(see illustration)**.

23 Screw the pilot jet into the carburettor **(see illustration)**.

24 Hook the float needle valve onto the tab on the float **(see illustration)**. Fit the float onto the carburettor, making sure the needle valve locates in the seat, then insert the pivot pin **(see illustrations)**.

25 To check the float height, hold the carburettor at an inverted angle so the needle valve just seats, and check that the float is roughly parallel to the float chamber mating surface (no actual specifications for float heights are available) **(see illustration 6.55a)**. If not, adjust the float height by carefully

6.24b . . . then fit the float . . .

6.24c . . . and insert the pin

6.26a Fit a new seal (arrowed) into the groove . . .

6.26b . . . then fit the float chamber

6.28 Undo the screws (arrowed) and remove the cover

6.30a This type of holder is a push fit . . .

6.30b . . . and this one you turn to release its tabs

6.30c Push the needle up and remove it

bending the tab for the needle valve up or down as required (see illustration 6.55b).

26 Fit the seal onto the float chamber, making sure it is seated properly. Fit the chamber onto the carburettor and tighten the screws (see illustrations).

27 Refit any hoses previously removed and secure them with clamps where fitted. Install the carburettor (see Section 5).

CV carburettor

28 Undo the top cover screws and remove the cover along with any bracket(s) fitted with it (see illustration). Remove the spring from inside the piston (see illustration 6.58c).

29 Carefully peel the diaphragm away from its sealing groove in the carburettor and withdraw the diaphragm/piston assembly (see illustration 6.58b).

30 If required release the needle holder assembly and withdraw it from the piston - some you pull out, some you turn anti-clockwise to release tabs, some are retained by small screws (see illustrations) – have a good look at how yours is fitted, and do not use force as these components are delicate. Note the spring that is usually fitted between the holder and the needle (see illustration 6.57a). Push the needle up from the bottom of the piston and withdraw it from the top (see illustration). Note the arrangement of any spacer, washer and E-clip on the needle, according to model (see illustration 6.57b).

Caution: Do not use a sharp instrument

to displace the diaphragm, as it is easily damaged.

31 Undo the float chamber screws and detach it from the base of the carburettor (see illustration). Note the seal and remove it if required - a new one should be used.

32 Push the float pivot pin out using a suitable tool and remove the float assembly, noting how it fits (see illustration 6.4). Unhook the needle valve from the tab on the float, noting how it fits (see illustration 6.24a). If the needle valve seat in the carburettor is retained by a screw (rather than being pressed in) remove the screw, along with any washer or retaining plate, then remove the seat – there may be a gauze fuel strainer underneath.

33 Unscrew the pilot jet (see illustration).

6.31 Undo the screws (arrowed) and remove the float chamber

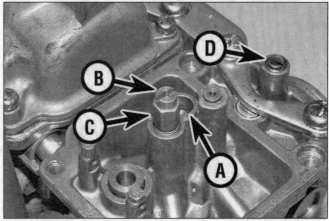

6.33 Pilot jet (A), main jet (B), needle jet (C), pilot screw (D)

6.36a Undo the screws . . .

6.36b . . . and remove the cover, spring and diaphragm . . .

6.36c . . . and where fitted the O-ring

34 Counter-hold the needle jet using a spanner and unscrew the main jet, noting any washer **(see illustration 6.6a)**. Unscrew the needle jet.

35 The pilot screw can be removed from the carburettor, but note that its setting will be disturbed (see **Haynes Hint**). Unscrew and remove the pilot screw along with its spring, washer and O-ring, which may need to coaxed out with a small screwdriver **(see illustration 6.33)**. Discard the O-ring, as a new one must be used.

36 Where fitted and if required undo the air cut-off valve cover screws and remove the cover, spring and diaphragm, noting how they fit **(see illustrations)**. Where fitted remove the small O-ring from the air passage and discard it **(see illustration)**.

37 Undo the choke plunger nut and withdraw the plunger – on twin carburettor assemblies you must first undo the linkage bar screws, withdraw the bar and remove the lifters **(see illustration)**.

Cleaning

Caution: Use only a dedicated carburettor cleaner or petroleum-based solvent for carburettor cleaning. Do not use caustic cleaners.

38 Clean the carburettor body, float chamber and individual components according to the

instructions on the cleaner container. Loosen and remove the varnish and other deposits using a nylon-bristle brush. Rinse then dry with compressed air.

39 Squirt carburettor cleaner through all of the fuel and air passages. Use a jet of compressed air to blow through all passages. *Caution: Never clean the jets or passages with a piece of wire or a drill bit, as they will be enlarged, causing the fuel and air metering rates to be upset.*

Inspection

Note: *The availability of spare parts for the carburettor varies according to manufacturer – from some all components are listed as available, but even so your dealer may not stock them, and only be able to supply a complete carburettor. Other manufacturers do not supply any spare parts and only offer the complete carburettor.*

40 Make sure the choke plunger slides up and down easily in its bore. Check the plunger spring for distortion and fatigue.

41 If removed from the carburettor, check the tapered portion of the pilot screw and the spring and O-ring for wear or damage **(see illustration)**.

42 Check the carburettor body, float chamber and top cover for cracks, distorted sealing surfaces and other damage.

43 Check the piston diaphragm for splits, holes, creases and general deterioration. Holding it up to a light will help to reveal problems of this nature. Check the spring for distortion and fatigue. Similarly check the air cut-off valve diaphragm and spring where fitted.

44 Insert the piston in the carburettor body and check that it moves up and down smoothly. Check the surface of the piston for wear.

45 Check the needle is straight. If you remove the E-clip (where fitted), note which groove it fits into first, and return it to the same one.

46 Check the tip of the float needle valve and the valve seat for wear which may affect their ability to form a seal against the flow of fuel into the carburettor **(see illustration 6.16)**. Check the spring loaded rod in the valve operates correctly. Where fitted clean the fuel strainer gauze.

47 Operate the throttle pulley to make sure the butterfly valve(s) open(s) and close(s) smoothly. If not, clean the throttle linkage, and also check the butterfly for distortion, or for any debris caught between the edge and the carburettor. Also check that the butterfly is central on the shaft – if the screws securing it to the shaft have come loose it may be catching **(see illustration)**.

48 Check the float for damage. This will usually be apparent by the presence of fuel inside the float.

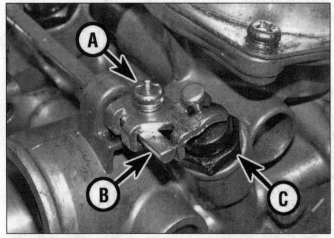

6.37 Undo the screw (A) on each lifter and withdraw the bar (B) on twin carb assemblies before unscrewing the plunger nut (C)

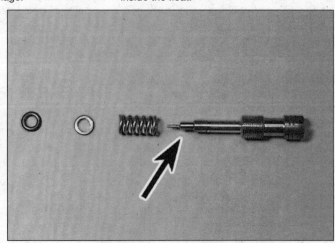

6.41 Check the pilot screw taper (arrowed)

6.47 Check the mechanism and the butterfly screws (arrowed)

6.52 Thread the pilot jet into its bore

6.53a Thread the needle jet into its bore . . .

6.53b . . . then thread the main jet into the needle jet

6.54a Fit the needle valve onto the float . . .

6.54b . . . then locate the float and insert the pin

Reassembly and float height check

Note: *When reassembling the carburettor(s), do not overtighten the carburettor jets and screws, as they are easily damaged.*

49 Fit the choke plunger into its bore and tighten the nut. On twin carburettor assemblies, after fitting both plungers locate each lifter plate under the plunger head, then slide the bar through and tighten the lifter screws (see illustration 6.37). Check the action of the plunger(s).

50 Where fitted and if removed fit the small O-ring onto the air cut-off valve air passage **(see illustration 6.36c)**. Fit the diaphragm so the tip on its inner face locates in the hole,

then fit the spring into the cover, fit the cover, and tighten the screws **(see illustrations 6.36b and a)**.

51 Fit the spring, washer and O-ring onto the pilot screw (if removed), then thread the screw in until it seats lightly **(see illustration 6.41)**. Now, turn the screw out the number of turns previously recorded, or as specified at the beginning of the Chapter.

52 Screw the pilot jet into the carburettor **(see illustration)**.

53 Screw the needle jet into the carburettor **(see illustration)**. Screw the main jet into the needle jet **(see illustration)**.

54 Where fitted locate the fuel strainer and

needle valve seat and secure them with the retainer, washer and screw according to fitment. Slide the float needle valve onto the slot on the float assembly **(see illustration)**. Position the float assembly onto the carburettor, making sure the needle valve locates in the seat, then insert the pivot pin **(see illustration)**.

55 To check the float height, hold the carburettor at an inverted angle so the needle valve just seats, and check that the float is roughly parallel to the float chamber mating surface (no actual specifications for float heights are available) **(see illustration)**. If not, adjust the float height by carefully bending the tab for the needle valve up or down as required **(see illustration)**.

6.55a Measuring float height

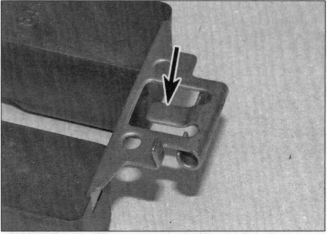

6.55b Bend the tab (arrowed) up or down as required to alter float height

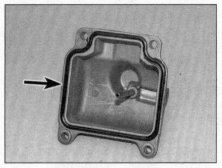

6.56a Fit a new seal (arrowed) into the groove . . .

6.56b . . . then fit the float chamber

6.57a Make sure the spring (arrowed) is in the holder

6.57b Fit the needle into the piston

6.57c On this push-fit holder align the cut-outs with the ribs (arrowed)

6.57d On this holder insert it so the tabs are offset . . .

6.57e . . . then turn it so they lock under

6.58a Fold the diaphragm down . . .

6.58b . . . then fit the piston, making sure the needle enters the jet and the tab (A) aligns with the cut-out (B)

56 Fit a new seal onto the float chamber, making sure it is seated properly **(see illustration)**. Fit the chamber onto the carburettor and tighten its screws **(see illustration)**.

57 Where fitted check that the spring is fitted to the needle holder **(see illustration)**.

Check that the washer, E-clip and spacer are correctly fitted on the needle as required according to model, then fit the needle into the piston **(see illustration)**. Fit the needle holder onto it, making sure it is correctly aligned and the spring end locates against the head of the needle, then press it gently down until either it

clicks into place, or you can turn it clockwise to secure its tabs, or fit the screws, according to model **(see illustrations)**.

58 Fold the diaphragm down over the piston **(see illustration)**. Fit the piston/diaphragm assembly into the carburettor, making sure the needle is correctly aligned with the needle jet, and any tab on the rim of the diaphragm is aligned with the cut-out in the carburettor, and hold the piston up with your finger **(see illustrations)**. Press the rim of the diaphragm into its groove, making sure it is correctly seated. Keeping the piston held up, fit the spring into it, making sure it locates correctly onto the needle holder, then fit the cover, making sure it is correctly aligned for the diaphragm tab where necessary, and locating the centre peg into the top of the spring **(see illustrations)**. Make sure the diaphragm rim stays in place and the cover is seated on

6.58c Fit the spring into the piston . . .

6.58d . . . and the cover onto the spring

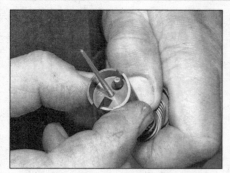

7.4a Release the cable end from the slide . . .

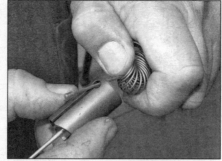

7.4b . . . and slip it out the side . . .

7.4c . . . and remove the spring

it, then locate any bracket(s) fitted with the cover and tighten the cover screws. Release the piston and check that it moves smoothly in the guide by pushing it up with your finger. Note that the piston should descend slowly and smoothly as the diaphragm draws air into the chamber – it should not drop sharply under spring pressure.

59 Refit any hoses previously removed and secure them with clamps where fitted. Install the carburettor (see Section 5).

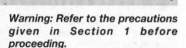

7 Throttle and choke cables

![warning] **Warning: Refer to the precautions given in Section 1 before proceeding.**

Throttle cable

Slide carburettor

1 Remove any body panels as required according to model (see Chapter 8).
2 Remove the fuel tank (see Section 2).
3 Unscrew the carburettor top cap and draw the slide out, taking care not to bend the needle (see illustration 5.3).

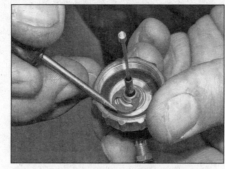

7.4d Lever the E-clip out (where fitted)

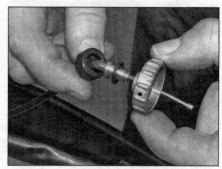

7.4e Draw the cable out of the cap

4 Draw the return spring up and hold it compressed, then push the cable into the piston to free its end and slip it out of the slot in the side (see illustrations). Remove the spring (see illustration). Where fitted release the E-clip securing the cable in the cap (see illustration). Draw the cable out of the cap (see illustration).
5 Withdraw the cable from the machine, carefully noting its correct routing – you can tie string to the end which can be drawn through with the cable and used as a guide to draw the new cable in when installing it.
6 Undo any cable retainer screw or locknut

on the switch housing on the handlebar (see illustration). Undo the switch housing screws and separate the halves. Detach the cable end from the pulley (see illustration). Draw the cable out of or unscrew it from the bottom half of the housing.

CV carburettor

7 Remove any body panels as required according to model (see Chapter 8).
8 Remove the fuel tank (see Section 2).
9 Where fitted unscrew the throttle cam cover screws and remove the cover (see

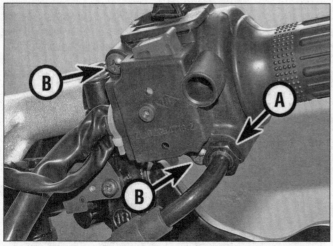

7.6a Undo the retainer screw or locknut (A) then the housing screws (B)

7.6b Split the housing and detach the cable end from the pulley

7.9 Undo the screws (arrowed) and remove the cover

7.10a Slacken the nuts (arrowed) . . .

7.10b . . . then slip the cable out of the bracket . . .

7.10c . . . and detach the end

7.14 Locate the peg (arrowed) in the hole in the handlebar

illustration). Where twin cables are fitted (one for opening the throttle, one for closing), mark each according to its position in the bracket, and also mark their upper ends according to their position in the switch housing.

10 Slacken the nuts securing the cable(s) in the bracket, then slip the cable(s) out and detach the end(s) from the cam **(see illustrations)**.

11 Withdraw the cable from the machine, carefully noting its correct routing – you can tie string to the end which can be drawn through with the cable and used as a guide to draw the new cable in when installing it.

12 Undo any cable retainer screw(s) or locknut(s) on the switch housing on the handlebar **(see illustration 7.6a)**. Undo the switch housing screws and separate the halves. Detach the cable end(s) from the pulley **(see illustration 7.6b)**. Draw the cable(s) out

of or unscrew it/them from the bottom half of the housing.

Installation – slide and CV types

13 Installation is the reverse of removal.
14 Make sure the cables are correctly routed – if string was used on removal tie it to the end of the cable and pull it through. The cable(s) must not interfere with any other component and should not be kinked or bent sharply. On models with twin cables make sure each is fitted in its correct location – if new cables are being installed match them according to the old cables. Lubricate the cable ends with multi-purpose grease. When fitting the switch housing halves onto the handlebar, locate the peg in the hole in the handlebar **(see illustration)**.
15 On slide carburettors feed the cable through the carburettor cap, and secure it with the E-clip where fitted **(see illustrations**

7.4e and d). Fit the spring over the cable and against the cap, then hold the spring up and fit the cable end into the slide **(see illustrations 7.4c, b and a)**. Fit the slide into the carburettor, making sure it is correctly aligned – normally one side of the slide is chamfered at the bottom, and this faces back towards the air intake, there is often a small guide pin in the carburettor which the cable removal slot locates over, and there is a short cut-out for the idle speed adjuster screw **(see illustration 5.10)**.
16 On CV carburettors make sure each cable is correctly located in the throttle cam according to its function (i.e. opening the throttle or closing it) **(see illustrations 7.10c, b and a)**. Fit the cam cover where applicable **(see illustration 7.9)**.
17 Adjust the cable freeplay (see Chapter 1). Operate the throttle to check that it opens and closes freely. Turn the handlebars back and forth to make sure the cable doesn't cause the steering to bind.
18 Start the engine and check that the idle speed does not rise as the handlebars are turned. If it does, the throttle cable(s) is/are routed incorrectly. Correct the problem before riding the motorcycle.

Choke cable

Removal

19 Remove the fuel tank (see Section 2).
20 Release the cable from its holder and free the cable end from the lever or linkage bar **(see illustrations)**.

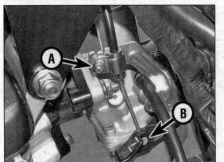

7.20a On this slide carb slacken the screw (A) and free the cable from the holder then detach the end (B) from the lever

7.20b On this CV carb slacken the screw (arrowed) and free the cable from the holder . . .

7.20c . . . then detach the end from the lever

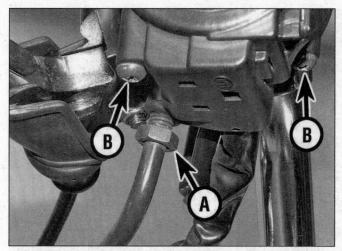

7.22a On this type slacken the nut (A), then undo the housing screws (B), detach the cable end from the lever, then thread the cable out of the housing

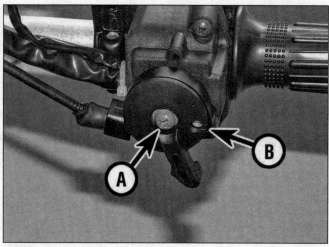

7.22b On this type undo the screw (A) and detach the lever, then free the cable end (B) from it

21 Withdraw the cable from the machine, carefully noting its correct routing – you can tie string to the end which can be drawn through with the cable and used as a guide to draw the new cable in when installing it.

22 Undo any cable retainer screw or locknut on the switch housing on the handlebar **(see illustration)**. Release the choke lever, either by undoing the switch housing screws and separating the halves, or by undoing the screw securing it on the underside, then detach the cable end from it **(see illustration)**. Where necessary draw the cable out of or unscrew it from the bottom half of the housing, according to type.

Installation

23 Installation is the reverse of removal.

24 Make sure the cable is correctly routed – if string was used on removal tie it to the end of the cable and pull it through. The cable must not interfere with any other component and should not be kinked or bent sharply. Lubricate the cable ends with multi-purpose grease. If fitting the switch housing halves onto the handlebar, locate the peg in the hole in the handlebar where fitted **(see illustration 7.14)**.

25 Adjust the cable freeplay (see Chapter 1).

8.5 Typical vacuum take-off point blanking screw (arrowed)

Operate the choke to check that it opens and closes freely. Turn the handlebars back and forth to make sure the cable doesn't cause the steering to bind.

26 Start the engine and check that the idle speed does not rise as the handlebars are turned. If it does, the choke cable is routed incorrectly. Correct the problem before riding the motorcycle.

---

8 Carburettor synchronisation (twin carburettors)

Note: *This procedure applies only to twin cylinder engines with a carburettor for each cylinder.*

⚠ *Warning: Petrol (gasoline) is extremely flammable, so take extra precautions when you work on any part of the fuel system. Don't smoke or allow open flames or bare light bulbs near the work area, and don't work in a garage where a natural gas-type appliance is present. If you spill any fuel on your skin, rinse it off immediately with soap and water. When you perform any kind of work on the fuel system, wear safety glasses and have a fire extinguisher suitable for a Class B type fire (flammable liquids) on hand.*

⚠ *Warning: Take great care not to burn your hand on the hot engine unit when accessing the gauge take-off points on the inlet manifolds. Do not allow exhaust gases to build up in the work area; either perform the check outside or use an exhaust gas extraction system.*

1 Carburettor synchronisation is simply the process of adjusting the carburettors so they pass the same amount of fuel/air mixture to each cylinder. This is done by measuring the vacuum produced in each cylinder. Carburettors that are out of synchronisation

will result in increased fuel consumption, increased engine temperature, less than ideal throttle response and higher vibration levels. Before synchronising the carburettors, make sure the idle speed is correct and that the valve clearances are properly set (see Chapter 1).

2 To properly synchronise the carburettors, you will need a set of vacuum gauges or calibrated tubes (manometer) to indicate engine vacuum. The equipment used should be suitable for a two cylinder engine and come complete with the necessary adapters and hoses to fit the take-off points.

3 Start the engine and let it run until it reaches normal operating temperature, then shut it off.

4 Remove any body panels as required according to models for access to the carburettors (see Chapter 8).

5 Remove the blanking screw from the vacuum take-off point on each intake duct **(see illustration)**. Thread the take-off adapter provided with the vacuum gauges into the blanking screw hole. If on one side there is a vacuum hose (for example for the AIS control valve if fitted) connected to a union in place of a blanking screw, detach the hose from it and use the union rather than an adapter.

6 Connect the vacuum gauge hoses to the intake ducts. Make sure they are a good fit because any air leaks will result in false readings.

7 Start the engine and make sure the idle speed is correct. If it isn't, adjust it. If the gauges are fitted with damping adjustment, set this so that the needle flutter is just eliminated but so that they can still respond to small changes in pressure.

8 The vacuum readings for both cylinders should be the same, or at least within 20 mmHg of each other.

9 If the vacuum readings vary, turn the synchronising screw situated in-between the carburettors in the throttle linkage **(see**

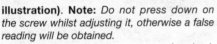

8.9 Carburettor synchronisation screw (arrowed)

9.4 Exhaust downpipe nuts (arrowed)

9.5a On this model unscrew the nut on the inner end . . .

illustration). Note: *Do not press down on the screw whilst adjusting it, otherwise a false reading will be obtained.*

10 When the carburettors are synchronised, open and close the throttle quickly to settle the linkage, and recheck the gauge readings, readjusting if necessary.

11 When the adjustment is complete, check the idle speed and adjust as required until the idle speed is correct. Stop the engine.

12 Remove the vacuum gauges. Fit the blanking screw(s) and/or connect the hose where removed. Install any removed body panels.

9.5b . . . then withdraw the bolt (arrowed)

9.5c On this twin cylinder model one bolt (arrowed) secures both silencers

9 Exhaust system

⚠ *Warning: If the engine has been running the exhaust system will be very hot. Allow the system to cool before carrying out any work.*

Note: *Before starting work on the exhaust system spray all the mounting bolts, and if they are to be removed the heat shield bolts, with penetrating fluid – many of them are exposed and are prone to corrosion.*

Removal

1 Remove any body panels or engine bars as required according to model (see Chapter 8).

2 On models with an air induction system that flows air directly into the exhaust, either release the hose clamp and detach the hose from its union on the reed valve housing, or

unscrew the reed valve housing bolts and detach it from the exhaust **(see illustration 10.10)**. Note that there will be a valve for each exhaust pipe on twin cylinder engines.

3 On models with a two-piece system (i.e. separate silencer and downpipe), if you want or need to remove the two sections separately, or only one of the sections, slacken the clamp bolt at the joint, then follow the applicable Steps only. On twin cylinder engines look for a joint pipe linking the exhaust pipe for each cylinder (some models have one, others don't) – if there is one slacken the clamp on the joint.

4 Unscrew the nuts or bolts securing the downpipe to the cylinder head **(see illustration)**.

5 Support the exhaust, then unscrew the silencer mounting bolt **(see illustrations)**.

6 On models with a two-piece system,

locate and unscrew any other mounting bolt – there could be one towards the back of the downpipe section and/or the front of the silencer.

7 Detach the downpipe from the cylinder head, noting how the flange locates on the studs where fitted, and how the half-ring spacers fit where present, and remove the exhaust system **(see illustrations)**.

8 Remove the gasket from the port in the cylinder head and discard it – a new one must be fitted **(see illustration)**.

9 On models with a two-piece system where you have separated the silencer and downpipe, and on twin cylinder engines with a joint between pipes, check the condition of the sealing ring at the joint – it could be in or on either section. If it is in reasonable condition it can be re-used – it is too easy to damage a new one when fitting it to make it

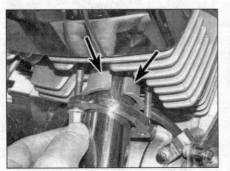

9.7a Where necessary draw the flange off the studs and remove the spacers (arrowed)

9.7b Removing one side of the exhaust system on a twin cylinder model

9.8 Use a screwdriver to remove the old gasket from the head

9.11 Always use a new gasket in the head port(s)

worthwhile replacing one just for the sake of it. If necessary dig the old one out, and be very careful when fitting the new one and joining the sections.

10 If required and where fitted remove any heat shields, note the arrangement of the washers.

Installation

11 Installation is the reverse of removal, noting the following:

- *It is advisable to apply some copper grease to the threads of all fasteners.*
- *Fit a new gasket into the cylinder head port(s) (see illustration) – apply a smear of grease to keep it/them in place if necessary.*
- *On models with a two-piece system and on twin cylinder engines with a joint between pipes, fit a new sealing ring to the section joint if necessary and take care not to distort it when joining the sections.*

Tighten the clamp bolt after tightening the downpipe nuts/bolts (if loosened), but before any mounting bolts, making sure the joint sections are parallel.

- *Align all mountings and finger-tighten the nuts/bolts, then fully tighten the downpipe nuts/bolts first.*
- *Do not forget to connect the AIS hose or fit the reed valve housing where applicable (see Section 10).*
- *Run the engine and check that there are no air leaks.*

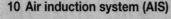

10 Air induction system (AIS)

Function and check

1 Refer to Chapter 1 for a description and routine checks of the system.

2 On models fitted with a control valve, if the valve is thought to be faulty, remove it (see below). With no vacuum applied to the vacuum hose union, it should be possible to blow air into the hose union from the air filter and it should exit via the reed valve through the union for the hose to the engine. If you then apply a vacuum it should not be possible to blow air through. If not, the diaphragm valve is faulty. Also it should not be possible to blow air through in the opposite direction via the engine hose union and for it to exit via the air filter hose union. If you can, then the reed valve is faulty.

3 On models with just a reed valve, locate the open end of the air inlet hose or detach the hose from the air filter housing, according to model **(see illustration)**. It should be possible to blow air into the hose and it should exit via the reed valve into the exhaust system. It should not be possible to suck air back. If not, the reed valve is faulty.

4 Availability of individual components for either of the valves will vary between manufacturers – check with your dealer, but it is likely you will have to buy the complete valve assembly. In the case of a faulty reed valve, note that sometimes a dirt particle can lodge between the valve and its seat preventing a good seal, so it is worth removing the valve and cleaning it before consigning it to the bin **(see illustration)**.

Control valve removal

5 Remove any body panels as required according to model (see Chapter 8).

6 Release the clamps securing the air inlet hose, the vacuum hose, and the outlet hose and detach them from their unions, noting which fits where **(see illustration)**. Unscrew the bolt(s) and remove the valve.

7 If the diaphragm valve or reed valve is faulty and is available separately, undo the valve cover screws and remove the cover and the valve, noting how it fits **(see illustrations)**. Fit the new valve, making sure it is correctly located, then fit the cover using a new O-ring.

8 To replace a hose, release the clamps securing it and disconnect it at each end. Note its routing. To detach the hose union

10.3 AIS air supply hose (arrowed)

10.4 Make sure the reed (arrowed) is making a good seal with its seat

10.6 Air inlet hose (A), vacuum hose (B) and air outlet hose (C)

10.7a Remove the covers to check the diaphragm (arrowed) . . .

10.7b . . . and the sealing ring (arrowed) for the air passage . . .

10.7c . . . and the reed valve (arrowed)

10.8 Intake pipe union bolts (arrowed)

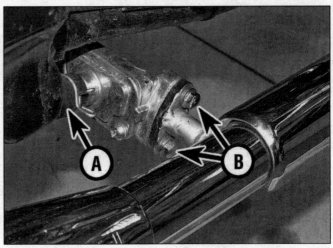

10.10 Air intake hose (A), reed valve housing bolts (B)

from the head or block unscrew its bolts **(see illustration)**. Discard the seal or gasket – a new one must be used.

Reed valve removal

9 Remove any body panels as required according to model (see Chapter 8).
10 Release the clamp securing the air inlet hose and detach it from the reed valve **(see illustration)**. Unscrew the bolt(s) and remove the valve.
11 If the reed valve is faulty and is available separately, undo the valve cover screws and remove the cover and the valve, noting how it fits **(see illustration 10.7c)**. Fit the new valve, making sure it is correctly located, then fit the cover.
12 To replace a hose, release the clamps securing them and disconnect them at each end. Note its routing. To detach the hose union from the head or block unscrew its bolts **(see illustration 10.8)**. Also note the filter canister on open-ended hoses that do not connect to the air filter housing, and make sure the hose or filter is not blocked **(see illustration 10.3)**.

Installation

13 Installation is the reverse of removal.
14 Make sure all the hoses are correctly routed and securely connected at each end and held by their clamps.

11 Catalytic converter

General information

1 On some models a catalytic converter may be incorporated in the exhaust system to minimise the level of exhaust pollutants released into the atmosphere.
2 The catalytic converter consists of a canister containing a fine mesh impregnated with a catalyst material, over which the hot exhaust gases pass. The catalyst speeds up the oxidation of harmful carbon monoxide, unburned hydrocarbons and soot, effectively reducing the quantity of harmful products released into the atmosphere via the exhaust gases.

Precautions

3 The catalytic converter is a reliable and simple device which needs no maintenance in itself, but there are some facts of which an owner should be aware if the converter is to function properly for its full service life.
● *DO NOT use leaded or lead replacement petrol (gasoline) – the additives will coat the precious metals, reducing their converting efficiency and will eventually destroy the catalytic converter.*
● *Always keep the ignition and fuel systems well-maintained in accordance with the manufacturer's schedule – if the fuel/air mixture is suspected of being incorrect have it checked on an exhaust gas analyser.*
● *If the engine develops a misfire, do not ride the bike at all (or at least as little as possible) until the fault is cured.*
● *DO NOT use fuel or engine oil additives – these may contain substances harmful to the catalytic converter.*
● *DO NOT continue to use the bike if the engine burns oil to the extent of leaving a visible trail of blue smoke.*
● *Avoid bump-starting the bike unless absolutely necessary.*

Chapter 5
Ignition system

Contents

Degrees of difficulty

Easy, suitable for novice with little experience	Fairly easy, suitable for beginner with some experience	Fairly difficult, suitable for competent DIY mechanic	Difficult, suitable for experienced DIY mechanic	Very difficult, suitable for expert DIY or professional

Specifications

General torque settings according to thread size

5 mm bolt/nut.	5 Nm
6 mm bolt/nut.	10 Nm
8 mm bolt/nut.	24 Nm
10 mm bolt/nut.	35 Nm
12 mm bolt/nut.	55 Nm

1 General information

All models are fitted with an electronic ignition system which, due to its lack of mechanical parts, and with the exception of the spark plug(s) is totally maintenance-free. The system comprises a trigger or triggers, a pick-up coil, electronic control unit (ECU), and ignition coil(s).

The ignition trigger(s), which is/are on the alternator rotor on the left-hand end of the crankshaft, magnetically operate the pick-up coil as the crankshaft rotates. The coil sends a signal to the electronic control unit, which then supplies the ignition coil with the power necessary to produce a spark at the plug.

The ECU incorporates an electronic advance system.

The system has a starter safety circuit, comprising the neutral switch and the clutch switch, and on some models the sidestand switch, that prevents the engine from being started unless it is in neutral, or if it is in gear unless the clutch lever is pulled in, and where applicable the sidestand is up.

Because of their nature, the individual ignition system components can be checked but not repaired. If ignition system troubles occur, and the faulty component can be isolated, the only cure for the problem is to replace the part with a new one. Keep in mind that most electrical parts, once purchased, cannot be returned. To avoid unnecessary expense, make very sure the faulty component has been positively identified before buying a replacement part.

Note that there is no provision for adjusting the ignition timing.

2.2a Where necessary undo the screws (arrowed) and remove the cover

2.2b Pull the cap off the spark plug

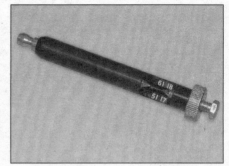

2.4 A typical spark gap testing tool

2 Ignition system check

⚠ **Warning: The energy levels in electronic systems can be very high. On no account should the ignition be switched on whilst the plug or plug cap is being held. Shocks from the HT circuit can be most unpleasant. Secondly, it is vital that the engine is not turned over or run with the plug cap removed, and that the plug is soundly earthed (grounded) when the system is checked for sparking. The ignition system components can be seriously damaged if the HT circuit becomes isolated.**

1 As no means of adjustment is available, any failure of the system can be traced to failure of a system component or a simple wiring fault. Of the two possibilities, the latter is by far the most likely. In the event of failure, check the system in a logical fashion, as described. First make sure the battery is fully charged and fuse has not blown (see Chapter 9).

2 Where fitted, and if it restricts removal of the spark plug cap, undo the side trim cover screws and remove the cover **(see illustration)**. Pull the cap off the spark plug **(see illustration)**. Fit a spare spark plug that is known to be good into the cap and lay the plug against the cylinder head with the threads contacting it. If necessary, hold the spark plug with an insulated tool.

⚠ **Warning: Do not remove the spark plug from the engine to perform this check – atomised fuel being pumped out of the open spark plug hole could ignite, causing severe injury! Make sure the plug is securely held against the engine – if it is not earthed when the engine is turned over, the ignition control unit could be damaged.**

3 Check that the transmission is in neutral, then turn the ignition switch ON, set the kill switch to RUN, and turn the engine over on the starter motor. If the system is in good condition a regular, fat blue spark should be evident at the plug electrodes. If the spark appears thin or yellowish, or is non-existent,

further investigation will be necessary. Turn the ignition off. On twin cylinder engines repeat for the other spark plug.

4 The ignition system must be able to produce a spark which is capable of jumping at least a 6 mm gap. Simple ignition spark gap testing tools are commercially available – follow the manufacturer's instructions **(see illustration)**.

5 If the test results are good the entire ignition system can be considered good. If the spark appears thin or yellowish, or is non-existent, further investigation is necessary.

6 Ignition faults can be divided into two categories, namely those where the ignition system has failed completely, and those which are due to a partial failure. The likely faults are listed below, starting with the most probable source of failure. Work through the list systematically, referring to the subsequent sections for full details of the necessary checks and tests. **Note:** *Before checking the following items ensure that the battery is fully charged and that the fuse(s) is/are in good condition.*

● *Loose, corroded or damaged wiring connections, broken or shorted wiring between any of the component parts of the ignition system (see Chapter 9, Section 2).*
● *Faulty HT lead(s) or spark plug cap(s), faulty spark plug(s), dirty, worn or corroded plug electrodes, or incorrect gap between electrodes.*
● *Faulty ignition switch (see Chapter 9).*
● *Faulty neutral, clutch or sidestand switch, or safety circuit (see Chapter 9).*

3.3a Disconnect the coil primary wiring connector . . .

● *Faulty pick-up coil or damaged trigger(s).*
● *Faulty ignition coil(s).*
● *Faulty electronic control unit (ECU).*

7 If the above checks don't reveal the cause of the problem, have the ignition system tested by a dealer.

3 Ignition coil and spark plug cap

Check

1 To locate the coil(s) trace the HT lead(s) from the spark plug(s), removing any body panels and the fuel tank as required according to model (see Chapters 8 and 4). Check the coil visually for loose or damaged connectors and terminals, loose mountings, cracks and other damage.

2 Make sure the ignition is off. The coil can be tested in situ, but remove it if preferred (see Steps 8 and 9).

3 Disconnect the primary wiring connector(s) **(see illustrations)**. Where fitted, and if it restricts removal of the spark plug cap, undo the side trim cover screws and remove the cover **(see illustration 2.2a)**. Pull the cap off the spark plug **(see illustration 2.2b)**.

4 Set an ohmmeter or multimeter to the ohms x 1 scale and measure the resistance between the primary terminal on the coil and one of the coil mounting bolts on models with a single wiring connector, and between both

3.3b . . . or connectors (arrowed), according to type

3.4a Testing the coil primary resistance on single terminal models

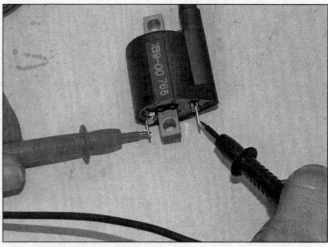

3.4b Testing the coil primary resistance on twin terminal models

the primary terminals on the coil on models with twin connectors **(see illustrations)**. This will give a resistance reading of the primary windings of the coil – depending on the manufacturer of the coil the reading could be anything from 0.5 ohm to 5 ohms.

5 To check the condition of the secondary windings, set the meter to the K-ohm scale. Unscrew the plug cap from the end of the HT lead **(see illustration)**. Connect one meter probe to the primary terminal on the coil (either of them on twin terminal coils), and insert the other in the end of the HT lead **(see illustration)**. Depending on the manufacturer of the coil the reading could be anything from 3 to 12 K-ohms.

6 If the readings are as specified, measure the resistance of the spark plug cap by connecting the meter probes between the HT lead socket and the spark plug contact **(see illustration)**. A cap usually has a resistance of about 5 K-ohms. If not, replace the spark plug cap with a new one.

Removal and installation

7 To locate the coil(s) trace the HT lead(s) from the spark plug(s), removing any body panels and the fuel tank as required according to model (see Chapters 8 and 4).

8 Disconnect the primary wiring connector(s)

3.5a To test the coil secondary resistance unscrew the cap from the lead . . .

from the coil **(see illustration 3.3a or b)**. Where fitted, and if it restricts removal of the spark plug cap, undo the side trim cover screws and remove the cover **(see illustration 2.2a)**. Pull the cap off the spark plug **(see illustration 2.2b)**. Release the lead from its guide on the intake duct where fitted, and/or from any other ties.

9 Undo the screws or bolts securing the coil **(see illustration)**, noting the earth wire on single terminal models, or release the coil sleeve from its mount **(see illustration 3.3b)**, as required.

10 Installation is the reverse of removal.

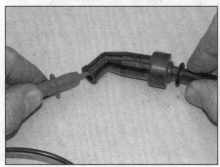

3.6 Measuring the resistance of the spark plug cap

3.9 Coil mounting screws (arrowed) – typical coil; note the earth wire

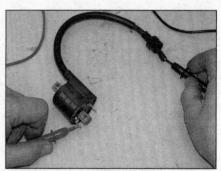

3.5b . . . and connect the multimeter leads between the primary circuit terminal (either terminal on coils with two) and the spark plug lead end

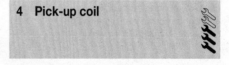

4   Pick-up coil

Check

1 Make sure the ignition is OFF.

2 The pick-up coil is in the alternator cover on the left-hand side of the engine. Trace the wiring from the cover and disconnect it at the 2-pin connector. Check the wiring and connectors for loose or broken wires and terminals. Using an ohmmeter or multimeter set to the ohms x 100 scale, measure the resistance between the terminals on the coil side of the connector. There should be a reading of anything between 15 and 150 ohms, depending on the manufacturer. If not, and in particular if there is zero or infinite resistance, replace the coil with a new one (Step 4).

3 If the result is good, and you have checked the wiring and connectors as described in Step 2, remove the alternator cover (see Chapter 2A, 2B, 2C or 2D) and check whether the sensor has come loose on its mounts.

4.4a Pick-up coil (arrowed) – OHV single cyl engine

4.4b Pick-up coil (arrowed) – OHC single cyl engine

Removal and installation

4 Make sure the ignition is OFF. Remove the alternator cover, then remove the stator and pick-up coil from it (see Chapter 2A, 2B, 2C or 2D, according to engine) – on most models the stator and coil come as an integrated assembly along with the wiring sub-loom, but on some the coil may be separate **(see illustrations)**.

5 Electronic control unit (ECU)

1 If the tests shown in the preceding or following Sections have failed to isolate the cause of an ignition fault, it is possible that the electronic control unit itself is faulty. No test details are available with which the unit can be tested. The best way to determine whether it

is faulty is to substitute it with a known good one, if available. Otherwise, take the unit to a dealer for assessment.

2 Before condemning the ECU make sure the wiring connector terminals are clean and none of the wires have broken. The ECU is usually located along the frame top rails, typically under the seat, but may also be mounted behind the side panels or under the fuel tank **(see illustration)**.

6 Ignition timing

General information

1 Since no provision exists for adjusting the ignition timing and since no component is subject to mechanical wear, there is no need

for regular checks: only if investigating a fault such as a loss of power or a misfire, should the ignition timing be checked.

2 The ignition timing is checked dynamically (engine running) using a stroboscopic lamp. The inexpensive neon lamps should be adequate in theory, but in practice may produce a pulse of such low intensity that the timing mark remains indistinct. If possible, one of the more precise xenon tube lamps should be used, powered by an external source of the appropriate voltage. **Note:** *Do not use the machine's own battery, as an incorrect reading may result from stray impulses within the machine's electrical system.*

Check

3 Warm the engine up to normal operating temperature, then stop it.

4 Unscrew the timing inspection cap and crankshaft end cap from the alternator cover

4.4c Pick-up coil (arrowed) – twin cyl engine

5.2 Typical electronic control unit (arrowed)

6.4a Timing inspection cap (A), crankshaft end cap (B) – OHV single cyl engine

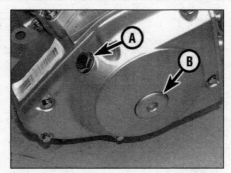

6.4b Timing inspection cap (A), crankshaft end cap (B) – K157FMI engine

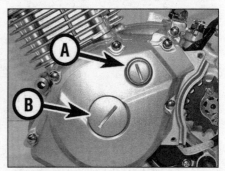

6.4c Timing inspection cap (A), crankshaft end cap (B) – 154FMI engine

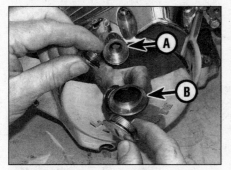

6.4d Timing inspection cap (A), crankshaft end cap (B) – twin cyl engine

6.5 Ignition timing mark, as on OHV single cyl engine

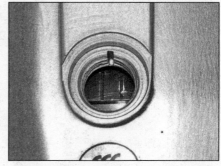

6.9 Full advance marks, as on OHV single cyl engine

on the left-hand side of the engine (see illustrations).

5 Turn the engine anti-clockwise using a suitable socket on the alternator rotor nut to find the mark on the rotor which indicates the firing point at idle speed – usually a line, often with an F next to it (see illustration) (this should

HAYNES HINT *The timing marks can be highlighted with white paint to make them more visible under the stroboscope light – turn the engine anti-clockwise using a socket on the alternator rotor bolt to find the marks.*

not be confused with the line that denotes the TDC position for the engine which may be a similar line, but often with a T next to it). The static timing mark with which this should align is a notch in the inspection hole rim or a pointer next to the hole on the crankcase.

6 Connect the timing light to the HT lead as described in the manufacturer's instructions.

7 Start the engine and aim the light at the inspection hole.

8 With the machine idling at the specified speed, the mark on the rotor should align with the static timing mark.

9 Slowly increase the engine speed whilst observing the mark – it should appear to move clockwise, increasing in relation to the engine

speed until it reaches full advance, which may be identified by two parallel lines, another single line, or sometimes there is no mark for it at all (see illustration).

10 As already stated, there is no means of adjustment of the ignition timing on these machines. If the ignition timing is incorrect, or suspected of being incorrect, one of the ignition system components is at fault, and the system must be tested as described in the preceding Sections of this Chapter.

11 Install the timing inspection cap, and crankshaft end cap if removed, using a new O-ring or sealing washer as required, and smear the O-ring(s) with grease.

Chapter 6
Frame and suspension

Contents

Degrees of difficulty

| Easy, suitable for novice with little experience | 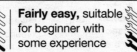 | Fairly easy, suitable for beginner with some experience | | Fairly difficult, suitable for competent DIY mechanic | | Difficult, suitable for experienced DIY mechanic | | Very difficult, suitable for expert DIY or professional | |

Specifications

General torque settings according to thread size

5 mm bolt/nut	5 Nm
6 mm bolt/nut	10 Nm
8 mm bolt/nut	24 Nm
10 mm bolt/nut	35 Nm
12 mm bolt/nut	55 Nm

1 General information

Most models have a tubular steel frame, though some sports models may have an aluminium beam frame.

Front suspension is by oil-damped telescopic forks, conventionally mounted on some models and upside down on others. Rear suspension is either by twin shock absorbers or by a single shock absorber and a rising rate linkage, on all models via a box-section or tube steel swingarm that pivots through the frame. On some models the rear shock absorber(s) is/are adjustable for spring pre-load.

2 Frame inspection and repair

1 The frame should not require attention unless accident damage has occurred. In most cases, fitting a new frame is the only satisfactory remedy for such damage. Frame specialists have the jigs and other equipment necessary for straightening a frame to the required standard of accuracy, but even then there is no simple way of assessing to what extent it may have been over-stressed.

2 After a high mileage, the frame should be examined closely for signs of cracking or splitting at the welded joints. Loose engine mounting bolts can cause ovaling or fracturing of the mounting points. Minor damage can often be repaired by specialised welding, depending on the extent and nature of the damage.

3 Remember that a frame that is out of alignment will cause handling problems. If, as the result of an accident, misalignment is suspected, it will be necessary to strip the machine completely so the frame can be thoroughly checked.

3.1a Remove the split pin (arrowed) . . .

3.1b . . . or the E-clip (arrowed) and washer

3.1c Where fitted note how the return spring ends locate

3 Footrests, brake pedal and gearchange lever

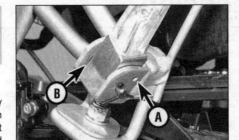

3.1d This footrest has a ball and spring above the hole (A), and a washer (B)

3.1e This footrest can be removed with its bracket by unscrewing the bolt (arrowed)

Footrests

1 The standard footrests fitted on many models are held to their bracket by a pivot pin that is retained either by an E-clip or a split pin. Either remove the E-clip or straighten and remove the split pin from the bottom of the pivot pin and collect the washer where fitted **(see illustrations)**. Withdraw the pivot pin and remove the footrest. On models fitted with a return spring on the rider's footrest note how the spring ends locate **(see illustration)**. The passenger footrests may be fitted with ball and spring, and on some a detent plate, to keep them in a raised position when required **(see illustration)** – take care when removing the footrest as the ball and spring are easily lost, and note how the plate locates. On some models, if required you can remove the footrest complete with its bracket **(see illustration)**.

2 On Custom models with footboards for the rider you can unbolt the individual boards **(see illustration)**.

3 Installation is the reverse of removal. Apply a small amount of multi-purpose grease to the pivot pin. Use a new split pin where fitted and bend its ends round the pivot pin to secure it.

4 If necessary it may be possible to fit a new rubber to the peg or footboard. On models with standard footrests the rubber is secured either by two screws on the underside of the peg **(see illustration)**, or the rubber can be simply slid off the peg. Footboard rubbers generally have rubber locating posts on their underside that fit into holes in the board **(see illustration 3.2)** – pull the old rubber off, and to make fitting the new one easier lubricate the posts with oil or grease.

Brake pedal

5 There are many different brake pedal arrangements – three common types are described and illustrated. The common features between all is that they have a method of pivoting, a method of connection to the rear brake and rear brake light switch, and a method of returning under spring tension. To remove the pedal it is necessary to detach it from whatever connects it to the rear brake and switch and to release it from the return spring and from its pivot. Take a moment to study how the pedal on your model works and how it connects.

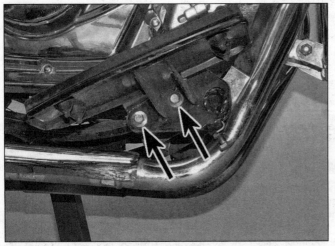

3.2 Unscrew the bolts (arrowed) and remove the board – typical example shown

3.4 Undo the screws (arrowed) to release the rubber

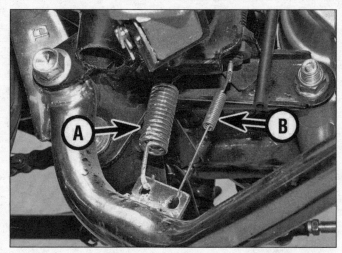

3.6 Unhook the return spring (A) and the switch spring (B)

3.7 Remove the split pin (A) and detach the brake rod. Pedal pivot bolt (B)

Type A

6 Unhook the brake light switch spring and pedal return spring from the pedal **(see illustration)**.

7 Straighten and remove the split pin securing the brake rod to the pedal, then remove the washer where fitted **(see illustration)**. Draw the pivot pin out and detach the rod. Discard the split pin – a new one should be used.

8 Unscrew the pivot bolt or nut and remove the pedal **(see illustration 3.7)**.

Type B

9 Straighten and remove the split pin from the pivot pin securing the brake and switch cables to the pedal, then draw the pivot pin out, collecting the washer where fitted, and detach the cables **(see illustration)**. Discard the split pin – a new one should be used.

10 Release the circlip securing the pedal on the pivot, then draw the pedal off along with the return spring, noting how its ends locate **(see illustration)**. Discard the circlip – a new one should be used.

Type C

11 Release and remove the pivot pin securing the brake pedal to the master cylinder pushrod **(see illustrations)**. Discard

3.9 Remove the split pin and withdraw the pivot pin to free the cables

the split pin where fitted – a new one should be used.

12 Unhook the brake pedal return spring and the brake light switch spring from the hook on the pedal **(see illustration)**.

13 Straighten and remove the split pin, or release the circlip, or unscrew the pivot bolt or nut, securing the brake pedal on its pivot and remove the pedal and any thrust washer(s) **(see illustration 3.12)**. Discard the split pin or circlip where fitted – a new one should be used.

3.10 Release the circlip (A) and remove the pedal, noting how the return spring (B) locates

Installation

14 Installation is the reverse of removal, noting the following:

● Apply grease to the pedal pivot – clean off any old grease first.

● Use new split pins and/or circlips as required and bend the ends of split pins round to secure them.

● Make sure the spring ends locate correctly **(see illustration 3.6, 3.10 or 3.12)**.

● Check the operation of the brake and the brake light switch (see Chapter 1).

3.11a Remove the split pin . . .

3.11b . . . then withdraw the clevis pin

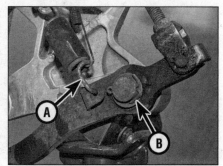

3.12 Release the springs (A) and the split pin (B), circlip or pivot nut or bolt

3.15 Unscrew the bolt (arrowed) and slide the lever off

3.16a Slacken the nuts (arrowed) then unscrew the rod

3.16b This lever is held on its pivot by a circlip (arrowed)

3.16c Unscrew the bolt and slide the linkage arm off

17 Installation is the reverse of removal, noting the following:

● *Align the slit in the lever or linkage arm with the mark made on the shaft.*
● *On models with a linkage apply grease to the lever pivot. Make sure the rubber boots for each end of the linkage rod are in good condition. Adjust the gear lever height as required by screwing the linkage rod in or out of the lever and arm. Tighten the locknuts.*
● *Use a new circlip to secure the lever where necessary.*

4	Sidestand and centrestand

Sidestand

1 Support the bike on its centrestand where fitted, or on an auxiliary stand. Where necessary displace the sidestand switch **(see illustration)**.

2 Unhook the stand springs, or where fitted the spring plate **(see illustrations)**.

Gearchange lever

15 On models with just a lever fitting onto the gearchange shaft, make a mark where the slot in the gearchange lever aligns with the shaft. Unscrew the pinch bolt and slide the lever off the shaft **(see illustration)**.

16 On models with a linkage arm and rod connecting the lever to the gearchange shaft, slacken the linkage rod locknuts, then unscrew the rod and separate it from the lever and the arm (the rod is reverse-threaded on one end and so will simultaneously unscrew from both lever and arm when turned in the one direction) **(see illustration)**. Note how far the rod is threaded into the lever and arm as this determines the height of the lever relative to the footrest. Unscrew the gearchange lever pivot bolt or release the circlip and remove the lever, noting any washers **(see illustration)**. If required make a mark where the slot in the linkage arm aligns with the shaft, then unscrew the pinch bolt and slide the arm off the shaft **(see illustration)**.

4.1 On this model undo the screw (arrowed) and displace the switch

4.2a Unhook the springs (arrowed) . . .

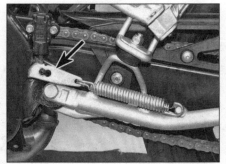

4.2b . . . or spring plate (arrowed)

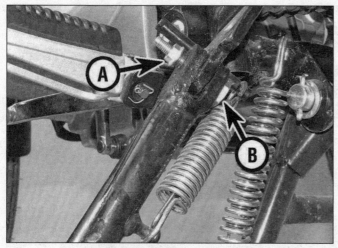

4.3a Sidestand nut (A) and pivot bolt (B) . . .

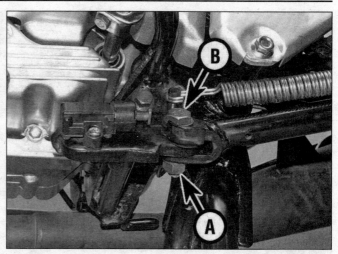

4.3b . . . are fitted in opposite direction on certain models

4.6 Unhook the springs (A). The pivot on this model is held by a split pin (B)

3 Unscrew the nut from the pivot bolt **(see illustrations)**. Unscrew the pivot bolt and remove the stand.

4 Installation is the reverse of removal. Apply grease to the pivot bolt shank. Do not overtighten the bolt, and check the stand pivots freely before fitting the nut. Counter-hold the bolt while tightening the nut.

5 Reconnect the springs, or where fitted the spring plate, and check that they hold the stand securely up when not in use – an accident could occur if the stand extends while the machine is in motion **(see illustration 4.3a)**. Check the operation of the

sidestand switch where fitted (see Chapter 1, Section 10).

Centrestand (where fitted)

6 Unhook the stand springs **(see illustration)**.

7 Either unscrew the pivot bolt and remove the stand, or straighten the ends of the split pin(s) securing the pivot, withdraw the pin(s), then withdraw the pivot, or release the circlip or E-clip securing the pivot and withdraw it, noting any washers, as required according to model.

8 Installation is the reverse of removal. Apply grease to the pivot. Check the stand pivots freely.

9 Reconnect the springs and check that they hold the stand securely up when not in use – an accident could occur if the stand drops while the machine is in motion.

5 Handlebars and levers

1 As a precaution, remove the fuel tank (see Chapter 4). Though not actually necessary, this will prevent the possibility of damage should a tool slip. Before removing the

assemblies from the handlebars make a note of their position and alignment on the bar, making marks where necessary, so everything can be installed in the same position. Look for any existing alignment marks, usually in the form of a punch mark aligned with the mating surfaces of clamps **(see illustrations 5.14a and b)**.

Note: *If required, for example if the top yoke is being removed to access the steering head bearings, the handlebars can be displaced without detaching any of the assemblies from them.*

Handlebars

Removal

2 Remove the mirrors (see Chapter 8). Release any ties from the handlebars, noting what is secured and how it is routed. Where fitted remove the end-weight from each end of the handlebar **(see illustration)**.

3 Either disconnect the brake light switch wiring connectors, or press the clip up on the underside of the switch and draw it out of its housing, according to type **(see illustrations)**.

4 Unscrew the brake master cylinder assembly clamp bolts and position the assembly clear of the handlebar, wrapping it in some rag, and making sure no strain is placed on the

5.2 Remove the end-weight (arrowed)

5.3a Either disconnect the wiring connectors (arrowed) . . .

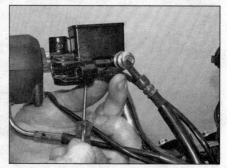

5.3b . . . or release and withdraw the brake light switch, according to type

5.4 Unscrew the master cylinder clamp bolts (arrowed) and displace the assembly

5.5a Undo the screws (arrowed) and split the housing . . .

5.5b . . . then detach the cable and remove the twistgrip

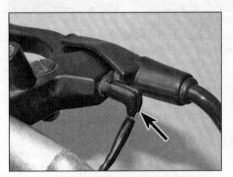

5.8a Either disconnect the wiring connectors (arrowed) . . .

5.8b . . . or release and withdraw the clutch switch (arrowed), according to type

5.9 Unscrew the bolts (arrowed) and displace the lever assembly

hydraulic hose **(see illustration)**. Keep the master cylinder reservoir upright to prevent possible fluid leakage.

5 Undo the right-hand switch housing screws and separate the halves, then free the throttle cable(s) from the twistgrip and slide the twistgrip off **(see illustrations)**.

6 Undo the left-hand switch housing screws and displace the switch.

7 Remove the grip from the left-hand end of the handlebar – if it has been glued on or is stuck feed a wooden or plastic tool up the inside and move it round the bar to release it, or squirt aerosol lube via the thin nozzle between the grip and bar, but wear eye protection as it may spray back into your face. At worst you will have to cut the grip off and fit a new one.

8 Either disconnect the clutch switch wiring connectors, or press the clip up on the underside of the switch and draw it out of its housing, according to type **(see illustrations)**.

9 If the clutch lever bracket has two bolts, unscrew them and position the assembly clear of the handlebar **(see illustration)**.

10 If the clutch lever bracket has one bolt detach the clutch cable (see Chapter 2). Slacken the bolt and slide the lever assembly off the handlebar **(see illustration)**.

11 Where fitted remove the handlebar clamp bolt blanking caps **(see illustration)**.

12 On models with one-piece handlebars, unscrew the handlebar clamp bolts and

5.10 Unscrew the bolt (arrowed) and slide the clutch lever bracket off

5.11 Carefully lever the caps off

5.12a Unscrew the clamp bolts (arrowed) . . .

5.12b . . . and displace or remove the handlebars

remove the clamp(s), then displace or remove the handlebars **(see illustrations)**. If required, and if separate from the top yoke, unscrew the handlebar holder nuts and draw them out of the yoke, noting the arrangement of the washers, collars and rubbers according to model **(see illustration)**.

13 On models with two-piece handlebars, unscrew the handlebar clamp bolt and/or positioning bolt according to model, and if fitted release any retaining clip from the top of the fork **(see illustrations)**. Lift the handlebar off the fork and yoke, noting how it aligns and locates if no positioning bolt is fitted.

Installation

14 Installation is the reverse of removal, noting the following.

● *On models with one-piece handlebars, if removed fit the handlebar holders onto the yoke along with any rubbers, collars and washers according to model, but do not fully tighten the holder nuts until the handlebars and top clamp(s) have been fitted so the holders are correctly aligned. Make sure the handlebars are central, and align the punch mark with the clamp mating surfaces where present, or as noted on removal if not **(see illustration)**. Generally clamps fit so the gap between it and the holder is at the back and you tighten the front clamp bolts first.*

● *On models with two-piece handlebars make sure they are correctly aligned with the lug or pin locating in its cut-out or hole if no positioning bolt is fitted **(see illustration 5.13b)**.*

● *Make sure the bracket clamps are*

5.12c Handlebar holder nut (arrowed)

5.13a Unscrew the positioning bolt (arrowed) . . .

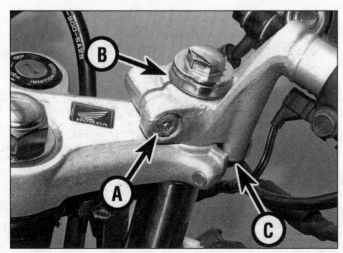

5.13b . . . and/or slacken the clamp bolt (A) and release the clip (B) where fitted, and noting how lug (C) locates

5.14a Handlebar alignment punch mark (arrowed)

5.14b Master cylinder alignment punch mark (arrowed)

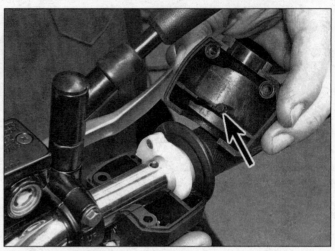

5.14c Locate the peg (arrowed) in the hole in the handlebar

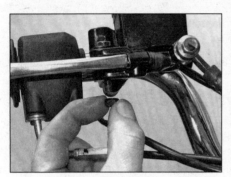

5.15a Undo the nut . . .

5.15b . . . then undo the pivot screw

16 To remove the clutch lever, where fitted pull the rubber boot of the cable adjuster, then loosen the adjuster lockring and thread the adjuster into the bracket to provide freeplay in the cable **(see illustration)**. Undo the lever pivot locknut, then undo the pivot screw or bolt and remove the lever, detaching the cable nipple as you do **(see illustration)**.

17 Installation is the reverse of removal, noting the following.

● *Apply silicone grease to the contact area between the front brake master cylinder pushrod tip and the brake lever.*
● *Apply lithium or molybdenum grease to the pivot shafts and the contact areas between the lever and its bracket, and to the clutch cable end.*
● *Make sure the levers move smoothly and freely.*
● *Adjust clutch cable freeplay (see Chapter 1).*

installed with the UP mark facing up **(see illustration 5.4)** and with the clamp mating surfaces aligned with the punch marks where present or as noted on removal **(see illustration)**. *Generally clamps fit so any gap between it and the bracket is at the bottom and you tighten the top clamp bolt first.*

● *When fitting the switch housings, where present locate the peg in the hole in the handlebar* **(see illustration)**.

Levers

15 To remove the front brake lever, undo the lever pivot locknut, then undo the pivot screw or bolt and remove the lever **(see illustrations)**.

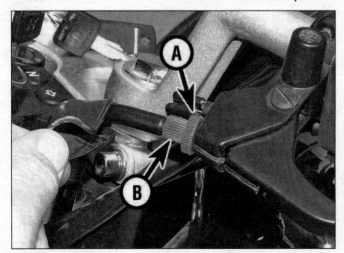

5.16a Slacken the lockring (A) and thread the adjuster (B) in

5.16b Unscrew the locknut (A) then undo the pivot screw (B) and remove the lever

6.4 Slacken the fork clamp bolt (arrowed) in the top yoke

6.5 Slacken the fork top bolt (arrowed) if the fork is to be disassembled

6.6a Slacken the fork clamp bolt (arrowed) in the bottom yoke

6 Fork removal and installation

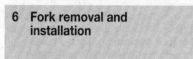

Removal

1 Note the routing of the cables, hose and wiring around the forks. Remove the fairing or body panels as required according to model (see Chapter 8).

2 Remove the front wheel (see Chapter 7) and the front mudguard (see Chapter 8). Tie the front brake caliper back so that it is out of the way.

3 Note the setting of the top of the fork in relation to the upper surface of the top yoke, or the handlebar clamp on models with two-piece bars (i.e. is the fork set flush or is there some protrusion, in which case measure the amount) so they can be installed in the same position – this is an important setting as it affects the overall geometry of the bike and therefore the handling.

4 Working on one fork at a time, slacken the fork clamp bolt in the top yoke **(see illustration)**. On models with two-piece handlebars that clamp around the top of the fork, slacken the handlebar clamp bolt, and where fitted remove any retaining ring **(see illustration 5.13b)**.

5 If the fork is to be disassembled, or if the fork oil is being changed, on models with a bolt on the top of the fork (as opposed to a rubber cap with plug and retaining ring beneath), slacken the top bolt now **(see illustration)**.

6 Slacken the fork clamp bolt(s) in the bottom yoke, and remove the fork by twisting it and pulling it down, where applicable noting how it fits through the headlight holder or any fork shroud(s) **(see illustrations)**.

> **HAYNES HiNT** *If the fork legs are seized in the yokes, spray the area with penetrating oil and allow time for it to soak in before trying again.*

Installation

7 Remove all traces of corrosion from the fork tube and the yokes. Make sure you install the forks the correct way round according to the lugs to carry the brake caliper.

8 Slide the fork up through the bottom yoke, through any shroud(s) and headlight holder where fitted, and into the top yoke, making sure all cables, hoses and wiring are routed on the correct side of the fork **(see illustration 6.6c and b)**. Set the top of the fork as noted on removal in relation to the top yoke or handlebar clamp. Tighten the clamp bolt(s) in the bottom yoke **(see illustration 6.6a)**.

9 If the fork has been dismantled or if the fork oil was changed, tighten the fork top bolt **(see illustration 6.5)**.

10 Tighten the fork clamp bolt in the top yoke **(see illustration 6.4)**. On models with two-piece handlebars that clamp around the top of the fork, tighten the handlebar clamp bolt, and where removed fit any retaining ring into its groove **(see illustration 5.13b)**.

11 Install the remaining components in a reverse of the removal procedure according to model, referring to the relevant Chapters.

12 Check the operation of the front forks and brake before taking the machine out on the road.

7 Fork oil change

1 After a high mileage the fork oil will deteriorate and its damping and lubrication qualities will be impaired. Always change the oil in both fork legs. Note that as no specifications for oil quantities are available it is important to tip the old oil out into a graduated jug so the volume can be measured to ensure correct refilling.

2 Remove the fork – where fitted make sure that the top bolt is loosened while the fork is still clamped in the bottom yoke (see Section 6).

3 On models with a top bolt support the fork leg in an upright position and unscrew the fork top bolt from the top of the fork tube – the bolt is under pressure from the fork spring, so use a ratchet tool so it does not need to be removed from the bolt as you unscrew it, and maintain some downward pressure on it, particularly as you come to the end of the threads, or alternatively hold the tool still and twist the fork tube to unthread it from the bolt **(see illustration)**. If the top bolt O-ring is damaged or deteriorated fit a new one **(see illustration 7.9)**.

6.6b Draw the fork down and out of the yokes, noting the headlight brackets where fitted . . .

6.6c . . . and on Custom models how any fork shroud(s) locate(s)

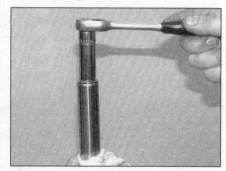

7.3 Unscrew the fork top bolt as described

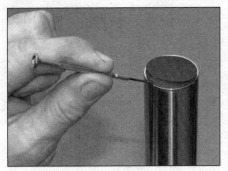

7.4a Prise out the top cap

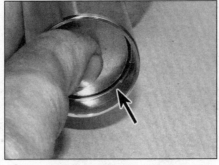

7.4b Push the top plug down, release the retaining ring (arrowed) . . .

7.4c . . . then remove the top plug, noting the O-ring (arrowed)

4 On models with a top cap support the fork leg in an upright position and carefully prise out the cap **(see illustration)**. Press down on the plug, noting it is under pressure from the fork spring, and release the retaining ring from its groove, then slowly release pressure on the plug and remove it **(see illustrations)**. If the plug O-ring is damaged or deteriorated fit a new one.

5 Compress the fork and remove any upper spring components, e.g. a short upper spring or spacer, followed by a washer or spring seat, noting their exact arrangement **(see illustrations)**. Withdraw the long fork spring, noting whether it has any closer wound coils at either the top or the bottom so it can be fitted the same way round **(see illustration)**. Wipe any excess oil off the spring.

6 Invert the fork leg over a suitable graduated container and pump the fork to expel as much oil as possible **(see illustration)**. Support the fork upside down in the container and allow it to drain for a few minutes. If the fork oil contains metal particles inspect the fork bush for wear (see Section 8). Note the volume of oil drained.

HAYNES HiNT *Fork oil is available in several different viscosities. If there is no recommendation in the owners manual, SAE10 would be a good choice for medium damping.*

7 Pour in the measured quantity of fresh fork oil, plus a little extra to account for any losses

on draining, then pump the fork several times to distribute it evenly and bleed out any air bubbles **(see illustration)**. Secure the fork leg upright with the inner tube compressed into the outer tube, and let it to stand for several minutes to allow the oil level to stabilise. Use a steel rule to measure the oil level from the top of the inner tube **(see illustration)**. Compare the level is each tube and if different add or subtract oil until it is the same in each fork.

8 Fit the long fork spring into the fork the same way round as noted on removal **(see illustration 7.5c)**. Draw the fork tubes apart until flush with the top of the spring, then fit the upper spring components as noted on removal **(see illustration 7.5b and a)**.

7.5a Remove the spacer . . .

7.5b . . . the spacer seat . . .

7.5c . . . and the spring

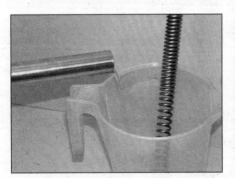

7.6 Invert the fork over a container and tip the oil out

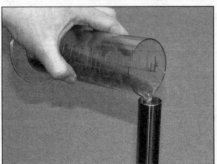

7.7a Pour fresh fork oil into the top of the tube and distribute and bleed it as described

7.7b Measuring the fork oil level

7.9 Smear the O-ring (arrowed) with oil before fitting the top bolt

7.10a Press the plug down and fit the retaining ring into the groove

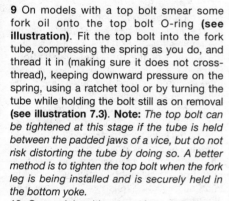

7.10b Press the cap into the top of the tube

9 On models with a top bolt smear some fork oil onto the top bolt O-ring **(see illustration)**. Fit the top bolt into the fork tube, compressing the spring as you do, and thread it in (making sure it does not cross-thread), keeping downward pressure on the spring, using a ratchet tool or by turning the tube while holding the bolt still as on removal **(see illustration 7.3)**. Note: *The top bolt can be tightened at this stage if the tube is held between the padded jaws of a vice, but do not risk distorting the tube by doing so. A better method is to tighten the top bolt when the fork leg is being installed and is securely held in the bottom yoke.*

10 On models with a top plug smear some fork oil onto the plug O-ring **(see illustration 7.4c)**. Fit the plug into the fork tube and press down on it, compressing the spring, and fit the retaining ring into its groove **(see illustration)**. Relax the pressure so the plug rests on the underside of the ring, which should remain secure in its groove. Fit the top cap **(see illustration)**.

11 Install the fork (see Section 6).

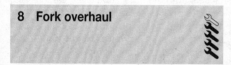

8 Fork overhaul

Note 1: *Before disassembling the fork for seal renewal or any other purpose check with your dealer on the availability of individual components. While on some models all fork components are available, on others, and in particular upside down forks, they only come as a complete assembly.*

Note 2: *Note that while most forks are very similar in construction to the types shown in this procedure, any differences seen in the layout or fitting of components on the forks on your model should be carefully noted to avoid confusion on installation. This is particularly the case with the fitting of washers on each side of the oil seal – most models will have one washer between the seal and the bush, but some have a washer on each side of the seal, and some have no washers at all.*

Disassembly

1 Remove the fork – where fitted make sure that the top bolt is loosened while the leg is still clamped in the bottom yoke (see Section 6). Where fitted remove the gaiter **(see illustration)**. Always dismantle the fork legs separately to avoid interchanging parts and thus causing an accelerated rate of wear. Store all components in separate, clearly marked containers.

2 Lay the fork flat on the bench, hold it down and slacken the damper rod bolt in the base of the fork **(see illustration)**. If the bolt does not slacken but instead the damper rod inside the fork turns with the bolt, try compressing the fork so that more pressure is exerted on the damper rod head, or if available use an air wrench. Otherwise, having removed the spring components as described in Section 7, use a holding tool (see your dealer), or a piece of wooden dowel rounded at the end, inserted in the fork and pressed against the top of the damper rod, to hold it.

3 Refer to Section 7, Steps 3 to 6 and drain the oil form the fork.

4 Fully unscrew and remove the damper rod bolt and its copper sealing washer from the bottom of the fork **(see illustration 8.18a)**. Discard the sealing washer as a new one must be used on reassembly. Tip the damper rod out of the top of the fork **(see illustration)**.

5 Try to withdraw the inner tube from the outer tube **(see illustration)**. If the tubes come apart easily follow Step 7. If the tubes do not come apart but come against a stop, follow Step 6.

6 Carefully prise out the dust seal from the

8.1 Release the clip and draw the gaiter off the top of the fork

8.2 Slacken the damper rod bolt

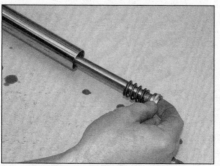

8.4 Tip the damper rod out of the inner tube

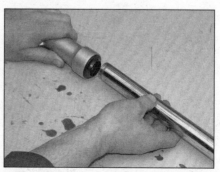

8.5 Draw the inner and outer tubes apart

8.6a Prise out the dust seal using a flat-bladed screwdriver

8.6b Prise out the retaining clip using a flat-bladed screwdriver

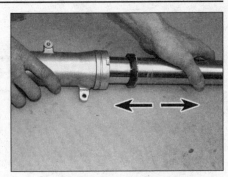

8.6c Repeatedly draw the tubes apart . . .

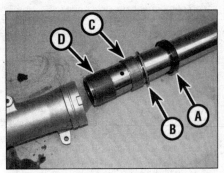

8.6d . . . to displace the oil seal (A), washer (B) and outer tube bush (C). Inner tube bush (D)

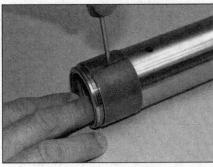

8.6e Remove the inner tube bush by levering its ends apart

outer tube **(see illustration)**. Discard the seal as a new one must be used. Carefully remove the retaining clip, taking care not to scratch the surface of the tube **(see illustration)**. Remove the washer if fitted. Grasp the inner tube in one hand and the outer tube in the other, then quickly and repeatedly draw the inner tube out until the oil seal, washer(s) and outer tube bush are displaced from the outer tube by the inner tube bush **(see illustrations)**. Draw the oil seal, washer and outer tube bush off the inner tube, then remove the inner tube bush from its cut-out by carefully levering its ends apart just as much as necessary **(see illustration)** – note that on upside down forks you will have to remove the inner tube bush first in order to slide the other components off. Discard the oil seal as a new one must be fitted on reassembly.

7 Carefully prise out the dust seal from the outer tube **(see illustration)**. Discard the seal as a new one must be used. Carefully remove the retaining clip, taking care not to scratch the surface of the tube **(see illustration)**. Remove the washer if fitted. Carefully prise the oil seal from the outer tube using either a seal hook or an internal puller with slide-hammer attachment **(see illustrations)**. If a seal hook is used take great care not to damage the rim of the tube. Remove the washer if fitted.

8 Tip the damper rod seat out **(see illustration)**.

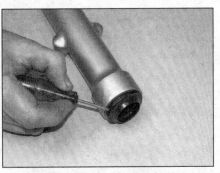

8.7a Prise out the dust seal using a flat-bladed screwdriver

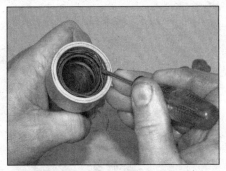

8.7b Prise out the retaining clip using a flat-bladed screwdriver

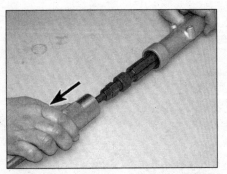

8.7c Locate the puller under the oil seal then expand the puller . . .

8.7d . . . and jar the seal out using the slide-hammer attachment

8.8 Tip the damper rod seat out

8.10 Measuring fork inner tube runout

8.11a Check the bushes (arrowed) for wear . . .

8.11b . . . on some models they will be in the outer tube

Inspection

9 Clean all parts in solvent and blow them dry with compressed air, if available. Check the inner fork tube for score marks, scratches, flaking of the chrome finish and excessive or abnormal wear. Look for dents in the tubes and replace the tubes in both forks if any are found. Check the fork seal seat for nicks, gouges and scratches. If damage is evident, leaks will occur.

10 Check the fork inner tube for runout using V-blocks and a dial gauge **(see illustration)**. If the amount of runout exceeds 0.2 mm, the tube should be replaced with a new one.

⚠ *Warning: If the tube is bent or exceeds the runout limit, it should not be straightened; replace it with a new one.*

11 Inspect the working surface of each bush for score marks, scratches and signs of excessive wear (in which case the grey Teflon outer surface will have worn away to reveal the copper inner surface) **(see illustrations)**. If available replace the bushes with new ones if damaged or worn – consult your dealer, but it is likely that on models where the forks come apart as in Step 5 the bushes will not be available and a new outer tube will have to be fitted (assuming that is available), whereas on models where the forks come apart as in Step 6 the bushes will be available (assuming that any parts at all are available).

12 Check the spring (both the main spring and the rebound spring on the damper rod, and where fitted the upper spring) for cracks and other damage. Measure the length of the main spring from each fork and compare their lengths **(see illustration)**. If a spring is deformed or has sagged limit, replace the main springs in both forks with new ones. Never replace only one spring.

13 Check the damper rod, and in particular the ring in its head, for damage and wear, and replace it with a new one if necessary **(see illustration)**. Check the damper rod seat for damage.

Reassembly

14 On forks that came apart as in Step 5 and 7, lay the washer (where fitted) against the bush in the outer tube **(see illustration)**. Smear the lips of the new oil seal with fork oil and press it squarely into its recess in the outer tube, with its markings facing out, then use a seal driver or a suitable socket and drive it in until it seats and the retaining clip groove is visible above it **(see illustrations)**. Once the seal is correctly seated lay the washer, where fitted, against the seal. Fit the retaining clip,

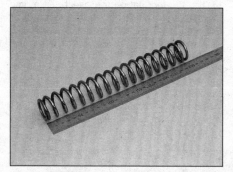

8.12 Measuring the fork spring length

8.13 Check the damper rod and spring for damage and the ring (arrowed) for wear

8.14a Fit the washer . . .

8.14b . . . fit the new oil seal . . .

8.14c . . . and drive it into place . . .

8.14d . . . until it seats – the retaining clip groove (arrowed) will be exposed

8.14e Fit the seal retaining clip into its groove

8.15a Fit the damper rod into the tube . . .

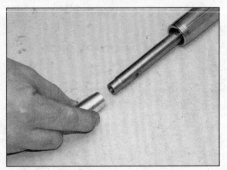

8.15b . . . so it protrudes from the bottom, then fit the damper rod seat . . .

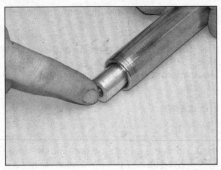

8.15c . . . and locate it in the bottom of the tube

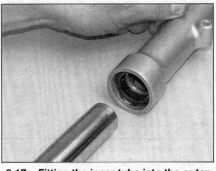

8.17a Fitting the inner tube into the outer tube – type with bushes in outer tube

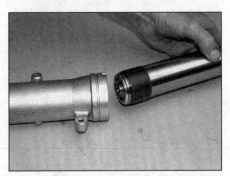

8.17b Fitting the inner tube into the outer tube – type with bushes on inner tube

making sure it is correctly located in its groove **(see illustration)**.

> **HAYNES HINT**
>
> *Place the old oil seal on top of the new one to protect it when driving the seal into place.*

15 If removed, fit the rebound spring onto the damper rod, and fit the ring into its groove in the head **(see illustration 8.13)**. Slide the damper rod into the top of the inner tube and all the way down so it protrudes from the bottom **(see illustrations)**. Fit the damper rod seat on the bottom of the rod, then push the

rod back into the tube so the damper rod seat fits into the bottom **(see illustration)**.

16 On upside down forks lubricate the inner and outer surfaces of the new oil seal and the bushes (if not fitted in the outer tube) with the specified fork oil. Slide the new dust seal, the retaining clip, washer (where fitted), oil seal, washer (where fitted), and, if not fitted permanently in the outer tube, the outer tube bush and then the inner tube bush (seating it in its cut-out), onto the inner tube in that order, making sure the seals are the correct way round with the outer side of the dust seal and the marked side of the oil seal facing the bottom of the tube, and with the exception of the inner tube bush slide them all along to the bottom.

17 Oil the inner tube and its bush (if not in the outer tube) with fork oil. Insert the tube into the outer tube, twisting it as you do, and push it fully down until it contacts the bottom **(see illustrations)**.

18 Lay the fork flat on the bench. Fit a new copper sealing washer onto the damper bolt and apply a few drops of a suitable non-permanent thread locking compound **(see illustration)**. Fit the bolt into the bottom of the fork and tighten it **(see illustration)**. If the damper rod rotates inside the tube as you tighten the bolt, either use the same holding method as on disassembly (Step 2), or wait until the fork is fully reassembled and tighten it then (the pressure of the spring on the rod

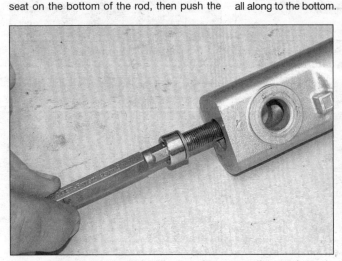

8.18a Fit the bolt using threadlock and a new sealing washer . . .

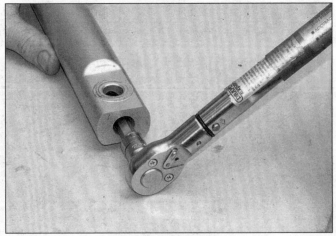

8.18b . . . and tighten it

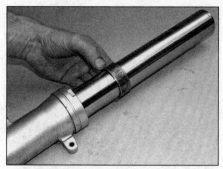

8.19a Slide the top bush into the outer tube . . .

8.19b . . . then rest the washer on top . . .

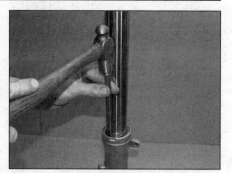

8.19c . . . to protect the bush as you drive it in

8.19d Make sure it has seated

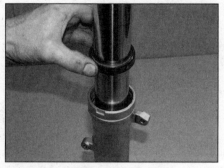

8.19e Fit the new oil seal . . .

8.19f . . . and drive it into the outer tube . . .

should prevent it from turning, especially if you compress the fork – Step 22).

19 On forks that came apart as in Step 6, lubricate the inner and outer surfaces of the outer tube bush with fork oil. Slide the bush along the inner tube and press it as far as possible into the outer tube by hand, making sure it fits squarely **(see illustration)**. Slide the washer, where fitted, onto the top of the bush, then carefully drive the bush into place until it seats using a suitable drift against the washer, using it as an interface to prevent damage to the exposed rim of the bush **(see illustrations)**. Take care not to mark the inner tube when driving the bush in. Lift the washer where fitted, and make sure the bush has fully entered, in which case its upper rim will be flush with the oil seal seat. Refit the washer. Lubricate the inner and outer surfaces of the new oil seal with the specified fork oil. Slide

the seal, making sure its marked side is facing away from the outer tube, along the inner tube and press it as far as possible into the outer tube by hand, making sure it fits squarely **(see illustration)**. Carefully drive the seal into place until it seats using a suitable drift **(see illustration)**. Take care not to mark the inner tube when driving the seal in. Make sure the seal has fully entered, in which case the groove for the retaining ring will be fully exposed. Lay the washer, where fitted, against the seal. Fit the retaining clip, making sure it is correctly located in its groove **(see illustration)**. Press the new dust seal into place **(see illustration)**.

20 On all fork types, lubricate the lips of the new dust seal then slide it down the fork tube and press it into position **(see illustration)**.

21 Refer to Section 7, Steps 7 to 10 and refill the fork with oil and finish reassembly.

22 If the damper rod bolt requires tightening (see Step 18), place the fork upside down on the floor, using a rag to protect it, then have an assistant compress the fork so that maximum spring pressure is placed on the damper rod head while tightening the bolt.

23 Install the fork (see Section 6).

9 Steering stem

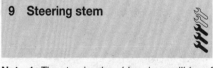

Note 1: *The steering head bearings will be of the uncaged or caged ball type. You cannot determine which type is fitted until the bearing adjuster nut and cover have been removed and the steering stem is loose in the head.*

Note 2: *The arrangement of the bearing adjuster nut, bearing cover and upper bearing*

8.19g . . . until the groove (arrowed) is visible

8.19h Fit the retaining clip into the groove

8.20 Fit the dust seal into position

9.6a Unscrew the nut or bolt and remove the washer (where fitted) . . .

9.6b . . . then lift the top yoke up off the stem

9.8a Unscrew the adjuster nut . . .

inner race will vary from model to model. On some they are three separate components, on some the adjuster nut will have the bearing cover incorporated, on some the bearing cover will have the inner race incorporated below it, and on some all three components are incorporated as one.

Removal

1 Remove the fuel tank (see Chapter 4).
2 Remove the front forks (see Section 6).
3 Check for anything bolted to the top and/or bottom yokes and either remove or displace them as required or preferred. Again as required or preferred displace or remove the instrument cluster and/or headlight assembly (see Chapter 9).

4 If the ignition switch is bolted to the top yoke, and you want to remove the yoke completely rather than just displace it, trace the wiring from the switch and disconnect it at the connector(s). Feed the wiring back to the switch, freeing it from any clips and ties and noting its routing.
5 If required displace the handlebars (see Section 5) – if you have a model with two piece handlebars, or if the one-piece handlebars on your model do not restrict access to the steering stem nut or bolt, and if you do not wish to remove the top yoke completely, you can leave them in place and displace the complete top yoke/handlebar assembly in one.
6 Unscrew and remove the steering stem

nut or bolt, and remove the washer where fitted **(see illustration)**. Lift the top yoke up off the steering stem and displace or remove it as required **(see illustration)**. On models with headlight holders that locate between the yokes take care to support them as you remove the top yoke, and note the fitment of any rubber bushes in the top and bottom of the holders.
7 Check for a locknut above the adjuster nut and see if there is a tabbed lockwasher locking them together. If there is a lockwasher above the locknut remove it then unscrew the locknut using either a C-spanner, a peg spanner or a drift located in one of the notches if required – though it should only be finger-tight. If the washer is between them, unscrew the locknut then remove the washer. In either case note how the washer locates.
8 Support the bottom yoke and unscrew the bearing adjuster nut using a C-spanner, a peg spanner or a suitable drift located in one of the notches if necessary **(see illustration)**. Remove the bearing cover if separate from the adjuster nut, then remove the inner race if separate from the bearing cover and adjuster nut, and at this point check the type of bearing fitted **(see illustrations)**.
9 If the balls are caged gently lower the bottom yoke and steering stem out of the frame **(see illustration)**. Remove the upper bearing from the top of the steering head **(see illustration)**. Remove the lower

9.8b . . . and remove the bearing cover . . .

9.8c . . . then remove the inner race and check whether caged balls . . .

9.8d . . . or un-caged balls are fitted

9.9a Draw the bottom yoke/steering stem out of the steering head

9.9b Remove the upper bearing from the top of the head . . .

9.9c . . . and the lower bearing from the bottom of the stem

9.10 Hold the container below the steering head as you draw the stem out

bearing from the steering stem **(see illustration)**.

10 If the balls are un-caged hold a container under the steering head, then gently lower the bottom yoke and steering stem out of the frame, hopefully catching any balls which drop out **(see illustration)**. Remove any balls that have stayed stuck in place from the inner race on the bottom of the stem or the outer race in the bottom of the head as necessary. Remove the bearing balls from the top of the steering head – it is wise to again hold the container below the head as you remove the race in case the balls drop down through it.

11 Wash all traces of old grease from the bearings and races using solvent or paraffin, then check them for wear or damage as described in Section 10. **Note:** *Do not attempt to remove the outer races from the steering head or the lower bearing inner race from the steering stem unless they are to be replaced with new ones (see Section 10).*

Installation

12 If the balls are un-caged smear a liberal quantity of multi-purpose grease onto the bearing races, then stick the bearing balls to the grease. Stick the balls to the inner race on the base of the steering stem and the outer race in the top of the steering head. Make

sure all the balls are pressed against the race to prevent them being dislodged by the opposite race when fitted. Carefully lift the steering stem/bottom yoke up through the steering head, making sure all balls stay in place, and when it has located turn it a few times to spread and seat the lower bearing balls, then support it **(see illustration 9.9a)**. Fit the inner race into the top of the steering head, taking care not dislodge the balls, and turn it to spread and seat the balls **(see illustration 9.8d)**. Fit the bearing cover where separate, then fit the adjuster nut and tighten finger-tight **(see illustrations)**.

13 If the balls are caged smear a liberal

quantity of multi-purpose grease onto the bearing races and bearings. Fit the lower bearing onto the steering stem **(see illustration 9.9c)**. Carefully lift the steering stem/bottom yoke up through the steering head and support it **(see illustration 9.9a)**. Fit the upper bearing onto the race **(see illustration)**. Fit the inner race and bearing cover **(see illustrations 9.8c and b)**. Fit the adjuster nut and tighten finger-tight **(see illustrations)**.

14 Using either a C-spanner, a peg spanner or a drift located in one of the notches, tighten the adjuster nut until all freeplay is removed, then tighten it a little more **(see illustration)**.

9.12a Fit the bearing cover . . .

9.12b . . . and the adjuster nut

9.13a Fit the upper bearing

9.13b Tighten the adjuster nut finger-tight

9.14 Tightening the adjuster nut using a C-spanner

9.15a Fit the forks and any spacers and rubbers for headlight holder/shrouds ...

9.15b ... then fit the holders/shrouds

9.15c Fit the top yoke ...

9.15d ... then tighten the nut or bolt

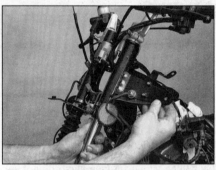

9.15e Position the forks correctly then tighten the clamp bolts

This pre-loads the bearings. Now slacken the nut, then tighten it again, setting it so that all freeplay is just removed, yet the steering is able to move freely from side to side.

Caution: Take great care not to apply excessive pressure because this will cause premature failure of the bearings.

15 Where removed fit the lock washer and the locknut in the reverse order of removal, and setting the washer tabs as noted. Temporarily install the forks, not forgetting any lower shrouds, and secure them by tightening the bottom yoke clamp bolts only (see Section 6). On models with headlight holders or fork shrouds that fit between the yokes slide them over the forks, making sure any rubber bushes are fitted and everything locates correctly **(see illustration)**. Fit the top yoke onto the steering

stem **(see illustration)**. Fit the washer where removed, then the steering stem nut or bolt, and tighten it **(see illustration)**. Now position the forks correctly in the yokes, setting the amount of protrusion as noted on removal in relation to the top yoke or handlebar clamp **(see illustration)**. Tighten all clamp bolts (see Section 6).

16 Install the remaining components in a reverse of the removal procedure, referring to the relevant Sections or Chapters where required. Make sure the wiring, cables and hose are correctly routed.

17 Refer to the freeplay check procedure in Chapter 1 to make a final assessment of the bearings with the leverage and inertia of all components taken into account, and if necessary readjust.

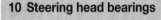

10 Steering head bearings

Inspection

1 Remove the steering stem (see Section 9).
2 Wash all traces of old grease from the bearings and races using paraffin or solvent, and check them for wear or damage.
3 The races should be polished and free from indentations **(see illustration)**. Inspect the bearing balls for signs of wear, damage or discoloration. If there are any signs of wear on any of the above components both upper and lower bearing assemblies must be replaced with a new set. Only remove the outer races in the steering head and the lower bearing inner race on the steering stem if they need to be replaced with new ones – do not reuse them once they have been removed.

Replacement

4 The outer races are an interference fit in the steering head – tap them from position using a suitable drift located on the exposed inner lip of the race **(see illustrations)**. Tap firmly and evenly around each race to ensure that it is driven out squarely. Curve the end of the drift slightly to improve access if necessary.
5 Alternatively, remove the races using a slide-hammer type bearing extractor – these can often be hired from tool shops.
6 Press the new outer races into the head using

10.3 Check the races for wear and damage

10.4a Drive the bearing races out with a brass drift ...

10.4b ... locating it on the exposed inner rim of the race (arrowed)

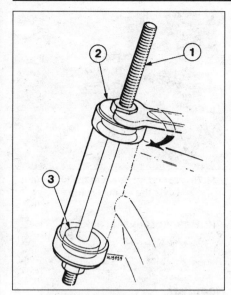

10.6 Drawbolt arrangement for fitting steering stem bearing races

1 Long bolt or threaded bar
2 Thick washer
3 Guide for lower race

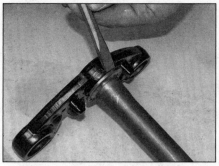

10.7a Remove the lower bearing race using a cold chisel . . .

10.7b . . . and screwdrivers . . .

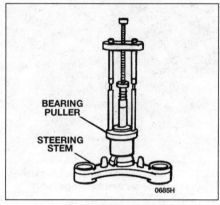

10.7c . . . or a puller if necessary

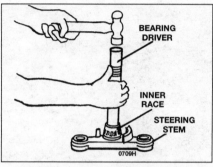

10.9 Drive the new bearing on using a suitable bearing driver or a length of pipe that bears only against the inner race and not against the bearing surface

a drawbolt arrangement (see illustration), or drive them in using a large diameter tubular drift (to do this the bike must be solidly supported as all the force needs to be transmitted to the race). Make sure that the drawbolt washer or drift (as applicable) bears only on the outer edge of the race and does not contact the working surface. Alternatively, have the races installed by a dealer equipped with bearing race installation tools.

 HAYNES HINT *Installation of new bearing outer races is made much easier if the races are left overnight in the freezer. This causes them to contract slightly making them a looser fit. Alternatively, use a freeze spray on the races just before you install them.*

7 Only remove the lower bearing inner race from the steering stem if a new one is being fitted. To remove the race, first thread the

steering stem nut onto the top and position the yoke on its front for stability, then tap under it using a cold chisel – the nut will protect the threads from the transmitted force of the impact of the chisel (see illustration). Next use two screwdrivers placed on opposite sides to work the race free, using blocks of wood to improve leverage and protect the yoke (see illustration). If the race is firmly in place it will be necessary to use a puller (see illustration). Take the steering stem to a dealer if required.
8 Where fitted remove the dust seal from the bottom of the stem and replace it with a new one. Smear the new one with grease.
9 Fit the new lower race onto the steering stem. Tap the new race into position using a length of tubing with an internal diameter slightly larger than the steering stem (see illustration).
10 Install the steering stem (see Section 9).

11 Rear shock absorber(s)

⚠ *Warning: Do not attempt to disassemble shock absorbers. Improper disassembly could result in serious injury. Spare parts are unlikely to be available for the damper unit, although you should be able to obtain replacement bushes for the upper and lower mountings.*

Removal

1 Where necessary remove the silencer or exhaust system (see Chapter 4).
2 Support the motorcycle on its centrestand or using an auxiliary stand or stands so that no weight is transmitted through any part of the rear suspension – tie the front brake lever to the handlebar to ensure the bike can't roll forward. Position a support under the rear wheel or swingarm so that it does not drop when the second shock absorber is removed, but also making sure that the weight of the machine is off the rear suspension so that it is not compressed.

Twin shock models

3 Unscrew the nuts or bolts and remove the washers where fitted securing the top and bottom of the shock absorber (see illustration).
4 Draw the shock absorber off its mounts (see illustration).

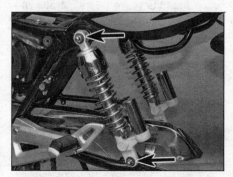

11.3 Unscrew the nuts or bolts (arrowed) . . .

11.4 . . . and remove the shock absorber

11.6 Remove the lower bolt . . .

11.7a . . . then the upper bolt . . .

11.7b . . . and manoeuvre the shock out via the easiest route

11.8 Check for signs of oil on the rod (arrowed) . . .

11.9 . . . and check for wear in the bushes or seals and bearings

Single shock models

5 Remove the seat and/or any body panels as required to access the upper mounting bolt (see Chapter 8).
6 Unscrew the nut and withdraw the bolt securing the bottom of the shock absorber, noting any washers **(see illustration)**.
7 Unscrew the nut and withdraw the bolt securing the top of the shock absorber, noting any washers, then manoeuvre the shock absorber out **(see illustrations)**.

Inspection

8 Inspect the shock absorber(s) for obvious physical damage and oil leakage, and the coil spring(s) for looseness, cracks or signs of fatigue **(see illustration)**.

9 Inspect the bush(es) and/or bearing(s) in the shock absorber mounts and the mounts themselves for wear or damage **(see illustration)**.
10 Old bushes and bearings can be driven or drawn out after removal of any seal and circlips retaining them (see Section 12, Steps 5 to 12). New ones should be drawn or pressed in. Where seal are fitted always use new ones – the old ones will be damaged on removal.

Installation

11 Installation is the reverse of removal, noting that multi-purpose grease to the shock absorber bush(es) and/or bearing(s).

12 Rear suspension linkage

Removal

1 Support the motorcycle so that no weight is transmitted through any part of the rear suspension – tie the front brake lever to the handlebar to ensure the bike can't roll forward. Position a support under the rear wheel or swingarm so that it does not drop when the shock absorber is detached, but also making sure that the weight of the machine is off the rear suspension so that the shock is not compressed.
2 Remove the silencer(s) or exhaust system as required according to model for access to the suspension linkage nuts and bolts.
3 Make a note of which side the bolts go in from and which way round the linkage arm and where fitted the linkage rods fit – it varies from model to model.
4 Unscrew the nuts and withdraw the bolts, noting any washers, securing the linkage rods (where fitted) and linkage arm to the swingarm, the bottom of the shock absorber, and to the frame, and remove them.

Inspection

5 Where fitted and as required according to model withdraw the spacers from the linkage arm and from the linkage rod mount in the swingarm, then lever out the grease seals, noting what fits where **(see illustrations)** – different sizes may be used in each mount and so each must be returned to its original place, and though new seals must be fitted keep the old seals as a guide for installation of the new.
6 Thoroughly clean all components, removing all traces of dirt, corrosion and grease.
7 Inspect all components closely, looking for obvious signs of wear such as heavy scoring, or for damage such as cracks or distortion. Slip each spacer back into its bearing(s) and check that there is not an excessive amount of freeplay between the two components. Replace worn or damaged components with new ones as required.

12.5a Withdrawn spacers from a typical linkage arm

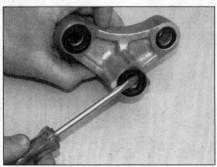

12.5b Lever the old seals out

12.8 Check the bearings

12.11 Press the new seals into place

● *Make sure the bolts are inserted from the correct side as noted on removal. Install all nuts and bolts before tightening any of them.*

13 Rear shock absorber adjustment

8 Check the condition of the bearings **(see illustration)**. They should turn smoothly and freely with little noise and no grittiness.

9 Worn bearings can be driven or drawn out of their bores after removal of any circlip(s) retaining them, but note that removal will destroy them; new bearings should be obtained before work commences. Before removing the bearings measure the set depth (i.e. how much space is left for the grease seal) of each one using a Vernier caliper. The new bearings should be pressed or drawn into their bores rather than driven into position. In the absence of a press, a suitable drawbolt tool can be made up using a suitable bolt (or length of threaded rod), nut(s) and washers. When fitting the new bearings make sure the marked end faces out, with the correct gap (as measured before removal) between each end and the rim of the bore for the seal. Note that a dealer may have a set of bearing

installation tools that will automatically set the bearings correctly, and if the components are taken loose and ready for assembly (i.e. clean) expense should not be excessive. It is best to use new circlips where fitted.

10 Lubricate the needle bearings, spacers and seals with grease.

11 Press the new seals into place in all the mounts where fitted, making sure each is in its correct place as noted on removal **(see illustration)**.

12 Where fitted and as required according to model slide the spacers into the bearing(s).

Installation

13 Installation is the reverse of removal, noting the following:

● *Apply grease to the bearings, spacers and seals.*

● *Make sure all components are fitted the correct way round as noted on removal.*

1 Spring pre-load is adjusted by turning the adjuster ring, which is usually on the bottom (though sometimes on the top) of the spring **(see illustrations)**. Use either a suitable C-spanner or a pin spanner or piece of rod as required according to the type of adjuster fitted – if you are lucky there may be one in the toolkit if provided.

2 Each pre-load setting is identified by cut-out seats in the adjuster ring which locate over (or under if the adjuster is at the top) the tab on the shock body. The amount of pre-load increases as the adjuster compresses the spring, and decreases as the adjuster lengthens it. If you have an owner's manual with the motorcycle, it may suggest a standard spring pre-load setting.

3 On models with twin rear shock absorbers, the pre-load setting must be set to the same position on each side.

14 Swingarm

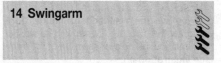

Removal

1 Support the motorcycle so that no weight is transmitted through any part of the rear suspension – tie the front brake lever to the handlebar to ensure the bike can't roll forward.

2 Remove the rear wheel (see Chapter 7).

3 Have a good look around the swingarm and remove or detach any component(s) connected to the swingarm or fitting around it as required according to model – these may include any of the following: silencer or exhaust system (see Chapter 4), shock absorber(s) (see Section 11), suspension linkage (see Section 12), chainguard, brake torque arm (drum brake models), brake hose (disc brake models) **(see illustrations)**.

13.1a Use a rod in the hole (arrowed) to turn this adjuster ring

13.1b Use a C-spanner in the cut-outs to turn this adjuster ring

14.3a Chainguard secured by two screws (arrowed)

14.3b Drum brake torque arm secured by a split pin (arrowed), nut and bolt

14.3c Hydraulic brake hose guide secured by a bolt (arrowed)

14.4a Unscrew the nut . . .

14.4b . . . withdraw the pivot bolt . . .

14.4c . . . and remove the swingarm

14.5 Remove the chain slider (arrowed) if required

14.6 Remove the pivot caps

14.9a Check for wear in the bushes or seals and bearings according to type . . .

4 Unscrew the swingarm pivot bolt nut and remove the washer **(see illustration)**. Withdraw the pivot bolt along with its washer, then manoeuvre the swingarm out of the frame **(see illustrations)**.

5 Remove the chain slider from the front of the swingarm if required, noting how it fits **(see illustration)**. Also remove any chain guide or guard not already removed if required. Check the condition of the slider and replace it with a new one if necessary.

Inspection

6 Remove the pivot cap from each side where fitted, noting any shims or washers fitted with them **(see illustration)**.
7 Thoroughly clean the swingarm, removing all traces of dirt, corrosion and chain grease.
8 Inspect the swingarm closely, looking for obvious signs of wear such as heavy scoring, and cracks or distortion due to accident damage.
9 Check the pivot components (spacers,

bushes, bearings and grease seals as fitted, according to model) **(see illustrations)**. If necessary replace any worn components with new ones – check with your dealer as to the availability. Lever out the old grease seals where fitted, then remove any circlip securing a bearing **(see illustrations)**. Refer to Section 12, Steps 5 to 12 for more detailed information.
10 Check the swingarm pivot bolt is straight by rolling it on a flat surface such as a piece of plate glass (first wipe off all old grease and remove any corrosion using wire wool). Replace the pivot bolt with a new one if it is bent.

Installation

11 If removed, install the chain slider **(see illustration 14.5)**.
12 Clean off all old grease, then lubricate the spacers, bushes, bearings and grease seals as fitted according to model, and the pivot bolt, with multi-purpose grease. Fit the

spacers back into the bushes or bearings where removed, and fit the pivot caps along with any shims or washers **(see illustration 14.6)**.
13 Position the swingarm and loop the drive around the front **(see illustration)**. Slide the pivot bolt through with its washer, then fit swingarm pivot nut with its washer and tighten it **(see illustrations 14.4b and a)**. Check the swingarm moves up and down smoothly and freely – if any binding is felt slacken the nut and check again, then re-tighten the nut a bit at a time, checking as you go. If necessary remove the swingarm and check that all components have been correctly installed.
14 Install the remaining components in reverse of the removal procedure. Where fitted secure the brake torque arm with a new split pin, bending the ends around the stud or bolt.
15 Check and adjust the drive chain slack (see Chapter 1). Check the operation of the rear suspension and brake before taking the machine on the road.

14.9b . . . withdraw the spacers . . .

14.9c . . . and lever out the seals where necessary

14.13 Make sure the drive chain is correctly looped over the front and routed through the chainguard

Chapter 7
Brakes, wheels and final drive

Contents

Degrees of difficulty

Easy, suitable for novice with little experience	**Fairly easy,** suitable for beginner with some experience	**Fairly difficult,** suitable for competent DIY mechanic	**Difficult,** suitable for experienced DIY mechanic	**Very difficult,** suitable for expert DIY or professional

Specifications

General torque settings according to thread size

5 mm bolt/nut	5 Nm
6 mm bolt/nut	10 Nm
8 mm bolt/nut	24 Nm
10 mm bolt/nut	35 Nm
12 mm bolt/nut	55 Nm

1 General information

Most models have an hydraulically operated single disc brake at the front and a drum brake at the rear, exceptions to this are models with a drum brake front and rear, or with a disc brake front and rear. Disc brake caliper types may also vary, with some models having a twin opposed piston caliper and some a single piston caliper, either opposed or sliding.

The drive to the rear wheel is by chain and sprockets on all models.

Some models have cast alloy wheels, others have steel spoked wheels.

Caution: Disc brake components rarely require disassembly. Do not disassemble components unless absolutely necessary. If a hydraulic brake hose is loosened or disconnected, the union sealing washers must be renewed and the system bled upon reassembly. Do not use solvents on internal brake components. Solvents will cause the seals to swell and distort. Use only clean brake fluid of the correct type for cleaning. Use care when working with brake fluid as it can injure your eyes and it will damage painted surfaces and plastic parts.

2 Disc brake pads

⚠ *Warning: The dust created by the brake system is harmful to your health. Never blow it out with compressed air and don't inhale any of it. An approved filtering mask should be worn when working on the brakes.*

Note 1: *There are many different brake calipers used across the range of models covered. Take a moment to study how the pads in your caliper fit.*

2.1a Unscrew the plug . . .

2.1b . . . then slacken the pin

2.2 Free the brake hose from its guide

Note 2: *Do not operate the brake lever or pedal while the pads are out of the caliper.*
1 Where fitted unscrew the pad retaining pin plug(s) **(see illustration)**. If the pad retaining pin(s) are threaded rather than a push fit, slacken them **(see illustration)**.

2 For maximum freedom of movement free the brake hose from any guide or unscrew the guide bolt **(see illustration)**.
3 Unscrew the caliper mounting bolts and slide the caliper off the disc **(see illustration)**.
4 On push-fit retaining pins remove the

clip(s). Withdraw the retaining pin(s) **(see illustration)**. Remove the pads from the caliper, noting how they locate **(see illustrations)**. Where fitted remove the shim from the back of each pad, noting how they fit **(see illustration)**.

2.3 Unscrew the bolts and slide the caliper off the disc

2.4a On this caliper remove the pins . . .

2.4b . . . then remove the inner pad, noting how its end locates against the post . . .

2.4c . . . then remove the outer pad

2.4d On this caliper remove the outer pad first, noting how it locates in the bracket . . .

2.4e . . . then tilt the inner pad and lift it off the posts . . .

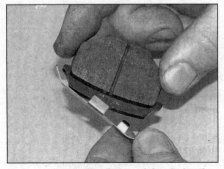

2.4f . . . noting the fitting of the spring for the outer pad . . .

2.4g . . . and the clip for the inner pad

2.4h Remove the shim from the back of the pad

2.5a Slide the caliper off the bracket . . .

2.5b . . . on this caliper you will need to unscrew the slider bolt (arrowed) after removing its cap

5 Separate the caliper from the bracket – on some calipers you need to unscrew one or both slider pins to do this **(see illustrations)**.

6 Inspect the surface of each pad for contamination and check that the friction material has not worn beyond its service limit (see Chapter 1, Section 8). If either pad is worn, is fouled with oil or grease, or heavily scored or damaged, fit a set of new pads. If required measure the thickness of the friction material to determine the extent of wear – the service limit is 1 mm. **Note:** *It is not possible to degrease the friction material; if the pads are contaminated in any way they must be replaced with new ones.* On twin piston calipers check the pad is wearing evenly across the friction material – uneven wear is a sure sign of a sticking or seized piston.

7 If the pads are in good condition clean them carefully, using a fine wire brush which is completely free of oil and grease to remove all traces of road dirt and corrosion. Using a pointed instrument, dig out any embedded particles of foreign matter. If required, spray with a dedicated brake cleaner to remove any dust.

8 Check the condition of the brake disc (see Section 4).

9 Remove all traces of corrosion from the pad pin(s) and check for wear and damage. Fit new ones if necessary.

10 Clean around the exposed section of the piston(s) to remove any dirt or debris that could cause the seals to be damaged. If new pads are being fitted, now push the piston(s) all the way back into the caliper to create room for them; if the old pads are still serviceable push the piston(s) in a little way. To push the piston(s) back use finger pressure or a piece of wood as leverage, or place the old pads back in the caliper and use a metal bar or a screwdriver inserted between them, or use grips and a piece of wood, with rag or card to protect the caliper body **(see illustration)**. Alternatively obtain a proper piston-pushing tool from a good tool supplier **(see illustration)**. If there is too much brake fluid in the reservoir It may be necessary to remove the master cylinder reservoir cover, plate (where fitted) and diaphragm and siphon some out (see *Pre-ride checks)*. If a piston is difficult to push back, remove the bleed valve cap, then attach a length of clear hose to the bleed valve and place the open end in a suitable container, then open the valve and try again (see Section 8). Take great care not to draw any air into the system. If in doubt, bleed the brake afterwards.

11 If a piston appears seized, apply the brake lever and check whether the piston in question moves at all – on models with two pistons first block or hold the other piston using wood or cable-ties. If it moves out but can't be pushed back in the chances are there is some hidden corrosion stopping it. If it doesn't move at all, or to fully clean and inspect the pistons, disassemble the caliper and overhaul it (see Section 3).

12 Clean off all traces of corrosion and hardened grease from the caliper slider pins and rubber boots. Replace the boots with new ones if they are damaged, deformed or

2.10a Push the piston(s) in using one of the methods described . . .

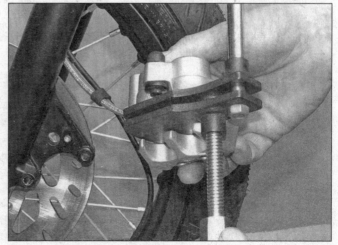

2.10b . . . or using a purpose built commercial tool

2.12 Make sure the boots (arrowed) are in good condition

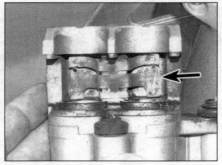

2.14a Make sure the pad spring (arrowed) is correctly in place

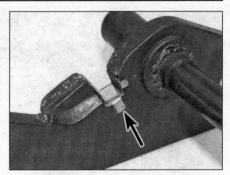

2.14b On some brackets there is a pad guide (arrowed)

deteriorated **(see illustration)**. Make sure the fitted slider pin(s) is/are tight. Apply a smear of silicone-based grease to the boots and slider pins.

13 Slide the caliper onto the bracket, making sure each boot seats correctly around the base of its pin **(see illustration 2.5a)**. Tighten the slider bolt(s) and fit any cap **(see illustration 2.5b)**.

14 Make sure the pad spring(s) and clip(s) are correctly located **(see illustrations and 2.4f and g)**. Where fitted make sure the shim is correctly located on the back of each pad, with the arrow pointing in the normal direction of disc rotation where present **(see illustration 2.4h)**.

15 Smear some copper grease onto the back of each pad, or its shim where fitted, and onto the retaining pins or around any pad locating post(s).

16 Fit the pads into the caliper, making sure they locate correctly against or over any post(s), and where necessary push them up against the spring to align the hole(s), then insert the pad pin(s), and if of the threaded type tighten them finger-tight at this stage **(see illustrations 2.4c, b and a or 2.4e and d)**.

17 Slide the caliper onto the disc making sure the pads locate correctly on each side **(see illustration 2.3)**. Fit the caliper mounting bolts and tighten them. Now tighten the pad retaining pin(s) **(see illustration 2.1b)**. Fit the pad pin plug(s) **(see illustration 2.1a)**.

18 Fit the brake hose into its guide or fit the guide onto the fork or mudguard as required according to model **(see illustration 2.2)**. Operate the brake lever until the pads contact with the disc. Check the level of fluid in the hydraulic reservoir and top-up if necessary (see *Pre-ride checks*).

19 Check the operation of the front brake before riding the motorcycle.

3 Brake caliper

⚠️ *Warning: If a caliper is in need of an overhaul all old brake fluid should be flushed from the system. Also, the dust created by the brake system may contain asbestos, which is harmful to your health. Never blow it out with compressed air and do not inhale any of it. An approved filtering mask should be worn when working on the brakes. Overhaul of the brake calipers must be done in a spotlessly clean work area to avoid contamination and possible failure of the brake hydraulic system components. Do not, under any circumstances, use petroleum-based solvents to clean brake parts. Use clean DOT 4 brake fluid, dedicated brake cleaner or denatured alcohol only, as described. To prevent damage from spilled brake fluid, always cover paintwork when working on the braking system.*

Removal

Note 1: *If the caliper is being overhauled (usually due to sticking piston(s) or fluid leaks) read through the entire procedure first and make sure that you have obtained all the new parts required (if available – check with your dealer), including some new DOT 4 brake fluid.*

Note 2: *Do not operate the brake lever or pedal while the caliper is off the disc.*

1 For maximum freedom of movement free the brake hose from any guide or unscrew the guide bolt as required according to model **(see illustration 2.2)**.

2 If the caliper is just being displaced from the forks as part of the wheel removal procedure unscrew the mounting bolts and slide the caliper off the disc **(see illustration 2.3)**. Tie the caliper back out of the way.

3 If the caliper is being completely removed or overhauled, have some rag to hand, then unscrew the brake hose banjo bolt and detach the banjo union, noting its alignment with the caliper **(see illustration)**. Wrap plastic foodwrap around the banjo union and secure the hose in an upright position to minimise fluid loss, or if available use a hose clamp **(see illustration)**. Discard the sealing washers, as new ones must be fitted on reassembly. Remove the brake pads (see Section 2).

Overhaul

4 Clean the exterior of the caliper and bracket with denatured alcohol or brake system cleaner. Have some clean rag ready to catch any spilled brake fluid. Clean off all traces of corrosion.

5 Clean off any hardened grease from the slider pins and rubber boots. Replace the boots with new ones if they are damaged, deformed or deteriorated **(see illustration 2.12)**. Make sure the slider pins are tight.

6 Make sure the bleed valve is tight. To remove the piston, cover it and the caliper with rag and apply compressed air gradually and progressively, starting with a fairly low pressure, to the fluid inlet in the caliper and allow the piston to ease out of the bore **(see**

3.3a Brake hose banjo bolt (arrowed)

3.3b Using a hose clamp to prevent fluid loss

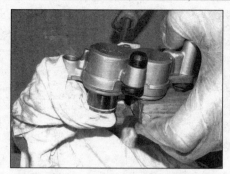

3.6a Apply compressed air to the fluid passage . . .

3.6b . . . until the pistons are displaced

3.8 Remove the seals and discard them

illustrations). On models with two pistons, if one is being pushed out before the other, you may need to block that one so more pressure is applied to the sticking one, but do not use your fingers. Always make sure the caliper is covered, with the pistons pointing down onto the bench so they cannot fly out and hit something.

7 If a piston is stuck in its bore due to corrosion, find a suitable bolt to block the fluid inlet banjo bolt bore and thread it in, then unscrew the bleed valve and apply the air to this in the same way – the narrower bore will allow more air pressure to be applied to the piston as less can escape. Do not try to remove a piston by levering it out or by using pliers or other grips. If the piston has completely seized you may have to replace the caliper with a new one.

8 Remove the dust seal(s) and the piston seal(s) from the piston bore(s) using a soft wooden or plastic tool to avoid scratching the bores **(see illustration)**. Discard the seals as new ones must be fitted.

9 Clean the piston(s) and bore(s) with clean DOT 4 brake fluid. If compressed air is available, blow it through the fluid galleries in the caliper to ensure they are clear (make sure it is filtered and unlubricated).

Caution: Do not, under any circumstances, use a petroleum-based solvent to clean brake parts.

10 Inspect the caliper bore and piston for signs of corrosion, nicks and burrs and loss of plating. If surface defects are present, the

pistons and/or the caliper assembly must be replaced with new ones.

11 Lubricate the new piston seal with new brake fluid and fit it into the inner (large) groove in the caliper bore **(see illustrations)**.

12 Lubricate the new dust seal with new brake fluid and fit it into the outer groove in the caliper bore **(see illustration)**.

13 Lubricate the piston with new brake fluid and fit it, closed-end first, into the caliper bore, taking care not to displace the seals **(see illustration)**. Using your thumbs, push the piston squarely all the way in.

14 Apply a smear of silicone-based grease to the boots and slider pins.

Installation

15 If removed, install the brake pads (see Section 2).

3.11a Lubricate the new piston seal with brake fluid . . .

16 Slide the caliper onto the brake disc, making sure the pads locate correctly on each side **(see illustration 2.3)**. Install the caliper mounting bolts and tighten them to the torque setting specified at the beginning of the Chapter.

17 If detached, connect the brake hose to the caliper, using new sealing washers on each side of the banjo fitting **(see illustration)**. Locate the hose elbow between or against the lug(s) on the caliper where present according to model. Tighten the banjo bolt.

18 Fit the brake hose into its guide or fit the guide onto the fork or mudguard as required according to model **(see illustration 2.2)**.

19 Top up the hydraulic reservoir with DOT 4 brake fluid (see *Pre-ride checks*) and bleed the system as described in Section 8. Check that there are no fluid leaks and test the operation of the brake before riding the motorcycle.

3.11b . . . then fit it into its groove . . .

3.12 . . . followed by the new dust seal

3.13 Fit the piston and push it all the way in

3.17 Always use new sealing washers and align the hose as noted on removal

4.2 Measure the thickness of the disc

4.3 Checking disc runout with a dial gauge

4 Brake disc

Inspection

1 Inspect the surface of the disc for score marks and other damage. Light scratches

4.5a Bend the tabs off the bolts to unlock them

are normal after use and won't affect brake operation, but deep grooves and heavy score marks will reduce braking efficiency and accelerate pad wear. If a disc is badly grooved it must be replaced with a new one.

2 The disc must not be machined, or allowed to wear down to a thickness less than the minimum stamped on the disc **(see illustration 4.5a)**. Check the thickness of the disc in the middle of the pad contact area using a micrometer **(see illustration)** – do not measure across the rim of the disc with a ruler. Replace the disc with a new one if necessary.

3 To check if the disc is warped, position the bike on an auxiliary stand with the wheel raised off the ground. Mount a dial gauge to the fork leg (front disc) or swingarm (rear disc), with the gauge plunger touching the surface of the disc about 10 mm from the outer edge **(see illustration)**. Rotate the wheel and watch the gauge needle, comparing the reading with the limit listed in the Specifications at the beginning of this Chapter. If the runout is greater than 0.2 mm, check the wheel bearings

for play (see Chapter 1). If the bearings are worn, install new ones (see Section 14) and repeat this check. If the disc runout is still excessive, a new disc will have to be fitted.

Removal

4 Remove the wheel (see Section 12 or 13). *Caution: Don't lay the wheel down and allow it to rest on the disc – the disc could become warped. Set the wheel on wood blocks so the wheel rim supports the weight of the wheel.*

5 If you are not replacing the disc with a new one, mark the relationship of the disc to the wheel, so it can be installed in the same position. Where fitted bend down the retainer plate tabs **(see illustration)**. Unscrew the disc bolts, loosening them evenly and a little at a time in a criss-cross pattern to avoid distorting the disc, then remove the disc **(see illustrations)**.

Installation

6 Before installing the disc, make sure there

4.5b This disc is secured by four bolts. Note how the retainer plates fit

4.5c This disc is secured by five bolts

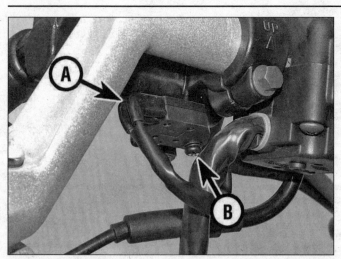

5.1 Brake switch wiring connectors (A) and retaining screw (B)

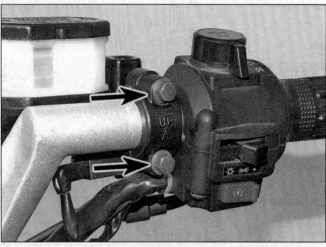

5.2 Unscrew the bolts (arrowed) and remove the master cylinder and its clamp

is no dirt or corrosion where it seats on the hub. If the disc does not sit flat when it is bolted down, it will appear to be warped when checked or when the front brake is used.

7 Fit the disc onto the wheel with its marked side facing out, aligning the previously applied matchmarks (if you're reinstalling the original disc), and making sure the arrow points in the direction of normal rotation.

8 Clean the threads of the disc mounting bolts, then apply a suitable non-permanent thread locking compound. Fit the bolts and tighten them evenly and a little at a time in a criss-cross pattern. Clean the disc using acetone or brake system cleaner. If a new disc has been fitted, remove any protective coating from its working surfaces and fit new brake pads.

9 Install the wheel (see Section 12 or 13).

10 Check the operation of the brake before riding the motorcycle.

5   Front brake master cylinder

> ⚠️ **Warning: If the brake master cylinder is in need of an overhaul all old brake fluid should be flushed from the system. Overhaul**

of the brake master cylinder must be done in a spotlessly clean work area to avoid contamination and possible failure of the brake hydraulic system components. Do not, under any circumstances, use petroleum-based solvents to clean brake parts. Use clean DOT 4 brake fluid, dedicated brake cleaner or denatured alcohol only, as described. To prevent damage from spilled brake fluid, always cover paintwork when working on the braking system.

Removal

Note: *If the master cylinder is being overhauled (usually due to sticking or poor action, or fluid leaks) read through the entire procedure first and make sure that you have obtained all the new parts required (if available – check with your dealer), including some new DOT 4 brake fluid. Before removing the master cylinder from the handlebars make a note of its position and alignment on the bar, making marks where necessary, so it can be installed in the same position. Look for any existing alignment mark, usually in the form of a punch mark aligned with the mating surfaces of the clamp (see illustrations 5.16a and b).*

1 Disconnect the brake light switch wiring connector(s), and if required remove the switch **(see illustration)**.

2 If the master cylinder is being overhauled, follow Steps 3 to 7. If the master cylinder is just

being displaced, follow this Step only: unscrew the master cylinder clamp bolts and remove the back of the clamp, noting how it fits, then position the master cylinder assembly clear of the handlebar **(see illustration)**. Ensure no strain is placed on the hydraulic hose. Keep the reservoir upright to prevent air entering the system.

3 Remove the brake lever (see Chapter 6). If mounted on the master cylinder bracket remove the mirror (see Chapter 8).

4 Slacken the reservoir cover screws **(see illustration)**.

5 Unscrew the brake hose banjo bolt and detach the banjo union, noting its alignment with the master cylinder **(see illustration)**. Wrap plastic foodwrap around the banjo union and secure the hose in an upright position to minimise fluid loss. Discard the sealing washers as new ones must be fitted on reassembly.

6 Unscrew the master cylinder clamp bolts and remove the back of the clamp, noting how it fits, then lift the master cylinder and reservoir away from the handlebar **(see illustration 5.2)**.

7 Remove the reservoir cover, diaphragm plate (where fitted), and diaphragm. Drain the brake fluid from the master cylinder and reservoir into a suitable container. Wipe any remaining fluid out of the reservoir with a clean rag.

Overhaul

8 Carefully remove the rubber boot from the master cylinder **(see illustration)**.

5.4 Slacken the cover screws

5.5 Brake hose banjo bolt (arrowed)

5.8 Remove the boot

5.9a Release the circlip . . .

5.9b . . . then draw out the piston
assembly and the spring

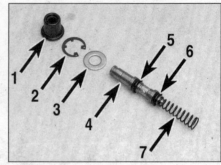

5.12 Typical master cylinder components

1	Rubber boot	5	Seal
2	Circlip	6	Cup
3	Washer	7	Spring
4	Piston		

9 Depress the piston and use circlip pliers to remove the circlip, then slide out the piston assembly and the spring, noting how they fit **(see illustrations)**. If they are difficult to remove, apply low pressure compressed air to the brake fluid outlet. Lay the parts out in the proper order to prevent confusion during reassembly.

10 Clean the master cylinder bore with clean brake fluid. If compressed air is available, blow it through the fluid galleries to ensure they are clear (make sure the air is filtered and unlubricated).

Caution: Do not, under any circumstances, use a petroleum-based solvent to clean brake parts.

11 Check the master cylinder bore for corrosion, scratches, nicks and score marks. If damage or wear is evident, the master

cylinder must be replaced with a new one. If the master cylinder is in poor condition, then the caliper should be checked as well.

12 If available all the necessary parts are included in the master cylinder rebuild kit. Use all of the new parts, regardless of the apparent condition of the old ones. Lay out the new parts in their correct order according to those removed **(see illustration)**.

13 Smear the piston, cup and seal and the master cylinder bore with new brake fluid. Slide the piston and spring assembly into the master cylinder **(see illustration 5.9b)**. Push the piston in, making sure the lips on the cup and seal do not turn inside out **(see illustration)**. Fit the washer (where fitted) and circlip over the end of the piston **(see illustrations)**. Push the circlip into

its groove, making sure it locates correctly **(see illustration)**.

14 Smear some silicone grease onto the lips and inside of the rubber boot. Fit the rubber boot onto the piston so its outer end lips locate in the groove and press the boot into place in the end of the cylinder **(see illustrations)**.

15 Inspect the reservoir diaphragm and fit a new one it if it is damaged or deteriorated.

Installation

16 Attach the master cylinder to the handlebar, aligning the clamp joint with the

5.13a Push the piston into the bore

5.13b Fit the washer . . .

5.13c . . . and the circlip . . .

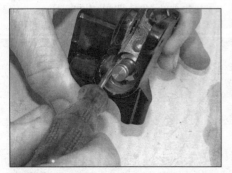

5.13d . . . and push it down into its groove

5.14a Fit the new boot . . .

5.14b . . . making sure it locates correctly

5.16a Align the master cylinder mating surface with the mark (arrowed) . . .

5.16b . . . and with the UP mark facing up

5.17 Always use new sealing washers

punch mark where present, or as noted on removal if not **(see illustration)**. then fit the back of the clamp with its UP mark facing up **(see illustration 5.2)**. Tighten the upper bolt first, then the lower bolt.

17 Connect the brake hose to the master cylinder, using new sealing washers on each side of the banjo fitting **(see illustration)**. Locate the hose elbow between or against the lug(s) on the master cylinder where present according to model. Tighten the banjo bolt.

18 Install the brake light switch if removed, and connect the wiring connectors **(see illustration 5.1)**.

19 Install the brake lever (see Chapter 6). Install the mirror if removed (see Chapter 8).

20 Fill the fluid reservoir with new DOT 4 brake fluid (see *Pre-ride* checks). Refer to Section 8 and bleed the air from the system.

21 Check the operation of the brake before riding the motorcycle.

6 Rear brake master cylinder

⚠️ *Warning: If the brake master cylinder is in need of an overhaul all old brake fluid should be flushed from the system. Master cylinder overhaul must be done in a spotlessly clean work area to avoid contamination*

and possible failure of the brake hydraulic system components. Do not, under any circumstances, use petroleum-based solvents to clean brake parts. Use clean DOT 4 brake fluid, dedicated brake cleaner or denatured alcohol only, as described. To prevent damage from spilled brake fluid, always cover paintwork when working on the braking system.

Removal

Note: *If the master cylinder is being overhauled (usually due to sticking or poor action, or fluid leaks) read through the entire procedure first and make sure that you have obtained all the new parts required (if available – check with your dealer), including some new DOT 4 brake fluid.*

1 Release and remove the pivot pin securing the brake pedal to the master cylinder pushrod **(see illustrations)**. If a split pin was fitted note that you should use a new one on installation.

2 Detach the fluid reservoir, then remove the cover, diaphragm plate (where fitted) and diaphragm **(see illustrations)**. Pour the brake fluid into a suitable container. Wipe any remaining fluid out of the reservoir with a clean rag.

3 Unscrew the brake hose banjo bolt and detach the banjo union, noting its alignment with the master cylinder **(see illustration)**. Once disconnected, wrap plastic foodwrap around the banjo union and secure the hose in an upright position to minimise fluid loss. Discard the sealing washers as new ones must be fitted on reassembly.

6.1a On this type remove the split pin then withdraw the pin

6.1b On this type release the clip (arrowed) then withdraw the pin

6.2a Undo the screw and displace the reservoir . . .

6.2b . . . then remove the cap, plate and diaphragm and drain the reservoir

6.3 Brake hose banjo bolt (arrowed) – note its alignment

6.4a Unscrew the bolts (arrowed) . . .

6.4b . . . and remove the master cylinder and reservoir

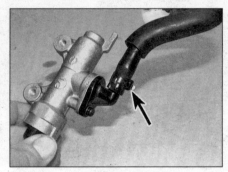

6.5 Release the clip (arrowed) and pull the hose off its union

4 Undo the bolts securing the master cylinder and remove it **(see illustrations)**.

Overhaul

5 Release the clip securing the reservoir hose to the union on the master cylinder and detach the hose, being prepared to catch any residual fluid **(see illustration)**. Inspect the hose for cracks or splits and replace it with a new one if necessary. If required undo the screw or release the circlip (according to type) and remove the union – discard the O-ring as a new one must be used.
6 Dislodge the rubber dust boot from the base of the master cylinder and from around the pushrod, noting how it locates **(see**

illustration). Push the pushrod in and, using circlip pliers, remove the circlip from its groove in the master cylinder and slide out the pushrod assembly, the piston assembly and the spring, noting how they fit **(see illustrations)**. Lay the parts out in order as you remove them to prevent confusion during reassembly.
7 Slacken the locknut holding the clevis on the bottom of the pushrod **(see illustration)**. If there is a roll pin fitted below the clevis, drive it out **(see illustration)**. Note how far the clevis is threaded up the pushrod, then thread it off, followed by the locknut **(see illustration)**. Remove the rubber boot and the circlip.
8 Clean the master cylinder bore with clean

brake fluid. If compressed air is available, blow it through the fluid galleries to ensure they are clear (make sure the air is filtered and unlubricated).
Caution: Do not, under any circumstances, use a petroleum-based solvent to clean brake parts.
9 Check the master cylinder bore for corrosion, scratches, nicks and score marks. If damage or wear is evident, the master cylinder must be replaced with a new one. If the master cylinder is in poor condition, then the caliper should be checked as well.
10 All the necessary parts are included in the master cylinder rebuild kit. Use all of the new parts, regardless of the apparent condition of the old ones. Lay out the new parts in their

6.6a Remove the rubber boot . . .

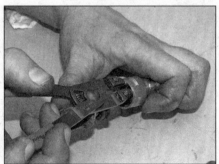

6.6b . . . then release the circlip . . .

6.6c . . . and remove the pushrod, piston and spring

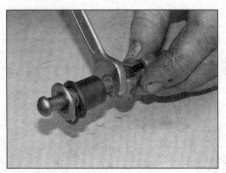

6.7a Slacken the locknut

6.7b Remove the roll pin, if fitted

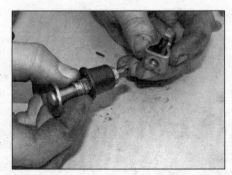

6.7c Thread the clevis and locknut off then remove the boot and circlip

6.10 Typical piston and spring assembly showing cup and seal fitted

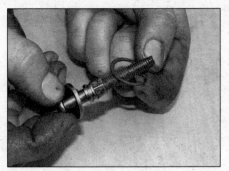

6.11a Fit the circlip . . .

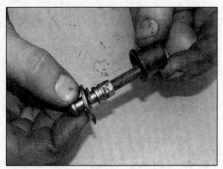

6.11b . . . boot . . .

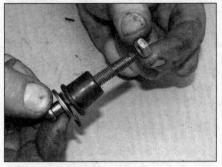

6.11c . . . locknut . . .

6.11d . . . and clevis

6.11e Drive the roll pin into the hole

6.11f Set the clevis position then tighten the locknut against it

6.12 Fit the assembly into the cylinder

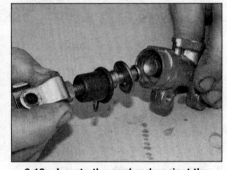

6.13a Locate the pushrod against the piston and push it in . . .

correct order according to those removed (see illustration).

11 Smear some silicone grease onto the lips and inside of the rubber boot and onto the rounded end of the pushrod. Make sure the washer is on the pushrod, then fit the new circlip and rubber boot onto the pushrod, then thread the locknut and clevis on (see

illustrations). Drive the roll pin into its hole if fitted (see illustration). Set the position of the clevis as noted on removal and tighten the locknut securely against it (see illustration).

12 Smear the piston, cup and seal and the master cylinder bore with new brake fluid. Slide the piston and spring assembly into the master cylinder (see illustration). Make sure

the lips on the cup and seal do not turn inside out.

13 Push the piston in using the pushrod and locate the circlip in the groove (see illustrations).

14 Press the rubber boot into place in the end of the cylinder (see illustrations).

15 If removed fit the reservoir hose union

6.13b . . . then fit the circlip into the groove

6.14a Fit the new boot into the cylinder . . .

6.14b . . . and locate it in its groove

using a new O-ring and secure it with its screw or circlip as fitted. Connect the hose to the union on the master cylinder and secure it with the clip (see illustration 6.5). Check that the hose is secured with a clip at the reservoir end as well. If the clips have weakened, use new ones.

Installation

16 Locate the master cylinder, then fit the bolts and tighten them (see illustration 6.4b and a).

17 Align the clevis with the brake pedal, then insert the pivot pin and secure it in place, using a new split pin where required (see illustration 6.1a or b).

18 Connect the brake hose to the master cylinder, using new sealing washers on each side of the banjo fitting (see illustration). Locate the hose elbow between or against the lug(s) on the master cylinder where present according to model. Tighten the banjo bolt.

19 Fill the fluid reservoir with new DOT 4 brake fluid (see *Pre-ride checks*). Refer to Section 8 and bleed the air from the system.

20 Fit the fluid reservoir onto its mount and tighten the bolt (see illustration 6.2a).

21 Check the operation of the brake carefully before riding the motorcycle.

7 Brake hoses and fittings

Inspection

1 Brake hose condition should be checked regularly and the hoses replaced with new ones at the specified interval (see Chapter 1).

2 Twist and flex the hoses while looking for cracks, bulges and seeping hydraulic fluid. Check extra carefully around the areas where the hoses connect with the banjo fittings, as these are common areas for hose failure.

3 Inspect the banjo fittings connected to the brake hoses. If the fittings are rusted, scratched or cracked, fit new hoses.

Removal and installation

4 Drain the old brake fluid from the system (see Section 8).

6.18 Always use new sealing washers

5 The brake hoses have banjo fittings on each end. Cover the surrounding area with plenty of rags and unscrew the banjo bolt at each end of the hose, noting the alignment of the fitting with the master cylinder or brake caliper (see illustrations 3.3a, 5.5 and 6.3). Free the hose from any clips or guides and remove it, noting its routing. Discard the sealing washers. **Note:** *Do not operate the brake lever or pedal while a brake hose is disconnected.*

6 Position the new hose, making sure it isn't twisted or otherwise strained, and ensure that it is correctly routed through any clips or guides and is clear of all moving components. Make sure the elbow locates correctly.

7 Check that the fittings align correctly, then install the banjo bolts, using new sealing washers on both sides of the fittings, and tighten the bolts (see illustrations 3.17, 5.17 and 6.18).

8 Refill the system with new DOT 4 brake fluid (see *Pre-ride checks*) and bleed the air from it (see Section 8).

9 Check the operation of the brakes before riding the motorcycle.

8 Brake system bleeding and fluid change

Note: *If bleeding the system using the conventional method does not work sufficiently well, you could try a commercially available vacuum-type brake bleeding tool, following the manufacturer's instructions for using the tool.*

8.2 Set-up for bleeding the brakes – this shows one of the commercially available one-man kits

Bleeding

1 Bleeding the brakes is simply the process of removing air from the brake fluid reservoir, the hose and the brake caliper. Bleeding is necessary whenever a brake system hydraulic connection is loosened, after a component or hose is replaced with a new one, or when the master cylinder or caliper is overhauled. Leaks in the system may also allow air to enter, but leaking brake fluid will reveal their presence and warn you of the need for repair.

2 To bleed the brakes, you will need some new DOT 4 brake fluid, a length of clear flexible hose, a small container partially filled with clean brake fluid, some rags, a spanner to fit the brake caliper bleed valve, and possibly help from an assistant (see illustration). Bleeding kits that include the hose, a one-way valve and a container are available relatively cheaply from a good auto store, and simplify the task as you don't need an assistant.

3 Cover painted components to prevent damage in the event that brake fluid is spilled.

4 Refer to '*Pre-ride checks*' and remove the reservoir cover, diaphragm plate (where fitted) and diaphragm and slowly pump the brake lever (front brake) or pedal (rear brake) a few times, until no air bubbles can be seen floating up from the holes in the bottom of the reservoir. This bleeds the air from the master cylinder end of the line. Temporarily refit the reservoir cover.

5 Pull the dust cap off the bleed valve (see illustrations). If using a ring spanner fit it onto the valve (see illustration). Attach one end of the hose to the bleed valve and, if not using a kit, submerge the other end in the clean brake fluid in the container (see illustration 8.2).

> **HAYNES HiNT** *To avoid damaging the bleed valve during the procedure, loosen it and then tighten it temporarily with a ring spanner before attaching the hose. With the hose attached, the valve can then be opened and closed either with an open-ended spanner, or by leaving the ring spanner located on the valve and fitting the hose above it.*

8.5a Brake caliper bleed valve (arrowed)

8.5b Fit the ring spanner before connecting the hose

6 Check the fluid level in the reservoir. Do not allow the fluid level to drop below the lower mark during the procedure.

7 Carefully pump the brake lever or pedal three or four times and hold it in (front) or down (rear) while opening the bleed valve. When the valve is opened, brake fluid will flow out of the caliper into the clear tubing, and the lever will move toward the handlebar, or the pedal will move down. If there is air in the system there will be air bubbles in the brake fluid coming out of the caliper.

8 Tighten the bleed valve, then release the brake lever or pedal gradually. Repeat the process until no air bubbles are visible in the brake fluid leaving the caliper, and the lever or pedal is firm when applied, topping the reservoir up when necessary. On completion, disconnect the hose, then tighten the bleed valve to the torque setting specified at the beginning of this Chapter and install the dust cap.

> **HAYNES HiNT**
> *If it is not possible to produce a firm feel to the lever or pedal, the fluid may be aerated. Let the brake fluid in the system stabilise for a few hours and then repeat the procedure when the tiny bubbles in the system have settled out.*

9 Top-up the reservoir, then install the diaphragm, diaphragm plate (where fitted), and cover (see *Pre-ride checks*). Wipe up any spilled brake fluid. Check the entire system for fluid leaks.

10 Check the operation of the brakes before riding the motorcycle.

Fluid change

11 Changing the brake fluid is a similar process to bleeding the brakes and requires the same materials plus a suitable tool (such as a syringe) for siphoning the fluid out of the reservoir. Also ensure that the container is large enough to take all the old fluid when it is flushed out of the system.

12 Follow Steps 3 and 5, then remove the reservoir cap, diaphragm plate (where fitted) and diaphragm and siphon the old fluid out of the reservoir. Wipe the reservoir clean. Fill the reservoir with new DOT 4 brake fluid, then carefully pump the brake lever or pedal three or four times and hold it in (front) or down (rear) while opening the caliper bleed valve. When the valve is opened, brake fluid will flow out of the caliper into the clear tubing, and the lever will move toward the handlebar, or the pedal will move down.

13 Tighten the bleed valve, then release the brake lever or pedal gradually. Keep the reservoir topped-up with new fluid to above the LOWER level at all times or air may enter the system and greatly increase the length of the

> **HAYNES HiNT**
> *Old brake fluid is invariably much darker in colour than new fluid, making it easy to see when all old fluid has been expelled from the system.*

task. Repeat the process until new fluid can be seen emerging from the caliper bleed valve.

14 Disconnect the hose, then tighten the bleed valve and install the dust cap.

15 Top-up the reservoir, then install the diaphragm, diaphragm plate (where fitted), and cover (see *Pre-ride checks*). Wipe up any spilled brake fluid. Check the entire system for fluid leaks.

16 Check the operation of the brakes before riding the motorcycle.

Draining the system for overhaul

17 Draining the brake fluid is again a similar process to bleeding the brakes. Follow the procedure described above for changing the fluid, but quite simply do not put any new fluid into the reservoir – the system fills itself with air instead.

---

9   Drum brake

> ⚠ **Warning: The dust created by the brake system may contain asbestos, which is harmful to your health. Never blow it out with compressed air and don't inhale any of it. An approved filtering mask should be worn when working on the brakes.**

Check

1 Remove the wheel (see Section 12 or 13). Lift the brake plate out of the drum **(see illustration)**.

2 Measure the thickness of material remaining at

the cam end (the thinnest point) of the shoe **(see illustration)**. The wear limit is typically 1.5 mm.

3 Inspect the surface of the friction material on each shoe for contamination **(see illustration)**. If either shoe is fouled with oil or grease, or heavily scored or damaged by dirt and debris, both shoes must be replaced as a set. Note that it is not possible to degrease the friction material; if the shoes are contaminated in any way they must be replaced.

4 If the shoes are in good condition clean them carefully, using a fine wire brush which is completely free of oil and grease, some sandpaper, to remove all traces of road dirt and corrosion. Using a pointed instrument, dig out any embedded particles of foreign matter. If the material appears glazed, roughen up the surface using course sandpaper, bearing in mind the *Warning* above.

5 Check the condition of the brake shoe springs – they should hold the shoes tight against the cam and post **(see illustration)**. Replace them with new ones if they appear weak or are obviously deformed or damaged. If the springs are different note which fits where.

6 Clean the brake drum lining using brake cleaner or a rag soaked in solvent. Examine the surface of the lining for scoring and excessive wear **(see illustration 9.3)**. While light scratches are expected, any heavy scoring or cracks will impair braking and there is no satisfactory way of removing them – the wheel should be replaced with a new one.

7 Check that the brake cam operates smoothly and to its full limits of travel by operating the lever arm. Clean off all traces

9.1 Lift the brake plate out

9.2 Check the amount of friction material on the shoe

9.3 Check the surface of the shoe and that of the drum

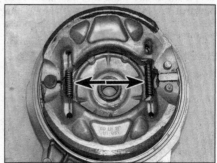

9.5 Check the springs (arrowed) and note which way round they fit

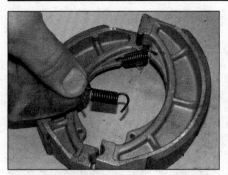

9.12a Fit the shoes together and join them with the springs

9.12b Locate the rounded ends around the post . . .

9.12c . . . and the flat ends on each side of the cam and fold them onto the plate

of old and hardened grease from the cam and pivot post – remove the shoes to do this (see Step 10). If the bearing surfaces of the cam are worn or damaged it should be replaced with a new one.

8 Make sure the brake actuating rod is straight and the pivot bush in the arm is clean and greased. Clean off any corrosion if necessary. If a cable is used see below.

Shoe replacement

9 Remove the wheel (see Section 12 or 13). Lift the brake plate out of the drum (**see illustration 9.1**).

10 Grasp the outer edge of each shoe and fold them upwards and inwards to form a 'V', noting that they are under the pressure of the springs, then remove them from the plate noting how they locate around the cam and the pivot post (**see illustration 9.12b**). Remove the springs from the shoes (**see illustration 9.12a**).

11 Check the shoes and the drum as outlined above.

12 Apply some copper grease to the bearing surfaces on the cam and pivot post. Fit the springs onto the shoes (**see illustration**). Position the shoes so that the rounded end of each shoe fits around the pivot post and the flat end against the flats on the cam (**see illustrations**). Fold the shoes flat onto the plate making sure the shoes sit correctly on each side of the pivot and the cam and the springs remain in place (**see illustration 9.5**). Operate the lever arm to check that the cam and shoes work correctly.

13 Fit the brake plate into the drum (**see illustration 9.1**). Install the wheel (see Section 13). Check the operation of the brake before riding the motorcycle.

Brake cable

Note: *For details of cable adjustment and lubrication see Chapter 1.*

14 Slacken the nuts securing the cable in its bracket just ahead of the drum. Thread the front nut up the cable and the rear nut off it.

15 Fully unscrew the adjuster nut on the drum end of the cable, then draw the cable out of the brake arm and the bracket. Remove the spring from the cable and the pivot bush from the arm for safekeeping.

16 Release the other end of the cable from the brake lever or brake pedal.

17 Free the cable from any clips or ties, then withdraw it carefully, noting its routing and any guides it passes through.

18 Install the new cable. Apply some grease to the ends of the inner cables before fitting them, and to the pedal and arm pivot points.

19 Adjust the cable freeplay (see Chapter 1). Check the operation of the brake before riding the bike.

10 Wheel inspection and repair

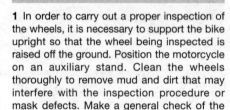

1 In order to carry out a proper inspection of the wheels, it is necessary to support the bike upright so that the wheel being inspected is raised off the ground. Position the motorcycle on an auxiliary stand. Clean the wheels thoroughly to remove mud and dirt that may interfere with the inspection procedure or mask defects. Make a general check of the

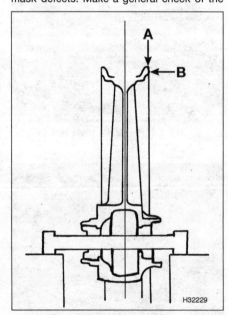

10.2 Check the wheel for radial (out-of-round) runout (A) and axial (side-to-side) runout (B)

wheels (see Chapter 1) and tyres (see *Pre-ride checks*).

2 Attach a dial gauge to the fork or the swingarm and position its tip against the side of the wheel rim. Spin the wheel slowly and check the axial (side-to-side) runout of the rim (**see illustration**). Runout should not exceed 2 mm.

3 In order to accurately check radial (out of round) runout with the dial gauge, remove the wheel from the machine, and the tyre from the wheel. With the axle clamped in a vice and the dial gauge positioned on the top of the rim, the wheel can be rotated to check the runout, which should not exceed 2 mm (**see illustration 10.2**).

4 An easier, though slightly less accurate, method is to attach a stiff wire pointer to the fork or the swingarm and position the end a fraction of an inch from the wheel rim where the wheel and tyre join. If the wheel is true, the distance from the pointer to the rim will be constant as the wheel is rotated. **Note:** *If wheel runout is excessive, check the wheel bearings very carefully before renewing the wheel.*

5 The wheels should also be inspected for cracks, flat spots on the rim and other damage. Look very closely for dents in the area where the tyre bead contacts the rim. Dents in this area may prevent complete sealing of the tyre against the rim, which leads to deflation of the tyre over a period of time. If damage is evident, or if runout in either direction is excessive, the wheel will have to be renewed. Never attempt to repair a damaged cast alloy wheel.

11 Wheel alignment check

1 Misalignment of the wheels due to a bent frame or forks can cause strange and possibly serious handling problems. If the frame or forks are at fault, repair by a frame specialist or renewal are the only options.

2 To check wheel alignment you will need an assistant, a length of string or a perfectly straight piece of wood and a ruler. A plumb bob or spirit level for checking that the wheels are vertical will also be required.

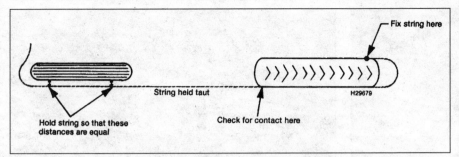

11.5 Wheel alignment check using string

3 In order to make a proper check of the wheels it is necessary to support the bike in an upright position, using an auxiliary stand. First ensure that the chain adjuster markings coincide on each side of the swingarm (see Chapter 1, Section 1). Next, measure the width of both tyres at their widest points. Subtract the smaller measurement from the larger measurement, then divide the difference by two. The result is the amount of offset that should exist between the front and rear tyres on both sides of the machine.

4 If a string is used, have your assistant hold one end of it about halfway between the floor and the rear axle, with the string touching the back edge of the rear tyre sidewall.

5 Run the other end of the string forward and pull it tight so that it is roughly parallel to the floor **(see illustration)**. Slowly bring the string into contact with the front edge of the rear tyre sidewall, then turn the front wheel until it is parallel with the string. Measure the distance from the front tyre sidewall to the string.

6 Repeat the procedure on the other side of the motorcycle. The distance from the front tyre sidewall to the string should be equal on both sides.

7 As previously mentioned, a perfectly straight length of wood or metal bar may be substituted for the string **(see illustration)**.

8 If the distance between the string and tyre is greater on one side, or if the rear wheel appears to be out of alignment, have your machine checked by a dealer or frame specialist.

9 If the front-to-back alignment is correct, the wheels still may be out of alignment vertically.

10 Using a plumb bob or spirit level, check the rear wheel to make sure it is vertical. To do this, hold the string of the plumb bob against the tyre upper sidewall and allow the weight to settle just off the floor. If the string touches both the upper and lower tyre sidewalls and is perfectly straight, the wheel is vertical. If it is not, adjust the stand until it is.

11 Once the rear wheel is vertical, check the front wheel in the same manner. If both wheels are not perfectly vertical, the frame and/or major suspension components are bent.

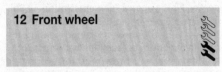

12 Front wheel

Removal

1 Position the motorcycle on its centrestand where fitted, or on an auxiliary stand, supporting it so that the front wheel is off the ground. Always make sure the motorcycle is properly supported. If a support is being placed under the engine, remove any body panel (such as a belly pan or sump guard) as required according to model (see Chapter 8), and do not support the bike through the exhaust pipe.

2 On disc brake models displace the front brake caliper (see Section 3). Support the caliper with a cable-tie or a bungee cord so that no strain is placed on the hydraulic hose. There is no need to disconnect the hose from the caliper. **Note:** *Do not operate the front brake lever with the caliper removed.*

3 On drum brake models detach the cable from the arm on the brake plate.

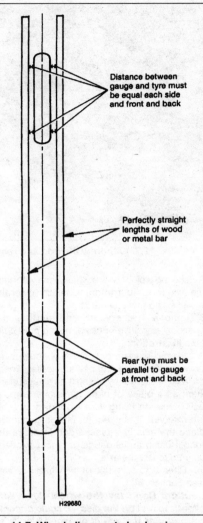

11.7 Wheel alignment check using a straight-edge

4 Detach the speedometer cable from the drive housing and draw the cable out **(see illustration)**. Alternatively leave the cable connected and displace the drive housing from the wheel as it is removed.

5 Where fitted remove the cap from each end of the axle **(see illustration)**.

6 Unscrew the axle nut and remove the washer where fitted **(see illustration)**.

12.4 Detach the speedo cable if required

12.5 Remove the axle caps if fitted

12.6 Unscrew the nut and remove the washer (if fitted)

12.7 Withdraw the axle and remove the wheel

12.8a Remove the spacer . . .

7 Take the weight of the wheel, then withdraw the axle **(see illustration)**. Carefully lower the wheel and draw it forwards.

8 Remove the spacer and detach the speedometer drive housing, noting how it fits **(see illustrations)**.

9 Clean all dirt and old grease off the spacer, drive housing, axle and bearing seal(s). Check the axle is straight by rolling it on a flat surface such as a piece of plate glass (first remove any corrosion using wire wool or a suitable alternative). If the equipment is available, place the axle in V-blocks and measure the runout using a dial gauge. If runout exceeds 0.2 mm renew the axle.

10 Check the condition of the wheel bearings (see Section 14).

Caution: Don't lay the wheel down and allow it to rest on the disc – it could become warped. Set the wheel on wood blocks so the disc doesn't support the weight of the wheel.

Installation

Note: *If a new tyre has been fitted, make sure the directional arrow on the tyre is pointing in the direction of normal rotation of the wheel.*

11 Smear some grease to the inside of the wheel spacer and to the lips of the bearing seal(s). Fit the spacer **(see illustration 12.8a)**.

12 Smear grease into the speedometer drive housing. Fit the drive housing, locating the tabs in the cut-outs **(see illustration 12.8b)**.

13 Manoeuvre the wheel into position between the forks, making sure the brake disc or drum is on the correct side. Apply a thin coat of grease to the axle.

14 Lift the wheel into place, making sure the spacer and speedometer drive housing remain in position, and that the drive housing is correctly positioned with the cable socket facing back **(see illustration 12.4)** – some housings have an UP mark and/or arrow which must be at the top or point upwards **(see illustration 12.6)**, and others may have a lug which seats against a stop on the fork or between tabs **(see illustration)**. Slide the axle in **(see illustration 12.7)**.

15 Fit the axle nut, with its washer where fitted, and tighten it, counter-holding the axle head if necessary.

16 If detached fit the speedometer cable into the drive housing, aligning the tab with the slot, and tighten the knurled ring or fit the screw **(see illustration 12.4)**. Fit the axle caps **(see illustration 12.5)**.

17 On disc brake models install the brake caliper (see Section 3). Apply the front brake a few times to bring the pads back into contact with the disc.

18 On drum brake models connect the brake cable, then adjust the freeplay (see Chapter 1).

19 Check for correct operation of the front brake before riding the motorcycle.

13 Rear wheel

Removal

1 Position the motorcycle on its centrestand where fitted, or on an auxiliary stand so that

12.8b . . . and the drive housing

12.14 On this model locate the lug (arrowed) between the raised tabs

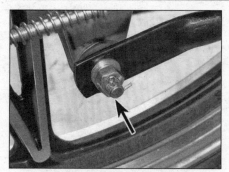

13.2a Remove the split pin (arrowed), then unscrew the nut and remove the washer(s) . . .

13.2b . . . then detach the arm

13.2c Remove the rubber washer and bolt

13.2d Unscrew the nut and draw the rod out

13.2e Remove the pivot bush . . .

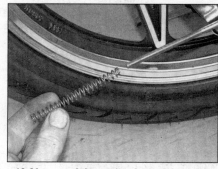

13.2f . . . and the spring for safekeeping

the rear wheel is off the ground. Always make sure the motorcycle is properly supported. Create some slack in the chain (see Chapter 1, Section 1).

2 On drum brake models remove the split pin from the brake torque arm bolt, then unscrew the nut, remove the washer(s), and detach the arm **(see illustrations)**. Remove the inner washer where fitted and withdraw the bolt if loose (some models have a fitted stud) **(see illustration)**. Unscrew the rear brake adjuster nut then draw the rod or cable out of the arm **(see illustrations)**. Remove the spring, and washer where fitted, from the rod or cable and the pivot bush from the arm for safekeeping **(see illustration)**.

3 Unscrew the axle nut and remove the washer, where fitted **(see illustration)**.

4 Take the weight of the wheel, then withdraw the axle and lower the wheel to the ground **(see illustration)**. If the axle is difficult to

withdraw, drive it through with a drift, making sure you don't damage the threads. Retrieve the wheel spacer(s) if they have dropped out.

5 Remove the chain adjusters from each end of the swingarm **(see illustration)**.

6 Disengage the chain from the sprocket and

draw the wheel back out of the swingarm **(see illustration)**. Remove the spacer(s) from wheel if not already done **(see illustration)**. Keep the wheel upright – if you need to lay it down, first lift the sprocket coupling out of the hub (where possible), and the brake plate out of the drum

13.3 Unscrew the axle nut

13.4 Withdraw the axle and lower the wheel

13.5 Remove the chain adjusters noting how they fit

13.6a Disengage the chain as the wheel is withdrawn

13.6b Remove the wheel spacers

13.7 Displace the caliper, noting how it locates. Note the hose in the guide (arrowed)

13.13 Position the wheel and fit the chain around the sprocket

13.14a Slide the axle through the chain adjuster and spacer . . .

on drum brake models, then lay the wheel on wooden blocks **(see illustrations 18.2a and b)**.

7 On disc brake models displace the rear brake caliper bracket from the swingarm, noting how it locates, and rest it on some rag on the swingarm **(see illustration)**. **Note:** *Do not operate the brake pedal while the caliper is off the disc.*

8 Clean all old grease of the spacer(s), axle and the seal(s).

9 Check the axle is straight by rolling it on a flat surface such as a piece of plate glass (if the axle is corroded, first remove any corrosion with wire wool or a suitable alternative). If the equipment is available, place the axle in V-blocks and check the runout using a dial gauge. If runout exceeds 0.2 mm, renew the axle.

10 Check the condition of the wheel bearings (see Section 14).

Installation

Note: *If a new tyre has been fitted, make sure the directional arrow on the tyre is pointing in the direction of normal rotation of the wheel.*

11 Apply a smear of grease to the inside of the wheel spacer(s), and also to the ends where they fit against the wheel and swingarm, and to the seal lips. Apply a thin coat of grease to the axle.

12 If removed fit the sprocket coupling into the hub, making sure the spacer is in place **(see illustrations 18.2b and a)**. On drum

brake models fit the brake plate into the drum **(see illustration 9.1)**. On disc brake models locate the caliper bracket on its guide, making sure the hose is correctly routed in relation to the swingarm **(see illustration 13.7)**.

13 Manoeuvre the wheel into position between the ends of the swingarm with the sprocket to the left. Engage the drive chain with the sprocket **(see illustration)**.

14 Lift the wheel into position, on disc brake models making sure the disc locates between the brake pads, and slide the axle through the chain adjuster, locating it against the swingarm as you do, the spacer, and fitting the other spacer and chain adjuster as the axle passes out the other side of the wheel **(see illustrations)**. Check that everything is correctly aligned, then fit the axle nut, with its washer where fitted, but leave it loose **(see illustration 13.3)**.

15 Check and adjust the drive chain slack (see Chapter 1). On completion tighten the axle nut, counter-holding the axle head if necessary.

16 On drum brake models fit the spring onto the brake rod or cable **(see illustration 13.2f)**. Fit the rod or cable pivot bush into the arm **(see illustration 13.2e)**. Fit the rod or cable into the bush and thread the nut on **(see illustration 13.2d)**. Fit the torque arm bolt and inner washer if removed **(see illustration 13.2c)**. Fit the arm and washer(s) and tighten the nut **(see illustration)**. Fit a new split pin through the hole in the end

of the bolt and bend its ends round **(see illustration 13.2a)**. Refer to Chapter 1, Section 8 and set the correct amount of brake pedal freeplay. Check the operation of the rear brake carefully before riding the bike.

17 On disc brake models operate the brake pedal several times to bring the pads into contact with the disc. Check the operation of the rear brake carefully before riding the bike.

14 Wheel bearings

Caution: *Don't lay the wheel down and allow it to rest on the disc or the sprocket – they could become warped. Set the wheel on wood blocks so the wheel rim supports the weight of the wheel, or keep the wheel upright.*

Note: *Always renew the wheel bearings in sets, never individually. Avoid using a high pressure cleaner on the wheel bearing area.*

1 Remove the wheel (see Section 12 or 13). Remove the sprocket coupling (see Section 18) and brake plate (see Section 9) as required.

2 Where fitted lever out the bearing seal(s) using a flat-bladed screwdriver or a seal hook **(see illustration)**. Take care not to damage the hub. Discard the seal as a new one must be fitted on reassembly. On the front wheel, where fitted remove the speedometer drive plate, noting how it locates **(see illustration)**.

13.14b . . . on each side

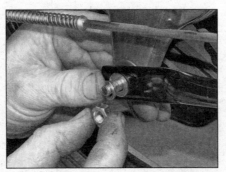

13.16 Fit the torque arm onto the brake plate

14.2a Lever out the bearing seal

14.2b Remove the speedo drive plate where fitted

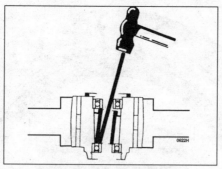

14.5a Locate the drift as shown . . .

14.5b . . . and drive the bearing out

3 Inspect the bearings – check that the inner race turns smoothly, quietly and freely and that the outer race is a tight fit in the hub. **Note:** *Do not remove the bearings unless they are going to be replaced with new ones.*

4 If the bearings are worn, first check for and if fitted remove any circlip securing them.

5 Remove the bearings using a metal rod (preferably a brass punch) inserted through the centre of the opposite bearing and locating it on the inner race, pushing the bearing spacer aside to expose it **(see illustration)**. Curve the end of the drift to obtain better purchase if necessary. Strike the drift with a hammer, working evenly around the bearing, to drive it from the hub **(see illustration)**.

6 If the bearings are difficult to remove as described in Step 5, remove them using an internal expanding puller with slide-hammer attachment, which can be obtained commercially **(see illustrations)**.

7 Remove the spacer which fits between the bearings. Turn the wheel over and remove the other bearing using the same procedure.

8 To remove the bearing(s) from the sprocket coupling (where fitted), first remove the seal, then support the coupling on blocks of wood, sprocket side down, and drive the bearing(s) out from the inside using a bearing driver or socket **(see illustrations)**.

9 Thoroughly clean the hub area of the wheel with a suitable solvent and inspect the bearing seats for scoring and wear. If the seats are damaged, consult a dealer before reassembling the wheel.

10 Install the bearings with the marked or sealed side facing outwards, using a bearing

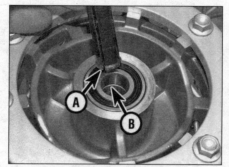

14.6a Locate the knife edges (A) under the lower edge of the bearing (B) and tighten the tool so they expand into the groove . . .

driver or socket to drive them in until they seat **(see illustration)**. Ensure the bearing is fitted squarely and all the way onto its seat.

11 Turn the wheel over then install the bearing spacer and the other new bearing. Where any

14.6b . . . and pull the bearing out

bearing has been secured by a circlip, fit a new one, making sure it locates correctly in its groove.

12 Press the new seal(s) into the hub and level it/them with the rim of the hub **(see illustrations)**. Smear the seal lips with grease.

13 Install the wheel (see Section 12 or 13).

14.8a Lever out the bearing seal

14.8b Drive the bearing out from the inside

14.10 Using a socket to drive the bearing in

14.12a Press the seal into place . . .

14.12b . . . and set it flush as shown

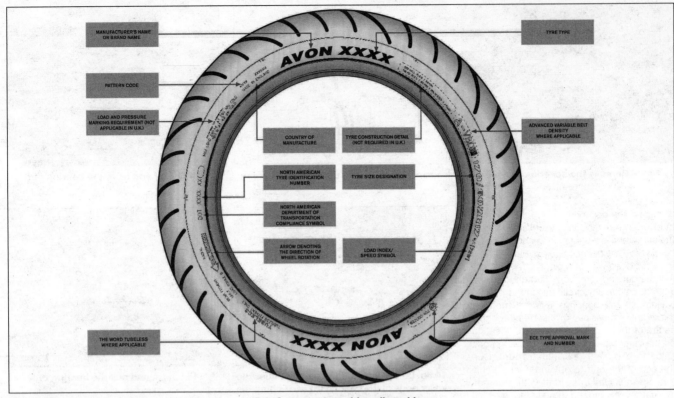

15.2 Common tyre sidewall markings

15 Tyres

General information

1 Refer to the *Pre-ride checks* listed at the beginning of this manual for tyre maintenance.

Fitting new tyres

2 When selecting new tyres, refer to the tyre information in the Owner's Handbook. Ensure that front and rear tyre types are compatible, the correct size and correct speed rating; if necessary seek advice from a dealer or tyre fitting specialist **(see illustration)**.

3 It is recommended that tyres are fitted by a motorcycle tyre specialist rather than attempted in the home workshop. The specialist will be able to balance the wheels after tyre fitting.

16 Drive chain

Cleaning

1 Refer to Chapter 1, Section 1, for details of routine cleaning with the chain installed on the sprockets.

2 If the chain is extremely dirty remove it from the motorcycle and soak it in paraffin (kerosene) for approximately five or six minutes, then clean it using a soft brush. Where an O-ring chain is fitted, care should be taken not to use solvents which might damage the sealing properties of the chain.

Removal and installation

3 Remove the chainguard **(see illustrations)**.
4 Remove the front sprocket cover (see Section 17).
5 Fully slacken the drive chain as described in Chapter 1.

16.3a Chainguard screws (arrowed) on a standard model

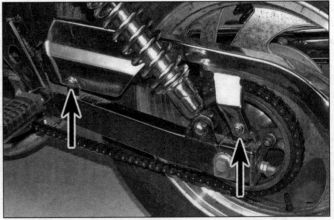

16.3b Chainguard screws (arrowed) on a Custom model

16.6 This is the joining link on an O-ring chain

16.8a Release the open end of the clip from around the pin . . .

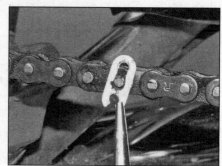

16.8b . . . then remove it

6 Before removing the chain identify the type fitted. Most models are fitted with a standard chain that has a clip-type master (split) link, which is identifiable by the open ended clip securing one of the outer side plates **(see illustration 16.8a)**. However on some models it is possible that an O-ring chain is fitted – this has a staked (soft) master link, which is identifiable by the master joining link side plate's identification marks (and usually its different colour), as well as by the staked ends of the link's two pins which look as if they have been deeply centre-punched, instead of peened over as with all the other pins **(see illustration)**.

Standard chain

7 Support the motorcycle so that the rear wheel is off the ground. Tie the front brake on. Identify the joining link and rotate the wheel so it is in a suitable position to work on.
8 Release and remove the clip from the master link **(see illustrations)**. Remove the side plate **(see illustrations)**. Withdraw the master link from the inside **(see illustrations)**. Remove the chain from the bike, noting its routing around the swingarm.
9 Route the new chain around the sprockets and swingarm, leaving the ends in the middle of the lower run **(see illustration)**. Fit the master link through each end of the chain **(see illustrations 16.8f and e)**. Fit the side plate, then slide the clip across the groove in each master link pin, making sure the open end of the clip points to the front of the bike so the

closed end points to the direction of chain rotation **(see illustrations 16.8d, c, b and a)**. Make sure the clip has located in the grooves and around then end of each pin.

O-ring chain

 Warning: Use ONLY the correct service tools to secure the staked-type of master link – if you do not have access to such tools, have the chain replaced by a dealer service department or bike repair shop to be sure of having it securely installed.

10 Support the motorcycle so that the rear wheel is off the ground. Tie the front brake lever to the handlebar. Identify the joining link and rotate the wheel so it is in a suitable position to work on.
11 Split the chain at the joining link using the chain cutter, following carefully the manufacturer's operating instructions (see

also Section 8 in *Tools and Workshop Tips* in the Reference Section). Remove the chain from the bike, noting its routing around the swingarm.
12 Fit the drive chain around the swingarm and sprockets, leaving the two ends mid-way between the sprockets along the bottom run.
13 Refer to Section 8 in *Tools and Workshop Tips* in the Reference Section. Install the new joining link from the inside with the four O-rings correctly located between the link plate and side plates. Install the new side plate with its identification marks facing out. Stake the new link using the drive chain cutting/staking tool, following carefully the instructions of both the chain manufacturer and the tool manufacturer. DO NOT reuse old joining link components.
14 After staking, check the joining link and staking for any signs of cracking. If there is any evidence of cracking, the joining link, O-rings

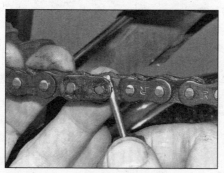

16.8c Lever the side plate off . . .

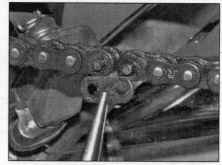

16.8d . . . then remove it

16.8e Separate the chain . . .

16.8f . . . and draw the master link out

16.9 Feeding the chain around the front sprocket

16.17 Make sure the chainguard is correctly located and chain correctly routed

17.1 Unscrew the pinch bolt and slide the lever or arm off the shaft

17.2a Sprocket cover bolts (arrowed) – OHV single

and side plate must be replaced. Make sure the ends are evenly staked. Check that the link pivots freely.

All types

15 Adjust and lubricate the chain following the procedures described in Chapter 1.
16 Install the sprocket cover (see Section 17).
17 Install the chainguard **(see illustration)**.

17 Sprockets

Front sprocket cover

1 If the gearchange shaft passes through the sprocket cover, the lever must be removed. Make a mark where the slot in the gearchange lever or linkage arm aligns with the shaft.

Unscrew the pinch bolt and slide the lever or arm off the shaft **(see illustration)**.
2 Unscrew the front sprocket cover bolts and remove the cover **(see illustrations)**.
3 Check the wear pattern on both sprockets (see Chapter 1, Section 1). If the sprocket teeth are worn excessively, replace the chain and both sprockets as a set – worn sprockets can ruin a new drive chain and vice versa. Whenever the sprockets are inspected, the drive chain should be inspected also (see Chapter 1).
4 Adjust and lubricate the chain following the procedures described in Chapter 1.

Sprocket removal and installation

Front sprocket

5 Remove the front sprocket cover (see Steps 1 and 2). Tie the front brake on using a cable-tie or suitable alternative.

6 As appropriate, unscrew the sprocket retainer plate bolts **(see illustration)**. Turn the sprocket retainer plate to unlock it from the splines then slide it off the shaft **(see illustration)**.
7 Alternatively, bend back the tabs on the sprocket nut lockwasher **(see illustration)**. Hold the rear brake on hard and unscrew the sprocket nut **(see illustration)**. Remove the washer – if it is weakened renew it.
8 If the drive chain is being removed as well do so now (see Section 16). If not, fully slacken the chain as described in Chapter 1. If the rear sprocket is being removed as well, remove the rear wheel now to create full slack (see Section 13). Otherwise disengage the chain from the rear sprocket if required to provide more slack.
9 Slide the sprocket off the input shaft, then if not removed slip the sprocket out of the chain **(see illustrations)**.

17.2b Sprocket cover bolts (arrowed) – Twin cylinder

17.6a Unscrew the bolts (arrowed) . . .

17.6b . . . and remove the retainer plate as described

17.7a Bend the tab back . . .

17.7b . . . then unscrew the nut and remove the washer

17.9 Draw the sprocket off the shaft and disengage the chain

17.10 Fit the sprocket into the chain and onto the shaft

17.11 Locate and lock the retainer plate then fit the bolts

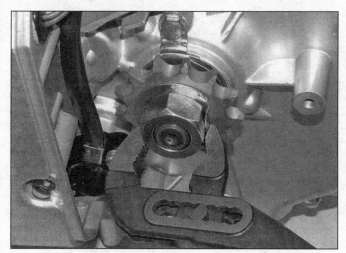

17.15 Bend the rim of the washer up against the nut

17.19 Bend back the tabs (arrowed), then unscrew the nuts or bolts

10 Engage the new sprocket with the chain if in situ, making sure the marked side of the sprocket is facing out, and slide it on the shaft **(see illustration)**.

11 On OHV single and Twin cylinder engines fit the retainer plate, then turn it in the groove so it is locked in the splines **(see illustration)**. Fit the bolts and tighten them finger-tight.

12 On SOHC single cylinder engines slide the (new) lockwasher on, then fit the nut and tighten it finger-tight **(see illustration 17.7b)**.

13 If the rear wheel was removed, change the sprocket now and install the wheel (see Section 13). If the chain was merely disengaged, fit it back onto the rear sprocket. Take up the slack in the chain. If the chain was removed fit it now (see Section 16).

14 Hold the rear brake on hard and tighten the bolts or nut.

15 On SOHC engines bend the rim of the lockwasher up against the nut **(see illustration)**.

16 Fit the sprocket cover (see Steps 2

and 1). Adjust and lubricate the chain (see Chapter 1).

Rear sprocket

17 Remove the rear wheel (see Section 13).

18 On drum brake models lift the brake plate out of the drum but leave the sprocket coupling in the hub **(see illustration 9.1)**.

19 Lay the wheel on blocks with the sprocket facing up. Where fitted bend the retainer plate tabs off the nuts or bolts **(see illustration)** and unscrew them. Remove the retainer plates (where fitted) and lift off the sprocket.

20 Check the condition of the sprocket nuts/bolts and replace them with new ones if any are damaged.

21 Fit the sprocket onto the hub with the stamped mark facing out. Fit the retainer plates (where fitted). Fit the nuts or bolts and tighten them evenly and in a criss-cross sequence. Bend up the retainer plate tabs against the nut/bolt flats **(see illustration 17.19)**.

22 Install the rear wheel (see Section 13).

18 Rear sprocket coupling/rubber dampers

Note: *Not all models are fitted with a sprocket coupling and rubber damping (or cush-drive) arrangement. Instead the sprocket is fitted directly to the hub of the rear wheel.*

1 Remove the rear wheel (see Section 13). Grasp the sprocket and feel for play between the sprocket coupling and the wheel hub by attempting to twist the sprocket in each direction. Any play indicates worn rubber damper segments.

Caution: Do not lay the wheel down on the disc as it could become warped. Lay the wheel on wooden blocks so that the disc is off the ground.

2 Lift the sprocket coupling out of the hub leaving the rubber dampers in position

18.2a Lift the sprocket coupling off the wheel

18.2b Remove the spacer from inside the coupling

18.3 Check the rubber dampers as described

18.4 Fit a new O-ring if necessary

(see illustration). Note any spacer inside the coupling and remove it if it is likely to drop out **(see illustration)**. Check the coupling for cracks or any obvious signs of damage.

3 Lift the rubber damper segments from the wheel and check them for cracks, hardening and general deterioration **(see illustration)**. Renew them as a set if necessary.

4 Where fitted check the condition of the hub O-ring – if it is damaged, deformed or deteriorated replace it with a new one and smear it with oil **(see illustration)**. Otherwise clean it and smear it with oil.

5 Checking and replacement procedures for the sprocket coupling bearing are in Section 14.

6 Installation is the reverse of removal. Make sure the spacer is still correctly installed in the coupling, or install it if it was removed **(see illustration 18.2b)**.

7 Install the rear wheel (see Section 13).

Chapter 8
Bodywork

Contents

Degrees of difficulty

Easy, suitable for novice with little experience	**Fairly easy,** suitable for beginner with some experience	**Fairly difficult,** suitable for competent DIY mechanic	**Difficult,** suitable for experienced DIY mechanic	**Very difficult,** suitable for expert DIY or professional

Specifications

General torque settings according to thread size

5 mm bolt/nut	5 Nm
6 mm bolt/nut	10 Nm
8 mm bolt/nut	24 Nm
10 mm bolt/nut	35 Nm
12 mm bolt/nut	55 Nm

1 General information

This Chapter covers the procedures necessary to remove and install bodywork. It is general in its approach as it has not been possible to cover specific model fitments – if you have an owner's handbook that covers removal of bodywork refer to it for specific details for your model.

In the case of damage to the bodywork, it is usually necessary to remove the broken component and replace it with a new (or used) one. The material that the body

panels are composed of doesn't lend itself to conventional repair techniques. Note that there are however some companies that specialize in 'plastic welding' and there are a number of DIY bodywork repair kits now available for motorcycles.

When attempting to remove any body panel, first study it closely, noting any fasteners and associated fittings (washers, collars, grommets etc), to be sure of returning everything to its correct place on installation. Once the evident fasteners have been removed, try to withdraw the panel as described but DO NOT FORCE IT – if it will not release, check that all fasteners have been removed and try again.

When installing a body panel, first study it closely, noting any fasteners and associated fittings removed with it, to be sure of returning everything to its correct place. Check that all fasteners are in good condition, including the rubber mounts; replace any faulty fasteners with new ones before the panel is reassembled. Check also that all mounting brackets are straight and repair them or replace them with new ones if necessary before attempting to install the panel.

Tighten the fasteners securely, but be careful not to overtighten any of them or the panel may break (not always immediately) due to the uneven stress.

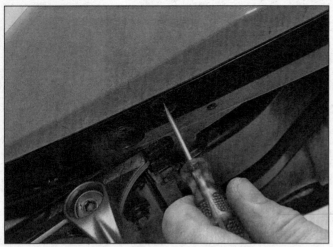

1.2a Push the centre into the body . . .

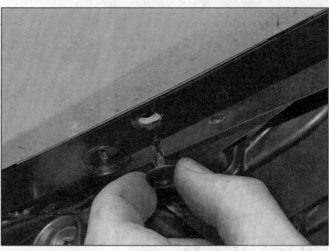

1.2b . . . then draw the body out

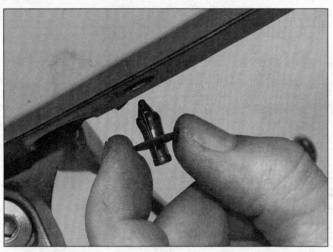

1.2c Reset the clip by drawing the centre out, then fit the body into the hole . . .

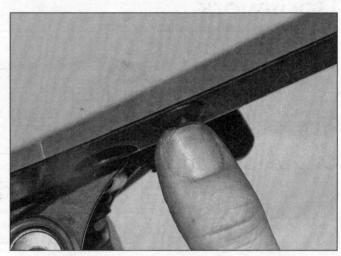

1.2d . . . and push the centre in flush to secure it

Trim clips

1 Three types of plastic trim clip are commonly used, so carefully note which type it may be before attempting to remove it.

2 The most commonly used type has a centre pin which you push into the body of the clip to allow the clip to be drawn out of the panel **(see illustrations)**. To install the clip, first expand the pawls of the clip body and push the centre pin back out **(see illustration)**. Now fit the clip body into its hole, then push the centre pin in so that it is flush with the clip head **(see illustration)**. The clip should now be locked in place.

3 Another type has a Phillips screw head. To release it unscrew the centre of the clip, then pull the body of the clip out of the panel **(see illustration)**. When installing them, unscrew the centre of the clip and insert it in the panel then push the centre fully into the body **(see illustration)**. As they are made of plastic, the threads easily become worn in which case the centres may not unscrew. If this happens, lever the centre out of the body using a small screwdriver and replace the trim clip with a new one.

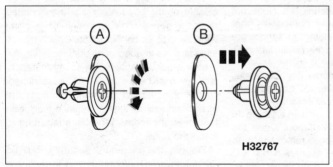

H32767

1.3a Unscrew the centre of the clip (A) then pull the clip body out (B)

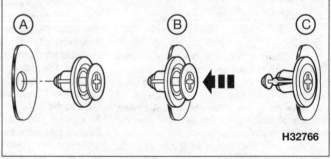

H32766

1.3b Fit the clip body into its hole (A), then push the centre into the body (B) so that its head is flush (C)

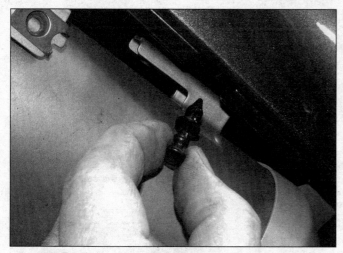

1.4 Removing a trim clip with a protruding centre pin

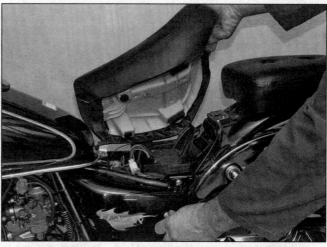

2.1 Unlock the seat using the ignition key then lift it off

4 Another has a protruding centre pin which you pull out of the body of the clip to allow the clip to be drawn out of the panel **(see illustration)**. To install the clip, fit the clip body into its hole, then push the centre pin in. The clip should now be locked in place.

2 Seat and seat cowling

Seat

1 If a seat lock is fitted, use the ignition key to unlock the seat, then lift it away noting how any tabs locate **(see illustration)**.

2 If there is no lock, unscrew the bolts securing the seat, then lift the seat away, noting how any tabs locate **(see illustrations)**. On dual seat models you may need to remove one seat before you can remove the other **(see illustration)**.

3 Installation is the reverse of removal. Make sure any tabs or hooks locate correctly.

Seat cowling

4 Remove the seat(s).

5 Where fitted and if necessary remove the luggage rack or passenger grab rail (see Section 8).

6 Check around the cowling to see what secures it, and whether you can remove the complete cowling in one piece or whether you have to remove each side individually. When

removing each side individually there will be tabs at the joint between each side or between the side and the centre trim section at the rear. These tabs are easily broken so take care.

7 Release any trim clips (see Section 1) and/ or undo any screws or bolts that secure the cowling **(see illustration)**. Carefully pull the cowling away where any pegs locate in grommets, and remove the cowling – if the

2.2a On this seat unscrew the bolt (arrowed) on each side . . .

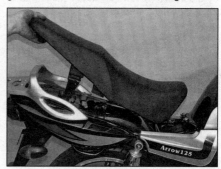

2.2b . . . then remove the seat, noting how it locates

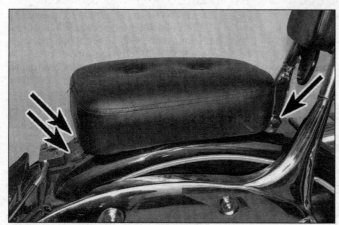

2.2c This passenger seat on a Custom model is secured by three bolts – the front two are obscured by the rider's seat which must be removed first

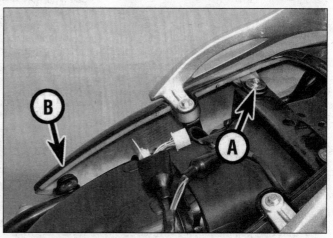

2.7 On this model first remove the luggage rack, then unscrew the bolt (A) and free the peg (B) on each side

3.2 Remove the side cover screw

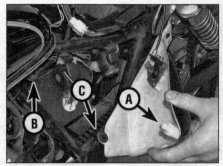

3.3a Pull the cover to free the peg (A) from the grommet (B), then lift it to free the grommet (C) from its peg . . .

3.3b . . . then free the seat lock cable

tail light is fitted in it disconnect the wiring connector(s).

8 Installation is the reverse of removal. Make sure any tabs locate correctly. Make sure the grommets are in good condition.

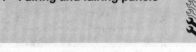

3 Side covers

1 It is usually necessary to remove the seat before removing a side cover (see Section 2).
2 Check to see whether the cover is secured by a screw or screws, in which case undo it/ them **(see illustration)**.
3 Feel around the cover to get an idea of where any locating pegs are, then carefully manoeuvre the cover as required to free them **(see illustrations)**.
4 Installation is the reverse of removal. Make sure the grommets are in good condition.

4 Fairing and fairing panels

Fairing side panels and lower fairings

1 Before removing a fairing panel first check around to see what secures it, and then whether you can remove it without first having to remove some other panel, for example

on some sports models, if they are separate you may have to remove a lower fairing panel before removing a fairing side panel, or there may be a cockpit trim panel covering one of the fairing panel screws. Where panels join together there may well be tabs at the joint – these tabs are easily broken so take care. Also check whether the turn signal is part of the panel, and whether you can access and disconnect its wiring connectors before removing the panel or whether you can only do it after displacing the panel.
2 Release any trim clips securing the panel to any other panel (see Section 1).
3 If necessary and if accessible disconnect the turn signal wiring connector(s).
4 Undo any screws securing the panel.
5 Carefully manoeuvre the panel as required to free any pegs from their grommets and tabs or slots from the slots or tabs of adjoining panels **(see illustration)**. If necessary and not already done disconnect the turn signal wiring connector(s). Remove the panel.
6 Installation is the reverse of removal.

Fairing

7 Before removing a fairing first check around to see what secures it, and then whether you can remove it without first having to remove some other panel, for example on some sports models you may have to remove the fairing side panels first, or there may be a cockpit trim panel covering one of the fairing screws. There will probably be tabs at the joint with any fairing side panel or cockpit trim panel – these

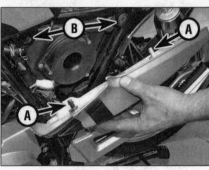

3.3c On this cover pull it away to free the pegs (A) from the grommets (B)

tabs are easily broken so take care. Also check whether the headlight is mounted to the fairing, and if so whether it is easier to disconnect its wiring connectors and bring the headlight with the fairing, or whether if the headlight is also mounted to the fairing stay you separate them and leave the headlight behind.
8 Release any trim clips securing the fairing to any other panel.
9 If necessary remove the windshield.
10 If necessary and if accessible disconnect the headlight wiring connector(s).
11 If the mirrors are mounted on the fairing remove them (see Section 5).
12 Undo any screws or bolts securing the fairing **(see illustration)**.
13 Carefully pull the fairing forwards to free any pegs from their grommets **(see illustration)**. If necessary and not already done

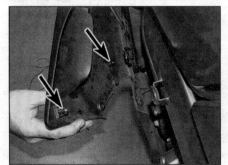

4.5 Carefully pull the panel away to free any pegs (arrowed) from their grommets

4.12 On this model with a simple cockpit fairing unscrew the bolt (arrowed) on each side and the screw on the underside . . .

4.13 . . . then draw the fairing forwards off the headlight

5.1a On handlebar-mounted mirrors, lift the rubber boot to access the hex . . .

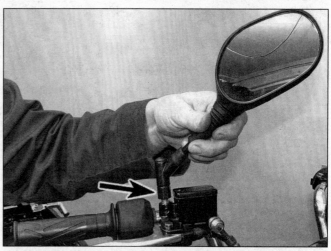

5.1b . . . or the base hex (arrowed) may be exposed

5.2a Fairing-mounted mirror bolts (arrowed) are accessed from the top . . .

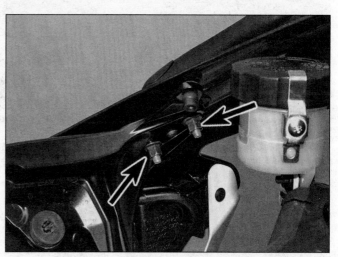

5.2b . . . and nuts from the underside

disconnect the headlight wiring connector(s). Remove the fairing.

14 Installation is the reverse of removal.

5 Mirrors

1 To remove handlebar mounted mirrors, lift any rubber boot or shroud covering the base of the mirror. Unscrew the mirror using the hex at the base of the stem **(see illustrations)**. Note that mirrors sometimes have a left-hand thread, meaning you have to turn it clockwise to unscrew it, and anti-clockwise to thread it in – if the mirror won't unscrew in the normal anti-clockwise direction, before doing any damage try unscrewing it clockwise.

2 To remove fairing mounted mirrors, check whether the mirror is secured from the top or the underside **(see illustrations)** – if its secured from the top lift any rubber boot or shroud

covering the base of the mirror. If the mirror has not nuts or bolts but is similar to a handlebar mounted mirror (see Step 1). Otherwise unscrew the nuts or bolts and remove the mirror, noting any rubber seat fitted with it.

3 Installation is the reverse of removal. Make sure handlebar mounted mirrors are tight

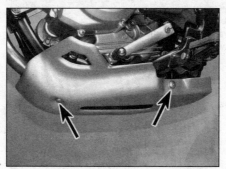

6.1 This sump guard is secured by a bolt at the front and one on each side at the back

enough to stop them from unscrewing it when moving.

4 Most handlebar mirrors have adjustable stems. On the mirror shown in illustration 5.1a, counter-hold the base hex and slacken the nut above it, reposition the mirror as required, then tighten the nut. On the mirror shown in illustration 5.1b remove the rubber cap from the top of the mounting stem, counter-hold the base hex and slacken the bolt inside the stem, reposition the mirror as required, then tighten the bolt.

6 Belly pan and sump guard

1 Identify what secures the belly pan or sump guard. Support the pan or guard while undoing the screws or bolts, then lower the pan or guard and remove it **(see illustration)**.

2 Installation is the reverse of removal.

7.2 Free the brake hose from its guide if necessary

7.3a Mudguard bolts (arrowed) accessed from the outside

7.3b Mudguard bolts (arrowed) on the inside which also secure the brake hose guide . . .

7 Front mudguard

1 If necessary, either for access to the mudguard bolts, or because the mudguard is shaped around the forks and so will not pass between them but must be lowered and removed from the bottom, remove the front wheel (see Chapter 7).
2 If necessary free the brake hose from its guide, or displace the guide from the mudguard **(see illustration)**.
3 Unscrew the nuts or bolts securing the mudguard and draw it forwards or down as required **(see illustrations)**. Note any hose

7.3c . . . and a fork brace

guide bracket or brace fitted inside the guard **(see illustration)**.
4 Installation is the reverse of removal.

8 Luggage rack, grab rail and protection bars

Luggage racks and grab rail

1 Remove the seat.
2 Unscrew the bolts and remove the rack/rails **(see illustration)**.
3 Installation is the reverse of removal.

Protection bars

4 Unscrew the nuts and bolts and manoeuvre the bars out **(see illustration)**.
5 Installation is the reverse of removal.

8.2 On this model the luggage rack incorporates a grab rail, and is secured by four bolts (arrowed)

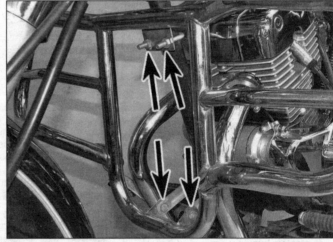

8.4 Typical engine protection bar mounting hardware (arrowed)

Chapter 9
Electrical system

Contents

Degrees of difficulty

Easy, suitable for novice with little experience	**Fairly easy,** suitable for beginner with some experience	**Fairly difficult,** suitable for competent DIY mechanic	**Difficult,** suitable for experienced DIY mechanic	**Very difficult,** suitable for expert DIY or professional

Specifications

General torque settings according to thread size

5 mm bolt/nut	5 Nm
6 mm bolt/nut	10 Nm
8 mm bolt/nut	24 Nm
10 mm bolt/nut	35 Nm
12 mm bolt/nut	55 Nm

1 General information

All models have a 12 volt electrical system charged by an alternator with separate regulator/rectifier.

The regulator maintains the charging system output within the specified range to prevent overcharging, and the rectifier converts the ac (alternating current) output of the alternator to dc (direct current) to power the lights and other components and to charge the battery. The alternator rotor is mounted on the left-hand end of the crankshaft.

The starter motor is mounted on the back of the crankcase on OHV single cylinder engines, and on the front on OHC single and Twin cylinder engines. The starting system includes the motor, the battery, the relay and the various wires and switches. Some of the switches are part of a starter safety circuit – see Chapter 1 for further information and checks on the system.

Note: *Keep in mind that electrical parts, once purchased, often cannot be returned. To avoid unnecessary expense, make very sure the faulty component has been positively identified before buying a replacement part.*

2 Electrical system fault finding

1 A typical electrical circuit consists of an electrical component, the switches, relays, etc, related to that component and the wiring and connectors that link the component to the battery and the frame.

2 Before tackling any troublesome electrical circuit consider whether other components related to that circuit are operating properly or not. If several components or circuits fail at one time, chances are the fault lies either in the fuse or in the common earth (ground) connection, as several circuits are often routed through the same fuse and earth (ground) connections.

3 Electrical problems often stem from simple causes, such as loose or corroded connections or a blown fuse. Prior to any electrical fault finding, always visually check the condition of the fuse, wires and connections in the problem circuit. Intermittent failures can be especially frustrating, since you can't always duplicate the failure when it's convenient to test. In such situations, a good practice is to clean all connections in the affected circuit, whether or not they appear to be good – where possible use a dedicated electrical cleaning spray along with sandpaper, wire wool or other abrasive material to remove corrosion, and a dedicated electrical protection spray to prevent further problems. All of the connections and wires should also be wiggled to check for looseness which can cause intermittent failure.

2.4a A digital multimeter can be used for all electrical tests

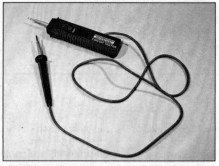

2.4b A battery-powered continuity tester

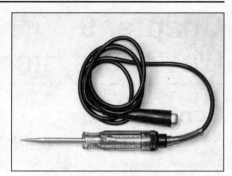

2.4c A simple test light is useful for voltage tests

4 If you don't have a multimeter it is highly advisable to obtain one – they are not expensive and will enable a full range of electrical tests to be made **(see illustration)**. Go for a modern digital one with LCD display as they are easier to use. A continuity tester and/or test light are useful for certain electrical checks as an alternative, though are limited in their usefulness compared to a multimeter **(see illustrations)**.

Continuity checks

5 The term continuity describes the uninterrupted flow of electricity through an electrical circuit. Continuity can be checked with a multimeter set either to its continuity function (a beep is emitted when continuity is found), or to the resistance (ohms / Ω) function, or with a dedicated continuity tester. Both instruments are powered by an internal battery, therefore the checks are made with the ignition OFF. As a safety precaution, always disconnect the battery negative (-) lead before making continuity checks, particularly if ignition switch checks are being made.

6 If using a multimeter, select the continuity function if it has one, or the resistance (ohms) function. Touch the meter probes together and check that a beep is emitted or the meter reads zero, which indicates continuity. If there

is no continuity there will be no beep or the meter will show infinite resistance. After using the meter, always switch it OFF to conserve its battery.

7 A continuity tester can be used in the same way – its light should come on or it should beep to indicate continuity in the switch ON position, but should be off or silent in the OFF position.

8 Note that the polarity of the test probes doesn't matter for continuity checks, although care should be taken to follow specific test procedures if a diode or solid-state component is being checked.

Switch continuity checks

9 If a switch is at fault, trace its wiring to the wiring connectors. Separate the connectors and inspect them for security and condition. A build-up of dirt or corrosion here will most likely be the cause of the problem – clean up and apply a water dispersant such as WD40, or alternatively use a dedicated contact cleaner and protection spray.

10 If using a multimeter, select the continuity function if it has one, or the resistance (ohms) function, and connect its probes to the terminals in the connector **(see illustration)**. Simple ON/OFF type switches, such as brake light switches, only have two wires whereas combination switches, like the handlebar switches, have many wires. Study the wiring diagram to ensure that you are connecting to the correct pair of wires. Continuity should be indicated with the switch ON and no continuity with it OFF.

Wiring continuity checks

11 Many electrical faults are caused by damaged wiring, often due to incorrect routing or chaffing on frame components. Loose, wet or corroded wire connectors can also be the cause of electrical problems.

12 A continuity check can be made on a single length of wire by disconnecting it at each end and connecting the meter or continuity tester probes to each end of the wire **(see illustration)**. Continuity (low or no resistance – 0 ohms) should be indicated if the wire is good. If no continuity (high resistance) is shown, suspect a broken wire.

13 To check for continuity to earth in any earth wire connect one probe of your meter or tester to the earth wire terminal in the connector and the other to the frame, engine, or battery earth (-) terminal. Continuity (low or no resistance – 0 ohms) should be indicated if the wire is good. If no continuity (high resistance) is shown, suspect a broken wire or corroded or loose earth point (see below).

Voltage checks

14 A voltage check can determine whether power is reaching a component. Use a multimeter set to the dc voltage scale, or a test light. The test light is the cheaper component, but the meter has the advantage of being able to give a voltage reading.

15 Connect the meter or test light in parallel, i.e. across the load **(see illustration)**.

16 First identify the relevant wiring circuit by referring to the wiring diagram at the end of

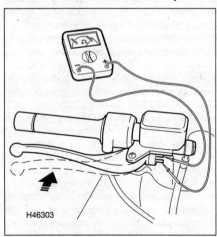

2.10 Continuity should be indicated across switch terminals when lever is operated

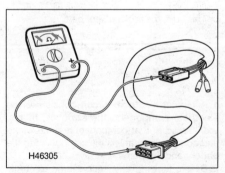

2.12 Wiring continuity check. Connect the meter probes across each end of the same wire

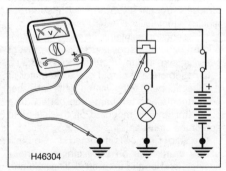

2.15 Voltage check. Connect the meter positive probe to the component and the negative probe to earth

this manual. If other electrical components share the same power supply (i.e. are fed from the same fuse), take note whether they are working correctly – this is useful information in deciding where to start checking the circuit.

17 If using a meter, check first that the meter leads are plugged into the correct terminals on the meter (red to positive (+), black to negative (-). Set the meter to the dc volts function, where necessary at a range suitable for the battery voltage – 0 to 20 vdc. Connect the meter red probe (+) to the power supply wire and the black probe to a good metal earth (ground) on the motorcycle's frame or directly to the battery negative terminal. Battery voltage should be shown on the meter with the ignition switch, and if necessary any other relevant switch, ON.

18 If using a test light, connect its positive (+) probe to the power supply terminal and its negative (-) probe to a good earth (ground) on the motorcycle's frame. With the switch, and if necessary any other relevant switch, ON, the test light should illuminate.

19 If no voltage is indicated, work back towards the fuse continuing to check for voltage. When you reach a point where there is voltage, you know the problem lies between that point and your last check point.

Earth (ground) checks

20 Earth connections are made either directly to the engine or frame (such as neutral switch, oil pressure switch etc. that only have a positive feed) or by a separate wire into the earth circuit of the wiring harness. Alternatively a short earth wire is sometimes run from the component directly to the motorcycle's frame.

21 Corrosion is a common cause of a poor earth connection, as is a loose earth terminal fastener.

22 If total or multiple component failure is experienced, check the security of the main earth lead from the negative (-) terminal of the battery, the earth lead bolted to the engine, and the main earth point(s) on the frame **(see illustration)**. If corroded, dismantle the connection and clean all surfaces back to bare metal. Remake the connection and prevent further corrosion from forming by smearing battery terminal grease over the connection.

2.22 Check common earth points on the engine and frame

23 To check the earth of a component, use an insulated jumper wire to temporarily bypass its earth connection **(see illustration)** – connect one end of the jumper wire to the earth terminal or metal body of the component and the other end to the motorcycle's frame. If the circuit works with the jumper wire installed, the earth circuit is faulty.

24 To check an earth wire first check for corroded or loose connections, then check the wiring for continuity (Step 13) between each connector in the circuit in turn, and then to its earth point, to locate the break.

3 Battery removal, installation and inspection

Caution: Be extremely careful when handling or working around the battery. The electrolyte is very caustic and an explosive gas (hydrogen) is given off when the battery is charging.

Removal and installation

1 Make sure the ignition is switched OFF. If available refer to your owner's handbook for the location of the battery. Remove the seat and/or side cover as required according to model for access (see Chapter 8).

2 Unscrew the negative (–) terminal bolt first and disconnect the lead from the battery **(see illustration)**. Lift up the insulating cover to access the positive (+) terminal, then unscrew the bolt and disconnect the lead.

3 Disconnect the vent hose **(see illustration)**.

2.23 A selection of insulated jumper wires

Where fitted release the battery strap or bracket.

4 Lift or draw the battery out, noting that it is quite heavy **(see illustration)**.

5 On installation, clean the battery terminals and lead ends with a wire brush, fine sandpaper or steel wool. Reconnect the leads, connecting the positive (+) terminal first.

> **HAYNES HiNT**
>
> *Battery corrosion can be kept to a minimum by applying a layer of battery terminal grease or petroleum jelly (Vaseline) to the terminals after the leads have been connected. DO NOT use a mineral based grease.*

6 Install the side cover or seat (see Chapter 8).

Inspection and maintenance

Note: *A standard type battery is fitted to most models, but a maintenance free (MF) battery may be fitted to some. The batteries are easy to distinguish – standard ones have removable caps across the top and electrolyte level lines (marked UPPER and LOWER or MAX and MIN), while MF batteries do not, and are usually marked MF on the front. Identify the type of battery fitted on your bike before proceeding.*

Conventional battery

Note: *Refer to Chapter 1 for electrolyte level check and top up.*

7 Check the battery terminals and leads

3.2 Disconnect the negative lead first, then disconnect the positive lead

3.3 Disconnect the vent hose from its union on a conventional battery

3.4 Remove the battery

3.11 Checking terminal voltage on a conventional battery

are tight and free of corrosion. If corrosion is evident, clean the terminals as described in Step 5, then protect them from further corrosion (see *Haynes Hint*).

8 Keep the battery case clean to prevent current leakage, which can discharge the battery over a period of time (especially when it sits unused). Wash the outside of the case with a solution of baking soda and water. Rinse the battery thoroughly, then dry it.

9 Look for cracks in the case and replace the battery with a new one if any are found. If acid has been spilled on the frame or battery box, neutralise it with a baking soda and water solution, dry it thoroughly, then touch up any damaged paint.

10 If the motorcycle sits unused for long periods of time, disconnect the cables from the battery terminals, negative (–) terminal first. Refer to Section 4 and charge the battery once every month to six weeks.

11 Measure the battery's terminal voltage with a multimeter set to the 0-20vdc scale. Connect the voltmeter positive (+) probe to the battery positive (+) terminal, and the negative (–) probe to the battery negative (–) terminal **(see illustration)**. When fully-charged there should be 12.8 to 13.2 volts present. If the voltage falls much below this remove the battery (see above), and recharge it as described below in Section 4.

12 The condition of the battery can be assessed by measuring the specific gravity of the electrolyte. To do this an hydrometer is needed. Remove the cell caps from the

4.1 Battery connected to a charger

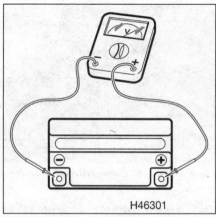

H46301

3.17 Checking terminal voltage on an MF battery

battery. Insert the hydrometer nozzle into each cell in turn and squeeze the hydrometer pump to draw some electrolyte from the cell. Check the reading on the float at the level of the electrolyte – it should be between 1.26 and 1.28. Charge the battery if the specific gravity is low.

Maintenance free battery

13 Check the battery terminals and leads are tight and free of corrosion. If corrosion is evident, clean the terminals as described in Step 5, then protect them from further corrosion (see *Haynes Hint*).

14 Keep the battery case clean to prevent current leakage, which can discharge the battery over a period of time (especially when it sits unused). Wash the outside of the case with a solution of baking soda and water. Rinse the battery thoroughly, then dry it.

15 Look for cracks in the case and replace the battery with a new one if any are found. The MF battery is sealed so its gel or electrolyte should never leak out.

16 If the motorcycle sits unused for long periods of time, disconnect the cables from the battery terminals, negative (–) terminal

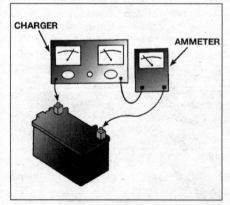

4.2 If the charger doesn't have an ammeter built in, connect one in series as shown. DO NOT connect the ammeter between the battery terminals or it will be ruined

first. Refer to Section 4 and charge the battery once every month to six weeks.

17 Check the condition of the battery by measuring the voltage present at the battery terminals. Connect the voltmeter positive (+) probe to the battery positive (+) terminal, and the negative (–) probe to the battery negative (–) terminal **(see illustration)**. When fully-charged there should be 12.8 to 13.2 volts present. If the voltage falls much below this remove the battery (see above), and recharge it as described below in Section 4.

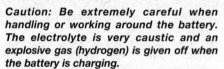

4 Battery charging

Caution: Be extremely careful when handling or working around the battery. The electrolyte is very caustic and an explosive gas (hydrogen) is given off when the battery is charging.

1 Remove the battery (see Section 3). Connect the charger to the battery, making sure that the positive (+) lead on the charger is connected to the positive (+) terminal on the battery, and the negative (–) lead is connected to the negative (–) terminal **(see illustration)**.

2 A battery should be charged according to its capacity, the rate being one tenth of its amp hour value – for example a 10Ah battery should be charged at 1 amp, a 7Ah battery at 0.7 amp, a 5Ah battery at 0.5 amp. Exceeding this figure can cause the battery to overheat, buckling the plates and rendering it useless. The battery rating is marked on the battery, usually on the front or the top. The amount of charging time required depends on the initial voltage, but generally 5 to 10 hours are required for a low battery to be fully charged. Few owners will have access to an expensive current controlled charger, so if a normal domestic charger is used check that after a possible initial peak, the charge rate falls to a safe level **(see illustration)**. If the battery becomes hot during charging **stop**. Further charging will cause damage. Note that there are many bike-specific chargers **(see illustration 4.1)** available from good suppliers that are designed for the maintenance and recovery of motorcycle batteries, in particular catering for the requirements of heavily discharged MF batteries. They are not too expensive, and are a worthwhile investment, especially if the bike is not used over winter. Follow the manufacturer's instructions.

3 If the recharged battery discharges rapidly if left disconnected it is likely that an internal short caused by physical damage or sulphation has occurred. A new battery will be required. A sound item will tend to lose its charge at about 1% per day.

4 Install the battery (see Section 3).

5 If the motorcycle sits unused for long periods of time, charge the battery once every month to six weeks and leave it disconnected.

5.1 Fuse holder (arrowed) as fitted to most models

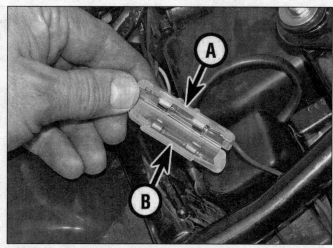

5.3 Unclip and open the holder to access the fuse (A) – this holder carries a spare (B) in the lid

5 Fuse

1 The electrical system on most models is protected by a single cartridge fuse, fitted in a holder and usually located close to the battery **(see illustration)**.

2 If available refer to your owner's handbook for the location of the fuse. Remove the seat and/or side cover as required according to model for access (see Chapter 8).

3 Unclip and open the fuse holder **(see illustration)**.

4 The fuse can checked visually in situ. A blown fuse is easily identified by a break in the element. The fuse is clearly marked with its rating and must only be replaced by a fuse of the correct rating.

5 You should be able to remove the fuse using your fingers, or use a small screwdriver to lever out one end if necessary – note that the glass on cartridge fuses breaks easily so do not lever it in the middle or try to grip it with pliers. Some models may carry a spare fuse – if the spare is used, always replace it with a new one so that a spare is carried on the bike at all times. If no spare is supplied it is wise to carry one with you.

> ⚠ **Warning: Never put in a fuse of a higher rating or bridge the terminals with any other substitute, however temporary it may be. Serious damage may be done to the circuit, or a fire may start.**

6 If the new fuse blows immediately check the wiring circuit very carefully for evidence of a short-circuit. Look for bare wires and chafed, melted or burned insulation.

7 Occasionally a fuse will blow or cause an open-circuit for no obvious reason. Corrosion of the fuse ends and fuse holder terminals may occur and cause poor fuse contact. If this happens, remove the corrosion with a wire brush or emery paper, then spray the fuse end and terminals with electrical contact cleaner.

6 Lighting system check

Note: *If available refer to your owner's handbook for a wiring diagram for your model.*

1 If a light fails first check the bulb (see relevant Section), the bulb terminals in the holder, and the wiring connector(s). If none of the lights work, check battery voltage – low voltage indicates either a faulty battery or a defective charging system. Refer to Section 3 for battery checks and Section 27 for charging system tests. If there is a problem with more than one circuit at the same time, or with all circuits, it is likely to be a fault relating to a multi-function component, such as the fuse or the ignition switch. When checking for a blown filament in a bulb, it is advisable to back up a visual check with a continuity test of the filament as it is not always apparent that a bulb has blown. When testing for continuity, remember that on single terminal bulbs it is the metal body of the bulb that is the earth (ground). Refer to Section 2 for details on testing electrical circuits.

Headlight

2 Most models have one twin filament bulb, one for high beam and one for low beam, although some sports models have two bulbs, either both twin filament, or both single filament with one bulb for the high beam and one for low – it will be obvious by operating the switches. Custom models are often fitted with auxiliary light units mounted on a bar under the main headlight – they are either connected to the sidelight circuit or headlight circuit.

3 If any beam fails to work, first check the bulb (see Section 7). If it is good, the problem lies in the wiring or connectors, the headlight switch where fitted, or the dimmer switch. Refer to Section 18 for the switch testing procedures, and also to the wiring diagrams at the end of this Chapter.

4 If a beam does not work, and the bulb is good, check for battery voltage on the loom side of the headlight wiring connector with the ignition ON, the light switch ON where fitted, and the dimmer switch set appropriately. If voltage is present, check for continuity to earth (ground) in the earth wire from the wiring connector. Repair or renew the wiring or connectors as necessary.

5 If there is no voltage check the headlight circuit wiring for continuity. Also make sure that all the terminals and connectors are clean and secure. Repair or renew the wiring or connectors as necessary.

Sidelight

6 If the sidelight fails to work, first check the bulb (Section 7). If it is good, disconnect the sidelight wiring connector(s), and check for battery voltage on the loom side of the connector with the ignition switch ON, and the light switch in the P or POS position. If voltage is present, check for continuity to earth (ground) in the earth wire from the wiring connector. If no voltage is indicated, check the wiring and connectors in the sidelight circuit.

Tail light

7 If the tail light fails to work, first check the bulb (Section 9). If it is good, remove the seat (see Chapter 8), disconnect the tail light wiring connector, and check for battery voltage on the loom side of the connector with the ignition switch ON, and the light switch ON. If voltage is present, check for continuity to earth (ground) in the earth wire from the wiring connector. If no voltage is indicated, check the wiring and connectors in the tail light circuit.

Brake light

8 If the brake light fails to work, first check the bulb (Section 9). If it is good remove the seat (see Chapter 8), disconnect the tail light wiring connector, and check for battery voltage on the loom side of the connector, first with the front brake lever pulled in, then

7.1a Undo the screw (arrowed) on each side . . .

7.1b . . . and release the beam unit

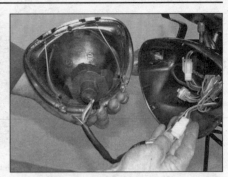

7.1c Disconnect the wiring connectors and remove the beam unit

with the rear brake pedal pressed down. If voltage is present with one brake on but not the other, then the switch or its wiring is faulty. If voltage is present in both cases, check for continuity to earth (ground) in the earth wire from the wiring connector. If no voltage is indicated, check the wiring and connectors between the brake light and the switches, then check the switches themselves. Refer to Section 14 for the switch testing procedures.

Turn signals

9 See Section 11.

Licence plate light

10 If the licence plate light fails to work, first check whether the tail light is working – they run off the same circuit. If it isn't refer to Step 7. If it is, check the bulb (Section 9). If the bulb and tail light are both good check the wire

between the connector on the tail light and that on the licence plate light for continuity.

---

7 Headlight bulb and sidelight bulb

Note: *When installing a new quartz-halogen bulb do not touch the glass as skin acids will shorten the bulb's service life. If the bulb is accidentally touched, it should be wiped carefully when cold with a rag soaked in methylated spirit and dried before fitting.*

HAYNES HiNT *Always use a paper towel or dry cloth when handling new bulbs to prevent injury if the bulb should break and to increase bulb life.*

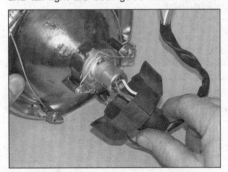

7.2a Remove the dust cover

7.2b Release the retaining clip . . .

Shell headlight

Headlight

1 Undo the screws securing the beam unit and draw it out of the shell (see illustrations). If required disconnect the headlight and sidelight wiring connectors and remove the beam unit to a bench (see illustration).
2 Pull the rubber cover off the bulb holder (see illustration). Either release the retaining clip and withdraw the bulb holder, or turn the bulb holder anti-clockwise to release its tabs then withdraw it (see illustrations).
3 Carefully push the bulb in and turn it anti-clockwise to release it from the holder, bearing in mind the information in the **Note** above (see illustration).
4 Fit the new bulb in reverse order.
5 When fitting the beam unit into the shell, locate the hook section(s) of the rim at the top behind the tab(s) in the shell (see illustration 7.1b).
6 Check the operation of the headlight.

Sidelight

7 Undo the screws securing the beam unit and draw it out of the shell (see illustrations 7.1a and b). If required disconnect the headlight and sidelight wiring connectors and remove the beam unit to a bench (see illustration 7.1c).
8 Carefully pull the bulb holder out of the beam unit, then pull the bulb out of the holder (see illustration).
9 Fit the new bulb in reverse order.
10 When fitting the beam unit into the shell,

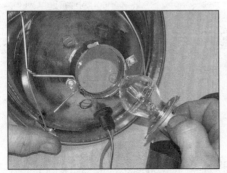

7.2c . . . withdraw the bulb holder . . .

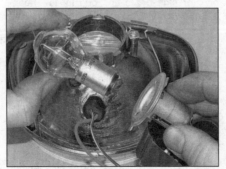

7.3 . . . and remove the bulb – 35/35W Tungsten bulb shown

7.8 Release the sidelight bulb holder and pull the bulb out

7.13 Disconnect the wiring connector

7.14a Remove the dust cover

7.14b Release the clip . . .

7.14c . . . and remove the bulb

7.18a Release the sidelight bulb holder . . .

7.18b . . . and pull the bulb out

locate the hook section(s) of the rim at the top behind the tab(s) in the shell **(see illustration 7.1b)**.

11 Check the operation of the sidelight.

Moulded headlight

Headlight

12 If required remove the fairing (see Chapter 8).

13 Disconnect the headlight wiring connector **(see illustration)**.

14 Pull the rubber cover off **(see illustration)**. Release the bulb retaining clip and withdraw the bulb, bearing in mind the information in the **Note** above **(see illustrations)**.

15 Fit the new bulb in reverse order.

16 Check the operation of the headlight.

Sidelight

17 If required remove the fairing (see Chapter 8).

18 Carefully pull the sidelight bulb holder out, then carefully pull the bulb out of the holder **(see illustrations)**.

19 Fit the new bulb, then fit the holder into the headlight.

20 Check the operation of the sidelight.

21 Install the fairing (see Chapter 8).

Auxiliary lights

22 Remove the nut and clamp screw from the base of the sidelight, then withdraw the rim and lens **(see illustrations)**.

23 Carefully push the bulb in and turn it anti-clockwise to release it from the holder set in the reflector unit **(see illustration)**.

24 Line up the pins on the new bulb with the

slots in the holder, then push the bulb in and turn it clockwise, making sure it locates correctly.

25 Ensure that the lens locates correctly in the rim and engage them on the sidelight shell. Insert the nut in the inner half of the rim clamp, then thread the screw into place and tighten it sufficiently to hold the assembly.

8   Headlight

Removal

Shell type headlight

1 Undo the screws securing the beam unit and draw it out of the shell **(see illustrations 7.1a and b)**. Disconnect the

7.22a Removing the auxiliary light rim clamp screw and nut . . .

7.22b . . . to free the rim and lens

7.23 Auxiliary light bulb is a bayonet fit

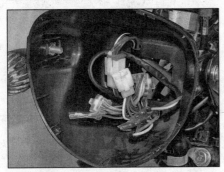

8.2a Disconnect, release and draw out all the wiring . . .

8.2b . . . then unscrew the bolt on each side

8.7 Slacken the bolt (arrowed) on each side before pivoting the headlight up or down

8.8a Adjuster screw (arrowed) on an off-road model

8.8b Adjuster screws (arrowed) on a sports model

usually ridden with a passenger on the back, have a second assistant to do this.

7 On some models adjustment is made by pivoting the headlight up or down in its brackets – this is typical of shell headlights, but check first for any other method of adjustment. If necessary slacken the headlight mounting bolts to ease adjustment **(see illustration)**.

8 On other models adjustment is made by turning the adjuster screw(s) **(see illustrations)**.

headlight and sidelight wiring connectors **(see illustration 7.1c)**.

2 If required release the wiring guides and disconnect all the wiring connectors, then feed the wiring out the back of the shell – note what routes where **(see illustration)**. Unscrew the nuts and withdraw the bolts securing the shell to the brackets and remove the shell **(see illustration)**. Note the collars in the grommets.

Models with fairing

3 Remove the fairing (see Chapter 8).
4 If the headlight is in the fairing undo the screws securing it. Otherwise disconnect the headlight wiring connector(s) then undo the screws securing it to its bracket and remove it.

Installation

5 Installation is the reverse of removal. Make sure all the wiring is correctly routed, connected and secured. Check the operation

of the headlight and sidelight. Check the headlight aim.

Headlight aim

Note: *An improperly adjusted headlight may cause problems for oncoming traffic or provide poor, unsafe illumination of the road ahead. Before adjusting the headlight aim, be sure to consult with local traffic laws and regulations – for UK models refer to MOT Test Checks in the Reference section.*

Note: *If available refer to your owner's handbook for specific adjustment details for your model.*

6 The headlight beam can adjusted vertically. Before making any adjustment, check that the tyre pressures are correct and the suspension is adjusted as required. Make any adjustments to the headlight aim with the machine on level ground, with the fuel tank half full and with an assistant sitting on the seat. If the bike is

9 Brake/tail light bulb

HAYNES HiNT *Always use a paper towel or dry cloth when handling new bulbs to prevent injury if the bulb should break and to increase bulb life.*

Brake/tail bulb

1 On models with a detachable lens undo the screws and remove the lens, noting any rubber seal **(see illustrations)**.
2 On models without a detachable len (i.e. no screws visible on the lens) remove the seat and if necessary any seat cowling as required to access the back of the tail light. Turn the bulb holder anti-clockwise to release it **(see illustration)**.
3 Carefully push the bulb in and turn it anti-

9.1a On this model undo the screw (arrowed) on each side . . .

9.1b . . . and remove the lens

9.2 Release the bulb holder from the tail light

9.3a Removing the bulb from the tail light

9.3b Removing the bulb from the holder

9.7a On this model undo the screw and detach the housing . . .

9.7b . . . then undo the screws (arrowed) . . .

9.7c . . . detach the bulb holder . . .

9.8 . . . and remove the bulb

clockwise to release it from the tail light or bulb holder **(see illustrations)**.

4 Line up the pins on the new bulb with the slots in the holder, then push the bulb in and turn it clockwise, making sure it locates correctly.

5 On models with a detachable lens, make sure any rubber seal is correctly in place, and take care not to overtighten the screws as it is easy to strip the threads or crack the lens.

6 On models without a detachable lens turn the bulb holder clockwise to secure it.

Licence plate bulb

7 On many models the tail light bulb also illuminates the licence plate. If your model has a separate light unit for the licence plate check to see if you can remove the lens to access the bulb, or whether you have to remove the cover, or displace the whole unit **(see illustrations)**.

8 Carefully either push the bulb in and turn it anti-clockwise to release it from the holder, or pull the bulb out of its socket, depending on the type fitted, and replace it with a new one **(see illustration)**.

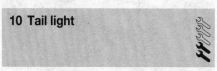

10 Tail light

1 Remove the seat and if necessary the seat cowling as required to access the tail light (see Chapter 8) – on some models the tail light may be mounted in the seat cowling.

2 Disconnect the wiring connector(s).

3 Undo the screws, nuts or bolts as required according to model and remove the tail light.

4 Installation is the reverse of removal. Check the operation of the tail and brake lights.

11 Turn signal circuit check

1 Most turn signal problems are the result of a burned out bulb or corroded socket. This is especially true when the turn signals function on one side (although possibly too quickly), but fail to work on the other side. If this is the case, first check the bulbs, the sockets and the wiring connectors. If all the turn signals fail to work, check the relay (see below). If it is good, the problem lies in the wiring or

11.2a Typical turn signal relay (arrowed) – block type

connectors, or the switch. Refer to Section 18 for the switch testing procedures.

2 To access the relay remove the seat or one of the side covers as required (see Chapter 8). Disconnect the relay wiring connector(s) **(see illustrations)**.

3 Check for battery voltage at the input wire terminal on the loom side of the connector with the ignition ON. If no voltage is present, check the wiring from the relay to the ignition switch for continuity.

4 If voltage was present, short between the terminals on the connector using a jumper wire. Turn the ignition ON and operate the turn signal switch, first in one direction, then the other. If the turn signal lights come on in each direction (they won't flash), the relay is confirmed faulty.

5 If none of the lights come on, check the wiring for continuity to the left-hand switch housing, and repair or renew the wiring or connectors as required.

11.2b Typical turn signal relay (arrowed) – cylinder type

12.1a Undo the screw(s) . . .

12.1b . . . and detach the lens

12.2 Release the bulb and replace it with a new one

6 If all is good so far, or if some of the lights work but not all, check the wiring for the lights concerned between the left-hand switch housing and the turn signals themselves. Repair or renew the wiring or connectors as necessary.

12 Turn signal bulbs

Always use a paper towel or dry cloth when handling new bulbs to prevent injury if the bulb should break and to increase bulb life.

1 Undo the screw(s) securing the lens and detach it from the housing, noting how it fits **(see illustrations)**.
2 Push the bulb into the holder and twist it anti-clockwise to remove it **(see illustration)**. Check the socket terminals for corrosion and clean them if necessary.
3 Line up the pins of the new bulb with the slots in the socket, then push the bulb in and turn it clockwise until it locks into place.
4 Fit the lens onto the housing, making sure it locates correctly, and install the screw. Do not over-tighten the screw as it is easy to strip the threads or crack the lens.

13 Turn signal assemblies

1 On models with a shell headlight the wiring connectors are usually inside – undo the screws securing the beam unit and draw it out of the shell **(see illustrations 7.1a and b)**. Trace the wiring from the turn signal and disconnect it at the connectors **(see illustration 8.2a)**.
2 On models with a fairing trace the wiring from the turn signal and disconnect it at the connectors. If the turn signal is mounted in a fairing panel and the screw(s) securing it are not accessible remove the panel (see Chapter 8).

3 To access the rear turn signal wiring connectors remove the seat, and if required the seat cowling (see Chapter 8). Trace the wiring from the turn signal and disconnect it at the connectors.
4 Undo the screw(s) or nut securing the turn signal and remove it, taking care not to snag the wiring as you draw it through where applicable **(see illustration)**.
5 Installation is the reverse of removal. Check the operation of the turn signals.

14 Brake light switches

Circuit check

1 Before checking the switches, and if not already done, check the brake light circuit (see Section 6).

Front brake lever switch

2 The switch is mounted on the bottom of the brake master cylinder if it is of the block type, or in the brake lever bracket if it is the cylinder type.
3 If a block type switch is fitted, disconnect the wiring connector(s) from it **(see illustration)**. If a cylinder type switch is fitted, either pull the boot off the switch and disconnect the connectors, or trace the wiring from the switch and disconnect it at the connector(s), according to type **(see illustration)**.
4 Using a continuity tester (see Section 2),

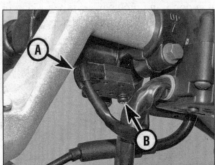

14.3a Front brake light switch wiring connectors (A) and mounting screw (B) – block type switch

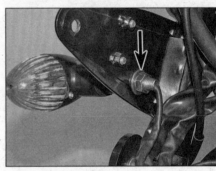

13.4 Many turn signal stems are secured by a nut (arrowed) on the inside

connect the probes to the terminals on the switch or to the terminals on the switch side of the connector according to type. With the brake lever at rest, there should be no continuity. With the lever applied, there should be continuity. If the switch does not behave as described, replace it with a new one (see below).
5 If the switch is good, check for voltage at the input wire terminal with the ignition switch ON – there should be battery voltage. If there's no voltage present, check the wiring between the connector and the ignition switch. If voltage is present, check the other wire for continuity to the brake light wiring connector. Repair or renew the wiring as necessary.

Rear brake pedal switch

6 Trace the wiring from the switch and disconnect it at the connector(s), removing

14.3b Cylinder type brake light switch with direct wiring connectors (arrowed)

14.6 Rear brake light switch (arrowed)

14.11 Release the clip and withdraw the switch

14.14 Unhook the spring (arrowed)

the seat, side cover or fuel tank as required according to model (see Chapter 8 or 4) **(see illustration)**.

7 Using a continuity tester, connect the probes to the terminals on the switch side of the wiring connector(s). With the brake pedal at rest, there should be no continuity. With the pedal applied, there should be continuity. If the switch does not behave as described, replace it with a new one, although check first that switch is adjusted correctly (see Step 16).

8 If the switch is good, check for voltage at the input wire terminal on the loom side of the connector with the ignition switch ON – there should be battery voltage. If there's no voltage present, check the wiring between the connector and the ignition switch. If voltage is present, check the other wire for continuity to the brake light wiring connector, referring to the relevant wiring diagram. Repair or renew the wiring as necessary.

Switch replacement

Front brake lever switch

9 The switch is mounted on the bottom of the brake master cylinder if it is of the block type, or in the brake lever bracket if it is the cylinder type.

10 If a block type switch is fitted disconnect the wiring connector(s) **(see illustration 14.3a)**. Undo the screw securing the switch.

11 If a cylinder type switch with direct connectors is fitted pull the boot off the switch and disconnect the connectors **(see illustration 14.3b)**. If a cylinder type switch with integral wiring loom is fitted trace the wiring from it and disconnect it at the connector(s), then feed the wiring back to the switch, noting its routing and releasing it from any ties. Press the switch retaining clip and draw the switch out of its housing **(see illustration)**.

12 Installation is the reverse of removal.

Rear brake pedal switch

13 Trace the wiring from the switch and disconnect it at the connector(s), removing the seat, side cover or fuel tank as required according to model (see Chapter 8 or 4) **(see illustration 14.6)**. Feed the wiring down to the switch, noting its routing and releasing it from any ties.

14 Unhook the switch spring from the pedal **(see illustration)**.

15 Thread the switch out of its adjustment nut, then remove the nut from the mounting.

16 Installation is the reverse of removal. Make sure the brake light is activated just before the rear brake pedal takes effect. If adjustment is necessary, hold the switch body and turn the adjustment nut as required until the brake light is activated correctly – if the brake light comes on too late or not at all, turn the ring clockwise (when looked at from the top) so the switch threads up the nut. If the brake light comes on too soon or is permanently on, turn the ring anti-clockwise so the switch threads down the nut.

15 Instruments and cables

Check

1 If there is a problem with an electronic instrument cluster, first check the wiring connector(s) is/are secure and that all wires and terminals are securely connected – refer below for access. On many models you will also need to remove the instrument cluster (see below), then unscrew the rear cover nuts and remove the cover and lift the bracket off, to access the connectors on the back of the individual instruments. Make sure the power supply to the cluster is good by checking for battery voltage at the input wire terminal in the loom side of the wiring connector with the ignition ON.

2 Next refer to Section 2 and to the Wiring Diagrams at the end of the Chapter and check the wiring and connectors in the relevant circuit. Also check the other components relevant to the circuit, e.g. neutral switch, dimmer switch, turn signals, fuel level sensor.

3 If there is a problem with a cable driven speedometer or tachometer first check the cable is securely connected at each end **(see illustrations)**. Next detach the cable and make sure the inner cable is not broken – if it is replace the cable with a new one.

15.3a Disconnect the speedometer cable at the wheel . . .

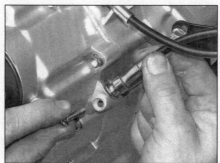

15.3b . . . the tachometer cable at the engine . . .

15.3c . . . and both cables at the instruments

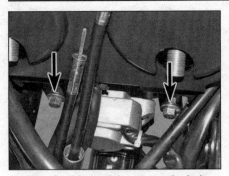

15.6a On this model unscrew the bolts (arrowed) . . .

15.6b . . . and remove the instruments

15.6c On fuel tank mounted instruments undo the screws (arrowed) to free the housing . . .

Removal and installation

4 Where fitted and if necessary remove the fairing (see Chapter 8), or the fuel tank if required on Custom models with a tank mounted instrument.

5 On instruments without a direct wiring connector trace the wiring from the instruments and disconnect it at the connector(s). On models with a shell headlight the wiring connectors are usually inside – undo the screws securing the beam unit and draw it out of the shell **(see illustrations 7.1a and b)**. On other models you may need to remove the fuel tank to access the connector(s) (see Chapter 4).

6 Check how the instruments are mounted and whether the speedometer cable and tachometer cable are accessible with the instruments in place or whether you need to displace the instruments first before disconnecting them **(see illustrations)**.

7 Check with your dealer as to the availability of individual instruments within a cluster.

8 Installation is the reverse of removal.

16 Instrument and warning light bulbs

1 Remove the instrument cluster (Section 15).

2 Remove the instrument lower cover and the mounting bracket **(see illustrations)**.

3 Carefully pull the relevant bulb holder out, then pull the bulb out of the holder and replace it with a new one **(see illustrations)**.

17 Ignition switch

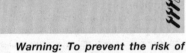

Warning: To prevent the risk of short circuits, disconnect the battery negative (–) lead before making any ignition switch checks.

Check

1 The ignition switch is bolted to the underside of the top yoke.

2 Trace the wiring from the switch and disconnect it at the connector(s). On models with a shell headlight the wiring connectors are usually inside – undo the screws securing the beam unit and draw it out of the shell **(see**

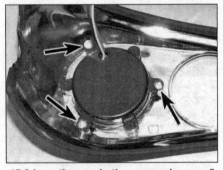

15.6d . . . then undo the screws (arrowed) to free the instrument

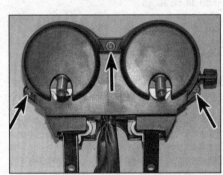

16.2a Undo the screws (arrowed) . . .

16.2b . . . and remove the lower cover

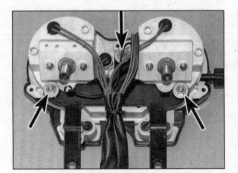

16.2c If necessary unscrew the nuts (arrowed) and remove the bracket

16.3a Carefully pull the bulb holder out . . .

16.3b . . . then remove the bulb

illustrations 7.1a and b). On other models you may need to remove the fairing (where fitted – see Chapter 8) or the fuel tank (see Chapter 4) to access the connector(s).

3 Using an ohmmeter or a continuity tester, check the continuity of the connector terminal pairs (see the wiring diagram in your handbook if available, or ask your dealer for one, and refer to Section 2 if necessary). Continuity should exist between the terminals connected by a solid line on the diagram when the switch is in the indicated position.

4 If you don't have access to a wiring diagram identify which is the main power input line on the loom side of the connector – it is often (but not always) a red wire and is usually thicker than the others, and there will be battery voltage present at all times (temporarily reconnect the battery to find out). Connect one probe of your continuity tester to the corresponding terminal on the switch side of the connector and check for continuity with the other wires in the connector with the switch in its ON position (refer to Section 2 if necessary).

5 If the switch fails the test, check for continuity in the wiring between the connector and the switch, and check the terminals on the switch. If necessary replace the switch with a new one.

6 If the switch is good, check for battery voltage at the power input wire terminal on the loom side of the connector (see Step 4). If there is none, check the fuse (Section 5). If that is good check for continuity in the wire to the battery.

Removal and installation

7 The ignition switch is bolted to the underside of the top yoke. Where fitted and if required remove the fairing (see Chapter 8).

8 Trace the wiring from the ignition switch and disconnect it at the connector(s). On models with a shell headlight the wiring connectors are usually inside – undo the screws securing the beam unit and draw it out of the shell **(see illustrations 7.1a and b)**. On other models you may need to remove the fuel tank to access the connector(s) (see Chapter 4). Feed the wiring back to the switch, freeing it from any clips and ties and noting its routing.

9 Check under the top yoke and see what sort of bolts secure the switch **(see illustration)** – on some models security bolts with shear-heads may be used, which have to be drifted round until loose using a punch in which case it is necessary remove the top yoke (see Chapter 6, Section 9, and follow the relevant steps). On some models security Torx screws may be used, for which a special Torx bit is needed. If the switch is secured by standard bolts that are accessible there is no need to remove the yoke, but remove the instruments if required (see Section 15).

10 Unscrew the bolts and remove the switch.

11 Installation is the reverse of removal. If shear head bolts are used fit new bolts and tighten them until the heads shear off. Make sure the wiring connector(s) is/are correctly routed and securely connected.

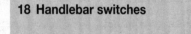

18 Handlebar switches

Check

1 Generally speaking, the switches are reliable and trouble-free. Most troubles, when they do occur, are caused by dirty or corroded contacts, but wear and breakage of internal parts is a possibility that should not be overlooked. If breakage does occur, the entire switch and related wiring harness will have to be replaced with a new one, as individual parts are not usually available.

2 The switches can be checked for continuity using an ohmmeter or a continuity test light. Disconnect the battery negative (–) lead, which will prevent the possibility of a short circuit, before making the checks.

3 Trace the wiring from the switch and disconnect it at the connector(s). On models with a shell headlight the wiring connectors are usually inside – undo the screws securing the beam unit and draw it out of the shell **(see illustrations 7.1a and b)**. On other models you may need to remove the fairing (where fitted – see Chapter 8) or the fuel tank (see Chapter 4) to access the connector(s).

4 Check for continuity between the terminals of the switch connector with the switch in the various positions (i.e. switch off – no continuity, switch on – continuity) – see the wiring

diagram in your handbook if available, or ask your dealer for one, and refer to Section 2 if necessary. Continuity should exist between the terminals connected by a solid line on the diagram when the switch is in the indicated position. If you don't have access to a wiring diagram undo the screws and displace the switch housing from the handlebar to identify which wires go to which switch, and test accordingly.

5 If the continuity check indicates a problem exists, displace the switch housing and spray the switch contacts with electrical contact cleaner (there is no need to remove the switch completely). If they are accessible, the contacts can be scraped clean with a knife or polished with crocus cloth. If switch components are damaged or broken, it will be obvious when the switch is disassembled.

Removal and installation

6 Trace the wiring from the switch and disconnect it at the connector(s). On models with a shell headlight the wiring connectors are usually inside – undo the screws securing the beam unit and draw it out of the shell **(see illustrations 7.1a and b)**. On other models you may need to remove the fairing (where fitted – see Chapter 8) or the fuel tank (see Chapter 4) to access the connector(s). Feed the wiring back to the switch, freeing it from any clips and ties and noting its routing. Also disconnect the wiring connector(s) from the brake light switch and clutch switch where fitted if the wiring is part of the handlebar switch loom.

7 To remove the right-hand switch, refer to Chapter 4 for removal of the throttle cable(s) from the switch housing, which involves detaching it from the handlebars.

8 To remove the left-hand switch undo the switch housing screws and free it from the handlebar by separating the halves **(see illustration)** – on models with a choke cable and lever in the housing refer to Chapter 4 if required to detach it.

9 Installation is the reverse of removal. Where present make sure the locating pin in the switch housing locates in the hole in the handlebar **(see illustration)**. Refer to Chapter 4 for installation of the throttle cable(s) and where fitted the choke cable and lever.

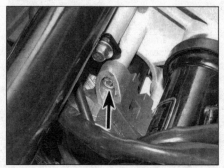

17.9 Ignition switch bolt (arrowed) – this is a standard bolt

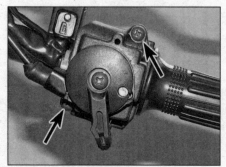

18.8 Left-hand switch housing screws (arrowed)

18.9 Locate the pin (arrowed) in the hole

19.3 Disconnect the single bullet connector in this cut-out

19.5 Check the contacts in the switch face and the plunger (arrowed) in the drum

19.12 Neutral switch screws (arrowed) – OHV engine

19 Neutral switch/gear position indicator

1 The neutral switch is part of the starter safety circuit (see Chapter 1). On some models the switch operates as a gear position indicator (see Step 5).

Check

2 Before checking the electrical circuit, check the neutral light in the instrument cluster (Section 16).
3 The switch is located in the left-hand side of the transmission casing. Remove the front sprocket cover (see Chapter 7). On single cylinder engines trace the wiring from the switch and disconnect it at the connector – remove the seat or side cover (see Chapter 8) or the fuel tank (see Chapter 4) as required. On twin cylinder engines disconnect the single bullet connector in the wiring housing above the front sprocket **(see illustration)**.
4 Make sure the transmission is in neutral. With the connector disconnected and the ignition switch ON, the neutral light should be out. If not, the wire between the connector and instrument cluster must be earthed (grounded) at some point.
5 On single cylinder engines the switch has six wires, one for neutral and one for each gear, but the wires for the gears are only used if there is a gear position indicator fitted. Identify which is the wire for neutral and

check for continuity between that terminal in the switch side of the wiring connector and the crankcase. With the transmission in neutral, there should be continuity. With the transmission in gear, there should be no continuity. If not remove the switch (see below) and check the contacts on the switch face and the plunger and spring in the end of the selector drum – make sure the plunger moves in and out smoothly and freely against spring pressure **(see illustration)**. Check for continuity between the neutral wire terminal in the connector and the neutral contact on the switch face (it is the smallest of the contacts) – if there is no continuity replace the switch with a new one.
6 On twin cylinder engines check for continuity between the switch wiring connector and the crankcase. With the transmission in neutral, there should be continuity. With the transmission in gear, there should be no continuity. If the tests prove otherwise, remove the alternator cover (see Chapter 2D) and check the wire terminal on the switch. If that is good remove the switch (see below) and check for continuity between the wiring terminal and the contact on the switch itself. If that is good then the contact on the selector drum could be distorted – try and make a visual check via the switch bore in the crankcase. Replace the switch with a new one if necessary.
7 If the continuity tests prove the switch is good, check for voltage at the neutral wire terminal on the loom side of the connector with the ignition on. If there's no voltage

present, check the wire between the switch and the instrument cluster.
8 If the switch is good, check the other components (sidestand switch (where fitted), clutch switch and diodes) and their wiring and connectors in the starter safety circuit as described in the relevant sections of this Chapter. If all components are good, check the wiring between the various components. Repair or renew the wiring as required.

Removal

Single cylinder engines

9 The switch is located in the left-hand side of the transmission casing. Drain the engine oil (see Chapter 1).
10 Remove the front sprocket cover (see Chapter 7). Access to the switch screws is restricted by the alternator cover – if you do not have the correct tools to access both screws remove the cover (see Chapter 2A, 2B or 2C).
11 Trace the wiring from the switch and disconnect it at the connector – remove the seat or side cover (see Chapter 8) or the fuel tank (see Chapter 4) as required. Feed the wiring back to the switch, freeing it from any clips and ties and noting its routing.
12 Clean the area around the switch. Undo the screws and remove the switch **(see illustration)**. Discard the O-ring – a new one must be used.
13 If required remove the contact plunger and spring from the end of the selector drum **(see illustrations)**.

Twin cylinder engines

14 The switch is located in the left-hand side of the transmission casing. Drain the engine oil (see Chapter 1).
15 Remove the alternator cover (see Chapter 2D). Remove the outer gasket and discard it – a new one should be used. Remove the starter motor (see Section 25). Remove the two dowels and carefully displace the backplate – if the inner gasket behind it is in any way damaged you will have to fit a new one. Rotate the plate so the neutral switch is exposed.
16 Clean the area around the switch. Unscrew the retainer plate bolt and remove

19.13a Remove the plunger . . .

19.13b . . . and spring

the retainer **(see illustration)**. Carefully withdraw the switch using needle nose pliers **(see illustration)**. Discard the O-ring – a new one must be used. Disconnect the wire from the switch, and/or free the wire grommet from its cut-out, as required **(see illustrations)**.

Installation

17 Installation is the reverse of removal – use a new O-ring and smear it with oil.

20 Sidestand switch

1 The sidestand switch is part of the starter safety circuit (see Chapter 1). It is not fitted on all models.

Check

2 On some models the switch is mounted on the stand pivot **(see illustration)**. On other models the sidestand switch is mounted next to the stand **(see illustration)**.
3 Trace the wiring from the switch and disconnect it at the connector – remove the seat or side cover (see Chapter 8) or the fuel tank (see Chapter 4) as required.
4 Check the operation of the switch using an ohmmeter or continuity test light. Connect the meter between the terminals on the switch side of the connector. With the sidestand up there should be continuity (zero resistance) between the terminals, and with the stand down there should be no continuity (infinite resistance). Make sure the switch post or plunger is clean and not stuck, and that it moves freely and smoothly.
5 If the switch does not perform as expected, it is faulty and must be replaced with a new one. If the switch is good, check the other components (clutch switch, neutral switch and diodes) and their wiring and connectors in the starter safety circuit as described in

the relevant sections of this Chapter. If all components are good, check the wiring between the various components. Repair or renew the wiring as required.

Removal and installation

6 On some models the switch is mounted on the stand pivot **(see illustration 20.2a)**. On other models the sidestand switch is mounted next to the stand **(see illustration 20.2b)**.
7 Trace the wiring from the switch and disconnect it at the connector – remove the seat or side cover (see Chapter 8) or the fuel

tank (see Chapter 4) as required. Feed the wiring back to the switch, freeing it from any clips and ties and noting its routing.
8 Make sure the sidestand is retracted. Undo the screw(s) and remove the switch.
9 Fit the new switch and tighten the screw(s).
10 Feed the wiring up to its connector, making sure it is correctly routed and secured by any clips and ties. Reconnect the wiring connector.
11 Check the operation of the switch.
12 Install the fuel tank (see Chapter 4), side cover or seat (see Chapter 8).

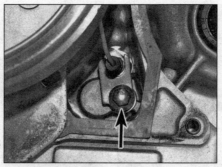
19.16a Unscrew the bolt (arrowed) and remove the plate . . .

19.16b . . . then withdraw the switch. Discard the O-ring (arrowed)

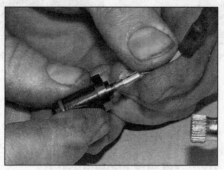
19.16c Disconnect the wiring connector . . .

19.16d . . . and/or free the wiring grommet

20.2a Pivot mounted sidestand switch and its screw (arrowed)

20.2a Frame mounted sidestand switch and its bolts (arrowed)

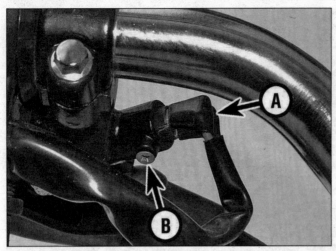

21.3 Clutch switch wiring connectors (arrowed) (A) and mounting screw (B)

22.1a Diode blocks (arrowed) can be taped into the loom . . .

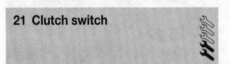

21 Clutch switch

1 The clutch switch is part of the starter safety circuit (see Chapter 1).

Check

2 The switch is mounted on or in the clutch lever bracket.
3 Disconnect the wiring connector(s) **(see illustration)**.
4 Using a continuity tester, connect the probes to the terminals on the switch or to the terminals on the switch side of the connector according to type. With the clutch lever at rest, there should be no continuity. With the lever applied, there should be continuity. If the switch does not behave as described, replace it with a new one (see below).
5 If the switch is good, check the other components (sidestand switch (where fitted), neutral switch and diodes) and their wiring

and connectors in the starter safety circuit as described in the relevant sections of this Chapter. If all components are good, check the wiring between the various components. Repair or renew the wiring as required.

Removal and installation

6 The switch is mounted on or in the clutch lever bracket.
7 Disconnect the wiring connector(s) **(see illustration 21.3)**. Undo the screw securing the switch, or unscrew the switch itself, or release the clip on the underside and withdraw the switch, according to type.
8 Installation is the reverse of removal.

22 Diodes

1 The diode(s) for the starter safety circuit are housed in a block, which plugs directly into the wiring loom, and is possibly wrapped

in insulating tape **(see illustrations)**. The location of the diode block varies from model to model – remove the seat, side covers and fuel tank to locate it (see Chapters 8 and 4).
2 Remove the diode block from the loom.
3 Test the diode(s) using an ohmmeter or continuity tester. A diode can pass a current in one direction only, and in that direction will show continuity, or a very small resistance if using an ohmmeter. In the other direction there should be no continuity or a very high resistance. Connect the meter or tester probes to the diode terminals, then reverse them, and check it behaves as described.
4 If it doesn't behave as stated, replace the diode block with a new one.
5 If the diode block is good, push it back into its socket, then check the other components (sidestand switch (where fitted), neutral switch and clutch switch) and their wiring and connectors in the starter safety circuit as described in the relevant sections of this Chapter.

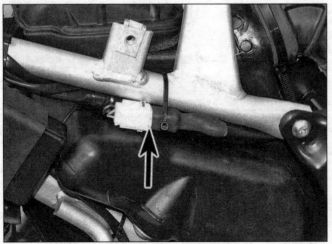

22.1b . . . plugged into an opening in the loom . . .

22.1c . . . or a separately mounted component

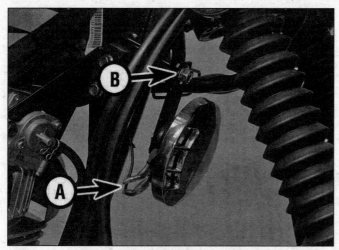

23.1 Horn wiring connectors (A) and mounting bolt (B) – typical example

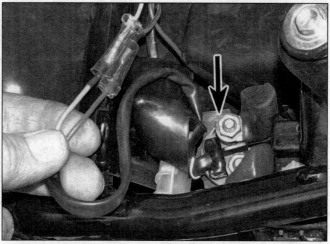

24.2 Typical starter relay (arrowed) and its wiring connectors

23 Horn

Check

1 The horn will be mounted at the front of the bike **(see illustration)**, typically on the frame downtubes, steering lower yoke or radiator. Remove any fairing panels as required for access according to model (see Chapter 8).
2 Disconnect the wiring connectors from the horn. Check them for loose wires. Using two jumper wires, apply voltage from a fully-charged 12V battery directly to the terminals on the horn. If the horn doesn't sound, replace it with a new one.
3 If the horn works check the wiring in the horn circuit for continuity.
4 If all the wiring and connectors are good, check the horn button contacts in the switch housing (see Section 18).

Removal and installation

5 Disconnect the wiring connectors from the horn **(see illustration 23.1)**. Unscrew the bolt and remove the horn.
6 Install the horn, connect the wiring, and check that it works.

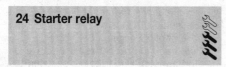

24 Starter relay

Check

1 If the starter circuit is faulty, first check the fuse (see Section 5). To test the relay you need a multimeter with a continuity function.
2 The starter relay is usually located near the battery **(see illustration)**. Remove the seat and/or side cover as required for access (see Chapter 8).
3 Lift the rubber terminal cover and detach

the starter motor lead (usually a black lead, the battery leads is usually red); position the lead away from the relay terminal. With the ignition switch ON, the engine kill switch in the RUN position, and the transmission in neutral, press the starter switch. The relay should be heard to click.
4 If the relay doesn't click, switch off the ignition and remove the relay as described below; test it as follows. First check the resistance of the coil by connecting an ohmmeter across the wiring connector terminals – there should be some resistance shown, and exact figure isn't available, but it could be anything from 5 to 100 ohms. The important thing is that there is some resistance.
5 Now connect a continuity tester across the relay's starter motor and battery lead terminals. There should be no continuity. Using a fully-charged 12 volt battery and two insulated jumper wires, connect the battery to the wiring connector terminals. At this point the relay should be heard to click and the multimeter read 0 ohms (continuity). If this is the case the relay is proved good. If the relay does not click when battery voltage is applied and indicates no continuity (infinite resistance) across its terminals, and reversing the battery connections to the relay makes no difference, it is faulty and must be replaced with a new one.
6 If the relay is good, check the main lead from the battery to the relay, and the lead from the relay to the starter motor – check that the terminals and connectors at each end are tight and corrosion-free.
7 Next check the wiring and connectors from the relay wiring connector to the switch housing, referring to Section 2, and then check the switches (see Section 18).
8 If all appears good check the starter safety circuit components (neutral switch, clutch switch, sidestand switch (where fitted) and diodes) and their wiring and connectors as described in the relevant sections of this Chapter.

Removal and installation

9 Disconnect the battery terminals, remembering to disconnect the negative (–) terminal first (see Section 3).
10 Disconnect the relay wiring connector(s) **(see illustration 24.2)**. Lift the insulating cover and detach the starter motor and battery leads. Remove the relay from its rubber sleeve.
11 Installation is the reverse of removal. Make sure the terminal nuts or bolts are securely tightened. Connect the negative (–) lead last when reconnecting the battery.

25 Starter motor removal and installation

Single cylinder engines

Removal

1 Disconnect the battery negative (–) lead (see Section 3). The starter motor is mounted on the top of the crankcase on OHV engines and on the front on OHC engines.
2 Peel back the rubber terminal cover on the starter motor. Undo the nut or screw securing the starter lead to the motor and detach the lead **(see illustration)** – if the terminal is

25.2 Pull back the terminal cover then undo the nut or screw and detach the lead

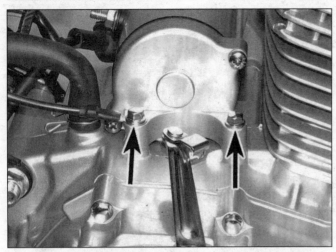

25.3a Starter motor bolts (arrowed) – OHV single engine

25.3b Starter motor bolts (arrowed) – OHC single engine

25.3c Removing the starter motor – OHV single engine

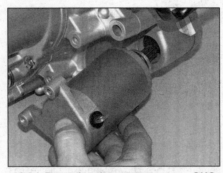

25.3d Removing the starter motor – OHC single engine

25.5 Fit a new O-ring and lubricate it

25.10 Pull back the terminal cover then undo the nut (arrowed) and detach the lead

25.11a Slide the gear off the shaft

25.11b Remove the gasket and fit a new one

corroded spray it with some penetrating fluid and leave it for a while before attempting to undo it.

3 Unscrew the two bolts securing the starter motor to the crankcase, noting the earth lead secured by one of the bolts where fitted **(see illustrations)**. Slide the starter motor out and remove it **(see illustrations)**.

4 Remove the O-ring on the end of the starter motor and discard it as a new one must be used **(see illustration 25.5)**.

Installation

5 Fit a new O-ring onto the end of the starter motor, making sure it is seated in its groove **(see illustration)**. Apply a smear of engine oil to the O-ring.

6 Manoeuvre the motor into position and slide it into the crankcase **(see illustration 25.3c or d)**. Ensure that the starter motor teeth mesh correctly with those of the starter idle/reduction gear. Install the mounting bolts, not forgetting the earth lead where fitted, and tighten them **(see illustration 25.3a or b)**.

7 Connect the starter lead to the motor and secure it with the nut or screw **(see illustration 25.2)**. Fit the rubber cover over the terminal.

8 Connect the battery negative (–) lead.

Twin cylinder engine

Removal

9 Disconnect the battery negative (–) lead (see Section 3). The starter motor is mounted on the front of the engine.

10 Peel back the rubber terminal cover on the starter motor. Undo the nut securing the starter lead to the motor and detach the lead – if the terminal is corroded spray it with some penetrating fluid and leave it for a while before attempting to undo it **(see illustration)**.

11 Remove the alternator cover (see Chapter 2D). Slide the drive gear and chain off the starter motor shaft **(see illustration)**. Remove the outer gasket and discard it **(see illustration)** – a new one should be used.

12 Unscrew the four bolts securing the starter

25.12a Unscrew the bolts (arrowed) ...

25.12b ... noting the clamp ...

motor to the crankcase, noting the lead clamp **(see illustrations)**. Slide the starter motor out and remove it **(see illustration)**.

13 Remove the O-ring on the end of the starter motor and discard it as a new one must be used **(see illustration 25.5)**.

Installation

14 Fit a new O-ring onto the end of the starter motor, making sure it is seated in its groove **(see illustration 25.5)**. Apply a smear of engine oil to the O-ring.

15 Manoeuvre the motor into position and slide it into the crankcase **(see illustration 25.12c)**. Install the mounting bolts, not forgetting the lead clamp and tighten them **(see illustration 25.12b)**.

16 Make sure the alternator cover dowels are fitted, then locate the new outer gasket onto them **(see illustration 25.11b)**. Slide the drive gear and chain onto the starter motor shaft **(see illustration 25.11a)**. Install the alternator cover (see Chapter 2D).

17 Connect the starter lead to the motor and secure it with the nut **(see illustration 25.10)**. Fit the rubber cover over the terminal.

18 Connect the battery negative (–) lead.

26 Starter motor overhaul

Check

1 Remove the starter motor (see Section 25). Cover the body in some rag and hold it down.

2 Prepare a fully-charged 12 volt battery and two insulated jump leads. Connect the negative (–) jump lead to one of the motor's mounting lug. Hold the starter motor down, then touch the positive (+) jump lead to the protruding terminal on the starter motor – there may be sparks **(see illustration)**. At this point the starter motor should spin. If this is the case the motor is proved good, though it is worth overhauling it if you suspect it of not

working properly under load. If the motor does not spin, disassemble it for inspection.

OHV single cylinder engine

Disassembly

3 Remove the starter motor (see Section 25).

4 Note any alignment marks between the main housing and the front and rear covers, or make your own if they aren't clear **(see illustration)**.

5 Undo the two long screws, noting the washers **(see illustration)**. Remove the front cover, noting the sealing ring **(see illustration)**. Remove the shim(s) from the shaft **(see illustration 26.21a)**.

25.12c ... and remove the starter motor

26.2 Testing a starter motor

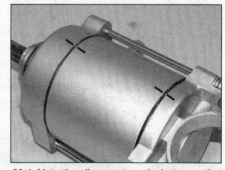

26.4 Note the alignment marks between the housing and the covers or make your own

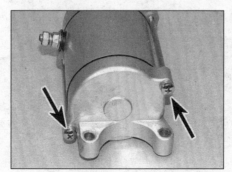

26.5a Undo and remove the two screws (arrowed) ...

26.5b ... then remove the front cover

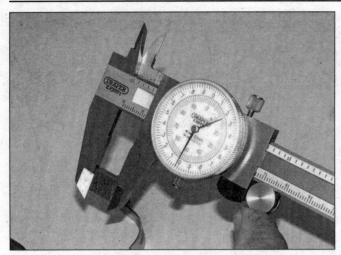

26.11 Measure the length of each brush

26.12a Check the bars for wear and damage . . .

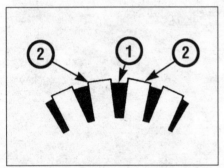

26.12b . . . and make sure the mica (1) is the correct depth below the bars (2)

6 Remove the rear cover, noting the sealing ring **(see illustration 26.22b)**. Remove the shim(s) from the shaft **(see illustration 26.22a)**.

7 Withdraw the armature from the back of the main housing **(see illustration 26.20a)**.

8 At this stage check for continuity between the terminal bolt and the brushes with insulation. There should be continuity (zero resistance). Check for continuity between the terminal bolt and the housing. There should be no continuity (infinite resistance). Also check for continuity between the brushes with uninsulated wire and the brushplate. There should be continuity (zero resistance). If there is no continuity when there should be or vice versa, identify the faulty component and replace it with a new one.

9 Slide the insulated brushes out of their holders. Remove the brushplate assembly, noting how it locates and how the insulated brush wires are routed **(see illustration 26.19g)**. Noting the correct fitted location of each component, unscrew the nut from the terminal bolt and remove the insulating piece and the dished O-ring **(see illustration 26.19f)**. Withdraw the terminal bolt from the main housing, noting how it locates, then remove the insulator, the brush piece and the holder **(see illustrations 26.19d, c, b and a)**.

10 Slide the brushplate brushes out of their holders.

Inspection

11 The parts of the starter motor that are most likely to require attention are the brushes. Measure the length of each brush – they should be about 12 mm when new **(see illustration)**. If any of the brushes are worn down to 6 mm fit a new set. If the brushes are not worn excessively, nor cracked, chipped, or otherwise damaged, they may be reused. Check the brush springs for distortion and fatigue. Check the brushplate for damage.

12 Inspect the commutator bars on the armature for scoring, scratches and discoloration **(see illustration)**. The commutator can be cleaned and polished with crocus cloth, but do not use sandpaper or emery paper. After cleaning, wipe away any residue with a cloth soaked in electrical system cleaner or denatured alcohol. Make sure the insulating Mica is at least 1 mm below the depth of each commutator bar **(see illustration)**. If necessary scrape it away.

13 Using an ohmmeter or a continuity tester, check for continuity between the commutator bars **(see illustration)**. Continuity should exist between each bar and all of the others. Also, check for continuity between the commutator bars and the armature shaft **(see illustration)**.

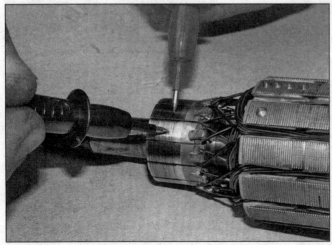

26.13a There should be continuity between the bars . . .

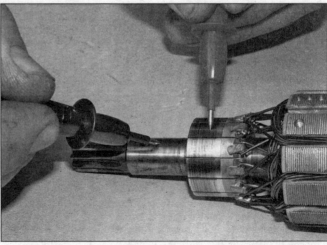

26.13b . . . and no continuity between the bars and the shaft

26.18 Hold the brush springs back using pieces of wire located as shown

26.19a Fit the holder . . .

26.19b . . . the brush piece . . .

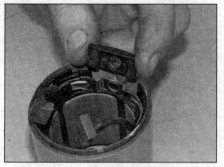

26.19c . . . and the insulator . . .

26.19d . . . then insert the bolt

26.19e Make sure the dished O-ring is the correct way round

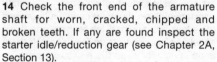
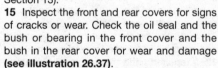

There should be no continuity (infinite resistance) between the commutator and the shaft. If the checks indicate otherwise, the armature is faulty.

14 Check the front end of the armature shaft for worn, cracked, chipped and broken teeth. If any are found inspect the starter idle/reduction gear (see Chapter 2A, Section 13).

15 Inspect the front and rear covers for signs of cracks or wear. Check the oil seal and the bush or bearing in the front cover and the bush in the rear cover for wear and damage **(see illustration 26.37)**.

16 Inspect the magnets in the main housing and the housing itself for cracks.

17 Inspect the housing sealing rings, the insulating pieces and O-ring for signs of damage, deformation and deterioration and replace them with new ones if necessary.

Reassembly

18 Get some short lengths of wire and locate them against the brush housings so they will hold the brush spring ends off the brushes **(see illustration)**. Slide the brushplate brushes back into position in their housings.

19 Fit the holder, brush piece and the insulator into the main housing **(see illustrations)**. Insert the terminal bolt through them and the housing **(see illustration)**. Fit the dished O-ring onto the terminal bolt with its dished side facing in so it locates in the gap between the gap and the housing **(see illustration)**. Fit the insulating piece with its wider side facing out, then fit the nut and tighten it **(see illustration)**. Fit the brushplate onto the housing, making

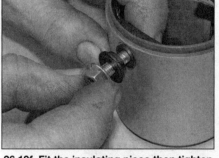

26.19f Fit the insulating piece then tighten the nut

26.20a Insert the armature . . .

sure its tab is correctly located in the housing slot and that the insulated brush wires are routed through the cut-outs in the plate **(see illustration)**. Slide the insulated brushes into their housings.

20 Insert the armature into the housing, taking

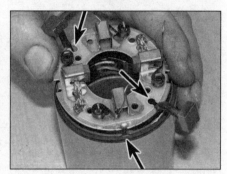

26.19g Make sure the tab and wires locate in the cut-outs (arrowed)

care as the magnets will want to forcefully pull it in **(see illustration)**. With the armature installed, remove the pieces of wire allowing each brush spring end to locate against the end of its brush and press it against the commutator bars **(see illustration)**.

26.20b . . . then remove the pieces of wire

26.21a Fit the sealing ring (arrowed) and the shim(s) . . .

26.21b . . . then fit the front cover

26.22a Fit the sealing ring (arrowed) and the shim(s) . . .

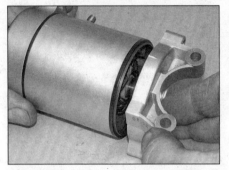

26.22b . . . then fit the rear cover

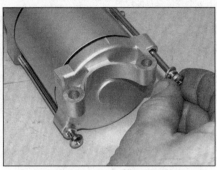

26.23 Fit the screws and tighten them

21 If removed fit the sealing ring onto the front of the housing. Slide the shim(s) onto the front of the armature shaft (see illustration). Apply a smear of grease to the front cover oil seal lip. Slide the front cover into position, aligning the marks made on removal (see illustration).

22 If removed fit the sealing ring onto the rear of the housing. Slide the shim(s) onto the rear of the armature shaft (see illustration). Apply a smear of grease to the end of the shaft. Fit the rear cover, aligning the marks made on removal (see illustration).

23 Check the marks made on removal are correctly aligned then fit the long screws with their washers and tighten them (see illustration).

24 Install the starter motor (see Section 25).

OHC single cylinder engine

Disassembly

25 Remove the starter motor (see Section 25).

26 Note any alignment marks between the main housing and the front and rear covers, or make your own if they aren't clear (see illustration). Also mark which is the shaft end of the main housing.

27 Unscrew the two long bolts, noting the O-rings, then remove the front cover from the motor (see illustration). Remove the tabbed washer, either from the cover or the shaft, and the shim (see illustrations 26.45a and 26.44).

28 Draw the main housing off the armature (see illustration 26.43) – it is held in by the attraction of the magnets, so take care not to lose your grip before the magnets lose theirs.

29 Withdraw the armature from the rear cover (see illustration 26.42).

30 At this stage check for continuity between the terminal and its brushes (the two not secured by screws) – there should be continuity (zero resistance). Check for continuity between the terminal and the cover – there should be no continuity (infinite resistance). Also check for continuity between the other brushes and the rear cover – there should be continuity (zero resistance). If there is no continuity when there should be or *vice versa*, identify the faulty component and replace it with a new one.

31 Slide the brushes out of their housings and remove the springs for safekeeping.

32 If required undo the two screws securing

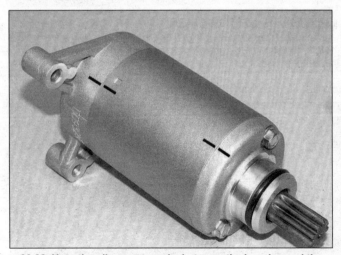

26.26 Note the alignment marks between the housing and the covers or make your own

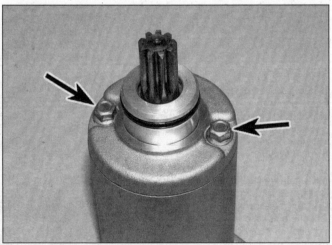

26.27 Unscrew the bolts (arrowed) and remove the front cover

26.32 Undo the screws (arrowed) and remove the brushplate

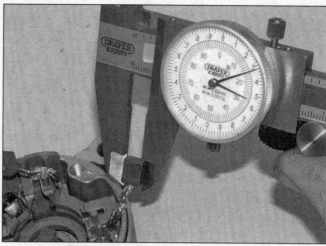

26.33 Measure the length of each brush

the brushplate, noting how they secure the brushes **(see illustration)**. Lift the brushplate out of the cover.

Inspection

33 The parts of the starter motor that are most likely to require attention are the brushes. Measure the length of each brush **(see illustration)**. If any of the brushes are worn significantly below their new length of 9 mm, fit a new set. If the brushes are not worn excessively, nor cracked, chipped, or otherwise damaged, they may be reused. Check the brush springs for distortion and fatigue. Check the brushplate for damage.

34 Inspect the commutator bars on the armature for scoring, scratches and discoloration **(see illustration 26.12a)**. The commutator can be cleaned and polished with crocus cloth, but do not use sandpaper or emery paper. After cleaning, wipe away any residue with a cloth soaked in electrical system cleaner or denatured alcohol. Make sure the insulating Mica is at least 1 mm below the depth of each commutator bar **(see illustration 26.12b)**. If necessary scrape it away.

35 Using an ohmmeter or a continuity tester, check for continuity between the commutator bars **(see illustration 26.13a)**. Continuity should exist between each bar and all of the others. Also, check for continuity between the commutator bars and the armature shaft **(see illustration 26.13b)**. There should be no continuity (infinite resistance) between the commutator and the shaft. If the checks indicate otherwise, the armature is faulty.

36 Check the front end of the armature shaft for worn, cracked, chipped and broken teeth. If any are found inspect the starter idle/ reduction gear (see Chapter 2B, Section 13).

37 Inspect the front and rear covers for signs of cracks or wear. Check the oil seal and the bush or bearing in the front cover and the bush in the rear cover for wear and damage **(see illustration)**.

38 Inspect the magnets in the main housing and the housing itself for cracks.

39 Inspect the housing sealing rings and long bolt O-rings for signs of damage, deformation and deterioration and replace them with new ones if necessary.

Reassembly

40 If removed fit the brushplate into the rear cover, making sure it locates correctly, then fit the brushes and screws **(see illustration 26.32)**.

41 Slide the springs back into their housings **(see illustration)**. Fit each brush into its

housing and push it in, then fit a small crocodile clip over each brush wire and the rim of the cover so that each brush is held back in its housing **(see illustration)** – this makes fitting the armature much simpler.

42 Apply a smear of grease to the rear end of the armature shaft. Insert the armature into the rear cover so that the shaft end locates in its bush, then release the brushes so they locate against the commutator **(see illustration)**.

43 If removed fit the sealing ring onto the rear of the main housing. Grasp both the armature and the rear cover in one hand and hold them

26.37 Check the bush and seal in the front cover

26.41a Fit the springs then push each brush into its housing . . .

26.41b . . . and fit crocodile clips to keep them retracted

26.42 Fit the armature into the rear cover making sure the brushes locate correctly

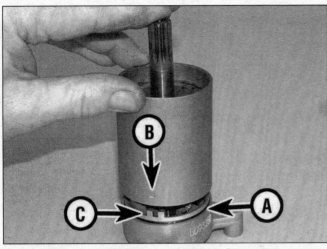

26.43 Make sure the sealing ring (A) is in place and fit the indent (B) between the tabs (C)

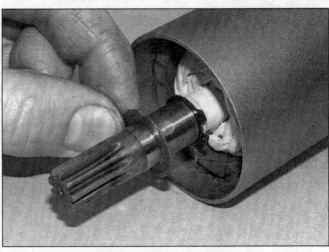

26.44 Slide the shim onto the shaft

26.45a Make sure the sealing ring (arrowed) is in place. Fit the washer locating the tabs in the cut-outs

26.45b Fit the cover . . .

together – this will prevent the armature being drawn out by the magnets in the housing. Note however that you should take care not to let the housing be drawn forcibly onto the armature or you will trap your fingers. Carefully allow the housing to be drawn onto the armature, making sure it is the correct way round and the marks between the cover and housing align (Step 26) **(see illustration)**.

44 Slide the shim onto the armature shaft **(see illustration)**.

45 Apply a smear of grease to the front cover oil seal lip **(see illustration 26.37)**. If removed fit the sealing ring onto the front cover. Fit the tabbed washer into the cover so that its tabs locate in the cut-outs **(see illustration)**. Slide the front cover into position, aligning the marks **(see illustration)**.

46 Check the marks made on removal are correctly aligned then fit the long bolts, not forgetting the O-rings (using new ones if necessary) and tighten them **(see illustration)**.

47 Install the starter motor (see Section 25).

Twin cylinder engine

Disassembly

48 Remove the starter motor (see Section 25).

49 Note any alignment marks between the main housing and the front and rear covers, or make some of your own if they aren't clear **(see illustration)**. Also make a mark to identify which way up the housing fits.

50 Unscrew the two long bolts, noting the washer(s) **(see illustration)**. Remove the front cover, noting the sealing ring. Note the locating pin between the ring gear and the front cover, and take care not to lose it **(see illustration 26.66c)**.

51 Remove the rear cover, noting the sealing ring **(see illustration 26.65c)**. Remove the shim(s) from the shaft or from inside the cover **(see illustration 26.65b)**.

52 Withdraw the armature from the main housing **(see illustration 26.64b)**. Remove the shim(s) from the shaft **(see illustration 26.64a)**.

53 Noting the correct fitted location of each component, unscrew the terminal nut and remove the washers, insulating piece and O-ring **(see illustration 26.63d)**. Remove the brushplate assembly and insulator from the rear cover **(see illustrations 26.63b and a)**.

54 Lift the brush springs and slide the brushes out from their holders, noting how they fit.

Inspection

55 The parts of the starter motor that are most likely to require attention are the brushes. Measure the length of each brush – they should be about 12 mm when new

26.46 . . . then fit the long bolts with their O-rings

26.49 Note the alignment marks between the housing and the covers or make your own

26.50 Unscrew the bolts (arrowed) and remove the front cover

26.55 Measure the length of each brush

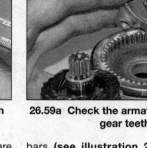

26.59a Check the armature shaft and ring gear teeth . . .

26.59b . . . and the drive shaft teeth

(see illustration). If any of the brushes are worn down to 6 mm fit a new set if available. If the brushes are not worn excessively, nor cracked, chipped, or otherwise damaged, they may be reused. Check the brush springs for distortion and fatigue. Check the brushplate for damage.

56 Inspect the commutator bars on the armature for scoring, scratches and discoloration **(see illustration 26.12a)**. The commutator can be cleaned and polished with crocus cloth, but do not use sandpaper or emery paper. After cleaning, wipe away any residue with a cloth soaked in electrical system cleaner or denatured alcohol. Check the insulating mica is at least 1 mm below the surface of the commutator bars **(see illustration 26.12b)**. If necessary scrape it away.

57 Using an ohmmeter or a continuity tester, check for continuity between the commutator

bars **(see illustration 26.13a)**. Continuity should exist between each bar and all of the others. Also, check for continuity between the commutator bars and the armature shaft **(see illustration 26.13b)**. There should be no continuity (infinite resistance) between the commutator and the shaft. If the checks indicate otherwise, the armature is defective.

58 Check for continuity between the positive brush and the terminal bolt. There should be continuity (zero resistance). Check for continuity between the terminal bolt and the housing (when assembled). There should be no continuity (infinite resistance).

59 Check the front end of the armature shaft, the ring gear assembly and the drive shaft on the front of the cover for worn, cracked, chipped and broken teeth **(see illustrations)**.

60 Inspect the end covers for signs of cracks or wear. Check the bush in the rear cover

and that in the main housing for wear **(see illustration)**. Inspect the magnets in the main housing and the housing itself for cracks.

61 Inspect the sealing rings, insulator pieces and terminal bolt O-ring for signs of damage and fit new ones if necessary.

Reassembly

62 Slide the brushes back into position in their holders on the brushplate and place the brush spring ends onto the brushes.

63 Fit the insulator into the rear cover, then insert the bolt and locate the brushplate assembly, making sure the bolt seats correctly in the cut-out in the insulator, and the tab locates between the ribs on the cover **(see illustrations)**. Fit the O-ring onto the bolt and fit it into the space between the bolt and the housing **(see illustration)**. Fit the insulating piece and the washers and secure them with the nut **(see illustration)**.

26.60 Check the bushes for wear

26.63a Fit the insulator into the hole . . .

26.63b . . . then fit the brushplate, seating the bolt in the insulator . . .

26.63c . . . and locating the tab between the ribs

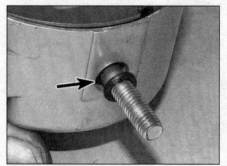

26.63d Fit the O-ring and push it into the gap (arrowed) . . .

26.63e . . . then fit the insulating piece, washers and nut

26.64a Fit the shims . . .

26.64b . . . then slide the armature into the housing

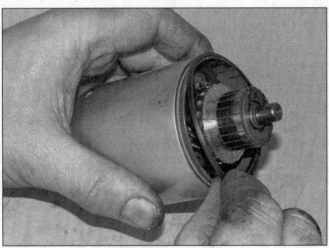

26.65a Fit the sealing ring . . .

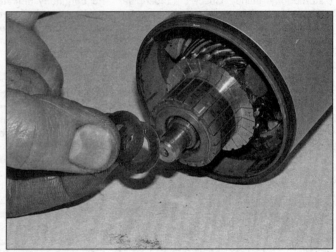

26.65b . . . and the shims . . .

64 Fit the shims onto the front of the armature (see illustration). Insert the armature into the main housing, noting that it will be drawn in by the magnets, locating the shaft in the bush (see illustration).

65 Fit the sealing ring onto the rear of the housing if removed (see illustration). Fit the shims onto the shaft (see illustration). Align the marks between the housing and rear cover, then fit the armature into the offset opening in the brushplate, locating the commutator bars against the brushes, then press the brushes back into the holders until the armature shaft end locates in its hole in the cover (see illustration). Take care not to damage the brushes.

66 Fit the sealing ring onto the front of the housing if removed (see illustration). Lift the small gears off their posts and grease them (see illustration). Check that the locating pin is in the front cover. Fit the front cover onto

26.65c . . . then fit the rear cover as described

26.66a Fit the sealing ring

26.66b Grease the posts, and make sure the locating pin (arrowed) is fitted . . .

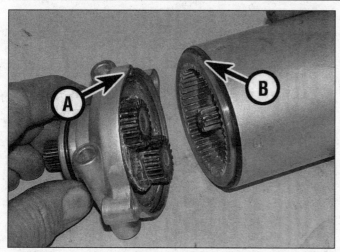

26.66c . . . then fit the front cover aligning the pin (A) with the cut-out (B)

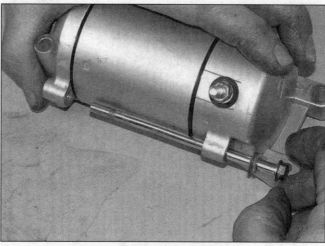

26.67 Fit the bolts and tighten them

the housing, aligning the pin with the cut-out **(see illustration)**.

67 Check the marks made on removal are correctly aligned, then install the long bolts with their washers and tighten them **(see illustration)**.

68 Install the starter motor (see Section 25).

27 Charging system testing

1 If the performance of the charging system is suspect, the system as a whole should be checked first, followed by testing of the individual components. **Note:** *Before beginning the checks, make sure the battery is fully charged and that all system connections are clean and tight.*

2 Checking the output of the charging system and the performance of the various components within the charging system requires the use of a multimeter (with voltage, current, and resistance functions). If a multimeter is not available, the job of checking the charging system should be left to a dealer.

3 When making the checks, follow the procedures carefully to prevent incorrect connections or short circuits resulting in irreparable damage to electrical system components.

Leakage test

Caution: Always connect an ammeter in series, never in parallel with the battery, otherwise it will be damaged. Do not turn the ignition ON or operate the starter motor when the ammeter is connected – a sudden surge in current will blow the meter's fuse.

4 Ensure the ignition is OFF, then disconnect the battery negative (-) lead (see Section 3).

5 Set the multimeter to the Amps function and connect its negative (-) probe to the battery negative (-) terminal, and positive (+)

probe to the disconnected negative (-) lead **(see illustration)**. Always set the meter to a high amps range initially and then bring it down to the mA (milli Amps) range; if there is a high current flow in the circuit it may blow the meter's fuse.

6 Battery current leakage should not exceed 0.1 mAmp. If a higher leakage rate is shown there is a short circuit in the wiring, although if an after-market immobiliser or alarm is fitted, its current draw should be taken into account. Disconnect the meter and reconnect the battery negative (-) lead.

7 Systematically disconnect individual electrical components and repeat the test until the source is identified.

Regulated output test

8 Refer to Section 3 to access the battery. Start the engine and warm it up.

9 To check the regulated (DC) voltage output, allow the engine to idle. Connect a multimeter set to the 0-20 volts DC scale across the terminals of the battery with the positive (+) meter probe to battery positive (+) terminal

and the negative (-) meter probe to battery negative (-) terminal **(see illustration)**. There should be a voltage reading of around 12 to 13 volts.

10 Slowly increase the engine speed to 5000 rpm and note the reading obtained – it should rise slightly and show between 13.5 to 15 volts. If the regulated voltage output is outside the specification, check the stator coil (see below) and the regulator (see Section 28).

> **HAYNES HiNT**
> *Clues to a faulty regulator are constantly blowing bulbs, with brightness varying considerably with engine speed, and battery overheating.*

Stator coil check

11 Trace the wiring from the alternator on the left-hand side of the engine and disconnect it at the connector with two or three wires the same colour (often yellow, sometimes white) – remove the seat or side cover (see Chapter 8) or the fuel tank (see Chapter 4) as

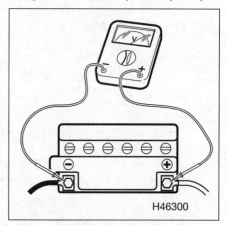

27.5 Checking the charging system leakage rate – connect the meter as shown

H46302

27.9 Checking regulated voltage output – connect the meter as shown

H46300

28.2a Regulator/rectifier mounted to the frame behind the engine (arrowed)

28.2b Regulator/rectifier mounted to the front of the frame – remove the fuel tank for access (arrowed)

required.Check the connector terminals for corrosion and security.

12 Using a multimeter set to the ohms x 1 (ohmmeter) scale measure the resistance of the stator coil(s) as described according to model, as follows:

13 On models with two wires, measure between the two wire terminals on the alternator side of the connector, then check for continuity between each terminal and earth.

14 On models with three wires measure between each pair of wire terminals on the alternator side of the connector, taking a total of three readings, then check for continuity between each terminal and earth.

15 If the coil windings are in good condition there should be a small resistance of 0.5 to 1 ohm, sometimes a bit more, and there should be no continuity (infinite resistance) between the terminals and earth. If not, the alternator stator coil assembly is at fault and should be replaced with a new one. **Note:** *Before*

condemning the stator coils, check the fault is not due to damaged wiring between the connector and the coils.

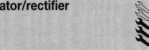

28 Regulator/rectifier

Check

1 No test details are given for the regulator/rectifier. If having checked the charging system as in Section 27 there is obviously a problem, and the alternator stator and the wiring is all good, the regulator/rectifier unit is probably faulty. Take it to a dealer for confirmation of its condition before replacing it with a new one.

Removal and installation

2 The regulator/rectifier is a finned grey block a few inches wide **(see illustrations)**. Its location varies from model to model – you have to look for it, removing the seat, side

covers and fuel tank as required according to model until you find it (see Chapters 8 and 4).

3 Disconnect the regulator/rectifier wiring connector(s).

4 Unscrew the bolts securing the regulator/rectifier, noting the earth wire where fitted.

5 Fit the new unit and tighten its bolts, not forgetting the earth wire if fitted. Connect the wiring connector(s).

29 Wiring diagrams

1 The following wiring diagrams relate to a selection of the models covered by this manual. The electrical circuits are fairly straightforward and the diagrams will be a useful guide when working on other models.

2 Note that a wiring diagram is often included at the back of the owner's handbook, provided with the machine when new.

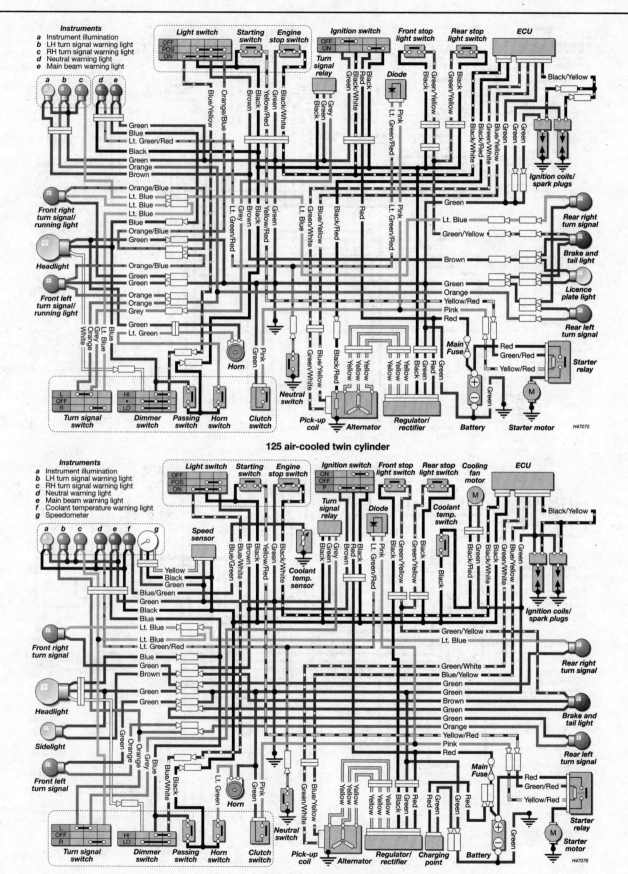

125 air-cooled twin cylinder

125 liquid-cooled twin cylinder

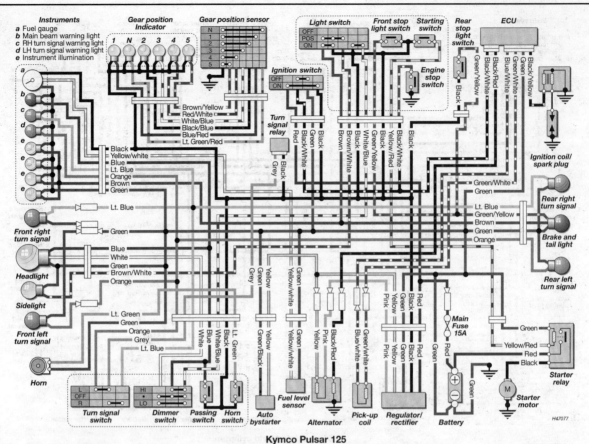

Kymco Pulsar 125

Kaisar XTR 125 (KS125-23) – early model

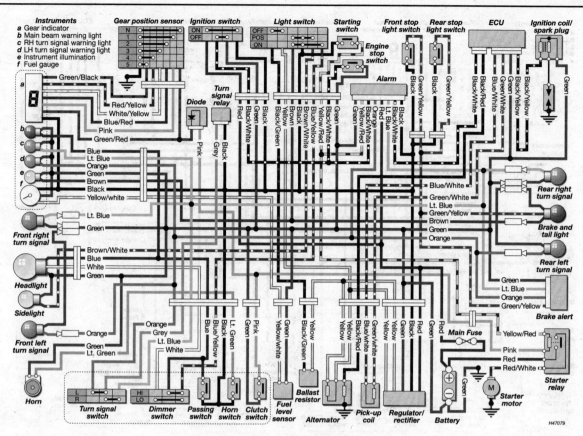

Lifan City X 125 (LF125-J)

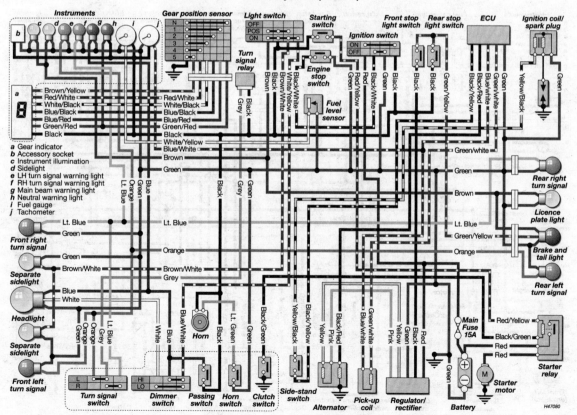

Pioneer Nevada 125 (XF125L-4B)

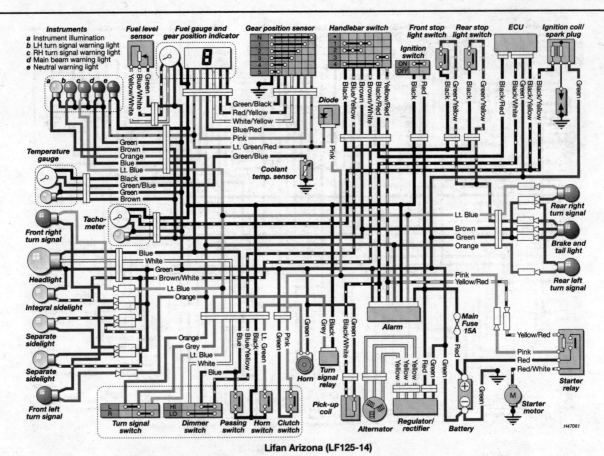

Lifan Arizona (LF125-14)

Lifan Arizona (LF125-14A)

Reference

Tools and Workshop Tips

Buying tools

A toolkit is a fundamental requirement for servicing and repairing a scooter. Although there will be an initial expense in building up enough tools for servicing, this will soon be offset by the savings made by doing the job yourself. As experience and confidence grow, additional tools can be added to enable the repair and overhaul of the scooter. Many of the specialist tools are expensive and not often used so it may be preferable to hire them, or for a group of friends or scooter club to join in the purchase.

As a rule, it is better to buy more expensive, good quality tools. Cheaper tools are likely to wear out faster and need to be renewed more often, nullifying the original saving.

 Warning: To avoid the risk of a poor quality tool breaking in use, causing injury or damage to the component being worked on, always aim to purchase tools which meet the relevant national safety standards.

The following lists of tools do not represent the manufacturer's service tools, but serve as a guide to help the owner decide which tools are needed for this level of work. In addition, items such as an electric drill, hacksaw, files, soldering iron and a workbench equipped with a vice, may be needed. Although not classed as tools, a selection of bolts, screws, nuts, washers and pieces of tubing always come in useful.

For more information about tools, refer to the Haynes *Motorcycle Workshop Practice Techbook* (Bk. No. 3470).

Manufacturer's service tools

Inevitably certain tasks require the use of a service tool. Where possible an alternative tool or method of approach is recommended, but sometimes there is no option if personal injury or damage to the component is to be avoided. Where required, service tools are referred to in the relevant procedure.

Service tools can usually only be purchased from a scooter dealer and are identified by a part number. Some of the commonly-used tools, such as rotor pullers, are available in aftermarket form from mail-order motorcycle tool and accessory suppliers.

Maintenance and minor repair tools

☐ Set of flat-bladed screwdrivers-
☐ Set of Phillips head screwdrivers
☐ Combination open-end and ring spanners
☐ Socket set (3/8 inch or 1/2 inch drive)
☐ Set of Allen keys or bits
☐ Set of Torx keys or bits
☐ Pliers, cutters and self-locking grips (Mole grips)
☐ Adjustable spanners
☐ C-spanners
☐ Tread depth gauge and tyre pressure gauge
☐ Cable oiler clamp
☐ Feeler gauges
☐ Spark plug gap measuring tool
☐ Spark plug spanner or deep plug sockets
☐ Wire brush and emery paper
☐ Calibrated syringe, measuring vessel and funnel

☐ Oil filter adapters (4-stroke engines)
☐ Oil drainer can or tray
☐ Pump type oil can
☐ Grease gun
☐ Straight-edge and steel rule
☐ Continuity tester
☐ Battery charger
☐ Hydrometer (for battery specific gravity check)
☐ Anti-freeze tester (for liquid-cooled engines)

Repair and overhaul tools

☐ Torque wrench (small and mid-ranges)
☐ Conventional, plastic or soft-faced hammers
☐ Impact driver set
☐ Vernier gauge
☐ Circlip pliers (internal and external, or combination)
☐ Set of cold chisels and punches
☐ Selection of pullers
☐ Breaker bars
☐ One-man brake bleeder kit
☐ Wire stripper and crimper tool
☐ Multimeter (measures amps, volts and ohms)
☐ Stroboscope (for dynamic timing checks)
☐ Hose clamp
☐ Clutch holding tool

Specialist tools

☐ Micrometers (external type)
☐ Telescoping gauges
☐ Dial gauge
☐ Stud extractor
☐ Screw extractor set
☐ Bearing driver set
☐ Valve spring compressor (4-stroke engines)
☐ Piston pin drawbolt tool
☐ Piston ring clamp

1 Workshop equipment and facilities

The workbench

● Work is made much easier by raising the bike up on a ramp - components are much more accessible if raised to waist level. The hydraulic or pneumatic types seen in the dealer's workshop are a sound investment if you undertake a lot of repairs or overhauls **(see illustration 1.1)**.

1.1 Hydraulic motorcycle ramp

● If raised off ground level, the bike must be supported on the ramp to avoid it falling. Most ramps incorporate a front wheel locating clamp which can be adjusted to suit different diameter wheels. When tightening the clamp, take care not to mark the wheel rim or damage the tyre - use wood blocks on each side to prevent this.
● Secure the bike to the ramp using tie-downs **(see illustration 1.2)**. If the bike has only a sidestand, and hence leans at a dangerous angle when raised, support the bike on an auxiliary stand.

1.2 Tie-downs are used around the passenger footrests to secure the bike

● Auxiliary (paddock) stands are widely available from mail order companies or motorcycle dealers and attach either to the wheel axle or swingarm pivot **(see illustration 1.3)**. If the motorcycle has a centrestand, you can support it under the crankcase to prevent it toppling whilst either wheel is removed **(see illustration 1.4)**.

1.3 This auxiliary stand attaches to the swingarm pivot

1.4 Always use a block of wood between the engine and jack head when supporting the engine in this way

Fumes and fire

● Refer to the Safety first! page at the beginning of the manual for full details. Make sure your workshop is equipped with a fire extinguisher suitable for fuel-related fires (Class B fire - flammable liquids) - it is not sufficient to have a water-filled extinguisher.
● Always ensure adequate ventilation is available. Unless an exhaust gas extraction system is available for use, ensure that the engine is run outside of the workshop.
● If working on the fuel system, make sure the workshop is ventilated to avoid a build-up of fumes. This applies equally to fume build-up when charging a battery. Do not smoke or allow anyone else to smoke in the workshop.

Fluids

● If you need to drain fuel from the tank, store it in an approved container marked as suitable for the storage of petrol (gasoline) **(see illustration 1.5)**. Do not store fuel in glass jars or bottles.

1.5 Use an approved can only for storing petrol (gasoline)

● Use proprietary engine degreasers or solvents which have a high flash-point, such as paraffin (kerosene), for cleaning off oil, grease and dirt - never use petrol (gasoline) for cleaning. Wear rubber gloves when handling solvent and engine degreaser. The fumes from certain solvents can be dangerous - always work in a well-ventilated area.

Dust, eye and hand protection

● Protect your lungs from inhalation of dust particles by wearing a filtering mask over the nose and mouth. Many frictional materials still contain asbestos which is dangerous to your health. Protect your eyes from spouts of liquid and sprung components by wearing a pair of protective goggles **(see illustration 1.6)**.

1.6 A fire extinguisher, goggles, mask and protective gloves should be at hand in the workshop

● Protect your hands from contact with solvents, fuel and oils by wearing rubber gloves. Alternatively apply a barrier cream to your hands before starting work. If handling hot components or fluids, wear suitable gloves to protect your hands from scalding and burns.

What to do with old fluids

● Old cleaning solvent, fuel, coolant and oils should not be poured down domestic drains or onto the ground. Package the fluid up in old oil containers, label it accordingly, and take it to a garage or disposal facility. Contact your local authority for location of such sites or ring the oil care hotline.

OIL CARE
FOLLOW THE CODE

Note: It is antisocial and illegal to dump oil down the drain. To find the location of your local oil recycling bank in the UK, call 03708 506 506 or visit www.oilbankline.org.uk

In the USA, note that any oil supplier must accept used oil for recycling.

2 Fasteners - screws, bolts and nuts

Fastener types and applications

Bolts and screws

● Fastener head types are either of hexagonal, Torx or splined design, with internal and external versions of each type **(see illustrations 2.1 and 2.2)**; splined head fasteners are not in common use on motorcycles. The conventional slotted or Phillips head design is used for certain screws. Bolt or screw length is always measured from the underside of the head to the end of the item **(see illustration 2.11)**.

2.1 Internal hexagon/Allen (A), Torx (B) and splined (C) fasteners, with corresponding bits

2.2 External Torx (A), splined (B) and hexagon (C) fasteners, with corresponding sockets

● Certain fasteners on the motorcycle have a tensile marking on their heads, the higher the marking the stronger the fastener. High tensile fasteners generally carry a 10 or higher marking. Never replace a high tensile fastener with one of a lower tensile strength.

Washers (see illustration 2.3)

● Plain washers are used between a fastener head and a component to prevent damage to the component or to spread the load when torque is applied. Plain washers can also be used as spacers or shims in certain assemblies. Copper or aluminium plain washers are often used as sealing washers on drain plugs.

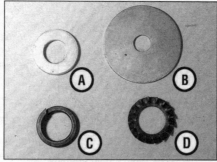

2.3 Plain washer (A), penny washer (B), spring washer (C) and serrated washer (D)

● The split-ring spring washer works by applying axial tension between the fastener head and component. If flattened, it is fatigued and must be renewed. If a plain (flat) washer is used on the fastener, position the spring washer between the fastener and the plain washer.

● Serrated star type washers dig into the fastener and component faces, preventing loosening. They are often used on electrical earth (ground) connections to the frame.

● Cone type washers (sometimes called Belleville) are conical and when tightened apply axial tension between the fastener head and component. They must be installed with the dished side against the component and often carry an OUTSIDE marking on their outer face. If flattened, they are fatigued and must be renewed.

● Tab washers are used to lock plain nuts or bolts on a shaft. A portion of the tab washer is bent up hard against one flat of the nut or bolt to prevent it loosening. Due to the tab washer being deformed in use, a new tab washer should be used every time it is disturbed.

● Wave washers are used to take up endfloat on a shaft. They provide light springing and prevent excessive side-to-side play of a component. Can be found on rocker arm shafts.

Nuts and split pins

● Conventional plain nuts are usually six-sided **(see illustration 2.4)**. They are sized by thread diameter and pitch. High tensile nuts carry a number on one end to denote their tensile strength.

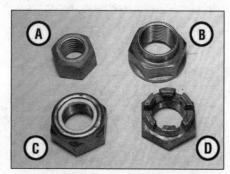

2.4 Plain nut (A), shouldered locknut (B), nylon insert nut (C) and castellated nut (D)

● Self-locking nuts either have a nylon insert, or two spring metal tabs, or a shoulder which is staked into a groove in the shaft - their advantage over conventional plain nuts is a resistance to loosening due to vibration. The nylon insert type can be used a number of times, but must be renewed when the friction of the nylon insert is reduced, ie when the nut spins freely on the shaft. The spring tab type can be reused unless the tabs are damaged. The shouldered type must be renewed every time it is disturbed.

● Split pins (cotter pins) are used to lock a castellated nut to a shaft or to prevent slackening of a plain nut. Common applications are wheel axles and brake torque arms. Because the split pin arms are deformed to lock around the nut a new split pin must always be used on installation - always fit the correct size split pin which will fit snugly in the shaft hole. Make sure the split pin arms are correctly located around the nut **(see illustrations 2.5 and 2.6)**.

2.5 Bend split pin (cotter pin) arms as shown (arrows) to secure a castellated nut

2.6 Bend split pin (cotter pin) arms as shown to secure a plain nut

Caution: If the castellated nut slots do not align with the shaft hole after tightening to the torque setting, tighten the nut until the next slot aligns with the hole - never slacken the nut to align its slot.

● R-pins (shaped like the letter R), or slip pins as they are sometimes called, are sprung and can be reused if they are otherwise in good condition. Always install R-pins with their closed end facing forwards **(see illustration 2.7)**.

2.7 Correct fitting of R-pin. Arrow indicates forward direction

Circlips (see illustration 2.8)

● Circlips (sometimes called snap-rings) are used to retain components on a shaft or in a housing and have corresponding external or internal ears to permit removal. Parallel-sided (machined) circlips can be installed either way round in their groove, whereas stamped circlips (which have a chamfered edge on one face) must be installed with the chamfer facing away from the direction of thrust load **(see illustration 2.9)**.

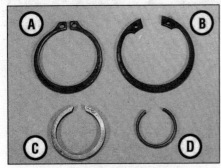

2.8 External stamped circlip (A), internal stamped circlip (B), machined circlip (C) and wire circlip (D)

● Always use circlip pliers to remove and install circlips; expand or compress them just enough to remove them. After installation, rotate the circlip in its groove to ensure it is securely seated. If installing a circlip on a splined shaft, always align its opening with a shaft channel to ensure the circlip ends are well supported and unlikely to catch **(see illustration 2.10)**.

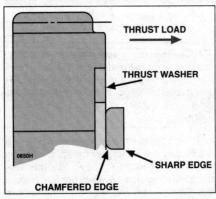

2.9 Correct fitting of a stamped circlip

THRUST LOAD
THRUST WASHER
SHARP EDGE
CHAMFERED EDGE
0650H

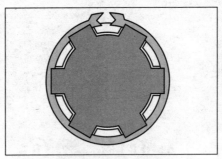

2.10 Align circlip opening with shaft channel

● Circlips can wear due to the thrust of components and become loose in their grooves, with the subsequent danger of becoming dislodged in operation. For this reason, renewal is advised every time a circlip is disturbed.

● Wire circlips are commonly used as piston pin retaining clips. If a removal tang is provided, long-nosed pliers can be used to dislodge them, otherwise careful use of a small flat-bladed screwdriver is necessary. Wire circlips should be renewed every time they are disturbed.

Thread diameter and pitch

● Diameter of a male thread (screw, bolt or stud) is the outside diameter of the threaded portion **(see illustration 2.11)**. Most motorcycle manufacturers use the ISO (International Standards Organisation) metric system expressed in millimetres, eg M6 refers to a 6 mm diameter thread. Sizing is the same for nuts, except that the thread diameter is measured across the valleys of the nut.

● Pitch is the distance between the peaks of the thread **(see illustration 2.11)**. It is expressed in millimetres, thus a common bolt size may be expressed as 6.0 x 1.0 mm (6 mm thread diameter and 1 mm pitch). Generally pitch increases in proportion to thread diameter, although there are always exceptions.

● Thread diameter and pitch are related for conventional fastener applications and the accompanying table can be used as a guide. Additionally, the AF (Across Flats), spanner or socket size dimension of the bolt or nut **(see illustration 2.11)** is linked to thread and pitch specification. Thread pitch can be measured with a thread gauge **(see illustration 2.12)**.

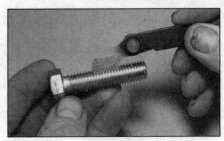

2.12 Using a thread gauge to measure pitch

AF size	Thread diameter x pitch (mm)
8 mm	M5 x 0.8
8 mm	M6 x 1.0
10 mm	M6 x 1.0
12 mm	M8 x 1.25
14 mm	M10 x 1.25
17 mm	M12 x 1.25

● The threads of most fasteners are of the right-hand type, ie they are turned clockwise to tighten and anti-clockwise to loosen. The reverse situation applies to left-hand thread fasteners, which are turned anti-clockwise to tighten and clockwise to loosen. Left-hand threads are used where rotation of a component might loosen a conventional right-hand thread fastener.

Seized fasteners

● Corrosion of external fasteners due to water or reaction between two dissimilar metals can occur over a period of time. It will build up sooner in wet conditions or in countries where salt is used on the roads during the winter. If a fastener is severely corroded it is likely that normal methods of removal will fail and result in its head being ruined. When you attempt removal, the fastener thread should be heard to crack free and unscrew easily - if it doesn't, stop there before damaging something.

● A smart tap on the head of the fastener will often succeed in breaking free corrosion which has occurred in the threads **(see illustration 2.13)**.

● An aerosol penetrating fluid (such as WD-40) applied the night beforehand may work its way down into the thread and ease removal. Depending on the location, you may be able to make up a Plasticine well around the fastener head and fill it with penetrating fluid.

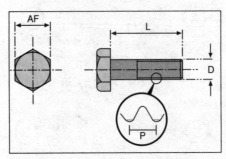

AF
L
D
P

2.11 Fastener length (L), thread diameter (D), thread pitch (P) and head size (AF)

2.13 A sharp tap on the head of a fastener will often break free a corroded thread

● If you are working on an engine internal component, corrosion will most likely not be a problem due to the well lubricated environment. However, components can be very tight and an impact driver is a useful tool in freeing them **(see illustration 2.14)**.

2.14 Using an impact driver to free a fastener

● Where corrosion has occurred between dissimilar metals (eg steel and aluminium alloy), the application of heat to the fastener head will create a disproportionate expansion rate between the two metals and break the seizure caused by the corrosion. Whether heat can be applied depends on the location of the fastener - any surrounding components likely to be damaged must first be removed **(see illustration 2.15)**. Heat can be applied using a paint stripper heat gun or clothes iron, or by immersing the component in boiling water - wear protective gloves to prevent scalding or burns to the hands.

2.15 Using heat to free a seized fastener

● As a last resort, it is possible to use a hammer and cold chisel to work the fastener head unscrewed **(see illustration 2.16)**. This will damage the fastener, but more importantly extreme care must be taken not to damage the surrounding component.

Caution: Remember that the component being secured is generally of more value than the bolt, nut or screw - when the fastener is freed, do not unscrew it with force, instead work the fastener back and forth when resistance is felt to prevent thread damage.

2.16 Using a hammer and chisel to free a seized fastener

Broken fasteners and damaged heads

● If the shank of a broken bolt or screw is accessible you can grip it with self-locking grips. The knurled wheel type stud extractor tool or self-gripping stud puller tool is particularly useful for removing the long studs which screw into the cylinder mouth surface of the crankcase or bolts and screws from which the head has broken off **(see illustration 2.17)**. Studs can also be removed by locking two nuts together on the threaded end of the stud and using a spanner on the lower nut **(see illustration 2.18)**.

2.17 Using a stud extractor tool to remove a broken crankcase stud

2.18 Two nuts can be locked together to unscrew a stud from a component

● A bolt or screw which has broken off below or level with the casing must be extracted using a screw extractor set. Centre punch the fastener to centralise the drill bit, then drill a hole in the fastener **(see illustration 2.19)**. Select a drill bit which is approximately half to three-quarters the diameter of the fastener

2.19 When using a screw extractor, first drill a hole in the fastener . . .

and drill to a depth which will accommodate the extractor. Use the largest size extractor possible, but avoid leaving too small a wall thickness otherwise the extractor will merely force the fastener walls outwards wedging it in the casing thread.

● If a spiral type extractor is used, thread it anti-clockwise into the fastener. As it is screwed in, it will grip the fastener and unscrew it from the casing **(see illustration 2.20)**.

2.20 . . . then thread the extractor anti-clockwise into the fastener

● If a taper type extractor is used, tap it into the fastener so that it is firmly wedged in place. Unscrew the extractor (anti-clockwise) to draw the fastener out.

Warning: Stud extractors are very hard and may break off in the fastener if care is not taken - ask an engineer about spark erosion if this happens.

● Alternatively, the broken bolt/screw can be drilled out and the hole retapped for an oversize bolt/screw or a diamond-section thread insert. It is essential that the drilling is carried out squarely and to the correct depth, otherwise the casing may be ruined - if in doubt, entrust the work to an engineer.

● Bolts and nuts with rounded corners cause the correct size spanner or socket to slip when force is applied. Of the types of spanner/socket available always use a six-point type rather than an eight or twelve-point type - better grip

2.21 Comparison of surface drive ring spanner (left) with 12-point type (right)

is obtained. Surface drive spanners grip the middle of the hex flats, rather than the corners, and are thus good in cases of damaged heads **(see illustration 2.21)**.

● Slotted-head or Phillips-head screws are often damaged by the use of the wrong size screwdriver. Allen-head and Torx-head screws are much less likely to sustain damage. If enough of the screw head is exposed you can use a hacksaw to cut a slot in its head and then use a conventional flat-bladed screwdriver to remove it. Alternatively use a hammer and cold chisel to tap the head of the fastener around to slacken it. Always replace damaged fasteners with new ones, preferably Torx or Allen-head type.

A dab of valve grinding compound between the screw head and screwdriver tip will often give a good grip.

Thread repair

● Threads (particularly those in aluminium alloy components) can be damaged by overtightening, being assembled with dirt in the threads, or from a component working loose and vibrating. Eventually the thread will fail completely, and it will be impossible to tighten the fastener.

● If a thread is damaged or clogged with old locking compound it can be renovated with a thread repair tool (thread chaser) **(see illustrations 2.22 and 2.23)**; special thread

2.22 A thread repair tool being used to correct an internal thread

2.23 A thread repair tool being used to correct an external thread

chasers are available for spark plug hole threads. The tool will not cut a new thread, but clean and true the original thread. Make sure that you use the correct diameter and pitch tool. Similarly, external threads can be cleaned up with a die or a thread restorer file **(see illustration 2.24)**.

2.24 Using a thread restorer file

● It is possible to drill out the old thread and retap the component to the next thread size. This will work where there is enough surrounding material and a new bolt or screw can be obtained. Sometimes, however, this is not possible - such as where the bolt/screw passes through another component which must also be suitably modified, also in cases where a spark plug or oil drain plug cannot be obtained in a larger diameter thread size.

● The diamond-section thread insert (often known by its popular trade name of Heli-Coil) is a simple and effective method of renewing the thread and retaining the original size. A kit can be purchased which contains the tap, insert and installing tool **(see illustration 2.25)**. Drill out the damaged thread with the size drill specified **(see illustration 2.26)**. Carefully retap the thread **(see illustration 2.27)**. Install the

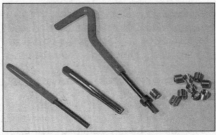

2.25 Obtain a thread insert kit to suit the thread diameter and pitch required

2.26 To install a thread insert, first drill out the original thread . . .

2.27 . . . tap a new thread . . .

2.28 . . . fit insert on the installing tool . . .

2.29 . . . and thread into the component . . .

2.30 . . . break off the tang when complete

insert on the installing tool and thread it slowly into place using a light downward pressure **(see illustrations 2.28 and 2.29)**. When positioned between a 1/4 and 1/2 turn below the surface withdraw the installing tool and use the break-off tool to press down on the tang, breaking it off **(see illustration 2.30)**.

● There are epoxy thread repair kits on the market which can rebuild stripped internal threads, although this repair should not be used on high load-bearing components.

Thread locking and sealing compounds

● Locking compounds are used in locations where the fastener is prone to loosening due to vibration or on important safety-related items which might cause loss of control of the motorcycle if they fail. It is also used where important fasteners cannot be secured by other means such as lockwashers or split pins.

● Before applying locking compound, make sure that the threads (internal and external) are clean and dry with all old compound removed. Select a compound to suit the component being secured - a non-permanent general locking and sealing type is suitable for most applications, but a high strength type is needed for permanent fixing of studs in castings. Apply a drop or two of the compound to the first few threads of the fastener, then thread it into place and tighten to the specified torque. Do not apply excessive thread locking compound otherwise the thread may be damaged on subsequent removal.

● Certain fasteners are impregnated with a dry film type coating of locking compound on their threads. Always renew this type of fastener if disturbed.

● Anti-seize compounds, such as copper-based greases, can be applied to protect threads from seizure due to extreme heat and corrosion. A common instance is spark plug threads and exhaust system fasteners.

3 Measuring tools and gauges

Feeler gauges

● Feeler gauges (or blades) are used for measuring small gaps and clearances (see illustration 3.1). They can also be used to measure endfloat (sideplay) of a component on a shaft where access is not possible with a dial gauge.

● Feeler gauge sets should be treated with care and not bent or damaged. They are etched with their size on one face. Keep them clean and very lightly oiled to prevent corrosion build-up.

3.1 Feeler gauges are used for measuring small gaps and clearances - thickness is marked on one face of gauge

● When measuring a clearance, select a gauge which is a light sliding fit between the two components. You may need to use two gauges together to measure the clearance accurately.

Micrometers

● A micrometer is a precision tool capable of measuring to 0.01 or 0.001 of a millimetre. It should always be stored in its case and not in the general toolbox. It must be kept clean and never dropped, otherwise its frame or measuring anvils could be distorted resulting in inaccurate readings.

● External micrometers are used for measuring outside diameters of components and have many more applications than internal micrometers. Micrometers are available in different size ranges, eg 0 to 25 mm, 25 to 50 mm, and upwards in 25 mm steps; some large micrometers have interchangeable anvils to allow a range of measurements to be taken. Generally the largest precision measurement you are likely to take on a motorcycle is the piston diameter.

● Internal micrometers (or bore micrometers) are used for measuring inside diameters, such as valve guides and cylinder bores. Telescoping gauges and small hole gauges are used in conjunction with an external micrometer, whereas the more expensive internal micrometers have their own measuring device.

External micrometer

Note: *The conventional analogue type instrument is described. Although much easier to read, digital micrometers are considerably more expensive.*

● Always check the calibration of the micrometer before use. With the anvils closed (0 to 25 mm type) or set over a test gauge

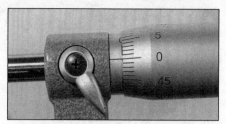

3.2 Check micrometer calibration before use

(for the larger types) the scale should read zero **(see illustration 3.2)**; make sure that the anvils (and test piece) are clean first. Any discrepancy can be adjusted by referring to the instructions supplied with the tool. Remember that the micrometer is a precision measuring tool - don't force the anvils closed, use the ratchet (4) on the end of the micrometer to close it. In this way, a measured force is always applied.

● To use, first make sure that the item being measured is clean. Place the anvil of the micrometer (1) against the item and use the thimble (2) to bring the spindle (3) lightly into contact with the other side of the item **(see illustration 3.3)**. Don't tighten the thimble down because this will damage the micrometer - instead use the ratchet (4) on the end of the micrometer. The ratchet mechanism applies a measured force preventing damage to the instrument.

● The micrometer is read by referring to the linear scale on the sleeve and the annular scale on the thimble. Read off the sleeve first to obtain the base measurement, then add the fine measurement from the thimble to obtain the overall reading. The linear scale on the sleeve represents the measuring range of the micrometer (eg 0 to 25 mm). The annular scale

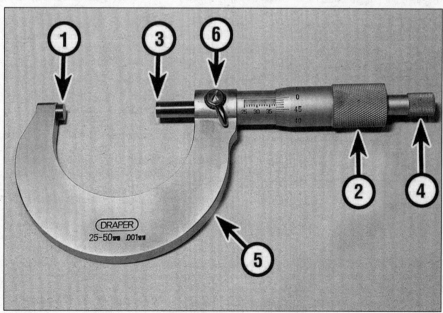

3.3 Micrometer component parts

1	Anvil	3	Spindle	5	Frame
2	Thimble	4	Ratchet	6	Locking lever

on the thimble will be in graduations of 0.01 mm (or as marked on the frame) - one full revolution of the thimble will move 0.5 mm on the linear scale. Take the reading where the datum line on the sleeve intersects the thimble's scale. Always position the eye directly above the scale otherwise an inaccurate reading will result.

In the example shown the item measures 2.95 mm **(see illustration 3.4)**:

Linear scale	2.00 mm
Linear scale	0.50 mm
Annular scale	0.45 mm
Total figure	2.95 mm

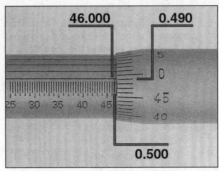

3.5 Micrometer reading of 46.99 mm on linear and annular scales . . .

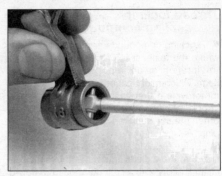

3.7 Expand the telescoping gauge in the bore, lock its position . . .

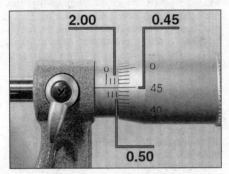

3.4 Micrometer reading of 2.95 mm

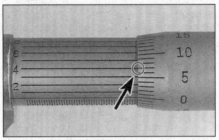

3.6 . . . and 0.004 mm on vernier scale

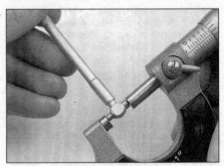

3.8 . . . then measure the gauge with a micrometer

Most micrometers have a locking lever (6) on the frame to hold the setting in place, allowing the item to be removed from the micrometer.
● Some micrometers have a vernier scale on their sleeve, providing an even finer measurement to be taken, in 0.001 increments of a millimetre. Take the sleeve and thimble measurement as described above, then check which graduation on the vernier scale aligns with that of the annular scale on the thimble **Note:** *The eye must be perpendicular to the scale when taking the vernier reading - if necessary rotate the body of the micrometer to ensure this.* Multiply the vernier scale figure by 0.001 and add it to the base and fine measurement figures.

In the example shown the item measures 46.994 mm **(see illustrations 3.5 and 3.6)**:

Linear scale (base)	46.000 mm
Linear scale (base)	00.500 mm
Annular scale (fine)	00.490 mm
Vernier scale	00.004 mm
Total figure	46.994 mm

Internal micrometer

● Internal micrometers are available for measuring bore diameters, but are expensive and unlikely to be available for home use. It is suggested that a set of telescoping gauges and small hole gauges, both of which must be used with an external micrometer, will suffice for taking internal measurements on a motorcycle.
● Telescoping gauges can be used to

measure internal diameters of components. Select a gauge with the correct size range, make sure its ends are clean and insert it into the bore. Expand the gauge, then lock its position and withdraw it from the bore **(see illustration 3.7)**. Measure across the gauge ends with a micrometer **(see illustration 3.8)**.
● Very small diameter bores (such as valve guides) are measured with a small hole gauge. Once adjusted to a slip-fit inside the component, its position is locked and the gauge withdrawn for measurement with a micrometer **(see illustrations 3.9 and 3.10)**.

Vernier caliper

Note: *The conventional linear and dial gauge type instruments are described. Digital types are easier to read, but are far more expensive.*
● The vernier caliper does not provide the precision of a micrometer, but is versatile in being able to measure internal and external diameters. Some types also incorporate a depth gauge. It is ideal for measuring clutch plate friction material and spring free lengths.
● To use the conventional linear scale vernier, slacken off the vernier clamp screws (1) and set its jaws over (2), or inside (3), the item to be measured **(see illustration 3.11)**. Slide the jaw into contact, using the thumbwheel (4) for fine movement of the sliding scale (5) then tighten the clamp screws (1). Read off the main scale (6) where the zero on the sliding scale (5) intersects it, taking the whole number to the left of the zero; this provides the base measurement. View along the sliding scale and select the division which

3.9 Expand the small hole gauge in the bore, lock its position . . .

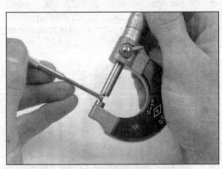

3.10 . . . then measure the gauge with a micrometer

lines up exactly with any of the divisions on the main scale, noting that the divisions usually represents 0.02 of a millimetre. Add this fine measurement to the base measurement to obtain the total reading.

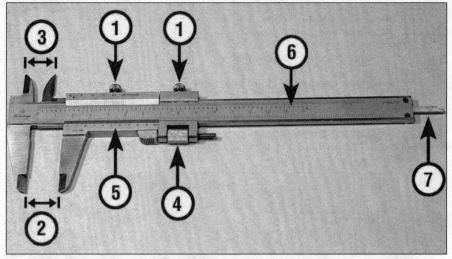

3.11 Vernier component parts (linear gauge)

1	Clamp screws	3	Internal jaws	5	Sliding scale	7	Depth gauge
2	External jaws	4	Thumbwheel	6	Main scale		

In the example shown the item measures 55.92 mm (see illustration 3.12):

Base measurement	55.00 mm
Fine measurement	00.92 mm
Total figure	55.92 mm

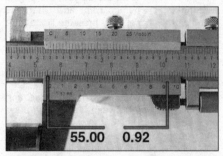

3.12 Vernier gauge reading of 55.92 mm

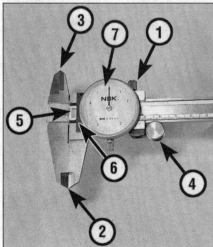

3.13 Vernier component parts (dial gauge)

1	Clamp screw	5	Main scale
2	External jaws	6	Sliding scale
3	Internal jaws	7	Dial gauge
4	Thumbwheel		

● Some vernier calipers are equipped with a dial gauge for fine measurement. Before use, check that the jaws are clean, then close them fully and check that the dial gauge reads zero. If necessary adjust the gauge ring accordingly. Slacken the vernier clamp screw (1) and set its jaws over (2), or inside (3), the item to be measured (see illustration 3.13). Slide the jaws into contact, using the thumbwheel (4) for fine movement. Read off the main scale (5) where the edge of the sliding scale (6) intersects it, taking the whole number to the left of the zero; this provides the base measurement. Read off the needle position on the dial gauge (7) scale to provide the fine measurement; each division represents 0.05 of a millimetre. Add this fine measurement to the base measurement to obtain the total reading.

In the example shown the item measures 55.95 mm (see illustration 3.14):

Base measurement	55.00 mm
Fine measurement	00.95 mm
Total figure	55.95 mm

3.14 Vernier gauge reading of 55.95 mm

Plastigauge

● Plastigauge is a plastic material which can be compressed between two surfaces to measure the oil clearance between them. The width of the compressed Plastigauge is measured against a calibrated scale to determine the clearance.

● Common uses of Plastigauge are for measuring the clearance between crankshaft journal and main bearing inserts, between crankshaft journal and big-end bearing inserts, and between camshaft and bearing surfaces. The following example describes big-end oil clearance measurement.

● Handle the Plastigauge material carefully to prevent distortion. Using a sharp knife, cut a length which corresponds with the width of the bearing being measured and place it carefully across the journal so that it is parallel with the shaft (see illustration 3.15). Carefully install both bearing shells and the connecting rod. Without rotating the rod on the journal tighten its bolts or nuts (as applicable) to the specified torque. The connecting rod and bearings are then disassembled and the crushed Plastigauge examined.

3.15 Plastigauge placed across shaft journal

● Using the scale provided in the Plastigauge kit, measure the width of the material to determine the oil clearance (see illustration 3.16). Always remove all traces of Plastigauge after use using your fingernails.

Caution: Arriving at the correct clearance demands that the assembly is torqued correctly, according to the settings and sequence (where applicable) provided by the motorcycle manufacturer.

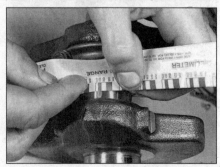

3.16 Measuring the width of the crushed Plastigauge

Dial gauge or DTI (Dial Test Indicator)

● A dial gauge can be used to accurately measure small amounts of movement. Typical uses are measuring shaft runout or shaft endfloat (sideplay) and setting piston position for ignition timing on two-strokes. A dial gauge set usually comes with a range of different probes and adapters and mounting equipment.

● The gauge needle must point to zero when at rest. Rotate the ring around its periphery to zero the gauge.

● Check that the gauge is capable of reading the extent of movement in the work. Most gauges have a small dial set in the face which records whole millimetres of movement as well as the fine scale around the face periphery which is calibrated in 0.01 mm divisions. Read off the small dial first to obtain the base measurement, then add the measurement from the fine scale to obtain the total reading.

In the example shown the gauge reads 1.48 mm (see illustration 3.17):

Base measurement	1.00 mm
Fine measurement	0.48 mm
Total figure	1.48 mm

3.17 Dial gauge reading of 1.48 mm

● If measuring shaft runout, the shaft must be supported in vee-blocks and the gauge mounted on a stand perpendicular to the shaft. Rest the tip of the gauge against the centre of the shaft and rotate the shaft slowly whilst watching the gauge reading (see illustration 3.18). Take several measurements along the length of the shaft and record the

3.18 Using a dial gauge to measure shaft runout

maximum gauge reading as the amount of runout in the shaft. **Note:** *The reading obtained will be total runout at that point - some manufacturers specify that the runout figure is halved to compare with their specified runout limit.*

● Endfloat (sideplay) measurement requires that the gauge is mounted securely to the surrounding component with its probe touching the end of the shaft. Using hand pressure, push and pull on the shaft noting the maximum endfloat recorded on the gauge (see illustration 3.19).

3.19 Using a dial gauge to measure shaft endfloat

● A dial gauge with suitable adapters can be used to determine piston position BTDC on two-stroke engines for the purposes of ignition timing. The gauge, adapter and suitable length probe are installed in the place of the spark plug and the gauge zeroed at TDC. If the piston position is specified as 1.14 mm BTDC, rotate the engine back to 2.00 mm BTDC, then slowly forwards to 1.14 mm BTDC.

Cylinder compression gauges

● A compression gauge is used for measuring cylinder compression. Either the rubber-cone type or the threaded adapter type can be used. The latter is preferred to ensure a perfect seal against the cylinder head. A 0 to 300 psi (0 to 20 Bar) type gauge (for petrol/gasoline engines) will be suitable for motorcycles.

● The spark plug is removed and the gauge either held hard against the cylinder head (cone type) or the gauge adapter screwed into the cylinder head (threaded type) (see illustration 3.20). Cylinder compression is measured with the engine turning over, but not running. The

3.20 Using a rubber-cone type cylinder compression gauge

gauge will hold the reading until manually released.

Oil pressure gauge

● An oil pressure gauge is used for measuring engine oil pressure. Most gauges come with a set of adapters to fit the thread of the take-off point (see illustration 3.21). If the take-off point specified by the motorcycle manufacturer is an external oil pipe union, make sure that the specified replacement union is used to prevent oil starvation.

3.21 Oil pressure gauge and take-off point adapter (arrow)

● Oil pressure is measured with the engine running (at a specific rpm) and often the manufacturer will specify pressure limits for a cold and hot engine.

Straight-edge and surface plate

● If checking the gasket face of a component for warpage, place a steel rule or precision straight-edge across the gasket face and measure any gap between the straight-edge and component with feeler gauges (see illustration 3.22). Check diagonally across the component and between mounting holes (see illustration 3.23).

3.22 Use a straight-edge and feeler gauges to check for warpage

3.23 Check for warpage in these directions

● Checking individual components for warpage, such as clutch plain (metal) plates, requires a perfectly flat plate or piece or plate glass and feeler gauges.

4 Torque and leverage

What is torque?

● Torque describes the twisting force about a shaft. The amount of torque applied is determined by the distance from the centre of the shaft to the end of the lever and the amount of force being applied to the end of the lever; distance multiplied by force equals torque.

● The manufacturer applies a measured torque to a bolt or nut to ensure that it will not slacken in use and to hold two components securely together without movement in the joint. The actual torque setting depends on the thread size, bolt or nut material and the composition of the components being held.

● Too little torque may cause the fastener to loosen due to vibration, whereas too much torque will distort the joint faces of the component or cause the fastener to shear off. Always stick to the specified torque setting.

Using a torque wrench

● Check the calibration of the torque wrench and make sure it has a suitable range for the job. Torque wrenches are available in Nm (Newton-metres), kgf m (kilograms-force metre), lbf ft (pounds-feet), lbf in (inch-pounds). Do not confuse lbf ft with lbf in.

● Adjust the tool to the desired torque on the scale (see illustration 4.1). If your torque wrench is not calibrated in the units specified, carefully convert the figure (see Conversion Factors). A manufacturer sometimes gives a torque setting as a range (8 to 10 Nm) rather than a single figure - in this case set the tool midway between the two settings. The same torque may be expressed as 9 Nm ± 1 Nm. Some torque wrenches have a method of locking the setting so that it isn't inadvertently altered during use.

4.1 Set the torque wrench index mark to the setting required, in this case 12 Nm

● Install the bolts/nuts in their correct location and secure them lightly. Their threads must be clean and free of any old locking compound. Unless specified the threads and flange should be dry - oiled threads are necessary in certain circumstances and the manufacturer will take this into account in the specified torque figure. Similarly, the manufacturer may also specify the application of thread-locking compound.

● Tighten the fasteners in the specified sequence until the torque wrench clicks, indicating that the torque setting has been reached. Apply the torque again to double-check the setting. Where different thread diameter fasteners secure the component, as a rule tighten the larger diameter ones first.

● When the torque wrench has been finished with, release the lock (where applicable) and fully back off its setting to zero - do not leave the torque wrench tensioned. Also, do not use a torque wrench for slackening a fastener.

Angle-tightening

● Manufacturers often specify a figure in degrees for final tightening of a fastener. This usually follows tightening to a specific torque setting.

● A degree disc can be set and attached to the socket (see illustration 4.2) or a protractor can be used to mark the angle of movement on the bolt/nut head and the surrounding casting (see illustration 4.3).

4.2 Angle tightening can be accomplished with a torque-angle gauge . . .

4.3 . . . or by marking the angle on the surrounding component

Loosening sequences

● Where more than one bolt/nut secures a component, loosen each fastener evenly a little at a time. In this way, not all the stress of the joint is held by one fastener and the components are not likely to distort.

● If a tightening sequence is provided, work in the REVERSE of this, but if not, work from the outside in, in a criss-cross sequence (see illustration 4.4).

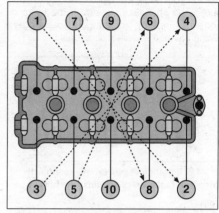

4.4 When slackening, work from the outside inwards

Tightening sequences

● If a component is held by more than one fastener it is important that the retaining bolts/nuts are tightened evenly to prevent uneven stress build-up and distortion of sealing faces. This is especially important on high-compression joints such as the cylinder head.

● A sequence is usually provided by the manufacturer, either in a diagram or actually marked in the casting. If not, always start in the centre and work outwards in a criss-cross pattern (see illustration 4.5). Start off by securing all bolts/nuts finger-tight, then set the torque wrench and tighten each fastener by a small amount in sequence until the final torque is reached. By following this practice, the joint

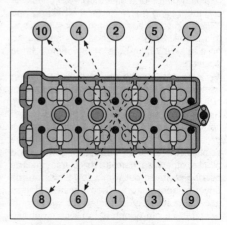

4.5 When tightening, work from the inside outwards

will be held evenly and will not be distorted. Important joints, such as the cylinder head and big-end fasteners often have two- or three-stage torque settings.

Applying leverage

● Use tools at the correct angle. Position a socket wrench or spanner on the bolt/nut so that you pull it towards you when loosening. If this can't be done, push the spanner without curling your fingers around it **(see illustration 4.6)** - the spanner may slip or the fastener loosen suddenly, resulting in your fingers being crushed against a component.

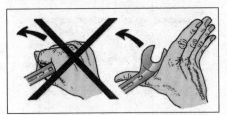

4.6 If you can't pull on the spanner to loosen a fastener, push with your hand open

● Additional leverage is gained by extending the length of the lever. The best way to do this is to use a breaker bar instead of the regular length tool, or to slip a length of tubing over the end of the spanner or socket wrench.
● If additional leverage will not work, the fastener head is either damaged or firmly corroded in place (see Fasteners).

5 Bearings

Bearing removal and installation

Drivers and sockets

● Before removing a bearing, always inspect the casing to see which way it must be driven out - some casings will have retaining plates or a cast step. Also check for any identifying markings on the bearing and if installed to a certain depth, measure this at this stage. Some roller bearings are sealed on one side - take note of the original fitted position.
● Bearings can be driven out of a casing using a bearing driver tool (with the correct size head) or a socket of the correct diameter. Select the driver head or socket so that it contacts the outer race of the bearing, not the balls/rollers or inner race. Always support the casing around the bearing housing with wood blocks, otherwise there is a risk of fracture. The bearing is driven out with a few blows on the driver or socket from a heavy mallet. Unless access is severely restricted (as with wheel bearings), a pin-punch is not recommended unless it is moved around the bearing to keep it square in its housing.

● The same equipment can be used to install bearings. Make sure the bearing housing is supported on wood blocks and line up the bearing in its housing. Fit the bearing as noted on removal - generally they are installed with their marked side facing outwards. Tap the bearing squarely into its housing using a driver or socket which bears only on the bearing's outer race - contact with the bearing balls/rollers or inner race will destroy it **(see illustrations 5.1 and 5.2)**.
● Check that the bearing inner race and balls/rollers rotate freely.

5.1 Using a bearing driver against the bearing's outer race

5.2 Using a large socket against the bearing's outer race

Pullers and slide-hammers

● Where a bearing is pressed on a shaft a puller will be required to extract it **(see illustration 5.3)**. Make sure that the puller clamp or legs fit securely behind the bearing and are unlikely to slip out. If pulling a bearing

5.3 This bearing puller clamps behind the bearing and pressure is applied to the shaft end to draw the bearing off

off a gear shaft for example, you may have to locate the puller behind a gear pinion if there is no access to the race and draw the gear pinion off the shaft as well **(see illustration 5.4)**.

> **Caution: Ensure that the puller's centre bolt locates securely against the end of the shaft and will not slip when pressure is applied. Also ensure that puller does not damage the shaft end.**

5.4 Where no access is available to the rear of the bearing, it is sometimes possible to draw off the adjacent component

● Operate the puller so that its centre bolt exerts pressure on the shaft end and draws the bearing off the shaft.
● When installing the bearing on the shaft, tap only on the bearing's inner race - contact with the balls/rollers or outer race with destroy the bearing. Use a socket or length of tubing as a drift which fits over the shaft end **(see illustration 5.5)**.

5.5 When installing a bearing on a shaft use a piece of tubing which bears only on the bearing's inner race

● Where a bearing locates in a blind hole in a casing, it cannot be driven or pulled out as described above. A slide-hammer with knife-edged bearing puller attachment will be required. The puller attachment passes through the bearing and when tightened expands to fit firmly behind the bearing **(see illustration 5.6)**. By operating the slide-hammer part of the tool the bearing is jarred out of its housing **(see illustration 5.7)**.
● It is possible, if the bearing is of reasonable weight, for it to drop out of its housing if the casing is heated as described opposite.

5.6 Expand the bearing puller so that it locks behind the bearing . . .

5.7 . . . attach the slide hammer to the bearing puller

If this method is attempted, first prepare a work surface which will enable the casing to be tapped face down to help dislodge the bearing - a wood surface is ideal since it will not damage the casing's gasket surface. Wearing protective gloves, tap the heated casing several times against the work surface to dislodge the bearing under its own weight **(see illustration 5.8)**.

5.8 Tapping a casing face down on wood blocks can often dislodge a bearing

● Bearings can be installed in blind holes using the driver or socket method described above.

Drawbolts

● Where a bearing or bush is set in the eye of a component, such as a suspension linkage arm or connecting rod small-end, removal by drift may damage the component. Furthermore, a rubber bushing in a shock absorber eye cannot successfully be driven out of position. If access is available to a engineering press, the task is straightforward. If not, a drawbolt can be fabricated to extract the bearing or bush.

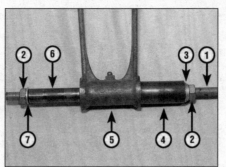

5.9 Drawbolt component parts assembled on a suspension arm

1 Bolt or length of threaded bar
2 Nuts
3 Washer (external diameter greater than tubing internal diameter)
4 Tubing (internal diameter sufficient to accommodate bearing)
5 Suspension arm with bearing
6 Tubing (external diameter slightly smaller than bearing)
7 Washer (external diameter slightly smaller than bearing)

5.10 Drawing the bearing out of the suspension arm

● To extract the bearing/bush you will need a long bolt with nut (or piece of threaded bar with two nuts), a piece of tubing which has an internal diameter larger than the bearing/ bush, another piece of tubing which has an external diameter slightly smaller than the bearing/bush, and a selection of washers **(see illustrations 5.9 and 5.10)**. Note that the pieces of tubing must be of the same length, or longer, than the bearing/bush.
● The same kit (without the pieces of tubing) can be used to draw the new bearing/bush back into place **(see illustration 5.11)**.

5.11 Installing a new bearing (1) in the suspension arm

Temperature change

● If the bearing's outer race is a tight fit in the casing, the aluminium casing can be heated to release its grip on the bearing. Aluminium will expand at a greater rate than the steel bearing outer race. There are several ways to do this, but avoid any localised extreme heat (such as a blow torch) - aluminium alloy has a low melting point.
● Approved methods of heating a casing are using a domestic oven (heated to 100°C) or immersing the casing in boiling water **(see illustration 5.12)**. Low temperature range localised heat sources such as a paint stripper heat gun or clothes iron can also be used **(see illustration 5.13)**. Alternatively, soak a rag in boiling water, wring it out and wrap it around the bearing housing.

> ⚠ **Warning: All of these methods require care in use to prevent scalding and burns to the hands. Wear protective gloves when handling hot components.**

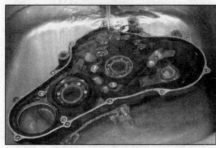

5.12 A casing can be immersed in a sink of boiling water to aid bearing removal

5.13 Using a localised heat source to aid bearing removal

● If heating the whole casing note that plastic components, such as the neutral switch, may suffer - remove them beforehand.
● After heating, remove the bearing as described above. You may find that the expansion is sufficient for the bearing to fall out of the casing under its own weight or with a light tap on the driver or socket.
● If necessary, the casing can be heated to aid bearing installation, and this is sometimes the recommended procedure if the motorcycle manufacturer has designed the housing and bearing fit with this intention.

● Installation of bearings can be eased by placing them in a freezer the night before installation. The steel bearing will contract slightly, allowing easy insertion in its housing. This is often useful when installing steering head outer races in the frame.

Bearing types and markings

● Plain shell bearings, ball bearings, needle roller bearings and tapered roller bearings will all be found on motorcycles (see illustrations 5.14 and 5.15). The ball and roller types are usually caged between an inner and outer race, but uncaged variations may be found.

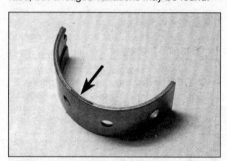

5.14 Shell bearings are either plain or grooved. They are usually identified by colour code (arrow)

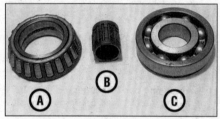

5.15 Tapered roller bearing (A), needle roller bearing (B) and ball journal bearing (C)

● Shell bearings (often called inserts) are usually found at the crankshaft main and connecting rod big-end where they are good at coping with high loads. They are made of a phosphor-bronze material and are impregnated with self-lubricating properties.
● Ball bearings and needle roller bearings consist of a steel inner and outer race with the balls or rollers between the races. They require constant lubrication by oil or grease and are good at coping with axial loads. Taper roller bearings consist of rollers set in a tapered cage set on the inner race; the outer race is separate. They are good at coping with axial loads and prevent movement along the shaft - a typical application is in the steering head.
● Bearing manufacturers produce bearings to ISO size standards and stamp one face of the bearing to indicate its internal and external diameter, load capacity and type (see illustration 5.16).
● Metal bushes are usually of phosphor-bronze material. Rubber bushes are used in suspension mounting eyes. Fibre bushes have also been used in suspension pivots.

5.16 Typical bearing marking

Bearing fault finding

● If a bearing outer race has spun in its housing, the housing material will be damaged. You can use a bearing locking compound to bond the outer race in place if damage is not too severe.
● Shell bearings will fail due to damage of their working surface, as a result of lack of lubrication, corrosion or abrasive particles in the oil (see illustration 5.17). Small particles of dirt in the oil may embed in the bearing material whereas larger particles will score the bearing and shaft journal. If a number of short journeys are made, insufficient heat will be generated to drive off condensation which has built up on the bearings.

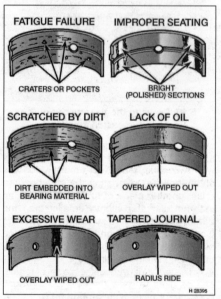

5.17 Typical bearing failures

● Ball and roller bearings will fail due to lack of lubrication or damage to the balls or rollers. Tapered-roller bearings can be damaged by overloading them. Unless the bearing is sealed on both sides, wash it in paraffin (kerosene) to remove all old grease then allow it to dry. Make a visual inspection looking to dented balls or rollers, damaged cages and worn or pitted races (see illustration 5.18).
● A ball bearing can be checked for wear by listening to it when spun. Apply a film of light oil to the bearing and hold it close to the ear - hold the outer race with one hand and spin the

5.18 Example of ball journal bearing with damaged balls and cages

5.19 Hold outer race and listen to inner race when spun

inner race with the other hand (see illustration 5.19). The bearing should be almost silent when spun; if it grates or rattles it is worn.

6 Oil seals

Oil seal removal and installation

● Oil seals should be renewed every time a component is dismantled. This is because the seal lips will become set to the sealing surface and will not necessarily reseal.
● Oil seals can be prised out of position using a large flat-bladed screwdriver (see illustration 6.1). In the case of crankcase seals, check first that the seal is not lipped on the inside, preventing its removal with the crankcases joined.

6.1 Prise out oil seals with a large flat-bladed screwdriver

● New seals are usually installed with their marked face (containing the seal reference code) outwards and the spring side towards the fluid being retained. In certain cases, such as a two-stroke engine crankshaft seal, a double lipped seal may be used due to there being fluid or gas on each side of the joint.

● Use a bearing driver or socket which bears only on the outer hard edge of the seal to install it in the casing - tapping on the inner edge will damage the sealing lip.

Oil seal types and markings

● Oil seals are usually of the single-lipped type. Double-lipped seals are found where a liquid or gas is on both sides of the joint.
● Oil seals can harden and lose their sealing ability if the motorcycle has been in storage for a long period - renewal is the only solution.
● Oil seal manufacturers also conform to the ISO markings for seal size - these are moulded into the outer face of the seal (see illustration 6.2).

6.2 These oil seal markings indicate inside diameter, outside diameter and seal thickness

7   Gaskets and sealants

Types of gasket and sealant

● Gaskets are used to seal the mating surfaces between components and keep lubricants, fluids, vacuum or pressure contained within the assembly. Aluminium gaskets are sometimes found at the cylinder joints, but most gaskets are paper-based. If the mating surfaces of the components being joined are undamaged the gasket can be installed dry, although a dab of sealant or grease will be useful to hold it in place during assembly.
● RTV (Room Temperature Vulcanising) silicone rubber sealants cure when exposed to moisture in the atmosphere. These sealants are good at filling pits or irregular gasket faces, but will tend to be forced out of the joint under very high torque. They can be used to replace a paper gasket, but first make sure that the width of the paper gasket is not essential to the shimming of internal components. RTV sealants should not be used on components containing petrol (gasoline).
● Non-hardening, semi-hardening and hard setting liquid gasket compounds can be used with a gasket or between a metal-to-metal joint. Select the sealant to suit the application: universal non-hardening sealant can be used on virtually all joints; semi-hardening on joint faces which are rough or damaged; hard setting sealant on joints which require a permanent bond and are subjected to high temperature and pressure. **Note:** *Check first if the paper gasket has a bead of sealant*

impregnated in its surface before applying additional sealant.
● When choosing a sealant, make sure it is suitable for the application, particularly if being applied in a high-temperature area or in the vicinity of fuel. Certain manufacturers produce sealants in either clear, silver or black colours to match the finish of the engine. This has a particular application on motorcycles where much of the engine is exposed.
● Do not over-apply sealant. That which is squeezed out on the outside of the joint can be wiped off, whereas an excess of sealant on the inside can break off and clog oilways.

Breaking a sealed joint

● Age, heat, pressure and the use of hard setting sealant can cause two components to stick together so tightly that they are difficult to separate using finger pressure alone. Do not resort to using levers unless there is a pry point provided for this purpose (see illustration 7.1) or else the gasket surfaces will be damaged.
● Use a soft-faced hammer (see illustration 7.2) or a wood block and conventional hammer to strike the component near the mating surface. Avoid hammering against cast extremities since they may break off. If this method fails, try using a wood wedge between the two components.

> **Caution: If the joint will not separate, double-check that you have removed all the fasteners.**

7.1 If a pry point is provided, apply gently pressure with a flat-bladed screwdriver

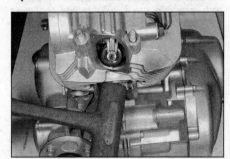

7.2 Tap around the joint with a soft-faced mallet if necessary - don't strike cooling fins

Removal of old gasket and sealant

● Paper gaskets will most likely come away complete, leaving only a few traces stuck

Most components have one or two hollow locating dowels between the two gasket faces. If a dowel cannot be removed, do not resort to gripping it with pliers - it will almost certainly be distorted. Install a close-fitting socket or Phillips screwdriver into the dowel and then grip the outer edge of the dowel to free it.

on the sealing faces of the components. It is imperative that all traces are removed to ensure correct sealing of the new gasket.
● Very carefully scrape all traces of gasket away making sure that the sealing surfaces are not gouged or scored by the scraper (see illustrations 7.3, 7.4 and 7.5). Stubborn deposits can be removed by spraying with an aerosol gasket remover. Final preparation of

7.3 Paper gaskets can be scraped off with a gasket scraper tool . . .

7.4 . . . a knife blade . . .

7.5 . . . or a household scraper

7.6 Fine abrasive paper is wrapped around a flat file to clean up the gasket face

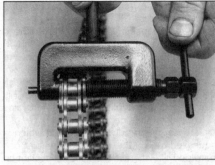

8.1 Tighten the chain breaker to push the pin out of the link . . .

8.4 Insert the new soft link, with O-rings, through the chain ends . . .

7.7 A kitchen scourer can be used on stubborn deposits

8.2 . . . withdraw the pin, remove the tool . . .

8.5 . . . install the O-rings over the pin ends . . .

the gasket surface can be made with very fine abrasive paper or a plastic kitchen scourer **(see illustrations 7.6 and 7.7)**.

● Old sealant can be scraped or peeled off components, depending on the type originally used. Note that gasket removal compounds are available to avoid scraping the components clean; make sure the gasket remover suits the type of sealant used.

8 Chains

Breaking and joining final drive chains

● Drive chains for all but small bikes are continuous and do not have a clip-type connecting link. The chain must be broken using a chain breaker tool and the new chain securely riveted together using a new soft rivet-type link. Never use a clip-type connecting link instead of a rivet-type link, except in an emergency. Various chain breaking and riveting tools are available, either as separate tools or combined as illustrated in the accompanying photographs - read the instructions supplied with the tool carefully.

⚠ **Warning: The need to rivet the new link pins correctly cannot be overstressed - loss of control of the motorcycle is very likely to result if the chain breaks in use.**

● Rotate the chain and look for the soft link. The soft link pins look like they have been

8.3 . . . and separate the chain link

deeply centre-punched instead of peened over like all the other pins **(see illustration 8.9)** and its sideplate may be a different colour. Position the soft link midway between the sprockets and assemble the chain breaker tool over one of the soft link pins **(see illustration 8.1)**. Operate the tool to push the pin out through the chain **(see illustration 8.2)**. On an O-ring chain, remove the O-rings **(see illustration 8.3)**. Carry out the same procedure on the other soft link pin.

Caution: Certain soft link pins (particularly on the larger chains) may require their ends to be filed or ground off before they can be pressed out using the tool.

● Check that you have the correct size and strength (standard or heavy duty) new soft link - do not reuse the old link. Look for the size marking on the chain sideplates **(see illustration 8.10)**.

● Position the chain ends so that they are engaged over the rear sprocket. On an O-ring

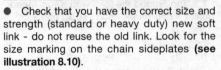

8.6 . . . followed by the sideplate

chain, install a new O-ring over each pin of the link and insert the link through the two chain ends **(see illustration 8.4)**. Install a new O-ring over the end of each pin, followed by the sideplate (with the chain manufacturer's marking facing outwards) **(see illustrations 8.5 and 8.6)**. On an unsealed chain, insert the link through the two chain ends, then install the sideplate with the chain manufacturer's marking facing outwards.

● Note that it may not be possible to install the sideplate using finger pressure alone. If using a joining tool, assemble it so that the plates of the tool clamp the link and press the sideplate over the pins **(see illustration 8.7)**. Otherwise, use two small sockets placed over

8.7 Push the sideplate into position using a clamp

8.8 Assemble the chain riveting tool over one pin at a time and tighten it fully

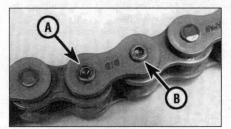

8.9 Pin end correctly riveted (A), pin end unriveted (B)

the rivet ends and two pieces of the wood between a G-clamp. Operate the clamp to press the sideplate over the pins.

● Assemble the joining tool over one pin (following the maker's instructions) and tighten the tool down to spread the pin end securely **(see illustrations 8.8 and 8.9)**. Do the same on the other pin.

 Warning: Check that the pin ends are secure and that there is no danger of the sideplate coming loose. If the pin ends are cracked the soft link must be renewed.

Final drive chain sizing

● Chains are sized using a three digit number, followed by a suffix to denote the chain type **(see illustration 8.10)**. Chain type is either standard or heavy duty (thicker sideplates), and also unsealed or O-ring/X-ring type.
● The first digit of the number relates to the pitch of the chain, ie the distance from the centre of one pin to the centre of the next pin **(see illustration 8.11)**. Pitch is expressed in eighths of an inch, as follows:

8.10 Typical chain size and type marking

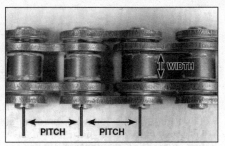

8.11 Chain dimensions

Sizes commencing with a 4 (eg 428) have a pitch of 1/2 inch (12.7 mm)
Sizes commencing with a 5 (eg 520) have a pitch of 5/8 inch (15.9 mm)
Sizes commencing with a 6 (eg 630) have a pitch of 3/4 inch (19.1 mm)

● The second and third digits of the chain size relate to the width of the rollers, again in imperial units, eg the 525 shown has 5/16 inch (7.94 mm) rollers **(see illustration 8.11)**.

9 Hoses

Clamping to prevent flow

● Small-bore flexible hoses can be clamped to prevent fluid flow whilst a component is worked on. Whichever method is used, ensure that the hose material is not permanently distorted or damaged by the clamp.

a) A brake hose clamp available from auto accessory shops **(see illustration 9.1)**.
b) A wingnut type hose clamp **(see illustration 9.2)**.

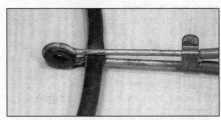

9.1 Hoses can be clamped with an automotive brake hose clamp . . .

9.2 . . . a wingnut type hose clamp . . .

c) Two sockets placed each side of the hose and held with straight-jawed self-locking grips **(see illustration 9.3)**.
d) Thick card each side of the hose held between straight-jawed self-locking grips **(see illustration 9.4)**.

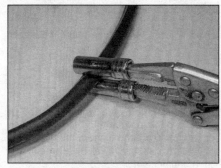

9.3 . . . two sockets and a pair of self-locking grips . . .

9.4 . . . or thick card and self-locking grips

Freeing and fitting hoses

● Always make sure the hose clamp is moved well clear of the hose end. Grip the hose with your hand and rotate it whilst pulling it off the union. If the hose has hardened due to age and will not move, slit it with a sharp knife and peel its ends off the union **(see illustration 9.5)**.
● Resist the temptation to use grease or soap on the unions to aid installation; although it helps the hose slip over the union it will equally aid the escape of fluid from the joint. It is preferable to soften the hose ends in hot water and wet the inside surface of the hose with water or a fluid which will evaporate.

9.5 Cutting a coolant hose free with a sharp knife

About the MOT Test

In the UK, all vehicles more than three years old are subject to an annual test to ensure that they meet minimum safety requirements. A current test certificate must be issued before a machine can be used on public roads, and is required before a road fund licence can be issued. Riding without a current test certificate will also invalidate your insurance.

For most owners, the MOT test is an annual cause for anxiety, and this is largely due to owners not being sure what needs to be checked prior to submitting the motorcycle for testing. The simple answer is that a fully roadworthy motorcycle will have no difficulty in passing the test.

This is a guide to getting your motorcycle through the MOT test. Obviously it will not be possible to examine the motorcycle to the same standard as the professional MOT tester, particularly in view of the equipment required for some of the checks. However, working through the following procedures will enable you to identify any problem areas before submitting the motorcycle for the test.

It has only been possible to summarise the test requirements here, based on the regulations in force at the time of printing. Test standards are becoming increasingly stringent, although there are some exemptions for older vehicles. More information about the MOT test can be obtained from the TSO

publications, *How Safe is your Motorcycle* and *The MOT Inspection Manual for Motorcycle Testing*.

Many of the checks require that one of the wheels is raised off the ground. If the motorcycle doesn't have a centre stand, note that an auxiliary stand will be required. Additionally, the help of an assistant may prove useful.

Certain exceptions apply to machines under 50 cc, machines without a lighting system, and Classic bikes - if in doubt about any of the requirements listed below seek confirmation from an MOT tester prior to submitting the motorcycle for the test.

Check that the frame number is clearly visible.

Electrical System

Lights, turn signals, horn and reflector

✔ With the ignition on, check the operation of the following electrical components. **Note:** *The electrical components on certain small-capacity machines are powered by the generator, requiring that the engine is run for this check.*

a) *Headlight and tail light. Check that both illuminate in the low and high beam switch positions.*

b) *Position lights. Check that the front position (or sidelight) and tail light illuminate in this switch position.*

c) *Turn signals. Check that all flash at the correct rate, and that the warning light(s) function correctly. Check that the turn signal switch works correctly.*

d) *Hazard warning system (where fitted). Check that all four turn signals flash in this switch position.*

e) *Brake stop light. Check that the light comes on when the front and rear brakes are independently applied. Models first used on or after 1st April 1986 must have a brake light switch on each brake.*

f) *Horn. Check that the sound is continuous and of reasonable volume.*

✔ Check that there is a red reflector on the rear of the machine, either mounted separately or as part of the tail light lens.

✔ Check the condition of the headlight, tail light and turn signal lenses.

Headlight beam height

✔ The MOT tester will perform a headlight beam height check using specialised beam setting equipment **(see illustration 1)**. This equipment will not be available to the home mechanic, but if you suspect that the headlight is incorrectly set or may have been maladjusted in the past, you can perform a rough test as follows.

✔ Position the bike in a straight line facing a brick wall. The bike must be off its stand, upright and with a rider seated. Measure the height from the ground to the centre of the headlight and mark a horizontal line on the wall at this height. Position the motorcycle 3.8 metres from the wall and draw a vertical

Headlight beam height checking equipment

line up the wall central to the centreline of the motorcycle. Switch to dipped beam and check that the beam pattern falls slightly lower than the horizontal line and to the left of the vertical line **(see illustration 2)**.

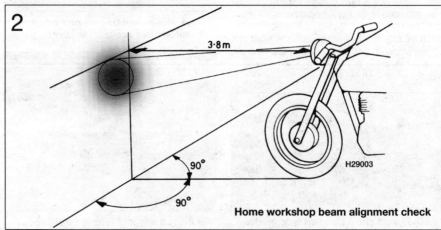

Home workshop beam alignment check

Exhaust System and Final Drive

MOT Test Checks

✔ Check that the exhaust mountings are secure and that the system does not foul any of the rear suspension components.

✔ Start the motorcycle. When the revs are increased, check that the exhaust is neither holed nor leaking from any of its joints. On a linked system, check that the collector box is not leaking due to corrosion.

✔ Note that the exhaust decibel level ("loudness" of the exhaust) is assessed at the discretion of the tester. If the motorcycle was first used on or after 1st January 1985 the silencer must carry the BSAU 193 stamp, or a marking relating to its make and model, or be of OE (original equipment) manufacture. If the silencer is marked NOT FOR ROAD USE, RACING USE ONLY or similar, it will fail the MOT.

Final drive

✔ On chain or belt drive machines, check that the chain/belt is in good condition and does not have excessive slack. Also check that the sprocket is securely mounted on the rear wheel hub. Check that the chain/belt guard is in place.

✔ On shaft drive bikes, check for oil leaking from the drive unit and fouling the rear tyre.

Steering and Suspension

Steering

✔ With the front wheel raised off the ground, rotate the steering from lock to lock. The handlebar or switches must not contact the fuel tank or be close enough to trap the rider's hand. Problems can be caused by damaged lock stops on the lower yoke and frame, or by the fitting of non-standard handlebars.

✔ When performing the lock to lock check, also ensure that the steering moves freely without drag or notchiness. Steering movement can be impaired by poorly routed cables, or by overtight head bearings or worn bearings. The tester will perform a check of the steering head bearing lower race by mounting the front wheel on a surface plate, then performing a lock to lock check with the weight of the machine on the lower bearing **(see illustration 3)**.

✔ Grasp the fork sliders (lower legs) and attempt to push and pull on the forks **(see illustration 4)**. Any play in the steering head bearings will be felt. Note that in extreme cases, wear of the front fork bushes can be misinterpreted for head bearing play.

✔ Check that the handlebars are securely mounted.

✔ Check that the handlebar grip rubbers are secure. They should by bonded to the bar left end and to the throttle cable pulley on the right end.

Front suspension

✔ With the motorcycle off the stand, hold the front brake on and pump the front forks up and down **(see illustration 5)**. Check that they are adequately damped.

✔ Inspect the area above and around the front fork oil seals **(see illustration 6)**. There should be no sign of oil on the fork tube (stanchion) nor leaking down the slider (lower leg). On models so equipped, check that there is no oil leaking from the anti-dive units.

✔ On models with swingarm front suspension, check that there is no freeplay in the linkage when moved from side to side.

Rear suspension

✔ With the motorcycle off the stand and an assistant supporting the motorcycle by its handlebars, bounce the rear suspension **(see illustration 7)**. Check that the suspension components do not foul on any of the cycle parts and check that the shock absorber(s) provide adequate damping.

Front wheel mounted on a surface plate for steering head bearing lower race check

Checking the steering head bearings for freeplay

Hold the front brake on and pump the front forks up and down to check operation

Inspect the area around the fork dust seal for oil leakage (arrow)

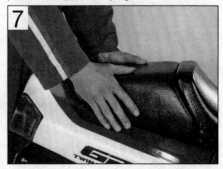

Bounce the rear of the motorcycle to check rear suspension operation

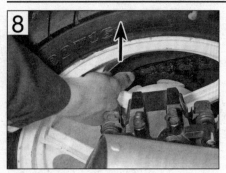

Checking for rear suspension linkage play

Worn suspension linkage pivots (arrows) are usually the cause of play in the rear suspension

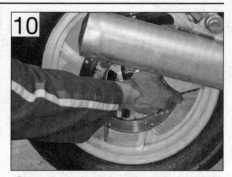

Grasp the swingarm at the ends to check for play in its pivot bearings

✔ Visually inspect the shock absorber(s) and check that there is no sign of oil leakage from its damper. This is somewhat restricted on certain single shock models due to the location of the shock absorber.

✔ With the rear wheel raised off the ground, grasp the wheel at the highest point and attempt to pull it up **(see illustration 8)**. Any play in the swingarm pivot or suspension linkage bearings will be felt as movement. **Note:** *Do not confuse play with actual suspension movement. Failure to lubricate suspension linkage bearings can lead to bearing failure* **(see illustration 9)**.

✔ With the rear wheel raised off the ground, grasp the swingarm ends and attempt to move the swingarm from side to side and forwards and backwards - any play indicates wear of the swingarm pivot bearings **(see illustration 10)**.

Brakes, Wheels and Tyres

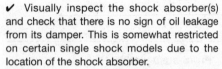

Brakes

✔ With the wheel raised off the ground, apply the brake then free it off, and check that the wheel is about to revolve freely without brake drag.

✔ On disc brakes, examine the disc itself. Check that it is securely mounted and not cracked.

✔ On disc brakes, view the pad material through the caliper mouth and check that the pads are not worn down beyond the limit **(see illustration 11)**.

✔ On drum brakes, check that when the brake is applied the angle between the operating lever and cable or rod is not too great **(see illustration 12)**. Check also that the operating lever doesn't foul any other components.

✔ On disc brakes, examine the flexible hoses from top to bottom. Have an assistant hold the brake on so that the fluid in the hose is under pressure, and check that there is no sign of fluid leakage, bulges or cracking. If there are any metal brake pipes or unions, check that these are free from corrosion and damage. Where a brake-linked anti-dive system is fitted, check the hoses to the anti-dive in a similar manner.

✔ Check that the rear brake torque arm is secure and that its fasteners are secured by self-locking nuts or castellated nuts with split-pins or R-pins **(see illustration 13)**.

✔ On models with ABS, check that the self-check warning light in the instrument panel works.

✔ The MOT tester will perform a test of the motorcycle's braking efficiency based on a calculation of rider and motorcycle weight. Although this cannot be carried out at home, you can at least ensure that the braking systems are properly maintained. For hydraulic disc brakes, check the fluid level, lever/pedal feel (bleed of air if its spongy) and pad material. For drum brakes, check adjustment, cable or rod operation and shoe lining thickness.

Wheels and tyres

✔ Check the wheel condition. Cast wheels should be free from cracks and if of the built-up design, all fasteners should be secure. Spoked wheels should be checked for broken, corroded, loose or bent spokes.

✔ With the wheel raised off the ground, spin the wheel and visually check that the tyre and wheel run true. Check that the tyre does not foul the suspension or mudguards.

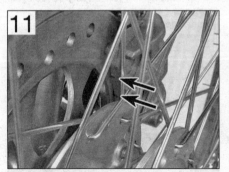

Brake pad wear can usually be viewed without removing the caliper. Most pads have wear indicator grooves (1) and some also have indicator tangs (2)

On drum brakes, check the angle of the operating lever with the brake fully applied. Most drum brakes have a wear indicator pointer and scale.

Brake torque arm must be properly secured at both ends

Check for wheel bearing play by trying to move the wheel about the axle (spindle)

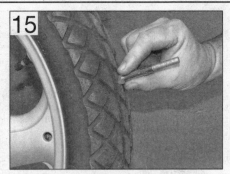

Checking the tyre tread depth

Tyre direction of rotation arrow can be found on tyre sidewall

Castellated type wheel axle (spindle) nut must be secured by a split pin or R-pin

Two straightedges are used to check wheel alignment

✔ With the wheel raised off the ground, grasp the wheel and attempt to move it about the axle (spindle) **(see illustration 14)**. Any play felt here indicates wheel bearing failure.

✔ Check the tyre tread depth, tread condition and sidewall condition **(see illustration 15)**.

✔ Check the tyre type. Front and rear tyre types must be compatible and be suitable for road use. Tyres marked NOT FOR ROAD USE, COMPETITION USE ONLY or similar, will fail the MOT.

✔ If the tyre sidewall carries a direction of rotation arrow, this must be pointing in the direction of normal wheel rotation **(see illustration 16)**.

✔ Check that the wheel axle (spindle) nuts (where applicable) are properly secured. A self-locking nut or castellated nut with a split-pin or R-pin can be used **(see illustration 17)**.

✔ Wheel alignment is checked with the motorcycle off the stand and a rider seated. With the front wheel pointing straight ahead, two perfectly straight lengths of metal or wood and placed against the sidewalls of both tyres **(see illustration 18)**. The gap each side of the front tyre must be equidistant on both sides. Incorrect wheel alignment may be due to a cocked rear wheel (often as the result of poor chain adjustment) or in extreme cases, a bent frame.

General checks and condition

✔ Check the security of all major fasteners, bodypanels, seat, fairings (where fitted) and mudguards.

✔ Check that the rider and pillion footrests, handlebar levers and brake pedal are securely mounted.

✔ Check for corrosion on the frame or any load-bearing components. If severe, this may affect the structure, particularly under stress.

Sidecars

A motorcycle fitted with a sidecar requires additional checks relating to the stability of the machine and security of attachment and swivel joints, plus specific wheel alignment (toe-in) requirements. Additionally, tyre and lighting requirements differ from conventional motorcycle use. Owners are advised to check MOT test requirements with an official test centre.

Conversion Factors

Length (distance)

Inches (in)	x 25.4	= Millimetres (mm)	x 0.0394	= Inches (in)
Feet (ft)	x 0.305	= Metres (m)	x 3.281	= Feet (ft)
Miles	x 1.609	= Kilometres (km)	x 0.621	= Miles

Volume (capacity)

Cubic inches (cu in; in³)	x 16.387	= Cubic centimetres (cc; cm³)	x 0.061	= Cubic inches (cu in; in³)
Imperial pints (Imp pt)	x 0.568	= Litres (l)	x 1.76	= Imperial pints (Imp pt)
Imperial quarts (Imp qt)	x 1.137	= Litres (l)	x 0.88	= Imperial quarts (Imp qt)
Imperial quarts (Imp qt)	x 1.201	= US quarts (US qt)	x 0.833	= Imperial quarts (Imp qt)
US quarts (US qt)	x 0.946	= Litres (l)	x 1.057	= US quarts (US qt)
Imperial gallons (Imp gal)	x 4.546	= Litres (l)	x 0.22	= Imperial gallons (Imp gal)
Imperial gallons (Imp gal)	x 1.201	= US gallons (US gal)	x 0.833	= Imperial gallons (Imp gal)
US gallons (US gal)	x 3.785	= Litres (l)	x 0.264	= US gallons (US gal)

Mass (weight)

Ounces (oz)	x 28.35	= Grams (g)	x 0.035	= Ounces (oz)
Pounds (lb)	x 0.454	= Kilograms (kg)	x 2.205	= Pounds (lb)

Force

Ounces-force (ozf; oz)	x 0.278	= Newtons (N)	x 3.6	= Ounces-force (ozf; oz)
Pounds-force (lbf; lb)	x 4.448	= Newtons (N)	x 0.225	= Pounds-force (lbf; lb)
Newtons (N)	x 0.1	= Kilograms-force (kgf; kg)	x 9.81	= Newtons (N)

Pressure

Pounds-force per square inch (psi; lbf/in²; lb/in²)	x 0.070	= Kilograms-force per square centimetre (kgf/cm²; kg/cm²)	x 14.223	= Pounds-force per square inch (psi; lbf/in²; lb/in²)
Pounds-force per square inch (psi; lbf/in²; lb/in²)	x 0.068	= Atmospheres (atm)	x 14.696	= Pounds-force per square inch (psi; lbf/in²; lb/in²)
Pounds-force per square inch (psi; lbf/in²; lb/in²)	x 0.069	= Bars	x 14.5	= Pounds-force per square inch (psi; lbf/in²; lb/in²)
Pounds-force per square inch (psi; lbf/in²; lb/in²)	x 6.895	= Kilopascals (kPa)	x 0.145	= Pounds-force per square inch (psi; lbf/in²; lb/in²)
Kilopascals (kPa)	x 0.01	= Kilograms-force per square centimetre (kgf/cm²; kg/cm²)	x 98.1	= Kilopascals (kPa)
Millibar (mbar)	x 100	= Pascals (Pa)	x 0.01	= Millibar (mbar)
Millibar (mbar)	x 0.0145	= Pounds-force per square inch (psi; lbf/in²; lb/in²)	x 68.947	= Millibar (mbar)
Millibar (mbar)	x 0.75	= Millimetres of mercury (mmHg)	x 1.333	= Millibar (mbar)
Millibar (mbar)	x 0.401	= Inches of water (inH₂O)	x 2.491	= Millibar (mbar)
Millimetres of mercury (mmHg)	x 0.535	= Inches of water (inH₂O)	x 1.868	= Millimetres of mercury (mmHg)
Inches of water (inH₂O)	x 0.036	= Pounds-force per square inch (psi; lbf/in²; lb/in²)	x 27.68	= Inches of water (inH₂O)

Torque (moment of force)

Pounds-force inches (lbf in; lb in)	x 1.152	= Kilograms-force centimetre (kgf cm; kg cm)	x 0.868	= Pounds-force inches (lbf in; lb in)
Pounds-force inches (lbf in; lb in)	x 0.113	= Newton metres (Nm)	x 8.85	= Pounds-force inches (lbf in; lb in)
Pounds-force inches (lbf in; lb in)	x 0.083	= Pounds-force feet (lbf ft; lb ft)	x 12	= Pounds-force inches (lbf in; lb in)
Pounds-force feet (lbf ft; lb ft)	x 0.138	= Kilograms-force metres (kgf m; kg m)	x 7.233	= Pounds-force feet (lbf ft; lb ft)
Pounds-force feet (lbf ft; lb ft)	x 1.356	= Newton metres (Nm)	x 0.738	= Pounds-force feet (lbf ft; lb ft)
Newton metres (Nm)	x 0.102	= Kilograms-force metres (kgf m; kg m)	x 9.804	= Newton metres (Nm)

Power

Horsepower (hp)	x 745.7	= Watts (W)	x 0.0013	= Horsepower (hp)

Velocity (speed)

Miles per hour (miles/hr; mph)	x 1.609	= Kilometres per hour (km/hr; kph)	x 0.621	= Miles per hour (miles/hr; mph)

Fuel consumption*

Miles per gallon, Imperial (mpg)	x 0.354	= Kilometres per litre (km/l)	x 2.825	= Miles per gallon, Imperial (mpg)
Miles per gallon, US (mpg)	x 0.425	= Kilometres per litre (km/l)	x 2.352	= Miles per gallon, US (mpg)

Temperature

Degrees Fahrenheit = (°C x 1.8) + 32   Degrees Celsius (Degrees Centigrade; °C) = (°F - 32) x 0.56

It is common practice to convert from miles per gallon (mpg) to litres/100 kilometres (l/100km), where mpg x l/100 km = 282

This Section provides an easy reference-guide to the more common faults that are likely to afflict your machine. Obviously, the opportunities are almost limitless for faults to occur as a result of obscure failures, and to try and cover all eventualities would require a book. Indeed, a number have been written on the subject.

Successful troubleshooting is not a mysterious 'black art' but the application of a bit of knowledge combined with a systematic and logical approach to the problem. Approach any troubleshooting by first accurately identifying the symptom and then checking through the list of possible causes, starting with the simplest or most obvious and progressing in stages to the most complex.

Take nothing for granted, but above all apply liberal quantities of common sense.

The main symptom of a fault is given in the text as a major heading below which are listed the various systems or areas which may contain the fault. Details of each possible cause for a fault and the remedial action to be taken are given, in brief, in the paragraphs below each heading. Further information should be sought in the relevant Chapter.

1 Engine doesn't start or is difficult to start

- [ ] Starter motor doesn't rotate
- [ ] Starter motor rotates but engine does not turn over
- [ ] No fuel flow
- [ ] Engine flooded
- [ ] No spark or weak spark
- [ ] Compression low
- [ ] Stalls after starting
- [ ] Rough idle

2 Poor running at low speed

- [ ] Spark weak
- [ ] Fuel/air mixture incorrect
- [ ] Compression low
- [ ] Poor acceleration

3 Poor running or no power at high speed

- [ ] Firing incorrect
- [ ] Fuel/air mixture incorrect
- [ ] Compression low
- [ ] Knocking or pinking
- [ ] Miscellaneous causes

4 Overheating

- [ ] Engine overheats
- [ ] Firing incorrect
- [ ] Fuel/air mixture incorrect
- [ ] Compression too high
- [ ] Engine load excessive
- [ ] Lubrication inadequate

5 Clutch problems

- [ ] Clutch slipping
- [ ] Clutch not disengaging completely

6 Gearchanging problems

- [ ] Doesn't go into gear, or lever doesn't return
- [ ] Jumps out of gear
- [ ] Overshifts

7 Abnormal engine noise

- [ ] Knocking or pinking
- [ ] Piston slap or rattling
- [ ] Valve noise
- [ ] Other noise

8 Abnormal driveline noise

- [ ] Clutch noise
- [ ] Transmission noise
- [ ] Final drive noise

9 Abnormal frame and suspension noise

- [ ] Front end noise
- [ ] Shock absorber noise
- [ ] Brake noise

10 Excessive exhaust smoke

- [ ] White smoke
- [ ] Black smoke
- [ ] Brown smoke

11 Poor handling or stability

- [ ] Handlebar hard to turn
- [ ] Handlebar shakes or vibrates excessively
- [ ] Handlebar pulls to one side
- [ ] Poor shock absorbing qualities

12 Braking problems – disc brake

- [ ] Brake is spongy or doesn't hold
- [ ] Brake lever or pedal pulsates
- [ ] Brake drags

13 Braking problems – drum brake

- [ ] Brake is ineffective
- [ ] Brake lever or pedal pulsates
- [ ] Brake drags

14 Electrical problems

- [ ] Battery dead or weak
- [ ] Battery overcharged

1 Engine doesn't start or is difficult to start

Starter motor doesn't rotate

☐ Main fuse blown. Check fuse (Chapter 9).

☐ Battery voltage low. Check and recharge battery (Chapter 9).

☐ Starter motor defective. Make sure the wiring to the starter is secure. Make sure the starter relay clicks when the start button is pushed. If the relay clicks, then the fault is probably in the wiring or motor.

☐ Starter relay faulty. Check it according to the procedure in Chapter 9.

☐ Starter button not contacting. The contacts could be wet, corroded or dirty. Disassemble and clean the switch (Chapter 9).

☐ Wiring open or shorted. Check all wiring connections and harnesses to make sure that they are dry, tight and not corroded. Also check for broken or frayed wires that can cause a short to earth.

☐ Ignition switch defective. Check the switch according to the procedure in Chapter 9. Replace the switch with a new one if it is defective.

☐ Faulty neutral/sidestand/clutch switch(es) or diode(s). Check the wiring to each switch and the switch itself, and check the diode(s), according to the procedures in Chapter 9.

Starter motor rotates but engine does not turn over

☐ Starter clutch defective. Inspect and repair or replace (Chapter 2A, 2B, 2C or 2D).

☐ Damaged idle/reduction or starter gears. Inspect and replace the damaged parts (Chapter 2A, 2B, 2C or 2D).

No fuel flow

☐ No fuel in tank.

☐ Fuel tap vacuum hose broken or disconnected (automatic tap only – Chapter 4).

☐ Tank cap air vent obstructed. Usually caused by dirt or water. Remove it and clean the cap vent hole.

☐ Fuel tap strainer or fuel filter clogged. Remove and clean the strainer or fit a new filter, according to type fitted (Chapters 1 and 4).

☐ Fuel hose clogged. Detach the fuel hose and carefully blow through it.

☐ Fuel passage clogged. For a passage to be clogged, either a very bad batch of fuel with an unusual additive has been used, or some other foreign material has entered the system. Many times after a machine has been stored for many months without running, the fuel turns to a varnish-like liquid and forms deposits on the inlet needle valve and jets. The carburettor should be removed and overhauled if draining the float bowl doesn't solve the problem.

Engine flooded

☐ Float height too high. Check as described in Chapter 4.

☐ Float needle valve worn or stuck open. A piece of dirt, rust or other debris can cause the inlet needle to seat improperly, causing excess fuel to be admitted to the float bowl. In this case, the float chamber should be cleaned and the needle and seat inspected. If the needle and seat are worn, then the leaking will persist and the parts should be replaced with new ones (Chapter 4).

☐ Starting technique incorrect. Under normal circumstances (e.g., if all the carburettor functions are sound) the machine should start with little or no throttle. When the engine is cold, the choke should be operated and the engine started without opening the throttle. When the engine is at operating temperature, only a very slight amount of throttle should be necessary. If the engine is flooded, hold the throttle fully open while cranking the engine. This will allow additional air to reach the cylinder.

No spark or weak spark

☐ Battery voltage low. Check and recharge battery as necessary (Chapter 9).

☐ Spark plug dirty, defective or worn out. Locate reason for fouled plug using spark plug condition chart on the inside rear cover and follow the plug maintenance procedures in Chapter 1.

☐ Spark plug cap or HT lead faulty. Check condition. Replace either or both components if cracks or deterioration are evident (Chapter 5).

☐ Spark plug cap not making good contact. Make sure that the plug cap fits snugly over the plug end.

☐ Pick-up coil defective. Check the unit, referring to Chapter 5 for details.

☐ Ignition HT coil defective. Check the coil, referring to Chapter 5.

☐ Ignition switch shorted. This is usually caused by water, corrosion, damage or excessive wear. The switch can be disassembled and cleaned with electrical contact cleaner. If cleaning does not help, replace the switch with a new one (Chapter 9).

☐ Wiring shorted or broken. Make sure that all wiring connections are clean, dry and tight. Look for chafed and broken wires (Chapters 5 and 9).

☐ Electronic control unit defective.

Compression low

☐ Spark plug loose. Remove the plug and inspect the threads (Chapter 1).

☐ Cylinder head not sufficiently tightened down. If the cylinder head is suspected of being loose, then there's a chance that the gasket or head is damaged if the problem has persisted for any length of time. The nuts and bolts should be tightened to the proper torque in the correct sequence (Chapter 2A, 2B, 2C or 2D).

☐ Improper valve clearance. This means that the valve is not closing completely and compression pressure is leaking past the valve. Check and adjust the valve clearances (Chapter 1).

☐ Cylinder and/or piston worn. Excessive wear will cause compression pressure to leak past the rings. This is usually accompanied by worn rings as well. A top-end overhaul is necessary (Chapter 2A, 2B, 2C or 2D).

☐ Piston rings worn, weak, broken, or sticking. Broken or sticking piston rings usually indicate a lubrication or carburetion problem that causes excess carbon deposits or seizures to form on the pistons and rings. Top end overhaul is necessary (Chapter 2A, 2B, 2C or 2D).

☐ Piston ring-to-groove clearance excessive. This is caused by excessive wear of the piston ring lands. Piston replacement is necessary (Chapter 2A, 2B, 2C or 2D).

☐ Cylinder head gasket damaged. If the head is allowed to become loose, or if excessive carbon build-up on the piston crown and combustion chamber causes extremely high compression, the head gasket may leak. Retorquing the head is not always sufficient to restore the seal, so gasket replacement is necessary (Chapter 2A, 2B, 2C or 2D).

☐ Cylinder head warped. This is caused by overheating or improperly tightened head nuts/bolts. Machine shop resurfacing or head replacement is necessary (Chapter 2A, 2B, 2C or 2D).

☐ Valve spring broken or weak. Caused by component failure or wear; the spring(s) must be replaced (Chapter 2A, 2B, 2C or 2D).

☐ Valve not seating properly. This is caused by a bent valve (from over-revving or improper valve adjustment), burned valve or seat (improper carburetion) or an accumulation of carbon deposits on the seat (from carburetion or lubrication problems). The valves must be cleaned and/or replaced and the seats serviced if possible (Chapter 2A, 2B, 2C or 2D).

1 Engine doesn't start or is difficult to start (continued)

Stalls after starting

☐ Improper choke action. Make sure the choke is getting a full stroke and staying in the out position.
☐ Ignition malfunction. See Chapter 5.
☐ Carburettor malfunction. See Chapter 4.
☐ Fuel contaminated. The fuel can be contaminated with either dirt or water, or can change chemically if the machine is allowed to sit for several months or more. Drain the tank and float bowl and check the strainer (Chapters 4 and 1).
☐ Intake air leak. Check for loose carburettor-to-intake connection, loose or missing vacuum hoses, or loose carburettor top (Chapter 4).
☐ Engine idle speed incorrect. Turn throttle stop screw until the engine idles at the specified rpm (Chapters 1 and 4).

Rough idle

☐ Ignition malfunction. See Chapter 5.
☐ Idle speed incorrect. See Chapter 1.
☐ Carburettor malfunction. See Chapter 4.
☐ Fuel contaminated. The fuel can be contaminated with either dirt or water, or can change chemically if the machine is allowed to sit for several months or more. Drain the tank and float bowl and check the strainer (Chapters 4 and 1).
☐ Intake air leak. Check for loose carburettor-to-intake connection, loose or missing vacuum hoses, or loose carburettor top (Chapter 4).
☐ Air filter clogged. Service or replace air filter element (Chapter 1).
☐ Air induction system (AIS) hose detached or faulty reed valve or control valve. Check the system (Chapters 1 and 4).

2 Poor running at low speed

Spark weak

☐ Battery voltage low. Check and recharge battery (Chapter 9).
☐ Spark plug fouled, defective or worn out. Refer to Chapter 1 for spark plug maintenance.
☐ Spark plug cap or HT lead defective. Refer to Chapters 1 and 5 for details on the ignition system.
☐ Spark plug cap not making contact.
☐ Incorrect spark plug. Wrong type, heat range or cap configuration. A cold plug or one with a recessed firing electrode will not operate at low speeds without fouling.
☐ Pick-up coil defective. See Chapter 5.
☐ Ignition HT coil defective. See Chapter 5.
☐ Electronic control unit defective. See Chapter 5.

Fuel/air mixture incorrect

☐ Pilot screw out of adjustment (Chapter 4).
☐ Pilot jet or air passage clogged. Remove and overhaul the carburettor (Chapter 4).
☐ Air bleed holes clogged. Remove carburettor and blow out all passages (Chapter 4).
☐ Air filter clogged, poorly sealed or missing (Chapter 1).
☐ Air filter housing poorly sealed. Look for cracks, holes or loose clamps and replace or repair defective parts.
☐ Fuel level too high or too low. Check the float height (Chapter 4).
☐ Fuel tank air vent obstructed. Make sure that the air vent passage in the filler cap is open.
☐ Carburettor intake duct loose. Check for cracks, breaks, tears or loose clamps. Repair or replace the rubber intakes.

Compression low

☐ Spark plug loose. Remove the plug and inspect the threads (Chapter 1).
☐ Cylinder head not sufficiently tightened down. If the cylinder head is suspected of being loose, then there's a chance that the gasket and head are damaged if the problem has persisted for any length of time. The nuts and bolts should be tightened to the proper torque in the correct sequence (Chapter 2A, 2B, 2C or 2D).
☐ Improper valve clearance. This means that the valve is not closing completely and compression pressure is leaking past the valve. Check and adjust the valve clearances (Chapter 1).

☐ Cylinder and/or piston worn. Excessive wear will cause compression pressure to leak past the rings. This is usually accompanied by worn rings as well. A top-end overhaul is necessary (Chapter 2A, 2B, 2C or 2D).
☐ Piston rings worn, weak, broken, or sticking. Broken or sticking piston rings usually indicate a lubrication or carburetion problem that causes excess carbon deposits or seizures to form on the pistons and rings. Top-end overhaul is necessary (Chapter 2A, 2B, 2C or 2D).
☐ Piston ring-to-groove clearance excessive. This is caused by excessive wear of the piston ring lands. Piston replacement is necessary (Chapter 2A, 2B, 2C or 2D).
☐ Cylinder head gasket damaged. If the head is allowed to become loose, or if excessive carbon build-up on the piston crown and combustion chamber causes extremely high compression, the head gasket may leak. Retorquing the head is not always sufficient to restore the seal, so gasket replacement is necessary (Chapter 2A, 2B, 2C or 2D).
☐ Cylinder head warped. This is caused by overheating or improperly tightened head nuts/bolts. Machine shop resurfacing or head replacement is necessary (Chapter 2A, 2B, 2C or 2D).
☐ Valve spring broken or weak. Caused by component failure or wear; the spring(s) must be replaced (Chapter 2A, 2B, 2C or 2D).
☐ Valve not seating properly. This is caused by a bent valve (from over-revving or improper valve adjustment), burned valve or seat (improper carburetion) or an accumulation of carbon deposits on the seat (from carburetion, lubrication problems). The valves must be cleaned and/or replaced and the seats serviced if possible (Chapter 2A, 2B, 2C or 2D).

Poor acceleration

☐ Carburettor leaking or dirty. Overhaul the carburettor(s) (Chapter 4).
☐ Timing not advancing. The pick-up coil or the electronic control unit may be defective. If so, they must be replaced with new ones, as they can't be repaired.
☐ Brakes dragging. With disc brakes usually caused by debris which has entered the brake piston seals, or from a warped disc or bent axle. Repair as necessary (Chapter 7). With drum brakes first check the freeplay adjustment, then the shoes, springs and actuating cam (Chapter 7).

3 Poor running or no power at high speed

Firing incorrect

☐ Air filter restricted. Clean or replace filter (Chapter 1).
☐ Spark plug fouled, defective or worn out. See Chapter 1 for spark plug maintenance.
☐ Spark plug cap or HT lead wiring defective. See Chapters 1 and 5 for details of the ignition system.
☐ Spark plug cap not in good contact. See Chapter 5.
☐ Incorrect spark plug. Wrong type, heat range or cap configuration. A cold plug or one with a recessed firing electrode will not operate at low speeds without fouling.
☐ Ignition HT coil defective. See Chapter 5.
☐ Electronic control unit defective. See Chapter 5.

Fuel/air mixture incorrect

☐ Main jet clogged. Dirt, water or other contaminants can clog the main jet. Clean the fuel tap strainer, the float bowl area, and the jets and carburettor orifices (Chapter 4).
☐ Air bleed holes clogged. Remove and overhaul carburettor (Chapter 4).
☐ Air filter clogged, poorly sealed, or missing (Chapter 1).
☐ Fuel level too high or too low. Check the float height (Chapter 4).
☐ Fuel tank air vent obstructed. Make sure the air vent passage in the filler cap is open.
☐ Carburettor intake duct loose. Check for cracks, breaks, tears or loose clamps. Repair or replace the rubber intakes (Chapter 4).
☐ Fuel valve strainer clogged. Remove the valve and clean it and the strainer (Chapter 1).
☐ Fuel hose clogged. Detach the fuel hose and carefully blow through it.

Compression low

☐ Spark plug loose. Remove the plug and inspect the threads (Chapter 1).
☐ Cylinder head not sufficiently tightened down. If the cylinder head is suspected of being loose, then there's a chance that the gasket and head are damaged if the problem has persisted for any length of time. The nuts and bolts should be tightened to the proper torque in the correct sequence (Chapter 2A, 2B, 2C or 2D).
☐ Improper valve clearance. This means that the valve is not closing completely and compression pressure is leaking past the valve. Check and adjust the valve clearances (Chapter 1).
☐ Cylinder and/or piston worn. Excessive wear will cause compression pressure to leak past the rings. This is usually accompanied by worn rings as well. A top-end overhaul is necessary (Chapter 2A, 2B, 2C or 2D).
☐ Piston rings worn, weak, broken, or sticking. Broken or sticking piston rings usually indicate a lubrication or carburetion problem that causes excess carbon deposits or seizures to form on the pistons and rings. Top-end overhaul is necessary (Chapter 2A, 2B, 2C or 2D).

☐ Piston ring-to-groove clearance excessive. This is caused by excessive wear of the piston ring lands. Piston replacement is necessary (Chapter 2A, 2B, 2C or 2D).
☐ Cylinder head gasket damaged. If the head is allowed to become loose, or if excessive carbon build-up on the piston crown and combustion chamber causes extremely high compression, the head gasket may leak. Retorquing the head is not always sufficient to restore the seal, so gasket replacement is necessary (Chapter 2A, 2B, 2C or 2D).
☐ Cylinder head warped. This is caused by overheating or improperly tightened head nuts/bolts. Machine shop resurfacing or head replacement is necessary (Chapter 2A, 2B, 2C or 2D).
☐ Valve spring broken or weak. Caused by component failure or wear; the spring(s) must be replaced (Chapter 2A, 2B, 2C or 2D).
☐ Valve not seating properly. This is caused by a bent valve (from over-revving or improper valve adjustment), burned valve or seat (improper carburetion) or an accumulation of carbon deposits on the seat (from carburetion, lubrication problems). The valves must be cleaned and/or replaced and the seats serviced if possible (Chapter 2A, 2B, 2C or 2D).

Knocking or pinking

☐ Carbon build-up in combustion chamber. Use of a fuel additive that will dissolve the adhesive bonding the carbon particles to the crown and chamber is the easiest way to remove the build-up. Otherwise, the cylinder head will have to be removed and de-carbonised (Chapter 2A, 2B, 2C or 2D).
☐ Incorrect or poor quality fuel. Old or improper grades of fuel can cause detonation. This causes the piston to rattle, thus the knocking or pinking sound. Drain old fuel and always use the recommended fuel grade.
☐ Spark plug heat range incorrect. Uncontrolled detonation indicates the plug heat range is too hot. The plug in effect becomes a glow plug, raising cylinder temperatures. Install the proper heat range plug (Chapter 1).
☐ Improper air/fuel mixture. This will cause the cylinder to run hot, which leads to detonation. Maladjusted pilot screw or clogged jets or an air leak can cause this imbalance. See Chapter 4.

Miscellaneous causes

☐ Throttle doesn't open fully. Check the cable (Chapter 1).
☐ Clutch slipping. May be caused by loose or worn clutch components. Refer to Chapter 2A, 2B, 2C or 2D for clutch overhaul procedures.
☐ Timing not advancing.
☐ Brakes dragging. With disc brakes usually caused by debris which has entered the brake piston seals, or from a warped disc or bent axle. Repair as necessary (Chapter 7). With drum brakes first check the freeplay adjustment, then the shoes, springs and actuating cam (Chapter 7).

4 Overheating

Engine overheats – liquid-cooled models

- [ ] Coolant level low. Check and add coolant (Pre-ride checks).
- [ ] Leak in cooling system. Check cooling system hoses and radiator for leaks and other damage. Repair or replace parts as necessary (Chapter 3).
- [ ] Thermostat sticking open or closed. Check and replace as described in Chapter 3.
- [ ] Faulty radiator pressure cap. Have it checked by a dealer.
- [ ] Coolant passages clogged. Drain, flush and refill with fresh coolant (Chapter 3).
- [ ] Water pump defective. Remove the pump and check the components (Chapter 3).
- [ ] Clogged radiator fins. Clean them by blowing compressed air through the fins from the rear of the radiator.

Firing incorrect

- [ ] Spark plug fouled, defective or worn out. See Chapter 1 for spark plug maintenance.
- [ ] Incorrect spark plug.
- [ ] Faulty ignition HT coil (Chapter 5).

Fuel/air mixture incorrect

- [ ] Main jet clogged. Dirt, water and other contaminants can clog the main jet. Clean the fuel tap filter, the float bowl area and the jets and carburettor orifices (Chapter 4).
- [ ] Main jet wrong size. The standard jetting is for sea level atmospheric pressure and oxygen content.
- [ ] Maladjusted pilot screw (Chapter 4).
- [ ] Air filter clogged, poorly sealed or missing (Chapter 1).
- [ ] Air filter housing poorly sealed. Look for cracks, holes or loose clamps and replace or repair.
- [ ] Fuel level too low. Check float height (Chapter 4).
- [ ] Fuel tank air vent obstructed. Make sure that the air vent passage in the filler cap is open.
- [ ] Carburettor intake duct loose. Check for cracks, breaks, tears or loose clamps. Repair or replace the rubber intakes (Chapter 4).

Compression too high

- [ ] Carbon build-up in combustion chamber. Use of a fuel additive that will dissolve the adhesive bonding the carbon particles to the piston crown and chamber is the easiest way to remove the build-up. Otherwise, the cylinder head will have to be removed and de-carbonised (Chapter 2A, 2B, 2C or 2D).
- [ ] Improperly machined head surface or installation of incorrect gasket during engine assembly.

Engine load excessive

- [ ] Clutch slipping. Can be caused by damaged, loose or worn clutch components. Refer to Chapter 2A, 2B or 2C for overhaul procedures.
- [ ] Engine oil level too high. The addition of too much oil will cause pressurization of the crankcase and inefficient engine operation. Drain to proper level (Chapter 1 and Pre-ride checks).
- [ ] Brakes dragging. With disc brakes usually caused by debris which has entered the brake piston seals, or from a warped disc or bent axle. Repair as necessary (Chapter 7). With drum brakes first check the freeplay adjustment, then the shoes, springs and actuating cam (Chapter 7).

Lubrication inadequate

- [ ] Engine oil level too low. Friction caused by intermittent lack of lubrication or from oil that is overworked can cause overheating. The oil provides a definite cooling function in the engine. Check the oil level (Pre-ride checks).
- [ ] Poor quality engine oil or incorrect viscosity or type. Oil is rated not only according to viscosity but also according to type (Pre-ride checks).

5 Clutch problems

Clutch slipping

- [ ] Cable freeplay insufficient. Check and adjust cable (Chapter 1).
- [ ] Friction plates worn or warped. Overhaul the clutch assembly (Chapter 2A, 2B, 2C or 2D).
- [ ] Steel plates worn or warped (Chapter 2A, 2B, 2C or 2D).
- [ ] Clutch spring(s) broken or weak. Old or heat-damaged (from slipping clutch) springs should be replaced with new ones (Chapter 2A, 2B, 2C or 2D).
- [ ] Clutch release mechanism defective. Replace any defective parts (Chapter 2A, 2B, 2C or 2D).
- [ ] Clutch centre or housing unevenly worn. This causes improper engagement of the plates. Replace the damaged or worn parts (Chapter 2A, 2B, 2C or 2D).
- [ ] Incorrect engine oil. Use of an engine oil designed for cars can cause clutch slip. Always use a motorcycle engine oil.

Clutch not disengaging completely

- [ ] Cable freeplay excessive. Check and adjust cable (Chapter 1).
- [ ] Clutch plates warped or damaged. This will cause clutch drag, which in turn will cause the machine to creep. Overhaul the clutch assembly (Chapter 2A, 2B, 2C or 2D).

- [ ] Clutch spring tension uneven. Usually caused by a sagged or broken spring. Check and replace the springs (Chapter 2A, 2B, 2C or 2D).
- [ ] Engine oil deteriorated. Old, thin, worn out oil will not provide proper lubrication for the discs, causing the clutch to drag. Replace the oil and filter (Chapter 1).
- [ ] Engine oil viscosity too high. Using too heavy an engine oil can cause the plates to stick together, putting a drag on the engine. Change to the correct weight oil (Pre-ride checks).
- [ ] Clutch housing seized on shaft. Lack of lubrication, severe wear or damage can cause the housing to seize on the shaft. Overhaul of the clutch, and perhaps transmission, may be necessary to repair the damage (Chapter 2A, 2B, 2C or 2D).
- [ ] Clutch release mechanism defective. Worn or damaged release mechanism parts can stick and fail to apply force to the pressure plate. Overhaul the clutch cover components (Chapter 2A, 2B, 2C or 2D).
- [ ] Loose clutch centre nut (not applicable to OHV engines). Causes drum and centre misalignment putting a drag on the engine. Engagement adjustment continually varies. Overhaul the clutch assembly (Chapter 2B, 2C or 2D).

6 Gearchanging problems

Doesn't go into gear or lever doesn't return

☐ Clutch not disengaging. See Section 5.

☐ Selector fork(s) bent or seized. Often caused by dropping the machine or from lack of lubrication. Overhaul the transmission (Chapter 2A, 2B, 2C or 2D).

☐ Gear(s) stuck on shaft. Most often caused by a lack of lubrication or excessive wear in transmission bearings and bushings. Overhaul the transmission (Chapter 2A, 2B, 2C or 2D).

☐ Selector drum binding. Caused by lubrication failure or excessive wear. Check the drum (Chapter 2A, 2B, 2C or 2D).

☐ Gearchange shaft centralising spring weak or broken (Chapter 2A, 2B, 2C or 2D).

☐ Gearchange lever or linkage broken. Splines stripped out of lever, linkage arm or shaft, caused by allowing the lever to get loose or from dropping the machine. Replace necessary parts (Chapter 6 and 2A, 2B, 2C or 2D).

☐ Gearchange mechanism stopper arm broken or worn. Full engagement and rotary movement of selector drum results. Replace the arm (Chapter 2A, 2B, 2C or 2D).

☐ Stopper arm spring broken. Allows arm to float, causing sporadic shift operation. Replace spring (Chapter 2A, 2B, 2C or 2D).

Jumps out of gear

☐ Selector fork(s) worn. Overhaul the transmission (Chapter 2A, 2B, 2C or 2D).

☐ Gear groove(s) worn. Overhaul the transmission (Chapter 2A, 2B, 2C or 2D).

☐ Gear dogs or dog slots worn or damaged. The gears should be inspected and replaced (Chapter 2A, 2B, 2C or 2D). No attempt should be made to service the worn parts.

Overshifts

☐ Stopper arm spring weak or broken (Chapter 2A, 2B, 2C or 2D).

☐ Gearchange shaft centralising spring or post broken or distorted (Chapter 2A, 2B, 2C or 2D).

7 Abnormal engine noise

Knocking or pinking

☐ Carbon build-up in combustion chamber. Use of a fuel additive that will dissolve the adhesive bonding the carbon particles to the piston crown and chamber is the easiest way to remove the build-up. Otherwise, the cylinder head will have to be removed and decarbonised (Chapter 2A, 2B, 2C or 2D).

☐ Incorrect or poor quality fuel. Old or improper fuel can cause detonation. This causes the piston to rattle, thus the knocking or pinking sound. Drain the old fuel and refill with fresh fuel.

☐ Spark plug heat range incorrect. Uncontrolled detonation indicates that the plug heat range is too hot. The plug in effect becomes a glow plug, raising cylinder temperatures.

☐ Improper air/fuel mixture. This will cause the cylinders to run hot and lead to detonation. Maladjusted pilot screw or clogged jets or an air leak can cause this imbalance. See Chapter 4.

Piston slap or rattling

☐ Cylinder-to-piston clearance excessive. Caused by improper assembly. Inspect and overhaul top-end parts (Chapter 2A, 2B, 2C or 2D).

☐ Connecting rod bent. Caused by over-revving, trying to start a badly flooded engine or from ingesting a foreign object into the combustion chamber. Replace the damaged parts (Chapter 2A, 2B, 2C or 2D).

☐ Piston pin or piston pin bore worn or seized from wear or lack of lubrication. Replace damaged parts (Chapter 2A, 2B, 2C or 2D).

☐ Piston ring(s) worn, broken or sticking. Overhaul the top-end (Chapter 2A, 2B, 2C or 2D).

☐ Piston seizure damage. Usually from lack of lubrication or overheating. Replace the piston(s) and bore the cylinder(s), as necessary (Chapter 2A, 2B, 2C or 2D).

☐ Connecting rod upper or lower end clearance excessive. Caused by excessive wear or lack of lubrication. Replace worn parts.

Valve noise

☐ Incorrect valve clearances. Adjust the clearances by referring to Chapter 1.

☐ Valve spring broken or weak. Check and replace weak valve springs (Chapter 2A, 2B, 2C or 2D).

☐ Camshaft, pushrods (OHV engines), rocker arms or cylinder head worn or damaged. Lack of lubrication at high rpm is usually the cause of damage. Insufficient oil or failure to change the oil at the recommended intervals are the chief causes (Chapter 2A, 2B, 2C or 2D).

Other noise

☐ Cylinder head gasket leaking. Fit new gasket and check head for distortion (Chapter 2A, 2B, 2C or 2D).

☐ Exhaust pipe leaking at cylinder head connection. Caused by improper fit of pipe or loose exhaust flange. All exhaust fasteners should be tightened evenly and carefully. Failure to do this will lead to a leak.

☐ Crankshaft runout excessive. Caused by a bent crankshaft (from over-revving) or damage from an upper cylinder component failure. Can also be attributed to dropping the machine on either of the crankshaft ends.

☐ Engine mounting bolts loose. Tighten all engine mount bolts (Chapter 2A, 2B, 2C or 2D).

☐ Crankshaft bearings worn (Chapter 2A, 2B, 2C or 2D).

☐ Cam chain tensioner defective. Replace according to the procedure in Chapter 2A, 2B, 2C or 2D.

☐ Pushrods (OHV engines), rocker arms (all engines), cam chain, sprockets or guides (OHC and Twin engines) worn (Chapter 2A, 2B, 2C or 2D).

8 Abnormal driveline noise

Clutch noise

- [ ] Clutch housing/friction plate clearance excessive (Chapter 2A, 2B, 2C or 2D).
- [ ] Loose or damaged clutch pressure plate and/or bolts (Chapter 2A, 2B, 2C or 2D).

Transmission noise

- [ ] Bearings worn. Also includes the possibility that the shafts are worn. Overhaul the transmission (Chapter 2A, 2B, 2C or 2D).
- [ ] Gears worn or chipped (Chapter 2A, 2B, 2C or 2D).
- [ ] Metal chips jammed in gear teeth. Probably pieces from a broken clutch, gear or shift mechanism that were picked up by the gears. This will cause early bearing failure (Chapter 2A, 2B, 2C or 2D).
- [ ] Engine oil level too low. Causes a howl from transmission. Also affects engine power and clutch operation (Pre-ride checks).

Final drive noise

- [ ] Chain not adjusted properly (Chapter 1).
- [ ] Front or rear sprocket loose. Tighten fasteners (Chapter 7).
- [ ] Sprocket(s) worn. Replace sprocket(s) (Chapter 7).
- [ ] Rear sprocket warped. Replace (Chapter 7).
- [ ] Sprocket coupling worn. Check coupling, dampers and bearing (Chapter 7).

9 Abnormal frame and suspension noise

Front end noise

- [ ] Low fluid level or improper viscosity oil in forks. This can sound like spurting and is usually accompanied by irregular fork action (Chapter 6).
- [ ] Spring weak or broken. Makes a clicking or scraping sound. Fork oil, when drained, will have a lot of metal particles in it (Chapter 6).
- [ ] Steering head bearings loose or damaged. Clicks when braking. Check and adjust or replace as necessary (Chapters 1 and 6).
- [ ] Fork clamp bolts loose. Make sure all fork clamp bolts are tight (Chapter 6).
- [ ] Fork tube bent. Good possibility if machine has been dropped. Renew both tubes (Chapter 6).
- [ ] Front axle nut loose (Chapter 6).

Rear suspension noise

- [ ] Shock damping fluid leak, caused by defective seal. Shock will be covered with oil. Renew shock (Chapter 6). If twin shocks are fitted, renew both of them.
- [ ] Defective shock absorber with internal damage. This is in the body of the shock and can't be remedied. The shock must be replaced with a new one (Chapter 6).
- [ ] Bent or damaged shock body. Replace the shock with a new one (Chapter 6).
- [ ] Worn, damaged or dirty suspension linkage components (where fitted). Remove, clean and check all components (Chapter 6).
- [ ] Worn, damaged or dirty swingarm pivot components. Remove, clean and check all components (Chapter 6).

Brake noise

- [ ] Squeal caused by dust on brake pads or shoes. Usually found in combination with glazed pads or shoes. Renew the pads/shoes (Chapter 7).
- [ ] Contamination of brake pads or shoes. Oil or brake fluid causing brake to chatter or squeal. Renew pads or shoes (Chapter 7).
- [ ] Pads or shoes glazed. Caused by excessive heat from prolonged use or from contamination. Do not use sandpaper, emery cloth, carborundum cloth or any other abrasive to roughen the pad surfaces as abrasives will stay in the pad material and damage the disc or drum. A very fine flat file can be used, but pad or shoe renewal is advised (Chapter 7).
- [ ] Disc or drum warped. Can cause a chattering, clicking or intermittent squeal. Usually accompanied by a pulsating lever or pedal and uneven braking. Check the disc runout and the drum ovality (Chapter 7).
- [ ] Loose or worn wheel (front) or transmission (rear) bearings. Check and renew as needed (Chapter 7).

10 Excessive exhaust smoke

White smoke

- [ ] Piston oil ring worn. The ring may be broken or damaged, causing oil from the crankcase to be pulled past the piston into the combustion chamber. Replace the rings with new ones (Chapter 2A, 2B, 2C or 2D).
- [ ] Cylinder worn, cracked, or scored. Caused by overheating or oil starvation. New components must be fitted (Chapter 2A, 2B, 2C or 2D).
- [ ] Valve oil seal damaged or worn. Replace oil seals with new ones (Chapter 2A, 2B, 2C or 2D).
- [ ] Valve guide worn. Perform a complete valve job (Chapter 2A, 2B, 2C or 2D).
- [ ] Engine oil level too high, which causes the oil to be forced past the rings. Drain oil to the proper level (Pre-ride checks).
- [ ] Head gasket broken between oil return and cylinder. Causes oil to be pulled into the combustion chamber. Replace the head gasket and check the head for warpage (Chapter 2A, 2B, 2C or 2D).
- [ ] Abnormal crankcase pressurisation, which forces oil past the rings. Clogged breather or hose usually the cause – check the hose first (Chapter 1).

Black smoke

- [ ] Air filter clogged. Clean or replace the element (Chapter 1).
- [ ] Choke stuck on, causing fuel to be pulled through choke circuit (Chapter 4).
- [ ] Fuel level too high. Check and adjust the float height as necessary (Chapter 4).
- [ ] Float needle valve held off needle seat. Clean the float bowl and fuel line and replace the needle and seat if necessary (Chapter 4).

Brown smoke

- [ ] Main jet clogged. Lean condition caused by a restricted orifice. Clean float bowl and jet (Chapter 4).
- [ ] Fuel flow insufficient. Either fuel inlet needle valve stuck closed due to chemical reaction with old fuel, float height incorrect, or restricted fuel line, or blocked fuel tap strainer or filter. Check and clean tap, strainer/filter, fuel hose and float chamber (Chapters 1 and 4).
- [ ] Carburettor intake duct loose (Chapter 4).
- [ ] Air filter poorly sealed or missing (Chapter 1).

11 Poor handling or stability

Handlebars hard to turn

- [ ] Steering stem nut or bolt too tight (Chapter 6).
- [ ] Bearings damaged. Roughness can be felt as the bars are turned from side-to-side. Replace bearings and races (Chapter 6).
- [ ] Races dented or worn. Denting results from wear in only one position (e.g., straight-ahead), from a collision or hitting a pothole or from dropping the machine. Replace races and bearings (Chapter 6).
- [ ] Steering stem lubrication inadequate. Causes are grease getting hard from age or being washed out by high pressure washers. Disassemble steering head and repack bearings (Chapter 6).
- [ ] Steering stem bent. Caused by a collision, hitting a pothole or by dropping the machine. Replace damaged part. Don't try to straighten the steering stem (Chapter 6).
- [ ] Front tyre air pressure too low (Pre-ride checks).

Handlebar shakes or vibrates excessively

- [ ] Tyres worn or out of balance (Pre-ride checks and Chapter 7).
- [ ] Swingarm bearings worn. Replace worn bearings by referring to Chapter 6.
- [ ] Rim(s) warped or damaged. Inspect wheels for runout (Chapter 7).
- [ ] Wheel bearings worn. Worn front or rear wheel bearings can cause poor tracking. Worn front bearings will cause wobble (Chapter 7).
- [ ] Handlebar clamp bolts loose (Chapter 6).
- [ ] Steering stem or fork clamp bolts loose (Chapter 6).
- [ ] Engine mounting bolts loose. Will cause excessive vibration with increased engine rpm (Chapter 2).

Handlebar pulls to one side

- [ ] Frame bent. Definitely suspect this if the machine has been dropped. May or may not be accompanied by cracking near the bend. Replace the frame (Chapter 6).
- [ ] Wheel out of alignment. Caused by improper location of axle spacers (Chapter 7) or from bent steering stem or frame (Chapter 6).
- [ ] Swingarm bent or twisted. Caused by age (metal fatigue) or impact damage. Replace the swingarm (Chapter 6).
- [ ] Steering stem bent. Caused by impact damage or by dropping the motorcycle. Replace the steering stem (Chapter 6).
- [ ] Fork leg bent. Disassemble the forks and replace the damaged parts (Chapter 6).
- [ ] Fork oil level uneven. Check and add or drain as necessary (Chapter 6).

Poor shock absorbing qualities

- [ ] Too hard:
  - a) Fork oil level excessive (Chapter 6).
  - b) Fork oil viscosity too high. Use a lighter oil.
  - c) Fork tube bent. Causes a harsh, sticking feeling (Chapter 6).
  - d) Shock shaft or body bent or damaged (Chapter 6).
  - e) Fork internal damage (Chapter 6).
  - f) Shock internal damage (Chapter 6).
  - g) Tyre pressure too high (Pre-ride checks).
  - h) Suspension linkage damage (where fitted) (Chapter 6).
- [ ] Too soft:
  - a) Fork oil insufficient and/or leaking (Chapter 6).
  - b) Fork oil level too low (Chapter 6).
  - c) Fork oil viscosity too light (Chapter 6).
  - d) Fork springs weak or broken (Chapter 6).
  - e) Shock internal damage or oil leakage (Chapter 6).

12 Braking problems – disc brake

Brake is spongy or doesn't hold

- [ ] Air in brake line. Caused by inattention to master cylinder fluid level or by leakage. Locate problem and bleed brakes (Chapter 7).
- [ ] Pads or disc worn (Chapters 1 and 7).
- [ ] Contaminated pads. Caused by contamination with oil, grease, brake fluid, etc. Clean or replace pads. Clean disc thoroughly with brake cleaner (Chapter 7).
- [ ] Brake fluid deteriorated. Fluid is old or contaminated. Drain system, replenish with new fluid and bleed the system (Chapter 7).
- [ ] Master cylinder internal parts worn or damaged causing fluid to bypass (Chapter 7).
- [ ] Master cylinder bore scratched by foreign material or broken spring. Repair or replace master cylinder (Chapter 7).
- [ ] Disc warped. Replace disc (Chapter 7).

Brake lever or pedal pulsates

- [ ] Disc warped. Replace disc (Chapter 7).
- [ ] Axle bent. Replace axle (Chapter 7).

- [ ] Brake caliper bolts loose (Chapter 7).
- [ ] Brake caliper sliders damaged or sticking, causing caliper to bind. Lube the sliders or replace them if they are corroded or bent (Chapter 7).
- [ ] Wheel warped or otherwise damaged (Chapter 7).
- [ ] Wheel bearings damaged or worn (Chapter 7).

Brake drags

- [ ] Master cylinder piston seized. Caused by wear or damage to piston or cylinder bore (Chapter 7).
- [ ] Lever balky or stuck. Check pivot and lubricate (Chapter 7).
- [ ] Brake caliper binds. Caused by inadequate lubrication or damage to caliper sliders (Chapter 7).
- [ ] Brake caliper piston seized in bore. Caused by wear or ingestion of dirt past deteriorated seal (Chapter 7).
- [ ] Brake pad damaged. Pad material separated from backing plate. Usually caused by faulty manufacturing process or from contact with chemicals. Replace pads (Chapter 7).
- [ ] Rear brake pedal freeplay insufficient.

13 Braking problems – drum brake

Brake is ineffective

- [ ] Lever or pedal incorrectly adjusted. Check the setting (Chapter 1).
- [ ] Shoes or drum worn (Chapter 7).
- [ ] Contaminated shoes. Caused by contamination with oil, grease etc. Renew shoes. Clean drum thoroughly with brake cleaner (Chapter 7).
- [ ] Brake arm incorrectly positioned, or cam excessively worn (Chapter 7).

Brake lever or pedal pulsates

- [ ] Drum warped. Renew drum (Chapter 7).
- [ ] Wheel axle bent. Renew axle (Chapter 7).
- [ ] Wheel warped or otherwise damaged (Chapter 7).

- [ ] Wheel/hub bearings (front) or transmission bearings (rear) damaged or worn (Chapter 7).

Brake drags

- [ ] Lever or pedal incorrectly adjusted or pivot requires lubrication (Chapters 1 and 7).
- [ ] Shoe return springs broken (Chapter 7).
- [ ] Brake arm or cam binds. Caused by inadequate lubrication or damage (Chapter 7).
- [ ] Brake shoe damaged. Friction material separated from shoe. Usually caused by faulty manufacturing process or from contact with chemicals. Renew shoes (Chapter 7).
- [ ] Shoes improperly installed (Chapter 7).

14 Electrical problems

Battery dead or weak

- [ ] Battery faulty. Caused by sulphated plates which are shorted through sedimentation, or on a conventional battery low electrolyte level. Also, broken battery terminal making only occasional contact (Chapter 9).
- [ ] Battery cables making poor contact (Chapter 9).
- [ ] Load excessive. Caused by addition of high wattage lights or other electrical accessories.
- [ ] Ignition switch defective. Switch either earths internally or fails to shut off system. Replace the switch (Chapter 9).
- [ ] Regulator/rectifier defective (Chapter 9).

- [ ] Stator coil open or shorted (Chapter 9).
- [ ] Wiring faulty. Wiring grounded (earthed) or connections loose in ignition, charging or lighting circuits (Chapter 9).

Battery overcharged

- [ ] Regulator/rectifier defective. Overcharging is noticed when battery gets excessively warm or boils over (Chapter 9).
- [ ] Battery defective. Replace battery with a new one (Chapter 9).
- [ ] Battery amperage too low, wrong type or size. Install manufacturer's specified amp-hour battery to handle charging load (Chapter 9).

Note: *References throughout this index are in the form "Chapter number" • "Page number". So, for example, 2A•10 refers to page 10 of Chapter 2A.*

Note: *References throughout this index are in the form* **"Chapter number"** • **"Page number"**. *So, for example, 2A•10 refers to page 10 of Chapter 2A.*

Note: *References throughout this index are in the form* **"Chapter number"** • **"Page number"**. *So, for example, 2A•10 refers to page 10 of Chapter 2A.*

Preserving Our Motoring Heritage

< The Model J Duesenberg Derham Tourster. Only eight of these magnificent cars were ever built – this is the only example to be found outside the United States of America

Almost every car you've ever loved, loathed or desired is gathered under one roof at the Haynes Motor Museum. Over 300 immaculately presented cars and motorbikes represent every aspect of our motoring heritage, from elegant reminders of bygone days, such as the superb Model J Duesenberg to curiosities like the bug-eyed BMW Isetta. There are also many old friends and flames. Perhaps you remember the 1959 Ford Popular that you did your courting in? The magnificent 'Red Collection' is a spectacle of classic sports cars including AC, Alfa Romeo, Austin Healey, Ferrari, Lamborghini, Maserati, MG, Riley, Porsche and Triumph.

A Perfect Day Out

Each and every vehicle at the Haynes Motor Museum has played its part in the history and culture of Motoring. Today, they make a wonderful spectacle and a great day out for all the family. Bring the kids, bring Mum and Dad, but above all bring your camera to capture those golden memories for ever. You will also find an impressive array of motoring memorabilia, a comfortable 70 seat video cinema and one of the most extensive transport book shops in Britain. The Pit Stop Cafe serves everything from a cup of tea to wholesome, home-made meals or, if you prefer, you can enjoy the large picnic area nestled in the beautiful rural surroundings of Somerset.

John Haynes O.B.E., Founder and Chairman of the museum at the wheel of a Haynes Light 12.   >

< The 1936 490cc sohc-engined International Norton – well known for its racing success

The Museum is situated on the A359 Yeovil to Frome road at Sparkford, just off the A303 in Somerset. It is about 40 miles south of Bristol, and 25 minutes drive from the M5 intersection at Taunton.

Open 9.30am - 5.30pm (10.00am - 4.00pm Winter) 7 days a week, *except Christmas Day, Boxing Day and New Years Day*

Special rates available for schools, coach parties and outings   Charitable Trust No. 292048